MW01530492

Indigenous Peoples in Asia
A Resource Book

Editor | **Christian Erni**

IWGIA Document No. 123

International Work Group for Indigenous Affairs (IWGIA)
Asia Indigenous Peoples Pact Foundation (AIPP)

Copenhagen/Chiang Mai 2008

The Concept of Indigenous Peoples in Asia
A Resource Book
Editor: Christian Erni

Cover and layout: Co-Kayan Media Team
Cover images: Christian Erni
Printed in Thailand by Co-Kayan Media Team
© if not otherwise stated, the authors, IWGIA and AIPP

Published by:

International Work Group for Indigenous Affairs (IWGIA)
Classensgade 11E, DK-2100
Copenhagen, Denmark
www.iwgia.org

IWGIA

Asia Indigenous Peoples Pact Foundation
108 Soi 6, Moo 5, Tambon Sanpranate,
Amphur San Sai, Chiang Mai
50210, Thailand
www.aippfoundation.org

Distribution in North America:

Transaction Publishers
300 McGaw Drive
Edison, NJ 08837
USA
www.transactionpub.com

transaction

HURRIDOCS CIP DATA
Title: The Concept of Indigenous Peoples in Asia. A Resource Book
Edited by: Christian Erni
Pages: 462
ISSN: 0105-4503
ISBN: 9788791563348
Language: English
Index: 1. Indigenous peoples – 2. Indigeneity – 3. Asian controversy
Geographical area: Asia
Publication date: November 2008

The articles contained in this book reflect the authors' own views and opinions and not necessarily those of IWGIA or AIPP.

This book has been produced with financial support from the Danish and Norwegian Ministries of Foreign Affair.

Contents

Part III   **329**
Country Profiles

Annex

Foreword

Jannie Lasimbang

On 13 September 2007, the global indigenous peoples' movement achieved a major success in its decade long struggle for international recognition of their rights when the General Assembly of the United Nations adopted the Declaration on the Rights of Indigenous Peoples. Except for Bangladesh, who abstained from voting, all Asian governments present voted in favour of the Declaration. Some of them have however expressed reservations regarding the applicability of the concept of indigenous peoples to their countries. Some pointed at the lack of a definition as a major problem for the application of the Declaration. Such reservations have been expressed by Asian governments already before the adoption of the Declaration.

Indigenous peoples of Asia who followed closely, and actively engaged in the international standard setting process on the rights of indigenous peoples therefore found it necessary to elaborate on the concept of "indigenous peoples" particularly for this region. It was necessary not only because of the need to explain to most Asian governments who are having difficulties with this concept, but to clarify confusion among indigenous peoples themselves, who have been subjected to many names or terms by others in their own countries.

The Workshop on the "Concept of Indigenous Peoples" co-organized by the Asia Indigenous Peoples Pact (AIPP), the International Workgroup for Indigenous Affairs (IWGIA) and Tebtebba Foundation in March 2006, and the discussions and deliberations that followed made it clear that a definition of indigenous peoples is not necessary and would be counterproductive in view of the many positive developments at the international level and the huge diversity of indigenous peoples in Asia.

This publication is therefore a first attempt to reflect on the discussions that ensued by compiling contributions by authoritative scholars and indigenous activists and leaders whose writings could enrich the process of reflection and help in generating further ideas for clarifying who the indigenous peoples of Asia are. It is envisaged that further inputs, particularly to update the articles on self-ascription, would help indigenous peoples and governments in the elaboration and implementation of the United Nations Declaration on the Rights of Indigenous Peoples to promote and protect indigenous peoples' rights.

I would like to take this opportunity to thank all the contributors, including authors who have agreed to allow reprinting of their articles, as well as to the Danish Foreign Ministry, through its support to IWGIA, for making it possible to publish this book. My appreciation goes particularly to Dr. Chris Erni who has worked hard in finalizing the manuscripts.

Jannie Lasimbang
Asia Indigenous Peoples Pact
October 2008

Introduction

The Concept of Indigenous Peoples in Asia

Christian Erni

Over the past decades the world has witnessed an increasing presence of indigenous peoples in international processes and institutions dealing with issues ranging from general human rights, to sustainable development, forest and biodiversity conservation, international trade or intellectual property rights. In all these processes the indigenous participants' main agenda is to ensure that indigenous peoples' rights are given due attention and respect in order to prevent further marginalization or outright destruction of indigenous peoples' livelihoods, cultures, and societies. The success of indigenous peoples in making their voice heard at the international level is reflected in Prof. Erica-Irene Daes' statement at the 19th session of the UN Working Group on Indigenous Populations, in which she called the indigenous peoples "the first grassroots movement to gain direct access to the UN" (cf. Karlsson 2003: 403). In the process, the United Nations system itself is being transformed.

The indigenous movement's struggle for international recognition and a space within the UN system had a major breakthrough in 2000 when the Permanent Forum on Indigenous Issues was established. The significant feature of this new body is that indigenous peoples and states are equally represented. This is a novelty in a system that has thus far been the exclusive domain of state governments. It reflects the extent to which, as Niezen (2002) observed, the global indigenous peoples' movement has been able to impact on the "structures and ethical orientation of the United Nation" (p. 47). The success of the international indigenous movement culminated in the recent adoption of the United Nations Declaration on the Rights of Indigenous Peoples by the United Nations General Assembly. The Declaration was adopted by vast majority vote of 144 states. 11 countries abstained and only four countries voted against it: the United States, Canada, Australia and New Zealand.

Yet, while the Declaration on the Rights of Indigenous Peoples is rightfully celebrated as a major achievement there are also reasons to doubt that worldwide recognition of indigenous peoples' rights by state governments will become a reality soon. The intransigence of certain governments with respect to key issues – like the "s" in "peoples", and closely connected to this, self-determination, the rights to land, territories and resources, or free and prior informed consent – during the negotiations on the final text of the Declaration makes it appear unlikely that these, and probably many of the governments that remained silent during the process, will be willing to implement the Declaration at home.

Several countries have indicated this in their comments right after the adoption of the Declaration. Thailand's representative Ms. Punkrasing, for example, stated

> "[   ] that her delegation had voted in favour of the text and was in agreement with its intent, despite the fact that a number of paragraphs raised some concerns. [   ] Thailand understood that the articles on self-determination would be interpreted within the framework of the principle set out in the Vienna Declaration. Thailand also understood that the Declaration did not create any new rights and that any benefits that flowed from the Declaration would be based on the laws and Constitution of Thailand." (United Nations General Assembly 2007)

Some Asian countries, like Bangladesh, India, Indonesia and Pakistan, pointed at the lack of a definition as a major obstacle for the implementation of the Declaration. Indonesia's representative Muhammad Anshor, for example, said

> "[   ] that several aspects of the Declaration remained unresolved, in particular what constituted indigenous peoples. The absence of that definition prevented a clear understanding of the peoples to whom the Declaration applied. In that context, the Declaration used the definition contained in the International Labour Organization Convention, according to which indigenous people were distinct from tribal people. Given the fact that Indonesia's entire population at the time of colonization remained unchanged, the rights in the Declaration accorded exclusively to indigenous people and did not apply in the context of Indonesia. Indonesia would continue to promote the collective rights of indigenous peoples." (ibid.)

This statement reveals that the current Indonesian government's position does not differ from that of the Suharto regime which maintained that "Indonesia is a nation which has no indigenous people, or that all Indonesians are equally indigenous" (Li 2000a: 1).

In fact, already early on in the drafting process several other Asian governments have also expressed their reservation with regards to the application of the concept of indigenous peoples to their countries. With reference to the still common usage of the term dating back to the 19th century colonial era the Bangladesh government argued that "all Bangladeshis are indigenous people who existed in the territory prior to British colonization and are now, fortunately, liberated". (Kingsbury 1998: 433, footnote 74, in this volume p. 152 [75]).

Speaking at the 53rd session of the United Nations Commission on Human Rights in 1997, the adviser of the Chinese delegation, Long Xuequn, argued along similar lines:

> "The indigenous issues are a product of special historical circumstances. By and large, they are the result of the colonialist policy carried out in modern history by European countries in other regions of the world, especially on the continents of America and Oceania." "As in the case of other Asian countries, the Chinese people of all ethnic groups have lived on our own land for generations. We suffered from invasion and occupation of colonialists and foreign aggressors," Long said. "Fortunately, after arduous struggles of all ethnic groups, we drove away those colonialists and aggressors. In China, there are no indigenous people and therefore no indigenous issues." (Embassy of the Peoples Republic of China in Switzerland 1997)

Until June 6, 2008, when Japan's parliament voted in favour of the recognition of the Ainu as the country's indigenous people, only two Asian countries had officially recognized the existence of indigenous peoples within their boundaries: the Philippines and Taiwan. In 1997, a comprehensive law on indigenous peoples was passed in the Philippines, Republic Act 8371, known also as the Indigenous Peoples Rights Act (IPRA). In this law, the term "indigenous peoples" is however used interchangeably with Indigenous Cultural Communities, which was used in previous legislations (see Annex 1, p. 461). Taiwan has several laws pertaining to its indigenous peoples. The term itself gained legal status through a constitutional amendment already in 1994 (see country profile of Taiwan p. 437ff).

The opposition of Asian governments to the concept of indigenous peoples has received tacit support from eminent scholars who are questioning its empirical validity and usefulness as analytical category, and consider it dangerous due to its supposed exclusionary and potentially chauvinistic undercurrent (see e.g. Béteille 1998, 2006; Rodrigues and Game 1998 for the Indian context; Bowen 2000 and

Kuper 2003 generally). Partly in response to these authors a prolific discourse ensued among social scientists over the past decade (Rosengren 2002; Kenrick and Lewis 2004; Barnard 2004, Dove 2006 at global level; Xaxa 1999, Karlsson 2003, Baviskar 2006 on India, Li 2000 on Indonesia) which left the academic controversy largely unresolved, but the concept nevertheless firmly entrenched in both popular and scholarly use.

Unexpected support to Asian government's denial of the applicability of the concept in Asia came from within the very institution that contributed so much to the popularization of the concept and with it the growth of a global indigenous movement. During the 16th session of the United Nations Working Group on Indigenous Populations in July 1998, Working Group member and Special Rapporteur Miguel Alfonso Martínez submitted his "Study on treaties, agreements and other constructive arrangements between States and indigenous populations". In paragraph 88 of his report he states that

> "[ ] in post-colonial Africa and Asia autochthonous groups/minorities/ethnic groups/peoples who seek to exercise rights presumed to be or actually infringed by the existing autochthonous authorities in the States in which they live cannot, in the view of the Special Rapporteur, claim for themselves, unilaterally and exclusively, the 'indigenous' status in the United Nations context."

And in paragraph 89 he continues:

> "These States – whose existence as such is, in the majority of cases, very recent – have not only the right but also the duty to preserve their fragile territorial integrity. The risk to such States of breaking up (or 'balkanization') which such unilateral claims to 'indigenousness' imply naturally cannot be taken lightly."

Representatives of indigenous peoples from Asia responded with outrage to Special Rapporteur Martínez' report, and insist on the universality of the concept (see Victorial Tauli-Corpuz in this volume; or Asia Indigenous and Tribal Peoples Network 1999). Even though the debate within the United Nations on the applicability of the concept to Asia and Africa died down quickly after the closing of the 16th session of the UN Working Group, it left a bitter aftertaste reminding indigenous representatives from these regions that the absence of a definition of the concept can and in fact is perceived by many as a vulnerability which critics are quick to exploit.

To define or not to define?

The United Nations do not have any official definition of "indigenous peoples". The issue of the definition was discussed during the second and third sessions of the Working Group on Indigenous Populations in 1983 and 1984, taking the work of Special Rapporteur José Martínez Cobo as a point of departure (Daes 1996: para 21, in this volume p.34). Although Martínez Cobo included a definition in his final report of 1986 "Study of the Problem of Discrimination against Indigenous Populations" (see Annex p. 459), no consensus was reached in the Working Group and it has henceforth and in line with the indigenous participants' recommendations adopted "a flexible approach to determining eligibility to participate in its annual sessions, relying upon organizations of indigenous peoples themselves to draw attention to any improper assertions of the right to participate as 'indigenous' peoples" (Daes op.cit.).

Indigenous representatives participating in various processes at the UN have repeatedly emphasized that a definition of indigenous peoples is not necessary, and insisted on self-identification as part of their right to self-determination (see the article by Victoria Tauli-Corpuz in this volume p. 77ff). The members of the UN Working Group on indigenous populations also concluded that it is neither realistic nor useful to try and adopt a definition. As E. Daes points out, "the Working Group itself had been a success despite not having adopted any formal definition of 'indigenous peoples'" (1996: para. 6, in this volume p. 31).

The opposite position held by many state governments is that indigenous peoples as objects of international law need to be "defined either by criteria formulated by states or through recognition by states" (Kingsbury 1998: 441, in this volume p. 130).

These two opposing positions result in a dilemma: Refraining to agree on a general definition or insisting on self-identification alone may provide governments with a reason to refuse the recognition of indigenous peoples. Or it may lead to only a selective recognition of indigenous peoples by governments and multilateral institutions. Agreeing on a definition on the other hand brings with it the danger that certain groups, who may identify themselves as indigenous but to whom some of the respective definitional criteria do not apply, are excluded.

Concerned scholars like Howitt, Connell and Hirsch (1996: 13) have recognized the difficulties, and above all implicit dangers of a strict definition, and they argue in favour of a more flexible and open approach:

> "In making our analyses, we recognize the difficulties arising from uncritical acceptance of state approaches to defining indigenous status, which have often been part of the sophisticated array of ideological hurdles placed in the path of indigenous autonomy and self-determination [ ]. So, rather than pursue any unrealistic universal or all-encompassing definitional approach, we have accepted a much less 'tidy' approach.

Awkward political realities are allowed to intrude in the interest of inclusiveness over exclusiveness, and holism over narrowness."

Indigenous organizations and in particular large, national-level alliances have to find ways to practically deal with the problem of identification and recognition since this relates to the question of membership admission. The Aliansi Masyarakat Adat Nusantara (AMAN), the national indigenous peoples' alliance in Indonesia, for example, adheres to the principle of self-identification and thereby does not draw a strict boundary. As Tania Li (2001: 649) points out, "From all I have read and observed, nothing about the movement is exclusive or chauvinistic. Indeed, as I suspected, it is so inclusive that the boundaries are not coherent, but that is not the point. Rather, diverse parties are being drawn into a struggle for an imagined future which is inspired by the past, but takes its shape from the injustices that need to be confronted in the present."

However, she also comes to conclude, "The absence of clear boundaries to the category masyarakat adat provides advocates with important room for maneuver, but it also permits a rather formidable array of forces to narrow and limit the places of recognition that masyarakat adat may fill." (ibid.: 670)

As we have seen, this is indeed happening, and Muehlebach (2003: 251) points out that "state representatives regularly seize the opportunity to discredit the entire exercise by pointing precisely at these [definitional] quibbles", that the focus is conveniently kept on difficulties in identification "rather than the substantive political and legal issues at stake" (ibid.). To her, "a broad definition of 'indigenous' is indispensable, because the problem addressed is universal" (ibid.:252).

While there seems to be a general consensus within the relevant bodies of the United Nations and the international indigenous peoples movement – supported by some scholars – that a definition of indigenous peoples is neither desirable nor necessary, the problem remains that the subjects, whom international or national legal instruments are supposed to apply to, need to be identified.

Toward practical application: Identification without formal definition

Without ever having given any formal definition in writing, indigenous delegates to international forums have over the past two decades developed a kind of informal, collective process of identification. Its point of departure is self-identification, but it is complemented by the recognition by others. The United Nations' "open-door policy" (Niezen 2003: 21) with respect to participation of indigenous delegates can be considered a practical application of this approach. And, as Niezen (ibid.) points out, even though it may appear to be paradoxical ("the definition of no definition"), "[ ] the real paradox is that it works: indigenous delegates come to meetings with little insecurity about their own status as 'indigenous', and few open doubts about the claims of others" (ibid.). There were, however, cases of collective non-recognition of others at the meetings of the UN Working Group on Indigenous Populations. This was expressed for example by a walk-out of hundreds of indigenous delegates during the speech of a representative of the delegate of the Rehoboth Basters from Namibia, descendants of indigenous Khoi and white settlers (ibid.: 21f). Such direct ways of asserting, negotiating or denying identity are however not always or easily possible. Advocacy and lobbying for recognition and legal rights happen at various levels and by a wide range of actors who, in Asia, hardly ever have the chance to get together in large forums where such processes are possible.

Therefore, and in light of the anticipated adoption of the Declaration on the Rights of Indigenous Peoples by the United Nations' General Assembly, indigenous peoples in Asia felt the need to have a more in-depth reflection on the concept of indigenous peoples and its practical application in the region. Thus, from March 1 to 3, 2006, a workshop on "The Concept of 'Indigenous Peoples' in Asia" was jointly organized by the Asia wide alliance of indigenous organizations Asia Indigenous Peoples Pact (AIPP), the Tebtebba Foundation (Indigenous Peoples' International Centre for Policy Research and Education), and the advocacy organization International Work Group for Indigenous Affairs (IWGIA) in Chiang Mai, Thailand. 54 participants – mostly indigenous activists and leaders from 14 Asian countries together with a few non-indigenous researchers and NGO staff – met with the hope to gain more clarity on the issue and thereby be able to advocate more effectively for the implementation of the Declaration by their governments.

The participants were unanimous in their agreement with the position taken by indigenous peoples' representatives in the various international forums that a general definition of the concept of indigenous peoples was neither desirable nor necessary. It was agreed that the identification of groups that are to be recognized as indigenous peoples had to be done at the country level in an open process of consultation and discussion. Only this approach, it was stressed, allows for the flexibility needed to do justice to the diverse social, cultural and political contexts encountered in the Asian region. The workshop participants were very much aware of the challenges any such attempt faces, not the least from their governments whom they expect to either oppose, deny legitimacy of or try and control such a process.

This book is a direct result of the workshop, and its nature was determined by the participants' call for a flexible, contextual approach to the identification of indigenous peoples in Asia. The book therefore does not intend to dwell or expand on the controversy on the applicability of the concept to Asia. Its point of departure is the simple fact that despite the still ongoing definitional controversy more and more groups in Asia identify themselves as indigenous peoples. The question therefore is not whether, but how indigenous peoples can be identified in Asia. In absence of a universal definition and in recognition of the conclusion of the workshop participants that no blueprint for identifying indigenous peoples exists and that this has to be done in each country separately, the purpose of this book is to provide some assistance in this endeavour. This is done by means of a compilation of key articles, both previously published and unpublished, which directly or indirectly address the issue from historical, anthropological, legal and indigenous rights advocates' perspectives, and at international, regional, national and local levels. The articles compiled are meant to be resources which the reader can draw on in forming an opinion relevant for the specific context he or she may be working in.

The book is divided into three parts. The first part contains three documents that provide the reader with an introduction to the discussion at the international level. It includes the working paper by *Erica-Irene Daes*, former Chairperson of the United Nations Working Group on Indigenous Populations, submitted at an early stage of the deliberations of the Working Group. Daes provides an historical review of the use of the concept in international law, followed by a critical legal analysis. In her conclusions she stresses that the Working Group's flexible approach with respect to determining the eligibility to participate in the annual session was successful. She points out that in view of an eventual adoption and the practical implementation of a Declaration on the Rights of Indigenous Peoples, it is necessary to make sure that in practice there is room for the reasonable evolution and regional specificity of the concept of indigenous peoples.

Jeff J. Corntassel's article addresses the dilemma in standard setting in international law in which the call for establishing definitional standards for indigenous peoples is opposed by the claim for an unlimited right of indigenous self-identification. After surveying definitions of indigenous peoples developed by academicians in the field of nationalism, in international law as well as by practitioners from intergovernmental organizations and NGOs, he concludes that a balance between self-identification and establishing a working definition of indigenous peoples is possible.

Victoria Tauli-Corpuz in her article gives us a vivid account of the emergence of, and her involvement in the international indigenous movement, and the debate on the definition of indigenous peoples that ensued in connection with the deliberation of the UN Working Group on Indigenous Populations and other international bodies concerned with standard-setting on the rights of indigenous peoples. She presents the position taken by indigenous leaders and activists against a definition and the reasons behind it, and concludes with identifying challenges for the practical application of the concept and the related international legal instruments, i.e. the identification of indigenous peoples in the context of particular countries.

The second part of the book includes articles directly or indirectly dealing with the concept of indigenous peoples or "indigeneity", and its application in

Asia. The article by *Benedict Kingsbury* was already published in 1998, but is still the most comprehensive scholarly reflection on this issue. Providing an overview of the Asian Controversy, arguments raised against the applicability of the concept in the region, (then) existing international legal norms and institutions concerned with indigenous peoples he proceeds to discuss objections against a broad concept at international level and suggested alternatives, and concludes with presenting a proposal on how to deal with the definitional challenges. He advocates for the use of flexible, but focused, international criteria based on a combination of requirements and indicia. And he suggests that these criteria are to be linked to processes of negotiation and legal analysis, institutional decision making and social interaction through which they are applied to specific cases.

The article by *James C. Scott* is not in any way concerned with the issue of indigeneity, and he neither uses N or addresses the concept of indigenous peoples. His article was included in this book because it discusses the nature of the historically evolved relationship between "hill" and "valley" populations in Southeast Asia and the distinct identities that emerged in the process, which have come to be key determinants in the experiences and resulting self-understanding of groups that now define themselves as "indigenous peoples" of the region.

The article by *Danilo Geiger* is the result of his attempt to develop a, what he calls, "practical diagnostic instrument" that can be used to distinguish indigenous groups from non-indigenous groups in the context of a research project on the relationship between indigenous peoples and settlers at contemporary colonization frontiers of South and Southeast Asia.

The subsequent five articles focus their reflections on the concept within the context of a particular country, or ethnic group. *Ian Baird* explores the connection between the concept of indigenous peoples and the experience of colonization, illustrating and underpinning his arguments with the example of the experiences made by the Brao, an ethnic group living on both sides of the border between southern Laos and north-eastern Cambodia. *Virginius Xaxa* presents his reflection on the concept of indigenous peoples for the context of India, *Tan Chee-Beng* for China, *John Bamba* for Indonesia and *Christian Erni* for the Philippines.

The country-specific articles are followed by a report on the human rights situation of indigenous peoples in Asia by (then) *Special Raporteur Rodolfo Stavenhagen,* submitted to the UN Human Rights Council in May 2007. The report shows that the patterns of discrimination and human rights violations experienced by groups of people in Asia, who identify themselves or have been identified as indigenous peoples, are similar to those experienced by indigenous peoples in other parts of the world.

The experience of occupation, dispossession, forced assimilation, discrimination and political marginalization is one of the key criteria in self-identification of indigenous peoples globally. This is also evident in the *joint statement made by the participants of the workshop* on the Concept on Indigenous Peoples in Asia, held in Chiang Mai, Thailand, in March 2007. In this statement, the participants try to summarize the result of their discussions and present the experiences that they have identified as being common to groups in the region who have come to call themselves indigenous peoples.

The last part of the book contains short *country profiles* which for each country give an overview of the terms used for the groups commonly identified as indigenous peoples, the present government's position regarding the recognition of indigenous peoples and their rights, and an overview of those groups who identify themselves or are commonly identified as indigenous peoples. The country profiles are partly based on the presentations made at the workshop in Chiang Mai, and have been further elaborated by various authors with the help of various sources. The country profiles do not claim to be authoritative. They were compiled with the intention of providing basic information that can help readers to conduct further, more specific and in-depth investigations on the matter.

References and further reading

Asia Indigenous and Tribal Peoples Network 1999. The Universality of Indigenous Peoples. Commentary and recommendations to the Special Rapporteur on the Study on treaties, agreements and other constructive arrangements between states and indigenous populations. http://www.aitpn. org/un.htm

Barnard, Alan 2004. Indigenous Peoples. A response to Justin Kenrick and Jerome Lewis. *Anthropology Today* Vol. 20 No. 5, October 2004

———— 2006. Kalahri revisionism, Vienna and the 'indigenous peoples' debate. Social Anthropology 14 (1)

Benjamin, Geoffrey 2002. "On Being Tribal in the Malay World", in: Geoffrey Benjamin and Cynthia Chou ed., *Tribal Communities in the Malay World. Historical, Cultural and Social Perspectives,* pp. 7-76. Singapore: Institute of Southeast Asian Studies.

Béteille, André 1998. The Idea of Indigenous People. Commentary. *Current Anthropology,* Volume 39, Number 2, April 1998

————What Should We Mean by "Indigenous People"?; in: Bengt G. Karlsson and Tanka B. Subba 2006. Indigeneity in India. London: Kegan Paul

Bowen, John R. 2000. *Should We Have a Universal Concept of "Indigenous Peoples' Right"?* Paper presented at the 2000 Symposium "Development and the Nation State", Washington University, St. Louis

Burman, B.K. Roy 2003. Indigenous and Tribal Peoples in World System Perspective. Studies on *Tribes and Tribals* 1(1)

Corntassel, Jeff J. 2003. Who is Indigenous? "Peoplehood' and Ethnonationalist Approaches to Rearticulating Indigenous Identity. *Nationalism and Ethnic Politics,* Vol. 9, No. 1, Spring 2003, pp. 75-100

Cultural Survival 1987. *Southeast Asian Tribal Groups and Ethnic Minorities.* Cultural Survival Report 22. Cambridge: Cultural Survival

Daes, Erica-Irene A. 1996. Standard-setting activities: Evolution of Standards Concerning the Rights of Indigenous People. *Working Paper by the Chairperson-Rapporteur, Mrs. Erica-Irene A. Daes. On the concept* of *"indigenous people".* United Nations Economic and Social Council, UN Document E/CN.4/Sub.2/AC.4/1996/2

————— 2008. Indigenous Peoples. Keepers of our Past – Custodians of our Future. Copenhagen: International Work Group for Indigenous Affairs

Dove, Michael R. 2006. Indigenous People and Environmental Politics. *Annual Review of Anthropology* Vol. 35, October 2006

Embassy of the Peoples Republic of China in Switzerland 1997. China Concerned with Protection of Indigenous Peoples' Rights. Web-site of the Embassy of the Peoples Republic of China in Switzerland, 1997/04/01. http:// ch.china-embassy.org/eng/ztnr/rqwt/t138829.htm

Erni, Christian (ed.) 1996. *"Vines That Won't Bind". Indigenous Peoples in Asia.* IWGIA Document No. 80. Copenhagen: International Work Group for Indigenous Affairs

Fernandes, Walter 1995. *Indian Tribals and Search for an Indigenous Identity;* in: A.K. Sing and M.K. Jabbi. Tribals in India. Development, Deprivation, Discontent. New Delhi: Har-Anand Publications

Evans, Grant 1992. Internal Colonialism in the Central Highlands of Vietnam. *Sojourn,* volume 7, Number 2, Singapore

Geiger, Danilo 2008. *Frontier Encounters. Indigenous Communities and Settlers in Asia and Latin America.* IWGIA Document No. 120. Copenhagen: International Work Group for Indigenous Affairs and Swiss National Centre of Competence in Research North-South

Gray, Andrew 1995. The Indigenous Movement in Asia; in: R.H. Barnes, A. Gray and B. Kingsbury. *Indigenous Peoples* of Asia. Association for Asian Studies, Inc. Monograph and Occasional Paper Series 48. Ann Arbor, Michigan

Guenther, Mathisa 2006. Discussion. The concept of indigeneity. *Social Anthropology* 14 (1)

Howitt, Richard, John Connell and Philip Hirsch 1996. Resources, Nations and Indigenous Peoples; in: Richard Howitt, John Connell and Philip Hirsch (eds.): *Resources, Nations and Indigenous Peoples.* Case Studies from Australasia, Melanesia and Southeast Asia. Melbourne: Oxford University Press

International Work Group for Indigenous Affairs [IWGIA] 2004. *The Indigenous World 2004.* Copenhagen: IWGIA

Keal, Paul 2003. *European Conquest and the Rights of Indigenous Peoples. The Moral Backwardness of International Society.* Cambridge Studies in International Relations: 92. Cambridge: Cambridge University Press

Kenrick, Justin and Jerome Lewis 2004. Indigenous peoples' rights and the politics of the term 'indigenous'. *Anthropology Today* Vol 20 No 2, April 2004

Kingsbury, Benedict 1998. "Indigenous Peoples" in International Law: A constructivist Approach to the Asian Controversy. *The American Journal of International Law*, Vol. 92, No. 3, July 1998

Karlsson, Bengt G. 2003. Anthropology and the 'Indigenous Slot'. Claims to and Debates about Indigenous Peoples' Status in India. *Critique of Anthropology*, Vo. 23(4). London, Thousand Oaks, CA and New Delhi

Kuper, Adam 2003. The Return of the Native. *Current Anthropology* Vol. 44, No.3, June 2003

Lao Front for National Construction 2005. *The Ethnic Groups in Lao P.D.R.* Department of Ethnics (sic!)

Li, Tania Murray 1999. *Transforming the Indonesian Uplands: Marginality, Power, and Production. Reading* UK Hardwood Academic Publishers

———— Articulating Indigenous Identity in Indonesia: Resource Politics and the Tribal Slot. *Comparative Studies in Society and History* 42(1):149-179.

———— 2001. Masyarakat Adat, Difference, and the Limits of Recognition in Indonesia's Forest Zone. *Modern Asian Studies* 35, pp 645-676

Martínez, Miguel Alfonso 1999. *Study on Treaties, Agreements and other Constructive Arrangements between States and Indigenous Populations. Final Report.* New York: United Nations Economic and Social Council, UN Document E/CN.4/Sub.2/1999/20

Muehlebach, Andrea 2003. What Self in Self-Determination? Notes from the Frontiers of Transnational Indigenous Activism. I*dentities: Global Studies in Culture and Power*, 10, pp.241-268

Nicholas, Colin 1996. A Common Struggle: Regaining Control; in: Colin Nicholas and Rajeen Singh 1996. *Indigenous Peoples of Asia. Many Peoples, One Struggle.* Bangkok: Asia Indigenous Peoples Pact

Niezen, Ronald 2003. *The Origins of Indigenism. Human Rights and the Politics of Identity.* Berkeley: University of California Press

Rodrigues, Eddie and John Game 1998. Anthropology and the Politics of Rep[resentation. *Economic and Political Weekly*, October 17-24, 1998

Rosengren, Dan 2002. On 'indigenous identities': Reflections on a Debate. *Anthropology Today* 18(3): 25

Sahlins, Marshall 1999. What is Anthropological Enlightenment? Some Lessons of the Twentieth Century, *Annual Review of Anthropology* 28

Scott, James. C. 2000. *Hill and Valley in Southeast Asia… or Why the State is the Enemy of People who Move Around… or … Why Civilization Can't Climb Hills.* Paper presented at the 2000 Symposium "Development and the Nation State", Washington University, St. Louis

Stavenhagen, Rodolfo 1994. Indigenous Rights. Some Conceptual Problems; in:

W.J. Assies and A.J. Hoekema. *Indigenous Peoples' Experiences with Self-Government.* IWGIA Document no. 76. Copenhagen: International Work Group for Indigenous Affairs and University of Amsterdam

United Nations General Assembly 2007. General Assembly Adopts Declaration on Rights of Indigenous Peoples. Press release. United Nations General Assembly, Department of Public Information, News and Media Division. New York. http://www.un.org/News/Press/docs/2007/ga10612. doc.htm

Xaxa, Virginius 1999. Tribes as Indigenous Peoples of India. *Economic and Political Weekly,* December 18, 1999

Part I

The Concept of Indigenous Peoples: The International Dimension

Standard-setting Activities: Evolution of Standards Concerning the Rights of
Indigenous Peoples

On the concept of "indigenous people"

Erica-Irene A. Daes

Working Paper by the Chairperson-
Rapporteur of the United Nations
Working Group on Indigenous
Populations

10 June 1996[a]

Contents

	Paragraphs
Introduction	**1 - 9**

[a] The paper was presented as item 4 of the provisional agenda at the 14th session (29 July - 2 August 1996) of the United Nations Working Group on Indigenous Populations. The Working Group was set up by the Economic and Social Council under the Commission on Human Rights' Sub-Commission on Prevention of Discrimination and Protection of Minorities. UN document number: E/CN.4/Sub.2/AC.4/ 1996/2

Note: The original layout and pagination of the document was not retained in this version. The original document can be accessed at: http://www.unhchr.ch/Huridocda/Huridoca. nsf/(Symbol)/E.CN.4.Sub.2.AC.4.1996.2. En?Opendocument

Introduction

1. At its thirteenth session, the Working Group on Indigenous Populations decided to recommend to the Sub-Commission on Prevention of Discrimination and Protection of Minorities that the Chairperson-Rapporteur, Mrs. Erica-Irene A. Daes, be entrusted with the preparation of a note on criteria for the definition of indigenous peoples based on information which might be submitted to her by Governments, intergovernmental organizations and indigenous peoples' organizations.[1]

2. The recommendation of the Working Group was subsequently approved by the Sub-Commission in paragraph 3 of its resolution 1995/38 of 24 August 1995.

3. In paragraph 7 of its resolution 1996/40 of 19 April 1996, the Commission on Human Rights took note of the recommendation of the Working Group that the Chairperson-Rapporteur address the concept of "indigenous people" and noted that any work should take into account the views of Governments and organizations of indigenous people. The Commission furthermore requested that the discussion of this issue take place during the fourteenth session of the Working Group, and that the report of the Working Group be transmitted to Governments and organizations of indigenous people prior to the next session of the open-ended inter-sessional Working Group of the Commission established in accordance with resolution 1995/32 to elaborate a draft declaration on the rights of indigenous people.

4. To date, the Chairperson-Rapporteur has received no comments from Governments or organizations of indigenous people regarding the issue of definition. She has been guided, however, in particular by the rich relevant discussions on this conceptual question at previous sessions of the Working Group, and has taken careful note of the extensive edge of views between Governments and indigenous people at the first session of the open-ended inter-sessional Working Group of the Commission established An accordance with the above-mentioned resolution, which took place An Geneva from 20 November-1 December 1995.[2] The Chairperson-Rapporteur was fortunately able to participate in the deliberations and to address this Working Group, as an observer and in her capacity as Chairperson-Rapporteur of the Working Group on Indigenous Populations.

5. It should also be noted that the Chairperson-Rapporteur prepared a comprehensive note (E/CN.4/Sub.2/AC.4/1995/3) on criteria which might be applied when considering the concept of indigenous peoples which was submitted to the Working Group on Indigenous Populations at its thirteenth session. The basic criteria identified in the note included questions relating to historical continuity, distinctive cultural characteristics, traditional lands, non-dominance, self-identification and group consciousness. The Chairperson-Rapporteur also mentioned in the note para. 7) that the attendance at the Working Group of certain persons

describing themselves as "indigenous peoples" had been challenged by other indigenous peoples' representatives in the Working Group.

6. The Chairperson-Rapporteur also raised the question of the desirability of a definition of the concept "indigenous people". She, and others, pointed out that the Working Group itself had been a success despite not having adopted any formal definition of "indigenous people". That forum had none the less become, in the view of almost all the participants, the major meeting point in the United Nations system for representatives of observer Governments, indigenous peoples intergovernmental and non-governmental organizations and other interested individuals, in particular members of the academic family - a real "community of peoples", as the Chairperson-Rapporteur called it. It was also contributing, systematically and constructively, to the promotion, protection and realization of the rights of the world's indigenous peoples.

7. Notwithstanding these observations, the Chairperson-Rapporteur expressed, inter alia, the view that some discussions regarding in particular a further analysis of the concept of "indigenous people" might be desirable both as a response to the growing interest of Governments and indigenous peoples themselves and as a "guide" for the United Nations system, in particular in the field of the implementation of international instruments relating to the promotion and protection of the rights of indigenous peoples.

8. In elaborating the present working paper the Chairperson-Rapporteur also took into consideration the examination of this question by the Special Rapporteur of the Sub-Commission, Mr. M. Alfonso Martinez, in his second progress report on the study on treaties, agreements and other constructive arrangements between States and indigenous populations

9. The following analysis of the concept of "indigenous people" is of a preliminary nature, and has the principal aim of promoting a more focused discussion of this question by the interested parties at the fourteenth session of the Working Group, as well as at the open-ended working group of the Commission. As further explained below, it is the considered opinion of the Chairperson-Rapporteur that the concept of "indigenous" is not capable of a precise, inclusive definition which can be applied in the same manner to all regions of the world. However, greater agreement may be achieved with respect to identifying the principal factors which have distinguished "indigenous peoples" from other groups in the practice of the United Nations system and regional intergovernmental organizations. The Chairperson-Rapporteur has accordingly devoted a part of this working paper to a historical review of international practice, in an attempt to extract, inter alia, recurring conceptual elements or themes.

I. Historical Review of International Practice

10. It should be acknowledged at the outset that the international discussion of the concept of "indigenous" evolved, from the late nineteenth century until

the establishment of the Working Group in 1982,[3] within the framework of European languages, notably English, Spanish, and German. English and Spanish share a common root in the Latin term indigenae, which was used to distinguish between persons who were born in a particular place and those who arrived from elsewhere (advenae). The French term autochtone has, by comparison, Greek roots and, like the German term Ursprung, suggests that the group to which it refers was the first to exist in the particular location. Hence, the semantic roots of the terms historically used in modern international law share a single conceptual element: priority in time.

11. A fruitful starting point for the consideration of international practice is the Berlin Africa Conference of 1884-1885, convened by the Great Powers with the aim of agreeing on principles for the assertion and recognition of their territorial claims in Africa. In article 6 of the Final Act of the Conference, the Great Powers made a commitment to the "protection of indigenous populations" of Africa. In this legal context, the term "indigenous" was meant to distinguish between citizens of nationals of the Great Powers and those persons in Africa who were under the colonial domination of the Great Powers. It should be born in mind that there was an implicit element of race in the use of the term "indigenous", as well. When the British Empire subjected the Dutch settlers in South Africa to British rule following the Boer War, for example, it was never conceived that article 6 of the Final Act was applicable to them.

A. League of Nations

12. In accordance with Article 22 of the Covenant of the League of Nations the Members of the League accepted as a "sacred trust of civilization" the duty of promoting the well-being and development of the "indigenous population" of those "colonies and territories" which remained under their control. Hence, the Covenant of the League of Nations also used the term "indigenous" to distinguish between colonial powers and peoples who were living under colonial domination. The Covenant added a second level of qualification, however, characterizing "indigenous populations" as "peoples not yet able to stand by themselves under the strenuous conditions of the modern world", as contrasted to more "advanced" societies. Both factors (that is, colonial domination and institutional capacity) were to be considered, under Article 22 of the Covenant, in determining the degree of supervision that was appropriate to particular territories and peoples.

13. The case of South Africa illustrates the meaning which attached to Article 22 of the Covenant, in the practice of the League. In 1919, South Africa was not yet an independent State. It was still a part of the British Empire and, albeit self-governing in its local or internal affairs, subordinate to the British Parliament in London. Nevertheless, the League entrusted South Africa with a mandate, under Article 22, over the territory and population of Namibia. Within the conceptual framework of the Covenant, Namibia was "indigenous", in contradistinction to

the "advanced" character of South Africa. The League did not conceive, however, that the African population of South Africa itself was "indigenous" in relation to recent Dutch and British settlers.

14. It is possible to identify one more important element of the evolving concept of "indigenous" in the case of South Africa. Article 22 of the Covenant was applied to *territories,* as demarcated by internationally recognized borders, rather than to peoples who could be distinguished by sociological, historical or political factors. Thus, Namibia, as a territory geographically defined by the Great Powers, was deemed to be "indigenous", while the African population within South Africa was not so considered.

B. Pan-American Union

15. Meanwhile, however, the Pan-American Onion, as the predecessor of the present-day Organization of American States, had begun to use the "indigenous" in a rather different manner. In its resolution XI of 21 December 1938, the Eighth International Conference of American States declared:

> "That the indigenous populations, as descendants of the first inhabitants of the lands which today form America, and in order to offset the deficiency in their physical and intellectual development, have a preferential right to the protection of the public authorities".

The objective of this preferential treatment was to be their "complete integration into the national life" of existing States. In this and subsequent official documents of the Pan-American Union, it should be noted that the terms "indigenous" and "Indian" were used interchangeably.

16. As a matter of regional practice in the Americas, therefore, the term "indigenous" was employed to identify marginalized or vulnerable ethnic, cultural, linguistic and racial groups within State borders, rather than the inhabitants of colonial territories that were distinct geographically from the administering Power.

C. Charter of the United Nations

17. The adoption of the Charter of the United Nations in 1945 did nothing to reconcile different usages of the term "indigenous" in international law. Article 73 of the Charter refers to "territories whose peoples have not yet attained a full measure of self-government", rather than "indigenous populations" as that term appears in the Covenant of the League of Nations. It was not until 15 December 1960 that the United Nations General Assembly, in resolution 1541 (XV), defined a "Non-Self-Governing Territory" for this purpose, using a two-tiered test. A territory which is "geographically separate and is distinct ethnically and/or culturally from the country administering it" falls, prima facie, under Article 73.

Evidence that the inhabitants suffer a "position or status of subordination" may be advanced to support this presumption, but is not required.

18. It has generally been presumed that the foregoing definition of a "Non-Self-Governing Territory", in respect to Article 73 of the Charter, is also applicable to the definition of "peoples" who are entitled to the exercise of the right of self-determination under common article 1 of the two International Covenants on Human Rights (hereinafter Covenants). However, the significance of the choice of the term "peoples", rather than "territories", by the drafters of the two Covenants should not be minimized. The shift from a geographical conception to a sociological one implies a broadening of the application of the principle of self- determination to include non-dominant groups within the boundaries of independent States.

19. Consistent with the foregoing analysis of the choice of the term "peoples" in the two Covenants, the 1970 Declaration on Principles of International Law concerning Friendly Relations and Cooperation among States in accordance with the Charter of the United Nations[4] prohibits the dismemberment of States "conducting themselves in compliance with the principle of equal rights and self-determination of peoples ... and thus possessed of a government representing the whole people belonging to the territory without distinction as to race, creed or velours. It would have been unnecessary to make such a qualification unless it was understood that the population of a State could consist of a number of "peoples", each possessing the right of self-determination. As the Chairperson-Rapporteur has analysed in her explanatory note concerning the draft declaration on the rights of indigenous peoples, the right of self-determination may be satisfied where a people enjoys an effective voice, through its own representatives, in the governing of a democratic State, and suffers no disadvantage or discrimination.

20. After the Second World War, by comparison, the term "indigenous" assumed the meaning it had previously been given by the Pan-American Onion, rather than the League of National The General Assembly, in resolution 275 (III) of 11 May 1949, recommended a study of the conditions of the "aboriginal population and other underdeveloped social groups" of the Americas, with a view to promoting their integration and development. Three years later, the Government of Belgium provoked a controversy by arguing that Article 73 of the Charter should be interpreted in the light of the concept of "indigenous" found in Article 22 of the Covenant of the League of Nations.[5] According to the delegation of Belgium, the reporting obligations of Article 73 applied not only to overseas colonies, but to "backward indigenous peoples" living within the borders of independent States in all regions of the world.

D. ILO Convention No. 107

21. The delegation of Belgium was not successful in bringing the concept of "indigenous peoples" into Article 73 of the Charter, but the ILO adopted the

Convention concerning the Protection and Integration of Indigenous and Other Tribal and Semi-Tribal Populations in Independent Countries, 1957 (No. 107). Article 1 of the Convention defines the term "tribal" in terms reminiscent of the League Covenant: their "social and economic conditions are at a less advanced stage" in comparison with their neighbours, and they live under separate laws, either of their own choosing or imposed by the State. Some "tribal" peoples, moreover, "are regarded as indigenous on account of their descent from the populations which inhabited the country, or a geographical region to which the country belongs, at the time of conquest or colonization" and remain socially, economically and culturally distinct.

22. In the terms set forth by Convention No. 107, then, both "tribal" and "indigenous" peoples are mainly characterized by social, cultural, economic, legal and institutional distinctiveness. Evidence of actual oppression or discrimination is not a criterion. The only factor that differentiates "indigenous" peoples from "tribal" peoples is a history of "conquest or colonization", but this distinction is of no practical consequence, since the Convention guarantees both categories of people exactly the same rights. According to Convention No. 107, all "indigenous" peoples are "tribal", but not all "tribal" peoples are "indigenous". Special rights attach equally to both groups. No advantage is gained by virtue of being "indigenous" in the sense of having been a victim, historically, of conquest or colonization. Hence, the source of rights is not (according to this ILO international instrument) a people's history of being conquered, colonized or oppressed, but its history of being distinct as a society or nation. 23. It is noteworthy that Convention No. 107 was not only ratified by 14 States in Latin America and 2 in Western Europe, but also by 11 States in Africa and Asia.

E. Study of the Problem of Discrimination against Indigenous Populations

24. In his monumental Study of the Problem of Discrimination against Indigenous Populations (E/CN.4/Sub.2/1986/7 and Add.1-4), the Special Rapporteur of the Sub-Commission, Mr. J. Martinez Cobo, offered a cautious, preliminary analysis of the concept of "indigenous" that reflects the fundamental elements already incorporated into article 1 of Convention No. 107.

> "Indigenous communities, peoples and nations are those which, having a historical continuity with pre-invasion and pre-colonial societies that developed on their territories, consider themselves distinct from other sectors of the societies now prevailing in those territories, or parts of them. They form at present non-dominant sectors of society and are determined to preserve, develop and transmit to future generations their ancestral territories, and their ethnic identity, as the basis of their continued existence as peoples, in accordance with their own cultural

patterns, social institutions and legal systems".[6]

25. This combines the element of distinctiveness, which characterizes both "indigenous" and "tribal" peoples according to article 1 of ILO Convention No. 107, with the element of colonialism, which in the Convention No. 107 is employed to differentiate "indigenous" from "tribal".

26. The Special Rapporteur proposed three additional elements for the concept of "indigenous", albeit in a way that suggests that these new elements are neither necessary nor sufficient to clarify a particular group. One element is "non-dominance at present", implying that some form of discrimination or marginalization exists, and justifies action by the international community. It would not follow, however, that a group ceases to be "indigenous" if, as a result of measures taken for the full realization of its rights, it were no longer non-dominant.

27. The Special Rapporteur referred also to the importance to the group of retaining a relationship with ancestral lands or territories, as well as the importance of ensuring that the distinctiveness of the group is voluntary, rather than imposed upon the group by the State. These two points were addressed when the ILO revised Convention No. 107.

F. ILO Convention No. 169

28. ILO Convention No. 107 has been revised and replaced by the Convention on Indigenous and Tribal Peoples in Independent Countries, 1989 (No. 169), which in article 1 has retained the distinction between "indigenous" and "tribal" peoples, while modifying the way in which these two terms are defined.[7] "Tribal peoples" are peoples "whose social, cultural and economic conditions distinguish them from other sections of the national community, and whose status is regulated wholly or partially by their own customs or traditions or by special laws or regulations". This formulation embraces the factor of "distinctiveness" as it appeared in ILO Convention No. 107, but deletes any implication that tribal peoples are inferior or less "advanced". "Indigenous peoples" are now defined in terms of their distinctiveness, as well as their descent from the inhabitants of their territory "at the time of conquest or colonization or the establishment of present state boundaries" (emphasis supplied). The addition of the underlined phrase has the effect of minimizing any logical differences between the concepts of "indigenous" and "tribal", since both concepts are now chiefly defined by the extent to which the group in question constitutes a distinct society.

29. The only concrete remaining difference between the definition of "indigenous" and "tribal" in ILO Convention No. 169 relates essentially to the principle of self-determination. A people may be "tribal", either by its own choice (that is, by maintaining its own laws and customs), or without its consent (as a result of special legal status imposed by the State). A people may be classified as "indigenous" only if it so chooses by perpetuating its own distinctive institutions and

identity.

30. Even this residual distinction appears to be vitiated by article 1.2 of the Convention, which provides that "self-identification" shall be a fundamental criterion when determining the status of particular groups.[8] In other words, the only objective or extrinsic criterion of the "indigenous" or "tribal" character of a group is distinctiveness. The remaining criterion is subjective: the choice of the group to be and remain distinct, which is an exercise of self-determination.

31. Like ILO Convention No. 107, moreover, Convention No. 169 accords the same rights to "indigenous" and "tribal" peoples, further eroding the usefulness of distinguishing between these categories of peoples.

32. It may justifiably be stated that, after two rounds of exhaustive negotiations on the problem of definition, first in 1957 and again 1988-1989, the ILO did not achieve greater semantic precision, but on the contrary succeeded only in merging the definition of "indigenous" and "tribal" into a single broad test of distinctiveness.

33. The draft inter-American declaration on the rights of indigenous peoples, prepared by the inter-American Commission on Human Rights for consideration by the General Assembly of the Organization of American States, adopts the conceptual approach of ILO Convention No. 169, defining "indigenous peoples" as descendants of the earliest inhabitants of the country.[9] Interestingly, however, the draft inter-American declaration suggests that cultural distinctiveness - the central element of the ILO definition of "tribal" - provides an alternative basis for establishing that a group is "indigenous". If adopted, this instrument would combine "indigenous" and "tribal", as defined in the above-mentioned ILO Conventions, into one concept, with two alternative tests.

34. The United Nations Development Programme (UNDP) has prepared draft guidelines for support to indigenous peoples.[10] Draft guidelines 4, 5 and 6 refer to the definition of indigenous peoples. In these draft guidelines mention is made, inter alia, to the fact that despite certain characteristics common to the world's indigenous peoples, no single accepted definition of indigenous peoples exists which captures their diversity. Therefore, "self-identification" as indigenous or tribal is usually regarded as a fundamental criterion for determining whether groups are indigenous or tribal, sometimes in combination with other variables such as language spoken and geographic location or concentration. These draft guidelines adopt the definition of ILO Convention No. 169.

G. Indigenous peoples' point of view

35. Indigenous representatives on several occasions have expressed the view, before the Working Group that a definition of the concept of "indigenous people" is not necessary or desirable. They have stressed the importance of self-identification as an essential component of any definition which might be elaborated by the United Nations system. In addition, a number of other elements were noted

by indigenous representatives, in particular during the thirteenth session of the Working Group.[11] For example, the Aboriginal and Torres Strait Islander Social Justice Commissioner, Mr. M. Dodson, stated: "there must be scope for self-identification as an individual and acceptance as such by the group. Above all and of crucial and fundamental importance is the historical and ancient connection with lands and territories. ...". A number of other indigenous representatives referred to the working definition developed by the Special Rapporteur, Mr. Martinez Cobo.[12] The representative of the Sami Council, for example, stated that "even without a definition it should be relatively easy to identify the beneficiaries (of the draft declaration) by using the criteria of the Cobo report which is adequate to determine whether a person or community is indigenous or not. Factors such as historical continuity, self-identification and group membership are cardinal criteria in this regard".

36. As mentioned earlier, indigenous groups insist on their right to define themselves both in terms of an individual's "self-identification" as an indigenous person and with respect to the community's right to define its members. This "subjective" approach – that indigenous peoples are those who feel themselves to be indigenous and are accepted as such by members of the group - has been widely supported, although it is not clear whether it would be sufficient if other "objective" criteria, such as ancestry, were absent.[13] The Human Rights Committee, in addressing this question, especially in connection with the Sandra Lovelace case, has found that denial of the legal right of an Indian woman to reside on the Indian Tobique Reserve, in Canada, because of her marriage to a non-Indian violated her right, "in community with the other members of her group", to enjoy her own culture as guaranteed by article 27 of the International Covenant on Civil and Political Rights. The Human Rights Committee did not directly address the issue of whether the author of the communication, Ms. Lovelace, had lost her status as an Indian. Nevertheless, it has implicitly decided that she remained a part of the Maliseet Indian band from which she came. The case of Sandra Lovelace was considered in the light of the fact that her marriage to a non-Indian has broken up. There was no evidence that the above-mentioned Indian band objected to her residing on the reserve.[14]

37. Article 27 of the Covenant has also been invoked by indigenous people. In this respect, it should be mentioned, for example, that in 1980, an Aboriginal delegation addressed the Sub-Commission on the Australian Government's failure to protect a sacred site on Aboriginal leasehold land at Noonkanbah from the Western Australian Government's insistence that exploratory drilling for oil should proceed.[15] Another case concerning Canadian Indians (communication No. 167/1984, BERNARD OMINAYAK, CHIEF OF THE LUBICON LAKE BAND V. CANADA). raised issues before the Human Rights Committee under article 27 of the Covenant with respect to the traditional rights to fishing and hunting, as well as issues of self-determination under article 1 of the Covenant. In

its review of this case, the Committee did, inter alia, find a violation of article 27. It recognized "that the rights protected by article 27, include the rights of persons, in community with others, to engage in economic and social activities which are part of the culture of the community to which they belong".[16]

38. It should be also mentioned that some indigenous representatives from Asia stated that, in view of the establishment of the new working group of the Commission on Human Rights, a formal definition was urgently needed to prevent Governments from denying the existence of indigenous peoples in their countries.[17]

H. Views expressed by governments

39. The representatives of the observer Governments of Bangladesh and India emphasized the need for a clear definition of "indigenous people" in the interest of an effective focus on the true indigenous people of the world. The representative of the observer Government of Bangladesh stated in particular that a procedure based on self-identification could be self-defeating and that it would be a great disservice to the true indigenous people if the agenda for indigenous people were allowed to be confused with the agenda of other subnational and tribal groups that constituted minorities within their respective countries.

I. Views expressed by members of the Working Group

40. Mr. R. Hatano, member of the Working Group, in one of his statements before the Sub-Commission regarding in particular the draft declaration on the rights of indigenous peoples, expressed the following views in connection with the definition of the concept "indigenous people": "...Even if [the declaration] was not a binding legal instrument, it none the less sets out the rights of indigenous peoples and the duties of States towards these peoples. However, nowhere did the declaration define the key expression 'indigenous people'. Apparently, indigenous organizations did not want the term to be defined for fear some indigenous persons would not be covered by the scope of the definition. However, such organizations had repeatedly affirmed that the world's population included approximately 300 million indigenous persons. How had they arrived at that figure without some yardstick or definition to distinguish between indigenous and non-indigenous persons?[18]

41. Mr. J. Bengoa, alternate member of the Working Group, stated that regarding the development of a concept of indigenous people, the discussion clearly had two sides: a theoretical one and a political one. Also, there was a difficult linguistic problem in view of the usage of the words "populations" and "peoples". The draft declaration which had been approved by the Sub-Commission used both words without making a clear distinction between them. A definition of the concept of "indigenous peoples" could be an important step towards the recogni-

tion of indigenous peoples and their rights and could well serve to make the very important distinction between indigenous groups and minorities. In that regard, the difference between defining peoples and establishing procedures to exercise the right of self-identification should be made. The procedures to exercise the right of self-identification had to have the following characteristics: first, they had to be operational in order to serve international objectives and in particular allow an understanding of the many different cultures; second, they had to be functional to allow participation of the indigenous peoples; third, they had to be flexible in order to be able to respond to new situations in the dynamic process of recognizing indigenous peoples' rights. Mr Bengoa stressed the fact that the principle of self-identification is inalienable and has to be part of the definition. The characteristic of being the first people and the strong ties to the land also constituted important elements of a possible definition. He pointed out the inherent danger of a requirement of historic continuity, as many indigenous peoples had been forcibly removed from their lands or were now living in urban areas but had kept their indigenous identity. Also, he stated that the element of having been subjected to colonization needed further discussion, as it seemed to reflect mainly the situations faced by indigenous groups in the Americas. The element of distinct culture which was recognized by all existing definitions should not constitute a decisive feature in order to allow for a more dynamic approach, taking into account processes of change in indigenous societies. Furthermore, he regarded the characteristic of non-dominance as an empirical reality but not necessarily a substantive feature.[19]

II. Critical Legal Analysis

A. Comparison with "Non-Self-Governing Territories"

42. It will be recalled that in General Assembly resolution 1541 (XV) the Assembly had defined "Non-Self-Governing Territories" in terms of three fundamental factors: cultural distinctiveness, geographic separateness, and actual subordination. The evolving concept of "indigenous" overlaps with the formal definition of "Non-Self-Governing Territories" with respect to the first factor (distinctiveness). We have seen that subordination, while suggested as a possible element of a definition in the Martinez Cobo study, was not included in the definition adopted by the ILO conventions in this field, although marginalization and oppression are unquestionably shared experiences of most indigenous peoples. It does not seem logical, moreover, that the presence or absence of oppression should be a factor distinguishing indigenous peoples from others heaving experienced so-called classic colonialism.

43. The third factor, geographic separateness, also merits a critical re-examination. The Special Rapporteur, Mr. Martinez Cobo, recognized that indigenous peoples tend to be characterized by their maintaining special relationship" with

their "ancestral territories". Although ILO Convention No. 169 does not include any geographical factor in its definition of "indigenous", it none the less affirms, in article 13, the "special importance" of the continuing relationship between indigenous peoples and their ancestral territories for continuing their "cultures and spiritual values". In other words, the cultural distinctiveness of indigenous peoples, which is central to the concept of "indigenous" in contemporary international law, is inseparable from "territory".

44. The inseparability of cultural distinctiveness and territory from the concept of "indigenous" was noted by the United Nations Conference on Environment and Development in paragraph 26.1 of Agenda 21, adopted by a consensus of Member States:

> "Indigenous people and their communities have a historical relationship with their lands and are generally descendants of the original inhabitants of those lands".[20]

45. The centrality of land tenure systems and ecological knowledge to the cultures of indigenous peoples was reaffirmed, again by consensus, at the International Conference on Population and Development at Cairo in 1994.[21]

46. The *World Bank Operational Manual* also identifies "a close attachment to ancestral territories and to the natural resources in these areas" as one of five factors which, in varying degrees, tend to characterize "indigenous peoples".[22]

B. Comparison with "minorities"

47. Acknowledging the significance of "territory" may be necessary to address another major logical and conceptual problem: differentiating "indigenous peoples" from "minorities". A strict distinction must be made between "indigenous rights" and "minority rights". Indigenous peoples are indeed peoples and not minorities or ethnic groups.[23]

48. The Permanent Court of International Justice (P.C.I.J.) did not define the concept "minority" but made an attempt to provide the meaning of the concept of "community" in the Greco-Bulgarian Communities case as follows:

> "...a group of persons living in a given country or locality having a race, religion, language and traditions of their own, and united by this identity of race, religion, language and traditions in a sentiment of solidarity, with a view to preserving their traditions, maintaining their form of worship, securing the instruction and upbringing of their children in accordance with the spirit and tradition of their race and mutually assisting one another.[24]

49. The above-mentioned formula contains four main elements: (a) biological distinctiveness; (b) cultural distinctiveness (religion, language, traditions); (c) the choice or desire to remain distinct (which may be implied in the perpetuation of the cultural distinctiveness of the group); and (d) social cohesiveness (which may be implied from the fact that the group seeks a recognition of its collective rights). The racial factor is, of course, no longer admissible as a matter of law or science.

50. The meaning of the concept of "minority" provided by the P.C.I.J. may therefore be collapsed into the same concept that lies at the heart of all recent attempts to define "indigenous" - that is, a distinctiveness which the people concerned wish to perpetuate.

51. In his important *Study on the Rights of Persons Belonging to Ethnic, Religious and Linguistic Minorities,* the Special Rapporteur of the Sub-Commission, Mr. F. Capotorti, argued that the size and power of a group are important considerations in determining whether it should be an object of special international protection. A "minority" from the viewpoint of sociology, he reasoned, is not necessarily the same as a "minority" within the context of international human rights law. From his perspective, he proposed the following definition:

> "A group numerically inferior to the rest of the population of a State, in a non-dominant position. whose members - being nationals of the State - possess ethnic, religious or linguistic characteristics differing from those of the rest of the population and show, if only implicitly, a sense of solidarity, directed towards preserving their culture, traditions, religion or language.[25]

52. Thus defined, a group must not only lack political power, but lack the numerical strength ever to gain power through democratic means, before it qualifies as a "minority". An oppressive group that constitutes a numerical minority of the national population would, accordingly, not qualify as a "minority", but in such as case the State concerned would not be entitled to invoke national unity and territorial integrity against legitimate national liberation movements.

53. At the request of the Sub-Commission, Mr. J. Deschenes made a great effort to improve upon the definition of "minority" but reached essentially the same conclusions as Mr. Capotorti. Be suggested one refinement that merits our attention, however. This was to place greater weight on the element of choice, since there would seem to be no need to be concerned with groups that did not wish to be protected, or to maintain their distinct identity as groups.[26]

54. In a more recent study, the Special Rapporteur of the Sub-Commission, Mr. A. Eide, was also inspired by the definition proposed by Mr. Capotorti, although he concluded that the size of the group and its distinctiveness are sufficient as tests of its character as a minority, thereby abandoning the element of non-dominance.[27]

55. At its first session in 1995, the new Working Group on Minorities of the Sub-Commission considered the possibility of elaborating a more precise definition of "minority" but the debate merely underscored the futility of such an endeavour, and the Working Group proceeded to discuss practical means of protecting minorities without agreeing on a definition.[28]

56. At the second session of the Working Group on Minorities a member, Mr. S. Chernichenko, presented a working paper on the definition of minorities (E/CN.4/Sub.2/AC.5/1996/WP.1 and Corr.1), in which he proposed a new definition of minorities. In this respect, he emphasized, inter alia, that his definition did not extend to indigenous populations and that the tasks of the Working Group on Minorities did not include the development of any definition of indigenous populations (para. 7).

57. The Human Rights Committee in its General Comment No. 23 (50) (art. 27) observes that "culture manifests itself in many forms, including a particular way of life associated with the use of land resources, specially in the case of indigenous peoples. That right may include such traditional activities as fishing or hunting and the right to live in reserves protected by law".[29] In any event, the "working definition" included in the Capotorti study does not help distinguish between the concepts of "indigenous" and "minority" since most groups that regard themselves as indigenous peoples could satisfy its tests.

58. The task of clarifying the concept of "indigenous" is accordingly complicated by the fact that the United Nations has previously failed to devise reasonably precise definitions of "peoples" or "minorities".[30]

59. Since the three concepts "indigenous", "peoples" and "minorities" are logically and legally related, it would be necessary to refine all of them simultaneously, lest our efforts to clarify the concept of "indigenous" add to the existing uncertainty in the meaning of the other related concepts.

C. The search for factors specific to "indigenous"

60. It is none the less possible to identify at least two factors which have never been associated with the concept of "minorities": priority in time and attachment to a particular territory. These factors do not, however, help to distinguish between the concept of "indigenous" and the concept of "peoples", since "peoples" are also ordinarily identified with a distinct territory to which they have a claim of historical precedence. In other words, it is possible to find points of differentiation between "indigenous" and "minority", but not between "indigenous" and "peoples", based upon the efforts of international organizations to define these terms in this century.

61. This is an appropriate stage at which to review the discussion of these issues by participants at the first meeting of the working group of the Commission on Human Rights which was established by resolution 1995/32. Several delegations of Member States maintained that it was essential to adopt a definition of

the concept "indigenous" before negotiating the substantive provisions of a declaration on the rights of these people. Some delegations, moreover, reasoned that the concept of "indigenous" is applicable only to situations in which the original inhabitants of the territory were subjugated and physically dispossessed by settlers from overseas, bearing alien cultures and values, and where these settlers, rather than the original inhabitants, have been the real beneficiaries of decolonization and independent statehood. These circumstances, the same delegations contend, have largely been restricted historically to the Americas and Oceania.

62. Further, in adopting its report, the working group stipulated that it was "solely a record of the debate and does not imply acceptance of the usage of either expression 'indigenous peoples' or 'indigenous people,. In this report both are used without prejudice to the positions of the particular delegations, where divergences of approach remain" (E/CN.4/1996/84, para. 3).

63. The advisability and feasibility of adopting a definition of the concept of "indigenous" may reasonably be judged from the conceptual framework proposed by concerned delegations. The definition which has been suggested differs in only one concrete aspect from the conceptual model presented in the Martinez Cobo study or the two ILO conventions in this field: conquest, colonization, subjugation or discrimination must be at the hands of persons from other regions of the world rather than neighbours. In the opinion of the Chairperson-Rapporteur, this makes an unjustified distinction between long-distance aggression and short-distance aggression, and it is logically impossible to establish a cut-off distance. Moreover, it assumes that the cultural differences that exist between peoples in a simple linear function of distance, such that mere proximity creates a presumption of shared values. The information provided to the Working Group on Indigenous Populations each year contradicts the validity of that assumption.

64. Underlying the arguments made by many observer Government delegations is a conceptual critique of the use of the term "indigenous" to distinguish between groups that have been neighbours for millennia. To the extent that the English and Spanish terms which are currently in official use in the United Nations system imply a distinction between persons originating in a country, as opposed to immigrants or settlers, the unease of many African and Asian Governments is understandable. Plainly, most of the persons who have control of the contemporary State are not less native to the soil of the country as a whole than groups that are identified as "indigenous" or "tribal". It should be pointed out, however, that this conceptual difficulty disappears if we think of "indigenous" peoples as groups which are native to their own specific ancestral territories within the borders of the existing State, rather than persons that are native generally to the region in which the State is located.

65. The purpose of the present document is not to minimize the concerns expressed by some Governments, but to demonstrate that their concerns cannot effectively be met through an exercise in definition. The result of undertaking such

an exercise would be a definition which lacked any scientific or logical credibility, thereby undermining (in turn) the credibility and usefulness of the declaration of principles to which it was attached.

III. Conclusions and Recommendations

66. It is an encouraging fact that Governments in the Latin American region have expressed confidence in their understanding of the meaning of "indigenous" in their own regional context, rendering an explicit, negotiated definition of this concept largely unnecessary. The Chairperson-Rapporteur is cognizant of the fact that, even in the Americas, disputes have often arisen regarding the "indigenous" status of particular groups. Within the United States, for example, more than 100 groups are still seeking formal acknowledgement of their status as "Indian tribes", under a 1978 law identifying seven historical and sociological criteria applicants must satisfy with scientific evidence.[31]

67. In practical terms, then, it would be foolhardy to disregard both the regional and the national dimensions of the concept of "indigenous" Regional research and consultations would be extremely useful for this purpose and, in the future, differences in practice must be recognized as long as they are broadly consistent with regional and international expert opinion. Where disputes occur, they should be addressed in the same way as other disputes involving both factual and legal issues in the field of human rights, that is to say, through a constructive dialogue between expert bodies and the representatives of indigenous peoples and Governments.

68. At its second and third sessions, the Working Group on Indigenous Populations discussed the definition of the concept of "indigenous" at great length, using the work of the Special Rapporteur as a point of departure.[32] No consensus was reached, but indigenous people who participated in these discussions stressed the need for flexibility and for respecting the desire and the right of each indigenous people to define itself. From that time the Working Group has indeed adopted a flexible approach to determining eligibility to participate in its annual sessions, relying upon organizations of indigenous peoples themselves to draw attention to any improper assertions of the right to participate as "indigenous" peoples. On the whole, this has been successful, and shows that the gradual evolution of the concept of "indigenous" in practice, and in cooperation with indigenous peoples themselves, is sufficiently practical and effective as a method of screening the claims of groups whose legal character may be challenged.

69. In summary, the factors which modern international organizations and legal experts (including indigenous legal experts and members of the academic family), have considered relevant to the understanding of the concept of "indigenous" include:

(a) Priority in time, with respect to the occupation and use of a specific territory;

(b) The voluntary perpetuation of cultural distinctiveness, which may include the aspects of language, social organization, religion and spiritual values, modes of production, laws and institutions;

(c) Self-identification, as well as recognition by other groups, or by State authorities, as a distinct collectivity; and

(d) An experience of subjugation, marginalization, dispossession, exclusion or discrimination, whether or not these conditions persist.

70. The foregoing factors do not, and cannot, constitute an inclusive or comprehensive definition. Rather, they represent factors which may be present, to a greater or lesser degree, in different regions and in different national and local contexts. As such, they may provide some general guidance to reasonable decision-making in practice.

71. The United Nations system should be mindful of the conclusion of the managers of the World Bank that "no single definition can capture (the) diversity" of indigenous peoples worldwide.[33] It would also be wise to heed the words of the Special Rapporteur, Mr. Capotorti, who warned that precise universal definition, while of philosophical interest, would be nearly impossible to attain in the current state of global realities, and would in any event not contribute perceptibly to the practical aspects of defending groups from abuse.[34]

72. In presenting this analysis, the Chairperson-Rapporteur wishes to stress that she can find no satisfactory reasoning for distinguishing between "indigenous" and "tribal" peoples in the practice or precedents of the United Nations. Nor is she persuaded that there is any distinction between "indigenous" peoples, and "peoples" generally, other than the fact that the groups typically identified as "indigenous" have been unable to exercise the right of self-determination by participating in the construction of a contemporary nation-State.

73. The Chairperson-Rapporteur is compelled to conclude that any inconsistency or imprecision in previous efforts to clarify the concept of "indigenous" was not a result of a lack of adequate scientific or legal analysis, but due to the efforts of some Governments to limit its globality, and of other Governments to build a high conceptual wall between Indigenous and "peoples" and/or "Non-Self-Governing Territories". No one has succeeded in devising a definition of "indigenous" which is precise and internally valid as a philosophical matter, yet satisfies demands to limit its regional application and legal implications. All past attempts to achieve both clarity and restrictiveness in the same definition have in fact resulted in greater ambiguity.

74. The only immediate solution, based on the experience of the Working Group on Indigenous Populations, is a procedural one: we must ensure that the eventual implementation of a declaration on the rights of indigenous peoples is

entrusted to a body which is fair-minded and open to the views of indigenous peoples and Governments, so that there is room for the reasonable evolution and regional specificity of the concept of "indigenous" in practice.

Notes

[1] E/CN.4/Sub.2/1995/24, para. 162.

[2] See E/CN.4/1996/84.

[3] The creation of the Working Group on Indigenous Populations was recommended by the Sub-Commission on Prevention of Discrimination and Protection of Minorities in its resolution 2 (XXXIV) of 8 September 1981, endorsed by the Commission on Human Rights in its resolution 1982/19 of 10 March 1982, and authorized by the Economic and Social Council in its resolution 1982/34 of 7 May 1982.

[4] General Assembly resolution 2625 (XXV) of 24 October 1970, annex.

[5] See A/2361 (1952).

[6] E/CN.4/Sub.2/1986/7/Add.4, United Nations Publication, Sales No. E.86.XIV.3, para. 379.

[7] In connection with the definition employed in ILO Convention No. 169, see, I. Brownlie, "Treaties and Indigenous Peoples". *The Robb Lectures,* F.M. Brookfield (ed.), Clarendon Press, Oxford, 1992, pp. 60-67. For an analysis of the provisions of this Convention, see R.L. Barsh, "An Advocate's Guide to the Convention on Indigenous and Tribal Peoples", 15 *Oklahoma University Law Review* 209 (1990), L. Swepston, "A New Step in the International Law on Indigenous and Tribal Peoples: ILO Convention No 169 of 1989", 15 *Oklahoma University Law Review* 677 (1990) and S.J. Anaya, "Indigenous Rights Norms in Contemporary International Law", *Arizona Journal of International and Comparative Law,* vol. 8, No. 2, Fall 1991, pp 6-15.

[8] So formulated, art. 1.2 of ILO Convention No. 169 provides that "self-identification" should be given great weight, although it is not sufficient in itself.

[9] OEA/Ser/L/V/II.90, Doc. 9 rev. 1 (21 September 1995).

[10] Guidelines for Support to Indigenous Peoples, United Nations Development Programme, Draft V, January 1995. These draft Guidelines should be adopted by the Executive Board of UNDP.

[11] See E/CN.4/Sub.2/1995/24, para. 41-51.

[12] Ibid., para. 29-32.

[13] See H. Hannum, "New Developments in Indigenous Rights", *Virginia Journal of International Law,* vol. 28, No. 3, Spring 1988, p. 663.

[14] Communication No. R.6/24, SANDRA LOVELACE V. CANADA, in *Official Records of the General Assembly, Thirty-sixth Session, Supplement No. 40 (A/36/40),* annex XVIII. For a comprehensive analysis of the relevant Views, expressed by the Human Rights Committee, see G. Alfredsson and A. de Zayas, "Minority Rights: Protection by the United Nations", *Human Rights Law Journal* 26 February 1993, vol. 14, No. 1-2, pp. 5-6.

[15] H. McRae, G. Nettheim and L. Beacroft, *Aboriginal Legal Issues,* The Law Book Company Limited, Sydney, 1991, p.320.

[16] Ibid., *Forty-fifth Session Supplement No. 40 (A/45/40),* vol. II, annex IX, para 32.2.

[17] E/CN.4/Sub.2/1995/24, para. 41.

[18] E/CN.4/Sub.2/1992/SR.31/Add.1, para. 36.

[19] See E/CN.4/Sub.2/1995/24, paras. 45-51.

[20] *Record of the United Nations Conference on Environment and Development* (Rio de Janeiro, 3-4 June 1992), vol. I, resolution 1, annex II. United Nations Publication, Sales No. E.93.I.8. See also chapter 26 of Agenda 21 on "Recognizing and strengthening the role of indigenous people and their communities".

[21] A/CONF.171/13, para. 6.27.

[22] Operational Directive 4.20, para. 5 (a), September 1991. Other factors listed are self-identification, a distinct language, customary social and political institutions, and a subsistence-oriented economy.

[23] E.-I. A. Daes, "On the Relations Between Indigenous Peoples and States", *Without Prejudice,* vol. III, p. 44.

[24] See Greco-Bulgarian Communities (Advisory Opinion), P.C.I.J. Series B. No. 17, p. 22 (31 July 1930). In this respect, see also P. Thornberry, "The UN Declaration on the Rights of Persons Belonging to National or Ethnic, Religious and Linguistic Minorities: Background, Analysis, Observations, and an Update", *Universal Minority Rights,* A. Phillips and A. Rosas (eds.), Abo Akademi University Institute for Human Rights, 1995, pp. 16-17.

[25] F. Capotorti, *Study on the Rights of Persons Belonging to Ethnic, Religious and Linguistic Minorities,* United Nations publication, Sales No. E.91.XIV.2, Geneva, 1991, para. 568.

[26] E/CN.4/Sub.2/1985/31, paras. 74 and 181.

[27] E/CN.4/Sub.2/1993/34, para. 29.

[28] E/CN.4/Sub.2/1996/2, paras. 76-90.

[29] CCPR/C/21/Rev.1/Add.5. See in particular para. 7.

[30] For an analysis of the meaning of the concepts "indigenous", "peoples" and "minorities", see M.N. Shaw, "The Definition of Minorities in International Law", *Israel Yearbook on Human Rights,* vol. 20 (1991) pp. 13-43; E.-I.A. Daes, "Some Considerations on the Right of Indigenous Peoples to Self-Determination", *Transnational Legal and Contemporary Problems,* vol. 3 (1993), pp. 2-11; Daes, "Dilemmas Posed by the UN Draft Declaration on the Rights of Indigenous Peoples", *Nordic Journal of International Law,* 63:205-212 (1994); Daes, "The United Nations Declaration on Minority Rights: Necessary, Urgent and Overdue", *International Geneva Yearbook,* vol. IX, 1995, in particular pp. 91-92; R.L. Barsh, "Indigenous Peoples in the 1990s: From Object to Subject of International Law?", *Harvard Human Rights Journal,* vol. 7, Spring 1994, in particular pp. 36-41 and 78-82; D. Sanders, "Indigenous Peoples at the United Nations" (on file with the author), September 1995, pp. 1-17; G. Alfredsson, "Group Rights, Preferential Treatment and the Rule of Law", Discussion Paper for Consultation on Group Rights at the University of Cambridge, Law and Society Trust, Colombo, August 1995, p. 21.

[31] See W.C. Canby, Jr., *American Indian Law* (second edition), St. Paul, Minn., West Publishing Co., 1988, pp. 5-8.

[32] E/CN.4/Sub.2/1983/22, paras. 109-119; E/CN.4/Sub.2/1984/20, paras. 99-110.

[33] *World Bank Operational Manual,* op. cit., Operational Directive 4.20 (1991).

[34] Capotorti, op. cit., paras. 561-562.

Who is Indigenous?

"Peoplehood" and Ethnonationalist Approaches to Rearticulating Indigenous Identity

Jeff J. Corntassel[1]

Reprinted from Nationalism and Ethnic Politics, Vol. 9, No. 1, Spring 2003, pp. 75-100. Published by Frank Cass, London[a]

Debate within global forums over establishing definitional standards for indigenous peoples versus an unlimited right of indigenous self-identification has exposed something of a dilemma over standard setting in international law. Requiring strict, definitional standards excludes some indigenous groups from the very protections they need, while reifying their identities. Yet failure to establish an accepted definition of indigenous peoples leads to host-state concerns over applying international legal instruments to the world's indigenous populations. After surveying indigenous definitions developed by academicians in the field of nationalism/international law as well as practitioners from IGOs and NGOs, it is determined that a balance between self-identification and establishing a working definition of indigenous peoples is possible. Utilizing a model of 'Peoplehood' refined by Holm, Pearson and Chavis (2003), the article presents a new working definition of indigenous peoples that is both flexible and dynamic.

The question of 'who is indigenous?' is best answered by indigenous communities themselves. As testament to this, 'self-identification' policies for indigenous nations have increasingly become an accepted international legal practice beginning in 1977, when the second general assembly of the World Council of Indigenous Peoples (WCIP) passed a resolution stating that 'only indigenous peoples could define indigenous peoples'.[2] Since that time, two of the most active global organizations promoting indigenous rights, the United Nations Working Group on Indigenous Populations (WGIP)[3] and the International Labor Organization (ILO),[4] have advocated an unlimited right to 'self-identification'[5] for indigenous peoples in order to counter possible actions of 'host' states[6] who might deny indigenous claims within their borders.

Despite the accepted practice of unlimited self-identification for indigenous peoples within global forums, states 'hosting' indigenous peoples[7] within their borders have generally contested such an open policy.[8] They claim that if standard setting is to continue, declarations and treaties concerning indigenous peoples must clearly define the people these global policies are designed to protect. Debate over establishing definitional standards versus an unlimited right of indigenous self-identification has exposed something of a dilemma over the construction of indigenous identity.[9]

On the one hand, requiring strict, definitional standards could exclude some indigenous groups from the very protections they need and would also conform to state-centric, bureaucratic decision-making practices, which are antithetical to most indigenous belief systems. As Kanien'kehaka (Mohawk) scholar Taiaiake Alfred points out, 'Demands for precision and certainty disregard the reality of the situation: that group identity varies with time and place.'[10] Additionally, establishing an indigenous/non-indigenous dichotomy may 'serve to mask the diversity of interests that indigenous people have, silence debate among indigenous peoples, and/or support arguments against greater self-determination.'[11] Finally, a strict definitional approach may obstruct the process of community-building, as nationalist scholar Anthony D. Smith asserts: 'A crucial element in the formation of nations is the process of self-identification as distinct cultural populations through naming and self-definition.'[12]

On the other hand, failure to establish an accepted definition of indigenous peoples could lead other ethnic groups to position themselves as 'indigenous' solely to obtain expanded international legal status and protections enumerated in both ILO treaty No.169 and the 'Draft Universal Declaration on the Rights of Indigenous Peoples'. This concern was expressed by indigenous participants at previous WGIP meetings, who reported 'that certain of the participants claiming status as indigenous were not in fact so'.[13] Recently, Afrikaner (South Africa) delegations, which are actually descendants of Dutch settlers who colonized the region, attended the WGIP meetings claiming to be 'indigenous', causing great concern among delegations who had legitimate claims to indigenous status.[14]

The dilemma over 'who is indigenous' has become increasingly politicized as indigenous peoples have attained a distinct legal standing under international law. Consequently, international organizations, host states, non-governmental organizations and researchers have each attempted to develop their own definitional standards of native peoples. Yet while a definitional debate has developed almost exclusively within enclaves of academia, indigenous organizations, and inter-governmental organizations, little discourse has taken place between these communities of experts regarding 'who is indigenous'. Thus, a proliferation of indigenous definitions by practitioners and academies has not fostered consensus or cumulative integration across disciplines and communities. As Maori scholar Manuhuia Barcham explains:

> Theorists and practitioners alike have created and reified an ahistorical idealization of the indigenous self whereby the constitution of oneself as an 'authentic' indigenous self has been conflated with special ahistorical assumptions concerning the nature of indigeneity, a process intricately linked to the continued subordination of difference to identity.[15]

Additionally, current conceptual and theoretical research on indigenous groups in the field of ethnonationalism tends to be ahistorical and reified when distinguishing indigenous from ethnonationalist groups. For example, the Minorities at Risk project, which is a comprehensive dataset examining the status of some 275 politically active ethnopolitical groups around the world, makes conceptual distinctions between ethnonationalist and indigenous groups in terms of whether or not they seek to establish their own independent state. As the above quote from Barcham suggests, such an approach may be ahistorical while prioritizing identity over cultural and political variance between indigenous groups.

Even indigenous scholars who understand the differences between indigenous peoples and other minority groups have developed conceptualizations of indigenous peoples that are incomplete. Therefore, previous theories on nationalism and identity, whether primordial or circumstantial, may help to inform how one approaches the conceptualizations of indigenous peoples. Additionally, interdisciplinary work stressing the concept of 'Peoplehood' may also lend insights to this conceptual discussion. I begin by surveying various definitions that have been proffered by academicians, indigenous organizations and intergovernmental organizations to highlight existing conceptual disparities. The final section of the article evaluates the prospects for conceptualizing 'who is indigenous' using the concept of peoplehood as a guide to reconceptualize native identity from an interdisciplinary, self-identification framework.

Academicians Define Indigenous

While there have been several scholarly works examining global indigenous rights, I will focus on indigenous definitions developed by the most prominent researchers in the social sciences given their high visibility and impact on the field. In her acclaimed work, *The Indigenous Voice in World Politics,* Franke Wilmer was among the first social scientists to systematically examine the global historical process of moral exclusion undertaken by Western powers against indigenous peoples.[16] She defines indigenous in its broadest sense as peoples:

1. With tradition-based cultures;
2. Who were politically autonomous before colonization;
3. Who, in the aftermath of colonization and/or decolonization, continue to struggle for the preservation of their cultural integrity, economic self-reliance, and political independence by resisting the assimilationist policies of nation-states.[17]

Establishing a list of core components of indigenous identity, such as the three above, allows for maximum flexibility when identifying the approximately 5,000 indigenous groups worldwide. However, the above referenced definition is so general that it is difficult to ascertain whether indigenous peoples are different in terms of their cultural worldviews and goals from other minority groups throughout the world. In a more recent article co-authored with Alfred, a revised version of Wilmer's original three-part definition corrects some of the earlier ambiguities:

1. They are descended from the original inhabitants of the geographic areas they continue to occupy, hence, they are aboriginal;
2. They wish to live in conformity with their continuously evolving cultural traditions;
3. They do not now control their political destiny, and consequently, are frequently subjected to policies arising from the cultural hegemony originally imposed by an 'outside' force.[18]

The above three-part definition emphasizes the importance of geographic homelands and evolving cultural traditions for indigenous peoples.[19] However, Part 3 narrowly focuses on their political destiny and implies that lack of 'control' is part of being indigenous. Also, there is no mention of group or collective rights stressed by indigenous peoples as well as specific cultural traditions, such as language and ceremonial cycles, which set them apart from other populations. On the other hand, this definition of indigenous peoples is broad enough to encompass the approximately 350 million indigenous peoples throughout the world. Indigenous scholars, such as Alfred and S. James Anaya, tend to advocate broad and inclusive definitions of indigenous groups in order to avoid de-emphasizing variation between and within groups. For example, Anaya refers to indigenous peoples as:

The living descendants of pre-invasion inhabitants of lands now dominated by others... They are *indigenous* because their ancestral roots are imbedded in the lands in which they live, or would like to live, much more deeply than the roots of more powerful sectors of society living on the same lands or in close proximity. Furthermore, they are *peoples* to the extent they comprise distinct communities with a continuity of existence and identity that links them to communities, tribes or nations of their ancestral past.[20]

Anaya's definition of indigenous peoples highlights the continued colonial domination of indigenous homelands as well as the ancestral roots of these 'pre-invasion inhabitants'. He also acknowledges indigenous peoples as distinct communities with extensive kinship networks, which clearly distinguishes them from minority groups. However, unlike the Alfred and Wilmer definition, there is little discussion of culture or distinct worldviews in Anaya's version. Overall, both Alfred/Wilmer and Anaya's definitions, while ultimately incomplete, are inclusive and demonstrate a strategic flexibility in terms of defining the world's indigenous peoples.

John Bodley, who is an anthropologist by training, develops an even more inclusive definition of indigenous peoples by simply describing them as 'a group of people who identify themselves with a specific, small-scale cultural heritage'.[21] Such an overly generalizable approach excludes key indigenous identifiers, such as ancestral homelands and cultural continuity. For other researchers in the social sciences, defining indigenous more rigorously becomes critical to operationalizing concepts of indigeneity and ethnonationalism in order to study 'people versus state' conflicts more systematically.

For example, Ted Gurr, an eminent scholar in international relations, first began work on his Minorities at Risk (MAR) project in 1988.[22] One of the most comprehensive and detailed datasets on ethnopolitical conflicts currently available, MAR has tracked the activities of 275 ethnopolitical groups from 1980 to 1999. After working extensively with Gurr's dataset, I found the utility of his conceptual scheme, which divides indigenous and ethnonationalist phenomenon into mutually exclusive categories, questionable. For Gurr, 'ethnonationalist' and 'indigenous' are distinctive classifications under the general heading of 'national peoples'. Indigenous peoples are defined as:

> Conquered descendants of earlier inhabitants of a region who live mainly in conformity with traditional social, economic, and cultural customs that are sharply distinct from those of dominant groups... Indigenous peoples who had durable states of their own prior to conquest, such as Tibetans, or who have given sustained support to modem movements aimed at establishing their own state, such as the Kurds, are classified as ethnonationalists, not indigenous peoples.[23]

Under Gurr's definition/operationalization of indigenous peoples, being 'conquered' and being dominated by another group are preconditions for indigenous status. However, not all indigenous peoples were conquered militarily by colonial powers. For example, treaty-making, rather than outright military conquest, took place in North America on a wide scale between colonial powers, such as Great Britain, Holland, and France, and the native peoples of Canada and the U.S.[24] Nor are all indigenous peoples non-dominant, even when they are numerical minorities within the host state, such as the native Fijians in Fiji, the Inuit peoples in the autonomous region of Nunavut (Canada) or the East Timorese peoples who recently realized their goal of statehood. Additionally, one can easily think of ethnonationalist groups, such as the Tamils (Sri Lanka), and Chechens (Russia) who are not dominant in their region but would not necessarily be considered indigenous.[25]

Differentiating ethnonationalists from indigenous peoples may be problematic when the distinction is based solely on the group's overarching group objectives. In general, indigenous peoples do seek greater self-rule as autonomous entities within the framework of their host state(s).[26] Gurr's conceptualization of indigenous becomes problematic when a group, such as the East Timorese, could conceivably stop being considered indigenous under the MAR coding scheme when they achieve independent statehood. For that matter, if a group even pursues statehood, as the Mohawk nation (Canada, U.S.) or Jumma (Chittagong Hill Tracts in Bangladesh) have advocated at various points in their history, they cease to be indigenous under a 'Minorities at Risk' classification. Such an approach de-emphasizes the historical continuity of native peoples within a given region. The MAR conceptual scheme also reifies groups as being the sum total of the demands put forward by ethnic kindred who may or may not accurately represent the greater indigenous population. In other words, indigenous peoples are identified according to the highest level of aggregation possible - i.e. 'Mayans' versus specific cultural communities within the Mayan family, such as Tzeltal, Tzotzil, Tojolobal, Mam etc. Nonetheless, the MAR dataset is one of the most comprehensive currently available and may be useful for examining particular causes of intrastate conflicts rather than indigenous community variation and historical struggles.

In a departure from the MAR methodology, political scientist Fred Riggs contends that a definition indigenous should include the following four variables:

1. Cultural level, ranging from primitive to more complex societies;
2. Historical sequence (age), who came first and who followed;
3. Political position (power), i.e. marginalized vs. dominant communities; and
4. Geographic area (place).[27]

Riggs's definitional scheme is somewhat consistent with Alfred/Wilmer and Anaya's, although his discussion of cultural factors appears to be narrowly based on an economic mode of production (i.e. Bodley), versus other critical factors, such as changing community values and traditions.

As the above definitions of indigenous illustrate, attempts to formulate a single, over-arching definition of this term have not been successful and may even be futile given indigenous inter- and intra-community differences worldwide. Additionally, strict definitional approaches, labelled 'positivist' by legal scholar Benedict Kingsbury, run the risk of reducing the 'fluidity and dynamism of social life to distorted and rather static formal categories'.[28] For Kingsbury, a more feasible alternative is something he terms a 'constructivist' approach, which:

> Takes the international concept of 'indigenous peoples' not as one sharply defined by universally applicable criteria, but as embodying a continuous process in which claims and practices in numerous specific cases are abstracted in the wider institutions of international society,

then made specific again at the moment of application in the political, legal and social processes of particular cases and societies.[29]

In order to avoid excluding peoples in Asia and other regions from claiming indigenous status, Kingsbury advocates maximum flexibility while establishing four 'essential requirements':

1. Self-identification as a distinct ethnic group;
2. Historical experience of, or contingent vulnerability to, severe disruption, dislocation or exploitation;
3. Long connection with the region;
4. The wish to retain a distinct identity.

In addition to the four essential requirements for indigenous status listed above, Kingsbury includes other relevant indicators may include 'nondominance', 'historical continuity', 'socioeconomic and sociocultural differences', 'characteristics such as language, race, and material or spiritual culture', and 'regarded as indigenous'. While each of the four essential requirements has a reasonable basis for inclusion, previous definitions which are also deemed inclusive and flexible have offered much stronger language in terms of outlining indigenous status. For example, indigenous peoples have asserted the right to self-determination or greater autonomy in international legal documents, such as the UN Draft Declaration, which is much more comprehensive and precise than Kingsbury's criterion regarding 'the wish to retain a distinct identity'. As former chairperson and Special Rapporteur of the WGIP, Erica-Irene Daes points out:

> For indigenous peoples everywhere in the world today, self-determination is the central tenet and main symbol of their movements. They demand that it be addressed squarely, and insist that it is not negotiable... On objective, ethnological or historical grounds, their position is strong.[30]

In this case, the right to self-determination denotes greater autonomy for indigenous communities on their traditional homelands, which may include, but is certainly not limited to, the right to 'retain a distinct identity'.

Furthermore, Kingsbury's identification of indigenous peoples as 'ethnic groups' diminishes their identity as nations. Lowell Barrington discusses this as a 'loose use' of terminology, given that 'a nation is more than an ethnic group'.[31] Nationalist scholar Walker Connor makes a further distinction, contending that ethnic groups are identified by 'outside' observers, such as anthropologists, while indigenous groups are self-defined. Until group members become aware of their cultural, political and ancestral uniqueness, they are an ethnic group and not a nation.[32] To stress their status as ethnic groups may diminish the importance of indigenous homeland claims and cultural practices by reducing them to 'placeless minorities within a state'.[33]

Given the above-referenced insights from nationalism scholars, previous conceptualizations of nations and their formation may inform contemporary debates over 'who is indigenous?' There appears to be a growing consensus in the nationalism literature over what a nation entails. For example, nations or ethnonationalist groups are commonly defined as 'a community of self-identifying people who believe they share a common ancestry, culture and a historically common territory'.[34] Similar to the controversy over how indigenous is defined, a disagreement exists between those scholars who view the nation a 'self-defined' and those who see the nation as 'other-defined'.[35] In this light, the question of 'when is a nation?' is just as important as 'what is a nation?'[36] With a convergence of recent findings on what a nation entails, how might nationalist researchers inform the debate regarding 'who is indigenous'?

Nationalism Research and Indigenous Identity

Nationalism researchers differ substantially over how nations come into existence. Consequently, two distinct lines of inquiry have developed to explain nationalist group formation, which may provide insights into indigenous identity. The first theoretical body of work, broadly known as the primordialist school,[37] posits that ethnic identity is the essential component leading to political and military separatism regardless of any social, political and economic context in which the group operates. While conditions of social, political, and economic discontent may precede separatist violence, only discontent founded on ethnically-driven symbols, such as language, speeches, religion, origin myths, or cultural practices, can precipitate separatist movements.[38]

Essentially, primordialists focus on the historical ties shared by the ethnic group and how affective symbols, such as political speeches and language use, may evoke deep, emotional responses within individuals and collectivities.[39] Primordialists generally assume that ethnicity's shared belief in a common ancestry and ability to govern social relations is a historical artifact. It is suggested that ethnic 'life attachments', such as kinship relations, religion, language, and social practices, are natural and provide the basis for 'easy affinity' with peoples from the same background.[40]

Perennialists, such as Anthony D. Smith (who falls within a primordialist classification), view ethnonationalist groups as recurring (and sometimes universal) entities that regroup and adapt throughout history, often forming as contemporary nations from an historically-conceived ethnic group. Applying a perennialist perspective to indigenous peoples seems logical given the existence of their distinct, cultural communities since time immemorial. For Anthony D. Smith, a nation can be said to exist if it exhibits the following five features:[41]

1. A collective proper name;
2. Myths and memories of communal history;
3. A common public culture;
4. Common laws and customs;
5. A historic territory or home land.

Smith would concede that the above five factors are broadly conceived, but his typology does neglect the importance of language and oral traditions while emphasizing the importance of written literature and legal codes, which are predominantly Euro-centric or non-indigenous constructs. Also, while the primordial approach can explain the persistence of ethnic identity over time, it does not adequately address the issue of why such identity can, and often does, change or fluctuate in its intensity.[42] In this case, why did indigenous rights claims intensify locally and globally during the 1970s and 1980s?

As a reaction to primordialist shortcomings, the constructivist or instrumentalist[43] school emerges.[44] In stark contrast to perennialist views of 'ethnicity as a given', instrumentalists claim that ethnonationalist movements form in reaction to state dominance of a particular group of people. In other words, ethnicity is capable of being invented. Rather than view ethnicity as a natural entity, instrumentalists maintain that national groups are social constructs formed in relation to peoples' immediate needs and their relationships with others. Group solidarity results from certain social circumstances, whether internal or external, which group members experience. These circumstances, ranging from relative deprivation to state repression, enhance group solidarity as individuals rationally select an ethnic identity to attain desired political, economic and social goals.[45] Ethnic identity only becomes resurgent when it is invoked by entrepreneurial political leaders in the instrumental pursuit of material benefits for group members.

> In discussing potential indigenous land claims, Hobsbawm describes how an 'invention of tradition' takes place within host states:

> Students of peasant movements know that a village's claim to some common land or right' 'by custom from time immemorial' often expresses not a historical fact, but the balance of forces in the constant struggle of village against lords or against other villages.[46]

According to Hobsbawm, 'all invented traditions, so far as possible, use history as a legitimator of action and cement of group cohesion'.[47] In addition to a created history, these communities are often 'imagined', whose creation is facilitated by market forces and communication technologies.[48] Thus, while understanding the nature of religious communities and historical remnants of previous communities can be useful for examining nation formation (i.e. primordialists), instrumentalists focus on contemporary societal conditions which prompt group mobilization.[49]

Based on the writings of the instrumentalists,[50] context matters when discussing ethnonationalist identity. For indigenous peoples, the nature of their political, economic and social relationship with the host state(s) may determine the duration and intensity of their claims for self-determination. It is no coincidence that the contemporary global indigenous rights claims and social movements had their origins in Western democracies (U.S., Canada, Norway etc.) as an outgrowth of domestic civil rights movements and diffused to other regions during the height of decolonization efforts around the world.

While the instrumentalist approach has merit, it does not accurately depict indigenous nations who have existed for 10,000 years or more on their homelands. Clearly these first nations do not fit the instrumentalist scheme of being 'the products of developments of the last two centuries'.[51] On the other hand, local and global indigenous identities have become much more salient with the establishment of host states and resulting policies that are deemed threatening to indigenous community survival.[52]

Based on the above discussion, neither the perennialist nor the instrumentalist perspectives give a full picture of the origins or conceptualization of indigenous peoples. Perhaps there is a middle ground, as Gurr suggests:

> Ethnic identities are not 'primordial' but nonetheless based on common values, beliefs and experiences. They are not 'instrumental' but usually capable of being invoked by leaders and used to sustain social movements that are likely to be more resilient and persistent than movements based solely on material or political interests.[53]

Aside from the primordialist/instrumentalist debate, another recent subfield has emerged that examines the impact of gender on ethnonationalist identity.[54] Given that indigenous nations around the world tended to be historically matrifocal/lineal, understanding gendered relations in this dynamic yields important insights into the biological and cultural reproduction of the nation. Therefore, gender and nationalism, coupled with the ideas of historical continuity (perennialists) and invention of tradition (instrumentalists) may provide some key insights into a comprehensive, definitional approach to indigenous nations.

Overall, the conceptual development of indigenous identity has become increasingly sophisticated among various academic fields, but, for the most part, has little in common with those definitions devised by indigenous organizations and IGOs. I now proceed to evaluate indigenous definitions offered by intergovernmental organizations (IGOs) in order to offer a comparative perspective of 'who is indigenous'.

Intergovernmental Organizations Define Indigenous

Most of the conceptual development of indigenous peoples by practitioners has occurred within IGOs, such as the World Bank group and the WGIP. IGO conceptualizations of indigenous peoples have generally established checklists or composites of indigenous features to be considered either in full or in part as essential components of indigenous identity. This multipart definitional approach is best illustrated by the World Bank's composite of five indigenous indicators. According to the World Bank's original operational directive 4.20,[55] indigenous peoples are to be identified by Task Managers in assessing the degree of a population's 'indigenousness' 'by the presence in varying degrees of the following characteristics':

> A. A close attachment to ancestral territories and to the natural resources in these areas;
> B. Self-identification and identification by others as members of a distinct cultural group;
> C. An indigenous language, often different from the national language;
> D. Presence of customary social and political institutions; and
> E. Primarily subsistence-oriented production.

The multi-part definition above highlights the fact that the World Bank has provided policymakers with a wide latitude for identifying indigenous populations. While Part B of the definition allows for self-identification, indigenous groups are ultimately subject to verification by Task Managers for indigenous status. Given the conceptual ambiguity of terms such as 'culture', 'distinct cultural group', and 'customary social and political institutions', one could imagine a wide variability among World Bank Task Managers in determining a group's indigenous status. For example, Part C of the above definition discusses the presence of an indigenous language. Yet recent studies by Krauss,[56] Nettle and Romaine,[57] and UNESCO demonstrate that more than 3,000 languages currently spoken in the world may not survive the next century. While some indigenous groups around the world are losing the ability to speak their original languages,[58] they continue to express themselves as indigenous through their artwork and by using distinct dialects and/or uniquely indigenous expressions. Overall, the variability in interpreting indicators of indigenousness, such as language, seems to encourage subjectivity when assessing indigenous populations.

Recently the World Bank group attempted to update their definition of indigenous peoples and submitted the following proposal entitled 'Draft Operational Policies (OP 4.10)' for comment by indigenous delegations and academics. As with OD 4.20, indigenous peoples are identified by 'the presence, in varying degrees, of some of the following distinctive characteristics':

A. Close attachment to ancestral territories and the natural resources in them;

B. Presence of customary social and political institutions;

C. Economic systems primarily oriented to subsistence production;

D. An indigenous language, often different from the predominant language; and

E. Self-identification and identification by others as members of a distinct cultural group.[59]

At first glance, there are a few subtle changes between the World Bank group's 1991 and currently proposed definitions, but no real substantial changes. First, the criterion of self-identification now appears last on the list of determinants (E), while indigenous delegates contend that it should be listed first as a primary component of identity. Second, there is further clarification of 'subsistence production' (C), now described as 'economic systems primarily oriented to subsistence production'. Such an approach most closely resembles the above-referenced indigenous definition of 'small-scale cultures' provided by Bodley. Third, an indigenous language is now 'different from the predominant language' (D), versus being 'different from the national language', perhaps indicating that language difference continues to be a key criterion for Task Managers. Fourth, indigenous peoples' claims to natural resources appear more limited in the currently proposed definition (A); indigenous peoples now have 'close attachments to ancestral territories and to the natural resources in them' versus 'natural resources in these areas.' Aside from de-emphasizing cultural ties to their ancestral homelands, which have been extensively documented in a new United Nations report on 'Indigenous Peoples and their Relationship to Land',[60] this new definition seems to confine any natural resource use to clearly defined territorial holdings, rather than natural resources claims on or near indigenous home lands. Perhaps most strikingly absent in the newly revised World Bank definition (OP 4.10) is the notion of distinct community cultural traditions or worldviews, which were featured prominently in several of the above-referenced academic conceptualizations of indigenous.

Upon further scrutiny, the most significant change proposed in the World Bank definitional attempts to qualify who is considered indigenous based on one's place of residence in Part 6:

> The requirements of this policy do not apply to groups who (a) have left their communities of origin and (b) move to urban areas and/or migrated to obtain wage labor.[61]

Essentially, for the sake of policymaking, the proposed World Bank definition suggests that one's very identity as indigenous is lost upon entering an urban area. Have indigenous peoples living in cities lost their 'close attachment to ancestral territories' (A)? While this approach may be bureaucratically efficient for identifying indigenous communities, it appears to penalize freedom of movement or even changing cultural traditions by removing them from consideration as indigenous. The realities of indigenous refugees caused by war or even state policies of resettlement belie establishing such a policy. Consider the case of the Chittagong Hill Tracts, which are a confederacy of 16 different indigenous nations collectively called Jumma, in Bangladesh. Since Bangladesh statehood in 1971, the CHT region has been besieged by over 400,000 government-induced Bengali settlers who have sought to dislocate Jumma peoples from their homelands.[62] A 1997 agreement between the government of Bangladesh and the Parbatya Chattagram Jan Samhati Samiti (PCJSS), the political party of the Jumma indigenous peoples, was negotiated to end the ongoing intrastate conflict. However, Jumma homeland autonomy has not yet been restored as over 3,055 Jumma refugee families have yet to have their original homelands restored to them.[63] Does this mean that these 3,055 families would not be considered indigenous under the revised World Bank definition despite their illegal removal from this region? During the consultation process with regard to the newly proposed indigenous definition, most indigenous delegations voiced a similar concern, believing that 'this provision should be deleted or at least clarified'.[64]

Some indigenous delegations offering comments on the World Bank group's proposed definition suggested that the definition offered by ILO Convention No.169 be adopted instead. In contrast with the World Bank definition, ILO No.169 stresses the right of indigenous peoples to self-identify as a 'fundamental criterion' for being indigenous while also providing a rudimentary definition of indigenous peoples:

A. Tribal peoples in independent countries whose social, cultural and economic conditions distinguish them from other sections of the national community, and whose status is regulated wholly or partially by their own customs or traditions or by special laws or regulations;

B. Peoples in independent countries who are regarded as indigenous on account of their descent from the populations which inhabited the country, or a geographical region to which the country belongs, at the time of conquest or colonization or the establishment of present State boundaries and who, irrespective of their legal status, retain some or all of their own social, economic, cultural and political institutions.[65]

The ILO definition above emphasizes the notion of social and cultural distinctiveness based on traditions, which are not mentioned by the World Bank as a consideration of indigenous. Additionally, the ILO definition holds much broader recognition of 'some or all of their own social, economic, cultural and political institutions'.

Despite a wide variation in definitional approaches to indigenous peoples by the World Bank and ILO, the 1986 definition of indigenous peoples developed by the WGIP is the most thorough and widely-used. The UN never officially adopted this definition as a prerequisite for participation in the WGIP, mainly due to an adamant insistence by indigenous participants on an unrestricted self-identification policy. The 1986 WGIP 'working definition' of indigenous peoples is:

> The existing descendants of the peoples who inhabited the present territory of a country wholly or partially at the time when persons of a different culture or ethnic origin arrived there from other parts of the world, overcame them and, by conquest, settlement or other means, reduced them to a non-dominant or colonial condition; who today live more in conformity with their particular social, economic, and cultural customs and traditions than with the institutions of the country of which they now form part, under a State structure which incorporates mainly the national, social and cultural characteristics of other segments of the population which are predominant.[66]

The above UN working definition is fraught with difficulties, as I have pointed out in previous research.[67] For example, indigenous peoples are not always in a 'non-dominant' condition numerically or politically within their host state(s). According to most census estimates, the Quechua and other indigenous groups constitute 51-71 per cent of the overall population of Bolivia, while indigenous Fijians comprise approximately 51 per cent of Fiji's population, and the Inuit make up over 80 per cent of the total population of Greenland. Other potential problems with the UN working definition stem from the identification of 'existing descendants', the absence of an outright conquest by colonial powers among some indigenous groups around the world, and the general inability to distinguish indigenous peoples from other national groups. Yet despite its shortcomings, the UN working definition represents a starting point among international organizations for establishing an emerging global dialogue on 'who is indigenous'. After reviewing definitions of indigenous peoples proffered by academicians and intergovernmental organizations, how do indigenous organizations approach the question? I examine the definitions of two prominent indigenous organizations below.

Indigenous Organizations Define Indigenous

Robert Coulter, a lawyer and director of the Indian Law Resource Center, once said, 'Indigenous peoples are Indians and people like them.'[68] Definitions created by indigenous organizations generally share Coulter's philosophy by establishing very broad, minimal guide lines for identifying indigenous populations. For example, the International Work Group for Indigenous Affairs (IWGIA), which has consultative status with the United Nations, defines indigenous peoples as:

> The disadvantaged descendants of those peoples that inhabited a territory prior to the formation of a state. The term indigenous may be defined as a characteristic relating the identity of a particular people to a particular area and distinguishing them culturally from other people or peoples.[69]

The above-referenced definition closely resembles Kingsbury's conceptualization of indigenous peoples (discussed in a previous section), which outlined very general identity, territorial and cultural claims of indigenous nations. It differs from the United Nations' working definition in that indigenous peoples are said to have inhabited a particular territory prior to the 'formation of a state' versus being confronted by persons of a 'different culture or ethnic origin'. While the IWGIA definition does acknowledge the process of state building in terms of disadvantaging native peoples, it fails to adequately describe the colonial process that often reduces indigenous peoples to 'disadvantaged descendants'.

A working definition created by the World Council of Indigenous Peoples (WCIP), which was established in 1975 and has consultative status with the United Nations, offers another examination of the contemporary political/legal status of indigenous peoples:

> Indigenous peoples shall be people living in countries which have populations composed of different ethnic or racial groups who are descendants of the earliest populations which survive in the area, and who do not, as a group, control the national government of the countries in which they live.

The WCIP working definition closely mirrors the UN working definition, which illustrates its close relationship with the UN as a forerunner of the global indigenous rights movement in the 1970s. As with the UN, the WCIP stresses self-identification as its official policy while providing very little discussion of cultural, land claims and identity of indigenous peoples in its working definition. As with the other academic and IGO definitions that have been reviewed in this article, any definition of indigenous peoples runs the risk of being incomplete historically, culturally, politically and economically while reifying native peoples in a 'continued subordination of difference to identity'.[70]

Based on the preceding, comprehensive review of several IGO and indigenous organizations' approaches to defining indigenous, it is clear that a more dynamic and flexible strategy is warranted to more accurately conceptualize native peoples. To date, researchers and practitioners have had great difficulty overcoming the definitional problem identified by Alfred regarding the variance of group identity over time and place. Prior work examining the concept of 'Peoplehood' (along with work with nationalist and indigenous scholars/practitioners) may yield some important, new insights into this definitional quandary.

Rearticulating Indigenous Identity

The concept of 'peoplehood' has its roots in anthropologist Edward H. Spicer's work on 'enduring peoples'.[71] Spicer's discussion of an 'Indian sense of identity' centred on three key factors: their relationship to the land, common spiritual bond, and language use.[72] Distinct from 'ethnic groups', peoplehood was identified as a unique social category by Spicer given their persistence over time and sense of solidarity based on territory, religion and language. Cherokee anthropologist Robert K. Thomas added a fourth factor, sacred history, to the emerging concept of peoplehood as he elaborated on Spicer's original typology.[73] Thomas also described the four peoplehood components as being interwoven and dependent on one another.

Current work by Holm, Pearson and Chavis revives the original peoplehood concept and touts it as a foundational concept for the future of indigenous nations studies programmes.[74] In order to 'demonstrate how a group's religion is inseparably linked to language, sacred history, and to a particular environment',[75] Holm et al. slightly modify the original factor of 'religion' and replace it with 'ceremonial cycles'. Overall, their model yields great promise as an explanatory, interdisciplinary tool for understanding indigenous identity. Unlike the multi-part, ahistorical definitions of indigenous peoples proffered by most academicians and practitioners in the preceding sections, Holm et al.'s model views identity as dynamic and interlocking, as 'No single element of the model is more or less important than the others.'[76]

In light of the potential of Holm et al.'s revised peoplehood conceptualization, and after a comprehensive review of academic and IGO/NGO definitional approaches to indigenous peoples, it is possible to build on existing works to develop a more all-encompassing and interrelated working definition of indigenous peoples. While self-identification is still regarded as the most compelling factor in indigenous identity, my proposed working definition serves a similar function as ILO No.169 - a working reference for practitioners and indigenous peoples in documenting the impact of historical and colonial legacies on contemporary indigenous communities and as a policy guide in the current global indigenous rights discourse. By utilizing Holm et al.'s version of the peoplehood model, my proposed indigenous definition includes all four, interlocking concepts of sacred history, ceremonial cycles, language and ancestral homelands, while elaborating somewhat on their complex interrelationships:

1. Peoples who believe they are ancestrally related and identify themselves, based on oral and/or written histories, as descendants of the original inhabitants of their ancestral homelands;
2. Peoples who may, but not necessarily, have their own informal and/or

formal political, economic and social institutions, which tend to be community-based and reflect their distinct ceremonial cycles, kinship networks, and continuously evolving cultural traditions;

3. Peoples who speak (or once spoke) an indigenous language, often different from the dominant society's language - even where the indigenous language is not 'spoken', distinct dialects and/or uniquely indigenous expressions may persist as a form of indigenous identity;

4. Peoples who distinguish themselves from the dominant society and/or other cultural groups while maintaining a close relationship with their ancestral homelands/sacred sites, which may be threatened by ongoing military, economic or political encroachment or may be places where indigenous peoples have been previously expelled, while seeking to enhance their cultural, political and economic autonomy.

While the above-listed definition is not as compact as previous attempts, it gets away from a checklist or linear approach to conceptualizing indigenous by emphasizing self-identification as well as the interrelationships between identity and key cultural perspectives. My approach as an indigenous scholar also represents an attempt at cumulative integration with previous research by fusing the literature on nationalism, international law and indigenous rights into a comprehensive conceptual framework. For example, the phraseology in Part 1 of the above definition relies on work by prior ethnonationalist researchers, such as Connor and Smith, when discussing a collective belief that 'they are ancestrally related'. Part 2 utilizes the terminology of Alfred and Wilmer regarding 'continuously evolving cultural traditions', thus providing a dynamic rather than static or fixed model of indigenous peoples belief systems. Part 3 discusses language use, which is often taken as a given, but is clearly in need of elaboration as traditional language use dwindles and even disappears, which has been extensively documented by the findings of Ethnologue and Nettle and Romaine (2000). While language may not be spoken in some native societies on a daily basis, it may be reflected in other forms, such as artwork, dialects, unique community expressions and indigenous place names.

Finally, Part 4 of the definition ties into the notion of protecting one's ancestral homeland, which illustrates indigenous peoples special relationship to the land. For example, the land tenure system in Nepal, known as Kipat, is viewed as the core of indigenous existence and deemed inseparable from culture, ceremonial life and sacred history. The Limbu indigenous community of Nepal view the Kipat as 'fused with and articulates the culture and any assault on Kipat is seen as a threat to the very existence of the Limbu as a separate community within the society'.[77] Such an interdependent kinship with the land is often misunderstood by political theorists and nationalist scholars, whose writings often focus on the tension s between collective and individual worldviews.[78]

Differentiating indigenous peoples from 'dominant societies' is somewhat problematic in countries such as Fiji, where the indigenous population's power is elevated over other non-indigenous groups within existing governmental structures. In this case, the above definition attempts to account for differences that may be reflected in cultural perspectives as well as existing power relations - in the cases of Fiji or Thailand, indigenous group may be distinct from 'other cultural groups' within the host state(s). However, most of the world's indigenous peoples are non-dominant, which is why this phrase has become a critical part of the UN Working definition and subsequent definitions of indigenous peoples.

In terms of comparing my newly-created definition with others in the field, it probably comes the closest to either Smith or Kingsbury's. However, as mentioned previously, Kingsbury's approach does not maintain much definitional precision when discussing 'ethnic groups' or a 'long connection with the region'. When compared to a peoplehood model, Kingsbury's four 'essential' factors fail to account for ceremonial cycles, sacred history, language, and to some degree, ancestral homelands. Instead, factors such as 'language, race and material or spiritual culture' are relegated to being 'other relevant indicators'. In the end, however, one is never certain where and when these other relevant indicators might apply when discussing the world's indigenous peoples. Even with its parsimony, Kingsbury's definitional approach does not offer many guidelines for indigenous identities that vary according to time and place.

Smith's five-part definition comes the closest to approximating peoplehood as it documents the features of 'myths and memories of a communal history', 'a common public culture', 'common laws and customs', and a 'historic territory or homeland'. However, Smith neglects to discuss the importance of language in any detail as well as the salience of oral versus written sacred histories. More importantly, Smith's checklist approach is linear in its construction and fails to account for the interrelationships between key factors.

In sum, a somewhat modified peoplehood approach offers the most promise when defining indigenous communities given its non-linear construct and flexibility across time and place. In closing, several possible conclusions can be drawn from the application of nationalist and peoplehood conceptual frameworks to a rearticulation of indigenous identity.

Conclusions

Dilemmas over self-identification policies versus established definitional approaches to documenting indigenous peoples will continue, whether in global/regional forums, host state/indigenous group interactions, or among indigenous groups themselves. Can a self-identification policy work in tandem with a working definition of indigenous peoples? Certainly this has been the case with key global instruments and policies relating to indigenous peoples, such as ILO No.169, the UN Working Group, the Organization of American States Declaration, and the World Council on Indigenous Peoples. Thus far, however, established working and academic definitions have not allowed for maximum flexibility across time and space (Alfred 1999), accounted for inter and intra-group diversity, and avoided the pitfalls of reification (Barcham 2000). Unfortunately, the discourse over defining indigenous peoples has thus far been dominated by concerns of host states within international forums while de-emphasizing indigenous goals of political, cultural, economic and social autonomy. However, as my newly-created definition has demonstrated, one can develop conceptual approaches that balance self-identification policy with a comprehensive yet flexible working definition. If such definitions of indigenous peoples attain more global acceptance, indigenous human rights treaties, such as ILO No.169, are more likely to be ratified - currently, only 17 countries have ratified this treaty.

After surveying several existing conceptual frameworks of indigenous peoples, it is clear that Holm et al.'s model of peoplehood offers the most promise in terms of its non-Western approach to identity, its flexibility, comprehensiveness, and allowance for cultural continuity and change. Using a somewhat modified version of peoplehood and drawing on previous ethnonationalist research, one can devise a conceptual framework of indigenous identity, such as the one developed in this article, that has utility for both practitioners and theorists. Clearly the gap between praxis and theory must be closed if the global indigenous rights discourse is to move beyond technical, definitional approaches and towards more substantive issues of self-determination, land rights, and promoting cultural integrity. A new definitional framework not only documents the interrelationship between these key factors but it voices indigenous peoples' community-based priorities regarding homeland autonomy, language rights, importance of oral histories, and ceremonial cycles.

Given the emergence of new global and regional legal instruments to protect the rights of indigenous peoples, it is imperative that some consensus develops around global indigenous identity. As Kingsbury points out, a positivist approach to defining indigenous treats groups as 'distorted and rather static formal categories'.[79] However, even with a dynamic and fluid working definition of indigenous peoples, it is difficult to overcome some of the regional differences that groups face, especially in Asia, as host states deny the very relevance of indigenous identity. Such issues should be approached cautiously as attempts to confine indigenous peoples solely to regional contexts will disrupt an ongoing global indigenous rights discourse over the passage of key human rights protections, such as the 'Draft Universal Declaration on the Rights of Indigenous Peoples'. For example, Special Rapporteur Miguel Alfonso Martinez in his comprehensive 'study on Treaties, Agreements and Other Constructive Arrangements between States and Indigenous Populations' attempts to point out that given the different colonial and treaty-making contexts in Africa and Asia versus other regions of the world, peoples in Africa and Asia should pursue their rights as 'minority' populations rather than 'indigenous'.[80] Such erroneous distinctions lend further confusion to an already contentious debate and can be overcome somewhat with flexible and dynamic working definitions that account for such historical and contemporary differences.

Few may realize that a discussion over 'who is indigenous?' is taking place against the backdrop of the United Nations' 'International Decade of World's Indigenous People, 1995-2004', which has outlined one of its eventual goals as ratifying the 45-article Draft Declaration by 2004. However, since being adopted by the Sub-Commission on Prevention of Discrimination and Protection of Minorities in 1994, discussions over revising the Draft Declaration have disproportionally focused (and stalled) on host state concerns regarding defining indigenous. It is hoped that flexible definitional approaches to indigenous peoples can enhance the human rights protections of some 350 million peoples located in 70 different countries throughout the world. While international law is currently at a crossroads regarding the full recognition of global indigenous rights, indigenous peoples themselves are rearticulating their goals and reaffirming their identities for future generations.

Acknowledgements

An earlier version of this paper was presented at the joint conference of the Mexican International Studies Association and International Studies Association, Manzanillo, Mexico, 11-13 December 1997. This article is dedicated to the memory of R. Leon Corntassel, who inspired this work and passed over on 19 December 2002. Special thanks to Laura Parisi, Eda Saynes-Vazquez, Taiaiake Alfred, Cindy Holder, Tom Holm, J. Cedric Woods, Sam Cook, Laurie Comings, Tomas Hopkins Primeau and the anonymous reviewers of *Nationalism and Ethnic Politics* for their comments on earlier drafts of this work.

Notes

[1] Jeff J. Corntassel is a Tsalagi (Cherokee Nation) and currently Associate Professor at the School of Indigenous Governance, University of Victoria, Canada.

[2] John H. Bodley, *Victims of Progress,* 4th edn. (California: Mayfield Publishing Company, 1999). p.146.

[3] Established in 1982, the WGIP is probably the most important global facilitator of indigenous rights today. One of the WGIP's most pressing matters is revising the Draft Universal Declaration on the Rights of Indigenous Peoples for ratification by the UN General Assembly, preferably before the 'International Decade of the World's Indigenous People' ends in 2004. The Draft Declaration, which was authored by over 700 indigenous peoples and scholars, states unequivocally in Article 8 that indigenous peoples have the 'right to identify themselves as indigenous and be recognized as such.' 'Draft Universal Declaration on the Rights of Indigenous Peoples', Twelfth Session of the Working Group on Indigenous Peoples, 23 August 1994, E/CN.4/Sub.2/AC.4/1994/4/Add.1.

[4] As ILO Convention 169 'Concerning Indigenous and Tribal Peoples in Independent Countries', which went into force in 1989, states in Article 1, Section 2: 'Self-identification as indigenous

or tribal shall be regarded as a fundamental criterion for determining the groups to which the provisions of this Convention apply.' As of this writing, 14 states have ratified ILO Convention NO.169: Argentina, Bolivia, Colombia, Costa Rica, Denmark, Ecuador, Fiji, Guatemala, Honduras, Mexico, Netherlands, Norway, Paraguay, and Peru.

5   Based on a report by the Independent Commission on International Humanitarian Issues (1987), self-identification was deemed one of four critical elements in defining indigenous peoples; the other three were pre-existence, non-dominance and cultural difference. Additionally, a regional intergovernmental organization, the Organization of American States, has also advocated self-identification as a fundamental criterion in the recently approved 'Draft American Declaration on the Rights of Indigenous Peoples' (1997); See Article 1(2) in OAS doc. OEA/Ser.L/V/II.95, doc 6.

6   The term 'host' state is the most grammatically precise and widely used phrase describing those countries containing indigenous peoples within their borders. However, this term should not be construed to imply a sense of undue state cordiality, especially given the severe treatment that several indigenous populations have received at the hands of their 'host' states.

7   State governments have adamantly insisted that the term 'peoples' be eliminated from all international legal instruments involving global indigenous rights due to the term's implications for self-determination in international law, which has been construed by most legal scholars and state governments as the right to independent statehood. Debate over ratifying the UN Draft Declaration on the Rights of Indigenous Peoples has stalled over the document's use of the word 'peoples' and 'self-determination', which states such as Argentina, Brazil, Colombia, Japan, Mexico, Morocco and Russia contend would disrupt the territorial integrity of countries. Several states have suggested the use of the term 'people' or 'populations' along with a disclaimer, such as the one contained in International Labor Organization Treaty No.169 (1989), which asserts that use of the term peoples 'shall not be construed as having any implications as regards the rights which may attach to the term under international law'. In response to these criticisms, indigenous organizations have asserted that the right to self-determination does not necessarily entail a right to secession but rather a right to greater self-rule and autonomy; any compromise of this right is deemed detrimental to indigenous rights. For more on this extensive debate, see S. James Anaya, *Indigenous Peoples in International Law* (New York: Oxford University Press, 1996), esp. pp.48-9; Russel Lawrence Barsh, 'Indigenous Peoples and the UN Commission on Human Rights: A Case of the Immovable Object and the Irresistible Force', Human Rights Quarterly, No.18 (1996), esp. pp.796-800.

8   See specific examples in Barsh, pp.782-813; Sharon Helen Venne, *Our Elders Understand our Rights: Evolving International Law Regarding Indigenous Rights* (British Columbia: Theytus Books, 1998), pp.l58-60; Julian Burger, 'Indigenous Peoples and the United Nations', in Cynthia Price Cohen (ed.), *The Human Rights of Indigenous Peoples* (New York: Transnational, 1998), pp.10-11.

9   Jeff Corntassel and Tomas Hopkins Primeau, 'The Paradox of Indigenous Identity: A Levels-of-Analysis Approach', *Global Governance*, No.4 (1998), pp.139-56.

10 Taiaiake Alfred, *Peace, Power, Righteousness: An Indigenous Manifesto* (New York: Oxford University Press, 1999), p.85.

11 John and Susan Dodds Bern, 'On the Plurality of Interests: Aboriginal Self-Government and Land Rights', in Duncan Ivison, Patt Patton and Will Sanders (eds.), *Political Theory and the Rights of Indigenous Peoples* (Cambridge: University of Cambridge Press, 2000), p.165.

12 Anthony D. Smith, 'When is a Nation?', *Geopolitics*, No.7 (2002), pp.5-32.

13 Paragraph 7, 'Standard Setting Activities: Evolution of Standards Concerning the Rights of Indigenous People', Thirteenth Session of the Working Group on Indigenous Peoples, 21 June 1995, E/CN.4/Sub.2/AC.4/1995/3.

14 The WGIP is the most open forum within the United Nations system. To participate, indigenous delegates merely require a letter from their indigenous nation designating them as official indigenous representatives to the UN Working Group on Indigenous Populations.

[15] Manuhuia Barcham, '(De)Constructing the Politics of Indigeneity', in Ivison, Patton and Sanders, pp.137-8.

[16] See also: George Manuel and Michael Posluns, *The Fourth World: An Indian Reality* (New York: The Free Press, 1974); Julian Burger, *Report from the Frontier: The State of the World's Indigenous Peoples* (London: Zed Books, 1987).

[17] Franke Wilmer, *The Indigenous Voice in World Politics* (Newbury Park, CA: Sage, 1993), p.97.

[18] Gerald R. Alfred and Franke Wilmer, 'Indigenous Peoples, States and Conflict', in, David Carment and Patrick James (eds.), *Wars in the Midst of Peace* (Pittsburgh: University of Pittsburgh Press, 1997), p.27.

[19] Political Science scholar Alison Brysk points out: 'Most parties to the debate employ cultural rather than racial definitions, since racial identity is difficult to determine, subject to abuse, and socially superseded by cultural identity in any case,' in Alison Brysk, *From Tribal Village to Global Village* (Stanford: Stanford University Press, 2000), p.5, footnote 9.

[20] S. James Anaya, *Indigenous Peoples in International Law* (New York: Oxford University Press, 1996), p.3.

[21] Bodley, *Victims of Progress,* p.4.

[22] For access to information regarding the 275 ethnopolitical groups included in the 'Minorities at Risk' dataset, visit the following website: www.bsos.umd.edu/cidcm/mar.

[23] Ted Robert Gurr, *Peoples versus States: Minorities at Risk in the New Century* (Washington, D.C.: United States Institute of Peace Press, 2000), p.17.

[24] For more on this, see, Jeff Corntassel and Tomas Hopkins Primeau, 'Indigenous 'sovereignty' and International Law: Revised Strategies for Pursuing "Self Determination"', *Human Rights Quarterly,* No.17 (1995), pp.343-65.

[25] Ibid., pp.346-7.

[26] This has created a great deal of confusion among host states given indigenous claims to 'self-determination' in the Draft Declaration. As former WGIP chairperson Erica-Irene Daes points out, indigenous peoples 'do not usually assume that the right to self-determination is exercised by the creation of new nation-states', Erica-Irene A. Daes, 'Protection of the World's Indigenous Peoples and Human Rights', in Janusz Symonides (ed.), *Human Rights: Concepts and Standards* (Burlington: UNESCO, 2000), pJ03. See also, Erica-Irene A. Daes, 'Some Considerations on the Right of Indigenous Peoples to SelfDetermination', *Transnational Law and Contemporary Problems,* No.3 (1993), pp.1-11.

[27] Fred W. Riggs, 'Who's Indigenous? A Conceptual Inquiry', Proceeds from a panel discussion on ethnic nationalism at the annual meeting of the International Studies Association, Toronto, 18-21 March 1997. http://www2.hawaii.edu/~fredr/indig.htm [accessed 15 February 2001].

[28] Benedict Kingsbury, '"Indigenous Peoples" in International Law: A Constructivist Approach to the Asian Controversy', *American Journal of International Law,* No.92 (1998), pp.414-57.

[29] Kingsbury, 'Indigenous Peoples', p.415.

[30] Daes, 'Protection of the World's Indigenous Peoples', p.303.

[31] Lowell W. Barrington, '"Nation" and "Nationalism": The Misuse of Key Concepts in Political Science', *PS: Political Science and Politics* (1997), pp.712-16.

[32] Walker Connor, 'The Politics of Ethnonationalism', *Journal of International Affairs,* No.27 (1973), pp.1-21.

[33] Bernard Nietschmann, 'The Fourth World: Nations Versus States', in George J. Demko and William B. Wood (eds.), *Reordering the World: Geopolitical Perspectives on the 21ˢᵗ Century* (Boulder: Westview Press, 1995), pp.225-42.

[34] Author's additions in italics; Walker Connor, *Ethnonationalism: The Quest for Understanding* (Princeton: Princeton University Press, 1994), p.197; Nietschmann, 'The Fourth World', p.226.

[35] Umut Özkirimli, *Theories of Nationalism: A Critical Introduction* (New York: St. Martin's Press, 2000), p.58.

[36] Connor, *Ethnonationalism,* pp.210-26.

37 See, for example, works by: Clifford Geertz, 'The Integrative Revolution: Primordial Senti-ments and Civil Politics in New States', in, Clifford Geertz (ed.), *Old Societies and New States* (New York: The Free Press ofGlencoe, 1963), pp.104-57; Harold R. Isaacs, *Idols of the Tribe: Group Identity and Political Change* (Cambridge: Harvard University Press, 1975); Pierre L. van den Berghe, 'Race and Ethnicity: A Sociobiological Perspective', *Ethnic and Racial Studies,* No.1 (1978), pp.401-11; Anthony D. Smith, *The Ethnic Origins of Nations* (UK: Basil Blackwell, 1987); Walker Connor, *Ethnonationalism: The Quest for Understanding* (Princeton: Princeton University Press, 1994).

38 Alexis Heraclides, *The Self-Determination of Minorities in International Politics* (London: Frank Cass, 1991), pp.7-8.

39 Thomas Spear, 'Introduction', in Thomas Spear and Richard Waller (eds.), *Being Maasai: Ethnic-ity and Identity in East Africa* (Athens: Ohio University Press, 1995), pp.1-18.

40 Paul R. Brass, 'Elite Competition and Nation-Formation', in John Hutchinson and Anthony D. Smith (eds.), *Nationalism* (Oxford: Oxford University Press, 1994), pp.83-9.

41 Smith, 'When is a Nation?', p.17.

42 George M. Scott, Jr., 'A Resynthesis of the Primordial and Circumstantial Approaches to Ethnic Group Solidarity: Towards an Explanatory Model', *Ethnic and Racial Studies,* No.13 (1990), pp.147-71.

43 This body of research has alternatively been referred to as 'circumstantial approaches' and 'mod-ernists'. However, for the sake of clarity and consistency, the term instrumentalist will be used in this research to best describe the process of ethnonationalist group formation.

44 See, *for* example, works by: Fredrik Barth, 'Introduction', in Fredrik Barth (ed.), *Ethnic Groups and Boundaries* (London: George Allen & Unwin, 1969), pp.9-38; Michael Hechter, *Internal Colonialism: The Celtic Fringe in British Naval Development,* 1536-1966 (Berkeley: University of California, 1975); Charles Tilly, *From Mobilization to Revolution* (Springfield, MA: Addison-Wesley, 1978); Benedict Anderson, *Imagined Communities: Reflections on the Origin and Spread of Nationalism* (London: Verso, 1983);, Eric Hobsbawm and Terence Ranger (eds.), *The Inven-tion of Tradition* (Cambridge: Cambridge University Press, 1983).

45 Scott, 'A Resynthesis', p.148.

46 Hobsbawm, *The Invention of Tradition,* p.2.

47 Hobsbawm, *The Invention of Tradition,* p.12.

48 Anderson, *Imagined Communities,* p.103

49 Ibid., p.18.

50 It should be pointed out that there is a great deal of variation among instrumentalist theorists over the 'myth' of nationhood and the type of conditions that facilitate nationalism (i.e. de-pendency, political upheaval, collective insecurities, etc.). To address this variation, Özkirimli (2000) points to a third category of scholarship, which he calls 'ethno-symbolists' .

51 Özkirimli, *Theories of Nationalism,* p.220.

52 See Nietschmann, pp.232-8.

53 Gurr, *Peoples versus States,* p.5.

54 See, for example, Jayawardena's *Feminism and Nationalism in the Third World* (1986) and Yuval-Davis' *Gender and Nation* (1997).

55 The World Bank Operational Manual, September 1999, 'Indigenous Peoples', OD 4.20.

56 Michael Krauss, 'The World's Languages in Crisis', *Language,* No.68 (1992), pp.4-11.

57 Daniel Nettle and Suzanne Romaine, *Vanishing Voices: The Extinction of the World's Languages* (New York: Oxford University Press, 2000).

58 The Katukina nation of Brazil, for example, has only one native speaker remaining out of a com-munity of 300 people; the Bikya (aka Furu) of Cameroon have one speaker left in their com-munity; the Tagish in Canada have two speakers left out of a community of 400. According to the comprehensive 'Ethnologue.com' database, 416 languages throughout the world are nearly extinct. Ethnologue classifies languages as nearly extinct when 'only a few elderly speakers are still living'. http://www.ethnologue.com/nearly_extinct.asp, accessed 28 February 2002.

59 World Bank Group, 23 March 2001, 'Draft Operational Policies (OP 4.10)', http://[RTF bookmark start: _Hlt538023]/[RTF bookmark end: _Hlt538023]Inweb18.worldbank.org., accessed 29 January 2002.

60 Erica-Irene A. Daes, 11 June 2001, 'Indigenous Peoples and their Relationship to Land: Final Working Paper Prepared by the Special Rapporteur Mrs. Erica-Irene A. Daes', Commission on Human Rights, E/CN.4/Sub.2/2001/21.

61 World Bank Group, 'Draft Operational Policies (OP 4.10)'.

62 James Minahan, *Nations without States* (Westport, CT: Greenwood Press, 1996), pp.259-61.

63 'Intervention by Mangal Kumar Chakma', 18th Session of United Nations Working Group on Indigenous Populations, Geneva, Switzerland, 24-28 July 2000.

64 'Public Update #2 on Consultations with External Stakeholders', 15 December 2001. http:///Inweb18.worldbank.org., accessed 29 January 2002.

65 Article I, ILO Convention 169, 1989, 'Concerning Indigenous and Tribal Peoples in Independent Countries'.

66 Jose R. Martinez Cobo, 1986, *Study of the Problem of Discrimination Against Indigenous Populations,* Sub-Commission on Prevention of Discrimination and Protection of Minorities, E/CN.4/Sub.2/L.566, Paragraph 34.

67 Corntassel and Hopkins Primeau, 'Indigenous Sovereignty', pp.346-8.

68 Gerald R Alfred and Franke Wilmer, p.27.

69 IWGIA, 'Indigenous Issues', http://www.iwgia.org., accessed 17 October 2001.

70 Barcham, '(De)Constructing the Politics of Indigeneity', pp.137-8.

71 Edward H. Spicer, *Cycles of Conquest: The Impact of Spain, Mexico and the United States on the Indians of the Southwest, 1533-1960* (Tucson: The University of Arizona Press, 1962).

72 Ibid., p.576-8.

73 Robert K. Thomas, 'Colonialism: Classic and Internal', *New University Thought,* No.6 (1966-67a), pp.44-53.

74 Tom Holm, J. Diane Pearson and Ben Chavis, 'Peoplehood: A Model for American Indian Sovereignty in Education', *Wicazo Sa Review,* No.18 (Spring 2003), pp.7-24.

75 Ibid., p.4.

76 Ibid., p.5.

77 Lionel Caplan, 'Tribes in the Ethnography of Nepal: Some Comments on a Debate', *Nepalese Studies,* No.l7 (1990), and cited in Erica-Irene A. Daes, 11 June 2001, 'Indigenous Peoples and their Relationship to Land'.

78 Cindy L. Holder and Jeff J. Corntassel, 'Indigenous Peoples and Multicultural Citizenship: Bridging Collective and Individual Rights', *Human Rights Quarterly,* No.24 (2002), pp.127-51.

79 Kingsbury, "Indigenous Peoples", p.414.

80 United Nations Commission on Human Rights, 22 June 1999, *Study on Treaties, Agreements and Other Constructive Arrangements between States and Indigenous Populations: Final Report by Miguel Alfonso Martinez, Special Rapporteur.* E/CN.4/Sub.2/1999/20. See pp.12-15.

| **The Concept of Indigenous Peoples at the International Level:** Origins, Development and Challenges | Victoria Tauli-Corpuz[1] |

Introduction

I have been part of the indigenous peoples' movement in the Cordillera region of the Philippines since the early 1970s and at the national, regional and global levels in the 1980s up to the present. Having been engaged with the movement for more than three decades I participated in the debates around the definition and concept of indigenous peoples at the national, regional and global arenas. Most of these debates took place during the drafting of and negotiations on the various instruments on the rights of indigenous peoples, foremost of which is the UN Declaration on the Rights of Indigenous Peoples (UNDRIP). Other processes where such debates took place were at the International Labour Organization (ILO), during the formulation and adoption of Conventions No. 107 and 169, in the World Bank when it adopted its Operational Directive 4.20 and revised it to Operational Policy 4.10 on Indigenous People, and in the Asia Development Bank when it also adopted its Policy on Indigenous Peoples.[2]

The definition of indigenous peoples, the right to self-determination, collective rights and rights to lands, territories and resources and cultural rights are the most controversial issues in the evolution of instruments and policies on indigenous peoples and their rights. These five sets of issues are very much interlinked as peoples are the ones entitled to have the right to self-determination, and this is clearly a collective right. Indigenous peoples' identities and cultures are intricately linked with their lands, territories and resources. A discourse on the concept or definition of indigenous peoples, therefore, cannot be complete without referring to self-determination, collective rights, cultural rights and rights to lands, territories and resources.

It is important to look back into why and how the concept of indigenous peoples came into the global discourse, and at the contributions it made in the evolution of international human rights law.

Since the colonization era up to the present, indigenous peoples challenged the colonial and hegemonic discourses which denigrated their worldviews and ways of life. These contributions may not be very visible as history books are written, mainly, by the victors who represent the dominant thinking. Thus, discussing and writing about the evolution of the concept of indigenous peoples are important if only to give justice to those struggled to maintain the world's remaining cultural diversity.

The strength of the political movements of indigenous peoples from the local to the global level, which converged to finally get the United Nations to adopt a UN Declaration on the Rights of Indigenous Peoples can no longer be underestimated and ignored. Most of these struggles began with the basic denial of our ancestors' right to be different and distinct from those who colonized them. These are continued by us, of the present generations, again because of our desire to protect whatever remains of our lands, territories and resources and of the values and cultures which have kept us distinct and are important for us to continue co-creating the societies which we would like our future generations to live in.

In Asia, the identity question remains as a major concern of indigenous peoples because most states do not recognize their identities as distinct peoples. In fact, some Asian governments[3], in addition to the US[4] and several African countries, were the ones who constantly raised the need for the Declaration to define indigenous peoples. We, the few Asian indigenous representatives present in the negotiations, held several meetings with member-states from Asia to explain why a global definition of indigenous peoples cannot be done. Our main point has been that it is more feasible to make such a definition at the national level, while having one at the global level will risk excluding other indigenous peoples, as one definition cannot capture the diversity of indigenous peoples. Obviously, this worked because we finally got most of them to vote for the adoption of the Declaration. However, some of them still insist that there are no indigenous peoples in their countries or that the whole population is indigenous.

This paper will present an historical overview of how the concept of indigenous peoples has evolved at the regional and global levels, the content of the debates around it and how these were handled until the adoption of the Declaration in 2007. It will trace the way the definition of indigenous peoples was addressed in different global and regional processes. The concluding section will identify the key challenges which remain around this issue.

The Colonial Past and the Construct of Indigenous Peoples

The concept of indigenous peoples is a social construct which is mainly a result of colonial and post-colonial history including the building of new nation-states. Colonization and post-colonialism took various forms and these shaped the ways in which the concept of indigenous peoples evolved. This is not to say that all indigenous peoples suffered from colonization. There are those which were not directly colonized but who were still discriminated against by the populations who assumed economic, political and cultural dominance and thus suffered from the same problems as the others who went through colonization. But the majority of indigenous peoples experienced colonization whether from colonizers coming from overseas or from those from nearby territories.

The classic form of colonialism was European colonial invasions of independent peoples and nations which took place since the 15th century. The colonizers established their rule and imposed their political, economic, social and cultural systems for tens to hundreds of years. They and their descendants settled in these colonies, created the new nation-states and continued to be the political and economic rulers. These states are referred to as the settler states.

In most cases, the indigenous peoples became the minority because their populations were decimated by the colonialists' genocidal actions. Historical records will show that the populations of indigenous peoples were significantly reduced as a result of colonization.[5] Post-colonial governments facilitated the movement of huge numbers of the dominant populations into indigenous peoples' territories which effectively minoritized them. This is what happened in the United States, most countries in Latin America and the Caribbean, Canada, Australia and New Zealand. In situations where the indigenous peoples remained the majority of the population, the minority white people who decided to settle in their ex-colonies, continued to be the political and economic elites ruling the nation-state, like e.g. in Greenland and South Africa.

In these countries it is less complicated to identify who are the indigenous peoples as their differences from the settlers (skin colour, language, culture, etc.) are obvious. The problem is that there are those who deny their identities because of racism and discrimination. So the mixed-bloods can self-identify as non-indigenous. In Latin America, with the growth of the class-based Marxist movements, some indigenous persons identified themselves as *campesinos,* the Spanish term for peasants.

The initial reports on how indigenous peoples were maltreated by the European colonizers were done by Spanish priests such as Fray Bartolome de las Casas and Fray Francisco Vitoria in Latin America. Spanish colonizers debated whether the natives in their colonies had souls and therefore could be considered as human beings. If the natives do not have souls then they are categorized as sub-humans. Vitoria argued that the *indios* and *infieles* (non-believers, heathens) had their own politics and religion and therefore are essentially human and rational. Thus, they have original rights and they possess dominion over their territories. He also rejected the granting of legal titles, through Papal edicts of Pope Alexander VI, to the Spanish royalty over Indian lands which conquistadores claim to have "discovered".[6] De las Casas criticized the system in which the Spanish government granted, as rewards to the Spanish *conquistadores*, tracts of lands and slave labour of Indians living in these territories. This is the hated *encomienda* system which was not only imposed in Latin America but in the Philippines as well.

The colonization experience of the peoples in countries now known as the Philippines, Indonesia, Malaysia, Vietnam, small islands in the Pacific and the Caribbean and several African countries, was different in some ways. The colonizers[7] came and ruled over the native populations, but there was no large-scale inflow of settlers. And most of them left after struggles for freedom and independence of the natives succeeded. During the colonial era there were natives who were assimilated into the colonial rule and who were groomed to become the post-colonial elite and the rulers. There were also those who refused to be assimilated and others who simply were not reached because they live in the most remote and inaccessible territories. These were the ones who maintained the indigenous pre-colonial cultures, economic systems, social and political systems.

Because they were not colonized and assimilated, unlike the dominant population, they have been and still are subjected to systematic racism and discrimination by the colonizers and by the post-colonial governments as well as by the assimilated dominant populations. It is in the countries which went through this experience that the concept of indigenousness is very much contested. The post-colonial rulers, who were the ones who mainly fought for independence, found it difficult to accept that the ones who were least assimilated under the previous colonial regimes should be considered indigenous peoples. However, it has been shown in history that these least assimilated peoples still continued their struggles to have their collective rights over their cultures, lands, territories and resources, their customary governance systems and laws respected by the nation-state. In the past 30 years they have self-identified as indigenous peoples, established their own movements and converged their national and regional movements into a global indigenous peoples' movement.

This is what happened in the Philippines. Some peoples were not effectively assimilated or resisted integration into the dominant colonial society ruled for more than 300 years by the Spanish. While many of them eventually got reached by the American colonizers, including us, the Igorot of the Cordillera Region, the almost 300 years of not being under Spanish colonization before that spelled a world of difference in the cultures, worldviews, and economic and political systems of the assimilated population and those of the unassimilated ones. The latter are the ones who are now considered as indigenous peoples in the Philippines.

There is yet another experience of colonization. This is what is usually referred to as internal colonization. Making a differentiation between internal and external colonization does not make much sense, though. Colonization, whoever does it, is still colonization. It does not matter if the one who colonizes you is of a different colour or the same colour. One situation is the continuation of colonization even after the colonizers from overseas left or were driven away. The natives who were the victors of the anti-colonization struggles established the independent nation-state and often rallied the people within its boundaries to establish one nation, one culture and one language. Some nation-states forcibly integrated territories of indigenous peoples or included these as part of their territorial claims. Such is the case of the Naga of Northeast India. The Naga territory has never been a part of India but they also got colonized by the British. When the British left, the new nation-state called India decided to include them as part of the nation, against their will. Modern nation-state building contributed to the creation of indigenous peoples.

The Saami of Norway, Sweden, Finland and Kola Peninsula of Russia were not colonized from overseas. Thus, the "blue-water theory"[8] of colonization does not apply to them. This does not diminish their identity as indigenous peoples, however. They were included within the boundaries of the nation-states of which they are now considered national citizens. But they are distinct from the dominant population and they have struggled to maintain their identity, their cultures and their lands, territories and resources. They were subjugated by the expansion northward of the Swedish, the Norwegians, the Danes and even the Russians.

Neo-colonialism, Treaty-making and International Law

In the developing world (otherwise called the Third World), even after most colonies became independent nation-states, these states were not totally out of the clutches of the colonial powers. Their economies, political systems and socio-cultural systems were shaped to serve the political and economic interests of the former colonial masters. Many of the so-called "developing countries" remained as the providers of raw materials to feed the highly industrialized rich economies of the North and also as source of cheap labour for the manufacturing and service sectors of the same. Before the colonizers left they successfully negotiated economic, trade and military treaties supporting the perpetuation of their economic, military and cultural interests in their ex-colonies. This is what is now referred to as neo-colonialism. Indigenous peoples still suffer from such prevailing arrangements because their territories were reduced to resource-bases where their natural resources are extracted for export to the rich countries. Their indigenous economies, which were mainly for subsistence, were denigrated and illegalized in some countries because these were seen as impediments to modernity and development.

Indigenous peoples in some countries like the US, Canada, Australia, New Zealand negotiated treaties with their former colonizers which to a certain degree contained elements recognizing their rights as indigenous peoples. Some of these provided elements for the development of early international law in support of indigenous peoples' rights. In the main, however, the prevailing treatment of indigenous peoples remained in the protection mode. Douglas Sanders, an expert in International Human Rights Law cited, as an example, the Royal Proclamation of 1763 of the British which describe the tribes as those "with whom we are connected with and who live under our protection". He observed that "Protection is the historical basis for centralized jurisdiction over 'Indians and Lands Reserved for the Indians' in the Canadian Constitution of 1867".[9]

While the history of colonization of indigenous peoples varies from region to region, from country to country and from people to people, they have many things in common. Despite the oppression and discrimination they faced in the hands of the colonizers and the post-colonial nation-states, they persisted in asserting their identities as distinct peoples. They still practice their own cultures and speak their own languages, maintain wholly or partially their original territorial bases, practice their traditional livelihoods and natural resource management practices and still maintain some aspects of their customary political institutions and laws. The degrees of erosion and persistence of these vary from people to people but they have common aspirations to assert their identities and protect and further develop whatever remained of their territories, cultures and languages.

Recognition of Plurality and Establishment of Self-governing Structures

Nation-state building generally undermined the multi-cultural and multi-ethnic character of peoples within the country. In Latin America, the indigenous peoples who represent diverse nationalities, ethnicities and cultures were the ones who rallied around the need for the governments to constitutionally recognize the multi-ethnic and multi-cultural of the nation-state and to stop the actions taken by governments to assimilate them into the dominant system. Some indigenous peoples succeeded in getting national constitutions revised to recognize these pluralities and diversities. This happened in Ecuador, Peru, Colombia, Bolivia, Guatemala and other nation-states in Latin America. However, the hundreds of years old institutionalized and systematic discrimination which regarded indigenous peoples as inferior beings and indigenous cultures, religions and spirituality as backward, primitive or pagan still persists not only in Latin America but in most parts of the world.

The situation for some indigenous peoples in such countries changed through time due to actions taken by them jointly with others or in some cases on their own. For instance in South Africa apartheid was defeated and the blacks came to power. However, there are indigenous peoples like the Khoi-khoi and the San who still suffer from marginalization and discrimination. In Greenland, the Greenland Home Rule Government was established and now the Inuit are the ones ruling their own country, albeit as an autonomous unit of the Danish nation-state. The Saami have asserted their right to self-determination and now have self-governments, the Sami Parliaments in Sweden, Norway and Finland.

The coming to power of Evo Morales, an Aymara Indian, as President of Bolivia, is unique in the whole history of indigenous peoples. After the adoption of the UNDRIP the Bolivian Parliament adopted it in full as the National Law on Indigenous Peoples' Rights. Morales is now facing serious challenges from the white and mestizo population who refuse to surrender their power and privileges which they gained because of colonization. This illustrates how entrenched racism is among the settler populations, that any threat to their power will unleash the worst behaviour one can ever imagine.

There are indigenous territories declared as Autonomous Regions like by the Regional Autonomy Act for the Atlantic Coast of Nicaragua, the Autonomy Law of West Papua in Indonesia, of the legislation on the creation of Nunavut in Canada, among others. In Asia, two national laws that explicitly recognize the rights of indigenous peoples came into existence in the Philippines[10] and Taiwan[11]. These laws identify who are the indigenous peoples in these countries. This is not to say that these legal instruments are being implemented in a satisfactory way. Suffice it to say that such laws and arrangements exist as a result of indigenous peoples' struggles.

A look at the various historical accounts of indigenous peoples' responses to the impunity of colonialism shows that indigenous peoples did not accept the rule of the colonizers without fierce opposition. There are numerous accounts of resistance wars waged by indigenous peoples against the colonizers. Again, many of these stories have not been included in history books, many of which were written by the colonizers or the domestic elite who took over from them. Even if these stories remain unrecorded in books, the collective memories of indigenous peoples of what their ancestors did to stand up against colonialism and neo-colonialism will never be erased.

Racism, discrimination, inequality and oppression are the main drivers for indigenous peoples' stubborn assertion of their right to self-determination, rights to their identities and cultures and their rights over their lands, territories and resources. At an early stage of their struggles, some indigenous peoples already recognized the potentially important role that International Law will play in supporting their claims. Some of them also recognized that the international community, particularly the UN system, will be the main vehicle they can use to champion the establishment of norms and standards for their rights.

Several legal and human rights experts observed that a reciprocal relationship between indigenous peoples and international law has been developed and continues to evolve. Indigenous peoples used and continue to use international law to gain legitimacy for their claims. While indigenous peoples are invoking international law, they are also contributing to its enrichment. The adoption of the UN Declaration on the Rights of Indigenous Peoples, by itself, already is a major contribution for the further elaboration of international human rights law.[12]

Initial Engagements with the International Community

Early in the 20th century, in 1921, the Cayuga Chief Deskaheh, speaker of the Council of the Iroquois Confederacy, went to the League of Nations in Geneva to raise his complaints about the violation of their Treaties by the Canadian government. He was not provided an audience by the League, which considered his complaints as matters of domestic concern. Several years later, in 1925, a Maori leader named T. Ratana also went to the same body to complain about the violation of New Zealand of the Treaty of Waitangi. He got the same treatment. These incidents did not stop both these leaders from pursuing their cases. Both proceeded to England to further expose the situations their peoples faced and gained coverage in the media.

Around the same time that Deskaheh and Ratana were knocking at the doors of the League of Nations, the International Labour Organization (ILO)[13] received reports on the situation of indigenous peoples of Bolivia and Peru who were virtually slaves of foreign mining companies. In response to this, it conducted a study on this situation and in 1926 it created the Committee of Experts on Native Labour. This body was mandated to look into the situation of indigenous workers. By 1953 it released the study "Indigenous Peoples: Living and Working Conditions of Aboriginal Populations in Independent Countries".

After World War Two, in 1945, the United Nations was established to replace the League of Nations. A few years later, in 1949, the first UN debate on aboriginal peoples took place. A Bolivian proposal for the establishment of a sub-commission of the Economic and Social Council (ECOSOC) to study the aboriginal situation in the Americas was tabled and discussed. This resolution, together with the ILO study of 1953, led the UN to set up the Andean Indian Programme, which was jointly implemented by an inter-agency mechanism under the general management of the ILO.[14] The goal of this programme was to integrate indigenous peoples and to bring them development.

The ILO then proceeded to formulate and adopt its 1957 Convention No. 107 "Concerning the Protection and Integration of Indigenous and Other Tribal and Semi-Tribal Populations in Independent Countries". This was the first legally-binding international instrument addressing indigenous peoples. Its solution to the problem of indigenous peoples, however, was also to integrate and assimilate them with the nation-state and the dominant society. This approach was not acceptable to most indigenous peoples. Due to the harsh criticisms from indigenous peoples, Convention No. 169 was negotiated and eventually adopted in 1989. The assimilationist contents of the earlier Convention were removed.

ILO Convention No. 107 provided definitions of the populations that it will cover. Such definitions reflect the mindset of the experts during that period. They regarded indigenous and tribal peoples as backward, and the yardstick used to measure this was the stage of civilization and development reached by the West and by the dominant populations in the budding nation-states. The European political system and development model as well as their concepts of progress and modernity were the standards for assessing indigenous peoples economic, cultural and political systems. The Convention divided indigenous and tribal peoples into two categories. The first one includes;

> " [ ] members of tribal and semi-tribal populations in independent countries, whose social and economic conditions are in a less advanced stage than the stage reached by the other sections of the national community and whose status is regulated wholly or partially by their own customs and traditions or by special laws and regulations."[15]

The second category refers to:

> "[ ] members of tribal and semi-tribal populations in independent countries which are regarded as indigenous on account of the descent from the populations which inhabited the country or a geographical region to which the country belongs, at the time of conquest of colonization and which, irrespective of their legal status, live more in conformity with the social, economic and cultural institutions of that time than with the institutions of the nation to which they belong."[16]

There were objections by governments on these definitions and the act of differentiating populations within a nation-state. For example, Indonesia objected that it was "... not appropriate to consider tribals and semi-tribals as populations...", and that the act of differentiating goes against their national laws, which apply to all.[17] The view of the ILO Committee of Experts on the Application of Convention and Recommendations[18] (CEAR), however, is that the absence of differentiation in national legislations does not justify the claim that the Convention is not applicable in particular countries.

Resurgence and Growth of Indigenous Peoples' Movements: From the Local to the Global

The 1960s and 1970s saw the resurgence of movements of indigenous peoples, from the Americas and in other parts of the world. I use the word "resurgence" because I consider the protests of indigenous peoples against the colonial governments as the beginnings of indigenous peoples' movements. These movements were mainly concerned about the gross violations by the new nation-states of indigenous peoples' collective and individual human rights. Most of the time, these took the form of mass protests against the human rights violations committed against them as communities and as individuals. They also asserted their right to their distinct identities and cultures and their rights to own, control and manage their ancestral lands, territories and resources, and their right to practice their traditional livelihoods.[19] These common aspirations led them to build up their own movements and to develop their counter- discourses against the discriminatory and hegemonic views and practices of the ruling elites. The indigenous peoples also participated in processes where international standards for the respect, protection and fulfilment of their collective and individual rights were being developed.

In the Western hemisphere, the indigenous peoples were already reaching out to each other to establish a global movement. The World Council of Indigenous Peoples (WCIP) was established in 1975 in a founding congress which saw the participation of indigenous peoples from 19 countries.[20] This body obtained consultative status in the Economic and Social Council of the UN in 1979. In 1977, the NGO Summit on Indigenous Peoples in the Americas was convened by the NGOs sympathetic to indigenous peoples' issues which had ECOSOC Consultative Status, together with existing indigenous peoples' networks. Before that, various NGOs working on indigenous peoples' issues were also established. These were Survival International in the United Kingdom and the International Workgroup on Indigenous Affairs (IWGIA) based in Copenhagen, Denmark.

While mobilizations and organizing were taking place in the West, indigenous peoples in the Third World were also engaged in similar activities. The 1970s saw the upsurge of authoritarian regimes in Asia, Latin America and in Africa. The Cold War was used as a pretext by the US to strengthen its anti-communist campaign among its allies in the Third World. In several of these countries, national liberation movements against US imperialism, feudalism and bureaucrat capitalism gained strength and some indigenous peoples took part in these. While some became part of the open and armed liberation movements, others were used by the States for its counter-insurgency activities. Other indigenous peoples just wanted to be left alone and concentrated on their struggles for their most basic rights to land and resources, culture and identities.

Dictatorial regimes such as the Marcos Regime in the Philippines, the ones in Guatemala, Bolivia, Brazil, Peru, Nicaragua, to mention just a few, were supported by the United States as long as these were engage in anti-communist counter-insurgency programmes. The 1960s to the 1980s were the dark years of dictatorships, which led to the worst massacres and other egregious human rights violations against indigenous peoples. It is no surprise that in the Third World, it was in these same countries where indigenous peoples' movements started to develop and gain strength.

In the Philippines, for instance, a few indigenous persons became activists for the national liberation movement in the late 1960s and early 1970s. I myself, together with other Igorot activists, was involved in organizing the Kilusang Kabataan ng Kordilyera (Youth Movement of the Cordillera). This was an organization of Igorot students studying in Manila, and its objective is to raise the students' political and social awareness so they can be recruited to become part of the national liberation movement. The Highland Activists (a counterpart youth and student organization in Baguio City) merged with KKK after the First Cordillera Conference for National Liberation held in 1972.

The KKK was mainly organized as an anti-imperialist youth and student organization, but its members were Igorot students and youth. Thus, it tackled the issue of discrimination against "national minorities" (the term used at that time due to Marxist influence). This started the development of an indigenous peoples' movement in the Cordillera region in the Philippines. The KKK was short-lived, however, because Martial Law was declared in September 1972 and all mass organizations were illegalized and forced to go underground. This did not stop us from doing organizing work with our people, and in the process we learned that some of the problems we faced were not simply because of US imperialism but also because of discrimination against indigenous peoples, institutionalized in the state structures. We called this the national oppression of national minorities.

We received information that several projects were being planned by the Marcos Dictatorship, which would affect our ancestral domain, the Cordillera region. These were the World Bank funded Chico River Dam Hydroelectric Project and the Cellophil Resources Corporation (logging concession over our pine forests given by President Marcos to one of his cronies). By l983, the Cordillera Peoples' Alliance was born, and this was the body which pursued the campaigns. As a result of our success in stopping the building of the Chico River Dam, along with the campaign of the indigenous peoples of Brazil against the Polonoreste Highway, the World Bank developed their Operational Manual Statement 2.34: Tribal People in Bank-Financed Projects (OMS 2.34). This was their first ever guideline developed by institution on how to deal with indigenous peoples.

The experience of massive violations of indigenous peoples' collective and individual rights was not unique to the Philippines. The upsurge of the Maya movement in Guatemala emerged from the anti-dictatorship struggle as well as the fight against a hydroelectric dam called the Chixoy Dam. The movement of the Misquito in the Atlantic Coast of Nicaragua was also in conjunction with the rise of the national liberation movement led by the Sandinistas. In fact, in the Philippines we got inspired by the formation of the Autonomous Region in the Atlantic Coast. The Regional Autonomy Act of Nicaragua was studied by us to see if it can be used in our own struggle for regional autonomy.

It was during the campaigns against dictatorships and militarization, against so-called "development projects" ranging from dams, logging concessions, mineral extraction, among others, that some indigenous peoples in Asia learned of the UN Working Group on Indigenous Populations (WGIP), and the UN in general. Thus, during the first meeting of the WGIP, we in the Cordillera region decided to send a representative to the first meeting of this body in 1982. At this first meeting, it was only the Igorot of the Philippines and the Jumma of the Chittagong Hill Tracts of Bangladesh who came from Asia to participate. The

Jumma, at that time, were similarly subjected to massive human rights violations and their struggle for self-determination was also spurred by the building of the Kaptai Hydroelectric Dam.

The United Nations and International Standard Setting on Indigenous Peoples' Rights

Among the various international bodies, the most important space which indigenous peoples decided to engage with was the United Nations system. The degree of engagement with the various bodies, programmes and agencies of the United Nations vary. Since the main standard-setting body for human rights is the Commission on Human Rights and its independent expert bodies, this was where the biggest participation of indigenous peoples took place. Its establishment of the UN Working Group on Indigenous Populations opened the space for, us and this became the arena for the drafting of the UN Declaration on the Rights of Indigenous Peoples. Through indigenous peoples' active intervention, the rules of participation were changed to go beyond the traditional UN practice where the only observers allowed to take part in working groups were the ECO-SOC-accredited NGOs, observers from governments and from UN bodies and specialized agencies as well as regional intergovernmental bodies.

A UN Voluntary Fund for Indigenous Populations was also established through a General Assembly Resolution passed in 1985, which provided assistance to representatives of indigenous peoples to participate in the WGIP. I became a member and was Chair of the Board of Trustees of this Fund from 1994 until 2003. The process of identifying who should be the beneficiaries of this Fund involved making judgements on who were indigenous peoples from the various regions. Sometimes, we made mistakes because we cannot possibly know all the diverse indigenous peoples living in our regions. But in the main, through our networks and contacts in the various countries, we managed to bring in the right representatives.

While the ILO was the first body which developed legally binding instruments on indigenous peoples, its tripartite composition – governments, employers and trade unions – did not provided much space for indigenous peoples. We can only take part through the graces of the governments (if we become government delegates), through the trade unions or through the employers confederations. Very few indigenous representatives managed to take part in the ILO processes, in particular the revision of ILO Convention No. 107 toward ILO Convention No. 169. In the countries where the governments ratified ILO Convention No. 169,[21] the indigenous peoples invoked the Convention in their legal battles. Even in countries which did not ratify this, some legal cases filed within those countries and in the inter-regional courts used the Convention No. 169 to support the arguments in favour of indigenous peoples.

The drafting of the UN Declaration on the Rights of Indigenous Peoples was started in 1985 by an expert body, the Working Group on Indigenous Popula-tions. After the draft was completed it had to be adopted by the Sub-Commission on the Prevention of Discrimination and the Protection of Minorities. As these two bodies are expert bodies, which means that they are not intergovernmental entities, the Draft Declaration still had to go through a process of being negoti-ated and officially adopted by the member-states of the Commission on Human Rights and by the General Assembly.

The Commission on Human Rights established the Ad-Hoc, Open-ended Working Group on the Draft Declaration which started to negotiate in 1995. This body ended its existence in 2006 after it completed its negotiations on the Draft which it submitted to the newly established Human Rights Council.[22] By June 29, 2006, the Draft was adopted by the Human Rights Council which transmitted it to the Third Committee of the UN General Assembly. This highest decision-making body of the UN finally adopted the UN Declaration in Septem-ber 13, 2007 at its 61st Session.

While the end product, the UN Declaration on the Rights of Indigenous Peoples, was important, the spaces established and the processes leading to-wards its adoption were equally important. These were where we developed our counter-arguments against States who still were very much operating within the framework of the inviolability of national sovereignty and territorial integrity of nation-states. These spaces and processes provided the opportunities for the local, national and regional movements of indigenous peoples to link up and network with each other. In the absence of these, it would have been difficult to forge the formidable global movement of indigenous peoples which persisted in getting the UN Declaration on the Rights of Indigenous Peoples adopted.

The Evolution of Working Definitions of Indigenous Peoples

Around the same time that the indigenous peoples were flexing their muscles several things were happening within the UN system. The UN Commission on Human Rights[23] appointed Special Rapporteurs to examine how various minority groups were being subjected to discrimination. The first report which mentioned indigenous peoples was done by Hernán Santa Cruz, a Chilean, who made a re-port on economic, social and cultural discrimination of minorities.[24] This report described indigenous peoples as;

> "Disadvantaged in relation to the rest of the population: in some coun-tries they are victims of de facto discrimination and continue to suffer from prejudice."[25]

In 1971, the ECOSOC passed a resolution authorizing the Sub-Commis-sion to undertake a "Study on the Problem of Discrimination Against Indigenous Populations". Jose Martínez-Cobo, a delegate of Ecuador, was appointed as the

Special Rapporteur to do this study. It took place between 1972 and 1983. There were other processes which led towards resolutions or conclusions related to indigenous peoples. The World Conference to Combat Racism and Discrimination in 1978 came up with a final statement which endorsed the rights of indigenous peoples to

> "[ ] maintain their traditional structure of economy and culture, including their own language and also recognizes the special relationship of indigenous peoples to their land and stresses that their land rights and natural resources should not be taken away from them."[26]

After the World Council on Indigenous Peoples (WCIP) was established, one of the actions it took was to prepare for a draft Convention on the Rights of Indigenous Peoples. They hired Douglas Sanders, a professor of Law in Canada, to prepare the draft, and this says:

> "The term Indigenous People refers to people living within states which have a population composed of differing ethnic or racial group, who are descendants of the earliest population living in the areas and who do not as a group control the national government of the state in which they live."[27]

This was made more comprehensive by the Martínez-Cobo report,[28] which came out in 1983. His working definition established the standard reference within the UN and elsewhere on indigenous peoples.

> "Indigenous communities, peoples and nations are those which, having a historical continuity with pre-invasion, pre-colonial societies that developed on their territories, consider themselves distinct from other sectors of the societies now prevailing in those territories or parts of them. They form at present non-dominant sectors of the society and are determined to preserve, develop and transmit to future generations their ancestral territories, and their ethnic identity, as the basis of their continued existence as peoples, in accordance with their own cultural patterns, social institution and legal systems."

This working definition had evolved considerably from the one used at the beginning. His first working paper in 1972 used the term populations only. Now the terms indigenous communities, peoples and nations are applied. While the issues of historical continuity, colonization, and distinctiveness were there in the first working paper, the subsequent paragraphs regarding the aspiration of indigenous peoples to preserve, develop and transmit to future generations their territories and identities were only introduced in the later and final versions.

When asked what a working definition means, Willemsen-Díaz[29], the head of the Secretariat which assisted Martínez-Cobo and the Secretariat of the WGIP, said that it was a point for departure which can be subjected to criticism and further modification.

The common characteristics of most indigenous peoples are captured by this working definition. It acknowledges that indigenous peoples, compared to the settler populations and the dominant society, still retain some of their pre-colonial identities and values, cultural, social, economic and political systems, and that they are keen to transfer these to the future generations. It has to be stressed that in some cases, while they are numerically more than the others, they still occupy a position of non-dominance in economic, political, cultural and social terms.

These different features, which are used to identify who indigenous peoples are, have to be used as a whole package. It is not enough, for example, to assert one's identity based on culture and language alone. This should be linked with the history of oppression and discrimination from colonization up to nation-state building which is accompanied by the ideology of one-nation, one-culture, one language, as well as modernity and "development". Failure to approach the indigenous peoples' concept in this fashion de-historises the realities faced by them and can lead to the weakening of the human rights argument, which is the beginning and the end of indigenous peoples' struggles and movements.

Contesting a Global Definition

During the drafting and negotiations of the UN Declaration, there was a strong push by some states for a definition of the term indigenous peoples. In the second year of the WGIP, in 1983, the strong words from some Asian and South American observer governments were heard, demanding that a comprehensive and restrictive definition of indigenous peoples be made as this will determine who should take part in the WGIP.

The persistent call for a definition was resisted by all of us, the indigenous representatives who were engaged in these various processes. In spite of this resistance, the issue kept popping up at the UN-Working Group on Indigenous Peoples (UN-WGIP), the Commission on Human Rights' Ad-Hoc, Open-ended Working Group on the Draft Declaration, and at the Third Committee of the General Assembly. In fact, the adoption by the General Assembly was delayed,[30] and one of the reasons was the demand by the African Group of Countries that a definition of indigenous peoples had to be included in the Declaration.

There is a view from some Asian and African governments that the problematique of indigenous peoples is only applicable to settler nations like the US, Canada, Australia and New Zealand. This view was further reinforced by the "Study on Treaties, Agreements and other Constructive Arrangements with Indigenous Peoples" done by Miguel Alfonso Martínez, in his capacity as the Special Rapporteur for this study. He mentions in this study that indigenous peoples were mainly those who have undergone colonization from overseas, and that therefore the Declaration can only apply to these peoples. The others, especially many of those from Asia and Africa, are considered minorities, and he concludes that it is more appropriate for them to use the Declaration on Ethnic, Linguistic and Religious Minorities.

Martínez was strongly criticized by indigenous peoples from Asia and Africa. In a side event where he initially presented the results of his study in 2000 I argued that in the Philippines there is no question that there are indigenous peoples. He replied that he agrees with me that there are indigenous peoples in the Philippines as we went through the same colonization as those in Latin America. However, this is an exception rather than the rule in Asia and Africa. We appealed to some of our indigenous colleagues from North America, who helped research and write his study, to ask him to revise this conclusion. Unfortunately, this did not happen, so it remained in his final report. This did not deter the efforts of indigenous peoples from these two regions to assert their own identities and claim their rights as indigenous peoples and not as minorities.

We developed our arguments against a global definition in the Declaration and some of these include the following:

- Having a global definition will risk exclusion of some indigenous peoples because it can never adequately capture the diversity of indigenous peoples;
- A definition will write in stone indigenous peoples' characteristics, thereby not taking into account that these are constantly evolving and developing; and
- The insistence on a definition itself is an act of discrimination. The terms "peoples" and "minorities" were not defined by the other instruments of the UN. Why is it that when it comes to "indigenous peoples" states insist that a definition be made?

Because of these efforts to contest the need for a definition at the global level, the UN Declaration on the Rights of Indigenous Peoples does not contain any. The working definition of the Martínez-Cobo[31] report was used as reference whenever this issue was raised. This remained the case until the African Group of Countries, led by Namibia and Botswana, made their last ditch attempt to have a definition included in the Declaration. Their Aide-Memoire, which they brought out in November 2006, almost led to the non-adoption of the Declaration by the UN General Assembly. To convince the African States to support the adoption of the Declaration several compromises had to be made both by the States who were the sponsoring the adoption within the UN General Assembly, and by indigenous peoples, represented through the regional caucuses and the global caucus.

The first compromise was the deletion of Article 8 of the Sub-Commission Draft which says:

"Indigenous peoples have the collective and individual right to maintain and develop their distinct identities and characteristics, including the right to identify themselves as indigenous and to be recognized as such."

This article contains the principle of self-identification. As mentioned earlier, most Asian States did not like this Article. I remember discussing this issue with the Japanese delegate as he was one of those resisting the idea of self-identification. According to him this was the main reason why his delegation was not ready to accept the Declaration. When the indigenous peoples' caucus discussed this, there was an agreement that this could be deleted as long as Article 9 remained.

Article 9 of the Sub-Commission Draft was retained in the final adopted version, still with the same number.[32] It reads:

"Indigenous peoples and individuals have the right to belong to an indigenous community or nation, in accordance with the traditions and customs of the community or nation concerned. No discrimination of any kind may arise from the exercise of such a right."

The second compromise was in relation to the proposed change by the African Group which was to include a paragraph in the preambular part. It states:

"Recognizing that the situation of indigenous peoples varies from region to region, country to country and from community to community, every country or region shall have the prerogative to define who constitutes indigenous people in their respective countries or regions taking into account its national or regional peculiarities."

This was absolutely rejected by us, the representatives of the Asian regional caucus of indigenous peoples. We saw this as another attempt to give the State the right to determine and define who are indigenous peoples. We had to find another compromise language on this. What was finally agreed upon and which is now the preambular paragraph 23 of the final adopted version is the following[33]:

"Recognizing also that the situation of indigenous peoples varies from region to region and from country to country and that the significance of national and regional particularities and various historical and cultural backgrounds should be taken into consideration."

We finally got the support of the majority of the African and Asian States to adopt the UN Declaration on the Rights of Indigenous Peoples after these two compromises were made, and after an agreement was reached on the inclusion of

Article 46 which includes he following safeguard clause:[34]

> "Nothing in this Declaration may be interpreted as implying for any State, people, group or persons any right to engage in any activity [ ] construed as authorizing or encouraging any action which would dismember, totally or in part, the territorial integrity and political unity of sovereign or independent states."

The experience we went through in the process of negotiating the Declaration illustrates how difficult and complex the issue of the definition is. This will remain a challenge in the years to come for both indigenous peoples and states at the national level. The general agreement among indigenous peoples is that definition and identification will be done at the national level and in some cases, the regional or sub-regional level because there are indigenous peoples who were artificially divided and separated by the formation of nation-states and the establishment of national boundaries. At the Workshop on the Concept of Indigenousness in Asia, which was held in 2006, this general agreement was also reached.

Challenges Ahead

The process of defining and identifying indigenous peoples, especially at the national and regional levels, will entail continuous negotiations between states and indigenous peoples. Self-identification will remain the basic principle, but cannot be the sole process of identifying who indigenous peoples are. This principle has to be supplemented by a process of recognition by the indigenous peoples themselves. This is one challenge which has to be addressed. Not anybody can just come and claim an indigenous identity without recognition by the peoples he or she is identifying with. It is not far-fetched to imagine that with the adoption of the UN Declaration on the Rights of Indigenous Peoples there will be individuals, who are not necessarily indigenous, who will come out of the woodworks and self-identify as indigenous. In fact, there are already a few cases like this.

The other situation is when there is a collective claim by a group or a people that they are indigenous peoples. This happened at one session of the UN Working Group on Indigenous Population in 1996 which was attended by South Africa's Afrikaner nationalists and they claimed that they were an indigenous people. Most of us, representatives of indigenous peoples present in that meeting, rejected their claim. That was the first and last time that they attempted to do this. So, one factor which can regulate the false claims of a group or a people is their acceptance or rejection by other indigenous peoples, within the respective country and at the international level.

We are going through similar experiences at the UN Permanent Forum on Indigenous Issues. Some persons and groups who have participated in some sessions are requesting that the Forum provides a certificate that they are recognized as belonging to an indigenous people. In such cases I, as the chairperson of the Forum, have to explain that the Forum is not mandated to do this. If the ones claiming such identity are individuals it is first of all the indigenous peoples whom they are identifying with who can give them the legitimacy. If it is a group seeking recognition as an indigenous people, one way of dealing with this is through a process of collective recognition referred to earlier. The indigenous peoples in the country or region where the claimants reside can have a say in whether they are to be recognized as an indigenous people or not. For instance, there are African-Americans belonging to different organizations who claim that they are indigenous peoples. I had to consult with Native American representatives on where this claim is coming from and what they think of it. We were also faced with a complicated situation when the Basques from Spain and France and some people from Ireland participated in the sessions of the Forum and asserted that they are indigenous peoples. This issue has not yet been discussed more in-depth by the members of the Forum, but will have to be addressed in the near future.

Of course, a basis for determining whether they are indigenous could be the working definitions of the ILO Convention No. 169 and the Martínez-Cobo report. While I propose that those claiming indigenous identities should meet most of the different elements of the working definition, we cannot apply these, or any other definition rigidly for the reasons explained above. Erica Irene-Daes, the long-time Chairperson of the UN Working Group on Indigenous Populations suggested in one of her reports that

> "[   ] the ideal type of an 'indigenous people' is a group that is aboriginal (autochthonous) to the territory where it resides today and chooses to perpetuate a distinct cultural identity and distinct collective social and political organization within the territory."[35]

It is important to point out that she is referring to the territory of the respective people, and not that of a nation state, as explicitly or implicitly demanded by many state governments. There are however many cases, especially in Asia, where historical circumstances forced people to leave their ancestral territories and even cross national boundaries (or, rather, came to settle in places which became part of a nation-state in the wake of colonization and decolonization). Denying them their indigenous identity would amount to adding insult to injury. Again, there is no way that any global definition would do justice to the diversity of circumstances and conditions faced by indigenous peoples across the world.

In other cases, there are persons who did not know that they belong to an indigenous people, or who opted to hide or not to claim their indigenous identity because of discrimination and racism. Now, there is a growing desire among them to self-identify as indigenous. For as long as their peoples accept them, there should be no problem. I have met some persons from the coastal areas of Norway who now are now identifying themselves as Saami. Their parents have deliberately brought them up to be Norwegians because of the policy of assimilation in the past and the experiences of racism and discrimination. Because of the upsurge of the Saami peoples' movement, some of them started tracing their genealogies and they discovered that their grandparents are Saami. Now, they are reclaiming their identity and are trying to learn the Saami language. They are accepted by the established Saami organizations, such as the Saami Council or the Norwegian Sami Association, as Saami.

However, there are persons who are just opportunistic, who will claim indigenous identities, even if they are not, because they see some advantages in doing this. To prevent the misuse or abuse of the UN Declaration on the Rights of Indigenous Peoples by such persons, there need to be both non-formal and formal mechanisms established at different levels, which can deal with such incidents. How these mechanisms will look like and how these will assert their authority will depend in each case on the indigenous peoples concerned.

The other challenge is the continuing denial of states that there are indigenous peoples in their countries, or that all their peoples are indigenous. This is what India stated after the adoption of the Declaration; that all people in India are indigenous. Such assertions are attempts to justify the non-application of the Declaration within the respective country. However, the claim that all are indigenous peoples still cannot be an excuse for them not to implement the Declaration.

The Chinese government, for example, claims that they do not have indigenous peoples, that they only have ethnic minorities. In the past, however, the term used for these peoples are minority nationalities, which is a recognition that they are distinct nationalities or nations. Through the years this term was changed into ethnic minorities, which certainly was a political decision made by the State. But there is an admission by some of the authorities that the problems faced by their minorities are similar to the issues addressed by the Declaration.

Whatever claims countries have in terms of presence or absence of indigenous peoples, what is clear is that there are groups of peoples who still continue to practice their own cultures and traditions and their livelihoods which are closely linked with nature, their lands, territories and resources. They still suffer from racism and discrimination which are institutionalized in policies and laws and practiced by those from the dominant populations. These peoples aspire to pass on their lands, territories and resources as well as their languages, identities, cultures and traditions and also their social and political governance systems to the future generations. Even if they are not recognized by the State as indigenous peoples they can still assert their identities and claim their rights as contained in the Declaration. And these aspirations and demands have to be addressed by the States and the international community.

The policies of other multilateral bodies, like the Operational Directive 4.20 of the World Bank on indigenous peoples, the Asian Development Bank's policy on indigenous peoples as well as the UN Development Group Guidelines on

Indigenous Peoples' Issues, can help in supporting the identity claims of indigenous peoples. The World Bank policy applies to borrower countries which have indigenous peoples, whether they are officially recognized or not. So, for instance, if India or Kenya borrows from the World Bank and the project which they are using the World Bank loan is used for a territory with indigenous peoples, the Indian and Kenyan governments are obliged to identify who are these peoples and to apply the policy.

With the adoption of the UN Declaration on the Rights of Indigenous Peoples the road ahead for indigenous peoples looks brighter. The Declaration is an important instrument for indigenous peoples for their liberation from discrimination and oppression. Its implementation, however, will be an uphill struggle. Edmund Burke's exhortation that the "price of freedom is eternal vigilance" very much applies to us, indigenous peoples, and to our supporters. Indeed, the price for our assertion to be recognized as distinct peoples, and to have our rights, as contained in the UN Declaration on the Rights of Indigenous Peoples, protected, respected and fulfilled is eternal vigilance.

References

Anaya, S. James 2004. *Indigenous Peoples in International Law.* Oxford: Oxford University Press

Daes, Erica-Irene 2000. Working paper on the relationship and distinction between the rights of persons belonging to minorities and those of indigenous peoples. Geneva: Sub-Commission on Human Rights. UN Document No. E/CN.4/Sub.2/2000/10. 19 July 2000

Martínez, Miguel Alfonso 1999. *Study on Treaties, Agreements and other Constructive Arrangements between States and Indigenous Populations. Final Report.* New York: United Nations Economic and Social Council, UN Document E/CN.4/Sub.2/1999/20

Martínez-Cobo, José 1981. *Study of the Problem of Discrimination Against Indigenous Populations.* Geneva: United Nations. UN Doc. E/CN.4/Sub.2/1986/7/Add.4

Minde, Henry 2007. The Destination and the Journey. Indigenous Peoples and the United Nations from the 1960s to 1985; in: H. Minde, A. Eide and M. Ahren. *The UN Declaration on the Rights of Indigenous Peoples; What made it possible? The work and process beyond the final adoption,.* Galdu Cala. Journal of Indigenous Peoples' Rights No. 4/2007. Kautokeino: Galdu Resource Center for the Rights of Indigenous Peoples

Minde, Henry (ed.) 2008. *Self-determination, Knowledge, Indigeneity.* Delft, The Netherlands: Eburon Academic Publishers)

Sanders, Douglas 1999. *Developing a Modern International Law on the Rights of Indigenous Peoples.* University of British Columbia. Retrieved on 20 August 2008 at www.ubc.ca

United Nations Commission on Human Rights 1971. *Study on Racial Discrimination in the Political, Economic, Social and Cultural Spheres.* UN Doc. E.71 X1V

United Nations General Assembly 2007. Resolution adopted by the General Assembly. 61/295. United Nations Declaration on the Rights of Indigenous Peoples. UN Document A/RES/61/295. Accessed at: http://www2. ohchr.org/english/issues/ indigenous/declaration.htm

Weisner, Siegfred.1999 *Rights and Status of Indigenous Peoples:A Global Comparative and Legal Analysis.* Harvard Human Rights Journal 12.

Xanthaki, Alexandra 2007. *Indigenous Rights and the United Nations Standards: Self-determination, Culture and Land.* New York: Cambridge University Press

Notes

[1] The author is the Chairperson of the United Nations Permanent Forum on Indigenous Issues; Executive Director, Tebtebba (Indigenous Peoples' International Centre for Policy Research and Education) and the Convenor of the Asian Indigenous Women's Network (AIWN)

[2] I mentioned both the World Bank and the ADB as their respective policy documents contained their own description of indigenous peoples.

[3] These countries include India, Bangladesh, Pakistan.

[4] The US, in its interpretative statement after the adoption by the UN General Assembly of the UNDRIP in 13 Sept. 2007, cited the failure of the Declaration to define who constitutes indigenous peoples as one reason why it voted against the adoption of the Declaration.

[5] For example, the Maori population was around 125,000 to 135,000 when they were first colonized by the British. By 1886 their population dropped to 42,660. (Weisner 1999)

[6] For a more extensive discussion on the roles played by Vitorio and de las Casas, see Anaya 2004: p.17-18.

[7] Colonizers varied from country to country but these included the British, German, Spanish, Portuguese, Dutch, French, Americans and the Japanese.

[8] This refers to colonization from Europe across the ocean. Anaya:1996,p.43.

[9] Sanders 2008: p. 1

[10] The Philippine Indigenous Peoples Rights Act (IPRA) was enacted in 1997. This was the enabling law for the 1987 Constitutional provision which recognized the rights of indigenous peoples to their ancestral domains.

[11] A number of national laws protect the rights of Taiwan's indigenous peoples, the most important being the Indigenous Peoples' Basic Act of 2005. The Constitutional Amendments of 2005 provides for indigenous representation in the Legislative Assembly and protection of language and culture.

[12] Xanthaki 2007: p.6.

[13] The ILO was established in 1919, one of the first intergovernmental bodies, established even before the UN. When the UN was born in 1945 the ILO became one of its Specialized Agencies.

[14] The other UN agencies involved were WHO, UNESCO and FAO. UNICEF was brought in later. Countries covered included Bolivia, Peru and Ecuador. Argentina, Chile, Colombia and Venezuela were added at a later stage.

[15] Xanthaki 2007: p.52

[16] Ibid. p.17

[17] Ibid. p.53

[18] This is composed of 20 independent experts on labour law and social problems which is mandated to address problems related to the implementation of Conventions and Recommendations. The members are appointed by the Governing Body of the ILO on the basis of recommendations of the Director-General.

[19] The National Indian Youth Council of the United States got organized in l961 after they gate-crashed the Conference on Indian Policy of the University of Chicago and declared the inherent right of the Indian people to self-government and to their lands (Anaya 2004).

[20] Minde 2007: p.7

[21] As of now there are 19 countries which ratified ILO Convention No. 169. These are Argentina (2000), Bolivia (1994), Brazil (2002), Colombia (1991), Costa Rica (1993), Denmark, Dominica (2002), Ecuador (1998), Fiji, Guatemala (1996), Honduras (1993), Mexico (1990), Nepal (2007), the Netherlands, Norway, Paraguay (1993), Peru (1993), Spain (2007), Venezuela (1999).

[22] The Human Rights Council was the successor of the Commission on Human Rights.

[23] The Sub-Commission is an independent expert body consisting of appointed experts by the Commission.

[24] Minde 2007: p.13. The study by Hernán Santa Cruz done between 1966 and 1970 is found in UN Doc. E.71 X1V: *Study on Racial Discrimination in the Political, Economic, Social and Cultural Spheres.* Chapter IX: "Measures taken in connection with the protection of indigenous peoples", and Chapter XIII, para 1094-1102, "Problem of Indigenous Populations."

[25] UN Commission on Human Rights 1971: Chapter XIII, para 1094.

[26] Minde 2007: p.22. This is Article 21 of the UN Declaration and Programme of Action to Combat Racism and Racial Discrimination, Geneva, 1978.

[27] Ibid.: Attachment. This is Part 1, Article 2 of Draft prepared by Sanders for the WCIP.

[28] Martínez- Cobo 1981. *Conclusions: Study of the Problem of Discrimination Against Indigenous Populations* (Geneva: United Nations, 1981) para 379.

[29] Augusto Willemsen-Díaz is fondly referred to as the father of indigenous peoples issues in the United Nations. He, in his capacity as a member of the Secretariat of the UN, was the one who persisted in bringing to the attention of the UN the indigenous peoples problematique. He was the one who mainly did the research and writing of the Martínez-Cobo Study. He is now retired lives in Guatemala, his home country.

[30] Those of us, under the Global Indigenous Peoples' Caucus, who were doing the lobbying at the General Assembly, assumed that after the Human Rights Council submitted the finalized Draft to the GA at its Fall 2006 Session it will be approved without much fanfare. We did not foresee that the African Group of Countries, through the leadership of Namibia and Botswana, would go for radical amendments to the text. This move led the sponsors of the Resolution for the adoption to withdraw their resolution because if they insisted on pushing through with this they would lose the vote for its adoption. This pushed us to revisit our strategy, and plan other moves which were aimed at convincing the African Group of Countries not to block the resolution, which would be presented again before the end of the 61st Session of the GA in September 2007. The compromise text, which brought them on board, was Article 46 which mentioned that nothing in the Declaration may be interpreted as giving the right to any state, people, group or person to perform any act contrary to the UN Charter or construed as authorizing actions which will dismember or impair territorial integrity and political unity.

[31] Martínex-Cobo 1981

[32] United Nations General Assembly 2007

[33] Ibid.

[34] Ibid.

[35] Daes 2000: para 48

Part II
Toward Identifying Indigenous Peoples in Asia

"Indigenous Peoples" in International Law:
A Constructivist Approach to the Asian Controversy

Benedict Kingsbury[1]

Reprinted from The American Journal of International Law, Vol. 92, No. 3. July 1998. Reproduced with permission from The American Society of International Law©

Over a very short period, the few decades since the early 1970s, "indigenous peoples" has been transformed from a prosaic description without much significance in international law and politics, into a concept with considerable power as a basis for group mobilization, international standard setting, transnational networks and programmatic activity of intergovernmental and nongovernmental organizations.[2]

The development of "indigenous peoples" as a significant concept in international practice has not been accompanied by any general agreement as to its meaning, nor even by agreement on a process by which its meaning might be established. As the concept becomes increasingly important, international controversy as to its meaning and implications is acquiring greater legal and political significance. This article considers how to understand "indigenous peoples" as an international legal concept. To sharpen the focus, the discussion concentrates on the current practical dispute as to whether and how the concept of "indigenous peoples," formed and shaped in regions dominated by the history and effects of European settlement, might or should be adapted and made applicable in Asia and elsewhere. Both elements of the term – "indigenous" and "peoples" – are contentious, but the discussion here will focus on indigenousness.

Two broad approaches to relatively underspecified concepts such as "indigenous peoples" may be identified. The first, here termed a positivist approach, treats "indigenous peoples" as a legal category requiring precise definition, so that for particular operational purposes it should be possible to determine, on the basis of the definition, exactly who does or does not have a particular status, enjoy a particular right, or assume a particular responsibility. Once established, such definitions theoretically ground the interpretive process of determining the scope of application of particular legal instruments and rules. It will be argued that the experience of international agencies and associations of indigenous peoples demonstrates that it is impossible at present to formulate a single globally viable definition that is workable and not grossly under- or overinclusive. Any strict definition is likely to incorporate justifications and referents that make sense in some societies but not in others. It will tend to reduce the fluidity and dynamism of social life to distorted and rather static formal categories. One possible conclusion, that "indigenous peoples" as a global concept is unworkable and dangerously incoherent, has some adherents. But it is a concept of great normative power for many relatively powerless groups that have suffered grievous abuses, and it bears the imprimatur of representatives of many such groups who are themselves shaping it while being shaped by it. As a concept designating a locus of groups and issues, albeit with some imprecision and uncertainties, it has proved remarkably serviceable, and there is no contending replacement. The aspiration for perfect positivist coherence is unachievable, but there is another way to understand the concept.

This second approach, here termed constructivist, takes the international concept of "indigenous peoples" not as one sharply defined by universally applicable criteria, but as embodying a continuous process in which claims and practices in numerous specific cases are abstracted in the wider institutions of international society, then made specific again at the moment of application in the political, legal and social processes of particular cases and societies.

Neither approach suffices entirely on its own. It will be argued that the constructivist approach to the concept better captures its functions and significance in global international institutions and normative instruments. In most cases the terminology and indicative definitions in global or regional instruments are too abstract and remote to provide a sufficient basis to resolve the infinite variety of questions that arise in specific cases, and it is misguided to expect that these global instruments can even purport to resolve all such detailed problems. These instruments often contain relevant principles and criteria abstracted from the specifics of past cases and debates, and each has stimulated a body of practice concerning its scope of application and the meaning of concepts it employs. But many specific problems as to the meaning of "indigenous peoples" and related concepts can be solved only in accordance with processes and criteria that vary among different societies and institutions. Only in such specific contexts is it possible adequately to answer such questions as: Is a waning traditional authority or a popular, but state-created, political body the proper representative of an indigenous group in a land claim?[3] Are children of a marriage between a group member and a nonmember entitled to be full members?[4] Who are the legal successors to a group whose leaders signed a treaty in the eighteenth century?[5] Does organization of a new political body by one clan from a larger indigenous community make the clan an indigenous people?[26] Which group is part of which other group for purposes of representation?[27] Who ought to benefit from royalty payments for a therapeutic drug derived from a plant known and used by several groups?[28] Can local villagers close a forest that is the supply of fuel wood for a community of landless migrants nearby?[29] To which groups in a particular country does the World Bank's policy on indigenous peoples apply?[10] Who will be eligible to represent indigenous peoples if, as is currently proposed, a permanent forum for indigenous peoples is established in the United Nations?[11] Such questions can be resolved only through specific contextual decisions, often referring to detailed functional definitions that are influenced by and influence, the more abstract global concept.

Before the argument is developed, a caveat must be entered about the scope and generality of this article. It focuses on issues arising in east, south eastern and south Asia. Even with much of western and central Asia omitted, this region is so diverse as to issues pertaining to "indigenous peoples" that generalizations must be treated with the utmost caution.[12] There are overlapping themes, as well as considerable variation, between Asia and Africa in this regard, and the relevance or irrelevance of the concept of "indigenous peoples" in Africa is of great importance. Although to a lesser extent than Asian groups, a small number of African groups have become involved in the international indigenous peoples' movement,[13] and governments of a few African states have expressed concerns similar to those of Asian state governments considered in this article.[14] For clarity, specific issues concerning the concept of "indigenous peoples" in Africa are not considered in this article.

I. The Asian Controversy: Separating Justifications, Norms and Institutions

One of the central questions in the current controversy is whether the concept of "indigenous peoples" has any application to people in the group of major Asian states whose governments deny its relevance, Following the pattern of group mobilization established in states dominated by European settlement–in the Americas, Australasia and the Nordic countries–groups based in different Asian states have more recently begun to participate in international institutions and gatherings of "indigenous peoples," and transnational networks have been formed in Asia under the rubric "indigenous peoples."[15] The concept of "indigenous peoples," or its local cognates, has become an important unifying connection in transnational activist networks, linking groups that were hitherto marginal and politically unorganized to transnational sources of ideas, information, support, legitimacy and money.[16] International institutions increasingly apply to parts of Asia policies, programs and specific rules concerning "indigenous peoples." The World Bank, for example, first adopted a policy on tribal peoples arising out of the dismal experience of projects in Latin America, but seeks as a global organization to apply its current policy on indigenous peoples to some of its projects in Asia; the relevant

World Bank policies have also provided an influential model for the Asian Development Bank. The international activity has begun to shape national practice in many states, influencing political discourse, government policy, and some judicial and legislative action. The attitudes of governments in Asia to the application to their states of the concept of "indigenous peoples" differ considerably, but strong opposition has been expressed by China, India, Bangladesh, Myanmar and (for the most part) Indonesia.

The core of the current international controversy may be captured by juxtaposing two quotations, both originating in the context of ongoing efforts in the United Nations to draft a normative declaration on the rights of indigenous peoples. Each is representative of strongly held recurrent positions.

The first quotation is from a statement made in 1991 to the United Nations Working Group on indigenous populations in the names of members of the West Papuan Peoples' Front the Karen National Union, the Jumma Network in Europe, the Indian Council of Indigenous and Tribal Peoples, the Alliance of Taiwan Aborigines, the National Federation of Indigenous Peoples of the Philippines (KAMP), Lumad–Mindanao, the Cordillera Peoples Alliance, the Ainu Association of Hokkaido, the Asia Indigenous Peoples Pact, the Naga Peoples Movement for Human Rights, the Homeland Mission 1950 for South Moluccas, and the Hmong People:

> First and foremost, we want to bring to your attention the denial of some Asian governments of the existence of indigenous peoples in our part of the world. This denial presents a significant obstacle to the participation of many indigenous peoples from our region in the Working Group's deliberations. The denial also seeks to withhold the benefits of the Declaration from the indigenous, tribal, and aboriginal peoples of Asia. We hereby urgently request that peoples who are denied the rights to govern themselves and are called tribal, and/or aboriginal in our region, be recognized, for the purpose of this Declaration, and in accordance with I.L.O. practice, as equivalent to indigenous peoples.[17]

The second quotation is from comments sent in 1995 by the People's Republic of China to a working group of the UN Commission on Human Rights:

> The Chinese Government believes that the question of indigenous peoples is the product of European countries' recent pursuit of colonial policies in other parts of the world. Because of these policies, many indigenous peoples were dispossessed of their ancestral homes and lands, brutally oppressed, exploited and murdered, and in some cases even deliberately exterminated. To this day, many indigenous peoples still suffer from discrimination and diminished status. . . . As in the majority of Asian countries, the various nationalities in China have all lived for aeons on

Chinese territory. Although there is no indigenous peoples' question in China, the Chinese Government and people have every sympathy with indigenous peoples' historical woes and historical plight. China believes it absolutely essential to draft an international instrument to protect their rights and interests. . . . The special historical misfortunes of indigenous peoples set them apart from minority nationalities and ethnic groups in the ordinary sense. For this reason, the draft declaration must clearly define what indigenous peoples are, in order to guarantee that the special rights it establishes are accurately targeted at genuine communities of indigenous people and are not distorted, arbitrarily extended or muddled.[18]

As the first quotation indicates, representatives of a large number of groups in Asia are actively participating in international activities of indigenous peoples, and take the view that their groups fall within the international rubric of "indigenous peoples" even if a cognate expression has not hitherto been used in local politics. Conversely, several governments of Asian states argue that the concept of "indigenous peoples" is so integrally a product of the common experience of European colonial settlement as to be fundamentally inapplicable to those parts of Asia that did not experience substantial European settlement. The dispute as to the meaning and scope of this concept is of considerable importance to contemporary efforts in the United Nations to negotiate a declaration on the rights of indigenous peoples, and it has important implications for operational policy in institutions ranging from the World Bank to the Biodiversity Convention.

The controversy about the meaning and application of "indigenous peoples" as an international concept encompasses conflicting views about the *norms* applicable to indigenous peoples and their relationships with states and with individuals, and struggles over the potentially potent roles of *international institutions;* but the most fundamental problem is deep–seated differences over the *justifications* for institutional and normative programs based on recognition of a distinct category of "indigenous peoples." It will be argued that the best possibility of progress toward broad international agreement among different states and groups--an agreement that by no means exists at present--will be through continued bargaining on norms applicable to indigenous peoples, the continued evolution of distinct practices in different types of institutions, and a definition of "indigenous peoples" that is sufficiently flexible to accommodate a range of justifications.

In the area of international human rights, diplomatic negotiations have long utilized distinctions between norms, institutions and justifications as a means to facilitate consensus. A recurrent feature of international human rights instruments since 1945 has been the articulation of norms in universal terms, albeit with margins for different local interpretations and some acknowledgment of the relevance of cultural difference, accompanied by acceptance of wide discretion for states in choices of national and international institutional mechanisms to protect and promote human rights, and openness of international normative texts to divergent justifications of the norms concerned. At the same time, this pattern has been continuously contested by those seeking universality through convergence around tightly drafted norms, standardized court-centered national and international institutions for enforcement, and explicit endorsement of Enlightenment type justifications to be used to enhance interpretation of norms and effectiveness of institutions.

In relation to questions concerning indigenous peoples, I argue that, while there are conflicts of interests and values relating to norms and institutions, the most fundamental and problematic disagreement is over the justifications inherent in the concept of "indigenous peoples" as currently understood. Controversy arises in particular from the implication that distinctive rights of indigenous peoples are justified by the destruction of their previous territorial entitlements and political autonomy wrought by historic circumstances of invasion and colonization. The best possibility of progress is to interpret the concept with sufficient flexibility to make clear that it accommodates a wider range of justifications. The next part examines the issues of justification through consideration of existing international definitions, views advanced by indigenous peoples, views held in a range of European settler states, and practice in various Asian states, concluding with analysis of the arguments advanced by the governments of China and India. The two subsequent parts briefly consider issues of norms and institutions as they bear on the controversy over the meaning of "indigenous peoples." Part V will defend a particular–and contested–constructivist view of how such international legal concepts as "indigenous peoples" work, and make the case for broadening the concept of "indigenous peoples" to accommodate a wider range of justifications. This is a difficult issue of philosophy and of judgment; there is an appreciable risk for the indigenous peoples' movement that the existing and highly functional international political distinction between indigenous peoples and ethnic and other minorities will erode, galvanizing opposition to claims of indigenous peoples. Building on the premises developed in part V, a specific proposal as to definition is presented in part VI.

II. The Concept of "Indigenous Peoples" and its Justifications

International Definitions of "Indigenous Peoples"

Three different approaches to the problems of definition are found in texts of the United Nations, the International Labour Organization (ILO) and the World Bank. The level of controversy and the perceived political stakes are highest in the United Nations, and no UN definition of "indigenous peoples" has been adopted. UN practice has to some extent been guided by a working definition in the 1986 report of UN Special Rapporteur Martínez Cobo:

Indigenous communities, peoples and nations are those which, having a historical continuity with pre-invasion and pre-colonial societies that developed on their territories, consider themselves distinct from other sectors of the societies now prevailing in those territories, or parts of them. They form at present non-dominant sectors of society and are determined to preserve, develop and transmit to future generations their ancestral territories, and their ethnic identity, as the basis of their continued existence as peoples, in accordance, with their own cultural patterns, social institutions and legal systems.

This historical continuity may consist of the continuation, for an extended period reaching into the present, of one or more of the following factors:

(a) Occupation of ancestral lands, or at least of part of them;
(b) Common ancestry with the original occupants of these lands;
(c) Culture in general, or in specific manifestations (such as religion, living under a tribal system, membership of an indigenous community, dress, means of livelihood, life-style, etc.);
(d) Language (whether used as the only language, as mother-tongue, as the habitual means of communication at home or in the family, or as the main, preferred, habitual, general or normal language);
(e) Residence in certain parts of the country, or in certain regions of the world;
(f) Other relevant factors.[19]

This definition takes a potentially limited, and controversial, view of "indigenous peoples" by requiring "historical continuity with pre-invasion and pre-colonial societies that developed on their territories." By contrast, the ILO has a more diffuse historical requirement, and includes in its legal definition an additional category of "tribal peoples"; it has firmly established the applicability of its treaties in all regions.[20] The World Bank has dispensed altogether with criteria based on historical continuity and colonialism, instead taking a functional view of "indigenous peoples" as "groups with a social and cultural identity distinct from the dominant society that makes them vulnerable to being disadvantaged," an approach dearly applicable in much of Asia.[21]

The contrasts between the approaches in these three interstate institutions suggest that "indigenous peoples" is not a precise term of art with a single fixed meaning. Numerous variations in relevant categories and rules of participation are evolving to meet different functional requirements, political conditions and regional mores. Nevertheless, in the absence of any unifying global concept, this functional divergence may come at the price of unsustainable fragmentation and inconsistency. I will argue that a constructivist approach makes a global concept of "indigenous peoples" possible, while allowing functional specificity to meet diverse social circumstances and institutional requirements.

Approaches Taken by Indigenous Peoples

The early effort to build a vibrant international indigenous peoples' movement in the 1970s was driven primarily by groups from areas of European invasion and settlement. The World Council of Indigenous Peoples (WCIP), for example, was founded in 1975 at the initiative of George Manuel of the National Indian Brotherhood of Canada; its initial scope and the sources of its momentum are indicated by its early five-region structure, covering North, Central, and South America, the Nordic region and Australasia.[22] Asian groups were included under the umbrella of the international indigenous peoples' movement as such groups became more organized and active in international fora. Despite the initial hesitation of some individuals active in the "founding" regions of the World Council of Indigenous Peoples – people living in Japan, India and Thailand were permitted to speak only as observers at the Third General Assembly of the WCIP in 1981[23] – the WCIP subsequently decided to broaden its geographic scope, and a Pacific-Asia Council of Indigenous Peoples was established. While the WCIP is no longer as active as in its early years, the international indigenous peoples' movement is burgeoning, with numerous networks and loose organizational structures in which many groups from Asia are now involved.

The existence of an indigenous peoples' movement is a major factor in the diffusion and impact of "indigenous peoples" as an international legal concept. Groups and individuals participating in this movement have focused on elements of commonality that have helped the movement to cohere: connections with land and territory, aspirations for autonomy and self-determination, renewed interest in distinct cultures and languages, the historical experience of incursions by other groups, continuing consequences of dispossession and subordination, concerns over health and education, and relative disadvantages in child welfare, mortality, nutrition and income levels. A further element is the shared effects of modernity.[24] While the indigenous peoples' movement was made possible in some respects by modern communications, economy and politics, it is also a form of resistance to modernization and globalization, particularly to the convergence and homogenization they threaten to bring on. All of these factors affect the formulation of international normative programs and credos various groups of organizations participating in the indigenous peoples' movement. Not surprisingly, structured political settings such as the UN negotiations on drafting a declaration on the rights of indigenous peoples have been heavily influenced by the agendas and demands of a small number of representatives of politically dominant groups skilled in the methods, politics and working languages of the United Nations, relatively few of whom are Asian.

The choice and evolution of an overarching self-conception to unify the international political movement of indigenous peoples has necessarily involved abstracting from a highly diverse range of self-understandings and political discourses among different groups. The social and political concepts available to the movement are influenced by the concepts carried in its principal working languages. "Indigenous peoples" is now a well-established usage in English and Spanish, but it conveys an element of novelty even in French and is difficult to capture nonpejoratively in Chinese, Japanese or Thai except by new usages or translation from other languages. In ordinary language "indigenous peoples" connotes priority in time, if not immemorial occupancy. It also suggests continuity of group identity over a very long period, even as conditions have been altered by colonialism, influx, migration, or the frequent changes in group structures and ethnic identities.[25] These elements of historical priority and group continuity have acquired significance as "indigenous peoples" has evolved from ordinary language into a specialized term in transnational mobilization and normative instruments.

A comparison of two texts from the international indigenous peoples' movement illustrates the point, notwithstanding that the texts themselves proved evanescent. A preparatory meeting in 1974 to plan the 1975 conference that established the WCIP used a provisional working definition (for determining who qualified as delegates) that contains elements of priority and historical continuity, but also seems to acknowledge their fluidity and imprecision:

> The term indigenous people refers to people living in countries which have a population composed of differing ethnic or racial groups who are descendants of the earliest populations living in the area and who do not as a group control the national government of the countries within which they live.[26]

By 1984, the developing collective political consciousness and confidence of the international indigenous peoples' movement produced, in the draft International Covenant on the Rights of Indigenous Peoples prepared for the WCIP, a sharpened and more reified view of these elements. An indigenous people is one:

> a) who lived in a territory before the entry of a colonizing population, which colonizing population has created a new state or states or extended the jurisdiction of an existing state or states to include the territory, and
> b) who continue to live in the territory and who do not control the national government of the state or states within which they live.[27]

This construction of a collective self-representation simultaneously challenges dominant conceptions of the State as the political embodiment of a nation comprising all of the people within that state, and emulates the representation of historical "nations" connected to particular territory as a foundation for many modern "nation-states."

The impacts on political consciousness of the modem territorial state, and the concepts of "nation" that have buttressed it, have been so strong that it is scarcely surprising that in some usages the concept of "indigenous peoples" has taken on a parallel structure.

"Indigenous peoples" challenges totalizing views of "nation" and the "nation-state" that have frequently made it difficult for identities other than the "nation" to secure recognition and acceptance. "Indigenous peoples" would legitimize such cultural and political units in the way nation-states have been legitimized by "nations." "History" has often seemed to leave indigenous peoples not so much as participants and subjects but as marginal objects contained within a much broader account of the nation, prominent perhaps as to customs and folk dances but peripheral in national politics and national law.

In a reaction against this view, the rhetoric of some international conceptions of "indigenous peoples" implies an approach to history similar to those nationalistic histories of "nations" probed skeptically by Elie Kedourie, Benedict Anderson and many others.[28] These approaches have proved highly functional for certain purposes. As Prasenjit Duara argues in a discussion of Chinese historiography:

> [N]ational history secures for the contested and contingent nation the false unity of a self-same, national subject evolving through time. . . . It allows the nation-state to see itself as a unique form of community which finds its place in the oppositions between tradition and modernity, hierarchy and equality, empire and nation. Within this schema, the nation appears as the newly realized, sovereign subject of [Enlightenment] History embodying a moral and political force that has overcome dynasties, aristocracies, and ruling priests and mandarins, who are seen to represent merely themselves historically. In contrast to them, the nation is a collective historical subject poised to realize its destiny in a modern future.[29]

James Clifford captures exactly this element in his observation of the trial of a Native American land rights claim that under U.S. law was deemed to depend on establishing simple linear historical continuity of the group over hundreds of years—a romanticized continuity demanded by Western history with little regard to tribal history. In history,

> [tribal] societies are always either dying or surviving, assimilating or resisting. Caught between a local past and a global future, they either hold on to their separateness or "enter the modern world." . . . But the familiar paths of tribal death, survival, assimilation, or resistance do not catch the specific ambivalence of life in places like Mashpee over four

centuries of defeat, renewal, political negotiation, and cultural innovation.[30]

In struggles to put into question totalizing views of the "nation," it may be
inevitable that the concept of "indigenous peoples" takes on some of the same
characteristics. But such approaches risk some of the same hazards as extreme
varieties of nationalism, and are likely in the future to meet with similar skeptical
reconsideration. However, just as national projects have evolved or metamor-
phosed in many places, so the concept of "indigenous peoples" is often espoused
flexibly both in international institutions and in more local politics.

The existence and recognition of "indigenous peoples" in international and
transnational practice provides a legitimacy, perhaps even a language, for the
pursuit of aspirations and grievances that may otherwise struggle for purchase or
vocabulary. It provides access to transnational benefits supplied by private groups
such as Oxfam, intergovernmental agencies such as the World Bank, and foreign
governments such as the Netherlands and Norway, which have policies specifically
targeted to overseas indigenous peoples;[31] and to political and institutional fora
such as the United Nations, the UN Commission on Sustainable Development,
the Conference of the Parties to the Biodiversity Convention, and associations of
museum directors and national parks administrators. The category certainly has
international purchase: publications and Internet postings of nongovernmental
organizations (NGOs) seeking to appeal to a Western/Northern audience regularly emphasize adverse impacts of projects on ethnic minorities or indigenous
groups with distinct cultures. Nevertheless, the precise justifications on which
the concept of "indigenous peoples" depends for its appeal and effectiveness vary
across different groups, societies and issues.

Attitudes in States Dominated by European Settlement

Not surprisingly, proponents of "national" projects in many states have resisted concepts of "indigenous peoples" that seem to challenge the unity of the
"nation." This "national" view is evident in ILO Convention No. 107 of 1957, in
which indigenous and tribal populations are identified as distinct social groups
whose conditions of life ought to be ameliorated to promote their assimilation
into the ambient population, leading eventually to national integration. Numerous adherents of such views can still be found in Europe, the Americas and
Australasia, but it is remarkable how far the governments of many states in these
regions have shifted to endorse a concept of "indigenous peoples" as enduring and
distinctive collectivities internationally and within the polity. Many hesitations
and exceptions remain, in these regions as elsewhere. The governments of France,
Japan, Sweden, the United States and other states have expressed strong misgiv-
ings about international recognition of collective rights.[32] Several states argue
that their constitutions do not permit the possibility of more than one "people"

within the national territory,[33] and object to the use of such terms as "indigenous nations,"[34], or in some cases to recognition of autonomous indigenous legal and political systems. [35]

Nevertheless, the shift in government attitudes, for purposes of multilateral negotiations but often in specific dealings with indigenous peoples as well, has been substantial. Although to date such deep-rooted, nuanced, complex and in some cases contradictory developments is simplistic, significant shifts in formal policies of state governments concerning indigenous peoples in regions of European settlement have been evident in the United States (episodically), Peru (marred by subsequent violence), Canada, Denmark and to some extent Australia since the beginning of the 1970s; Colombia, New Zealand, Norway, Finland, and (more equivocally) Sweden, Brazil and Nicaragua since the mid1980s; and Russia, Chile, Bolivia, Mexico, Argentina, Guatemala and other states from the late 1980s onward.

Explaining the generality of this largely contemporaneous shift in so many states remains a conjectural enterprise at present. In many states it has been facilitated by political and ideological changes accompanying democratic transitions. Over more than a century appreciable, if spasmodic, parallel shifts have taken place in government policies concerning indigenous peoples among clusters of states in these regions of European settlement. These parallels doubtless reflect similarities in demands of dominant political groups far access to land and resources, and to some extent are a natural consequence of the logics common to similar legal and political systems.[36] It is a plausible hypothesis that the recent shifts were also influenced by such factors as transnational linkages among indigenous peoples, pressures and incentives from international institutions, a degree of borrowing and mimesis, and the incipient emergence .of common norms. However, little comparative social scientific work has yet been done on the causal impacts of such factors in this regard or the precise pathways through which they operate.

The dynamics of the international debate about "indigenous peoples" differ from those of the "human rights" debate in that the relation of Western states to indigenous peoples is much mare ambivalent than their commitment at least to civil and political rights.[37] Similarly, the transnational connections of indigenous peoples are not quite like those of human rights groups or environmental activists; for different people they involve a commitment to a self-constituted "Fourth World," and much experience with conditions associated with the "Third World," as well as some elements of the more "First World" style of the major transnational NGOs.

It would be a misleading oversimplification to suggest that there is a consensus in the political West, or in the European settler states or the prosperous countries of the Organisation for Economic Co-operation and Development, as to the position of indigenous peoples in national polities and legal systems. First, the view of indigenous peoples as long-existing nations, as ancient collectivities with special entitlements arising from distant historical priority, is resisted by adherents of several of the strands of state nationalism that remain strong in most Western states.

Second, claims of indigenous peoples are presumptively dubious to those liberals who believe ethnic nationalism and ethicized politics are dangers to be avoided. As a Ukrainian government representative put it, "claims for preferential treatment for indigenous peoples would not contribute to inter-ethnic peace and understanding in any society.[38] A powerful strand of Western liberalism takes the individual as the essential self-determining or at least freely chasing subject, is mistrustful of group-based claims extending beyond nondiscrimination, and calls for neutrality of the state and other social institutions with respect to competing substantive views among groups as to what is good and how to live.[39] Nevertheless, many political theorists in this tradition have resorted to some conception of "the people" at the least to define the boundaries of a society,[40] and there is a close fit between such "liberal" concepts as the colour-blind constitution and some varieties of nationalist projects.

Third, while many members of indigenous peoples are imbued with liberal values, Western liberals have struggled to give coherent accounts of issues posed for liberalism by indigenous peoples.[41] Quite apart from pervasive problems of ignorance and translation, many issues concerning, indigenous peoples do not fit readily into structures of liberal thought. In a somewhat murky way, most liberals see something distinctive in "indigenous peoples," something that is not adequately captured in the standard human rights program, though most assert that the human rights program should be applicable, more or less. There are conflicting basic tendencies in contemporary liberal opinion. In one liberal view, indigenous peoples embody premodern cultural forms that are slowly being shed en route to liberal individualism, unmarked modernity and the puzzles of nationalism. In an alternative view, indigenous peoples attest that identity is not simply a matter of individuals and nations, and that life ordered by cosmology, hierarchy and status is still possible and intelligible. Another strand finds in indigenous peoples the possibilities of sustainable development and ecological alternatives to consumptive capitalism. In many settler societies, indigenous peoples are seen as offering something to make the society whole. More legalistic liberal models probe the meaning for indigenous peoples of the ambient society's commitment to equal concern and respect, the realization of pluralism and voice, and the extent of legal structures that value historic claims to property, honour, treaty promises and the righting of old wrongs. Finally, a liberal commitment to transnational civil society often coincides with the expectation that networks of indigenous peoples help to constitute that society, to embed the state through operating in part outside it.[42] At present there is considerable political support among Western liberals for "indigenous peoples," especially those in distant countries; but this support is tempered by unresolved concerns about consistency with other liberal precepts, and these concerns appear quickly in the face of such concrete issues as relations between group autonomy and individual human rights.

Differing Impacts of Colonialism in Asia

The use of "indigenous peoples" or cognate terms in political discourse, and attitudes of state governments toward the concept, vary considerably among Asian countries. Differences in the impacts and legacies of European, Japanese and United States colonialism, political dynamics, nationalist ideologies, and understandings of history all contribute to this variation. The concept of "indigenous peoples" has multiple lineages. In the era of decolonization, the term was regularly used by Afro-Asian state governments and colonial governments to refer to the non-European majority populations of European colonies in Asia and Africa; the international indigenous peoples' movement draws, in part, on the discourses and legal principles (especially self-determination) given currency by the Afro-Asian decolonization movement.[43] The concept of "indigenous peoples" also has roots in colonial administrators' practice of establishing special laws and policies relating to distinct nonmajority groups, Security and the pursuit of cost-effective, if very rough, governance were often more reasons for establishing inner lines, scheduled areas, frontier zones and other special arrangements,[44] although the conscious motives of such administrators were in some cases also welfarist or religious.[45] In the nineteenth and early twentieth centuries especially, standards of good colonial administration were identified, espoused and disseminated to different parts of the world through metropolitan colonial offices and legislatures, missionary societies, NGOs such as the Aborigines Protection Society, and intergovernmental activity such as the 1884-1885 Berlin Conference and the 1889-1890 Brussels Conference. The impact of this diffusion of norms is evident, for example, in apparently mimetic colonial programs relating to aborigines adopted during Japan's rule in Formosa, which Japanese authorities publicized in a carefully produced English-language publication.[46] Such norms became more formal under the League of Nations mandate system and the rarely invoked provision in Article 23 (b) of the League of Nations Covenant requiring just treatment of native inhabitants.

Colonial policies had enduring impacts on understandings of ethnicity and patterns of ethnic relations in postcolonial states:[47] Benedict Anderson defines a polar position in his contention that in contemporary southeast Asia "the politics of ethnicity have their roots in modern times, not ancient history, and their shape has been largely determined by colonial policy. "[48] According to this thesis, the concept of ethnic minority was virtually introduced, and many ethnic identities largely created, by the imaginings of European colonial powers concerned in the late nineteenth and twentieth centuries with building majority coalitions to assuage their own vulnerability as minority rulers in an age when majority rule was increasingly a principle of legitimacy. Thus, groups favored by European rulers in the eighteenth century on the ground of having elevated themselves from others through embracing Christianity were by the late nineteenth century favored instead in census-defined ethnics as Moluccas or Karens. Such groups were cast. Stereotypically as honest and loyal, as opposed to larger and more threatening groups stereotyped as treacherous and feudal. As evidence for the thesis that ethnic classifications were designed to further coalition-building goals of the European colonists, Anderson asserts that in the last years of colonial administration, ethnic minorities were accorded disproportionate numbers of seats in "representative" bodies, these being occupied by individuals likely to act consistently with preferences of the colonial power.

The legacy of colonial experiences has been the distinctive identification of "alien" minorities (particularly Chinese, who have been integrated into non-Chinese elites much more easily in uncolonized Thailand than in Indonesia), the presence in many states of local "coalition minorities" with modem and evolving identities who are able to exercise influence in statewide coalition building, and a category of what in international terms might now be called "indigenous peoples." These are "groups which, because they are small in numbers, geographically remote from the political center, marginal to the national economy and lacking in Western education, are insignificant to any conceivable majority."[49] In some cases these groups were mobilized by the colonial power to resist advancing nationalist causes, though more often they were left unincorporated into the coalition-building arrangements. Whether they were wholly unincorporated or belatedly mobilized and ineffectually incorporated, the colonial legacy continues to the present in their pronounced underrepresentation in military officer corps, universities, large state enterprises, private corporations and the senior civil service. Their leverage with the state government and elites is small. One strategy for such groups is to combine forces with other local groups and form a larger ethnic identity, but willingness to do this may be inhibited by the necessity of religious conversion (e.g., to Islam to join the broad Malay identity in Malaysia. to Buddhism to integrate with Thai identity or to Christianity to build other coalitions) and reluctance to accept cultural fusion and a surrender of autonomy.[50] Another possible strategy, pursued in tandem with or instead of this larger-ethnic strategy, is to join the international category of "indigenous peoples" Whether this international movement provides sufficient legitimation and leverage to shape national political outcomes varies with the state and groups involved, but in some circumstances this alternative has begun to prove attractive.

Attitudes in Asian States and Impacts of International Legal Developments

Practice within states, including not only governmental and judicial policy but the terms used by civil society organizations and aspiring claimants. is of central importance in shaping the future development of the international concept of "indigenous peoples" and in determining its utility. Recent practice of governments and claimant groups in different Asian states concerning recognition and identities of distinct groups shows wide variation and, in some cases, rapid evolution. In some states, such as the Philippines and Japan, the development of the international concept of "indigenous peoples" has begun to have a political and legal impact. In others the international concept has had little demonstrable impact, but distinct groups are recognized under other conceptual categories and may enjoy entitlements in legal or political practice comparable to those claimed by indigenous peoples elsewhere. In a few states recognition of separate group identities with political and legal status is not accorded or has limited political and legal salience. In many states concerns persist about the ethnicization of politics, disturbing political balances, and the hazards of encouraging or accepting some types of group based claims. The positions taken by state governments within the United Nations and in dealings with international organizations broadly correspond with policies pursued within the state, although there may be disjunctions where different ministries are handling different aspects of the issue. The following very brief survey of practice within various Asian polities is intended merely to illustrate some of the problems of "indigenous peoples" as a global legal concept, and to indicate its potential as a constructivist concept with a more flexible range of justifications titan those it currently encompasses.

The Philippines. In relation to indigenous peoples, the process of state formation in the Philippines shows some commonality with experience in the Americas. Spanish colonial rule left a significant number of groups "un-Hispanicized" or "non-Christian," and distinctions of this sort were reinforced by the U.S. regime, which established a Bureau of Non-Christian Tribes and drew on administrative policies relating to Indians in the United States. The category of indigenous cultural communities (ICC), covering between 10 and 20 percent of the population, has become well established in Philippine politics. In the Marcos era, resistance by indigenous groups in northern Luzon to large projects such as the Chico dams (which were eventually canceled) and the Cellophil pulp and processing operations in Abra increased political mobilization among Kalinga, Bontoc, Tinggians and others;[51] these projects were also associated with militarization of the region, considerable brutality and some tribal support for the New Peoples Army.[52] In Mindanao, in-migration and dispossession have long fueled militancy among Lumad and especially Moro groups, but the conflict intensified in the early 1970s with the rise of the Muslim separatist movement. An agreement on autonomy in Mindanao, reached in 1976 under the auspices of the Islamic Conference, was not fully implemented.

The political and legal dynamics of issues concerning indigenous peoples have changed since the Marcos period, and numerous highly effective civil society organizations dedicated to indigenous peoples' causes are flourishing, including the internationally prominent Cordillera Peoples' Alliance and other northern groups, Lumad Mindanaw and several other organizations in Mindanao, and national bodies such as the National Federation of Indigenous Peoples of the Philippines.

The 1996 peace agreement in Mindanao establishes a renewed framework for the evolution of regional autonomy, but it is not yet clear that a workable balance has been struck between the majority and the various minorities. Bitter disputes about development projects continue, such as the opposition of Cordilleran groups to the Newcrest and Newmont mining explorations, the controversy concerning the operations of Western Mining Corp. in Mindanao,[53] and resistance to forced land sales and the exclusion of indigenous peoples by commercial plantation projects. The international concept: of "indigenous peoples" is currently influential, and is accepted by the government as applicable to the ICCs. The 1997 Indigenous Peoples Rights Act amalgamates the Philippine category of ICCs with the international category of indigenous peoples, and was heavily influenced by both the UN draft declaration and ILO Convention No. 169. Full implementation of the ambitious provisions of this statute would be a remarkable feat, although it builds on a preparatory process of issuing Certificates of Ancestral Domain Claim to groups among the ICCs that has proceeded apace for several years, albeit with some problems and unevenness.[54]

Japan Substantial Japanese northward movement in Hokkaido in the Edo and Meiji periods had a major impact on Ainu. An assimilationist philosophy was embodied in the principal Meiji legislation, the Hokkaido Former Indigenes Protection Act of 1899. Until the late 1980s, the government of Japan remained unwilling to accept that Ainu constituted even an ethnic minority under the International Covenant on Civil and Political Rights.[55] In subsequent years the government acquiesced to interacting domestic and international pressures and abandoned its insistence on the homogeneity of Japan. It has accepted de facto that the Ainu people are a distinct group properly associating themselves with the international indigenous peoples' movement. The 1899 statute was finally replaced in 1997, but this new legislation did not satisfy all concerns expressed by Ainu groups. In particular, while the legislation charts a clearly nonassimilationist policy, it reflects the government's continuing reluctance formally to accept that Ainu should be regarded as "indigenous" or an "indigenous people."

Malaysia. In Malaysia a concept of indigenousness features prominently in political discourse as an underpinning for the *bumiputera* (son of the soil) policy. In peninsular Malaysia this policy is designed to maintain and advance the position of Malays. "Malay" is defined in the Constitution as "a person who professes the religion of Islam. Habitually speaks the Malay language, conforms to Malay custom" and descends from one who at the date of independence had been born in or was domiciled in the Federation.[56] In a separate constitutional category are "aborigines" of the peninsula, usually known collectively as Orang Asli, whose legal status has been regulated (in the exercise of federal rather than state power) primarily by a series of Aboriginal Peoples' Acts.[57] The philosophy of the legislation and of the administration of the relevant government agency, the Jabatan Hal Ehwal Orang Asli, has been protectionist, with some aspiration of long-term assimilation of Orang Asli into Malay communities and very little endorsement of active self-determination. However, since the 1980s Orang Asli Organizations, led in particular by members of the growing cadre of Orang Asli who have gone through state educational institutions but supported also by non-Orang Asli, have been increasingly active in urging new approaches and initiatives.[58]

As to East Malaysia, the Constitution identifies a category of "natives" of Sabah and Sarawak, and in the case of Sarawak lists a large number of "races indigenous to Sarawak" who count as "native."[59] This category includes Malays, and formally these "native" groups are on much the same footing as Malays in Malaysia as a whole. In practice, the legal and political dynamics in East Malaysia have differed markedly from those obtaining in the center of federal power on the peninsula, and considerable opposition to deforestation and land alienation has emerged, involving numerous organizations including the Sarawak Indigenous Peoples' Alliance,[60] as well as debate about the direction and effects of rapid economic development.[61] Constitutional recognition of Orang Asli and natives of Sarawak and Sabah as indigenous is in some respects a continuation of British practice, overlain by the *bumiputra* policy. This policy actively privileges, on grounds of indigenousness, a politically dominant and economically influential Malay group and confers juridical recognition, if more limited practical benefits, on native groups in Sabah and Sarawak where they collectively constitute numerical majorities but wield an uneven degree of political influence and economic power. Against this complex background, it is not surprising that the final position of the Malaysian government on the developing concept of "indigenous peoples" in the United Nations has yet to emerge.

Thailand. A category of "hill tribe" people in north and northwest Thailand has been recognized and actively addressed as a subject of government policy since the 1950s, initially in response to concerns about opium cultivation and insurgency related to the Cold War, and more recently as part of forest policy and community development schemes. The complex demography of the hill regions includes many groups who moved into forest areas they now occupy within historical memory, often during the past century, and who came mainly from presentday Burma, Laos, and in some cases China.[62] At present the discourse of "indigenous peoples" appears scarcely to figure in national politics or in claims made by non-ethnic, Thai tribal groups. Nevertheless, many points of similarity can be found between issues in northern Thailand and those arising in other parts of the world. A major concern in northern Thailand is lack of recognized rights to the land that a particular group may have occupied or used for many decades; often the state has purported to obliterate such land claims through the proclamation of forest reserves or national parks.[63] Chayan reports that a 1995 demonstration by hill tribe people, mainly Karen, against Forest Department programs to depopulate watershed areas and relocate the inhabitants was "the first such event in modem Thai history."[64] In 1992 the government indicated to the

United Nations its view that hill tribes are ethnic groups but "are not considered to be minorities nor indigenous people but as Thais who are able to enjoy fundamental rights . . . as any other Thai citizen."[65] However, the government seems not to have taken a final position on the application to Thailand of the international concept of · 'indigenous peoples."

Taiwan. The position of indigenous peoples in Taiwan has changed appreciably with the end of martial law and the democratization of politics, spurring the recent proliferation of indigenous organizations. The impact of these changes is illustrated by the campaign of Yami people against the Taiwan Power Company's use of Lanyu Island to store nuclear waste from power generation. Little progress was made under martial law, but in 1996 Yami succeeded in turning away a ship bringing more waste, and Taipower promised to remove all the waste by 2002.[66] This achievement of such a small group fewer than four thousand people are officially classified as Yami—reflects the growing political salience of environmental activism in Taiwan, reinforced to some extent by the involvement of international NGOs such as Greenpeace. There are clear connections between the developing international concept of "indigenous peoples" and the political and legal demands of some groups in Taiwan,[67] although many of the most active groups within Taiwan do not seem to attach great importance to the international concept. The most frequent participant in international gatherings of indigenous peoples has been the Alliance of Taiwan Aborigines (ATA), organized in 1984. It has met with mixed success in its objective of coordinating political action among the nine major indigenous groups, whose combined populations by official estimates exceed 350,000.[68] Campaigns have focused on such issues as land rights and land use, political status and representation, education, cultural protection and autonomy, economic opportunities, sexual exploitation of women and girls, and names. The requirement to signify personal names was reversed by the Taiwan authorities in 1995. In 1994 the Constitution of the Republic of China was amended to excise references to *shan-pao* (mountain compatriots, also *shanti tung-pao*); the official constitutional usage is now *yuan-chu min* (the people who lived here first). The ATA has made a similar argument in the United Nations Working Group on indigenous populations, challenging the UN translation of "indigenous peoples" as *tuzu renmin.* This usage is apparently supported by the People's Republic of China (PRC) in the United Nations, but is widely regarded as connoting "primitive" or "low cultural level." The ATA has urged the United Nations to adopt *yuanzu minzu* (indigenous peoples) or *yuanzu min* (indigenous people) instead.[69]

Bangladesh. The major questions shaping attitudes toward the concept of "indigenous peoples" in Bangladesh relate to the Chittagong Hill Tracts (CHT). From the early 1970s a government program to resettle in the CHT large numbers of people from other parts of Bangladesh has encountered fierce resistance by members of tribal groups who regard the land as theirs and see their economic circumstances deteriorating in the transformation from Sweden agriculture to plantation wage labour. The conflict became heavily militarized, causing large refugee flows and numerous deaths before a peace agreement was finally reached in December 1997.[70] Deliberately isolated from Bengali settlement during British rule, the diverse groups who have long inhabited the area have sought to build unity among themselves in the face of increasing interactions with the Pakistani and Bangladeshi states and massive Bengali settlement. This unity has been constructed around the term *jumma* as a new collective self-designation of these inhabitants of the CHT, and there are now frequent references among CHT people to the Jumma people or the Jumma nation. In Van Schendel's assessment, *jumma*, "[a]n old pejorative term for a Sweden cultivator in the Chittagonian dialect of Bengali," was appropriated by the Jana Samhati Samiti (the main nonsettler CHT political organization, whose military wing is the Shanti Bahini) "in an attempt to unify all the hill people under one social umbrella."[71] Externally, however, the issues raised by the CHT groups are increasingly being couched as issues of indigenous peoples. As one CHT activist put it prior to the peace agreement:

> The Government of Bangladesh does not recognize us as indigenous peoples in the constitution. We have no constitutional rights as indigenous peoples. The government is very carefully trying to avoid the international recognition of indigenous peoples in Bangladesh. The constitution has recognized the rights of citizens in general, but we have clear linguistic, cultural and socio-political distinctiveness from the majority Bengali people. That is why we want the right to a "separate status" in the constitution as indigenous peoples.[72]

The peace agreement concluded under the Awami League administration accords some recognition to "tribal" groups in the CHT, who together are allocated the majority of seats in the new Regional Council. Whether this will affect Bangladesh's position in UN negotiations concerning "indigenous peoples" is not yet clear.

Like that of Bangladesh until 1997, the government of Burma/Myanmar has been engaged in military conflicts with ethnically based groups for almost all of the country's post independence history. Myanmar, like Bangladesh, has argued against any United Nations definition that would legitimate claims by particular south Asian ethnic groups to be "indigenous peoples."[73] The most fully elaborated of these arguments have been made by the governments of India and China, and these will now be examined.

Arguments against Applicability of "Indigenous Peoples" to Asia

Since the establishment of the UN Working Group on indigenous populations in 1982, India has espoused the position that the concept of "indigenous peoples" does not apply within its borders.[74] In recent years, the People's Republic of China has taken assertive public positions against the applicability of the concept in China. In legal terms, the major controversy in the United Nations concerns the proposed requirement of historical continuity with a preinvasion or precolonial society established on the territory. Maintenance of a strict requirement of such continuity—a requirement that owes at least part of its inspiration to perceptions and experience in areas of European settlement—would be likely both to complicate and to restrict,[75] without altogether excluding, the applicability of the concept of "indigenous peoples" in other parts of the world.

The precise grounds for opposition among Asian governments vary and have not all been made fully explicit. At least three kinds of arguments are involved: definitional, practical and policy. The definitional arguments are lexical, resting on a view of "indigenous" as entailing prior occupancy, and stipulational, associating "indigenous peoples" with the deleterious effects of European colonialism. The practical argument is that it is impossible or misleading to seek to identify the prior occupants of countries and regions with such long and intricate histories of influx, movement and melding. The policy argument is the powerful one that recognizing rights on the basis of prior occupation for particular sets of groups will spur and legitimate mobilization and claims by a vast range of groups, undermining other values with which the state is properly concerned.

Definitional arguments. The views of the PRC government on the meaning of the concept of "indigenous peoples" are exemplified by its 1995 comments concerning a draft UN declaration, quoted above.[76] China's position is that the concept is inextricably bound up with, and indeed a function of, European colonialism. This is in one way a continuation of the UN General Assembly's practice of treating the entire nonsettler or non-European population of European colonies (e.g., the entire local population of Mozambique under Portuguese rule) as indigenous peoples. In this respect, indigenous peoples are those who, not having obtained liberation from European rule, are continuing victims of sufferings caused by the settlers' colonialism-the losers, in a sense, in the formation by Europeans of states outside Europe. China has thus supported in general terms a definition under which indigenous peoples were "living on their lands before settlers came from elsewhere; . . . descendants . . . of those who inhabited a country or a geographic region at the time when peoples of different cultures or ethnic origins arrived, the new arrivals becoming dominant through conquest, occupation, settlement or other means.[77]

India, Bangladesh and Myanmar have made similar arguments, stressing that indigenous peoples are descendants of the original inhabitants who have suffered from conquest or invasion from outside.[78] While these arguments do not refer expressly to the notion of "saltwater colonialism," used by the Group of 77 developing nations to distinguish European colonialism from practices by non-Europeans that might share some characteristics with it, China's approach strongly suggests that the "historical misfortunes of indigenous peoples" that set them apart are the misfortunes of saltwater settler colonialism. China's position is in one sense a continuation of the rejection by G-77 states of the "Belgian thesis," an assertion in the early 1950s that United Nations scrutiny of treatment of nonautonomous peoples under Chapter XI of the UN Charter should not be confined to the indigenous inhabitants of European colonies, but ought to extend to indigenous peoples in independent states, who were just as deserving of international protection. Peoples in many of the anticolonial states, including India, Indonesia, the Philippines and the Soviet Union, were described by Belgium as falling within this category.[79] The Belgian thesis was plausibly regarded at the time as a somewhat cynical aspect of the rearguard defense of European colonialism.[80]

Implicit in the contemporary position of China and other Asian states is the suggestion that the attempt to impose the concept of "indigenous peoples" upon various states in the region is a form of neocolonialism. In this view, the concept, which was made relevant and necessary in Western states (including Latin America) by the enduring human consequences of the European incursion and settlement that gave these states much of their present form and character, is now applied at the initiative of many of these same states to Asian states that either staved off Western colonialism or rid themselves of its most direct effects in the struggle for decolonization.

Practical arguments. Building on the notion of indigenous peoples as the peoples who can be first (or at least earlier than the others who are now dominant), representatives of the government of India have made the practical argument that the concept cannot apply there because, after centuries of migration, absorption and differentiation, it is impossible to say who came first. (This position is echoed in China's argument that all of the nationalities in China have lived there for aeons.) Thus, in 1991 the representative of India in the Working Group on indigenous populations commented that most of the tribes in India share ethnic, racial and linguistic characteristics with other people in the country, and that three to four hundred million people there are distinct in some way from other categories of people in India.[81]

Prescription of ethnicity by administrative fiat or self-designation involves numerous problems and is open to much criticism, and there are difficult cases under any approach. Nonetheless, it has proved possible as a practical matter to enumerate detailed lists of scheduled tribes under the fifth and sixth schedules to the Indian Constitution; these constitutional categories have provided a practical starting point for identification of groups to whom policies of international agencies relating to "indigenous peoples" have been applied in India.[82] Similarly, in China, in a major project conducted largely in the 1950s, the Nationalities Commission has identified fifty-five minorities to whom various preferential policies are supposed to apply.[83] Whether this was as much a process of enumerating preexisting groups as of creating identities in accordance with particular his historico-political views, and what the effects of distinctive treatment have been, are serious questions, but of policy rather than practicalities. This is not to down play the practical problems, which in many areas may be severe. But the practical objections seem to respond to the imposition of a foreign concept to which strong policy objections are made.

Policy arguments. The Indian government's position contains an implied argument that a forensic inquiry into who appeared first in India would be unhelpful and undesirable, for two reasons. First, some groups meriting special protection would be excluded, while others not in need of such protection might be included. Second, recognition of special rights and entitlements for having been the earliest or original occupants might spur and legitimate chauvinist claims by groups all over India, many of which might be very powerful locally while in some sense "nondominant" nationally. Claims to historical priority already feature in some "communal" conflicts, and incipient chauvinist movements abound, as with the pro-Marathi, Hindu-nationalist Shiv Sena party in Maharashtra.[84] In effect, if some people are "indigenous" to a place, others are vulnerable to being targeted as nonindigenous, and groups deemed to be migrants or otherwise subject to social stigma may bear the brunt of a nativist "indigenist" policy. Once indigenousness or "sons of the soil" becomes the basis of legitimation for a politically or militarily dominant group, restraints on abuses of power can be difficult to maintain.[85]

This has been a crucial issue in the national politics of states such as Malaysia and Fiji, and is a potential source of bitter division in many other polities. Strong policy arguments militate against legitimating the opening of fissures that may engulf an entire society in violence and intimidation. Perhaps because of the sensitivity of what it involves, this second point is not often developed explicitly in government statements, but it seems to have animated India's long-standing concern to keep the concept of "indigenous peoples" at a safe distance.

Even in societies that do not face imminent risks of division and heightened violence through legitimation of one powerful group as against others, the active privileging of the historically prior inhabitants carries risks. More recent arrivals, or seasonal migrant working families who themselves live at the very margins, can be lost from view in public policy and legal advocacy. Enthusiasm for the local and the historical can undercut desirable arrangements for taking some decisions at other levels to protect other deserving interests, and for valuing innovative and hybrid forms that do not qualify as traditional.

All these considerations underpin the point that a functional concept of "indigenous peoples" applicable in all regions will be viable only if it is broad enough to permit of alternative justifications. A concept that depends wholly on arguments of priority in time and historical continuity from ancient times to the present may work well enough in some regions but is unlikely to be adequate and workable in all regions.

III. International Legal Norms and "Indigenous Peoples"

Many claims made by indigenous peoples or their members do not depend directly on any particular status of the group as an "indigenous people," and juridical responses to these claims likewise need not depend on an exact definition of "indigenous peoples" or cognate categories. Claims involving indigenous peoples may draw on the law of the sea;[86] the law of treaties;[87] the law of diplomatic protection;[88] rules pertaining to title to territory;[89] international environmental law;[90] procedural doctrines such as those relating to estoppel, acquiescence, good faith, abuse of rights and laches;[91] and a host of other principles and rules of general international law.

Three well-established structures of general international law are used with great frequency in claims involving indigenous peoples: human rights, minority rights and, self-determination.[92] Thus, claims arising from slavery, genocide, discrimination, infant malnutrition and pollution of water supplies are cognizable under the general international law of human rights.[93] Claims against state action preventing the practice and enjoyment of a group's religion, culture and language draw upon international law standards concerning minorities. In current international negotiations, general claims by indigenous peoples to self-determination are often based not on particular rights of *indigenous* peoples, but on entitlements that pertain, it is argued, equally to all peoples; proponents frequently argue that the most deep-seated problem for indigenous peoples in contemporary international law is unjustified discrimination with respect to enjoyment of the right to self-determination.[94]

Yet, when tested in practice, many of the issues raised as matters of human rights or minority protection or self-determination display distinctive elements vis-à-vis indigenous peoples. Among these distinctive elements, four in particular may be noted: the central importance of land and territory to group identity and culture; the emerging view of self-determination in relation to indigenous peoples as referring more often to autonomy and control of the group's own destiny and development than to formation of independent states; the development of norms concerning participation by the group and its members in decisions affecting them; and the increasing support for self-identification as a basis of group definition. These four sets of norms, and the practices of claim, application and contestation relating to them, implicate some of the main justifications, for "indigenous peoples" as a distinct legal category.

Land and Culture

The special relations of many indigenous peoples to land is a recurrent theme in reports of international human rights institutions, which focus on such matters as racial and cultural discrimination in state treatment of indigenous peoples' land rights,[95] the violence associated with attempts to dispossess indigenous groups of land, the social and economic deprivation that results from dispossession, and the problems of securing and regaining enforceable rights to land and territory.[96] The close connections between the cultures of indigenous peoples and issues of use and control of land and natural resources have been recognized as adding a different dimension to minority rights decisions under Article 27 of the International Covenant on Civil and Political Rights (ICCPR). In its final views in the *Lubicon Lake Band* case, the Human Rights Committee opined that a violation of Article 27 was entailed because the band's way of life and culture were threatened by a combination of the inequitable historical failure to assure the band a land base to which it had a strong claim, and current large-scale extractive resource development by outsiders, which together are associated with miserable economic and social conditions of band members.[97]

National tribunals have followed this interpretation of Article 27 in cases involving indigenous peoples.[98] The Sapporo District Court held in 1997 that, in taking Ainu lands for a dam on the Saru River in Hokkaido, the government had failed to meet the duty under Article 27 to consider the impact on Ainu culture. The court's finding that the article created obligations cognizable in a Japanese court was consistent with other lower court decisions on the ICCPR in Japan, although the status of the Covenant in general and Article 27 in particular in Japanese Law has not yet been conclusively settled. For present purposes, the notable feature of the decision is that the court did not regard it as sufficient simply to determine that Ainu are a minority under Article 27 (a view the Japanese government now accepts), but made the further finding that Ainu are an indigenous people (a view not currently accepted by the Japanese government). Apparently drawing its understanding of "indigenous peoples" *(senju minzoku)* from international instruments, particularly ILO Convention No. 169, the court found:

> The Ainu people are the original inhabitants of Hokkaido and its adjacent areas and constituted a distinct culture before Japan extended jurisdiction over their land. Their land was incorporated by the Japanese government and they suffered economic and social dispossession under the governmental policies imposed by the majority Japanese. Even under these circumstances, the Ainu still maintain their distinct identity as an ethnic group. Thus, they may well be regarded as indigenous people.[99]

In making this finding, the court may have intended to pave the way for further legal recognition of rights held by Ainu but not accorded to other minorities.

Self-Determination

Notwithstanding the strong rhetorical and textual support for the proposition that self-determination is an equal right of all peoples, the reality is that during European decolonization international law was concerned less with "peoples" as social collectivities than with "peoples" as juridically defined groups associated with territorial units. Real engagement with the interests and aspirations of social collectivities involves a much more complex actualization of self-determination than the law of decolonization has established. The claims made by indigenous peoples and the development of practical resolutions in a myriad of cases involving these groups are beginning to contribute to normative development in this area.[100] A few examples may illustrate how the practice and meaning of self-determination are evolving in response to the claims and circumstances of indigenous peoples. In the Philippines, the Indigenous Peoples Rights Act of 1997 provides for recognition of communal and individual rights of indigenous peoples to ancestral lands and ancestral domains, continued state support for autonomy arrangements in the Cordilleras and Mindanao, and the recognition by the state of "the inherent right of ICCs/IPs to self-governance arid self-determination," and thus "the right of ICCs/IPs to freely pursue their economic, social and cultural development" within the framework of the Constitution and national unity and development. In Canada, claims settlement agreements between state authorities and indigenous peoples have incorporated increasingly extensive commitments to self-government for indigenous groups. In Australia, the 1997 report of a government commission on the ordeals of thousands of aboriginal children deliberately removed from aboriginal families over the past century recommended that self-determination for aboriginal people be a core principle for the future.[101] In each case, self-determination is envisaged as operating within existing states.

Participation and Consultation

Closely related to self-determination is the question of the ability of indigenous peoples to shape decisions affecting them. The 1989 ILO Convention No. 169 on Indigenous and Tribal Peoples, which has been strongly criticized by indigenous groups and other advocates for not referring to the right of self-determination and for focusing more on duties of states than rights of indigenous peoples,[102] has nevertheless had an impact on this question by providing that indigenous and tribal peoples "shall have the right to decide their own priorities for the process of development as it affects their lives, beliefs, institutions and spiritual well-being and the lands they occupy or otherwise use. "[103] In February 1997, the Colombian Constitutional Court, in a decision on oil operations affecting U'Wa people, held that an exploration license should not have been granted because the indigenous people had not been properly consulted, contrary to the right of participation contained in the Colombian Constitution and in ILO Convention No. 169.[104] The 1993 UN Draft Declaration on the Rights of Indigenous Peoples goes further than Convention No. 169, asserting:

> Indigenous peoples have the right to determine and develop priorities
> and strategies for the development or use of their lands, territories and

other resources, including the right to require that States obtain their free and informed consent prior to the approval of any project affecting their lands, territories and other resources, particularly in connection with the development, utilization or exploitation of mineral, water or other resources. Pursuant to agreement with the indigenous peoples concerned, just and fair compensation shall be provided for any such activities and measures taken to mitigate adverse environmental, economic, social, cultural or spiritual impact.[105]

The central importance to indigenous peoples of involvement in decision making, of having weight attached to their viewpoints and concerns, is often undervalued in popular Western imagery of these peoples as victims of "development,"[106] and in some of the more romantic attachments to cultural diversity and saving indigenous peoples from "vanishing." In some cases indigenous peoples may have cause to feel themselves victims as much of "conservation" as of "development" -when confronted, for example, with the restrictions on swidden agriculture introduced in most Southeast Asian countries, the displacement of people to make room for national parks, the blanket protection of depleted wildlife stocks, the denial of access to minor forest produce to prevent deforestation. But in either case the imagery of passive victims living at one with nature and beset by unwelcome modernity is misleading as a general account of the practices and aspirations of many of the groups participating in the indigenous peoples' movement. Most of these groups are active agents and practitioners of "development" and "conservation," and they vary considerably in their practices and attitudes relating to resource exploitation and environmental maintenance.[107] This reality is explicitly recognized in programs ranging from community forestry and biodiversity maintenance to opium crop substitution and peoples-and-parks. Nevertheless, while aspirations for self-determination and a substantial role in development decisions seem to be widely shared by indigenous groups, they are often far from being realized in practice. There remains, in Asia as elsewhere, a gulf between the self-determination advocated by indigenous peoples in the United Nations-or even the doctrines of consultation, participation and choice espoused in some international institutions-and the actual experiences of indigenous peoples with externally driven development and conservation.

Self Identification

The historical experience of many such groups of being defined, disparaged or treated as nonexistent by others adds to the strength of arguments by indigenous peoples for self-identification as the essential solution to the problem of definition. Self-identification is also buttressed by the ethos of self-determination. ILO Convention No. 169 provides that self-identification as indigenous or tribal is a "fundamental criterion" for determining the groups to whom the Convention

applies, and a similar statement appears in the Draft American Declaration on the
Rights of Indigenous Peoples proposed by the Inter-American Commission on
Human Rights.[108] The diametrically opposed approach adheres to the traditional
view of indigenous peoples as objects of international law, to be defined either by
criteria formulated by states or through recognition by states. The government
of the People's Republic of China has advocated a position of this sort.[109] The
antinomy between self-identification and state recognition obscures distinctions
among the situations in which problems of identification arise. The general right
of each indigenous people to recognition as a distinct group defined in terms of
its conception of itself in relation to other groups is increasingly accepted among
states, although national legislation is highly variable on this issue, and states
frequently take active positions when controversies over identity arise between or
within groups. A power to determine at the intergroup or international level which
groups are indigenous peoples, through either general rules or specific decisions,
has also been claimed by many indigenous peoples' groups. Some have begun to
seek the exclusion of certain groups (e.g., Reheboth Basters, a group of European
descent living in Namibia) from participation as indigenous peoples in the UN
Working Group on indigenous populations, a perilous venture that the United
Nations has not for the time being hazarded to undertake. States are less likely to
surrender the power to influence institutional decisions about participation and
entitlements, but some sharing of power in this regard seems likely. A separate set
of self-identification issues concerns the formation of political institutions and representative structures within indigenous groups. Structures of representation are
seldom purely autochthonous-in many cases they will continue to be influenced
by states, NGOs, interstate institutions and other indigenous groups with which
these political representatives deal. Finally, the view that self-identification entails
the power of the group to set and apply membership rules receives some support
in practice but is tempered by international human rights standards and by some
involvement of state legal and administrative agencies. In summary, norms of
self-identification are important, but they do not obviate the need for some agreed
criteria or for institutional procedures of assessment in certain situations.

Experience confirms the view of many representatives of indigenous peoples
that not all of their claims can be totally subsumed without adaptation into such
established generic legal structures as human rights, minority rights and self-determination, even while such claims draw heavily on these and other areas of legal
doctrine. The distinctive *sui generis* concept of "indigenous peoples" is important
to the development of international legal norms and institutional practice; its
nature and meaning therefore require careful consideration.

IV. International Institutions and "Indigenous Peoples"

The ILO and the World Bank have each been able to adopt broad and flexible
indicative definitions of "indigenous peoples" in terms that have met the practi-

cal needs of these agencies without provoking unmanageable state opposition. Nevertheless, each of the functional agencies has found issues of "indigenous peoples" to pose distinctive challenges in the practical operations of the institution. Each is required to engage in difficult negotiations with recalcitrant state governments while endeavoring to be somewhat responsive lo constituencies of indigenous peoples and their supporters. The leverage available to the Bank is typically greater, but it often has conflicting interests, especially in dealing with very large borrowers needed by the Bank, above all China. Neither in the World Bank nor even in the ILO have Indigenous Peoples been nearly as fully involved in the processes of formulating and implementing normative standards as many such groups would wish. In the UN Working Group on indigenous populations, by contrast, indigenous peoples have been more extensively involved, together with state governments, but the highly politicized setting and the realization that any definition adopted could have very wide ramifications have hitherto rendered any serious negotiation on the question of definition impossible.[110] In the World Bank policies are drafted mainly by the staff, with some external consultation as well as involvement of the executive directors, and focus directly on the lending and other development-related functions of the World Bank Group, whereas in the United Nations the drafting and adoption of normative instruments and work programs ordinarily are heavily influenced by member states and, increasingly, other actors such as NGOs and indigenous peoples' groups. With regard to issues concerning indigenous peoples, the United Nations as an institution enjoys less autonomy from both the member states and indigenous peoples, and its practice concerning a definition potentially has more potent political implications.

The only general, binding interstate treaties concerning indigenous peoples have been adopted by the International Labour Organization.[111] Convention No. 107 of 1957 remains in force for twenty-one states, including Bangladesh, India and Pakistan.[112] Convention No. 169 of 1989 was intended to supersede No. 107,[113] but by May 1998 had only twelve states parties,[114] with none in Asia, although the Philippines has seriously considered ratification. Acting under Convention No. 107, the ILO Committee of Experts on Conventions and Recommendations has raised concerns with Bangladesh about abuses in the Chittagong Hill Tracts, and with India about the Narmada dams and other natural resource projects.[115] The ILO has undertaken a program to promote Convention No. 169 in south and southeast Asia and southern Africa, convening workshops with the governments of Thailand and the Philippines. ILO technical assistance programs concerned with titling and demarcation of indigenous peoples' lands perforce involve taking positions on specific problems of group identity, but in dealing with broad categories of groups the ILO has sought to harmonize the classifications in the two Conventions with categories accepted by the member governments whose consent is required. Thus, projects in India deal with the constitutional category of "scheduled tribes," a project in Cambodia works with the Inter-Ministerial Committee on Highland Peoples Development.

Under Operational Directive 4.20, promulgated in 1991, the World Bank imposes special requirements on certain projects affecting indigenous peoples.[116] The normative positions taken by the Bank significantly affect project design and wider policies of borrowing countries. The operational directive promotes "legal recognition [by the state] of the customary or traditional land tenure systems of indigenous peoples." and "participation by indigenous people in decision making throughout project planning, implementation, and evaluation." The broad and in some respects contentious objective is to qualify, but not to displace, the Bank's general policies on financing projects: the aim is thus "to ensure that indigenous peoples do not suffer adverse effects during the development process . . . and that they receive culturally compatible social and economic benefits." The aspirations of the policy go further than minimization of harmful impacts of Bank projects, requiring active measures, including in many cases preparation of an "indigenous peoples development plan," Drawing upon its own experience and that of the World Bank, the Asian Development Bank in April 1998, adopted a similar policy. Both use the term "indigenous peoples" in a wide and inclusive way. With emphasis on cultural distinctiveness and special attachments to land and With recognition of the need for a definition capable of sensible application in diverse social contexts. Nevertheless, the policies differ slightly in their definitional sections. In particular, the World Bank notes that classifications of groups by states provide only a "preliminary basis" for identifying indigenous peoples to whom the Bank's policy applies. The ADB omits the "preliminary" element but refers to international law and to objective criteria, softening earlier indications of greater (and potentially excessive) deference to state governments.[117] ILO Convention No. 169 is indicative of a different approach in intern national law, providing in Article 1 (1)(b) that groups satisfying the prescribed criteria shall be regarded as indigenous peoples under the Convention "irrespective of their legal status [under national law]."

Internal procedures of the World Bank endeavor to assure compliance with its policies in projects in which it is involved, although there have been several cases, in Asia and elsewhere in which the operational directive on indigenous peoples was applicable but was not fully respected, partly because of uncertainties of interpretation and significant practical difficulties of implementation, but partly also because of the innovative character of the policy and the unfamiliarity of some task managers With indigenous peoples' issues. The situation is rendered substantially more difficult in countries such as Indonesia and the People's Republic of China where the government does not accept that there are many or any "indigenous peoples" to whom the Bank's policy applies. Where standard internal procedures do not secure the requisite result, the matter may be referred to the Bank's internal but independent Inspection Panel, which has proved more vigorous than many of the executive directors and borrowing countries seem to have wished in calling for full inspections and in pointing to violations of the

Bank's normative standards.[118] The World Bank's policies thus have considerable practical importance, although their effective application in particular cases depends heavily on the borrowing state and on the Bank staff involved.

The political salience of debates about the concept of "indigenous peoples," and much of the legal controversy, have been heightened by conflicts over land, forests, mineral resources, fishing rights and other valuable natural resources. These conflicts arise in the context of rapid economic change, often precipitated by government-supported "development" projects in which international institutions such as the World Bank are involved. If "indigenous peoples" are deemed in international practice to have particular entitlements to land, territory and resources, based on historical connections, customary practices, and the interdependence of land and culture, the question whether a particular group is an indigenous people may take on great political and legal importance. Even where governments do not accept that any of the groups in their states are indigenous peoples, international agencies, multinational corporations and the governments of foreign states may continue to press a particular case on the basis that relevant international standards apply. The Narmada River projects in western India illustrate the potential significance of the policies of the World Bank and comparable financing agencies.

The World Bank initially played a major role in international financing of the Sardar Sarovar dam and canal project, together with related projects in the Narmada River Basin. These projects have met with strong opposition from a wide variety of groups since they began to take clear shape in the early 1980s.[119] Groups subjected to or threatened with involuntary displacement, particularly tribal people whose undocumented customary land holdings did not meet the Indian states' requirements to prove title and who were thus deemed ineligible for land-for-land compensation, have engaged in direct protests such as peaceful occupations and hunger strikes.[120] Investigations, reports and litigation have been organized by these and many other Indian groups, including well known social activists, students and environmental NGOs, as well as numerous foreign NGOs and transnational networks.

Following intense criticism in India and abroad, withdrawal of support for the project by the government of Japan, and the 1992 independent review commissioned by the World Bank that found the project to fall far short of the Bank's own policies regarding resettlement of oustees, compensation to affected people and environmental protection, the Bank in 1993 ceased further participation.[121] The authors of the review took the position that the Bank had adopted explicit policies for the benefit of indigenous and tribal peoples in development projects, that "[c]oncern for such groups is an aspect of the world's increased awareness of how isolated cultures have all too often paid an appalling price for development," and that as a functional matter many aspects of tribal culture involved distinctive issues that required special consideration in implementing the project.

A basic disjunction was at the heart of this element of the project:

> From the point of view of the people themselves, the intent of the Indian
> Constitution, basic anthropological findings, and the criteria embedded
> in World Bank policy directives for tribals and indigenous peoples in
> Bank-aided projects, a substantial proportion of those likely to be af-
> fected by Sardar Sarovar Projects are tribal people and entitled to the
> benefit of special measures that will defend and secure their distinctive
> interests. . . . [Yet] no policies have been devised by the Governments
> of Gujarat, Maharashtra, or Madya Pradesh that pay attention to the
> particular needs and concerns of Sardar Sarovar tribals.[122]

In a bold decision, assisted by the expertise of the Indian NGOs in gathering
data and presenting arguments, and perhaps facilitated somewhat by the previous
developments in international bodies, the Supreme Court of India in December
1995 issued a temporary order restraining continued construction of the Sardar
Sarovar dam pending full judicial consideration of resettlement, environmental
impact and other issues, although the Indian government and the state governments remained more or less committed to the scheme.

Technocratic functional agencies such as the World Bank and even the
ILO have not moved so far in this direction, but participation by indigenous
peoples in international institutions dealing with issues of direct concern to them
is becoming an important criterion of legitimacy, spurring rapid innovation in
institutional design. For certain organizations of indigenous peoples, the Arctic
Council has established a category of "permanent participants," which imparts a
status higher than that of NGOs and comparable to that of member states, apart
from exclusion from the right to vote when consensus decision making breaks
down. In 1997 the Conference of the Parties to the Convention on Biological
Diversity inaugurated an intercessional workshop on Article 8(j) of tile Convention, in which "indigenous and local communities" were able to play a substantial
role.[123] The United Nations is beginning to consider establishing a permanent
forum for indigenous peoples; it is proposed that indigenous peoples and states be
represented in the forum on the same terms and in equal numbers.[124]

The rapidly rising status and involvement of indigenous peoples' groups in
international institutions, and the requirements of consistency where the same
states and groups are dealing with each other in multiple fora, probably will eventually require some unity in the underlying concepts and increasingly specific
rules of eligibility, membership, representation and accountability. The competing pressures for highly diverse and functional institutional practice, on one hand,
and for some unity across different fora, on the other, together make a case for
the dynamic constructivist view of the concept of "indigenous peoples" advanced
here.

V. How Expansive Should the Concept of "Indigenous Peoples" Be?

Representatives of both states and nonstate groups in Asia continue to suggest, albeit in radically different ways, that the international concept of "indigenous peoples," as commonly understood, does not adequately incorporate their interests or their social realities.

Undoubtedly, there are elements of cynicism and opportunism in the debate. The total refusal or failure of some state governments to recognize and take account of the distinctive histories, needs, vulnerabilities and aspirations of indigenous peoples has long been a cause of immense destruction, dispossession, misery and death for a great many people. In some cases such nonrecognition forms part of a deliberate strategy of denial to facilitate outrages against clear international and national legal standards. Nonrecognition may also be designed to cut groups off from the kinds of transnational and international support (not all of it benign), identity and solidarity increasingly associated with "indigenous peoples." Some states pursue an international policy of denial even while their domestic agencies recognize distinctive identities of individual indigenous groups at the national level.

Nevertheless, many societies find it difficult to accept priority based on continuity with a "precolonial" or "preinvasion" society as the foundation for a locally applicable concept of "indigenous people," and in these circumstances nonrecognition is not necessarily motivated by malevolence, particularly when other bases of social identity and of recognition of distinctive cultures, histories and needs are resonant and well established within the policy. Each of the main positions in this debate encompasses persuasive substantive concerns that must be addressed if the concept of "indigenous peoples" is to evolve and enjoy sustained useful application in situations where the modern social context is not structured in a European-type pattern of colonial settlement or invasion.

But should the concept be understood in the broad and open-ended terms necessary to encompass a wide range of societies and circumstances? The approach advocated in this article potentially involves losses and risks, as well as gains. This part weighs some of these difficult balances.

Possible Objections to a Broad Concept of "Indigenous Peoples"

The modern development of the concept of "indigenous peoples" has been conditioned by the history, circumstances and political discourses of states shaped by European settlement. The justifications for special claims and legal entitlements have turned on the perceived continuing Impact of colonialism on precolonial peoples inhabiting the territory, who even now remain discrete and identifiable and continue to suffer the effects of long historical processes of land deprivation, resource depletion, loss of political autonomy and erosion of cultural distinctiveness. Indigenous peoples are distinguished from other numerical minorities on grounds of having been lawful occupants of the land before European colonization, having sustained close cultural ties with particular land over many generations, and having political organizations that now pursue a self-governance that existed, albeit in different ways, before colonization. This set of justifications supports tolerable precise criteria for the identification of indigenous peoples in these societies, although the passage of time, shifts in economic patterns, the evolution of cultures, processes of melding and ethnogenesis, and the incentives for the emergence of new claims and claimants – all pose problems for the nexus between historically grounded justifications and contemporary law and politics. The justifications also support a set of normative claims that are intelligible to, and shaped by, Western political and legal traditions, however much those claims may vary among indigenous groups and be contested or even forcibly opposed by other interests. Broad similarities in the forms of European colonization and state formation contribute to commonality. The relevant practice and evidence are spread over several centuries, but the full construction of the state and the most disruptive interactions with indigenous peoples frequently date from the recent past, so that crucial historical periods are not only more proximally connected to the present, they are often well documented and carried within enduring memories and oral traditions.

Some groups in Asia fit this pattern, but "indigenous peoples," as the concept has evolved elsewhere, is not well tailored to many Asian situations. If the concept has evolved primarily in Asia, its justifications and perhaps its terminology would be significantly different. But a separate, regionally oriented concept with normative power now seems unlikely to emerge. Strategically, the principal options are interpreting "indigenous peoples" broadly enough to apply in much of Asia, or taking a narrow approach that will make it difficult for nonstate Asian groups to find alternatives on which to build the levels of legitimation, transnational support and normative claims currently offered by the concept.

Is there a risk that broadening the concept of "indigenous peoples" will weaken it?

One issue is whether the international indigenous peoples' movement, from which the international law concept derives much of its dynamism and impact, might become less cohesive with a wide array of groups and opinions to accommodate. Differences in interests will widen with heightened diversity. For example, many members of hill tribes who have lived in northern Thailand for several generations are not registered as citizens of Thailand but would like to be so as to secure political rights and access to government services. This position contrasts radically with that of some Native American groups in the United States, who assert a continuing separate tribal sovereignty as against U.S. federal jurisdiction and issue their own passports.[125] Divergences of this sort make it difficult to formulate positions in the international indigenous peoples' movement and illustrate the need for care in identifying the sources and representativity of normative pronouncements by international networks. In general, however, diverse groups have found that on many issues-including the problems and opportunities of emerging legal regimes for "traditional knowledge," genetic research, biodiversity, intellectual property, toxic wastes, international trade and transnational investment-they have much in common and have learned from each other.

The initial uncertainty among leaders of some groups in the areas of European settlement, particularly the Americas, about extending the category of "indigenous peoples" to Asia still recurs, and some of these leaders are undoubtedly tempted to acquiesce in a narrower definition in return for the agreement of Asian states to stronger substantive provisions in a UN declaration. It seems most likely, however, that such temptations will continue to be overwhelmed by the commitment to universality and solidarity within the internationally active indigenous peoples' movement, especially in view of the global scope of the United Nations agencies and the presumptions of universality inherent in the UN human rights culture. There presumptions are evident in the practice of the UN Voluntary Fund for indigenous populations, which has funded travel for people in all regions to participate in UN meetings of indigenous peoples.

A second issue arises from the evidence that, notwithstanding the aspiration for universality that pervades much of the literature of international law, more substantial and more effective commitments can sometimes be achieved by limiting the number participants and requiring commonality of values or capacity.[126] Thus, a global institution such as the World Bank might be able to adopt a more robust policy on indigenous peoples if it applied only to a set of borrowing countries with similarly expansive national commitments. But international institutions have been effective agents in the diffusion of policies, transmitting values and expertise, financing law reform and training of officials, and providing leverage to civil society organizations. In their day-to-day practice, international institutions continuously trade off perfect implementation for overall effectiveness in pursuit of their goals, but seldom will these global institutions fulfill their mandates adequately by deciding in principle to confine their policies concerning indigenous peoples and such matters as involuntary resettlement and environmental assessment to the like-minded. Optimizing participation and effectiveness is a more difficult conceptual problem with regard to the adoption by states of international normative instruments such as the UN draft declaration or international treaties pertaining to indigenous peoples. A constructivist approach offers the flexibility necessary to tackle such problems of optimization.

A third issue is the obvious significance the opposition of several major Asian state governments to application of the concept of "indigenous peoples" in their territories might have for the politics of matters relating to indigenous peoples in the United Nations. Having called for a clear, scientific, objective and practical definition of indigenous peoples that can clearly be interpreted as not applying to any groups in the PRC, China commented: "Until a clear definition of indigenous peoples has been established, the Chinese Government cannot formulate specific opinion on individual clauses of the draft declaration. . . ."[127] The PRC's position makes clear what is implicit: at least some Asian governments may support–or at a minimum not block–stronger provisions in the UN draft declaration if they are reasonably confident that those provisions will not be applied to groups within their states. A negotiating position is thus indicated: a draft declaration with a wide or open–ended definitional provision, or with no definitional provision at all, may well meet with opposition or proposals for severe attenuation, whereas a draft declaration with a narrow and precise definitional provision may well be supported.

Questions about the applicability of the international concept of "indigenous peoples" in various Asian states are, in part, questions about the suitability of the international concept in the context of competing visions of identities of particular groups and of national societies and polities.[128] Much of this complex problematique has to do with the evolving dynamics of identities and politics in these changing societies, but I argue that it also involves the terms of the international concept, and that the justifications of this concept are a central issue. China, like India, disputes the applicability of the concept while maintaining substantial policy programs intended to benefit constitutionally recognized categories of ethnic groups thought to face risks of disadvantage. In the early 1930s, drawing on Soviet nationalities theory, the Chinese Communist Party adopted a policy favoring self-government for minority peoples with the possibility even of independence. This policy was attenuated from the late 1930s, but recognition of various freedoms for minorities was incorporated in the first Constitution of the PRC.[129] The Anti Rightist Movement and the Cultural Revolution had severe impacts on minorities,[130] but in Yunnan province, for example, current official policy favors some provision for education in minority languages,[131] scholarships and special admission arrangements to promote minority involvement in higher education,[132] some preferential recruitment of minorities to government jobs,[133] some leniency and weighing of minority customs in judicial proceedings,[134] and special measures for political representation of minority areas and for the provision to members of minorities of positions in local government, as well as some involvement at higher levels of government.[135] Yunnan researchers have noted minority issues broadly similar to those faced by indigenous peoples in many parts of the world, such as disruption of land-use cycles because of diminishing land bases, unrestituted dispossession of natural resources, limited access to lands due to encroachment of rubber plantations and other industries, uneven terms of economic exchange with the Han majority, Han control of major economic activities, and neglect of health problems facing women.[136]

It seems unlikely that the PRC's objection to application of the concept of "indigenous peoples" to China is an objection in principle to the identification of distinct groups facing special problems. Nor is it necessarily a permanent objection to international law's touching "domestic" affairs: the PRC is considering accepting the norms of the International Covenant on Civil and Political Rights and is negotiating entry into the World Trade Organization, an institution much more intrusive than those pertaining to indigenous peoples. The PRC has concerns similar to those of India about the extension to nonstate groups of norms of self-determination, especially in relation to Tibet and Xinjiang, and some uneasiness about religious groups and cross-border ties of coreligionists.[137] The PRC may for some time take the view that its interests are better served by resisting application of the normative and institutional elements of the indigenous peoples' program, but interests change. More far-reaching is the conflict between views of China's history and the concept of "indigenous peoples" as victims of settler colonialism and oppression from an externally derived state constructed in their territories. The strong orthodoxy is of China not as colonizer but as a victim of colonialism, liberated by the revolution. As Zhou Enlai put it:

> [T] he whole country was one that suffered imperialist aggression, one that had become a semi-colony, or, in some regions, a colony. . . . [A]mong our various nationalities, they have shared weal and woe and cemented a militant friendship in the revolutionary wars, culminating in the liberation of this big family of nationalities.[138]

It is possible, without gravely weakening the concept of "indigenous peoples," to broaden the range of justifications it accommodates so as to avoid its interdependence with the historical patterns of European colonial settlement. This kind of broadening depends on understanding the global concept of "indigenous peoples" not primarily in positivist terms, but as a dynamic construct that itself has a shaping effect on social meanings and legal development. The international concept of "indigenous peoples" may be understood as an abstraction from a vast set of complex particular realities. These realities involve divergent self-perceptions and political discourses of groups and national societies, and diverse state-society relations. The abstract international concept of "indigenous peoples" has the potential to be drawn from international society back into national society; the abstract concept is worked out and made particular in a specific context.[139] This happens most obviously in those national societies where legal and political decision making gives weight to international practices and texts referring to indigenous peoples, and to decisions and models in other countries that are understood as involving indigenous peoples.[140] In different ways this concretization also occurs where groups draw upon the international concept of "indigenous peoples" in constructing their own identities: thus, groups whose self-concept might not have centered on prior possession may come to identify themselves as indigenous peoples with experiences and worldviews shared with other indigenous peoples.

The vitality of the concept of "indigenous peoples" in states such as Canada, Chile and Norway will not be eroded by an understanding of the global concept in broad constructivist terms, for the legitimacy of group claims within each society depends on interaction between a relatively amorphous global concept and the types of justification that resonate within that polity. A more open-ended global concept lacks certainty in its application but has the advantage of allowing scope for some variation when the concept is instantiated for purposes of positive law in different societies and institutional contexts. The effective application of such global concepts requires some overall indication of meaning and content, but beyond that depends much more on dynamic processes of claim, legitimation, and political and legal endorsement than on a single rigid definition.

Are "Local Communities" Functional Alternatives to "Indigenous Peoples" in Asia?

It remains to consider possible alternatives to the concept of "indigenous peoples." Alternative global concepts, such as "tribe" and "minority," have some legal purchase. "Tribal peoples" are specifically included in the relevant instruments of the ILO and the World Bank, but "tribal" is not easy to define, and its implicit emphasis on social structure does not mesh well with the dynamic societies, cultures and political forms of many of the groups in the internationally active indigenous peoples' movement. "Minority" is long established as a legal category but because of its generality and ubiquity is unlikely to be the basis for the kind of ambitious normative program, international institutional commitments and transnational networks that have built up around the concept of "indigenous peoples."

One broad alternative to a focus on "indigenous peoples" is a focus on local communities. Enhancing the salience of local residents' interests has been a major strategy in the field of international development, advocated even by environmental NGOs whose preferences and priorities may diverge sharply from those expressed by local people.[141]

Support for an "indigenous peoples" approach to enhancing local influence, however, may be tempered by concerns that the category of "indigenous peoples" is underinclusive or inequitable. Thus, in a village in India affected by land encroachments from a coal mine, people from one or more "scheduled tribes" may be interspersed with nontribal Hindus, some of whom are almost equally disadvantaged in economic vulnerability and social status under the caste system.[142]

Special factors relating to means of consultation and to compensatory development initiatives may apply to tribal families but not to others; but many of the economic and social issues may be similar. Tania Murray Li comments with reference to Indonesia that most "rural areas, both on and off Java, are complex mosaics of cultural groups and social classes, products of diverse agrarian histories and centuries of interaction with market and state."[143]

Reacting to concerns that "indigenous" or "tribal" is too narrow for certain functional purposes, some practitioners and policy activists concerned with sustainable development in Asia instead emphasize the role of local "communities" in such activities as development planning, common property management and sustainable forestry.[144] As a practical matter, in many situations local "communities" are in much the same position vis-à-vis the state or vis-à-vis development projects whether or not these communities or portions of them might be described as "indigenous." In practice, there will often be no sharp line between policies applicable wherever indigenous peoples are involved and policies applicable in cases of similarly situated "communities." Common to the concepts of "indigenous people" and a defined "community" are the challenging problems of how such abstract concepts are rendered operational in practice. As Li notes, the interests and voices of women, distress migrants and underclasses may be submerged in a focus on community that "leaves begging the central question of who is enabled or constrained: whose economic circumstances or security of tenure is at stake.[145] Internationally controversial projects, such as the enormous Arun III dam project in Nepal and logging of tropical forests in Sarawak, may attract the support of some members, on occasion even most members, of indigenous or local groups, whether on grounds of inevitability, the best interests of the community, or more personal benefits realized or hoped for.[146] Evaluating the cancellation in 1995 of the Arun III project, notwithstanding the apparent support of most residents of the remote Arun Valley for the roads and communications the project would bring, Ann Armbrecht Forbes comments that "the search for the real 'local' is an incomplete and thus a potentially misguided search. . . . Factors such as who speaks up, who claims to speak for whom, who chooses to remain silent and why, all influence which voice is eventually labeled as the 'local'."[147] Whether the focus is on local communities or indigenous peoples, complex issues arise as to decision making and representation in communities that may be undemocratic in structure, poorly informed about the long-term consequences of proposed projects, diverted by disputes with other groups, and vulnerable to suborning and coercion.[148]

For some purposes "local" is highly imprecise, and it is not very helpful to rely on an underspecified unit of "community" as somehow bounding legitimate involvement and concern. The sheer scale of large projects and the transformations they effect can overwhelm not only small groups with distinctive cultures, but much larger and more distant communities as well. As Forbes argues with respect to Nepal, a small country subject to enormous impact from such a project: "A 'local' in the Arun controversy. . . includes those living within an hour's walk of the dam site, as well as those in Kathmandu whose work is disrupted by electric shortages, as well as those worried about Nepal's foreign debt." [149]

Both local communities and indigenous peoples face the difficulty that their viewpoints may become minor elements, sometimes manipulated, of larger struggles. Where large projects draw on capital and support from intergovernmental agencies or foreign corporations, international campaigners have found points of leverage outside the host state that generate publicity and intensify pressure. In such cases issues arise as to who knows best and whose voice counts, entailing problems of representation, accountability and decision making in NGOs and in overseas lawsuits, as well as in governments and international organizations. High-visibility transnational campaigns against development projects attract the attention of many outside the area directly affected, but the objectives of such campaigns and their criteria of success may be radically different for national NGOs, transnational groups and local residents. In some cases campaigns of national and transnational NGOs and foreign governments on a specific develop-ment issue may be part of a wider political struggle concerning national leader-ship, in which indigenous peoples may or may not be active participants and in which their claims may be used to further quite different interests of others. National groups may focus on achieving victories in national courts, and thus set precedents requiring public access to environmental information or obliging the government to ensure consultation with affected groups. Transnational groups may seek to secure critical rulings from bodies such as the World Bank Inspection Panel and courts in the United States and elsewhere, and to change the broad policies of institutions such as the World Bank, the Export-Import Bank and the Overseas Private Investment Corporation. Campaigns are often directed at canceling projects; it is much more difficult for campaigners to promote and deliver positive alternatives that meet the development needs of local people. The actual consequences of a court victory, a policy change or cancellation of a project are not necessarily experienced in the same way by the local populace as by more distant NGOs, which can declare the battle over and move on. The indigenous peoples' program, with the status it confers on groups and the recognition of their active agency through institutions and the normative emphasis on participation and self-determination, may offer more potential for overcoming these problems than a focus on "local communities," which may lack socio-political individua-tion and capacities to act.

Promotion of the interests and agency of "local communities" is broadly compatible with the international indigenous peoples' program. Despite acute conflicts, as between settlers and natives in transmigration schemes, the two conceptual programs coexist and overlap. The concept of "local communities," however, is not a sufficient substitute for "indigenous peoples." The international concept of "indigenous peoples" connotes emphasis on self-determination and the role of groups in decisions affecting them, respect for different cultures shaped over long periods of history, recognition of special relations with land and terri-tory and unique knowledge about their use and management, and awareness of the disastrous consequences for these peoples of many prior policies of states and international institutions. The concept thus bears a range of justifications, vari-ously based on equity, history, the value of diversity, functional criteria, politics and law. Some of these are undervalued by an exclusive focus on "local communities." In particular, "local communities" is not so clearly a concept of history, of long association with territory, of cultural distinctiveness, of the political agency of autonomy and self-determination. By dint of its diffuse nature, it is unlikely ever to attain the normative purchase or institutional commitment of "indigenous peoples," and is a complement rather than a substitute.

VI. A Proposal Concerning Definition: Requirements and Indicia

For the purposes of international legal instruments intended to have general rather than regional or highly specific application, four factors seem relatively unproblematic as requisites for a group to be an "indigenous people" self-identi-fication as a distinct ethnic group; historical experience of, or contingent vulner-ability to, severe disruption, dislocation or exploitation; long connection with the region; and the wish to retain a distinct identity. These four criteria establish a set narrower than ethnic group" and more focused than "ethnic minority," but still overly broad to delimit the category of "indigenous peoples" as it is employed in contemporary practice. Three further criteria are highly relevant, but in each case some flexibility is required if special cases are not to be arbitrarily excluded.

The first of these is non dominance in the state or region. This criterion is virtually a requisite, but the exact meaning of "dominance" is difficult to cap-ture in many situations. Most obviously, numerical dominance is not ipso facto exclusionary where a group has little political or economic power. More complex situations arise where small groups are part of uneasy ruling political coalitions but have little power; or where a very few members of a group exercise consider-able national political power but most are entirely marginal to this process. Even where a group is numerically and politically dominant in a state, the state may be so small that, vis-à-vis international lending agencies, transnational mining and logging corporations, dumpers of hazardous waste, foreign fishing fleets, merce-naries and other powerful actors, the people of the state may face many of the same problems as "indigenous peoples" within states.[150]

Second is the requirement that a group have close cultural affinity with a particular territory or area of land. Many indigenous peoples regard this feature as essential to their own identities. It is not necessary for the group to have been associated with the particular land or territory for countless generations; groups have often moved, joined with other groups, or been forcibly relocated. Yet to make this requirement strict would argument about the concept of "human rights." Like the human rights argument, the charge of Eurocentrism is politically colorable when made against aggressive global assertion of Western concepts by governments and transnational networks based in the West, but it depends on notions of false consciousness, manipulation or opportunism when made against claims by local groups identifying themselves as indigenous peoples.

Some of the legal texts formulated under the *normative program,* particu-larly the UN draft declaration, assert rights of indigenous peoples or rights of individual members of indigenous peoples, and related duties of states and other obligées; but on these issues debate about the suitability of the language of rights does not simply oppose "Asia" to "the West." Objections to the substantive norms by some Asian states pertain mainly to self-determination and rights to land and resources, but these are unlikely to be more severe than those of some European settler states in which the concept of "indigenous peoples" is now uncontested (e.g., Brazil). The normative program does not formally depend at the global level on a precise definition of "indigenous peoples"; the disputes over relevant norms of land and resource rights, autonomy and self-determination, and equality and equity involve clashes of interests and values within states in all regions. Nevertheless, some formulations of elements of the normative program are bound up with particular views about justifications of the norms that are deeply contested.

The complexity of issues raised by indigenous peoples is reflected in the range of national, transnational and interstate *institutional mechanisms* deployed. International mechanisms include formal judicial or rule-governed approaches, special commissions, joint decision-making bodies, fact-finding and mediating bodies, consultative groups and negotiating fora. These overlap with individual human rights mechanisms, and additional mechanisms confer status on non state groups.[151] Not surprisingly, some states object to the institutional elements, particularly the availability of international platforms to criticize the state, the potential "meddling in internal affairs" by international agencies, the energetic activities of extensive transnational networks of indigenous peoples and interested NGOs, and extraterritorial proceedings in foreign courts.[152] But the give-and-take of bargaining within such institutional structures is the ordinary stuff of international law and politics, and it is to be expected that practical accommodations (however much open to criticism) can be reached, as has been demonstrated in the practice of some of the functional agencies such as the ILO and the World Bank, and in the evolution of the innovative practices of the UN Working Group on indigenous populations.

The concept of "indigenous peoples" carries within it grounds of *justification* related to prior occupancy, dispossession and group identity. While conceptual issues and more instrumental political and legal concerns are inevitably mixed, the principled objection, for example, of the Indian government to applying international instruments concerning indigenous peoples to India is above all an objection to a specific justification perceived to be inherent in the concept of "indigenous peoples," a justification that is not simply a product of European expansion but that nevertheless does not accurately capture identities and outlooks in some regions not structured by waves of recent invasion and migration.[153] Two paths are currently open. One is to adhere to the requirement of historical continuity of prior occupants, which would assure the political viability of the international concept of "indigenous peoples" and perhaps open the way for greater normative and institutional development, while avoiding some of the serious policy problems of a potent, but uncircumscribed and open-ended, category.

The other is to treat historical continuity as an indicator rather than a requirement. This approach emphasizes the commonality of experiences, concerns and contributions made by groups in many different regions, and argues that functional matters such as dispossession of land, cultural dislocation, environmental despoliation and experiences with large development projects establish a unity that is not dependent on the universal presence of historical continuity. This approach recognizes that the concept of "indigenous peoples" must be circumscribed to be useful but proposes to achieve this delimitation through a different means of definition, as set forth in this article. Where a broader range of groups is potentially involved, normative and institutional development will be more complex and more flexibility may be necessary, but the ILO and the World Bank have established that such an approach is, at a minimum, possible.

The flexible approach to definition advocated here would be problematic if the concept of "indigenous peoples" were understood as operating primarily in the positivist sense of defining and delimiting a category of right holders. Although this is one of its functions, the concept must be viewed not simply in static terms. The, basic question is how a single concept of "indigenous peoples," potentially global in scope, can be both abstracted from and germane to the enormous variety of local self-conceptions and political contexts to which its relevance is asserted. It has been argued here that such concepts are better understood in the constructivist fashion sketched in this article, and that on balance more is gained than lost by adopting a flexible approach. This article therefore advocates setting forth flexible, but focused, international criteria as to the meaning of "indigenous peoples," with a combination of requirements and indicia, and relying on the dynamic processes of negotiation, politics, legal analysis, institutional decision making and social interaction to work out the application of these criteria to the innumerable nuances of specific cases.

Notes

[1] Benedict Kingsbury is Murry and Ida Becker Professor of Law, Chair of the Graduate Division and Director of the Institute for International Law and Justice at the New York University School of Law.

[2] For overviews, see, e.g., Douglas Sanders, *The Re-Emergence of Indigenous Questions* in International Law. 1 CAN. HUM. RTS. Y.B. 3 (1983); Chris Tennant, *Indigenous Peoples, International Institutions, and the International Legal Literature from 1945-1993,* 16 HUM. RTS. Q. I (1994); and S. James anaya INDEGENOUS PEOPLES IN INTERNATIONAL LAW (1996). The history of international activity evolving or relating to indigenous peoples is much longer, encompassing, inter alia, bilateral diplomacy by indigenous peoples, as well as attempts to petition and appear at the League of Nations, transnational operations of church groups and NGOs such as the Aborigines Protection Society and the Anti-Slavery Society in the 19th century, and the activities of the International Labour Organization from the 1920s onward.

[3] For differing views on the adequacy of state created aboriginal institutions to represent indigenous people in Australia, see Mick Dodson, *Towards the Exercise of Indigenous Rights: Policy, Power, and Self-Determination,* RACE & CLASS, Apr–June 1994, at 65; and Paul Coe, ATSIG:

Self-Determination or otherwise, id. at 35.

4 Santa Clara Pueblo v. Martinez, 436 U.S. 49 (1978).

5 Cayuga Indians (Gr. Brit. v. U.S.), 6 R.I.A.A. 173 (1926).

6 U.S. Bureau of Indian Affairs, Branch of Acknowledgment and Research, Proposed Finding for Federal Acknowledgment of the Mash-she-pe-nash-she-wish Indian Tribe (visited Feb. 23, 1998) (http:/ /www.doi.gov/ bia/matchsum.html).

7 UN Hum. Rts. Comm., Communication No. 205/1986, Mikmaq Tribal Society v. Canada, UN Doc. CCPR/C/43/D/205/1986 (1991).

8 Sarah Laird, A. B. Cunningham & Estherine Lisinge, *Forests, Drugs, and Benefit sharing: Putting the Formula to the Test–The Cameroon Case of* Ancistrocladus Korupensis, in PEOPLE, PLANTS, AND JUSTICE (Charles Zerner ed., forthcoming).

9 Jesse Ribot, *Rebellion, Representation and Enfranchisement in the Forest Villages of Makacoulibantang, Eastern Senegal, in id.*

10 *See infra p.* 420 and pp. 441–45.

11 Report of the Second Workshop on a Permanent Forum for Indigenous People within the United Nations System, UN Doc. E/CN.4/Sub.2/1998/11 (1997).

12 See the thoughtful discussion in Yash Ghai, *Human Rights and Governance: The Asia Debate,* 14 AUSTL. Y.B. INT'L. L. 1 (1994).

13 A Member or the Tanzanian Parliament, Moringe Parkipuny, made two statements entitled "The Indigenous Peoples Rights Question in Africa" at the UN Sub-Commission Working Group on indigenous populations in 1989 and 1991 (see INTERNATIONAL WORK GROUP FOR INDIGENOUS AFFAIRS [IWGIA], NEWSLETTER, No. 59, 1989, at 92-94, and *id.,* Sept./Oct. 1991, at 48), and an increasing number of groups from Africa have attended subsequent meetings of the working group. Organizations such as IWGIA have assisted such involvement. See *generally*". . . NEVER DRINK FROM THE SAME CUP": PROCEEDINGS OF THE Conference ON INDIGENOUS PEOPLES IN AFRICA (Copenhagen, Hanne Veber, Jens Dahl, Fiona Wilson & Espen Waehle eds., 1993). Ken Saro Wiwa was one of the most prominent African participants in the international indigenous peoples' movement; his writings include GENOCIDE IN NIGERIA: THE OGONI TRAGEDY (Port Harcourt, 1992), and collections of short essays such as NIGERIA: THE BRINK OF DISASTER (Port Harcourt, 1991). He was a vice president of the Netherlands-based Unrepresented Nations and Peoples Organization. He was executed, with other Ogoni, by the Nigerian government in 1995. In a solemn session that year at the UN Commission on Human Rights Inter-Sessional Working Group on the draft declaration on the rights of indigenous peoples. "the Chairperson Rapporteur, at the request of many governmental and indigenous delegations, paid tribute to the Nigerian writer and human rights activist, Mr Ken Saro Wiwa, who had given his life for the cause of human rights." Report of the Working Group Established in accordance with Commission on Human Rights resolution 1995/ 32 of 3 March 1995, 1st Session, UN Doc. E/CN.4/1996/84, para. 17.

14 It may be indicative of the Nigerian government's sensitivity to the issue that Nigeria was the only sub-Saharan state not then a member of the Commission on Human Rights to have chosen to participate in both the first and second sessions of the intercessional working group. For an example of express governmental concern, see the comment of Niger on a UN report: "the absence of a definition of 'indigenous people' invited subjective interpretations, which poses dangers for those emerging nation-states in Africa that face recurrent tribal conflicts." Erica-Irene Daes, Protection of the Heritage or indigenous people: Final report. UN Doc. E/CN.4/ Sub.211995/26, para. 6,

15 For example, the Pacific-Asia Council of Indigenous Peoples, which has connections with the pioneering World Council of Indigenous Peoples, and the Asia Indigenous Peoples Pact (AIPP), established in the early 1900s, and active as an international network. In 1996 the primary membership of the AIPP numbered 18 organizations, including the Naga Peoples Movement for Human Rights, DIRSA (Ranchi, India), Nepal Federation or Nationalities Federal Council,

Chittagong Hill Tracks Peoples Council, Inter Mountain Peoples Education and Culture in Thailand Association, Partner of Community Organization (PACOS, Sabah), Arakhan Human Rights Centre. Kachin Land Foundation, Cordillera Peoples' Alliance, National Federation of Indigenous Peoples of the Philippines (KAMP). Lumad Mindanaw (Mindanao), Homeland Mission 1950 Maluku (Amsterdam), Alliance of Taiwan Aborigines, Adivasi Solidarity (Bombay) and Centre for Orang Asli Concerns (Petaling Jaya).

[16] See INDIGENOUS PEOPLES OF ASIA, esp. chs. 1–4 (R. H. Barnes, Andrew Gray &: Benedict Kingsbury eds., 1995) [hereinafter PEOPLES OF ASIA).

[17] *Reprinted as Declaration of the Asiain Delegation,* in IWGIA, NEWSLETTER, Sept./Oct. 1991, at 40.

[18] Consideration of a Draft United Nations Declaration on the Rights of Indigenous Peoples, UN Doc. E/CN.4/WG.l5/2 (l995) [hereinafter PRC Consideration]. In this and other statements, the PRC government chastises the UN Secretariat for inaccuracy:

> In the materials it prepared for the World Conference on Human Rights, the [UN] Centre for Human Rights presumptuously categorized ordinary minority nationalities in many Asia countries as "indigenous peoples" and refused, despite collective and individual clarifications from the Asian countries, to rectify its mistake. This example amply demonstrates the necessity of an established definition of an indigenous people.

[19] Jose Martínez Cobo, Study of the Problem of Discrimination against indigenous populations, UN Doc. E/CN.4/Sub.2/1986/7/Add.4, paras. 379–80.

[20] Article 1(1) of the Convention concerning Indigenous and Tribal Peoples in Independent Countries stipulates that the Convention applies to:

> (a) tribal peoples in independent countries whose social, cultural and economic conditions distinguish them from other sections of the national community, and whose status is regulated wholly or partially by their own customs or traditions or by special laws or regulations;
>
> (b) peoples in independent countries who are regarded as indigenous on account of their descent from the populations which inhabited the country, or a geographical region to which the country belongs, at the time of conquest or colonisation or the establishment of present state boundaries and who, irrespective of their legal status, retain some or all of their own social, economic, cultural and political institutions.

ILO Convention No. 169, June 27,1989,28 ILM 1382,1384-85 (1989).

[21] The World Bank Operational Directive 4.20 states:

> The terms "indigenous peoples," "indigenous ethnic minorities," "tribal groups," and "scheduled tribes" describe social groups with a social and cultural identity distinct from the dominant society that makes them vulnerable to being disadvantaged in the development process. For the purposes of this directive, "indigenous peoples" is the term that will be used to refer to these groups.

In providing more details to operations staff about groups to which the policy applies, the operational directive states:

> Because of the varied and changing contexts in which indigenous peoples are found, no single definition can capture their diversity. Indigenous people are commonly among the poorest segments of a population. They engage in economic activities that range from shifting agriculture in or near forests to wage labour or even small-scale market-oriented activities. Indigenous peoples can be identified in particular geographical areas by the presence in varying degrees of the following characteristics:
>
> (a) a close attachment to ancestral territories and to the natural resources in these areas;
> (b) self-identification and identification by others as members of a distinct cultural group;
> (c) an indigenous language, often different from the national language;

(d) presence of customary social and political institutions; and

(e) primarily subsistence-oriented production.

    Task managers (TM) must exercise judgment in determining the populations to which this directive applies and should make use of specialized anthropological and sociological experts throughout the project cycle.

    Operational Directive 4.20. reprinted in IWGIA, NEWSLETTER, Nov./Dec. 1991, at 19. This operational direct is at present being considered for revision under a reorganization of governance instruments within the Bank.

[22] See *generally* DOUGLAS SANDERS, THE FORMATION OF THE WORLD COUNCIL Of INIDIGENOUS PEOPLES (Copenhagen, 1977).

[23] IWGIA, NEWSLETTER, June 1981, at 5.

[24] These commonalities result from, e.g., the ubiquity of state interests in economic moderniza-tion and exploitation of resources, often in response to global demands for such commodities as timber, electricity, copper and gold; the transnational operation and global technologies of industries such as mining, nuclear power, large dams, tropical forestry and oil recovery; simi-larities among modern monetarized economies, and their connections through markets, brand names and tastes fostered by advertising; shared social technologies for the organization of important sectors from educational institutions and censuses to banking and insurance; and the global communications that simultaneously facilitate transnational connections of markets and networks of indigenous peoples.

[25] The CONCISE OXFORD DICTIONARY 692 (9th ed. 1995). defines "indigenous" as "I. *a* (esp. of flora or fauna) originating naturally in a region *b* (of people) born in a region 2. (foll. by *to*) belonging naturally to place.

[26] See SANDERS, *supra* note 21, at 12.

[27] World Council of Indigenous Peoples, Draft Covenant (mimeo 1984).

[28] See, e.g., ELIE KEDOURIE, NATIONALISM (4th ed. 1993); BENEDICT ANDERSON, IMAGINED COMMUNITIES: REFLECTIONS ON THE ORIGIN AND SPREAD OF NATIONALISM (rev. ed. 1991). The Solemn Declaration adopted at the 1975 WCIP meeting has a striking narrative line:

    We the Indigenous Peoples of the world, united in this corner of our Mother Earth in a great assembly of men of wisdom, declare to all nations: We glory in our proud past. when the each was our nurturing mother, when the night sky formed our common roof, when Sun and Moon were our parents, when all were brothers and sisters, when our great civilizations grew under the sun, when our chiefs and elders were great leaders, when justice ruled the law and its execution. Then other peoples arrived: thirsting for blood, for gold, for land and all its wealth, carrying the cross and the sword, one in each hand, without knowing or waiting to learn the ways of our worlds, they considered us to be lower than animals, they stole our lands from us and took us, from our lands, they made slaves of the sons of the sun. However, they have never been able to eliminate us, nor to erase our memories of what we were, because we are the culture of the earth and the sky, we are of ancient descent and we are millions, and although our whole universe be ravaged, our people will live on for longer even than the kingdom of death. . . . We vow to control again our own destiny and recover our complete humanity and pride in being Indigenous People.

SANDERS, *supra* note 21. at 17.

[29] PRASENJIT DUARA, RESCUING HISTORY FROM THE NATION 4 (1995).

[30] JAMES CLIFFORD. THE PREDICAMENT OF CULTURE 342 (1988).

[31] See Memorandum from the Minister of Foreign Affairs, P.H. Kooijmans, and the Minister of Development Cooperation, J.P. Pronk, to the Netherlands Parliament, Indigenous Peoples in the Netherlands Foreign Policy and Development Cooperation (Mar. 29, 1993) (Eng. trans.,

mimeo).

[32] Report of the Second Session of the Working Group Established in accordance with Commission on Human Rights resolution 1995/32 of 3 March 1995, UN Doc. E/CN.4/1997/102, paras. 107–13 (1996) [hereinafter WG Second Report]. For comments by the U.S. government, see UN Doc. E/CN.4/1995/WG.15/ 2/Add.l (1995).

[33] See, e.g., the decision of the French Conseil constitutional holding that a statute referring to the Corsican people is unconstitutional under Article 2 of the 1958 Constitution. Law no. 91-428 of May 13, 1991, J.O., May 14, 1991, p. 6318 (portant statut de la collectivé territoriale de Corse); Cons. const 1991, Dec. No. 91-290.

[34] WG Second Report. supra note 31, paras. 132 (Brazil), 134 (Malaysia), 137 (Ecuador). *See also id.,* paras.133 (Australia), 142 (Japan).

[35] *Id.,* paras, 233 (Brazil), 230 (Malaysia); see also id., para. 239 (Japan).

[36] On parallel legislation concerning individualisation of indigenous peoples' land holdings in the United States and several South American states from the 1860s to the 1880s, see Sanders, supra note 1. For a comparison between post-1945 evolutions of U.S. government policy concerning federal relations with Indian Groups in Alaska and Swedish state policy in relation to Sami, showing convergence in the early 1970s and divergence in the 1980s, see Fae L. Komso, Empowerment or Termination: Native Resource Rights in Alaska and Swedish Lapland (1992) (unpublished Ph.D. dissertation, University of New Mexico).

[37] On the human rights debate, see the literature and perspectives considered in Ghai, supra note 11; and Daniel Bell. *The East Asian Challenge to Human Rights: Reflection on all East-.West Dialogue,* 18 HUM. Rts. Q.641 (1996).

[38] WG Second Report. *supra* note 31. para. 187.

[39] *See, e.g.,* RONALD DWORKIN, TAKING RIGHTS SERIOUSLY (l977); JOHN RAWLS, A THEORY OF JUSTICE (1971).

[40] E.g., John Rawls, *The Law of People,* in ON HUMAN RIGHTS 41 (Stephen Shute & Susan Hurley eds., 1993), For the concept of "the people" in a theoretical explanation of written constitutions as commitments operating over many generations, see Jed Rubenfeld, *Reading the Constitution as Spoken,* 104 YALE L.J. 1119, 1143–69 (1995). On the history or "the people" as a concept of U.S. constitutionalism, see EDMUND MORGAN, INVENTING THE PEOPLE: THE RISE OF POPULAR SOVEREIGNTY IN ENGLAND AND AMERICA (1988).

[41] For a variety of approaches, see, e.g., JAMES TULLY, STRANCE MULTIPLICITY: CONSTITUSIONALISM IN AN AGE OF DIVERSITY (1995); WILL KYMLICKA, MULTICULTURAL Citizenship: A LIBERAL THEORY OF MINORITY RIGHTS (1995); and ANDREW SHARPE, JUSTICE, AND THE MAORI: THE PHILOSHOPHY AND PRACTICE OF MAORI CLAIMS IN NEW ZEALAND SINCE THE 1980s (2d ed. *1997*).

[42] Benedict Kingsbury, *Whose International Law? Sovereignty and Non-State* Groups, 88 ASlL PROC. I (1994).

[43] The general association between the Afro- Asian decolonization movement and contemporary UN activity concerning indigenous peoples has become more attenuated, but the anticolonial and antidiscrimination elements of the indigenous peoples' program have continued to find some resonance with governments of states active in the decolonization movement For example, the Zambian government stated in 1994 that it

> welcomes the establishment of a permanent forum in the United Nations for indigenous peoples. At the international level Zambia has traditionally been a strong supporter of the rights of indigenous peoples. This is evidenced by action taken in respect of the liberation of southern Africa and the eradication of apartheid in South Africa.
>
> UN Doc. E/CN.4/Sub.2/AC.4/1995/7/Add.1. Whether this support will endure if it appears that the concept of "indigenous peoples" is being used to confer international legitimacy on groups and alchemies within such states is another matter.

[44] E.g.. British designation of scheduled tribes and scheduled areas in India, *see, e.g.,* CHRISTOPH VON FORERHAIMENDORF, TRIBES OF INDIA: THE STRUCGLE FOR SURVIVAL (1982), scheduled areas in Burma, and the frontier districts subject to the Frontier Crimes. Regulations in what is now Pakistan.

[45] See. *e.g.,* VERRIER ELWIN, INDIA'S NORTH-EAST FRONT1ER, IN THE NINE-TEENTH CENTURY (1959); VERRIER ELW1N, A PHILOSOPHY FOR NEFA, (Shillong, 2d ed. 1959); and Peter Robb, *The Colonial State and contractions of Indian Identity: An Example on tile Northeast Frontier in the 1880's,* 31 MOD. ASIAN STUD. 245 (1997).

[46] FORMOSA, BUREAU OF ABORIGINAL AFFAIRS, REPORT ON THE CONTROL OF THE ABORIGINES IN FORMOSA (1911).

[47] For a detailed survey, see DONALD L. HOROWITZ., ETHNIC GROUPS IN CONFLICT (1985).

[48] Benedict Anderson, *Introduction* to SOUTHEAST ASIAN TRIBAL GROUPS AND ETHNIC MINORITIES I (Cambridge, Mass., 1987). This paragraph and the next focus on Anderson's account, but there is a considerable corpus of literature on histories of colonialism developing similar themes.

[49] *Id.* at 10–11.

[50] *Id.* at 1–11.

[51] See e.g.. Richard Dorall, *The Dialectic of Development: Tribal Responses to Development Capital in the Cordillera Central, Northern Luzon. Philippines,* in TRIBAL PEOPLES AND DEVELOP-MENT IN SOUTHEAST ASIA 37 (Kua1a Lumpur, Lim Teck Ghee & Alberto G. Gomes eds., 1990) hereinafter TRIBAL PEOPLES].

[52] For a historical survey, see Maria Elena R. Regpala. *Resistance in the Cordillera: A Philippine Tribal People's Historical Response to Invasion and Change Imposed from Outside,* in *id.* al 112.

[53] The Philippine Mining Act of 1995, the 1996 Implementing Rules and Regulations of the Philippine Mining Act, the Financial, or Technical Assistance Agreement made with Western Mining, and other instruments were challenged on constitutional and other grounds in judicial proceedings launched in the Philippines Supreme Court in 1996-1997.

[54] See OWEN LYNCH & KIRK TALBOTT, BALANCING ACTS: COMMUNITY BASED FOREST MANAGEMENT AND NATIONAL LAW IN ASIA AND THE PACIFIC (Wash-ington, 1995); DAVID Daoas, *The Rights of Cultural Communities in the Philippines,* in ". . . VINES THAT WON'T BIND. . ,"; INDIGENOUS PEOPLES IN ASIA 97 (Copenhagen, Christian Erni ed.. 1997); WG Second Report, *supra* note 31. para. 314.

[55] Article 27 of the Covenant, Dec. 16, 1966, 999 UN1S 1/1, refers to ethnic, religious and linguistic minorities. The Japanese government stated in 1980 that "minorities of the kind men-tioned in the covenant do not exist in Japan." UN Doc. ICCPR/C/l0/ Add.1 (1980). In 1988 the government "adopted a delicate formulation stating with respect to "the people of the Ainu" that "it is recognized that these people preserve their own religion and maintain their own culture." UN Doc. ICCPR/C/42/Add.4 (1988). See *infra* p. 438.

[56] CONST. Art. 160(2).

[57] For a brief overview, see Sothi Rachagan, *Constitutional and Statutory* Provision *Governing the Qrang As1i,* in TRIBAL PEOPLES, supra note 50, at 101. see also ISKANDAR CAREY, ORANG ASLI: THE ABORIGINAL TRIBES or PENINSULAR MALAYSIA (1976), The Malaysian Constitution, ninth schedule, allocates "welfare of the aborigines" to the federal power, whereas "native law and custom" is a matter of state power for Sabah and Sarawak.

[58] Several works of Colin Nicholas address this issue, e.g., *In the Name of the Semai: The State and Semai Society in Peninsular Malaysia,* in TRIBAL PEOPLES, *supra* note 50, at 68.

[59] CONST, Art. 161A.

[60] See, e.g., remarks by a leader of this organization, Anderson Muutang Urud, *Statement to the United Nations General Assembly, 10 December* 1992, in VOICE OF INDEGENOUS PEOPLES: NATIVE PEOPLE ADDRESS THE UNITED NATIONS 103 (Santa Fe, N.M., 1994). For a summary by a community organizer from PACOS in Sabah, see Jannie Lasimbang, Juridical

Rights of Indigenous Peoples and Their Relations to the State and Non-Indigenous Peoples: The Case of Sabah, in VINES THAT WON'T BIND, supra note 53. at 109.

[61] Victor King, *Indigenous Peoples and Land Rights in Sarawak, Malaysia:* To be or not To be a Bumiputra, in PEOPLE OF ASIA, supra note 15, at 289.

[62] Some implications of population movements are discussed in Cornelia Ann Kammerer, *Territorial Imperatives: Akha Ethnic Identity and Thailand's National Intergration,* in ETHNICITIES AND NATIONS 274 (Remo Guidieri, Francesco Pellizzi & Stanley Tambiah eds., 1988).

[63] See the powerful1973 statement against this government practice by King Bhumibol, *quoted* in LYNCH & TALBOTT, *supra* note 53, at iii.

[64] Chayan Vaddhanuphuti, *The Present Situation of Indigenous Peoples in Thailand,* in VINES THAT WON'T BIND, supra note 53, at 79, 83.

[65] Thailand government statement, Hill-Tribe Welfare and Development, UN Doc. E/CN.4/AC.211992/4.

[66] Taipower's 1997 proposal to export the waste to North Korea, a country in desperate need of revenue but unlikely adequately to manage such waste, led to strong protests in South Korea and from international NGOs, and caused disquiet among Yami and other campaigning groups in Taiwan. A further contentious issue for Yami arises from plans to turn a cleaned-up Lanyu into a national park, threatening to limit Yami economic opportunities and to promote a commodity-oriented tourist culture.

[67] See, e.g., Alliance of Taiwan Aborigines, I Chiang & Lava Kau, *Report on the Human Right Situation of Taiwan's Aborigines, in* PEOPLES OF ASIA, *supra* note 15, at 357.

[68] Also increasingly active are the Union of Native Taiwanese Villages founded in 1994 and other social movements.

[69] Statement by the Delegation of Taiwan Aborigines, United Nations Working Group on indigenous populations, 11th Sess. (July 1993) (mimeo, UN files). Although the Romanization differs, the Chinese characters in *yuan-chu min* and *yuanzu min* are identical.

[70] Peace Agreement between the Government of Bangladesh National Committee on Chittagong Hill Tracts Affairs and the Parhatya Chattagram Jana Sanghati [Samhati] Samiti, Dec, 2, 1997, DAILY STAR (Dhaka), Dec. 3, 1997 (Eng. trans.). On the conflict, see CHITTAGONG HILL TRACTS COMMISSION [a nongovernmental outside group], LIFE IS NOT OURS: LAND AND HUMAN RIGHTS IN THE CHITTAGONG HILL TRACTS, BANGLADESH (London, 1991). The Peace Agreement is opposed by the main opposition Bangladesh Nationalist Party.

[71] Willem Van Schendel, *The Invention of the 'Jummas:' State Formation and Ethnicity in Southeasthern Bangladesh,* in PEOPIES OF ASIA, supra note 15, at 121, 139. Van Schendel notes, at 139: "It is remarkable that this term was adopted at a time when many hill people had been forced to give up Sweden cultivation."

[72] Sanchay Chakma, *The Legal Right Situation of the Indigenous Peoples* in *Bangladesh,* in VINES THAT WON'T BIND, *supra* note 53, at 151. Chakma, a student in Dhaka, is General Secretary of the Greater Chiuagong Hill Tracts Hill Students' Council.

[73] U Win Mra, Statement on Behalf of the Delegation of Myanmar to the United Nations Working Group on Indigenous Populations {July 31,1991) (UN files, mimeo). Members of Karen and other groups in Burma have participated in UN fora and other international activities relating to indigenous peoples. See, e.g., the statement by a Chin student, Zo Tum Hmung, *The Juridical Rights of the Indigenous Peoples in Burma, in* VINES THAT WON'T BIND, *supra* note 53, at 89. However, this participation has been modest in relation to the numerical size of such groups and the scale of the issues involved. The impact in Burma of the international concept of "indigenous peoples" does not appear to have been great. On the conflicts in Burma, see BURMA: THE CHALLENGE Of CHANGE IN A DIVIDED SOCIETY (Peter Carey ed., 1997).

[74] See, e.g., Lakshmi Puri, Statement on Behalf of the Delegation of India to the United Nations Working Group on indigenous populations (Aug. 12, 1983) (UN files. mimeo).

[75] Alternatively, the Bangladesh government has argued that all Bangladeshis are indigenous people

who existed in the territory prior to British colonization and are now, fortunately, liberated.

[76] PRC Consideration, *supra* note 17.

[77] *Id.; See also* WG Second Report, *supra* note 31, para. 106: Report of the Third Session of the Working Group Established in accordance with Commission on Human Rights resolution 1995/32 of 3 March 1995, UN Doc. E/CN.4/1998/106, para. 37 (1997).

[78] Government of India, Observations, UN Doc. E/CN.4/Sub.2/1984/2/Add.2; Government of Myanmar, Observations, UN Doc. E/CN.4/Sub.2/1989/33/Add.1. For Bangladesh, see Report of the Working Group on indigenous populations on its fourteenth session, UN Doc. E/CN.4/Sub.2/1996/21. para. 34.

[79] BELGIAN GOVERNMENT INFORMATION CENTER, THE SACRED MISSION OF CIVILIZATION: TO WHICH PEOPLES SHOULD THE BENEFITS BE EXTENDED? THE BELGIAN THESIS (1953).

[80] INIS L CLAUDE, NATIONAL MINORITIES: AN INTERNATIONAL PROBLEM 172 (1955).

[81] Prabhu Dayal, Statement on Behalf of the Delegation of India to the United Nations Working Group on indigenous populations (July 31, 1991) (UN files, mimeo).

[82] CONST, Arts. 244, 342; and numerous presidential designating orders, e.g., Constitution (Scheduled Tribes) Order 1950. On some of the complexities of these categories in practice, see MARC GALANTER, Group *membership and Group Preferences in India,* in LAW AND SOCIETY IN MODERN INDIA 108 (1989).

The constitutional classifications of "scheduled tribes" and "tribal areas" are utilized explicitly by the World Bank *Group* in the International Development Association-Government of India Development Credit Agreement, Dec. 22, 1994, for the India: Andhra Pradesh First Referral Health System Project (C2663), Art. I & schedule 2, pt. C. They are utilized implicitly by the same parties in requirements that the borrower ensure implementation of a "Tribal Development Plan" (this being a mutually acceptable means to satisfy the World Bank's internal policy requirement for an Indigenous Peoples Development Plan) in the Agreement, Mar. 9. 1994, for the India: Andhra Pradesh Forestry Project (C2573), schedule 2. pt. B; and the Agreement, Aug. 12, 1993, for the India: Rubber Project (C2409), Art. III §3.08.

[83] For consideration of some of the consequences of this process, see CULTURAL ENCOUNTERS ON CHINA'S ETHNIC FRONTIER (Steven Harrell ed., 1994).

[84] MARY FAINSOD KATZENSTEIN, ETHNICITY AND EQUALITY THE SHIV SENA PARTY AND PEFERENTIAL POLICIES IN BOMBAY (1979); Clare Talwalker, *Shivaji's Armyy and Other "Natives"* in *Bombay,* 16 COMP. STUD. S. ASIA, AFR. & MIDDLE E. 114 (1996).

[85] See HOROWITZ, *supra* note 46, at 201-16.

[86] E.g., Muriwhenua Fisheries, Wai-22 (Waitangi Tribunal, NZ, 1988).

[87] E.g., the "Lapp Codicil" to the Norway-Sweden Treaty of 1751, discussed by the SAMERETSUTVALGET [Norwegian Sami Rights Committee], OM SAMENES RETTSSTILLING (NOU No. 18,1984).

[88] *E.g.,* Cayuga Indians (Gr. Brit. v. U.S.), 6 R.I.A.A. 173 (1926).

[89] Some of the issues are discussed in José Woehrling, *les Revendications du Canada sur les eaux de archipel de l'Arctique et l'utilisation immémoriale des glaces par les Inuit,* 30 GER. Y.B. INT'L L 120 (1987); and W. Michael Reisman, *Protecting Indigenous Rights* in *International Adjudication,* 89 AJIL 350 (1995).

[90] A prominent example of transnational environmental litigation in Australia relates to harm to the Ok Tedi and Maun Rivers and to the well-being of local people arising from the operation, by a company partly owned and controlled by the Australian mining company BHP, of the Ok Tedi mine in Papua New Guinea. Preliminary rulings in the Supreme Court of Victoria in 1995 struck out some of the plaintiffs' causes of action but left open a possibility that the case would reach a trial on the merits. Dagi v. BHP (No, 2), [1997] 1 V.R 428; Dagi v, BHP (Nov. 10, 1995) (Byrne, J.), 1995 VIC LEXIS 1182. Following public pressure on BHP and the company's

alleged involvement in a proposal to amend Papua New Guinea's criminal law to prevent civil suits in Australia, *see* [1996] 2 V.R 117, a settlement was reached in 1996 under which BHP paid compensation and look ameliorative measures in the affected areas. An example of increasingly frequent cases in which environmental and human rights arguments are combined is opposition to the Freeport-McMoRan mining and metal milling operation at Grasberg, West Irian. The western portion of Papua, a generally Melanesian area colonized by the Netherlands but not greatly developed under Dutch rule, was incorporated into Indonesia only during the 1960s, by which time a distinctive self-identity had begun to evolve, Armed conflict continues on a limited scale between the Indonesian army and the Free Papua Movement (Organisasi Papua Merdeka). Civil conflicts connected in some way to the Grasberg project have been frequent, and concerns about human rights abuses and environmental problems have been expressed within Indonesia by groups such as the Indonesian Human Rights Commission and church organizations; but the main pressure has come from outside. The U.S. government investment promotion agency, the Overseas Private Investment Corp., terminated its political risk guarantee to Freeport in 1995, reinstating it temporarily in 1996 with some encouragement from environmental NGOs keen to see Freeport held to stronger environmental conditions. Lawsuits against Freeport-McMoRan alleging human rights violations and breaches of international environmental obligations were filed in state and federal courts in Louisiana (where Freeport's corporate head office is located) in 1996 and 1997. Yosofa Alomang,v. Freeport-McMoRan, 1996 U.S. Dist. LEXIS 15,908 (E.D. La. Oct. 17, 1996) (declining Freeport's motion to remove the case from state court to federal court); Tom Beanal v. Freeport-McMoRan. 1997 WL 178,637 (E.D. La. Apr. 10, 1997) (dismissing plaintiff claim), An amended complaint was thereafter filed in the latter case in which an Amungme tribal organization, Lembaga Musyawarah Adat Suku Amungme, was also a plaintiff. but problems in the pleading of the plaintiffs' claims in this case continued. 1997 U.S. Dist LEXIS 12.001 (E.D. La. Aug. 8.1997).

[91] Some such procedural issues were considered in Cayuga Indians, 6 R.I.A.A. 173 (1926).

[92] Benedict Kingsbury, *Claims by Non-State Groups* in *International Law*, 25 CORNELL INT'L L.J. 481 (1992).

[93] An example is litigation concerning the projected Yadana natural gas pipeline, which runs from the Yadana offshore field under the Andaman Sea and through the Tenasserim region of Burma to the Thai border, where it will meet projects on the Thai side. The onshore portion passes through areas populated by non-Burman ethnic groups that have often been in conflict with the military regime, and opposition to the pipeline is bound up with opposition to the regime. A civil suit brought in the United States against the oil company Unocal and other defendants focused not on issues particular to indigenous peoples but on general human rights violation of Union of Burma v. Unocal, 176 F.R.D. 329 (C.D. Cal. 1997).

[94] This is the view taken by Erica-lrene Daes, *Dilemmas Posed by the UN Draft Declaration on the Rights of Indigenous Peoples,* 63 NORDIC. J. INT'L L. 205 (1994); Erica-Irene Daes, *Equality of Peoples under the Auspices of the United Nation Draft Declaration on the Rights of Indigenous Peoples,* 7 ST. THOMAS L. REV. 493 (1995).

[95] *E.g.,* Committee on the Elimination of All Forms of Racial Discrimination, Concluding Observations: Mexico, UN Doc. A/50/18, paras. 353–98 (1996).

[96] *See, e.g.,* Inter-American Commission on Human Rights, Report on the Situation of Human Rights in Brazil 93–113, OEA/Ser.L/V/II.97 (1997).

[97] Communication No. 167/1984, Ominayak v. Canada, UN Doc. A/45/40, Annex IX.A, at 27 (1990). *See also* Communication No. 197/1985, Kitok v. Sweden, UN Doc. A/43/40, at 221 (1988). In its General Comment on Article 27, the Committee observed that "culture manifests itself in many forms, including a particular way of life associated with the use of land resources, especially in the case of indigenous peoples. That right may include such traditional activities as fishing or hunting and the right to live in reserves protected by law." General Comment No. 23(50), UN Doc. A/49/40, Annex V, at 109 (1994).

[98] *E.g.,* Kashvasi Reindeer Herders' Cooperative v. Ministry of Trade & Industry (Sup. Admin.

Ct., Fin., May 15, 1996) (slip op. trans. Heljà Tilli & Martin Scheinin). The court held that the Ministry's decisions to issue a mining company certain deeds enabling mining in Sami reindeer-herding areas should be quashed for failure to consider the legal obligations of Finland arising from Article 27 of the ICCPR, and that reindeer herding was part of Sami culture under Article 27.

[99] Nibutani Dam Jiken Hanketsu [Kayano & Kaizawa v. Government of Japan] , HANREI JIHO, No. 1598, 1997, at 33 (Sapporo Dist. Ct. Mar. 27, 1997). This translation is an amalgam of work by Professors Sonohara Toshiaki, Hosokawa Komei, and Oota Hiroyuki. For commentary, see Sonohara Toshiaki, *Toward a Genuine Redress for an Unjust Past: The Nibutani Dam case,* MUR-DOCH ELECTRONIC L.J., June 1997.

[100] See S. James Anaya, *A Contemporary Definition of the International Norm of Self-Determination,* 3 TRANSNAT'L L. & CONTEMP. PROB. 131 (1993); Russel Lawrence Barsh, *Indigenous Peoples and the UN Commission on Human Rights: A Case of the Immovable Object and the Irresistible Force,* 18 HUM. RTS. Q. 782, 796–800 (1996); Erica-Irene Daes. Some consideration on *the Right of Indigenous Peoples to Self-Determination,* 3 TRANSNAT'L L. &: CONTEMP. PROP. 1 (1993); Hurst Hannum, rethinking *Self-Determination,* 34 VA. J. INT'L L. 1 (1993); Catherine Iorns, *Indigenous Peoples and Self-determination: Challenging State Sovereignty,* 24 CASE W. RES. J. INTL L. 199 (1992); Benedict Kingsbury, Self-Determination and "Indigenous Peoples," 86 ASIL PROC. 383 (1992); MODERN LAW OF SELF-DETERMINATION (Christian Tomuschat ed., 1993); Mary-Ellen Turpel, *indigenous Peoples' Rights of Political Participation and Self-Determination: Recent International Legal Developments and the Continuing Struggle for Recognition,* 25 CORNELL. INTL L.J. 579 (1992).

[101] HUMAN RIGHTS AND EQUAL, OPPORTUNITY COMMISSION, BRINGING THEM HOME (1997).

[102] For a forceful statement of this view, see Howard Berman. *Indigenous peoples and the right to self – determination ,87 ASIL PROC. 190 (1993)*

[103] ILO Convention No. 169, *supra* note 19, Art. 7.

[104] Petition of Jaime Córdoba Triviño, Defensor del Pueblo, en representación de varias personas intrigantes del Grupo Etnico Indigena U'Wa, Sentencia No. SU–039/97 (Corte constitutional, Feb. 3, 1997).

[105] UN Doc. E/CN.4/Sub.2/1993/29, Annex 1.

[106] E.g., JOHN H. BODLEY, VICTIM OF PROGRESS (2nd ed. 1990); and TRIBAL PEOPLES AND DEVELOPMENT ISSUES: A GLOBAL OVERVIEW (John H. Bodley ed.. 1988).

[107] For a mixture of assessment and advocacy, see PETER BROSIUS. AFTER DUWAGAN: DEFORESTATION, SUCCESSION AND ADAPTATION IN UPLAND LUZON, PHILIPPINES (Ann Arbor, 1990); THE STRUGGLE FOR LAND AND THE FATE OF THE FORESTS (Penang, Marcus Colchester &: Larry Lohmann eds., 1994); and INDIGENOUS PEOPLES AND PROTECTED AREAS (London. Elizabeth Kemf ed., 1993). The image of indigenous peoples as active consumers is evident in advertising in many of the places where the cash economy and mass commercial communication reach. See, e.g., NATION MAKING: EMERGENT IDENTITIES IN POSTCOLONIAL MELANESIA (Robert J. Foster ed., 1995), and Foster's forthcoming work on advertising in Papua New Guinea and other parts of Melanesia.

[108] OAS Doc. OEA/Ser.L/V/11.95, doc. 6. Art. 1(2) (1997).

[109] See UN Doc. E/CN.4/1998/106, para. 37 (1997).

[110] The consensus among the five members of the UN Working Group on indigenous populations appears to be that it is not realistic or useful to try to adopt a definition at present. See Report of the Working Group on indigenous populations on its fifteenth session. UN Doc. E/CN.4/Sub.2/1997/14. Earlier, Chair-Rapporteur Daes had suggested that the solidarity and experience built up in gatherings of indigenous peoples, states and working group members since 1982 might provide a platform on which that body might construct an agreed definition in the future. Erica-Irene Daes, Note on Criteria Which Might be Applied when considering the

concept of indigenous peoples, UN Doc. E/CN.4/Sub.2/AC.4/1995/3 [hereinafter Daes, Criteria). It is most improbable that the working group would confine the concept of "indigenous peoples" to areas of European settlement. Daes, Working Paper on the Concept of "Indigenous People," UN Doc. E/CN.4/ Sub.2/AC.4/1996/2 [hereinafter Daes, Working Paper]. However, one long-serving member, Miguel Alfonso Martinez, bas advocated distinguishing European colonialism from invasions by a group's neighbors, and has expressed skepticism about the broad applicability of the concept of "indigenous peoples" in much of Africa and Asia, while conceding that it may be pertinent in special circumstances. Miguel Alfonso Martinez, Study on Treaties, Agreements and Other Constructive Arrangements between States and indigenous populations: Second progress report, UN Doc. E/CN.4/Sub.2/1995/27, paras. 94–129.

[111] The ILO has a specialized mandate but for historical reasons has become involved in a broad range of indigenous peoples' issues that extend beyond the scope of other ILO activities.

[112] The others are Angola. Argentina, Belgium, Brazil, Cuba, the Dominican Republic, Ecuador, Egypt, El Salvador, Ghana, Guinea-Bissau, Haiti, Iraq, Malawi, Panama, Portugal, Syria and Tunisia. See the ILO Web site (visited May 18, 1998) (http://ilolex.ilo.ch:1567/public/english/50normes/infleg/iloeng/index.html). For Convention No. 107, see l ILO, INTERNATIONAL LABOUR CONVENTIONS AND RECOMMENDATIONS 1919 –1991, at 627 (1992).

[113] For an overview by an ILO official closely associated with Convention Nos. 107 and 169, see Lee Swepston. *A New Step in the International Law on indigenous and Tribal Peoples: ILO Convention No. 169 of* 1989, 15 OKLA CITY U. L. REV. 677 (1990).

[114] In order of ratification: Norway, Mexico, Colombia, Bolivia, Costa Rica, Paraguay, Peru, Honduras, Denmark, Guatemala, the Netherlands and Fiji. As the ratification pattern suggests, Convention No. 169, *supra* note 19, has been particularly influential in Latin America. Its provisions on definition were a model for the Inter-American Commission on Human Rights. In 1995 the Commission was unable to agree on a definition in its Draft Declaration on the Rights of Indigenous Peoples, partly because of disagreements about particular free communities founded by people brought involuntarily from Africa, to the Americas by the slave trade. In 1997 it reached a compromise that avoided any definition of "indigenous peoples," while making clear that the prescribed norms applied not only to the undefined category of indigenous peoples, but also to a category of groups corresponding to those treated as "tribal" in Article 1 (1) (a) of the ILO Convention, which apparently includes the free communities in question. See OEA/Ser.L/V /11.95. doc. 6, *supra* note 107.

[115] ILO, REPORT OF THE COMMITTEE OF EXPERTS ON THE APPLICATION OF CONVENTIONS AND RECOMMENDATIONS. Report III (Part 4A). IL Conf.. 83d Sess. 265–67, 268–69 (1996).

[116] Operational Directive 4.20, *Supra* note 20. The Bank is considering converting this directive to conform it to the Bank's new system of internal policy instruments, leading to complex discussions about the conversion process, the formulation of key principles, and the level and type of standards that arc normatively proper and operationally and politically viable.

[117] Asian Development Dank, Working Paper on Indigenous Peoples, paras. 6–8 (mimeo OCI. 25. 1994).

[118] Such a recommendation was made to the executive directors in December 1996 in the case of the Argentina/Paraguay Yacretá Hydroelectric Project, which involved numerous issues, including disruptive treatment and inadequate resettlement of indigenous peoples. For a brief overview, see Richard E. Bissell, *Resent Practice of the Inspection Panel of the World Bank,* 91 AJIL 741 (1997).

[119] The way was cleared for the projects after the 1979 decision of the Narmada Water Disputes Tribunal allocated water rights among the interested riparian and nonriparian slates. The tribunal also set a basic requirement of land-for-land compensation, as well as modest compensation for "landless" oustees. On the Narmada projects, see TOWARD SUSTAINABLE DEVELOPMENT? STRUGGLIJNG OVER INDIA'S NARMADA RIVER (William F. Fisher ed., 1995). For a critical view of the World Bank's involvement, see, e.g., Sumi Kazuo, SEIKAI GINKO

KAIBATZU KINYIN TO KONKYO: JINKEN MONDAI [The World Bank: Development Finance and the Issue of Human Rights) 265-69 (Tokyo, 1994) (kindly translated from the Japanese by Funahashi Junko).

[120]For example, the Bargi Bandh Visthapit Aur Prabhavit Sangh (an association of oustees displaced by the already-complete Bargi Dam) organized a satyagratha on the banks of the reservoir to try to prevent a further rise in its level in 1996; and litigation has been pursued by the Narmada Bachao Andolan. Groups organized around the issues of displacement and resettlement take a wide range of positions; many do not oppose, indeed support, the dam and canal projects, but are concerned about specific features of the projects or gross inadequacies in their implementation.

[121] This action followed a request from the government of India to end further disbursements, made in the context of the Bank's concerns about the project and the government's concerns about external pressure.

[122]BRADFORD MORSE & THOMAS BERGER, SARDAR SAROVAR: REPORT OF THE INDEPENDENT REVIEW 77-78 (Ottawa, 1992). The two authors of the review are, respectively, a U.S. citizen who served as a prominent international civil servant and formerly as head of the United Nations Development Programme, and a well known Canadian jurist who has been involved extensively in indigenous issues relating to development, projects in North America.

[123]Report of the Workshop on Traditional Knowledge and Biological Diversity. UNEP Doc. UNEP/CBD/TKBD/l/3 (1997).

[124]Report of the Second Workshop on a Permanent Forum for Indigenous People within the United Nations System. *supra* note 10.

[125] For an account of travels by an Onondaga leader from the United States to Switzerland on a Haudeno-saunee passport, see Oren Lyons, Remarks, 87 ASIL PROC. 195 (1993).

[126] *See generally* GEORGE DOWNS & DAVID ROCKE. OPTIMAL. IMPERFFECTION? DOMESTIC UNCERTAINTY AND INSTITUTIONS IN INTERNATIONAL. RELATIONS (1995); Benedict Kingsbury. *The Concept of Compliance as a Function of Competing Conceptions of International Law,* 19 MICH. J. INTL L. 345 (1998).

[127] PRC Consideration, *supra* note 17.

[128] *See, e.g.,* Tania Murray Li, *Images of Community: Discourse and Strategy* in *Property Relations,* 27 DEV. & CHANGE 501 (1996).

[129] ZHANG XIAOHUI, ZHONGGUO FALU ZAI SHAOSHUMINZU DIQU DE SHI SHI [The Enforcement of Law in Minority Areas in China] 27-29 (Kunming, 1994); WALKER CONNOR, THE NATIONAL. QUESTION IN MARXISTLENINIST STRATEGY 67-100 (1984). Thanks to Hu Jun for translating Chinese-language sources referred to here

[130]ZHANG XIAOHUI, *supra note* 128. at 92-93; WANG LIANFANG MINZU WENTI LUN-WENJI [Essays on the Problems among Races] 335-40 (Kunming. 1993).

[131] ZHANG XIAOHUI. *supra note* 128, at 16-17.

[132] MA QU, YUNNAN MINZU GONGZUO SISHI NIAN [Forty Years of Yunnan Minority Administration] 97 (Kunming, 1994).

[133] of. the problems noted in 1988 by WANG TIANXI. MINZU FA GAI LUN [Introduction to Nationalities Law] 247 (Kunming, 1988).

[134]ZHANG XIAOHUI, *supra note* 128, al 36-39.

[135] MINZU QUYU ZIZHI JIANMING DUBEN [Pamphlet on Minority Autonomous Districts] 37 (Kunming, Zhou Ruihai & Ha Jian eds., 1993).

[136] WANG LIANG FANG, *supra note* 129, at 90-128; YUNNAN LONGCUN FUNU XIAN-ZHUANG YANJIU [Analysis of the Reality of Women in Yunnan} 199-261 (Kunming, He Zhonghua & Qiao Hengrui eds., 1995).

[137] As to concerns about foreign religious penetration. see, e.g.. WEIHU JUGUO TONGYI BAO-CHI SHEHUI WENDING [Sustain the Unity of China, Maintain the Stability of Society] 62 (Kunming, Feng Dazhen & Yang Faren eds., 1993).

[138] Zhou Enlai, *Some Questions.* BEIJING REV. (1980). *quoted* in CONNOR, *supra* note 128, at 90-91.

[139] *See* PHILIP ALLOTT, EUNOMIA: NEW ORDER FOR A NEW WORLD. chs. 10. 16 {1990).

[140] On Australia. Canada, and New Zealand, see Kingsbury, supra note 41.

[141] *Note.* for example, Rangan's observation of differences in the Garhwal Himalayas, home of the Chipko tree-protection movement made famous and celebrated by international environmentalists, between "images of self-contained village communities living in harmonious ecological utopias" and the desire of many residents 10 resume their long-standing involvement in the commercial use of the forests and other activities necessary' to make a living. Haripriya Rangan, *Romancing the Environment: Popular Environmental Action* in the Garhwal Himalayas. in IN DEFENSE OF LIVELIHOOD: COMPARATIVE STUDIES *ON* Environmental, ACTION 151, 162 (John Friedman & Haripriya Rangan an eds.. 1993).

[142] Issues of this sort have arisen in the operations of Coal India Ltd. covered by the World Bank's India Coal Sector Rehabilitation Project. For comments on this project, see Ratnakar Bhengara, *Coal.Mining Displacement* ECON. & POL. WKLY., Mar. 16, 1996, at 647.

[143] Li, *supra* note 127, at 508.

[144] *See, e.g.,* the debate between Owen Lynch and James Anderson, in CRITICAL DECADE: PROSPECTS FOR DEMOCRACY IN THE PHILIPPINES IN THE 1990's (Berkeley, Cal., Dolores Flamiano &: Donald Goertzen eds., 1990). See also, e.g., LYNCH & TALBOTT. supra note 53, at 23, whose "definition" of "community" seems underspecified for many practical purposes; it is so broad as to encompass virtually any enduring mutual benefit arrangement. The relevant features are: "I) extensive participation by its members in the decisions by which its life is governed; 2) the community as a whole takes responsibilities for its members; and 3) this responsibility includes respect for the diverse individuality of these members." *See further* HERMAN DALY & JOHN COBB. FOR THE COMMON GOOD: REDIRETING THE ECONOMY TOWARD COMMUNITY, THE Environment, AND A SUSTAINABLE FUTURE 168-75 (1989).

[145] Li, *supra* note 127, at 505 (quoting Melissa Leach, Endangered Environments: Understanding Natural Resource Management in the west African Forest Zone IDS [Inst, Dev. Stud.] Bull. Oct. 1991, at 17, 18).

[146] Ann Armbresht Forbes, *Defining the "Local"* in the Arun *Controversy: \Villager, NGOs, and the World Bank in the* Arun Valley, *Nepal,* CULTURAL Survival. Q., Fall 1996, at 31]; Peter Brosius, *Prior Transcripts, Divergent Paths: Resistance and Acquiescence to Logging in Sarawak, East Malaysia,* 39 COMP. STUD. SOCY &: HIST. 468 (1997).

[147] Forbes, *Supra* note 145, at 31.

[148] Marcus Colchester, *Indigenous Peoples' Rights and Sustainable Resource Use* in *South and Southeast Asia,* in PEOPLES OF ASIA, *supra* note 15, at 59, 73-76.

[149] Forbes. *supra* note 145, at 31.

[150] The government of Fiji suggested .in the Commission on Human Rights working group that a self-identifying group whose members arc historically prior occupants with a unique cultural bond with the land may be an indigenous people even though they suffer no repression. The intended implication that the declaration will apply to groups controlling the government and the military in a state is highly problematic. If the nondominance criterion is relaxed as Fiji suggests, there are almost insuperable risks that dominant groups in deeply divided societies who regard themselves as threatened will use the declaration to bolster their chauvinist claims. Fiji itself opposed a proposal by the government of Bangladesh that all peoples threatened by globalization and Westernization. including those controlling postcolonial governments in Africa and Asia should be covered by the declaration. *See* Barsh, *supra* note 99, at 792-93.

[151] *See* Kingsbury, *supra* note 91.

[152] *See* RALPH LITZINGER, THE WORK OF CULTURE AND MEMORY IN CONTEMPORARY' CHINA 7 -8 (Duke University Working Papers in Asian/Pacific Studies No. 95-03, 1995).

[153] This argument about India may well apply also to the position of the Chinese government; and the views or the governments of Bangladesh and Myanmar may follow this track, but are difficult to analyze independently of issues of insurgency, state building and central political/ military control.

Hill and Valley in Southeast Asia

...or Why the State is the Enemy of People who Move Around...or... Why Civilizations Can't Climb Hills

James C. Scott

This article is the manuscript of a lecture given at the Symposium on Development and the Nation State at Washington University, in St. Louis in the year 2000.

It should not be quoted without permission from the author.

This article will be superceded by a book tentatively entitled "The Last Great Enclosure: The State and Autonomous Peoples in Mainland Southeast Asia", to be published in 2009.

One of the major shortcomings in my work, as I see it, – others will have many more objections, and more telling too – is that I seem always to forget the main itinerary and take the first interesting detour that presents itself. My talk today is a case in point.

My initial destination was the relationship between hill and valley peoples in Southeast Asia, particularly mainland Southeast Asia. As you know, it's a worthy destination. Of all the social divisions in the region, the cultural and political abyss between hill peoples (often, and I think, erroneously called "hill-tribes"), is perhaps the most enduring, the most likely to produce conflict, and the thorniest for national elites bent on national integration. Your neighbor and one-time-province in colonial days, Burma, has been beset by rebellious hill-peoples ever since its independence in 1948. Now that the Eritreans have won their independence, I believe that the hill-insurgencies in Burma (particularly that of the Karen) are the oldest, continuous, secessionist rebellions in this (oops last) past century.

My quarry in its crude – but original – form, was to understand why the state –not just the Southeast Asian state – was generally the enemy of "people who move around". I thought there was something generic about the state's desire to fix people geographically – whether bedouins, gypsies, wandering Jews, hunter-gatherers, nomadic pastoralists, slash-and-burn cultivators (typical of the hills in Southeast Asia), the so-called "sea-gypsies" of Southeast Asia (the *orang laut*), masterless men, vagrants and sturdy beggars, the homeless. Why has it been the project of nearly every state to concentrate and fix its population in space – in settlements where they can be more easily monitored? I could put it somewhat differently: what is it about a state that fears and suppresses (when it can) "unauthorized movement"? Or could we put it in still another way? Why is sedentarization just about the oldest state project in the world? The obvious fact that a sedentary population is easier to count, tax, conscript, and survey than a fugitive population is only the beginning of the story.

In the case of Burma, for example, very, very different lowland states – the pre-colonial kingdoms, as we shall see, the colonial state, and independent Burma – have pursued remarkably similar objectives in the hills. The means and the results have differed wildly, but the rhetoric and the policies were strikingly similar.

Here, then, were the crude facts that caught my attention. Why this continuity through history and through regimes? Upon closer inspection there is, I think, a somewhat deeper paradox and it is this: *First:* I believe that I can show that the categories "hill tribes" and "valley peoples" (say, Kachin and Burmans) are very leaky vessels when one takes a long historical view. People are *continually* moving from the valley to the hills. And the reverse is true as well: People are continually moving from the hills to the valleys. Their movement is, over time, also associated with a change of identity: hill people are becoming valley people all the time, *and, valley* people are becoming hill people all the time. To make things even more complicated, there are intermediate statuses: people who have one foot, culturally and ecologically speaking, in the hills and another foot in the valley. Thus the very terms "hill tribes" and "valley peoples" seem to lose much of their substance when examined closely or over any long period of time. And here is the full paradox: Despite this constant exchange of populations across this permeable membrane, there is an extraordinary stable, durable civilization discourse about hill and valley that treat each of these peoples as essentially different; one cultured, the other barbaric; one refined, the other primitive; one advanced and cosmopolitan and the other backward and parochial. These pairs, of course, are the pairs as valley elites see them. If we adopt a hill perspective we get different pairs: one is free and autonomous, the other is in bondage and subordinate; one is nominally an equal of others, the other is socially inferior; one is physically mobile, the other is hemmed in by officials and state institutions.

How does this happen? People moving back and forth constantly through this geographical membrane – so much so that over centuries the 'human material', in DNA terms, has been freely exchanged – while, magically, the *lived essentialism* between hill tribes and valley civilization remains intact as a powerful organizer of people's lives and thoughts.

This paradox has not escaped historians of Europe. Fernand Braudel wondered at the great rates of migration between the shifting Christian and Islamic religious frontiers in the Mediterranean, coupled with the durability of the distinction. He wrote:

> "For at bottom, a civilization is attached to a distinct geographical area and this is itself one of the indispensable elements of its composition. Before it can manifest its identity which is expressed in its art and which Nietzsche saw as its major truth … a civilization exists fundamentally in a geographical area which has been structured my men and history. This is why there are cultural frontiers and cultural zones of amazing permanence: all the cross fertilization in the world will not alter them" (Braudel 1966:33).

What's missing here is an appreciation of diaspora civilizations: people who move and, as it were, carry their civilization with them. Jews, Armenians, gypsies. And yet, if we occasionally allow civilizations to come unstuck, geographically, Braudel's major point about how brisk human traffic across cultural boundaries not necessarily threatening the perceived solidity of the boundary itself is well taken. Let me offer a brief example that may interest you: the gypsies of Europe. Linguistically, we can trace them back, definitively, to this part of the world and even establish something of their long itinerary. But, this is not a story they tell about themselves, nor do they have a "Promised Land" toward which that are headed (unlike the Jews). The gypsies are the quintessentially homeless people. They have a good claim to being the most scourged as well. From 15th century pogroms and expulsions, to 17th century "gypsy hunts" *(Zegeuner Jakt)* – in which the 'bag' of 'game' was noted at the end of the day as with stags – to the Gypsy Holocaust under the Nazis, they have been perhaps the most despised and persecuted group in Europe. And yet, it is perfectly clear that since at least the 14th century, people have been slipping in and out of "gypsiness" in huge numbers: through intermarriage, sedentarization, and through the state-classification of people who are itinerant as "gypsies". I am told that the DNA of "gypsies" in the Netherlands is virtually indistinguishable from the DNA of the surrounding Dutch population.

Here then is a population that is, genetically-speaking, completely assimilated and yet, always, and seemingly forever, culturally marked off. It's that way, as I'll try to explain, with the "tribal peoples" of Hill Burma and their lowland neighbors (Burmans mostly).

In considering these puzzles, I have been led to take two detours. The first is try to understand *"the hills"* as a geographical, cultural, demographic, ecological, and above all *positional* space vis-à-vis the lowland state. Here "the hills" are less distinctive as topography than their relative inaccessibility: an inaccessibility or illegibility that can be mimicked by marshes, deserts, mangrove swamps, dense forests. Together such out-of-the-way places, to use Anna Tsing's (1993) term, they might be called: *non-state spaces*. I propose something of a history and anthropology of such spaces. The second detour, following hard on the heels of the first, is an effort to imagine what a *non-state-centric history* of, say the area now called Burma might look like. It's fair to say that virtually all histories are histories of states or state-like entities inasmuch as they leave the paper trail. Unless we are very careful and practice a brilliant version of 'subaltern history' we see such history as the chronicle of the waxing and waning of dynasties – the consolidation of the Pagan kingdom; its collapse in the 13th century, the first Taung-nyu dynasty in 1486... and so on through the Kon-baung dynasty founded by Alaung-hpaya and its final demise in 1885. The dirty little secret, of course, is that for most of "Burmese" history there was no state in any robust sense of the term. There were, instead, small-scale local chiefs, confederations of villages, warlords, bandits, multiple sovereigns contending, millennial pretenders, etc.

We know this from the dynastic chronicles deploring such conditions. Might it be possible to imagine a history written systematically from this perspective – a kind of anarchist history in which a certain celebration of 'collapse', 'flight' and the 'elementary units of social life' creeps in? A history of the state's "blank pages" in which the deplorable exception is the paper trail and the officialdom that creates it? Not easy. It presents some of the same problems as a history of the peasantry. As I have long been fond of saying, "The job of peasants is to *stay out of the archives!*" Once they figure in the archives, once they have caught the attention of the court scribes as something more than aggregate calculations of conscripts, taxable inhabitants, producers of so many bushels of grain...you know something has gone terribly wrong. What would a non-state – perhaps even an anti-state – history look like?

I can't promise to follow these two detours to some grand and satisfying destination today. The best I can do is to say something provisionally about what I imagine the road might look like.

First, let me say something more about the cultural gulf between hill and valley. It is a real gulf, easily discernible, even if it were not so morally charged. Societies in the hills *are* different from valley societies in systematic ways which we shall examine later. For the time being, however, it is worth noting that most of major lowland religions have not made it to the hills in good order. The major exception in Burma are the Shan, a Tai, people who *are* Buddhists and are, in fact, situated midway – in terms of ecology, agriculture, social structure – between the lowland Burmans and the highland Kachin.

Writing of early Southeast Asian kingdoms, Oliver Wolters (1982: 32) notes how hard it is for civilizations to climb hills.

> "Many people lived in the distant highlands and were beyond the reach of the centers where records survive. The Mandalas were a phenomenon of the lowlands, and even where geographical conditions encouraged under-government. Paul Wheatley puts it well when he notes that 'the Sanskrit tongue was chilled to silence at 500 meters'. One cannot assume that powerful overlords in the plains always ignored the natural resources and manpower in the hills and mountains, but the historian, relying on written records, has to remove vast territories from the historical map of earlier Southeast Asia."

It was to this difference, I believe, that Edmund Leach (1954) was referring when he typified hill society as following a "Chinese model" while lowland society followed an "Indian" or Sanskritic model.

To return to Braudel once again. He also notes in even stronger terms (terms I find far too strong) the unbridgeable civilization gap between the plains and the mountains. He writes:

> "The mountains are as a rule a world apart from civilizations, which are an urban and lowland achievement. Their history is to have none, to remain always on the fringes of the great waves of civilization, even the longest and most persistent, which may spread over great distances in the horizontal plane but are powerless to move vertically when faced with an obstacle of several hundred meters." (Braudel 1966:33, emphasis added)

Why might this be so? Why have the hills in Southeast Asia been so relatively resistant to Sanskritization, then to Buddhism, then to Islam, and, in the Philippines, to Christianity? And, why, when the hills *do* embrace lowland religions are they likely to do so with a degree of heterodoxy and millennial fervor that makes lowland officials wish they hadn't tried in the first place.

There are other important cultural differences between the hills and the plains. We begin here only because the religious difference is longstanding and indicative. Before turning to other differences, let alone trying to account for them, let us return to the moral loading these differences carry.

For valley people – and here I mean largely growers of wet rice – hill peoples are typically seen as "wild" (the British distinguished between the "wild" Wa and the "tame" Wa), barbaric, primitives, whose mobility, dress, rude shelters, and archaic forms of hunting-gathering-and shifting cultivation mark them out as inferior in every respect (except for their control over the 'dark arts' of magic) to lowlanders. Even where they are looked at with some sympathy, as they are by current "development regimes", they are seen as backward, disorderly, and benighted: "our living ancestors", "what we were like before we discovered and embraced Buddhism/Islam, padi rice cultivation, sedentary life, and civilization". In Indonesian official parlance, such peoples are termed *suku terasing or:* "isolated peoples". The implication being that the developmental state plans to ease their loneliness by clasping them more firmly to the national bosom.

Such distinctions are strongly naturalized in official and popular discourse in the lowlands – *despite* the *fact,* that we *know* them to be *wrong*. Far from being "left behind", most hill populations are largely the descendants of valley and coastal peoples who migrated to the hills. That does not prevent the development of a strong sense of ethnic identity and solidarity from developing among, say, the Kachin, the Chin, the Hmong, the Karen: identities for which many have been willing to die.

How to reconcile a strongly 'constructivist' understanding of "hill tribes" as 'made up' societies of 'immigrants' who are seen from the valley's as "ur" primitives and also have an essentialist understanding of themselves to boot? The analogy from Western history I find instructive is that of the Cossacks. We know that the Cossacks were nothing more and nothing less than a maroon community of serfs from all over European Russia who fled to the frontiers of empire to escape bondage. There, in a new setting characterized by common property, physical dispersion, and rough equality they adapted the social structure and horseback habits of the Tatars, and constituted themselves as, say, the "Don Cossacks", the Cossacks who lived in the Don River Basin. Over time, they became a people (a "martial minority" like the Gurkha or the Karen) and, today, they are perhaps the strongest most solidaristic "ethnic" group in Russia. In short, the nub of my claim is that we do better to consider hill tribes as maroon societies than as "tribes" in the classical, strong sense of the term.

Now to return to the first of my two detours – the understanding of the hills as a *position* constituted by the state and yet not firmly within it. Two dynamic and antagonistic principles – of Southeast Asian state-craft on the one hand, and of what we might call "peasant cunning" of resistance on the other – will help us understand how the hills make the valleys and how the valleys make the hills.

I.   The first principle of Southeast Asian statecraft until well in to the 19th century has been the control of manpower – and its twin, slavery. This was dictated by demography. In 1700 there were roughly six people per square kilometer on average in Southeast Asia as compared to something like thirty per square kilometer in India or China. Rounding up people and concentrating them in a particular place was the central preoccupation of statecraft in the region. [The Red River Delta of northern Vietnam may be the exception that proves the rule]. Since the creation of a population base could rarely be achieved by persuasion alone, all Southeast Asian states, even the mini states in the hills, were states. Without exception. No people, no state. A series of Malay coastal kingdoms thus scoured the strands and islands of Eastern Indonesia and the Philippines for captives whom they could sell or resettle closer to the court. Piracy in the Malay world was centered on the region's main cargo – slaves. The agrarian kingdoms of Southeast Asia were slaving states as well – though the friction of distance slowed them down a bit.

Any state-making enterprise on the plains or at the coast, required a reliable supply of manpower and foodstuffs close at hand. This was true whether the state in question was bent on expansion through warfare or on building temple complexes for the glory of the dynasty. Simple demography, the logic of transportation, and 'central-place theory' of Johann Heinrich von Thünen, Walter Christaller, and G. William Skinner make it clear that only wet rice agriculture within a reasonable radius of the court provides the reliable tax base necessary to found and maintain a state.

Important exceptions are the Malay trading states like Jambi, Palembang, Srivijaya, or Melaka, mini states controlling key choke points in straits or navigable rivers or on overland trade routes, or site-specific resources such as gold or gems.

It's hardly surprising, then, that most state-formation in the region has classically been in the wet-rice cores: Mandalay, Ava, Pegu, Pagan, Ayuddhaya, Bangkok. The hills, with their dispersed population, their characteristically extensive form of agriculture, and their physically mobile population were decidedly unpromising sites for state-formation.

Evidence of the unending quest for manpower may be read from sources – only a few of which I will note in passing.

1. Proverbs and sayings about statecraft:

   a) 17th Century Malay Court History: "It is the custom of kings that they call themselves kings if they have ministers and subjects: if there are no subjects, who will render homage to the king?"

   From the ruler of Palembang (1747): "It is very easy for a subject to find a lord, but it is much more difficult for a lord to find a subject."

   b) Two Thai proverbs from the early Bangkok period (1782-1873):
   "In a large house with many servants, the door may be safely left open; in a small house with few servants, the doors must be shut."

   "To have too many people (as clients under a lord) is better than to have too much grass (uncultivated land)."

   c) And instructions for the king's officials:

"The governor should appoint loyal officials to go out to them (the population living outside the core) and persuade them to come and settle down in an inhabited area so that the area will be wealthy."

d) Finally, a lament from the Glass Palace Chronicle of the Kings of Burma:

"Yes, a soil, but no people. A soil without people is but a wilderness."

2. Warfare was, under the circumstances, rarely a war over territory. Rather it was a campaign for captives. The mark of success of a military expedition was the enumeration of captives returned to the court who would, in turn, represent a future base for food and manpower. By 1800, up to 350,000 people, perhaps on fifth of the agricultural population of Upper Burma, consisted of military deportees and their descendants, concentrated on royal service lands. A kingdom defeated was a kingdom whose population was quickly swept up by its neighbors. After the 1569 Burmese sacking of Ayudhya and the deportation of tens of thousands of captives, the Khmers rushed in and, in the next two decades, took all the captives they could find. In 1767, after sacking Ayudhya once again, the Burmese left with at least 30,000 captives, including much of the court and the nobility. Soon after, the booty of King Bow-daw-hpaya's conquest of Arakan was 20,000 captives who, along with their Buddhist images, were marched back to the capital, Ava, and settled there. In fact you could say that, in insular Southeast Asia, much of eastern Indonesia was scoured clean of manpower which, as Anthony Reid (1983:27) has pointed out, moved "from weak states to strong states, from politically fragmented states to strong, centralized states, from swidden and hunter-gatherer areas to lowland wet-rice cores."

3. The emphasis on manpower is obvious in the aesthetics of official discourse. The majesty of a ruler is directly proportional the size and affluence of his entourage: an entourage described in line after line of loving detail. The titles which officials bear are more likely to refer to the size of their entourage rather than to a territorial jurisdiction. Hence the Thai titles *Kun Pan,* "Lord of a Thousand Men", or *Kun Sen* "Lord of a Hundred Thousand Men".

The very core of Southeast Asian statecraft consisted in policies designed to attract and/or capture, and hold a densely settled population around the court. The Southeast Asian state was, in this sense, a vast centripetal population machine, endeavoring to maximize what I would call a "state space". Such a state space is characterized by surplus-producing, sedentary, grain cultivators settled densely within easy reach of the court. It was a rare thing for this machine to function very well for very long. In fact, the machine was in an important way, self-liquidating. The tendency was for the court to press hardest on the productive, legible population close at hand – this was the efficient "tax-corvée-and conscription" strategy for it to follow. If something went wrong – a bad harvest, overzealous conscription, rapacious officials – the state might find its precious tax base leaking away.

II. This brings us to the second, and antagonistic, dynamic: *flight*. The basis of popular freedom in Southeast Asia was physical mobility – the capacity to vote with one's feet. This is the centrifugal dynamic working constantly against the centripetal dynamic of taking captives, and slaves and population control. If slaving was the state-making principle; flight was the state breaking principle. If the endeavor of statecraft was to create legible "state spaces", flight was directed toward existing "non-state spaces" – primarily in the hills – and the creation of new "non-state spaces".

Let me outline with inexcusable brevity the logic of flight.

1. The most obvious reasons for running away were the burdens, in state-spaces, of taxes in all its forms: coin, grain, labor, and military service. Such burdens fell heaviest on the 'core peasantry' settled near the court capital and its officialdom. In a good year, blessed with a monarch or colonial ruler whose fiscal ambitions were modest, this pressure might be tolerable. Such years were, however, few and far between. The incapacity of the court to accurately assess crop yields district by district and year by year, coupled with the fiscal pressures of warfare (internal of external), large ambitions for 'public works' – whether pagoda complexes or new court centers, and rapacious tax collectors intent on their own take, produced a large volume of tax resistance and, above all, flight. The short-term logic of state consolidation and expansion dictated extracting resources and manpower from the densely-settled population around the court. The further this strategy was pressed, however, the greater the leakage of the tax base to locations out of easy range of the tax man and the press-gang. The most successful regimes maintained a precarious equilibrium between rates of extraction and rates of flight. These are the regimes we mostly hear about. Any long historical view would regard these regimes as minor miracles of statecraft, as the rare exceptions punctuating a political history more notable for warlordism, political fragmentation, and self-liquidating dynasties.

Warfare, which we recall was about taking captives and returning them to the core, drove people away from the core as well. Those who did not manage to escape conscription could, when the opportunity presented itself, desert. Alaung-hpaya's famous and successful invasion of Siam in 1767 involved some 200,000 troops. He returned, after sacking Ayudhaya, with roughly 100,000 men – of whom at least 30,000 were captives. What became of the other 130,000 conscripts? There were certainly battlefield losses and deaths due to the scourge of all pre-modern armies: cholera. But it is unlikely that they accounted for any more than, say, twenty percent of the total losses. The rest, we must surmise, deserted, staying along the routes of march, hiding out in the hills, and perhaps eventually making their way back. The demographic impact was not trivial. One careful calculation of the losses from Burma's core area as a result of Bod-aw-hpaya's unsuccessful invasions of Siam in 1785-6 and his subsequent mania for pagoda building in the 1790s (Min-gun pagoda which would have been the largest in the world at the time) claims that 17% of the population had fled. Most had headed for the hills. No 19th century commentary on Burma fails to note the huge 'floating population', dislodged oppression, war, disease, and famine. The Spanish, the colonial valley kingdom in the Philippines, recognized a comparable pattern of flight: the fugitives were called "remontados" (those who went *back* up into the hills) and away from the labor and taxes in the lowlands and on the Friar estates.

If we follow the subaltern studies instructions to "read against the grain" we can discern the political mobility of the southeast Asian subject. It is echoed in the classical texts' repeated emphasis on personal oaths of loyalty *(kyei-zu-thit-sa-daw-saung* in Burmese) and the harsh injunctions against treason *(durhaka,* in the Malay world). Why this endless preaching against treason and in praise of personal loyalty to the ruler? Like Puritan sermons against fornication and adultery, they tell us less about the rectitude of the population, than the elite's view of the major social ill – and, in this case, the great threat to statecraft. Sermons against treason tell us how very common it was for subjects to run away to the hills and/or to another ruler. Even the Thai practice of tattooing subjects (like cattle) with their lord's mark was of little avail and bounty hunters coursed the forests to capture runaways and return them to their owners. As the Thai proverb has it: "Subjects are hard to find."

2. Epidemics and famines were other common reasons for physical flight. Lowland wet-rice cultivation, compared to hill swiddening, was more restricted. While quite productive in a good year it was, due largely to mono-cropping, more vulnerable to crop failures. And when crops did fail, there was less in the way of subsistence alternatives than in the hills. Famine, in other words, though no stranger to the hills, was more widespread and devastating than in the hills. When it struck, dispersal was the rule. If the famine was severe enough, as it was for example in 1805-12 in Upper Burma, the decline in population might prompt a wholesale shift to shifting cultivation (Koenig 1990:143). Here was a case of the *un*making of a previously state space as the concentration of population declined.

As is nearly always the case, hill populations were, other things equal, healthier than dense valley populations. Their diet was more varied. Their very dispersal made them less vulnerable to epidemics than valley peoples who represented not only a concentration of subjects but a concentration of rodents, insects, and domestic animals who were the vectors of disease amidst a more vulnerable population. When famine and epidemics hit simultaneously, those who could, headed for the hills and comparative safety as they did in 17th century London as described by Defoe in his Journal of the Plague Year.

The Southeast Asian mainland state, then, both gathered in new populations by slaving, taking war-captives, and the episodic attractions of its culture and commerce. At the same time it was disgorging populations by its own rapacity as well as by its demographic and ecological vulnerability.

3. To this point, political-economy and epidemiology would seem to explain the 'reflux' of population to the hills. If it were entirely so, the hill population might more closely resemble the valley populations except for their elevation and the shifting cultivation that such elevations required. But they don't. The hill peoples are different: they tend to be animists who do not follow the 'great tradition' religions of the lowland peoples; they produce a surplus, but do not use it to support kings and monks. What is missing from the story thus far is the *cultural refusal of civilizational projects in the valleys* that characterizes hill populations.

"The hills", I must emphasize again, are meant both literally and metaphorically in this context. Literally, they were the destination for those fleeing valley polities; metaphorically "the hills" represented any space effectively outside the ambit of valley kingdoms: "the hills" in this last sense could be marshes, mangrove swamps *(sundarbans)*, or the sea itself as in the case of the "sea gypsies" or *orang laut* of archepelagic Southeast Asia.

Most of the peoples who lived at the margins of state power had either moved there or stayed there because they were positioned in a certain relation to large polities. Seen from the perspective of such large polities, to move upland, inland, and toward the margins, to move away from wet rice *(sawah)* cultivation, was to move down some hypothetical ladder of prestige, power, and civilization. But, as Tanya Li (1999:8) insists, location was a *choice*, "people who lived in the uplands did so not by default, bypassed by history, but for positive reasons of economy, security, and cultural style formed in dialogue with lowland agendas."

For a moment, let us concentrate on hill-dwellers as a cultural style. We have evidence of cultural choices of this kind from the earliest chronicles from the Malay world: the *Hikayat Raja Raja Pasai*. The local Raja of the Pasai Confederacy, Merah Silu, after a prophetic dream in which the Prophet came to him, converted from Buddhism to Islam. [Incidentally, the episode corresponds with the Mogul ascendancy in India and the trade ties between Sumatra and the Coromandel coast.] The chronicle tells us that some 'tribes' in Merah Silu's confederacy did not want to convert to Islam, and returned to the forest from the coast. Maybe they didn't want to give up their pigs, maybe they didn't want to give up their ritual life, saturated as it was with Hindu-Buddhist-animist rites, maybe it was a matter of political factions – maybe all three. In any case, the forest-hill peoples remained non-Muslim generally, though they remained firmly linked in trade and exchange with the coastal Muslim polities. Similarly, in Negri Sembilan on the Malay Peninsula, there seems to have been the same cultural dichotomy: some choosing to become Muslims and live in clearings near the banks of rivers and others moving upriver, outside this sphere of political power, but likewise connected to it by trade and exchange (Hall 1977). In the course of time many of these upstream peoples came to be considered – and to consider themselves – separate ethnic groups.

In the Spanish Philippines, the flight to the hills from the Chrisianization and labor-bondage mimicked and overlapped a still older pattern of flight from the Malay slaving raids that plagued the coasts. The Christian faith and baptism were inseparable from settled life in villages and labor bondage, and the flight from one was flight from the other. Keesing, in his pioneering Ethnohistory of Northern Luzon, concludes that the hills were only lightly populated when the Spanish arrived and that they were peopled by a flight from lower elevations and from the Spanish civilizational project. Living in the hills was a political and cultural choice.

This brings us back to the subtitle of my talk: "why civilizations can't climb hills." Here I want to modify Braudel's largely ecological observation: He writes:

> "The feudal system as a political, economic, and social system, and as an instrument of justice, failed to catch in its toils most of the mountain regions and those it did reach it only partially influenced [e.g. Corsica, Sardinia]. The observation could be confirmed anywhere where the population is so inadequate, thinly distributed, and widely dispersed as to prevent the establishment of the state, dominant languages, and important civilizations." (1966:38]

It is largely true as the Baron de Tott, quoted by Braudel, wrote that "The steepest places have always been the asylum of liberty." (ibid.:40) But what I want to suggest here is not simply that civilizations can't climb hills, but that people, sometimes collectively, sometimes individually, climb hills in order to get beyond the reach of the civilizational projects of the valleys.

Taking religion in particular, the hills are either "colored" pagan or animist, or, they are host to heterodox and dissident variants of valley orthodoxies. Here there are also parallels between Europe and Southeast Asia. Again, Braudel:

> "Everywhere in the 16th century, the hilltop world was very little influenced by the dominant religion at sea level."

> "The mountains were the favored refuge of these aberrant cults...at the end of the 16th century there were innumerable 'magic' mountains stretching from Germany as far as the Milanese or Piedmontese Alps, from the Massif Centrale to the healing soldiers of the Pyrenees, from the Franche-Comte to the Basque country." (1966: 35, 37)

Of course, geography is at work here too. The hills with their dispersed population, mobile, and diverse livelihoods, were not much more attractive to institutional, surplus-absorbing religions than they were to institutional, surplus absorbing states. Thus it should not be surprising that the Cevennes should have been the redoubt of the Hugenots in the 16th century, the Tyrol the redoubt of the Anabaptists, and that English dissenting traditions flourished in the fen and forest areas. It was not just that the church had not fully penetrated these areas but also that religious heterodoxy headed for the hills in the same way as valley 'criminals', social outcasts, beleaguered pretenders, and other stigmatized and persecuted lowlanders sought refuge outside the ambit of the state.

Just as Sanskritic tongues seldom made it into the hills in Southeast Asia, so have the hills remained the major geographical redoubt of non-Buddhist, non-Christian, non-Islamic beliefs. This is *not* to say that fragments of great tradition religious do not circulate in the hills; they most certainly do. Just as do elements of lowland systems of political and social stratification. They are, however, often confected into quite exotic hybrids. The Shan Hills of Burma are a case in point. Culturally intermediate in some ways between the relatively unstratified, non-Buddhist peoples nearby (e.g. the Kachin, Karen, Wa, Akha, and Hmong) and the more hierarchical, Burman Buddhist kingdoms in the valleys, the Shan *are* Buddhists. But with a difference, or rather many differences. What strikes one about Shan Buddhism is its stunning diversity and eclecticism. To tour the Buddhist monasteries of the Shan Hills is, in effect, to take an historical survey of dissident Buddhist sects expelled or, if that is the right word, excommunicated from lowland Burman kingdoms. Such forms of Buddhism did not simply prove attractive to hill peoples, they were brought to the hills in large part by religious refugees from "Burma proper".

One might map out other places in Southeast Asia that, because they lie athwart different cultural areas, offer both cultural and geographical room for maneuver. The patch of Cambodia sticking into southern Vietnam, known as "The Parrot's Beak", is a case in point. Because of its location between Khmer and Vietnamese cultures, and its marginal, out-of-the-way location, it became a 'no-man's land', host to a large floating population, and a long-reputed cradle of religious heterodoxy and millenarianism. Most recently, in the 20th century, it was home to the large and politically powerful Cao Dai syncretic religion and its "Pope"... among whose saints numbered Jesus Christ, the Buddha, and Victor Hugo.

There are other reasons to repair to the hills, forests, marshes, and trackless wastes: as elsewhere, there are bandits, petty traders, losers in valley feuds and factional fights, rebels and royal pretenders, adventurers, etc. These are the "stock cast of characters on any frontier". They are, in some senses, less important than the systemic forces of dispersion. It would, for example, be hard to understand the social composition of the "Wild West" in the United States from, say, 1865 to 1890, solely in terms of random 'drifters' and pioneers without the economic and social havoc wreaked by the Civil War in the Confederate States and the subsequent Northern policies of Reconstruction.

The Political Ecology of Hillness and of Freedom

Think for a moment of the standard narrative of civilization. It is a picture, in its high idealist form, of cultural and geographical "in-gathering", of the *pull* – both coercive and persuasive – of states and their cultural and economic attraction. Sanskritization, the glories of Han civilization, Buddhism, fixed abodes, town life, literature, arts, entertainments, dress, cosmopolitanism.

What I have tried briefly to portray are the forces of dispersion, of the centrifugal, repulsive pressures that represent a countervailing power. I hope that I've indicated why people might be moving, over time, up-hill, out-of-reach, and away from valley projects of statemaking. What remains to explore is how we might understand hill society, hill ethnicity, and hill ecology in this context.

Ecologically, the hills have typically – not always – meant slash-and-burn, shifting cultivation, while the valleys – when densely settled – have meant wet rice or *sawah* cultivation. To put this difference boldly and outrageously, I'd like you to consider the possibility that shifting cultivation is the agriculture of freedom and wet-rice the agriculture of subordination. On this view, swiddening is as much a political choice as a technical decision.

From an older, valley-centric, perspective the superiority of wet rice over shifting cultivation is self-evident. Surely, anyone who had a choice would cultivate wet rice in *padi* fields: it is far more productive per unit of land and it facilitates far denser settlement. The only reason people might practice shifting cultivation, this argument goes, would be because nothing else was feasible ecologically or because they had not yet learned the technique.

Even technically, matters are not that simple. Shifting cultivation, when land is abundant, is typically more efficient *per unit of labor*. If the scarce factor of production is labor, as it is in the hills, rather than land, swiddening is more advantageous. Swiddening is, furthermore, polyculture. It produces a far more varied and nutritious diet particularly when, as is usually the case, it is mixed with hunting and gathering. Its bio-diversity is, at the same time, an insurance policy against the crop-failures that so often strike valley-monocultures. Depending, then, on the relative supply of land and labor, the nature of the soil, the availability of water, one technique *or* the other may make most sense technically. Not a few Southeast Asian populations practice both forms of agriculture simultaneously or switch back and forth as conditions warrant. Neither one, we may conclude, is technically superior across the board.

Politically, however, the difference is massive. Shifting cultivation by a dispersed population is, from a state-making perspective, unpromising. Its diversity makes its yields and surplus hard to assess, its mobile population is hard to grab for corvée labor or military service, and the territory required to sustain a given tax yield in grain or men is large. Even an energetic, competent state would find the returns paltry. Consider the crops themselves. The prominence of root crops of different maturity in shifting cultivation; crops which can remain in the ground safely for some time as compared with wet-rice which must be gathered promptly when ripe and which officials can confiscate in one fell swoop, is another factor. Guerrillas plant root crops here and there, like shifting cultivators. Specific grain crops facilitate political flight. Maize, a new word crop adopted with alacrity in Southeast Asia, grows, as in the Andes, at a higher altitude than hill rice. For hill peoples, maize made it possible to push even higher in a watershed, out of the reach of the state.

From a tax-collector's eye-view, shifting cultivation is illegible, making appropriation difficult if not a losing proposition altogether. The classical Southeast Asian states treated such areas, when possible, as tributary states and ruled them tenuously and indirectly, occasionally threatening punitive expeditions. There were also zones of "no-tribute" and zones of "multiple-tribute" as hill societies strove to position themselves strategically among valley powers (Winichakul 1994).

Slash-and-burn agriculture represents, then, a non-state space. What I want to suggest, further, is that this non-state, illegible space is often a social creation, a political decision. Where various forms of cultivation are possible, swiddening promises relative freedom by its diversity, the mobility and autonomy it affords, by its relative economic (not necessarily social) egalitarianism. Many Southeast Asians have, historically, consciously chosen swiddening or have moved from wet-rice to swiddening zones as a political choice.

The Political Ecology of Freedom and Ethnicity

Ethnicity in the hills was and is deeply confusing, to states and ethnographers alike. The precolonial kingdoms were not much concerned with ethnic affiliation as a permanent, essential identity. Instead, they were more attentive to whether various hill populations were tributary or hostile: not an easy assessment until the chips were down. The colonial powers and, in Southwest China, Han administrators, were far more concerned to map out a reliable ethnoscape for their projects of rule. To read many of the early reports is to read the ethnographic equivalent of a "field-guide" to plants or birds. That is, the function of the knowledge being generated is to allow officials to discriminate, on the fly, the *field characteristics* of various peoples. For example: "The Lisu women wear black leggings, neck rings, and wear red hats." The assumption was that such groups were reasonably uniform, coherent, and stable over time. In the long run, of course, colonial administration with its codified "native law", distinct school systems, courts, and reinforced 'tribal' authority could go a long way towards actually *making,* tribes by creating and enforcing the social "traffic patterns" that fostered distinct group identities.

The imperial taxonomies of the hill tribes were, it is fair to say, radically wrong. The groups they discerned in the landscape were not uniform, coherent, or stable through time. What one encounters ethnographically in the hills are usually bewildering and intercalated "gradients" of cultural traits. Often there are no sharp boundaries of linguistic practice (tri-lingualism, for example, is common in the hills), dress, ritual, diet, body decoration. Where there *are* such sharp boundaries for *one* such trait, they are likely *not* to coincide with other cultural boundaries. Cultural hybridity is ubiquitous. As an objective matter of cultural traits (the older way of looking at ethnicity), any line of demarcation drawn by an ethnic taxonomist is more or less arbitrary. Nor, to make matters more complex, do the phenomenological tribal 'differences' in use among the inhabitants coincide with 'objective cultural boundaries.

Looking at this luxuriant and tangled variety, one astute observer of Northern Thailand has been moved to conclude that: "...tribal divisions were essentially political in origin" (Moerman 1965:1219).

On this view, we should abandon the mosaic of traits for phenomenology. People are what they call themselves. This is the least ambiguous way of determining where one social unit stops and another begins. [I say "least ambiguous" rather than "unambiguous" because there is no perfect correspondence between what people call themselves and what they are called and because people often call themselves by different designations in different contexts]. One advantage of a point of departure that takes those who call themselves Lisu as Lisu, those who call themselves Kachin as Kachin, is that it accords far better with the experienced world of hill peoples.

Once we adopt this perspective, however, the ethnographic ground is not much firmer under our feet. Given time to percolate, some ethnic self-identifications are born, others disappear, and substantial numbers of people move from one self-identification to another. The Karen*ni* (the *"red"* Karen) split from the Karen in the late 19th century, it has been claimed, because their patch of the hills, they realized, contained the most valuable stands of mature teak which they wanted for themselves. The split was, on this reading, an act of political entrepreneurship. The great contribution of Edmund Leach's justly famous book *The Political Systems of Highland Burma,* was to show that Shan-ness and Kachin-ness as tribal identities were not so much ethnic differences as varying political conditions of the same people. Given an economic surplus, elites began aping valley aristocrats and became "Shans"; but let the surplus disappear, the more egalitarian population dispersed and became "Kachin". Shanness, put another way, is an episodic political project among Kachin to build a small state.

Ethnicity is, as Moerman notes, "impermanent in that individuals, communities, and areas change their identifications" (ibid.:1222). Those in a position to alter some of the "markers" of hill ethnicity: forms of cultivation, religion, dress, dialect, diet, marriage alliances, are in a position to shift their self-identifications. Stable ethnic identities thus require as much explanation as shifting identities.

If we grant that ethnicity is political, a collective choice within a field of power relations; if we grant that the choice of livelihood, of cultivation, may also well be a political choice, one with important implications for state appropriation. *And,* if we

grant that hill populations have always been receiving refugees from the valleys...
then, why is it not reasonable to see a certain relationship to state power as *one* (not
the only) of the main organizing principles behind ethnic identifications?

This principle is most obviously at work in the Shan-Kachin model of oscillation made famous by Leach and elaborated by Friedman (1975, 1998), Nugent
(1982), and Kirsch (1973). The Kachin are the stateless, or state-fleeing, variant
of the Shan. Better put, the Kachin are the elementary social particles or units
which, once in a while, an ambitious man can confect into a statelet by mobilizing
a surplus and creating a fragile hierarchy. Those lineages who don't like it (no one
will take their women to bride) often leave – to Kachinness – and when and if the
statelet falters, it splinters into Kachin fragments.

Much of Felix Keesing's *Ethnohistory of Northern Luzon* rests squarely on the
connection between flight, ecology, and ethnicity. Before the Spanish, he reckons,
the hills were sparsely populated. As the Spanish pressures for taxes, forced labor,
Christianization, and fixed-settlement increased, people fled – some fled as the
Spanish advanced, others submitted and then ran away (apostates), and still others rebelled and then fled. Keesing's persuasive thesis is that hill and valley peoples
in Northern Luzon shared a common lowland origin. His simplest model goes
like this: An original group (similar linguistically, culturally, and ecologically)
split – one part remains in the lowlands and another part moves (flees?) into the
mountains. Each then undergoes, over time, ethnic reformulation, so that they
take on different ethnic identities. The upland migrating group might split and
reside in different ecological settings – say at different elevations, diversifying the
mountain opportunities for further ethnic reformulation.

Keesing works this out in convincing detail for group after group. The Isnegs,
the Tinguians, the Igorot, are the hill fragment of a lowland population. What is
crucial to the scenario, however, is its deep, long history in most cases. Although
the first nucleus of a hill population might have been established by a single migration event – mass flight, a rebellion, an epidemic – there is often a long process
of accretion as new fragments, perhaps from different areas, drift into the hills.

Such is the case with the ethnographically famous Kalinga. The Kalinga are
an enormously diverse group, as Beyer said in 1916:

> "They consist of several distinct peoples who are by now exceedingly
> mixed in physical type, language, and cultures that it is difficult if not
> impossible... to separate the constituent groups and define their distin-
> guishing characteristics." (Keesing 1962:336)

Much the same could be said as well for the Ilongot. They too are a long
historical amalgam of different streams of migrants from the lowlands. It is worth
remembering in this connection that hill communities are also manpower-short.
Hence, they have been brilliant at reworking genealogies and absorbing new migrants in short order while maintaining a collective tradition of continuity and

historical depth. Hill societies, like the Malay coastal states, have been what the French called, under Napoleon, a "career open to talent". If you dress the part, speak the language, and observe the rituals you are easily incorporated. In just this fashion have hill ethnic groups assimilated new arrivals while retaining, and even reinforcing their identity.

I hope I've made it clear that the same spatial relation to stateness occurs in the hills as it does between valley and hills. Thus large migrating groups might push weaker societies further up the watershed, further into the hills. There is strong evidence that many Negrito groups in the Philippines and so-called aboriginals *(orang asli)* in Malaysia were living at lower elevations and retreated to higher altitudes – and often to more hunting-and-gathering – as a result of pressure. The same pattern of avoidance by retreat was repeated for the orang asli during the Second World War and the revolutionary war known as the Malayan Emergency which followed.

The Wa in Burma are a case in point. They are divided conventionally into the "Wild Wa",reputed to take heads, and "Tame Wa". The "Wild Wa" live at higher elevations, farther away from valley kingdoms, more dispersed, more egalitarian, more mobile. It is reasonably clear that the split represented a *choice,* one that is still open to small groups of Wa.

Here, then, is the crude logic of the gradients of stateness in much of Southeast Asia: The farther away from core populations in the valleys, the higher in altitude, the more characterized by slash-and-burn cultivation or hunting-and-gathering, the more dispersed, the more mobile,.... the more illegible, the more egalitarian, and, of course, the less "civilized" as seen by valley states.

And yet, the view I want to urge is that the hills are, to a considerable extent, the product of state-making projects in the valleys.

Mainland Southeast Asian history could better be written in terms of the ebb and flow from valley to hill and vice-versa. At rare times of dynastic consolidation in the valleys, of growing commercial exchange, of relative peace, the flow of population – of assimilation – was toward "valleyness". From one perspective, *a valley perspective,* this marked progress in the "civilizing project",...becoming Thai, Burman, Malay, Vietnamese.

At the more common times of dynastic fragmentation, war, oppression, epidemics, crushing taxation, religious dissidence, the flow was preponderantly in the opposite direction. One could see it as protest – as voting-with-one's feet. One could also see it as a homeostatic device, setting sharp limits to oppression in valley kingdoms. The harder the dynasty pressed its core population, the more it leaked away to safety, to the hinterlands, to the hills (see Lieberman 1984 and his other work, and that of Koenig op.cit.).

In the valley histories these periods were lamentable episodes of backslid-ing, disintegration, anarchy, a retreat of civilization, Buddhism, political order, settled agrarian life. Told another way, it is also a story of liberty, freedom, and autonomy. While the Vietnamese have always seen their hill peoples (literally called *"montagnards"* by the French colonial administrators) as rude and uncivilized- as left behind – the montagnards characterize themselves as "Free in the Forest" (see Gerald Hickey's two volumes).

Let's try looking at this through the hill lens for a change. Let's try, for once, to adopt a non-state perspective. What I'm urging is something like Richard Cobb's celebration of the fatal desertions from Napoleon's armies after the invasion of Russia.

> "There could have been no more eloquent referendum on the universal unpopularity of an oppressive regime; and there is no more encouraging spectacle for a historian than a people that has decided it will no longer fight and that, without fuss, returns home...the common people, at least in this respect, had their fair share in bringing down France's most appalling regime." (Cobb, The Police and the People, pp.96-97.

What would an anti-dynastic, non-state-centric history of freedom look like, if it were written? This could be extended to contemporary efforts to construct state-space from non-state space: plantations, strategic hamlets, agent orange, resettlement and transmigration. Two features link the hills to freedom. The first is obvious. The dispersion, mobility, autonomy, and common-property regimes of hill life work against huge, permanent economic inequality. State-making is wellnigh impossible in this setting, and when, against the odds, it is tried seriously, its subjects have the easy option of removing themselves from the experimental terrain.

The second feature of hill freedom, however, is the one I have been urging. Like the Cossacks, the hill peoples of Southeast Asia are substantially a *maroon community*. A community of runaways. As Hegel and Orlando Patterson remind us, the concept of freedom is conceived only in societies of bondage and slavery. Freedom is the reciprocal of unfreedom. The hills in Southeast Asia represent more of an anti-state than a "non-state" or a "not-yet-state". They are filled with deserters from armies, runaways from taxes and corvée, refugees from bondage, losers in factional fights, outcasts, and religious dissidents, forest monks, hermits, heterodox sects...."the organic intellectuals" of the frontier or periphery who make a symbolic case against the center by their practices.

Much of the hill periphery of Southeast Asia is a shadow-society – in terms of its ecology, its religious practices, its social structure, its governance, and, above all, its fugitive dissident population. Ideas about rule and symbols of authority do, most certainly circulate in the hills, one might even say they saturate the hills, but they travel without the institutional battalions which accompany them on the plains.

References

Adas, Michael. 1981. "From Avoidance to Confrontation: Peasant Protest in Precolonial and Colonial Southeast Asia", *Comparative Studies in Society and History* 23, pp. 217-247.

_____1986. "From Footdragging to Flight: The Evasive History of Peasant Avoidance Protest in South and Southeast Asia", *Journal of Peasant Studies,* Special Issue, 13(2), pp. 64-86.

Braudel, Fernand 1966. *The Mediterranean World in the Age of Philipp II.* Translated by Sian Reynolds. New York: Harper and Row

Cobb, Richard C. 1970. *The Police and the People: French Popular Protest, 1789-1820.* New York: Oxford University Press

Defoe, Daniel 1722. *A Journal of the Plague Year.* London: E. Nutt

Friedman, Jonathan 1975. Tribes, States, and Transformations; in: Maurice Bloch (ed.), *Marxist Analyses and Social Anthropology,* pp. 161-202. London: Tavistock

_____1998 (1979). *System, structure and contradictions. The evolution of Asiatic social formations.* Walnut Creek, London, New Delhi: Alta Mira Press/ Sage. 1998. Second edition

Hall, Kenneth R. 1977. The Coming of Islam to the Archipelago: A Reassessment, in: Karl Hutterer (ed.), *Economic Exchange and Social Interaction in Southeast Asia.* Ann Arbor: Papers on South and Southeast Asia, 1977, pp. 216-223

Hickey, Gerald C. 1982. *Sons of the Mountains: Ethnohistory of the Vietnamese Central Highlands to 1954.* New Haven: Yale University Press

_____*Free in the Forest: Ethnohistory of the Vietnamese Central Highlands, 1954-1976.* New Haven: Yale University Press

Keesing, Felix 1962. *The Ethnohistory of Northern Luzon.* Stanford: Stanford University Press

Kirsch, A. Thomas 1973. *Feasting and social oscillation: Religion and society in upland Southeast Asia.* Data Paper. No. 92. Cornell University, Department of Asian Studies, Southeast Asia Program

Koenig, William J. 1990. *The Burmese Polity, 1752-1819. Politics, Administration and Social Organisation in the Early Konbang Period.* Centre for Southeast Asian Studies, The University of Michigan

Leach, Edmund R. 1960. The Frontiers of "Burma". *Comparative Studies in Society and History,* Vol. 3, No. 1, (Oct., 1960), pp. 49-68

Li, Tanya Murray (ed.) 1999. "Marginality, Power and Production: Analysing Upland Transformations", in Tania Murray Li ed., *Transforming the Indonesian Uplands: Marginality, Power, and Production,* pp. 1-44. Amsterdam: Harwood Academic Publishers

Lieberman, Victor B. 1984. *Burmese Administrative Cycles: Anarchy and Conquest. c. 1580-1760.* New Jersey: Princeton University Press

Moerman, Michael 1965. Ethnic Identification in a Complex Civilization. *American Anthropologist,* 67 (1965), pp. 1215-1230)

Nugent, David 1982. Closed Systems and Contradiction: The Kachin in and out of History. *Man* 17(3): 508-527

Reid, Anthony 1983. *Slavery Bondage and Dependency in Southeast Asia.* New York: St. Martin's Press

Tsing, Anna Lowenhaupt 1993. *In the Realm of the Diamond Queen: Marginality in an Out-of-the-Way Place.* Princeton University Press

Winichakul, Thongchai. 1994. *Siam Mapped: A History of the Geobody of a Nation.* Honolulu: University of Hawaii Press

Wolters, Oliver 1982. *History, Culture, and Religion in Southeast Asian Perspectives.* Singapore: Institute of Southeast Asian Studies

Notes

[1] James C. Scott is Sterling Professor of Political Science and Professor of Anthropology at Yale University, USA.

[2] On avoidance as a form of protest among Southeast Asian peasants refer to the work of Michael Adas (1981, 1986)

Some Thoughts on "Indigeneity" in the Context of Migration and Conflicts at Contemporary Asian Frontiers

Danilo Geiger[1]

The article is not so much an essay meant to capture general truths about indigenous peoples and how they need to be defined. It was written as a context-bound and ultimately unambitious attempt to remove terminological obstacles for an upcoming study[2] on settler migration and its attendant conflicts at contemporary colonization frontiers of South and Southeast Asia. Our research team had no difficulty defining what a settler was – in the main (but not exclusively) an agriculturalist who has advanced from the consolidated heartland of a national territory to its thinly-populated margins. It however proved much more complicated to spell out what an indigenous person, and, in extension, an indigenous community or people was. The sample of local situations that we studied[3] presented us with difficult choices. In some instances, not only the small-scale, kin-based local communities that were the most obvious candidates for "indigenous" status claimed indigeneity, but so did their neighbours of long standing, the locally hegemonic populations whose princely elites had ruled, taxed and sometimes enslaved the indigenous community through much of the pre-colonial and colonial eras. Similarly, there were cases where the settlers, too, referred to themselves as being indigenous, albeit with an ancestral territory hundreds of miles away, across a state or even an international boundary. Finally, while some dubious claims were pressed most noisily, certain communities upon which the label could be pinned most easily did not bother (or know how) to define themselves as "indigenous" in a political arena dominated by others, or indicate in other ways their concern with the preservation of their ethnic identity and territorial right, an often-cited criterion of "indigeneity".

A practical diagnostic instrument was called for that would allow us to assess the nature of the communal contenders in our study areas, and shine light on questions such as the following: Does a change in residence (in the sense of relocation across political boundaries) affect a group's "indigeneity"? Does the fact that it is confronted with settler migration give a group with a past (and often present) of domination (and sometimes oppression and exploitation) of indigenous communities a legitimate claim to "indigeneity"? And should a group's political history – notably the presence or absence of traditions of political centralizations – be made to matter when we have to tell "indigenous" from "non-indigenous"?

Definition of "Indigenous Peoples/Communities"

The word "indigenous" has no fixed meaning; like other key concepts in the realm of anthropology and international law, it is "essentially contested" (Lukes 1974) and has continuously stimulated debate and scepticism (Gray 1995:40). Especially pronounced is the fiery resistance against the notion on the part of states – both in the developed and the developing world – because under emerging international law, conferring "indigeneity" upon a group may imply binding rights which can be enforced against the states in question (Gray 1995:41; Keal 2003:11).

Although there is no single accepted definition that captures the diversity of indigenous peoples the world over, the usual reference point for any discussion of "indigeneity" is that of the UN's Special Rapporteur José Martinez Cobo. The definition which informs and guides the United Nations and its various sub-bodies in their work (Keal 2003:14f.), states that "indigenous communities, peoples and nations" are

> "those which, having a historical continuity with pre-invasion and pre-colonial societies that developed on their territories, consider themselves distinct from other sectors of the societies now prevailing in those territories or parts of them. They form at present non-dominant sectors of society and are determined to preserve, develop, and transmit to future generations their ancestral territories and their ethnic identity, the basis of their continued existence as peoples, in accordance with their cultural patterns, social institutions and legal systems" (Cobo 1986:Add 4, paragraph 379);

Cobo's definition stresses five key interrelated factors: 1) subjection to colonial invasion and settlement; 2) historical continuity with pre-invasion or pre-colonial societies; 3) an identity which is distinct from that of the encapsulating society; 4) non-dominance, the situation of being out-of-power locally and on the national level; and 5) a concern with the preservation of their ethnic identity, cultural traditions and territorial rights. These five key factors are joined by a sixth:

self-definition[4]. In order to keep states from using definitions based on so-called 'objective' criteria, self-definition by those concerned – the putatively 'indigenous' individuals – has come to be regarded as the most acceptable means of defining indigenous peoples (Keal 2003:12).

With a view to the difficulty of applying the 'indigenous peoples' concept to Asia – a difficulty, which is both empirical and political, as the continent's most economically successful and politically powerful states steadfastly refuse to grant the concept validity –, Benedict Kingsbury (1990, 1998, in this volume) advocates a flexible approach to definition. He comes up with a list of indicia which are graded according to whether they are truly indispensable and near-ubiquitous, or objectively contestable and frequently contested. He distinguishes essential requirements from traits which have strong indicative power from a comparative perspective, but are not required under special circumstances ('strong indicia'), and from simply familiar factors whose presence adds to the case, but is not in any sense required ('weaker indicia') (Kingsbury 1990:370-374). The main deviation from common definitional practice as exemplified by Cobo (1986) is that Kingsbury considers historical continuity with pre-invasion societies optional and negotiable rather than mandatory. His list looks as follows:

Essential requirements:

- self-identification as distinct ethnic group
- historical experience of, or contingent vulnerability to, severe disruption, dislocation, or exploitation
- long connection with the region
- wish to retain a distinct identity

Relevant indicia:

(a) strong:

- non-dominance in the national (or regional) society
- close cultural affinity with a particular area of land or territory
- historical continuity with prior occupants of land in the region

(b) weaker:

- socio-economic and socio-cultural differences from the ambient population
- distinct objective characteristics such as language, race, and material or spiritual culture
- regarded as indigenous by the ambient population or treated as such in legal and administrative arrangements

Of those writers who have tried to make the "indigeneity" concept relevant for Asia, Andrew Gray (1995) has probably pushed furthest in solving what he terms the "coherence and applicability dilemma" (Gray 1995:57). An important contribution is the insistence on the fact that "indigenousness is as much a concept of political action as it is of semantic reflection" (ibid.:41). One way to measure a group's indigeneity is to determine if it relates to the discourse propagated and popularized by indigenous organizations the world over – a discourse that revolves around the claims to self-determination, freedom of cultural expression and control over territories and resources (ibid.:57). However, making the definition contingent on the adoption of the discourse of self-determination will open the door for many groups that do not – at least not in the narrow sense – self-identify as "indigenous". The search for self-determination is a possible identifier of indigenous peoples, but it is not unique to them (Keal 2003:12). Ethnic and religious minorities as well as regionalist movements share in that demand, but may not want to compromise their political claims by associating with indigenous peoples. Crucially, therefore, self-identification as "indigenous" involves the selection of the same international fora where other indigenous peoples articulate their grievances. So far, the major fora for airing indigenous aspirations and grievances have been the United Nation's Working Group on Indigenous Populations (UN-WGIP) and the Permanent Forum on Indigenous Peoples' Issues (UNPFII)[5]. An emphasis on fora of struggle chosen by putative "indigenous" groups can help to maintain the "highly functional international political distinction between 'indigenous peoples' and ethnic and other minorities" (Kingsbury 1999:344).

Whereas the stress on venues for the articulation of grievances helps to draw the line between groups which espouse closely related, but not identical discourses, it ceases to be of help in all those cases where communities with the structural properties of indigenous peoples fail to articulate any "discourse" at all. This may be because they avoid contact with the world at large, are too busy with survival, too timid, too repressed or for other reasons unable to voice dissent. To his credit, Gray (1995:55) does not carry his case for an arena-bound "indigeneity" to its absurd consequence of excluding defensive, weak and isolated communities from coverage of the label. He insists that "peoples who are unaware of the indigenous peoples' movement but live in circumstances for which the term is appropriate" form an integral part of the category (Gray 1995:55).

In keeping with changing approaches to the understanding of ethnicity, definitions of indigeneity have moved away from a concern with "objective" cultural content (modes of production, social structures and world-views); instead, the emphasis now is on subjective, experiential factors (identity). However, the ascendancy of self-identification as "the most acceptable means of defining indigenous peoples" (Keal 2003:12) has its downsides. Not only does it invite misuse of definitional power by groups that claim indigenous status on the basis of little tangible evidence (Corntassel 2003:76; in this volume p. 52), but the desire to accommodate every possible permutation of indigenous cultural and social practice has started to obscure essential contours of large parts of the societies with which we are concerned. It serves us well to remind ourselves that for all the diversity of real life situations, indigenous peoples can most usefully be contrasted with other communal constituencies by describing them as "a group of people who identify themselves with a specific, small-scale cultural heritage" (Bodley 1999:4). That is, scale is an important gradient of indigeneity, excluding e.g. national peasantries where supra-local cultural orientations have replaced more strictly localized ones.

Furthermore, the cultural essence of a majority of these small-scale societies can still usefully be approximated by reference to the much-reviled term "tribal" (Gray 1995:39; Maybury-Lewis 2005:11)[6]. Tribes may be defined as kinship-based non-state societies that have traditionally lacked steep social hierarchies and are but loosely connected with the dominant national society (composite definition drawn from Goodland 1982:vii; Lewellen 1983:137; Maybury-Lewis 2005:11; Haller 2005:197). Especially useful is the reference to the absence of traditions of statecraft in these societies (Gurr 2000:17; IWGIA 2001, in Corntassel 2003:89f., in this volume p. 64ff; Maybury-Lewis 2005:11); political centralization – though undeniably existing in various degrees – has stopped short of producing courts, princes and kings. In regions like Southeast Asia, tribal societies have lived side by side with and were often subjugated by powerful kingdoms and smaller or larger princely states for centuries[7]. Insistence on the examination of political histories can help us avoid the error of lumping together the rulers and the ruled of old in one single category "indigenous peoples". We propose to refer to the descendants of such long-established hegemonic neighbour groups as "non-indigenous native communities", with "native" implying origin in the region (Goodland 1982:vii).

However, neither the introduction of more flexible criteria and the invocation of the interrelationship between identity and political practice, nor a call to the return to a more essentialist definitional practice provides a classificatory yardstick which is foolproof and unambiguous. In the following, we will discuss the shallows and pitfalls of the concept as they relate in particular to groups that have experienced settler migration to their territories. In a broader sense, these communities illustrate the vagaries of making sense of a general notion – "*indigenous peoples*" – to historically and ethnically complex regional contexts such as those encountered in Asia.

With regards to our immediate concern with migration-induced conflicts, the classificatory challenge arises not only with respect to the host communities that are exposed to immigration, but also to some of their neighbours of long standing – the locally-hegemonic populations whose princely elites ruled the former through the pre-colonial and colonial era –, and even some settler communities. Cobo's six definitional criteria and the two additional points raised above (articulation of political aspirations in certain fora, and "tribal" essence,

notably the absence of traditions of statecraft) will be taken up selectively when
they contain the seeds of controversy for the assessment of the nature of the communal contenders in conflicts of the sort of those that we have studied. Keeping
in mind inherent friction potential, we will concentrate on the experience of
colonization; historical continuity with pre-conquest societies; non-dominance;
shared tribal essence (notably absence of traditions of statehood); and the choice
of characteristic fora of struggle.

Colonial Experience

In various representations before human rights fora like the UN Working
Group on Indigenous Populations in the 1980s and 1990s, Asian states have
mounted fundamental challenges to the applicability of the concept of "indigenous peoples" by stating, among others, that it is historically associated with the
deleterious effects of European colonialism (Kingsbury 1999:350ff.).

Bound up as it is with the notion of "colonization", the "indigeneity" concept
has suffered the effects of the international community's practice of defining a
colonial situation as one involving only European colonizers (the so-called "saltwater settler colonialism" thesis, see Keal 2003:8). However, current legal opinion
is clearly in favour of interpreting Cobo's reference to "colonial invasion" in a
broader sense: The "colonizers" could be any "'alien' peoples who came to the
territory subsequently", and the indigenous peoples affected by such intrusion
"are 'colonized' in the sense of being disadvantaged and discriminated against"
(Gray 1995:37)[8].

The prevalent usage in deliberations of the United Nations is being refuted as
too narrow: To state that colonialism ended with decolonisation in the 1950s and
1960s and that "indigeneity" ceased to be a useful concept once the subjects of the
former European colonial dominions (all "indigenous" vis-à-vis the colonizers)
were given their freedom, amounts to a "failure to distinguish between different peoples contained within the boundaries of new states" (Keal 2003:8). Thus,
contradicting the state managers in Beijing, New Delhi, Yangoon and Dhaka,
most experts contend that for many indigenous peoples around the world, one set
of oppressors was replaced by another when the Caucasian colonizers left (ibid.;
Gray 1995:37). From the Ainu of Japan to the aboriginal peoples of Taiwan,
the *"Montagnards"* of Vietnam's Central Highlands of and the *Adivasi* of India,
the communities we are dealing with qualify as "indigenous" for virtue of being
exposed at present to various forms of "internal colonization".

Historical Continuity

The definitional requirement of historical continuity with pre-invasion or
pre-colonial societies is important in many contexts and often seen as a non-nego-
tiable criterion of "indigeneity". In a rigid interpretation of the criterion, a group
may be labelled "indigenous" only if it can give proof that it descends from the

"original" inhabitants of a contested territory (ICIHI 1987:6; see also the definition of the World Council of Indigenous Peoples in Corntassel 2003:90, in this
volume p. 65). However, in a number of cases it has been established that people
regarded as indigenous are not the original inhabitants of the contested area, but
in fact comparatively late arrivals who on their turn displaced or mingled with the
truly "aboriginal" populations of the area – populations that often (if not always)
belonged to a different racial stock and practiced other modes of production (like
hunting and gathering vs. agriculture).

To avoid "speculative history as to who are the 'original peoples' of an area", and
so as to better "concentrate on current patterns of colonialism", Gray (1995:38f.)
advocates using the term "prior" instead of "original". Indigenous peoples, then,
are the "prior occupants of lands colonised" (Keal 2003:9). Without softening
the requirement of historical continuity, many indigenous peoples in Asia would
fail the test. A case in point is the congeries of groups collectively designated as
"Jhumma" – the indigenous inhabitants of the Chittagong Hill Tracts. Most of
them migrated to the area during or after the 19th century and would not properly qualify as "indigenous" if the term were meant to signify "original" (Gray
1995:39). A more generous interpretation of the notion, however, allows us to
consider all of the 11 Jhumma groups as equally indigenous vis-à-vis the Bengali
settlers who arrived in dramatic numbers – notably, but not exclusively in the late
1970s and early 1980s – to transform the demography of the area. Similarly, the
Lumad of Mindanao consist of a wide array of groups, some of which – like the
foraging negritoid Mamanua – are known to belong to a distinctively earlier racial
sediment than most other Lumad communities, and had themselves been forced
from more favourable habitats by the latter long before the mass immigration of
settlers in the second half of the last century. Finally, every account of the history
of West Borneo would be utterly incomplete without mention of the conquests
of the Iban, a people of aggressive and expansive immigrants who from the 17th
century on became the scourge of the middle and upper Kapuas river basin in
West Kalimantan, striking fear into the hearts of (and displacing) earlier tribal
residents.

Admittedly for Asia, the question of whether or not a group can legitimately
claim to have arrived prior to a competitor group is often difficult to resolve[9].
On the Indian sub-continent, for example, the continuous migration of peoples
into the area over the past thousand years renders the issue of antecedence tricky
(ICHI 1987:6). Some of the so-called "hill tribes" of Northern Thailand would
be ill-advised to press their claim to times-immemorial occupancy of their current territories too hard, for they arrived there well within historical memory,
mainly during the second half of the 19th and the first half of the 20th century,
from areas in present-day Burma, Laos and China. On account of their relatively
recent migration into the area, many Hmong, Lisu Akha and other "hill tribes"
are being treated as foreign nationals by the Thai authorities, who routinely deny

their wishes for recognized land rights (Kingsbury 1990:356).

The situation is yet more twisted in Northeastern India. In British times, the tea plantations in Lower Assam recruited *Adivasi*[10](Oraon, Munda, Santhal etc.) in their tens of thousands as indentured labourers, many of whom settled in the vicinity of the plantations after their contracts expired. On the North bank of the Brahmaputra, they encountered the tribal Bodo, the original occupants of the area; after a longer period of surprisingly accommodative relations between the two groups, in recent decades the *Adivasi* were increasingly perceived (and finally attacked) as illegitimate intruders. The constellation is repeated in Arunachal Pradesh where the government of India in the mid-1960s offered a new home to an estimated 15.000 tribal Chakma from erstwhile East Pakistan (later Bangladesh) whose ancestral territories had been flooded by the Kaptai Dam (Chaudhury and Biswas 1997, Luithui-Erni, forthcoming). Initial local opposition to the settlement of the refugees was ignored by the central government, and since the early 1990s open hostility flared up repeatedly into ugly and partially violent anti-settler campaigns.

What these groups mentioned above, have in common is that they abandoned their original ancestral territories either of their own will or because they were forced to do so. All of them are "in historical continuity with pre-invasion or pre-colonial societies", but the continuity is not territorial in the sense that the groups continue to sit on the territories that their ancestors inhabited and cultivated. The "close cultural affinity with a particular area of land" which is said to be characteristic of indigenous peoples (Kingsbury 1990:372) may persist, but it is now – because of the groups' dislocation – with a distant (and often mythologized) homeland. Does the fact that a tribal group has migrated in recent memory deprive it of its claim to indigeneity?

The same question arises where individuals of tribal background have taken up residence in urban centres, and the prevailing sentiment of legal experts and commentators in both cases – voluntary migration to cities, and forced or voluntary migration to other rural locales – is that indigeneity is, so to speak, something "that you take with you" when you relocate. Among the arguments that have been put forward in support of this position is that residence in a city often reinforces rather than weakens a person's attachment to "traditional" culture in general and passionate ties to ancestral land in particular (see Kingsbury 1998:372f. and in this volume p. xx, Corntassel 2003:87 and in this volume p. xx)[11].

I strongly support the view that a change in residence does not affect an individual or a group's indigenous status, provided that it qualifies as such on other relevant counts. For our purposes, therefore, the *Adivasi* in Lower Assam and the Chakma of Arunachal Pradesh can be considered every bit as indigenous as the *autochthonous* indigenous groups of the likes of the Bodo, the Khamti and the Singpho. Putting indigenous immigrants and indigenous host communities on par terminologically does not automatically convey a judgment on these groups' relative entitlements to contested territory and civil and political rights. It does however, enable us to address the question: are the cultural affinities, which are supposed to exist between indigenous peoples, indeed perceived as such by indigenous locals when facing migrants who are from that same general social and political category?.

It is notably with respect to the relevant criteria for measuring historical continuity with pre-invasion populations that my notion of "indigeneity" diverges from the Indian government's definition of what a "tribal" person is ("tribal" being the terminological equivalent to "indigenous" in official bureaucratic usage). "Tribal" status confers certain privileges such as reserved civil-service jobs and access per quota to higher education; it does so, however, only in those districts and states where the group in question has been listed (in administrative parlance: "scheduled") as being "aboriginal" in the sense of having been first. Migrant communities that have branched off from the original population in more or less recent times are not accorded the constitutional protection that they enjoyed in their areas of origin. This leads to the paradoxical situation that an Oraon tribesperson, for instance, is for administrative purposes "tribal" in Jharkand and Orissa, but not in West Assam (Bosu Mullick 2001:100f., Devalle 1992:28, 80).

Non-dominance

The notion that indigenous peoples assume by necessity subaltern positions in regional and national fields of power follows directly from the definitional stress on descent from invaded, conquered or colonized groups. By help of the concept of "internal colonialism", this subjugation is declared to be perennial, so that we find indigenous peoples wherever there are "colonized peoples (...) who are prevented from controlling their own lives, resources, and cultures" (Gray 1995:35). However, while being out-of-power indeed characterizes the overwhelming majority of the world's indigenous communities, applying the criterion too strictly could have the bizarre effect that the very success of the struggle for the de-colonization of indigenous peoples' relations to the state – a common denominator of indigenous struggles worldwide – would cause a people to lose its indigeneity.

Papua Niugini, East Timor and Fiji are a few examples where tribal peoples have in relatively recent times acquired *external* self-determination in the form of a sovereign state; at least for those with privileged access to power among the multitude of tribal groups that make up (together with non-tribal groups, of course) the new nation-states, the days of subjugation have ended, but not necessarily the salience of tribal ways of life (Tanner 1992:25f.; Corntassel 2003:80 and in this volume p. 55). The same holds for cases where a group won itself *internal* self-determination, either in the form of territorial autonomy, or of institutions of protective discrimination by the help of which states legislate a disadvantaged group's privileged access to decision-making powers, employment and state benefits. The Inuit of the autonomous territory of Nunavut illustrate the first case, the Karbi and Dimasa of Karbi Anglong (Central Assam) as well as the various indigenous communities of the state of Arunachal Pradesh the second. With respect to all these groups, I believe, there are several good reasons for using the "out-of-power yardstick" cautiously[12].

As a general argument, I would advocate once more for tying our definition of indigeneity somewhat closer to cultural "essence" than this has been done in the literature over the last years. Thus, "tribal" polities, while structurally anti-thetical to statehood, will not change overnight in their basic texture simply by a change in their territories' administrative status – moreover since very few of these polities' members will share in regional and national power, the rest remaining entirely marginal to this process (Kingsbury 199:371). Moreover, not all of these administrative reconfigurations really end the subordination that Cobo's fourth criterion highlights.

While regimes of protective discrimination as they have been institutional-ized since colonial times in large parts of the Indian northeast *theoretically* shift the balance of power between locals and settlers in the former's favour, the lax ap-plication of the respective regulations by a dispassionate bureaucracy, the latter's ethnic favouritism in favour of settlers, and the settler's stronger economic clout *in practice* all but level out the competitive edge that the legal environment gives to the indigenous host communities. The reality of a continuing frontier situation, therefore, ensures that in important respects, the Karbi and Dimasa of Karbi Anglong and even most of Arunachal Pradesh's tribal constituency remain dis-empowered – in spite of state institutions that purportedly privilege their interests over those of others.

Like many of the defining characteristics of indigeneity, non-dominance is more a relational than an absolute quality: it emerges in situations of confronta-tion and conquest, and is defined against an expansive ‚Other'. Thus, a group's powerlessness, which may be hidden to the unknowing eye by the trappings of institutions of protective discrimination, stands out all the more clearly when viewed against the power of well-entrenched groups that have dominated and ruled their tribal neighbours throughout the pre-colonial and colonial periods. In comparatively rare cases, both the regional hegemonic group and their former tribal minions lay claim to "indigeneity". Here, the resort to the out-of-power/in-power gradient can help decide the relative merits of the competing positions.

In this regard the situations in West Kalimantan and West Assam are good examples. In pre-colonial West Kalimantan, Malay rulers in coastal mini-states exercised suzerainty over a tribal hinterland that provided the port centre and court with trade goods and tribute. Though deprived of much of their sovereign power after the Dutch colonialists consolidated their rule in the early part of the 19th century, the Malay have remained locally influential[13] far into the post-independence period, and continue to exert strong acculturative pressure on the Dayak population to this day. While they consider themselves to be *bhumiputra/*

putra daerah („sons of the soil'/'sons of the region') and have fraternized with and even fought alongside the Dayak during the riots against the Madurese migrants of 1997 and 1999, they have not to my knowledge staked public claims to being "indigenous" *(masyarakat adat)*, as that would diminish their claim to cultural superiority over the Dayak. The Malay, then, can be usefully distinguished from the properly indigenous Dayak by calling them a "non-indigenous native community", with "native" implying origin in the region (Goodland 1982:vii).

The same argument applies to the Axamiya – ethnic Assamese – who have dominated political relations in the middle and upper reaches of the Brahmaputra for the past nine centuries. The grip of their kings over the valley loosened in the latter part of the 18th and also the 19th century when their armies were defeated several times by invading Burmese forces. The British came to their help, but only at the price of assuming control of the valley and reducing the king's role to that of a ceremonial figurehead. Throughout the 19th and early 20th century, the British encouraged migrations into Assam that were to change the face of Assamese society. The inflow of predominantly Bengali migrants from West Bengal and Bangladesh continued after independence, triggering a powerful nativist protest movement that eventually captured power in the regional elections of 1985. While more radical forces[14] among the Axamiya nationalists continue to press for a socialist state outside the Union of India, there can be no doubt that Assam has for the past two decades essentially been ruled by Axamiya politicians, and that the Axamiya elite, at least, has had access to power. Not only since its revival in the course of the nativist agitation of the 1980s, Axamiya culture has defined itself as much in opposition to the tribal fringes as against the migrant element. For centuries, Bodo tribesmen on the Brahmaputra's north bank as well as the tribal Karbi and Dimasa in Central Assam had to endure strong pressure to adopt Vaishnavite Hinduism, the Assamese language and the Devanagri script. On a more material level, both the Himalayan foothills (the ancestral territory of the Bodo peoples) and the Karbi hills received Axamiya migrants, and the local state institutions are heavily dominated by the Axamiya. It is not surprising, therefore, that tribal activists in both areas decry what they call "Assamese colonialism" and "chauvinism", and violently demand their own homelands. In West Assam, the Bodo, Rabha and (probably to a lesser degree) Koch have come to define their cultural and ethnic identities in a way that shows them to be counter-cultures to the hegemonic Axamiya model. These subjective and objective realities are best accounted for by terminologically separating the subaltern and the dominant; it makes much sense to reserve the label "indigenous" for the former (the Bodo, Rabha, Karbi and Dimasa), while calling the latter (the Axamiya) a "non-indigenous native group". In the remainder of this article, two additional criteria: 1) stateness as part of an essentialist difference between regionally hegemonic groups and indigenous communities, and 2) the choice of different fora of struggle, will be examined in order to support this terminological choice.

Shared "Tribal" Essence, Notably: Lack of Traditions of Statehood

"Unfortunately", as the editor of a recent book on indigenous-state relations in the Malay world has observed, "political correctness (...) constantly deprives us of words that we need" (Benjamin 2002:12). None was so sorely missed as the word "tribal", he insisted, a term that he felt remained useful "precisely because it refers to a characteristic way of life and of social organization for which no other unambiguous label exists" (ibid.:13). Indigenous peoples are essentially tribal societies, i. e. kinship-based non-state societies that have traditionally lacked steep social hierarchies and are but loosely connected with the dominant national society. While more extensive lists of tribal characteristics can be had (e.g. Burger 1987:34), the above minimal definition is useful above all in drawing attention to the characteristic lack of traditions of statehood among these societies. Ted Robert Gurr, who authored an often-quoted classification of group types involved in communal conflicts, distinguished indigenous peoples proper from peoples with similar profiles, but with "durable states of their own" (such as the Tibetans), which he classified together with others as "ethnonationalists" (Gurr 2000:17). The Axamiya of Assam or the Meitei of Manipur in Northeast India belong to this category: peoples with centuries-old traditions of statehood. Where such a group raises the familiar demand of self-determination (such as in the case of ULFA's – the United Liberation Front of Assam, the most potent insurgent group in the state – constituency of radical Axamiya ethnonationalists), it does bear a resemblance with (politically mobilized) indigenous communities. Still, that resemblance is rather superficial, a matter of political rhetorics. We have already suggested that in such a case, a line needs to be drawn by pointing to the group's political dominance on the local and regional level; we can now add that the fact that the group produced kings and princely courts exclude it from coverage of the "indigeneity" label. While also of local origin, West Kalimantan's Malay and Assam's Axamiya are better termed "non-indigenous native" groups.

Choice of "Typical" Fora of Struggle

A final powerful indicator for "indigeneity" is whether a group seeks to voice its grievances in public fora which are typically selected for that purpose by indigenous peoples. Failure to do so may reveal that the group in question feels that it compromises its political demands by association with the latter[15]. There is yet another, more visceral reason why some leaders from groups that seek self-determination may not want to appear in the same places to air their grievances: if they come from a background that teaches them to despise tribal people, they may feel that any association with them is demeaning and, indeed, undermining established inter-ethnic power relations 'domestically'. This, I would argue, is one of the reasons why organizations such as the Moro National Liberation Front (MNLF) or the Moro Islamic Liberation Front (MILF) in Mindanao – who fight for self-determination over homelands that are inhabited by large tribal constituencies – have so far failed to make use of the common international fora which the peoples at their tribal periphery (in that case the Lumad) have used so often to press for homelands that would wrest power over their affairs from their former overlords' hands. Their selection of different venues for the internationalization of their cause, then, adds a third reason for not considering groups like the Moro or the Axamiya as "indigenous" in the proper sense of the word.

References

Benjamin, Geoffrey. 2002. "On Being Tribal in the Malay World", in: *Tribal Communities in the Malay World: Historical, Cultural and Social Perspectives.* Edited by Geoffrey Benjamin and Cynthia Chou, pp. 7-76. Leiden and Singapore: International Institute for Asian Studies (IIAS) and Institute of Southeast Asian Studies (ISEAS).

Mullick, Samar Bosu. 2001. "Indigenous Peoples and Electoral Politics in India: An Experience of Incompatibility", in : *Challenging Politics: Indigenous Peoples' Experiences with Political Parties and Elections.* IWGIA Document 104. Edited by Kathrin Wessensdorf, pp. 94-144. Copenhagen: International Work Group for Indigenous Affairs.

Burger, Julian 1987. Report from the Frontier: The State of the World's Indigenous Peoples. London: Zed Books.

Chaudhury, Sabyasachi Basu Ray, and Ashis K. Biswas. 1997. "A Diaspora is Made: The Jummas in North-East India", in: *Living on the Edge: Essays on the Chittagong Hill Tracts,* eds. Subir Bhaumik, Meghna Guhathakurta and Sabyasachi Basu Ray Chaudhury, pp. 139-166. Kathmandu: South Asia Forum for Human Rights and Calcutta Research Group.

Cobo, José Martinez. 1986. Study of the Problem of Indigenous Populations, Vol. 5, Conclusion, Proposals and Recommendations, UN Doc E/CN 4/Sub 2 1986.

Corntassel, Jeff J. 2003. Who is Indigenous? ,Peoplehood' and Ethnonationalist Approaches to Rearticulating Indigenous Identity. *Nationalism and Ethnic Politics 9(1):*75-100.

Devalle, Susana B. C. 1992. *Discourses of Ethnicity: Culture and Protest in Jharkand.* New Delhi: Sage Publications.

Falk, Richard. 1979. "The Rights of Peoples (In Particular Indigenous Peoples)", in: *The Rights of Peoples.* Edited by James Crawford,. Oxford. Clarendon Press

Goodland, Robert. 1982. Tribal Peoples and Development. Human Ecological Considerations. Washington D. C.: The World Bank.

Gurr, Ted Robert. 2000. *Peoples Versus States: Minorities at Risk in the New Century.* Washington D. C.: United States Institute of Peace Press.

Haller, Dieter. 2005. DTV *Atlas Ethnologie.* München: Deutscher Taschenbuch Verlag.

ICIHI. 1987. Indigenous Peoples: A Global Quest for Justice. A Report for the Independent Commission on International Humanitarian Issues. London: Zed Books.

IWGIA. 2001. "Indigenous Issues", http://www.iwgia.org, accessed 17 October 2001.

Keal, Paul. 2003. European Conquest and the Rights of Indigenous Peoples: The Moral Backwardness of International Society. Cambridge: Cambridge University Press, see "Defining indigenous peoples", pp. 6-16.

Kingsbury, Benedict. 1990. "The Applicability of the International Legal Concept of 'Indigenous Peoples' in Asia", in: The East Asia Challenge for Human Rights. Edited by J. R. Bauer and D. A. Bell, pp. 336-377. Cambridge: Cambridge University Press.

_____1998. "Indigenous Peoples in International Law: A Constructivist Approach to the Asian Controversy. American Journal of International Law 92(3):414-457.

Lewellen, Ted C. 1983. Political Anthropology: An Introduction. South Hadley, MASS: Bergin & Garvey.

Luithui-Erni, Shimreichon. Forthcoming. "Indigenous Peoples and Settlers in Arunachal Pradesh: Changing State Policies and Migration-Induced Conflicts in an Indian Frontier State", in: Colonization and Conflict: Contemporary Settlement Frontiers in South and Southeast Asia, ed. Danilo Geiger.

Maybury-Lewis, David. 2005. Defining ,Indigenous'. Cultural Survival Quarterly, Spring 2005:11.

Sills, Marc A. 1993. "Political Interaction between States and Indigenous Nations: A Point of Departure", in: Indigenous Peoples' Politics: An Introduction (Vol. I). Edited by Marc A. Sills and Glenn T. Morris, pp. 5-22. Boulder: University of Colorado, Fourth World Center for the Study of Indigenous Law and Politics [see ,The Fourth World of Indigenous Peoples and Nations', pp. 9f.]

Stavenhagen, Rodolfo. 1994. "Indigenous Rights: Some Conceptual Problems", in: Indigenous Peoples' Experiences with Self-Government. IWGIA Document No. 76. Edited by W. J. Assies and A. J. Hoekema, pp. 9-29. Copenhagen. International Work Group for Indigenous Affairs (IWGIA) and University of Amsterdam.

Tanner, Adrian. 1992. Le pouvoir et les peuples du quart monde. Anthropologie et Sociétés 16(3):17-35.

World Bank. 2005. Operational Policies 4.10 "Indigenous Peoples". Electronic Document, http://wbln0018.worldbank.org/Institutional/Manuals/OpManual.nsf/tocall/0F7D6F3F04DD70398525672C007D08ED?OpenDocument.

Notes

[1] Danilo Geiger is lecturer in Social Anthropology at the Institute of Social Anthropology, University of Zürich, Switzerland.

[2] Geiger, Danilo (ed.). forthcoming. *Colonization and Conflict: Contemporary Settlement Frontiers in South and Southeast Asia.* Zürich: University of Zürich. Another offshoot of the research project has come out recently in the IWGIA Documents series (Geiger, Danilo, ed., *Frontier Encounters: Indigenous Communities and Settlers in Asia and Latin America.* IWGIA Document No. 120. Subang Jaya, Malaysia and Copenhagen: IWGIA).

[3] The case studies included Lower Assam (Bodoland), Central Assam (Nagaon and Karbi Anglong Districts) and Arunachal Pradesh (Lohit District and the town of Tezu) in the Northeast of India; the Chittagong Hill Tracts of Bangladesh; Bukidnon province (Sinuda and surrounding municipalities) in the Philippines; and West Kalimantan (Sambas, Pontianak and Sanggau Districts) in Indonesia.

[4] An indigenous person, Cobo maintains, becomes such through self-identification as indigenous and by the fact that he/she is recognised and accepted by the populations concerned as one of their members (Cobo 1986: paragraph 381).

[5] The Permanent Forum on Indigenous Issues is not a standard-setting body but more a kind of overseeing and advisory body to the various UN organizations. While the UN Working Group on Indigenous Populations and the subsequent Open-ended Working Group on the Draft Declaration on Indigenous Peoples Rights did set standards opposing internal colonization, groups that seek secession from an existing state usually address fora like the United Nations Decolonisation Committee which hears cases pertaining to the dwindling number of remaining European colonies (examples: New Caledonia, East Timor). Groups that fell victim to acts of post-colonial invasion and the change of international boundaries through conquest (like the Tibetans) have preferred to speak to the United Nations Human Rights Commission (Gray 1995:54f.). Yet other groups have put their faith in fora that do not belong to the United Nations circuit at all, like the Moro of the Southern Philippines who took their case to a forum which is frequented by co-religionists (the Organisation of the Islamic Conference, OIC To a limited extent, indigenous organizations also started to make use of the former Human Rights Commission (now Human Rights Council) and some of its Treaty Bodies, like the Committee on the Elimination of Racial Discrimination (CERD).

[6] The outcry over our resurrection of this strongly contested term may be somewhat less when one considers that even the iconic Cobo definition (Cobo 1986: paragraphs 379-380) contains a reference to the groups in question "living under a tribal system". And even Robert Coulter, whose organization, the ‚Indian Law Resource Center', has been prominently involved in standard-setting activities at the United Nations, showed his infatuation with purely circumstantial understandings of "indigeneity" when he quipped – pressed to come up with a handy shorthand definition – "indigenous peoples are Indians and people like them" (Corntassel 2003:89).

[7] Examples are the countless Malay sultanates along the shores of Sumatra and Borneo, the Maranao and Maguindanao polities on Mindanao, the Meitei kingdom of Manipur and that of the Ahom in Assam in Northeast India, or the small princely states of Luang Prabang, Vieng Chan and Champassak in 18th and 19th century Laos.

[8] See also Stavenhagen (cited in Falk 1979:18) to whom indigenous peoples are „the original inhabitants of a territory who, because of historical circumstances (generally conquest and/or colonization by other people), have lost their sovereignty and have become subordinated to the wider society and the state over which they exercise no control"".

[9] Acknowledging this difficulty, Kingsbury (1999:373), for instance, resolved to de-emphasize the criterion of historical continuity by excluding it from the canon of „essential requirements"" for indigeneity.

[10] On the meaning of the term, see Xaxa in this volume, p. 227

[11] The World Bank in its Draft Operational Policies (the so-called OP 4.10) of 2001 has taken

the opposite view, and has drawn considerable criticism from indigenous organizations and indigenous rights advocates for that matter (World Bank 2001, quoted in Corntassel 2003:87, in this volume p. 62).

[12] Once again, Kingsbury (1998:371ff.) leads the way. He accounts for the complex nature of many local power situations and their being contingent on changing politico-legal environments by scaling down the comparative weight of ‚non-dominance' as an indicator, making it a „relevant indicia"" rather than an „essential requirement"".

[13] if not dominant, because both under the Sukarno and Suharto dispensations, they had to share power with the Javanese who were strongly over-represented both in the army and the bureaucracy on the Outer Islands.

[14] These forces are organized in ULFA, the United Liberation Front of Assam.

[15] As the United Nation's Permanent Forum on Indigenous Issues and the former Working Group on Indigenous Populations (UNWGIP) are usually concerning themselves with demands for *internal* self-determination, ethnonationalists who aspire to secession from existing nation-states usually choose to address different bodies (like the United Nations Decolonisation Committee) which more adequately reflect the nature of their cause.

Colonialism, Indigeneity and the Brao

Ian G. Baird[1]

Most native English speakers use the term "indigenous peoples " without thinking twice, let alone pondering the origin of the concept, questioning its meaning, or considering the political implications of its application. However, the reality is that the meaning of "indigenous" is far from obvious or simple, and is complex and frequently in flux. Like so many other identities, it is often contested. Some fully support the concept of "indigenous", others recognise that indigenous people exist but resist efforts by certain groups to be classified as "indigenous", and there are those who do not recognise the concept of "indigenous peoples" at all.

Even for those who accept the concept, there is not a universally recognised definition for "indigenous peoples", and it might come as a surprise to some that many indigenous activists do not advocate creating such a definition at the United Nations level (see Bowen 2000). Instead, they insist that indigenous people should be able to rely on "self-identification" to determine who is "indigenous" (see Erni 2006; Daes 1996 and in this volume). However, there are those who believe that a definition of "indigenous peoples" could be useful for securing peoples' rights[2]. Some see such definition as being useful for limiting those who can identify as "indigenous", because if anyone can claim to be "indigenous", the value of the designation would be greatly diminished, especially in relation to the land and resource rights claimed by those who identify as being indigenous (Kingsbury 1998; Corntassel 2003, both also in this volume).[3]

The meaning of the term "indigenous" has evolved since it was first applied by Europeans at the end of the nineteenth century. Initially, its use was fundamentally embedded within European colonialism, with all those "Others" from European colonies being classified as "indigenous" (Daes 1996, and in this volume). "Indigenous" was about separating the Europeans from non-Europeans, it was not about clarifying differences between peoples in the "colonies".

However, the use of "indigenous" has changed, and in 1938 it had already been given a different meaning by the Pan-American Union, the predecessor of today's Organization of American States. The Union declared that, "indigenous populations, as descendants of the first inhabitants of the lands which today form America, and in order to offset the deficiency in their physical and intellectual development, have a preferential right to the protection of the public authorities" (ibid.: para 15, in this volume p. 33).

Apart from referring to the first inhabitants of an area, "indigenous" has frequently been employed to denote marginalised and vulnerable peoples living within state borders dominated by other peoples, including those who may not be the "first peoples" to the particular geographical spaces where they presently live. The displacement of these peoples has frequently been associated with attempts by others to control them and their territories (Daes 1996, and in this volume).

As Christian Erni (2006) has pointed out, the two above-mentioned concepts of indigeneity—being the original inhabitants and being marginalised and vulnerable—have dominated conceptions of "indigenous peoples" for decades, and continue to have a significant influence in many parts—and an increasing number of parts—of the world today. Most Asian governments, however, do not explicitly recognise the concept of indigenous. They tend to either identify everyone as being indigenous, since all people are considered "first inhabitants", or they argue that there are no "indigenous peoples" in their countries, because European colonialism has ended, the existence of which "indigenous" is fundamentally rooted. This concept is known as the "salt water theory" because it postulates that only those who travel overseas are "colonial". This is the basis, for example, of China's position (Erni 2006).

Andrew Gray, the former director of International Work Group for Indigenous Affairs (IWGIA), considered the experience of being colonised to be fundamental to indigenous identities, but his position was quite different from that of the Chinese government. For him, the concept of indigenous,

> "refers to the quality of a people relating their identity to a particular area and distinguishing them culturally from other, 'alien' peoples who came to the territory subsequently. These indigenous peoples are 'colonized' in the sense of being disadvantaged and discriminated against. Their right to self-determination is their way of overcoming these obstacles" (1995: 37).

Gray's concept certainly expands the scope of what we consider to be "colonialism", going beyond "salt water theory", and including what some call "internal colonisation" (see Hechter 2007[1975]; Evans 1992), which is essentially the domination of marginalised groups by other groups of people who occupy the same nation state. Linking indigenous peoples with colonialism is useful for positioning people in the context of their relationships with others, rather than essentialising their place of origin. This is important, as many groups have been displaced from their "original places" by those who have tried to dominate them, thus putting them at a fundamental "geographical disadvantage" if only their place of origin is adopted as the primary means of categorising them. Forcing people to move from a particular area should not be grounds for extinguishing their "indigenous" rights.

Michael Watts, in the *Dictionary of Human Geography* (4th edition), defines colonialism as, "The establishment and maintenance of rule, for an extended period of time, by a sovereign power over a subordinate and alien people that is separate from the ruling power" (2000: 93). Colonisation, the physical settlement of people from the imperial centre to the colonial periphery, is frequently a part of colonialism, but not necessarily. Colonialism is, more fundamentally, characterised by political and legal domination, relations of economic and political dependence, imperial exploitation of colonies, and racially based inequality (Watts 2000).

Imperialism is a term closely associated with colonialism. Edward Said (1994: 9) defines imperialism as "The practice, the theory, and the attitudes of a dominating metropolitan center ruling a distant territory". He believes that colonialism is almost always the consequence of imperialism, but that it involves the "implanting of settlements on distant territories." In other words, colonialism always involves issues associated with gaining control of territory. In addition, imperialism and colonialism do not only involve "distant territories", but also groups that are closer to each other. Colonialism, therefore, involves one group gaining at least some control over territories apart from the ones where they come from. It seems that some have unnecessarily emphasised geographical distance when it comes to defining colonialism or imperialism.

Watts (2000: 93) understands colonialism to be "unequal territorial relationships among states based on subordination and domination...typically associated with distinct forms of contemporary capitalism such as the emergence of monopolies and transnational corporations." Moreover, as indicated by Gregory (2000: 612-3), post-colonial studies—the inquiry of the impacts of colonialism on peoples in the past and its ramifications for people in the present—have typically been concerned with "the period between the sixteenth and twentieth centuries, which has been marked by the expansion and contraction of European empires, the consolidation of a capitalist world-economy and the formation of a colonial, colonizing modernity."

In order to effectively link the concepts of "indigenous peoples" and colonialism, it is important to examine the concepts of "pre-colonial", "colonial" and "post-colonial", which are problematic when considering the experiences of many "indigenous peoples". That is because these terms are framed in ways that privilege European colonialism as opposed to other kinds of domination, including "internal colonialism". For example, "pre-colonial" is typically understood to represent the period before European arrival, "colonial" to represent the period of direct European domination, and "post-colonial" to represent the period after formal European domination has ended.

Scholars of "post-colonialism" typically emphasise the lingering impacts of colonialism long after it has formerly ceased to exist. As important as this work continues to be for understanding both the past and present circumstances, the idea of post-colonialism does not explicitly point to the various forms of colonialism, "internal" or otherwise, that frequently follow periods of European colonialism (Gregory 2000; Young 2003). Post-colonialism contrasts "the West" with the "the colonies", and while this dichotomy is important, it is crucial to consider attempts to dominate others closer to home. In other words, because post-colonialism clearly emphasises the long-term effects of European colonialism, it tends to privilege European colonialism without looking for other forms of colonialism. Similarly, "pre-colonial" suggests a period of relatively less domination before the Europeans arrived, something that is frequently far from the truth. As pointed out by Watts (2000), colonialism is generally considered to be the subjection of non-European societies as a result of European expansion, organisation and rule, although Japanese and American colonialisms are frequently recognised.

As I have argued in my doctoral dissertation in relation to the Brao ethnic group (see Baird 2008a), the above concepts of colonialism deserve to be analysed, deconstructed and reconstructed to better comprehend the experiences of small minority groups like the Brao, as they have tended to experience a series of colonialisms rather than just having been dominated by European powers. Even the concept of "internal colonialism" needs to be re-assessed, as while it is useful for making it clear that colonialism can occur at various scales, including within particular nation states, it continues to privilege the nation state by showing that colonialism can occur inside particular countries. In fact, colonialism can occur in ways that variously involve actors and spaces in one's own countries as well as those living in other countries.

In this article, I consider the ethnic Brao people of northeastern Cambodia and southern Laos, and argue that the framework encompassing the concepts of "pre-colonial", "colonial" and "post-colonial" are not particularly useful for understanding their experiences. Instead, these terms privilege European colonialism and in turn make it difficult to conceptualise other forms of colonialism that lie outside of this framework. The Brao people themselves do not view history in terms of pre-colonial, colonial and post-colonial. Instead, they see themselves as having been dominated over many historical periods, and by many different groups, beginning with the Khmer, Lao and Thai before the French arrived, taking place during the time they were in power, and continuing since Laos and Cambodia gained independence from France was achieved in 1953-1954. For the Brao, they have been affected by a series of colonialisms, each with its own objectives and methods for achieving them, and particular social and spatial implications. Thus, I argue that the present period should not be represented as "post-colonial" in the normative sense. It is simply a different period of colonialism, one of many that have come and gone in recent history.

The Brao

The Brao are a Mon-Khmer language-speaking ethnic group found mainly in Attapeu and Champasak Provinces in southern-most part of Laos, and Ratanakiri and Stung Treng Provinces in northeastern Cambodia. There are approximately 60,000 Brao people, of which about 35,000 live in northeastern Cambodia, 25,000 live in southern Laos. There is one Brao village in the Central Highlands of Vietnam. The Brao are broadly divided into nine sub-groups (see Figure 1). The Kreung, Umba, Brao Tanap, Kavet and Lun are found in Cambodia, while the Hamong, Ka-nying, Jree, Kavet and Lun are found in southern Laos. Until recently, the Brao were all Animists who were subsistence-oriented swidden cultivators who relied heavily on hunting, fishing and the collection of Non-Timber Forest Products (NTFPs). However, the livelihoods of Brao people have been variously altered over recent history (Baird 2008a).

The Brao and Colonialism

Here, the crux of my argument is that for members of ethnic groups like the Brao, who do not dominate any particular nation state, and have long been dominated by those from various ethnic or cultural groups in different periods over history, are people whose identities have been fundamentally shaped by various forms of colonialism. Each form of colonialism has had different objectives and has involved varying strategies, each with their concomitant social and spatial repercussions. However, colonialism began long before the French arrived, even if the colonialisms of the past were quite different from the colonialisms implemented by the French and others since them.

The following is a brief overview of some of the periods of colonialism that have affected the Brao in the past.

The Rise and Fall of the Khmer

It is difficult to know to what extent lowlanders influenced life in the highlands in the distant past. However, between the fifth and eighth centuries the Khmer of the Chenla Era inhabited and largely controlled present-day northeastern Cambodia and southern Laos. We know from the stone ruins that can still be found, but it is more difficult to understand the influence they had on the Brao. Still, the Khmer were almost certainly involved in the slave trade, and the Brao, like other highlanders, were most likely victimised (Bourotte 1955; Baird 2008a).

Between the ninth and the fourteenth centuries the Khmer of Angkor continued to dominate what is now northeastern Cambodia and southern Laos. Again,
it is difficult to know the exact nature of the relationship between the Brao and
the Khmer, but it likely that slave labour was used to build the amazing temples
of Angkor, and that Brao people made up some of these slaves. A Chinese visitor
to the Angkor court at Siem Reap in 1296-7, Chou Ta-Kuan (1987), mentions
the "savages" that fed the markets of the country and the capital, and the fierce
warriors that defended the highlands from outsiders. Ta-Kuan (1987) reported
that lowland Khmer had large numbers of slaves. Some wealthy families had more
than one hundred, and apparently only the poorest did not have any. These slaves
were captured in the mountains, and were considered to be of a different race. According to Ta-Kuan (1987: section 9, n.p.), "So looked down on are these wretches
that when, in the course of a dispute, a Cambodian is called "Chuang" [the name
used for highlanders] by his adversary, dark hatred strikes to the marrow of his
bones."

The fifteenth century saw the decline of the Angkor Kingdom and in 1432
Angkor in Siem Reap was abandoned as the Khmer capital, largely due to a series
of defeats at the hands of the Siamese (Chandler 1991; Coedes 1968). The Khmer
gradually withdrew from today's southern Laos and northeastern Cambodia, or
became assimilated with local Lao populations.

The Lao and the Siamese

The sixteenth and seventeenth centuries saw the Lao gradually gain control
in the lowlands of present-day southern Laos and northeastern Cambodia. However, it was not until the beginning of the eighteenth century that the Kingdom
of Champasak was established and *Chao* Soisysamout was appointed as its first
King. This marked the beginning of the "golden age" of independent Champasak,
but in 1778 Siamese troops marched in and forced Champasak to become its
vassal. The Siamese maintained control over Champasak for over a hundred years,
until it was finally forced to cede territories east of the Mekong River to France in
1893 (Archaimbault 1961).

During the pre-French Lao and Siamese periods, the slave trade proliferated
in the lowlands adjacent to Brao areas. This undoubtedly had a significant influence on the social and spatial organisation of the Brao, as they were frequently
victims of slave raids, either by the Lao or Siamese, or by other highlanders who
either wanted vengeance or hoped to gain wealth and power by capturing people
who could then be traded to the Lao and Siamese (Baird 2008a).

The Lao gained increasing influence over the highlanders, and managed to
convince or coerce at least some Brao villages to enter into tribute relations with
them. The Siamese wanted tribute to be paid to them by the Lao in gold, but most
highlanders did not have enough gold to do so. Therefore, in places like Attapeu
highlanders were allowed to pay in slaves instead, which the Lao nobles traded,

in turn, for gold that could then be sent to Bangkok. The Brao believe that this practice resulted in massive changes in life in the highlands, as it led to more attacks and insecurity in the uplands, and forced small communities to consolidate and locate themselves in large fortified villages in order to protect themselves against slave raids.

The slave trade had a profound influence on the Brao throughout the Siamese period, and while attempts were made by the Siamese to ban slave raiding in Champasak, Attapeu and Stung Treng a few years before the French gained control, those attempts led to considerable upheaval amongst the highland population and even increased slave raiding and general anarchy, as the Brao and other highlanders came to realise that the Lao were being prevented from slave raiding and controlling of the "trade" (Baird 2008a).

While the Lao and their Siamese minders did not attempt to control the highlands in the same way that others would in the future, they did gain some territorial control over the highlands. If they had not, it would have been impossible to elicit tribute from the highlanders. Also, at least partial control of the highlands was necessary to facilitate the slave raiding and trading, and other forms of commerce that took place at various times during the eighteenth and nineteenth centuries.

The periods outlined above are typically considered to be "pre-colonial", since they occurred prior to the arrival of European powers, in this case the French. However, were they really "pre-colonial"? On the one hand, the Lao were being dominated by the Siamese, but crucially for this article, the Lao and the Siamese both exerted certain levels of territorial control over the Brao in the highlands. While the circumstances were quite different from what would follow, for the Brao the Siamese and Lao are but some of the many players who have tried to dominate them over history. In relation to the Brao, and in terms of power relations, they were indeed colonial powers.

The French

The situation for the Brao changed dramatically when the French gained control over the territories east of the Mekong River. On the one hand, the French gradually brought an end to the slave trade and reduced the frequency of village-to-village attacks. This made it possible for the Brao to gradually abandon the fortified villages where they lived during the Siamese era, and organise themselves in small groups located in swidden areas spread throughout the land. For this reason, many Brao claim that the French period was relatively peaceful and "cool".

However, on the other hand, the French instituted their own particular forms of colonial control, as the Lao and Siamese had done before them. The tribute relations of the past were over. Instead, the French demanded that the Brao pay taxes and contribute two weeks of corvée labour annually. The French also hoped to "civilise" the highlanders, and to encourage them to engage more in trade and commerce. The French also encourage ethnic Chinese and Vietnamese people to immigrate in order to encourage commerce in the region (Guérin 2003; Baird 2008a).

Crucially, it was during the French period that the concept of nation-state became dominant, and the territorial boundaries between Siam and French Indochina became established (Winichakul 1994). The French also extracted Stung Treng Province and gave it to French Cambodia at the end of 1904 (Breazeale 2002). These administrative territorial changes were important. Whereas the uplands had been separated from the lowlands in the minds of many prior to the arrival of the French, during the French period both the lowlands and uplands became consolidated into particular political administrative systems that to at least some extent integrated the two spatially, thus providing a new and powerful form of spatial justification for lowland domination of those in the uplands.

The Japanese

In June 1940 France fell to Nazi Germany, and during the same year imperial Japan gained increasing control of mainland Southeast Asia. First, they demanded that the French Vichy government provide the Japanese military with access to their land, port and air space. Before long, Japanese troops occupied much of Indochina. The French could do little to counter Japanese power, and instead chose to abide by Japanese demands. However, in March 1945 the Japanese decided to change their strategy, abandon their tenuous relationship with Vichy, and use force to gain full control over French Indochina (Robbins 2000). But Japanese rule lasted just six months, and in August 1945 they surrendered and withdrew from Indochina (Dommen 1985).

While the particular variety of colonialism imposed by the Japanese was somewhat different from what the French demanded, the Japanese had relatively little impact on the Brao, because of the remote areas where the Brao mainly lived, and because the Japanese rule was short-lived. The most important impact of Japanese rule was to show the local population that the French were not invincible; that the Europeans could be beaten by other Asians. Nationalism was on the rise.

The Vietnamese

When the Japanese left Indochina, Lao and Khmer nationalists attempted to gain independence, thus preventing the French from returning. However, the French were able to re-establish their control over its former territories by the end of 1945.

The Viet Minh Communists under Ho Chi Minh were the main opposition to the French. After World War II they tried to develop the movement in neighbouring Laos and Cambodia, but they were initially not very successful in recruiting people to the movement. Between 1946 and 1948 there was little progress (Engelbert 2004; Heder 1979), but it was finally acknowledged by the Viet Minh that they had used inappropriate tactics. They had made little effort to consider important cultural and linguistic factors, thus making them largely ineffective outside of urban Vietnamese groups (Engelbert 2004; Baird 2008a). This changed in 1949, and as more Vietnamese Viet Minh operatives "went native", the movement gradually gained local support in southern Laos and northeastern Cambodia (Goscha 2005; Baird 2008a). Many Brao were amongst the first to cooperate with the Vietnamese Communists, both in Laos and Cambodia. Brao areas were also some of the first declared "liberated zones" in southern Laos. The first revolutionary district was established at Dakchung in 1949 (Engelbert 2004), which is a bit north of where the Brao live, in present-day Xekong Province, but by 1953 Phouvong Neua and Phouvong Tai Districts had been established in Brao areas in present-day eastern Attapeu Province (Baird 2008a). All the Party cadres and powerful political and military leaders at that time were Vietnamese, whereas the Brao occupied lower positions. The administrative system adopted came from Hanoi; it was not developed by the Brao, or even in consultation with them. Thus, the Viet Minh's control of Brao spaces along the Vietnamese/Lao/Cambodia border represents a particular variety of colonialism. Like those before them, Viet Minh control had its own particular social and spatial implications.

At the end of 1953, after the French attempted to end the military conflict by nominally handing control of Laos and Cambodia to pro-French local governments in each country, the Viet Minh remained dissatisfied with the situation and continued with the military struggle. Therefore, on December 30-31, 1953 a predominantly Vietnamese Communist force gained control of Attapeu town after fierce fighting, and over the next few months the Viet Minh were able to forcefully take Salavan in southern Laos and Veun Say, Siem Pang and Stung Treng in northeastern Cambodia (Baird 2008a). One observer noted that it was strange that the Viet Minh were fighting the French over a land that neither side had the right to control. Essentially, one colonial power (the Vietnamese) was fighting against another colonial power (the French), with both paradoxically claiming to represent the interests of the natives.

Khmer and Lao "Independence", Not "Post-Colonial" for the Brao

The 1954 Geneva Accords officially ended the French colonial period in Indochina. But was it really the beginning of "post-colonialism" for the Brao? On the one hand, the period of direct European control was coming to an end, even if the legacies of French colonialism, as with other forms of colonialism that pre-date the French, continue to be important for understanding present-day circumstances. In fact, Post-colonial theory frequently emphasises the enduring influences of European colonialism on their former colonies, at various levels (Young 2003). In this case, however, areas populated by Brao people were put under the nominal control of others who had somehow gained the political legitimacy required to manoeuvre themselves into power, but who were foreign to the places where the Brao lived. If one privileges the idea of the nation-state, one could say that external colonialism was replaced by "internal colonialism". But, in fact, I think the term "internal colonialism" gives too much legitimacy to dominate groups within particular countries to control the lives of others. The idea of "internal" suggests that it is an "internal" problem between different parties that are classified as being in the same national space. However, since the Brao had previously not considered themselves to be part of the Khmer state, and throughout history have frequently tried to remain outside the Khmer's dominion, their taking control over Brao spaces does not represent "internal colonialism" but rather another form of colonialism, with one group trying to gain a level of administrative and territorial control over another. The creation of nation-states serves to legitimise this kind of behaviour, in the name of "national unity" and "nation-building".

In Laos, the Geneva Accords provided the Pathet Lao (Lao Communists) with the provinces of Phongsaly and Sam Neua in northern Laos, which lead many Communists from Brao areas to travel to the Pathet Laos' new strongholds in the north. This included many Brao. However, some Communist Brao operatives continued to work secretly with the Pathet Lao gathering intelligence and otherwise monitoring the situation, as a fragile coalition government was established that brought communist, neutralist and rightist groups together. In any case, Brao areas came under the control of the rightists, led by Prince Boun Oum of the Champasak royal family. The Royal Lao Government's control over Brao areas represented yet another form of colonialism. For example, in Brao areas in southern Laos, American aid was used to launch a pilot project to try to "civilise" some Brao in Attapeu beginning as early as 1958. This included resettling three villages into a single community, and forcing them to adopt lowland wet-rice cultivation and teak plantation cultivation (Baird 2008a).

In Cambodia, the 1954 Geneva Accords did not allow the Communists to gain any autonomous areas like what was negotiated for the Lao. This led many Cambodian Communists to leave Cambodia and travel to Hanoi to receive further training under the tutelage of the Vietnamese Communists (Rathie 2006). Norodom Sihanouk gained the upper hand and established the *Sangkum Reastr Niyum* (People's Socialist Community) political Party, which gained full control over the newly independent Cambodia in the name of "neutralism" (Short 2004). As in Laos, Sihanouk's rule over the Brao in Cambodia represented yet another form of colonial expansion. His government moved many Brao from the northern highlands of northeastern Cambodia to the lowlands in the late 1950s, where efforts were made to teach them Khmer and convince them to adopt lowland forms of agriculture and livelihoods. Sihanouk's government also expropriated land and labour from the Brao to establish commercial rubber plantations in Brao areas of Ratanakiri Province. As might be expected, these actions were not appreciated by many highlanders, and would eventually be the fodder that would fuel the flame of revolution.

The Second Indochina War

In Laos, the coalition government of the late 1950s did not last long, and soon rightist elements seized control, leading the Pathet Lao and its Vietnamese allies to restart its military struggle in 1959. In response, President John F. Kennedy affirmed the US's support for Laos' neutrality, but the America's actions were far from neutral. Soon, they were militarily supporting the Royal Lao Government. On May 19, 1959, on Ho Chi Minh's birthday, the trail that borrowed his name began to be expanded significantly. Initially, multiple footpaths, roads, and river ways served mainly as lines of communication for communist couriers and small combat units, but by 1962 the network was transporting large quantities of supplies to the Viet Cong rebels in South Vietnam (Vongsavanh 1978).

In 1962 the second Geneva Accords were signed, a move that was supposed to keep Laos and Cambodia neutral and keep both countries from becoming increasingly embroiled in the armed conflict in Vietnam. Both the US and the North Vietnamese were prohibited from locating military personal in either country. But the stakes were too high, and both sides almost immediately violated the Accords. The North Vietnamese were already using the Ho Chi Minh Trail to transport people and supplies from North to South Vietnam via southern Laos, and this was not about to stop. The Americans were concerned about openly violating the Accords, but were not about to let the North Vietnamese gain the upper hand. Therefore, the Central Intelligence Agency (CIA) of the USA was given the job of supporting America's political and military interests in the country, and started placing non-uniformed operatives in Laos (Conboy 1995). Many were officially aid workers but were actually working to train and arm paramilitary units of highlanders to work against the Communists and particularly the Ho Chi Minh Trail. As "road watchers", many worked to support the aerial bombing campaign against the Communists, both in northern and southern Laos. The mountainous part of the Annamite Range in Laos began to be bombed by the Royal Lao Air Force (RLAF) and the US Air Force (USAF) in 1962, although initially at relatively low levels. Full-scale USAF bombing reportedly began on April 17, 1964, and over the coming years the intensity and scale of bombing would greatly increase. After the Ho Chi Minh Trail was extended into Cambodia in 1965-1966, named "Sihanouk Trail", bombing in Brao parts of southern Laos expanded even more (Van Staaveren 1993).

As the conflict intensified, the Pathet Lao and their Vietnamese mentors gained administrative control over the Brao populated areas in southern-eastern Laos, which overlapped with the territory necessary for maintaining the Trails. While many Brao supported them, the Vietnamese did not tolerate those who did not. They were determined to "liberate" South Vietnam, and any opposing objections by highlanders like the Brao were not going to prevent them from achieving their goal. In essence, the Vietnamese Communists, despite being fundamentally anti-imperialist, paradoxically imposed their own form of colonialism in Brao areas in southern Laos.

The Americans also imposed their own form of colonialism in Brao areas in southern Laos, especially after the establishment of the Sihanouk Trail in 1966. Kong Mi, a little-known Brao settlement in southeastern Attapeu Province, became the focus of the CIA in Brao areas. Hundreds of young Brao men were recruited and trained by the CIA to operate against the Communists. In particular, Brao "road-watchers" were employed to monitor activities along the Sihanouk Trail, so as to provide military intelligence useful for organising the bombing campaign against the Trail (Baird 2008a). Fully funded by the USA, they were flown near the Trail with American aircraft (see Robbins 2000). As with the Vietnamese, for the Americans the stakes were high, and while they were happy to cooperate with all the Brao willing to take their money and follow their lead, it was the American vision of things that was expected to prevail. Although the Brao aligned with the Americans were not particularly interested in fighting the Brao aligned with the Communists, the Brao view was not accepted by the Americans. For them communism was a threat that could not be tolerated. People were either with them or against them. US power represented yet another form of colonialism over the Brao, one that would last until the withdrawal of the US from the war was negotiated in 1973.

In Cambodia, the situation was somewhat different. Sihanouk was able to maintain a strong hold over the country for many years, and the Communists had many setbacks in the 1950s and 1960s. In fact, it was not until 1968 that the Cambodian Communists, who later became known as the Khmer Rouge, launched military activities against the Cambodian government, and even then, without the support of the North Vietnamese or the communist Chinese, who continued to support Norodom Sihanouk's neutralist policies. The Vietnamese Communists were particularly concerned to not upset Sihanouk, as they wanted to maintain their "sanctuary" bases in northeastern Cambodia, which Sihanouk had largely been tolerating (Short 2004; Caldwell and Lek 1973). However, the Brao were amongst the first strong supporters of the communist movement, and in the early 1960s the Khmer Rouge headquarters was located on Brao territory (Baird 2008a).

The situation changed in March 1970 when Sihanouk's cousin, Sirik Matak, and Sihanouk's long-time colleague, Lon Nol, orchestrated a bloodless coup that toppled Sihanouk from power when he was traveling in the Soviet Union. All of a sudden the Khmer Rouge's military campaign against the Cambodian government began to be supported by both the North Vietnamese and China (Short 2004). Within just a couple of months the Lon Nol government, which was suffering serious military losses, took the strategic decision to withdraw from the northeast, and essentially cede the region to communist forces (Sutsakhan 1978). This in turn opened up the northeast to intense US aerial bombardment, which had already begun in the late 1960s, but was significantly expanded once the northeast became a "free-fire zone" for B-52 carpet bombing, which continued until well into 1973 (Shawcross 1979).

Brao parts of northeastern Cambodia were amongst the first to be "liberated" by the Khmer Rouge. Although many were the trusted body guards of Pol Pot, no highlanders were among the top-echelon of the Khmer Rouge (Baird 2008a; Colm 1996). None were Brao, and before long directives from the top were being variably enforced on the Brao without any consultation with them. The details of how people were to organise their lives was being increasingly dictated from ethnic Khmer people above, turning the revolution originally supported by the Brao into something quite different, and not to their liking. The connections between many Brao revolutionaries and Vietnamese Communists also turned them into a threat in the eyes of some Khmer Rouge leaders. Ultimately, at around the same time that Phnom Penh fell to the Khmer Rouge, in April and May 1975, thousands of Brao people, mainly from Veun Say and Taveng, fled the increasingly draconian policies of the Khmer Rouge and fled en masse to Laos and Vietnam, where they became political refugees (Baird 2008a).

The Khmer Rouge and the Brao

The Brao who remained in Cambodia were forced to endure almost four years of the most draconian experiment in communist social-transformation that the world has ever known, eclipsing even Stalin's Soviet transformation and Mao's "Great Leap Forward" in China. Pol Pot and his cohorts attempted to socially and spatially alter all aspects of life of the people. They wanted rapid and dramatic changes to occur, but their idealised vision did not bring about the socialist utopia that they hoped for. Instead, illness, starvation and brutal repression and punishment of even the smallest infractions of their rules devastated the country (Short 2004; Chandler 1991).

The Khmer Rouge period may not be seen by most as a colonial period, especially considering the anti-imperialist ideology of Pol Pot, but the level of control administrated on the Brao by the Khmer Communists from other parts of Cambodia can certainly be categorised as a particular form of colonialism. Brao people were no longer to conduct animist rituals, and were mainly forced to do lowland wet-rice agriculture instead of swidden agriculture. Hunting, fishing and NTFP gathering activities fundamentally changed. Families were separated, and every aspect of life, including where one lived, what one did, or even who one married, was determined by *Angkar*.

The Pathet Lao and the Brao

Shortly after Phnom Penh fell to the Khmer Rouge, the Communist Pathet Lao also managed to increasingly gain control over Laos, and this was fully achieved by mid-1975. On December 2, 1975 the Lao People's Democratic Republic (Lao PDR) was officially established.

The Brao at the former-CIA base at Kong Mi were forced to give up, and its leaders were sent to "re-education camps" in Attapeu. The new government was not as draconian as the Khmer Rouge, but they too were full of revolutionary fervour, and hoped for radical and rapid change. In particular, the government wanted to transform highlanders like the Brao from being what they believed to be "backward", and decided to do so by radically altering their spatial circumstances. Thousands of Brao and other highlanders in Attapeu Province were forcibly re-settled to the lowlands, where they were expected to take up wet-rice lowland agriculture and other aspects of lowland Lao livelihoods. The consequences were dire, and the Brao did not adapt well to their new lives. Food shortages were severe, and poverty increased rapidly. Within a few years many had become disillusioned and had moved back to the mountains. Some were allowed to return; others were prevented from doing so.

The Vietnamese Invasion of Cambodia

Meanwhile, in Cambodia, the leadership of the Khmer Rouge had become increasingly paranoid and was brutally persecuting anyone even vaguely suspected of conspiring against them. The purges probably affected the highlanders of the northeast less than people in other parts of the country (Colm 1996), but still many died, and a pervasive atmosphere of fear persisted. Finally, at the end of 1978 the Vietnamese decided to invade Cambodia in order to oust the increasingly aggressive Khmer Rouge from power. They were supported by troops of the Khmer National United Front for National Salvation (FUNSK), a group created with Vietnamese support to oppose the Khmer Rouge. Its members were mainly Cambodians who had fled the Khmer Rouge and were living in Vietnam and Laos. They included many highlanders, most of whom were Brao.

While the invading Vietnamese army who entered northeastern Cambodia were supported by armed FUNSK units of mainly ethnic Brao people who had fled to Vietnam and Laos in 1975, it was the Vietnamese who did the bulk of the fighting. In fact, they did not want the FUNSK to suffer many casualties, as they needed them to help establish a new government once the Khmer Rouge were gone. By January 7, 1979 Phnom Penh had fallen to the Vietnamese, and the remnants of the Khmer Rouge had fled to the Thai border.

Upon gaining control of most of Cambodia, the Vietnamese established a government at least nominally headed by Cambodian members of FUNSK, including Heng Samrin, Chea Sim and Hun Sen, all ethnic Khmer. Since the Vietnamese could not trust those who lived under Khmer Rouge rule in the late 1970s, many Brao who had lived in Laos and Vietnam since fleeing Cambodia in 1975 were given senior positions in the government, including all the top provincial governor positions in the northeast, including Ratanakiri, Stung Treng, Mondolkiri and Preah Vihear Provinces. However, the Vietnamese continued to maintain control over the government. Another era of colonialism had begun, and as with other forms of colonialism, the Vietnamese had their own group of collaborating locals, including both Khmer and highlanders like the Brao.

The 1980s were a very difficult period for all sides involved in the Cambodia conflict, even if for most of the population they were generally better than the preceding Khmer Rouge period. Still, the geo-political circumstances left the country isolated, with only those countries aligned with the Soviet Union recognising the government. The Khmer Rouge remained the representative of Cambodia at the United Nations. Internally, civil war tore the country apart. The Vietnamese army continued to support the Cambodian government based in Phnom Penh, who fought against the armed forces of the Government of Democratic Kampuchea (CGDK), a loose coalition made up of the Khmer Rouge's National Army of Democratic Kampuchea (NADK)[4], the Sihanouk-supported National Army of Sihanouk (ANS)[5] and Son Sann's Khmer People's National Liberation Front (KPNLF), based along the border with Thailand.

Oddly enough, the Brao and other highlanders were very much involved in the civil war. On the one hand, many became soldiers in the Cambodian army and fought on the frontlines against the armed forces of the CGDK. On the other side, many highlanders were Khmer Rouge soldiers. Thus, it turned out that in many cases Brao fought Brao. Many died on both sides.

During the 1980s the Brao were subjected to yet another era of colonialism, albeit different again from anything that been had experienced by the Brao to date. They had more freedom to engage in traditional religious and livelihood activities. They also had considerable political power, and relatively high positions in government. Yet they still did not maintain full control over their lives. Even though they maintained a certain level of human agency, they were part of a system that was fundamentally created by the Vietnamese. Security issues associated with the continuing civil war prevented many of the Brao repatriated from Laos in the early 1980s from returning to the mountains along the border with Laos.

Present-Day Laos

Although the Pathet Lao has continuously governed Laos since 1975, the late 1970s were characterised by efforts to introduce a socialist state, including collective farming. The early years were also characterised by internal strife, including efforts by right-wing rebels to topple the communist Government of Laos.

However, the Government of Laos soon realised that collective agriculture was not working, and more importantly, that it was not popular with the people. Thus, by the end of the 1970s private agriculture was allowed. These initial reforms were followed, in the mid to late-1980s, by important changes in the economic system of the country, including opening the economy to private investment. These reforms were dubbed the "New Economic Mechanism", or "chinthankan mai" in Lao. This brought on a new form of colonialism, one grounded in a one-Party communist political system, but also increasingly neoliberal economic principles.

For the Brao, the present form of colonialism has brought on its own social and spatial changes, and unfortunately for many, considerable hardships. Most of the Brao in the mountains have again been resettled to the lowlands since the early 1990s, often with terrible results (see Baird and Shoemaker 2005; 2007). Furthermore, the Brao are facing other dramatic changes, including those caused by large-scale commercial logging, the development of large hydroelectric dams (Baird 2008a), and most recently the expansion of Vietnamese large-scale rubber plantations into their lands.

Present-Day Cambodia

In 1988 the Vietnamese began withdrawing their troops from Cambodia, a task that was apparently completed by September 1989. This ended a decade of direct Vietnamese military occupation of Cambodia. Thousands of Vietnamese had died fighting against the Khmer Rouge, and the Vietnamese finally tired of the conflict, which went on much longer than anyone expected (Tomodo 1997). The historic "Agreements on the Comprehensive Political Settlement of the Cambodia Conflict", signed on October 23, 1991 in Paris, marked the beginning of the "Development Era", or *"samai aphiwat"*. The United Nations Transitional Authority in Cambodia (UNTAC) arrived in Cambodia. They managed to generally keep the peace, and were able to organise democratic elections in May 1993 as planned (United Nations 2003).

The "Development Era" of Cambodia was, as in Laos, founded on neoliberal economic principles, but unlike Laos, by multi-party democratic reform as well. The United Nations intended to liberate the people from the quagmire that the country had been in, but for the Brao it was less about empowerment than about a changing of the guard. A new age of colonialism had arrived. As the Khmer filled the vacuum left by the Vietnam, they increasingly gained control, often at the expense of the highlanders who were rapidly losing the power they wielded in the 1980s. What has followed since the early 1990s has not been particularly good for the Brao. Many have suffered from large dams built in Vietnam that had negatively impacted downstream parts of Cambodia (Wyatt and Baird 2007), commercial logging in their forests (Bottomley 2002), and the establishment of Virachey National Park (Baird 2008b). Some have gained economically from taking up cashew nut cash cropping for the market (Baird 2008a), but many have suffered as a result of efforts by mainly Khmer people from the south to take control of their land. Land alienation is ongoing on a large scale, either through tricking people out of their land, buying it at low prices, using their power to gain control of it, or simply by grabbing it with impunity (NGO Forum 2006; Baird 2008a).

There is much more that could be written about the social and spatial changes forced on the Brao during the present period, but it is not the purpose of this section to do that. Instead, the intention is simply to show that even today the Brao are subjected to particular forms of colonialisms, even though these versions of colonialism are not concretely manifesting as they did in the past.

Conclusions

The purpose of this article has been to briefly map out the ways in which ethnic Brao people in southern Laos and northeastern Cambodia have been subjected to various forms of colonialism over history, beginning long before the French arrived, and continuing up to the present. The Brao themselves do not recognise the classification, "pre-colonial", "colonial", and "post-colonial". They do not privilege European domination over what others have forced on them. For them there are simply a series of colonialisms, a series of attempts to socially and spatially (re)organise Brao life.

In fact, this is in line with recent tendencies towards expanding the definition of colonialism and not privileging the European experience. Jones and Philips (2005), for example, make the case for including pre-modern non-European imperialism, while Gregory (2004) shows that colonialism still exists in present-day Iraq, Afghanistan and Palestine. Here, I argue that colonialism influenced the Brao long before the arrival of the French, and has continued since the French left, right up to the present.

Some may argue that "colonialism" is not an appropriate way of describing all the forms of domination that the Brao have had to face, because the term colonialism represents a particular form of European domination over other parts of the world. Others might suggest that imperialism might be a better way of describing more localised forms of Brao domination by lowland Lao and Khmer. However, I believe that colonialism is an appropriate way of describing the experience as understood by the Brao because all the forms of domination described in this article include an element of territorial control, of spatial domination, of attempts to gain power over space, and it is the spatial element of domination that is crucial for defining colonialism.

Ultimately, it is the colonial experience that defines the Brao in relation to "Others", and it is the land and resources rights that can potentially be gained through identifying as indigenous that are potentially particularly liberating. In other words, indigeneity has a role in the decolonising of particular peoples by providing them with more opportunities for self-determination. While the Brao themselves do not have a particular term for "indigenous," and therefore generally do not refer to themselves as such, they generally do recognise themselves as an unique ethnic group, as people who have been colonised and otherwise dominated by others over history. The experiences of the Brao are very similar to the social and political processes observed elsewhere, in which peoples are frequently identified as indigenous because of their previously self-governing, territorially concentrated, culturally distinct societies (Kymlicka 2001). But it is their status, as being "colonised" that defines their relationships with dominant peoples and nation states, and this is what ultimately led people like Andrew Gray (1995) to emphasise the link between colonialism and the concept of "indigenous peoples". In fact, the Brao are generally quick to accept the label of "indigenous peoples", especially when they learn that the concept is potentially empowering to them. Of course, the details of the histories of peoples will inevitably be different, but it is a group's history of incorporation—or lack of integration into nation states—that is ultimately the basis for the creation of ethnic identities (Kymlicka 1995), including those associated with colonialism and political concepts, like "indigenous peoples".

Acknowlegements

Thanks for the Christian Erni and Stefan Ehrentraut for providing comments regarding an earlier draft of this article.

References

Archaimbault, C. 1961. L'histoire de Campasak. *Journal Asiatique* 294(4): 519-595.

Baird, I. G. 2008a. *Various Forms of Colonialism: The Social and Spatial Reorganisation of the Brao in Southern Laos and Northeastern Cambodia*. PhD Dissertation, Geography Department, The University of British Columbia, Vancouver, B.C., Canada, 493 pp.

Baird, I.G. 2008b (In Press). Controlling the margins: nature conservation and state power in northeastern Cambodia. In: Bourdier, Frederic (ed.), *In the Name of Development: Indigenous Populations in South-East Asia* Under Command.

Baird, I.G. & B. Shoemaker 2005. *Aiding or Abetting? Internal Resettlement and International Aid Agencies in the Lao PDR*. Probe International, Toronto, 44 pp.

Baird, I.G. & B.P. Shoemaker 2007. Unsettling experiences: internal resettlement and international aid agencies in the Lao PDR. *Development and Change* 38(5): 865-888.

Bottomley, R. 2002. Contested forests: an analysis of the highlander response to logging, Ratanakiri province, northeast Cambodia. *Critical Asian Studies* 34(4): 587-606.

Bourotte, B. 1955. Essai d'historie des populations montagnards du Sud-Indochinois jusqu' à 1945. *Bulletin de la Societé des Étude Indochinoises* 30(1): 1-116.

Bowen, J. R. 2000. Should We Have a Universal Concept of "Indigenous Peoples' Right"? Paper presented at the 2000 Symposium "Development and the Nation State", Washington University, St. Louis.

Bryant, R.L. 2000. Politicized moral geographies: debating biodiversity conservation and ancestral domain in the Philippines. *Political Geography* 19: 673-695.

Caldwell, M. & K.H. Tan 1973. *Cambodia in the Southeast Asian War.* Monthly Review Press, New York and London, 446 pp.

Chandler, D. P. 1991. *The Tragedy of Cambodian History. Politics, War, and Revolution since 1945.* Yale University Press, New Haven, 396 pp.

Coedes, G. 1968. *The Indianized States of Southeast Asia.* Translated by Susan Brown Cowing. East-West Center Press, Honolulu, 403 pp.

Colm, S. 1996. *The Highland Minorities and the Khmer Rouge in Northeastern Cambodia 1968-1979.* Document Center of Cambodia, Phnom Penh, 107 pp.

Conboy, K. (with J. Morrison) 1995. *Shadow War: The CIA's Secret War in Laos.* Paladin Press, Boulder, CO, 454 pp.

Corntassel, J. J. 2003. Who is indigenous? "Peoplehood' and ethnonationalist approaches to rearticulating indigenous identity. *Nationalism and Ethnic Politics* 9(1): 75-100

Daes, E.-I. A. 1996. *Standard-setting activities: Concerning the Rights of Indigenous People. Working Paper by the Chairperson-Rapporteur, Mrs. Erica-Irene A. Daes. On the concept of "indigenous people".* United Nations Economic and Social Council, UN Document E/CN.4/Sub.2/AC.4/1996/2.

Dommen, A.J. 1985. *Laos. Keystone of Indochina.* Westview Press, Boulder and London, 182 pp

Engelbert, T. 2004. From hunters to revolutionaries. The mobilisation of ethnic minorities in Southern laos and North-Eastern Cambodia during the First Indochina War (1945-1954). Pages 225-270 in Engelbert, T. & H. Dieter Kubitscheck (eds.), *Ethnic Minorities and Politics in Southeast Asia,* Peter Lang, Frankfurt am Main, Berlin, Bern, Bruxelles, New York, Oxford, and Wien.

Erni, C. 2006. The concept of indigenous peoples in Asia. Working paper for the workshop in Chiang Mai, March 1-3, 2006

Evans, G. 1992. Internal Colonialism in the Central Highlands of Vietnam. *Sojourn* 7(2): 274-304.

Goscha, C.E. 2005. Vietnam and the world outside. The case of Vietnamese communist advisors in Laos (1948-1962). *South East Asia Research* 12(2): 141-185.

Gray, A. 1995. The Indigenous Movement in Asia. In R.H. Barnes, A. Gray and B. Kingsbury (eds.), *Indigenous Peoples of Asia.* Association for Asian Studies, Inc. Monograph and Occasional Paper Series 48. Ann Arbor, Michigan.

Gregory, D. 2000. Post-colonialism. Pages 612-615 in Johnston, R.J., D. Gregory, G. Pratt & M. Watts (eds.), *The Dictionary of Human Geography* (4th edition), Blackwell Publishers, Oxford and Malden, MA.

Gregory, D. 2004. *The Colonial Present: Afghanistan, Palestine, Iraq.* Blackwell Publishing, Oxford, 367 pp.

Guérin, M. 2003. *Des Casques Blancs sur le Plateau des Herbes. Les Pacification des Aborigènes des Hautes Terres du Sud-Indochinois (1858-1940)*. PhD Thesis, Université de Paris, Paris, 334 pp.

Hechter, M. 2007 [1975]. *Internal Colonialism: The Celtic Fringe in British National Development*. UBC Press, Vancouver, 390 pp.

Heder, S. 1979. Kampuchea's armed struggle. The origins of an independent revolution. *Bulletin of Concerned Asian Scholars* 11(1): 2-24.

Jones, R. & R. Phillips 2005. Unsettling geographical horizons: exploring premodern and non-European imperialism. *Annals of the Association of American Geographers* 95(1): 141-161.

Kingsbury, B. 1998. "Indigenous Peoples" in International Law: A constructivist Approach to the Asian Controversy. *The American Journal of International Law* 92(3): 414-457.

Kymlicka, W. 1995. *Multicultural Citizenship. A Liberal Theory of Minority Rights*. Oxford University Press, Oxford.

Kymlicka, W. 2001. *Politics in the Vernacular. Nationalism, Multiculturalism, and Citizenship*. Oxford University Press, Oxford.

NGO Forum on Cambodia 2006. *Land alienation from Indigenous minority communities, Ratanakiri province, Cambodia*. Phnom Penh, Cambodia, 46 pp.

Robbins, C. 2000[1988]. *The Ravens. Pilots of the Secret War of Laos*. Asia Books Co., Bangkok, 476 pp.

Said, E. 1994. *Culture and Imperialism*, Alfred A. Knopf, New York, 380 pp.

Shawcross, W. 1979. *Side-Show. Kissinger, Nixon and the Destruction of Cambodia*, Pocket Books, New York, 464 pp.

Short, P. 2004. *Pol Pot: Anatomy of a Nightmare*. Henry Holt and Company, New York, 537 pp.

Sutsakhan, S. (Lt. Gen.). 1978. *The Khmer Republic at war and the final collapse*. Indochina Monographs. Reprinted by Dalley Book Service, Christiansburg, VA.

Ta-Kuan, C. 1987. *The Customs of Cambodia*. Translated by J. Gilman d'Arcy Paul from the French translation by Paul Pelliot. The Siam Society, Bangkok.

Tomoda, S. 1997. Detaching from Cambodia. Pages 134-153 in Morley, J.W. & M. Nishihara (eds.), *Vietnam Joins the World*, M.E. Sharpe, Armonk and London.

United Nations 2003. Completed Peace Keeping Operations. United Nations Transitional Authority in Cambodia [UNTAC]. February 1992–September 1993. http://www.un.org/Depts/dpko/dpko/co_mission/untac.htm

Van Staaveren, J. 1993. *Interdiction in Southern Laos 1960-1968: The United States Air Force in Southeast Asia*. Center for Air Force History, Washington, D.C., 360 pp.

Vongsavanh, S. 1978. *RLG Military Operations and Activities in the Laotian Panhandle,* Indochina Monographs, U.S. Army Center of Military History, Washington, D.C., 120 pp.

Young, R.J.C. 2003. *Postcolonialism. A Very Short Introduction.* Oxford University Press, Oxford and New York, 178 pp.

Watts, M. 2000. Colonialism. Pages 93-95 in Johnston, R.J., D. Gregory, G. Pratt & M. Watts (eds.), *The Dictionary of Human Geography* (4th edition), Blackwell Publishers, Oxford and Malden, MA.

Winichakul, Thongchai 1994. *Siam Mapped: A History of the Geo-Body of a Nation.* University of Hawaii, Honolulu, 228 pp.

Wyatt, A. B. & I.G. Baird 2007. Transboundary impact assessment in the Sesan River Basin: The case of the Yali Falls Dam. *International Journal of Water Resources Development* 23(3): 427-442.

Notes

[1] Ian G. Baird, originally from Canada, holds a Ph.D. in Geography and is the director of the Global Association for People and the Environment, a Canadian NGO active in Laos.

[2] The World Bank and Asian Development Bank have special indigenous peoples policies (Erni 2006), thus allowing those defined as indigenous with special rights. In addition, special land rights accorded to indigenous peoples in the Land Law in Cambodia is a good Asian example (NGO Forum on Cambodia 2006), as are 'ancestral domain' rights given to indigenous peoples in the Philippines (Bryant 2000).

[3] In this article the legitimacy of the concept of 'indigenous peoples' is accepted. It is recognised that a large number of varied peoples identify as 'indigenous', thus making it an important identity marker even if its meaning frequently varies and can be questioned. The concept of 'indigenous peoples' is recognised by many governments internationally and the United Nations system, thus making it meaningful. Here, I see the concept as being fundamentally political, and useful for supporting those who have been politically disadvantaged or marginalised as a result of their minority statuses in increasingly powerful nation states. Even if frequently ambiguous, the concept is seen, theoretically, as a 'strategic essentialism', a concept that is helpful for evening the playing field where the majority populations tend to have more political power.

[4] Under the control of the Party of Democratic Kampuchea (PDK)

[5] Under the control of the *Front Uni National pour un Cambodge Indépendant, Neutre, Pacifique, et Coopératif* (FUNCINPEC).

The Concept of Indigenous Peoples in India

Virginius Xaxa[1]

The use of the term "indigenous" or its equivalent like "aboriginal" or "autochthon" to describe groups that were formerly called tribes or tribal people has been in practice in anthropology for quite some time. However, the use of "indigenous" has now gone beyond the discipline of anthropology. International agencies are increasingly and extensively making use of this term and concept in their deliberations and discussions. Until very recent times, there was hardly any unease or anxiety over the use of the term "indigenous" in India. Hardly was it thought of any merit for discussion. This is no longer true. Its use is increasingly being challenged and there is considerable debate over the use and applicability of the term. Yet an attempt to define and conceptualize it is lacking. The concept or definition of indigenous peoples has come primarily from international agencies such as the ILO and UNO and much of the writings on the indigenous peoples' issues revolve around the concept worked out by them.

The Concept of Indigenous Peoples

In the deliberations of the international agencies, the term indigenous people/population was used for the first time in 1957 in ILO Convention 107. It gained wide currency after 1993 with the declaration of that year as the International Year of the Indigenous People. The ILO convention 107 made a distinction between tribal and semi-tribal populations on the one hand and indigenous tribal populations on the other. The former were described as populations who were at a less advanced stage of development than those reached by the other sections of national community and whose status is regulated wholly or partially by their own customs and traditions. The latter (indigenous) were however referred to as those categories of tribal or semi-tribal population who traced their descent from the population which inhabited the country or a geographical region to which the country belonged to at the time of conquest or colonisation and which, irrespective of their legal status live more in conformity with the social, economic and cultural institutions of that time than with institution of the nation/country to which they belong (Daes 1996 and in this volume; ILO 1989; Roy Burman/undated).

The ILO convention 169 adopted in 1989 is different in substantive terms from convention 107 with respect to basic conceptualisation. Firstly, the convention speaks of tribal/indigenous *peoples* instead of tribal/indigenous *populations* and explicitly states their distinctiveness from other sections of the national community in social, cultural and economic terms. Secondly, it makes a distinction between tribal peoples and peoples regarded as indigenous. In general however, people, including scholars and activists, continue to use the term "tribal" along with "indigenous".

Notwithstanding the continuity in conceptualisation in convention 107 and 169 with regard to indigenous peoples there is a marked difference in the two conventions with respect to their general orientation towards tribal peoples. ILO Convention 107 of 1957 framed general international standards for facilitating government actions towards protecting and promoting progressive integration of these people into the respective national communities. By 1985 the ILO identified the need to revise the convention on account of changes in attitudes and approaches towards these peoples worldwide. The ILO had earlier proposed integration as the desired objective but this was no longer seen as appropriate. This was because the international organisations and increasing number of governments were moving toward greater recognition of the rights of indigenous and tribal peoples to retain their specific identities and to participate fully in the planning and execution of the activities affecting their way of life. Accordingly, the ILO adopted the revised Convention No 169 in 1989 after the expert committee appointed by the ILO gave its recommendation. The same was passed in consultation with other international bodies (Xaxa 1999). While the ILO was moving in the direction of revising convention 107 on tribal and indigenous peoples, the Working Group on Indigenous Populations, set up in 1982 by the Sub-commission on Prevention of Discrimination and Protection of Minorities of the Commission on Human Rights of the UNO, had already begun to employ the working definition of indigenous peoples developed in 1972 by Martinez Cobo, a Special Rapporteur of the UNO.

The definition was restated in 1986 by Cobo in his final report "Study of the Problem of Discrimination against Indigenous Populations", which reads as follows:

"Indigenous communities, peoples and nations are those which, having a historical continuity with pre-invasion and pre-colonial societies that developed on their territories, consider themselves distinct from other sectors of the societies now prevailing in those territories, or parts of them. They form at present non-dominant sector of society and are determined to preserve, develop and transmit to future generations their ancestral territories, and their ethnic identity, as the basis of their continued existence as peoples, in accordance with their own cultural patterns, social institutions and legal systems." (Cobo 1986, para 379).

The definitions given in both ILO conventions and in Cobo's report submitted to the Working Group on Indigenous Populations that was set up by the Human Rights Commission of the UNO refer to the indigenous peoples/populations as those tribal (and, in ILO Convention 107, "semi-tribal") peoples/populations that are regarded as having descended from the peoples/populations which inhabited the country or the geographical region to which the country belonged to at the time of conquest or colonisation. They are, in addition, also those who irrespective of their legal status live more in conformity with their own social, economic and cultural institutions than with the institution of the nation which they belong to.

Thus, there are two aspects that are central to the conceptualisation of the indigenous peoples. Firstly, the indigenous are the people who lived in the country which they belonged to before colonisation or conquest by people from outside the country or a particular geographical region. Secondly, the life of these people is governed more by their own social, economic and cultural institutions than the laws applicable to the society or the country at large. What is important here is that the notion of indigenous peoples, despite sharing attributes with the peoples described in ILO Convention 169 as the tribal peoples (in ILO Convention 107 as tribal and semi-tribal populations) is different from the latter in the sense that the indigenous peoples are invariably marked out as a distinct international entity. That is, the indigenous are invariably victims of conquest and colonisation from outside. Furthermore, the outsiders are easily identifiable. Being the descendants of the peoples who lived in their territory before the conquest or colonisation is the most important criterion for the definition of indigenous peoples, but it is not the only criteria. Other criteria include non-dominance or colonial situation, and living more in conformity with their own social, economic and cultural customs and traditions than the institutions of the country of which they now are part of. The context of the discourse on indigenous peoples, initiated by the ILO and later accepted by the UNO thus basically hinged on the twin concepts of "need right" and "power right" of a social category applicable to certain people all over the world. This category of people was progressively being marginalised and dispossessed from their sources of livelihood and was vulnerable to cultural shock and loss of their collective identity.

Tribal/Indigenous Peoples in India

As shown above, the concept of indigenous peoples is closely linked to that of tribal peoples. But before exploring this connection further in the context of India, it will be appropriate to give a brief outline of the tribal peoples in India. People belonging to groups and communities described as tribes, officially termed "scheduled tribes", are estimated to number 88.8 million, thus forming 8.6 percent of the country's population according to the 2001 census. An interesting aspect of the tribal peoples in India is that they represent an enormous diversity. This is evident from the fact that as per the Constitution order (Scheduled Tribes) 1950, as many as 212 tribal communities in as many as 14 states were declared to be scheduled tribes. As per the Scheduled Tribes Order (Amendment 1976), nearly 300 tribal communities were listed in the constitution. The Anthropological Survey of India under the People of India Project identified as many as 461 tribal communities in the country (Khubchandani 1992:2; Singh 1993:1-7).

The tribal communities in India are scattered over the length and breadth of the country. However their distribution is far from even. In fact, about 85 percent of the scheduled tribe population is concentrated in the central and western belt covering the nine states of Orissa, Madhya Pradesh, Chattisgarh, Jharkhand, Maharashtra, Gujarat, Rajasthan, Andhra Pradesh and West Bengal. About eleven percent inhabits the north-eastern region, three percent the southern region and about one percent inhabits the northern region (Verma 1990:15-16). In view of the wide geographical spread, it is not surprising to find a high diversity among them in terms of ecological conditions, physical features, language, social organisation and culture etc. They are also quite heterogeneous in terms of the size of their populations.

The use of the term indigenous peoples, though of recent coinage at the international level, has in fact been used in India for a long time. After all, groups and communities in India described as tribes have also been called *adivasis,* a term equivalent to indigenous people. The concept has now become part of the common consciousness of these people. The identity as expressed now by the term *adivasi* is indeed an expanded identity, cutting across tribes bearing different names, speaking different languages or dialects. It also goes beyond groups and communities that are listed in the constitution as scheduled tribes. However, there is a fundamental difference in the sense in which the term tribe is used and understood by the tribals themselves, and the sense of the term understood by others, especially by administrators, lawyers and academics. For the latter, communities are tribes only if they are listed in the constitution. Tribals themselves, on the other hand, do not view tribes in the sense of a politico-administrative category. Rather, they view them as people belonging to the same kind of community, irrespective of whether a group or segment of it is listed or not listed in the constitution. The term *adivasi* or indigenous peoples are generally used in the sense of the latter.

The Idea of Indigenous Peoples in India

As noted earlier, the use of the term indigenous people has become an issue of considerable contention in India today. This was hardly so until a few years ago. The difference is that earlier it was used only as a mark of differentiation and identification. In fact, social workers, missionaries and political activists have been using the term *adivasi,* the sanskritic term for indigenous peoples, to refer to the tribal peoples since the turn of the last century. It is they who took the term and along with it the prejudices and conjectures to the masses (Sengupta 1987: 1003). The term in conjunction with other related terms such as aborigines, autochthones etc., has also been extensively used by scholars and administrators in their writings and reports. Even Ghurye, who otherwise talks of tribes as the backward Hindus, refers to them as the "aborigines". He writes that it is possible to contend that even if the tribes are not aborigines of the exact area they now occupy, they are the autochthones of India and to that extent they may be called aborigines (Ghurye 1963:12). Hardly any unease was felt by them in the use of the term to refer to these groups of people.

The term, however, did not remain confined only to scholars, administrators, politicians and social workers, it also spread to the people. That is how the identity of adivasi entered into the consciousness of the tribal people. The identity that was forced upon from outside has now become internalised among the tribals at least in central India. And it no longer carries the sense of inferiority that was once associated with it but one of pride and dignity. The declaration of the year 1993 as the international year of the indigenous peoples has only sharpened this identity; an identity that now comes with certain rights and privileges. It is only with the internationalisation of the context and rights and privileges associated with it that the use of the term indigenous has come to be critically examined or even challenged in the Indian context.

The sense in which the term was used earlier and the sense in which it has come to be in use today are definitely not identical, though they overlap. Today, aspects of marginalisation are built into the definition of indigenous peoples. Only those people that have been subjected to domination and subjugation have come to constitute indigenous peoples. Yet the use of the term indigenous to designate certain people but not others, even though their ancestors may also have inhabited India prior to the coming of the Aryans, clearly reveals that these aspects were not altogether lost sight of. It may be noted that even earlier the term was confined to delineate people who were considered "backward" and cut off from the mainstream civilisation. The basic mark of differentiation was between those who were part of the civilisation and those who were not. Hence the use of the term indigenous to describe tribal people seems to have some validity also in the sense of marginalisation.

The historical antiquity may be a more distant criteria, but the most immediate and proximate is the fact that they were not part of the mainstream civilisation.

In a certain sense, then, it is the aspect of marginalisation that was taken note of while designating a group as indigenous. This seems all the more obvious when we take other aspects of the Indian society into account. The coming of the Aryans is invariably considered the decisive historical factor to determine the "original" people of India. Yet not all the original people have been called indigenous people. The Hinduized Dravidian language speakers are without doubt also descendants of inhabitants of India who lived there before the coming of the Aryans. Yet they have never been described as indigenous peoples, mainly because they do not constitute marginalised groups. The Government of India had in fact placed no objection to the use of the term indigenous populations when it was deliberated upon in the ILO in 1957 and was tied to the Convention 107. At that time, the term did not include such issues as empowerment and rights; rather it had articulated the need of integrating the indigenous and tribal people into the larger social and political system. By contrast, in ILO Convention 169 of 1989 the focus shifted from integration to rights and empowerment. And no sooner had the issue shifted that the argument was raised that a category such as this does not exist in the Indian context (Xaxa1999).

Arguments Against the Applicability

Much of the discussion questioning the applicability of the concept of indigenous peoples in India is centred on the complex historical processes of the movement of the populations and their settlement in the subcontinent. It is said that unlike in the Americas, Australia and New Zealand, where identification of indigenous peoples is easier on account of the recent history of conquest, immigration and colonisation, the same is not the case in the Indian context. Rather, in India there have been waves of movements of populations with different language, race, culture, or religion dating back to centuries and millennia. Even groups or communities described as tribes have not been outside of this process. Determining who are natives and who are immigrants therefore depends how far back one goes in history. Therefore any demarcation is going to be arbitrary and hence extremely contentious.

It is also maintained that the communities described as tribes have lived in close interaction with the non-tribal people for centuries, leading to much acculturation and even assimilation into the larger Hindu society. The Indian experience, it is often stated, is different from those of the New World where it was marked by conquest, subjugation and even decimation.

It is with the people described as tribes that the term indigenous peoples has come to be associated with in India. It is assumed that they have been the original settlers of India or at least people who inhabited the region before the Aryans arrived. They are said to belong to racial stocks other than Aryan and speak a variety of languages belonging presumably to two main linguistic families, i.e. the Dravidian and the Austroasiatic. That some Tibeto-Burman speaking groups are also original inhabitants in India is not altogether ruled out. Groups belonging to these three linguistic families are the ones that have generally been described as adivasis or original people by social workers, missionaries, political activists, scholars and administrators. Ray (1973:124-125), for example, writes, "The communities of people of today whom the anthropologists call tribals, happen to be the indigenous, autochthonous *(adivasis, adimjati)* people of the land, in the sense that they had long been settled in different parts of the country before the Aryan-speaking peoples penetrated India to settle down first, in the Kabul and Indus valleys and then within a millennium and half, to spread out in slow stages, over large areas of the country and push their way of life and civilisation over practically the entire area of the country along the plains and the river valleys." Ghurye (1963:12) writes that it is possible to contend that even if the tribes are not aborigines of the exact area they now occupy, they are the autochthones of India and to that extent they may be called the aborigines.

The questions that are raised in this context are: 1. Whether groups designated as tribes have been natives of India, and non-tribes immigrants, and 2. If they are not natives, whether their settlement is prior to that of the arrival of the major social groups viz. the Aryans. Most scholars are of the view that most tribes can hardly make a legitimate claim that they are the natives of India. Hutton (in Vidyarthi and Rai 1985), for example, is of the view that only the Negritos may be considered as the original inhabitants of India though they do not have any marked presence now. He considers groups belonging to the Austric and Dravidian categories etc. as much outsiders as the Aryans. Guha (in Shah 1992; Vidyarthi and Rai 1985) is also cited for making similar observation in the context of Austric speaking people. The oral traditions of the tribes themselves are however an authoritative source based on which such claims can be questioned. Dube (1977:2) writes, "it is difficult to speak of 'original' inhabitants, for tribal traditions themselves make repeated mention of migration of their ancestors. There is considerable evidence to suggest that several groups were pushed out of the areas where they were first settled and had to seek shelter elsewhere. And there are several groups, now absorbed in Hindu society, which can make an equally tenable claim to being original or, at any rate very old inhabitants".

If the proposition of tribes being natives is questionable, does this also apply to the second question? That is, are all tribal groups inhabitants that settled the territory before the coming of the Aryans? Would that then be the assumed cut-off point for demarcating the indigenous people in India? Whereas this in fact appears to be more or less the case, it cannot be said with utmost certainty for all the groups described as tribes in India. It is said that there are tribes in India, especially in the north-east, whose settlement in the territories they inhabit today is even a later phenomenon than that of the many non-tribals in other parts of India. The Nagas, for example, are stated to have come to India around the middle of the first millennium B.C., first to Tibet and later to the territory where they now live, a period much later than the arrival of the Aryans. The Mizos are said to have settled in their current territory only in the 16th century. The Kuki settlement is considered an even later phenomenon than that of the Mizos (Béteille 1993; Roy Burman undated). In contrast to this, the non-tribal groups such as the Bengalis, Gujratis, Oriyas etc. have a much longer history of settlement than those of the tribes referred to in the discussion (Béteille 1993; Roy Burman, undated). It is indeed problematic to say that all tribal people in India are earlier settlers than the Aryan and that tribals are indigenous and non-tribals non-indigenous.

It needs to be mentioned here that the tribal groups in India are not solely comprised of the Dravidian and Austro-Asiatic speaking groups. A very large number of the tribal groups in fact belong to Aryan and the Tibeto-Burman speaking group who can hardly be considered indigenous if the Aryan invasion is taken as the cut off mark to decide who is indigenous and who is not indigenous. To restrict the term indigenous to refer to only these groups of people means to exclude tribal groups speaking languages either of the Indo-Aryan family such as the Bhils and other related groups or the Tibeto-Burman family from the status of the indigenous people.[2] This means that people identified and described as tribals are not necessarily to be treated as the indigenous and that there are tribal groups who could be treated as indigenous and others could not. In contrast, many groups and communities especially those belonging to the Dravidian language speaking group such as the Tamilians, Telgus, Malyalis, could stake a claim of being indigenous people by virtue of the fact they have been inhabitants of India prior to the coming of the Aryans. They are however not recognised as the tribals and have few attributes in common with the tribals who are dispossessed, ex-ploited and marginalised. Instead these groups constitute a part of the dominant national community.

In terms of other criteria used to identify indigenous peoples, such as their marginalised status, loss of control over resources, they can hardly be considered sufficient. After all, they constitute not only numerically but also economically, politically and socially dominant communities in the regions they inhabit. The congruence between the term and the concept on which the tribal activists defend the application of the term does not stand valid in all situations.

The objections raised by the Indian governments through its delegation at UN bodies have been twofold. One is that tribal people in India do not have dis-tinct social, economic, political and cultural identities. To support this argument they draw on observations made by anthropologists, social reformers, govern-ment official census commissioners etc. In particular, they draw on G.S. Ghurye's observation that religion, occupation, or racial features have proved inadequate when attempting to distinguish the tribal people from non-tribal population in India (Prasad 1992). The same point is further articulated by dwelling upon the conceptual problem in defining tribal communities in India. To substantiate the argument the government draws on Béteille's observation that tribals show in varying degrees elements of continuity with the larger society of India (ibid.). The other observation made by Béteille in the same paragraph, i.e. that "groups which correspond closely to the anthropologists' conception of tribe, have lived in long association with communities of an entirely different type" is, however, conveniently overlooked by Prasad. And so has been Ghurye's (op.cit.) observation that *adivasis* as the original inhabitants of India.

There is still another argument that has been put forward by the government delegates in international fora: that the category tribe and more specifically scheduled tribe with which indigenous peoples are associated are a politico-administrative category and not a historical category, as the idea of indigenous peoples suggests. It is said that the identification of the groups as scheduled tribes has to do with the administration of social-welfare measures to ameliorate the condition of the tribal people. The point made is that the terms tribe/scheduled tribe and indigenous peoples are not synonymous and thus cannot be equated. They see no congruence between the two (Prasad 1992).

Interestingly, however, considerations or criteria on which scheduled tribes have been defined by the government, clumsy and esoteric though they may be, are concealed in the making of their argument. Scheduled tribe is not the only category based on which social policy measures have been directed. There are other categories, such as the scheduled castes ands other backward castes, which have also been brought under the ambit of social welfare policy. It needs to be explored on what ground certain groups of people are declared as scheduled tribes and others as scheduled castes or other backward castes.

Closer examination reveals that people are defined as tribes precisely because they are socially, culturally, linguistically and economically different from the other segments of the dominant population, and to that extent represent distinct social group vis-á-vis the larger society. This has generally been the sense in which tribes have historically been delineated. In fact, considerations (such as definite geographical area, distinctive culture, primitive traits, lack of education etc.) adopted by the Indian state for identification of groups as scheduled tribes in post-independence India emanate from the above-mentioned definitional characteristics of the tribal society.

Arguments in Defence of the Use of the Term

The applicability of the term indigenous peoples in India is strongly defended by activists and scholars, both tribal and non-tribal. This is done both on the basis of original settlement and other critical considerations. They trace the history of tribals in India to a time much before the coming of the Aryan people and argue that tribals, whose ancestors had lived here for some thousands of years prior to the Aryan invasion, a fact that can hardly be disputed, should be considered indigenous peoples so that certain international legal instruments can be applied to these marginalised and deprived social groups. But the case is made more forcefully on other grounds. Pathy (1992:8) for example writes that tribals in a way have been victims of conquest and colonisation and hence share all the attributes of the colonised people such as ethnic identity, loss of control over customary territorial resources, cultural annihilation and powerlessness. He makes the case despite the recognition that the original settlement in a territory is problematic. But even the issue of colonisation and colonised status remains far from being resolved.

The fact that there is no detailed and well-researched historical material on the nature of relations or encounters between groups that are designated as the indigenous peoples and the other social groups for the periods preceding the coming of the British, makes it impossible for us to say anything with certainty about the nature of the relations between the two social groups. In fact, this is the other important ground on which the term indigenous peoples is contested in the Indian context. It is maintained that most of the studies of the history of Indian civilisation show that the growth and expansion of Hindu society was a prolonged and complex process of assimilation. And the nature of interaction between the two groups has broadly been described as one of peaceful coexistence rather than one of conquest and subjugation, at least until the advent of the British rule (Bose 1975; Béteille 1998:189). Such an interpretation of the nature of interaction between tribals and non-tribals has also been endorsed by a scholar who otherwise talks of an aggressive absorption into the Hindu society with the onset of the colonial rule (Desai 1977:24). Pathy (1992b:51) himself elsewhere talks of a symbiotic relationship between the tribals and the non-tribals rather that one of colonisation and conquest. He writes, "Majority of the so-called tribals of India had developed class structure over a long period of time and therefore had interactions with the other communities. Up to the time of colonialism, it was largely not a relationship of domination and subjugation (Pathy 1992:51)." Thus not only the original settlement in the territory becomes problematic but also the question of colonisation and subjugation.

This means that the question of identification of indigenous people can only be raised with respect to the period of the arrival of the British and the subsequent process of colonization and subjugation in India. If the processes of British colonization are taken as the point of departure for demarcation of indigenous peoples, then it is generally argued that the issue of original settlement, which is so central to the notion of indigenous peoples, becomes redundant. From this perspective everyone is to be considered as indigenous. In other words, if the British colonisation of India is taken as the cut-off point for demarcation of the indigenous peoples, then the whole population living in the country would be indigenous. In my view such an argument stands flawed.

India was the colony of the British and the British exercised economic and political power over it. There was exploitation of the Indian people and appropriation of its resources for the over-all development of Great Britain. In other words, there was *colonialism* but no *colonisation* of India in the form of large-scale immigrant settlement by the British. In the case of the tribal people, however, both colonialism *and* colonisation was at work in colonial India. The colonialism in the context of tribes was external (British) as well as internal (dominant Indian population). There was control by the colonial state as well as by the dominant Indian population. The dominant Indian population in collusion with the colonial state embarked on alienating tribal people from their control over land, forest and other resources. In the course of this process there was also settler colonisation of the regions inhabited by the tribal people. The scale and degree of colonisation varied from region to region. Colonisation of tribal regions has gone on unabated in post-independent India.

In short, there has been domination and subjugation of the tribal people by the dominant Indian population resulting in increasing marginalisation and pauperization of the tribal people. And the processes through which this happened may not have been as violent as in the New World, for example, but has surely not been devoid of coercion, deceit, force and violence. Notwithstanding the difference, the end result has been spectacularly similar if not identical. The slow, gradual and refined process of marginalisation and subjugation is often more dangerous since it escapes indignation and condemnation.

However, even before the onset of this twofold colonialism, the interaction between tribes and non-tribes had been far from uniform and even. Sometimes the incorporation of tribes into the larger social structure had been through war, conquest and subjugation. At other times, the incorporation of tribes into the larger society had been through the process of mutual exchange and acculturation. All along there have been cases in which tribes either as a whole or in segments have defied their incorporation into the larger society by retreating into new frontiers from the fertile and accessible land they once occupied. That is how tribes in India came to maintain their distinctive identity at the arrival of the British. Indeed, much of the social, cultural and political situation in which they find themselves has not only to do with the British colonialism but also with earlier historical process. That is, historical processes prior to the British are as much responsible for their marginalisation (isolation, social and economic backwardness, being outside of the state institutions, coupled with distinct customs and traditions) of tribal people as the British rule. Such characteristics shared by the tribal people prior to the advent of the British colonialism are to a large extent identical to those that have been identified as key criteria for identifying indigenous peoples (see e.g. Cobo 1986; ILO 1989).

Indian society has grown and expanded through mutual interaction between tribals and non-tribals, the dominant section of the society. The contact of tribes with non-tribes prior to the British rule was on the whole either characterised by retreat from their original habitat after the arrival of the alien power and population, or by slow, gradual and – compared to what happened in the New World – less violent forms of domination and assimilation. In the latter case, through a long process of interaction tribals were drawn, incorporated and absorbed to varying degrees into the dominant society. Once they were incorporated they were usually assigned inferior positions in the structure of the larger society. This still-ongoing process of absorption is not recent but dates back to most ancient times.

Given this historical process, it is contended that it would be problematic to exclude those who were once part of the tribal community but who are by now absorbed in to the larger society from the claim of indigenous people status. This is this argument that the government has been using to justify its stand against the category of the indigenous peoples. Needless to say that those who moved into the dominant social and cultural fold of the larger society have ceased to maintain their distinct identity, and hence cease to be indigenous peoples of the country. Once they become part of the dominant and exploiting society, they have no legitimate claim to make their case as indigenous peoples.

One of the main thrusts of indigenousness as mentioned in the UN document "Study of the Problems of Discrimination against Indigenous Populations, of 1986 (Cobo 1986) is cultural distinctiveness, and people who have maintained their distinctiveness in spite of such long historical experiences with an expanding and dominant society have to be treated as indigenous peoples. Hence, only people who chose to remain outside of this process and maintained their distinct identity have legitimate claim to be considered and identified as the indigenous peoples.

In fact, the whole exercise of identification of groups and communities as tribes during the colonial period was to a great extent contingent upon the nature of relations the respective people had with the larger society. This dimension seems to have unconsciously continued to be one of the important considerations in identifying the tribes in independent India. By and large, tribes were considered as those outside "civilisation". This means that they not only remained outside the politico-administrative structure of the larger society or the kingdom but also the general social organisation and world-view of the larger society. In short, they continued to be distinct because they escaped colonisation and subjugation. That they lived in hills, plateaus or forests and lived on hunting, food-gathering or shifting cultivation was considered a result of being outside of the civilisation complex. This has been forcefully brought out by Béteille (1986:316). He writes that where tribes and civilisation coexist, as in India and the Islamic world, being a tribe has been more a matter of remaining outside the state and civilisation – whether by choice or necessity – than of attaining a definite stage in the evolutionary advance from the simple to the complex. The Indian practice of regarding as tribes a large assortment of communities, differing widely in size, mode of livelihood and social organisation cannot therefore be dismissed as unreasonable. They are all "tribals" because they all kept more or less outside the Hindu civilisation, and not because they all share the same socio-cultural and political characteristics and stand exactly at the same stage of "development". Therefore, in short, because the people described as tribes are those who escaped colonisation and subjugation prior to, during and after British colonial rule, they can legitimately be identified as indigenous peoples.

Though the question of indigenous people has generally been discussed in the context of the country as a whole, it has also been done with respect to particular regions or territories such as Eastern, Western, Southern region etc. within the country and the different populations living there side by side. It has generally been observed that there have been so many migrations in and out of these regions in the past centuries that no particular *jati* (caste) or group can have genuine grounds for claiming indigenous status (Béteille 1998: 189; Hardiman 1987: 15-16).

In the discussion of the concept of indigenous peoples in India it is important that we do not mix the problems arising at different levels. Often, the problem at the country-level is used as an argument against the identification of tribals as indigenous even at the regional or local level, and vice versa. Asking the question of whether tribals are indigenous peoples on the level of particular regions or territories within the country indeed gives rise to problems of a somewhat different nature.

The movement of the populations belonging to different races, ethnicity and linguistic groups, including those described as the tribals, from one place to another is something that has been in process within India for centuries. Thus, the groups who may be indigenous with respect to the country as a whole may not be indigenous with respect to their settlement in a given territory. It may also so happen that the same group may be indigenous and non-indigenous at the same time. The Oraons, Mundas and many other tribes living in Jharkhand, for example, may have legitimate claim to be called indigenous peoples with respect of their presence in what today is called India prior to that of the Aryans, or with respect to their settlement in the Jharkhand region, but it is not sure if they can claim to be indigenous in Assam or Bengal where they have moved in the course of the past century or so. Indeed, their claim of being indigenous is strongly contested in these places. Nowhere is this more true than in Assam where the migrant tribals' claim to be indigenous peoples is being disputed by tribal communities like the Bodos, Mishings and others who have a much longer history of settlement in that particular region than the tribals from Bihar, Orissa, Madhya Pradesh etc. If, however, one takes India as a whole, these migrant groups have a much longer history of settlement within the confines of present-day India than many of the tribes in the north-eastern region. The tribals from these states have also moved in large numbers to the Andaman Islands and have settled there as cultivators after reclaiming land from the forest and in the process have alienated the native Jarawas from their territories. Thus, the Oraons, Mundas and others are indigenous in the context of their claim to have lived in India before the Aryan invasion, and in the context of their being the first settlers of Jharkhand, but their indigenous claim becomes problematic with respect to places and territories outside the Jharkhand region where they have migrated to.

In the discussion on indigenous peoples in India critics have argued that there are groups such as Gujaratis or Maharastrians who have a longer history of presence in India than many tribal groups such as the Kukis, Mizos and others in the north-eastern states. The historical priority of the dominant group has primarily been made with reference to tribes of the northeast region of India. In my view such a reference is misplaced. After all, most of today's northeast region, e.g. Mizoram, Nagaland or the hill regions of Manipur, have in the past not been part of India either in the territorial or the cultural sense. They became part of India in the territorial sense only after the arrival of the British. Needless to say they were annexed into the British territory and subsequently to India only through war and conquest. And it was with the colonial rule that the process of colonisation of the northeast region by the dominant population of India began. The process of colonisation, which had begun during the colonial rule, has been checked to a limited extent only through various forms of, and often violent, political struggles. In light of situations such as these, questioning the indigenous status of the tribal people of northeast India is problematic.

Adivasi Consciousness

In the context of India as a whole the identification of indigenous peoples is indeed problematic and complex. This does however not mean that people of India representing different languages, physical features, cultures, modes of social organisations etc. do not identify and relate themselves in a special way with a given territory or region in the country.

In the course of history, different communities have come to develop distinct and definite associations with certain territories. These territories have been considered by the communities as their own, as against those of other communities. They consider themselves to have prior, if not exclusive, rights over the territory where they live either on account of prior historical settlement or the numerical and other dominance. In addition to that, they also tend to confer to their members special rights and privileges in the form of state power.

The creation of administrative states on the basis of major linguistic communities in India, can be seen as the culmination of this yearning by people with distinct identities living in particular territories. This in a way gives recognition to the fact, implicit though it may be, that certain people have prior rights over others in the territory that they occupy. This is almost paramount to saying that they are the original inhabitants. Nowhere is this identity with land or territory more crudely manifested than in the "sons-of-soil" theory that is raised from time to time by regionally dominant communities. Whereas such privileges and rights are recognised with respect to these dominant communities, the same has been denied to the tribal communities in India. The result is that they are progressively getting alienated from control over land, forest, water, minerals and other resources and in the process getting subjected to inhuman misery, injustice and exploitation.

If the tribal communities' status as indigenous peoples of India is problematic and the problem indeed is both empirical and conceptual, the least the dominant regional communities could do is to recognise the priorities of rights and privileges of these people in the territories and regions where they inhabit. It is in the absence of such powers and rights that a new form of identity, i.e. the identity as *adivasis* or indigenous peoples is crystallising among the tribes of central India. It has already been an important mark of identity in what is known as the Jharkhand region but it is also catching up in the tribal regions of Madhya Pradesh, Gujarat and Rajasthan, giving rise to a large number of organisations of different types both at the local/regional and the national level. The indigenous tribal communities of the Northeast, however, do not use the sanskritic term *"adivasi"* to refer to themselves. This does not mean that they do not articulate themselves as aboriginal peoples, but they prefer to use the English term "indigenous peoples" to describe themselves.

There are now several organisations that actively articulate the issue of the indigenous peoples at the national and the inter-national levels. The Indian Council of Indigenous and Tribal Peoples (ICITP) with its regional chapters has been one such prominent organization. The result is that the identity of tribal people as "indigenous peoples" has become a marked reality today notwithstanding the varied conceptual and empirical arguments brought to bear against the term.

References

Béteille, André 1986. The Concept of Tribe with Special Reference to India. European *Journal of Sociology*, XXVII.

_____1993. Myth of Indigenous People. *The Times of India*, 5 January.

_____1998. The Idea of Indigenous People. *Current Anthropology*,39(2).

Bose, N.K. 1975. *The Structure of the Hindu Society*. New Delhi: Orient Longman.

Cobo, José Martínez 1986. Study of the Problem of Discrimination against Indigenous Populations. UN Doc. E/CN.4/Sub.2/1986/7/Add.4.

Daes, Erica-Irene A. 1996. Standard-setting activities: Evolution of Standards Concerning the Rights of Indigenous People. Working Paper by the Chairperson-Rapporteur, Mrs. Erica-Irene A. Daes. On the concept of "indigenous people". United Nations Economic and Social Council, UN Document E/CN.4/Sub.2/AC.4/1996/2.

Desai, A.R. 1977, Tribes in Transition; in R. Thapar (ed.), *Tribe, Caste and Religion*. New Delhi: Macmillan.

Dube, S.C.1977. *Tribal Heritage of India*. Shimla: IIAS.

Ghurye, G.S.1963. *The Scheduled Tribes.* 3rd ed. Bombay: Popular Prakashan.

Hardiman, David 1987. *The Coming of the Devi: Adivasi Assertion in Western India.* Delhi: Oxford University Press.

International Labour Organization 1957. Indigenous and Tribal Populations Convention, 1957 (No. 107). Convention concerning the Protection and Integration of Indigenous and Other Tribal and Semi-Tribal Populations in Independent Countries. Geneva: ILO.

_____1989. Indigenous and Tribal Populations Convention, 1989 (No. 169). Convention concerning Indigenous and Tribal Peoples in Independent Countries. Geneva: ILO.

Khubchandani, L.M. 1992. *Tribal Identity. A Language and Communication Perspective.* Shimla: IIAS.

Pathy, Jaganath 1992. What is Tribe? What is Indigenous? Turn the Tables Toward the Metaphor of Social Justice. *Samata* 1/1992.

Prasad, Jayant 1992. Statement made on Behalf of the Delegation of India in the Working Group on Indigenous population at Geneva. Samata 1/1992.

_____1992. The Idea of a Tribe and the Indian Scene; in B. Chaudhuri (ed.), *Tribal Transformation in India.* Vol.3. New Delhi: Inter-India Publications.

Ray, Niharranjan 1973. Nationalism in India. Aligarh: AMU.

.Roy Burman, B.K. 1992. The Indigenous Peoples and their Quest for Justice; in: B. Chaudhuri (ed.), Tribal Transformation in India. Vol.3. New Delhi: Inter-India Publications.

_____1983. Transformation of Tribes and Analogous Social Formation. *Economic and Political Weekly* 18(27).

_____(undated). Indigenous and Tribal Peoples and the U.N. and International Agencies. Rajiv Gandhi Foundation (mimeographed).

Sengupta, Nirmal 1988. Reappraising Tribal Movement. *Economic and Political Weekly* 23 (17).

Shah, G. 1992. Tribal Issues: Problems and Perspectives. in B. Chaudhuri (ed.), *Tribal Transformation in India.* Vol.2. New Delhi: Inter-India Publications.

Singh, K.S. 1993. Marginalised Tribes. *Seminar* (412).

Verma, R.C. 1990. *Indian Tribes through the Ages.* New Delhi: Government of India Publication.

Vidyarthi, L.P. and Rai, B.K. 1985. *Tribal Culture of India.* New Delhi: Concept Publishing Company.

Xaxa, Virginius 1999. Tribes as Indigenous People of India., *Economic and Political Weekly* 34(51).

Notes

[1] Virginius Xaxa is an Oraon and currently professor of Sociology at the Department of Sociology, Delhi School of Economics, Delhi University.
[2] The literature on Bhils points to conflicting views with respect to the Bhils's racial and linguistic mark of identity. Some consider them belonging to Aryan / Indo-Aryan group and some to the Kolarian group.

The Concept of Indigenous Peoples and Its Application in China

Tan Chee-Beng[1]

Introduction

We begin by noting that the concept of "indigenous peoples" in English is a relatively new concept that has been accepted mainly by anthropologists and activists. There is a history to the present usage of this term as respectable, from savages and primitive people to aborigines and tribal people. Earlier, the term "natives" was also popular when referring to people in other lands, including the colonized people. Natives is a broad term that includes both the majority people and the "tribal people" that make up the "indigenous" peoples in an independent state today, such as the Malays and the non-Malay "natives" (see below) in Malaysia.

The concept of indigenous peoples needs to be considered together with the term "minority", whose presence is a common phenomenon in modern states. It is through the formation of nation states that minorities have been created. The indigenous minorities were mainly autonomous communities until they were incorporated into a state. They were made minorities by the state, were forced into a situation of unequal power relations with the majority people and with the state power. It is because of the need to protect the interests of such minorities from state oppression that researchers, non-governmental organizations and inter-governmental organizations are interested in defining and identifying indigenous peoples. While the term "indigenous" carries the dichotomy of the indigenous versus those who are not, anthropologists, activists and governmental as well as intergovernmental organizations are actually interested in the marginalized communities, which were once conveniently labeled tribal. Anthropologists have generally accepted the term indigenous peoples as a more respectful term for the people formerly known as tribal, and before that, primitive people.

When we refer to the Yao and Hmong in north Thailand as indigenous, we are actually just replacing the term "tribal". These peoples are comparably recent immigrants to Thailand, when compared to the Thai and other minorities such as the Lua and the Mlabri (who are called "tribal" in English, also by many anthropologists). While most anthropologists now prefer not to use the term "tribal" or at least put it within inverted commas, some like Benjamin (2002: 13) argues that it "remains useful precisely because it refers to a characteristic way of life and of social organization for which no other unambiguous label exists."

While I have argued against the use of the term "tribe" in Malaysia (Tan 1992), I do agree with Benjamin on this point. However, in the context of Malaysia, an Iban or a Kadazan is often qualified as tribal to portray them as belonging to more "backward" communities in contrast to the Malays, Chinese and Indians, and this is not appropriate. And it is precisely the implied derogatory meaning which is the reason for the general rejection of the term by many of these peoples as well as activists and concerned scholars, and their demand to replace it with "indigenous peoples".

The concept of "indigenous peoples" as "tribal peoples" nevertheless helps clarify that that the usage is not based solely on the issue of "indigenousness". The politics of indigenousness is very problematic, as can be seen in the case of Malaysia. The Malays, who are the majority people, claim to be indigenous, using the concept of *bumiputera* (literally "princes of the soil"), which excludes descendants of Chinese and Indian immigrants. Special rights and affirmative actions for the Malays are based on the concept of *bumiputera*. However, the earliest inhabitants in Malaysia were not Malays, and they were referred to as aborigines by the British colonial administrators and ethnologists, and called by the Malays by the derogatory term *Sakai* which connotes the meaning of "serf". Numbering around 90,000 and distributed in West Malaysia only, these aborigines comprise various groups most of which are Mon-Khmer speakers. Today they are known as Orang Asli (literally "original people") and they are administered by a special department, and, ironically, in practice do not enjoy the privileges of the *bumipuetra* (cf. Dentan, Endicott, Gomes and Hooker1997).

In East Malaysia (the states of Sarawak and Sabah in northern Borneo), there are many groups classified as *bumiputera* who are not Malays. Following earlier British usage, these peoples in East Malaysia are often referred to as "natives" in English, and they are officially so referred to in the Malaysian Constitution. For example, Article 153 of the Federal Constitution of Malaysia is about "Reservation of quotas in respect of services, permits, etc., for Malays and natives of any of the states of Sabah and Sarawak." With reference to the national level these "natives" of Sabah and Sarawak can in English be called "indigenous minorities," to distinguish them from the numerically and politically dominant Malays. Within East Malaysia, however, it is the Malays who are in fact numerically minorities in relation to, e.g., the Iban or Kadazan. In some official discourses in Malay, these indigenous minorities are described as pribumi, which actually also means "indigenous", although the discourse here carries the connotation of being "tribal" rather than "more indigenous". However, until recently in Indonesia, *pribumi* simply means people who are considered indigenous to the country, such as the Javanese, as opposed to the Chinese who are not considered indigenous. In July 2006 the Parliament of Indonesia abolished the distinction of indigenous and non-indigenous citizens (Yazhou Zhoukan 2007: 25). While this is good for the country (as it provides equal citizenship status and equal rights to all Indonesian citizens), it is still necessary to pay attention to the disempowered "tribal" people because of the continued marginalization and denied rights of these people.

If the term "indigenous peoples" is supposed to be used for marginalized and oppressed communities distinguished from the mainstream societies by their particular social organizations and ways of life it has to be divorced from the politics of indigenousness articulated by politicians who use the rhetoric of claiming to be indigenous or more indigenous than another ethnic category in a nation state to stir up ethnic nationalism or to treat the other ethnic group as second class citizens. In the Asian context, the concept needs to be discussed in relation to "tribal peoples" and "minorities". As minorities they need to be distinguished from new migrants and people whose migrant ancestors in recent history came from another country where they were majority people, such as the Chinese and Indians in Malaysia. Therefore the term indigenous peoples can best be applied to the "minorities" that have been referred to as "tribal", and are marginalized by the state. In other words there are indigenous minorities in relation to the dominant population who is in control of the state. The oppression of minorities deserves attention but that of the indigenous minorities deserve special attention as they are generally the most disempowered and marginalized in a country. Applying to them the term "indigenous" and thus the respective international instruments protecting the rights of indigenous peoples is the appropriate way to address the marginalization and disempowerment they are experiencing.

With this in mind I shall now proceed to discuss the situation in mainland China, Taiwan and Hong Kong SAR[2].

Minorities and Indigenous Peoples in Mainland China

In Chinese the term "indigenous people" is translated to *tuzhu* (natives, original inhabitants, aborigines) or *yuanzhumin* (original inhabitants). These terms are used in Taiwan but not in the People's Republic of China (PRC). That the terms are generally not used in PRC is due largely to historical and ethnological reasons. PRC recognizes 56 *minzu*, meta-ethno-categories, of which ethnic minorities make up 55, while all the Han people, who are the overwhelming majority of the population, form one *minzu*. Although based on many surveys and ethnological research, the recognition of only 56 *minzu* is still arbitrary. It is impossible to reduce the many diverse populations in such a big country to only 56 if the people are allowed to subjectively identify who they are. In fact, in the early post-liberation years, more than 400 names of nationalities were officially registered with the government. Of these 260 were from Yunnan alone (Fei 1981: 64). Such official classification reflects the perspective of the Han people who are one against the rest, the *shaoshu minzu* or nationality minorities. We note here that there is official recognition of ethnic minorities, and that non-Han communities were minorities in the Chinese state, but in specific regions where most of them reside, they may be a numerical majority in relation to the local Han people.

The classification of such diverse non-Han population into 55 categories is not just for state control, but also, and we need to recognize this, to realize the Chinese communist ideology of having representation from each *minzu,* hence the need to officially identify the number of minzu. It was, for example, not possible to have 400 *minzu* with each represented in the various levels of government. At issue here is the representation in autonomous areas. Autonomous regions, counties and prefectures were established in areas where there were concentrations of one or more minorities, taking into concentration local ethnic relations and economic development as well as historical conditions. At the provincial level, five autonomous regions were established, namely, Inner Mongolian Autonomous Region (already established in 1947), Xinjiang Uighur Autonomous Region (established in 1955), Guangxi Zhuang Autonomous Region (established in 1958), Ningxia Hui Autonomous Region (established in 1958), and Tibet Autonomous Region (officially inaugurated in 1965) (Fei 1981:34). Other than the five autonomous regions (provinces), there are 30 autonomous prefectures, and 120 autonomous counties (State Council 2005).

Despite the lack of democracy, minorities in China in fact have representatives in the local and provincial government, albeit not popularly elected. Article 113 of The Constitution of the People's Republic of China states that:

In the people's congress of an autonomous region, prefecture or county, in addition to the deputies of the nationality or nationalities exercising regional autonomy in the administrative area, the other nationalities inhabiting the area are also entitled to appropriate representation.

The chairmanship and vice-chairmanships of the standing committee of the people's congress of an autonomous region, prefecture or county shall include a citizen or citizens of the nationality or nationalities exercising regional autonomy in the area concerned.

The deputies of the nationality mentioned above means representatives *(daibiao)* of the nationality. Article 114 states that:

The administrative head of an autonomous region, prefecture or county shall be a citizen of the nationality, or of one of the nationalities, exercising regional autonomy in the area concerned.

In this way in a Yi autonomous county, for example, the county head should be a Yi (see below), and the other posts of the county government are to be filled by Yi and individuals of other *minzu*. The Han people form one *minzu,* and there are always Han people even in counties where they in fact form a minority. And in politically sensitive counties or provinces, it is not surprising that the *shuji* or the Party Secretary[3] goes to the cadre (not necessarily a Han Chinese) that has the trust of the central government.

State oppression of minorities in China needs to be seen in the context of local situations and in the context of Communist rule. Where there is a separatist movement, the communist government's handling of the situation is predictable, namely outright oppression. I do not think the intensity of oppression has to do with whether the people are minorities or not. Any group that tries to challenge the sovereignty or the power of the communist state will be suppressed, even ruthlessly. Similarly, over different periods of the communist rule, the fate of the minorities, as that of the Han majority, varied with the swings in leftist campaigns. For example, during 1949-1957, the government was keen to classify minorities and allocate seats according to minority representation. Expression of minorities' cultures and research on identifying minorities were encouraged, and nationality institutes were established to train minority cadres. From 1958-1976, the leftist politics discouraged the expression of minorities' distinction, and nationalities institutes were even closed down (cf. Schein 2000: 80-91). During the Cultural Revolution, the insults made by Han ultra-leftists on Muslims were so bad that to this day they still influence Muslim perception of and interaction with Han people in some regions. While there are stereotypes and general Han chauvinism, the oppression of minorities need above all to be seen in its historical context.

With economic liberalization since 1978, some minorities have done better than others, and in many places, they have to compete with Han for better economic opportunities, especially in counties and cities of minorities that have been opened up for tourism. While there is serious poverty in many Han areas in the interior, poverty among minorities in general is much more severe and of particular concern to activists and organizations concerned with indigenous peoples. Ethnic minorities in poor remote areas have little access to state and outside assistance. In fact, due to corruption and the derogatory attitude of some Han officials, they may not even get all the funds that the state has allocated to help them, as I learnt in the Tu Yao region of Guangxi[4].

The Han-centered Chinese imperial state had diverse relationships with the ancestors of the present-day minorities, in the form of tributary relationship, or ruling them directly or indirectly. The famous form of indirect rule of non-Han people is the tusi system, whereby a hereditary headman or chief called tusi was endowed with power by the Chinese imperial court, as in the case of the Dai people in Dehong, Yunnan (Yang 1997: 267-304). The Han view of these non-Han people may be characterized by the term "tribal" in English, in the sense of less civilized, and those who fought the court were described as fierce and ruthless. The non-Han people were also known by different labels connoting the "non-civilized others". In ancient China, the non-Han others were known as yi, *man, rong and di,* later associated with the non-Han people in the east, south, west and north respectively. Throughout Chinese history, as the expanding Han (themselves absorbing non-Han people) had more encounters with specific non-Han groups, there were specific names for specific group of non-Han people, the etymology of which is rather complicated. For example, the label "Yao" has a complex history, the study of which requires one to study not just the use of various Chinese characters for Yao in different periods of Chinese history but also to study the changing relationship between the Yao and the Chinese imperial state, as well as studying the ethnogenesis of the people that came to be known as Yao[5]. This is beyond the scope of this paper.

The so-called minorities in China today have co-exited in both friendly and hostile relationships for centuries in different dynasties of the Chinese empire, whose size varied from century to century. Chinese imperial rule over non-Chinese in the frontiers varied in intensity and space. As noted, the Han labels for the non-Han populations also varied from period to period. The Mongols today were in ancient times called Xiongnu, who harassed the Han Chinese from time-to-time, and in the 13th century ruled the Chinese empire. The Yi in Sichuan, who are non-Han Tibeto-Burman speaking people, having been living in Sichuan since ancient time, as do the Han people whose famous Shu Han Kingdom (A.D. 221 to A.D. 264) was also in Sichuan. Even though the Yi lived separately in the mountainous parts of Sichuan, as many still do, it does not make sense today to distinguish between the two peoples in terms of their indigenousness in its narrow sense, and argue over who is more indigenous. What distinguishes and defines them today is the power relation. Since centuries the Yi had to defend their territory against the intrusion of the Han people. Those groups of Yi who fought Han people stubbornly were portrayed as fierce and warlike, very similar to the British description of the Badeng Kenyah of Sarawak in Malaysia, for example, who were among the last to submit to the rule of the Brooke government (Tan 1993: xiii), which was established by James Brooke in 1841 until Sarawak was ceded to Britain in 1946.

To the credit of the Communist ideology of respecting minorities, and despite the continuing presence of Han prejudicial view of minorities as backward, the derogatory labels for minorities were abolished, and even new names were created. The Yi who today are distributed mainly in Sichuan, Yunnan, Guizhou and Guangxi[6] were called Luoluo (transcribed as Lolo in western works) written with a dog radical, which evoked among Han Chinese an image of fierce and uncivilized non-Han people. The communist government has popularized Yi as a label for Luoluo and other related groups classified under this *minzu* category, although a category of Yi in Yunnan continue to identify themselves as Luoluo. We need to note that the ethnic categories today reflect both the state policy of *minzu* identification and changing group alignments over time. As the late

Chinese anthropologist Fei Xiaotong (1999) has pointed out, the Yao of Jinxiu in Guangxi, for example, were likely formed from diverse ethnic communities, including Dong and Miao, who moved to the mountains and cooperated to fight off the government troops and Han people. To give another example, Zhuang is today the largest category of minorities in China, but this was not the case before the Communist government classified the diverse groups of people in Guangxi and Yunnan as such (cf. Kaup 2000).

Thus, in China, there is historical and ethnological reason why the term "indigenous" in the narrow sense of whether indigenous or not does not figure in the relations between the Han and the non-Han populations which are described as minorities today. However, "indigenous peoples" in the sense of peoples regarded as "tribal" has its equivalents in China, too, especially in the case of the marginalized others such as the Lahu and Jinuo in Yunnan but also the historically more known groups such as the Meo and the Yao. It is not difficult for scholars and tourists who have been to minority theme parks in China to see that the minorities are portrayed as "tribal". The mainstream Chinese (Han people) still see the minorities as "tribal".

For the purpose of adopting the UN usage on "indigenous peoples", the minorities recognized by the government of China may be regarded loosely as "indigenous people". What the NGOs and IGOs should be concerned with in PRC are the *conditions* of the non-Han minorities, which should not be assumed to be worse than the treatment of indigenous peoples in non-communist countries. In fact, the Chinese government does have some affirmative actions for minorities, including less stringent requirement for admission to nationality universities and colleges.

Minorities and Indigenous Peoples in Taiwan

In Taiwan the situation is quite different. Over the past centuries, and especially since the 17th century, Chinese mainly from Fujian had been migrating to the island, where they encountered the local inhabitants. They labeled them *fan,* which has a similar connotation as the concept "tribe" in English, and, above all the most derogatory notion of being "barbarians". Thus there has always been the recognition of *fan* people as the local original inhabitants, who were over time forced by the Han people to move to the hills. When Japan took over Taiwan in 1895, the Japanese colonial regime paid much attention to the separate administration of the "tribal" people to curb rebellion. Reservations were created for them whom the Japanese called *man-jin,* that is, "primitive people" (Hsu 1991: 13). The Japanese also established the "Department of Aboriginal Affairs" (Nagata 1995: 77).

After the Second World War, when Taiwan was returned to the Kuomintang government, the aborigines were administered as *tuzhu,* "aborigines"[7], who were officially and popularly referred to as *shanbao,* "hill comrades". The policy on the aborigines was described as *shandi xingzheng zhengce,* hill region administrative policy. A few years before the democratization of Taiwan in 1987, the aborigines were able to assert themselves, and demanded the removal of the term *shanbao,* and called for the adoption of the term *yuanzhumin,* indigenous peoples. This campaign for re-labeling is called *zhengming yundong* or "campaign to correct the label". On 23 June 1994, the aborigines organized a big demonstration in Taipei in conjunction with the 10th anniversary of this campaign. The "correcting the label" campaign at first encountered some objections from the Chinese, pointing out that the aborigines were themselves migrants from mainland China, albeit in ancient time. The Chinese opponents argued that if the aborigines were *yuanzhumin,* then what about Chinese who had settled down in Taiwan for generations? The re-labeling campaign had triggered discourse on the politics of indigenousness.

The government and scholars in Taiwan had used *tuzhu* as the Chinese equivalent of "aborigines" in English, so why was there objection to the use of the term *yuanzhumin?* While both terms are generally understood as indigenous peoples in English, the latter term carries the specific meaning of "original inhabitants" as indicated by the character *yuan* which means "original", while *tuzhu* literally connotes local inhabitants that migrants from afar have come into contact. Thus Chinese migrants referred to the people of the land they had come to trade or settle as *tuzhu.* There is also the distinction of three different understandings of the term "indigenous" and consequently different ways to translate it into Chinese: that is 1) indigenous as being the original inhabitants of the land *(yuanzhumin, tuzhu),* 2) indigenous as being of the local when colonial powers, invaders, and immigrants encountered the people *(tuzhu)*; and 3) indigenous as simply belonging to the local (bendiren, which can be translated as indigenous people or natives). In the last understanding of the term, descendants of migrants who have lived in a country for some generations can also claim to be "indigenous". As the usage of *tuzhu* arises from contact between immigrants who saw themselves as the civilized and the weaker local inhabitants who were seen as *fan,* not so civilized or tribal, there is an in-built unequal power relation in the term. It is thus easy for the Chinese to adopt the term *tuzhu* for the pre-existing local people. Nevertheless, the label *yuanzhumin* (original inhabitants of the land) is now used in Taiwan both officially and by the public, albeit it is still primarily perceived by the mainstream society as referring to "tribal people". The aborigines themselves certainly use the term, especially in articulating their demands for development and rights.

Minorities and Indigenous People in Hong Kong Special Administrative Region (SAR)

The concept of indigenous people is used in Hong Kong in a unique way. When scholars write about the rights of indigenous people in Hong Kong, they are not referring to a different ethnic category apart from the mainstream Chinese population. They are also not referring to "tribal" people. They refer to Chinese from the villages in the New Territory, who claim to be descendants of established lineages who inhabited the New Territories when it was leased to the British government in 1898. The British recognized the right of the local inhabitants, including their customs. This recognition of the special status of the original inhabitants continues to this day. Article 40 of the Basic Law states that "The lawful traditional rights and interests of the indigenous inhabitants of the 'New Territories' shall be protected by the Hong Kong Special Administrative Region." The Hong Kong case is special. While there are urban minorities such as the Nepalis, Pakistanis, and other peoples of South Asian origins, there are no indigenous minorities who need special protection. Thus the application of a UN endorsed term of "indigenous peoples" is not a problem since, in this sense, there are no indigenous peoples in Hong Kong.

Conclusion

The examples from China show that the English term "indigenous peoples" can have very different perceptions, implications, and problems of usage in different societies and contexts, and can be translated in different ways into Chinese. Corntassel (2003) has provided us with a comprehensive discussion of who is indigenous. There are many definitions of indigenous peoples; most emphasize the disadvantaged status in a country (e.g. IWGIA definition, see IWGIA 2006: 8) and being indigenous to a particular territory. Taking into consideration our discussion above, it is more practical to use "indigenous" to refer to the status of being indigenous to a region or country to distinguish from migrant population and their descendants from another country, without considering whether the indigenous people are the earliest population or debating which group is the earliest and therefore more indigenous.

We need to avoid getting paralyzed with the politics of indigenousness if understood in a narrow sense, and note that the term "indigenous" can be used by different ethnic categories in a country in different ways, including for political articulation. In addition, we need to understand indigenous peoples as such peoples who have separate cultural life and are marginalized in modern states, who generally need some kind of protection for their economic and cultural survival.

In the case of PRC, both Han and non-Han *minzu* are indigenous in its narrow sense, and our concern is not who is more indigenous in the sense of who was there first. It is unwise to stir up such a debate since there is no final conclusion that can be drawn. Our concern is the condition of the non-Han peoples who have been rendered minorities and disadvantaged in the Chinese state which is overwhelmingly dominated by the Han people. While in most places in Xinjiang, for instance, the Uighurs are numerically the majority people, nationally they are numerically a minority; even in Xinjiang they are economically and politically a minority in relation to the economic and political dominance of the Han people. With liberalization since 1978, the influx of Han migrants from other parts of China means that the local Uighurs have to compete even more with the Han Chinese for economic opportunities and resources, although this also provides economic opportunities for well-off Uighurs.

Thus for the international adoption of the term "indigenous peoples" to be applied to China, there are two approaches. One is, for convenience, to regard as indigenous peoples the populations that have been rendered minorities by the state, officially recognized by PRC as 55 *minzu*. The logic for this is that the state has identified these as "minorities" who are entitled to some special administration (such as entitlement to administration as autonomous counties, autonomous prefectures and autonomous regions), affirmative actions (special consideration for college education) or other special considerations (such as the less strict application of the one-child policy). Given such special considerations, there is no opposition to being classified as minorities. In fact there are requests by some groups to be reclassified as separate minzu rather than under an existing one, but the state so far does not entertain such requests.

The alternative is to identify which of these "minorities" are entitled to be "indigenous peoples" by studying their marginality and the need for special protection. This is no easy task, as the Chinese state has made all non-Han peoples minorities, and these "minorities" are very heterogeneous in terms of history, educational achievement, economic livelihood, and acculturation (cultural change in the direction of the Han). And they are all Indigenous as do the Han, in the sense that their homelands are in China[8].

To illustrate the complexity of identifying "indigenous peoples" from among the nationality minorities in China, we can take the example of the Manchus. Economically the Manchus are not much different from the Han people, but they can claim the need for protection in order to revive their language and culture, as they are already largely linguistically assimilated by the Han. It is also problematic to say that they do not qualify for special protection whereas the Chinese state has already allowed them the same special considerations as the other non-Han minorities. Then there is also the issue that the Manchu were descendants of a people who ruled China during the Qing dynasty, China's last imperial dynasty. There are also the Kinhs and Russians (more below) whose similar people in Vietnam and Russia are majority people within their own states. Are they "indigenous people"? Given such complexity and that the Chinese state has already made provisions for "minorities" which in other countries are generally for "tribal" people, and that many ethnocentric Han Chinese do regard most of these minorities as "tribal", I propose to regard the existing national minorities in China as loosely equivalent of indigenous peoples, i.e., as disadvantaged minorities whose economic and cultural rights need protection. One can then more strictly determine which among these "nationality minorities" need special attention as do those in other countries.

As discussed, neither the Chinese government nor the Han and non-Han minorities have used the term "indigenous people" to distinguish among themselves. Even Tibetans overseas who are fighting for a separate state have not articulated themselves as indigenous people, but rather as a people who had a state system albeit with various forms and intensity of rule by the central governments of imperial China. The Tibetan case is too complicated to be discussed here[9]. Putting aside the issue of a separate state, which is hardly an option for those in China, there is no opposition to providing affirmative actions for minorities. This does not mean that there is no opposition to specific policies which may have hidden agendas. While special consideration for college entrance is welcome, the policy of financing Tibetan students to study in secondary schools in different Chinese cities outside Tibet is controversial because it is likely to cause many young Tibetans to be less competent in their own language and traditions or even assimilated by the Han[10]. It should also be noted that the Tibetans in Tibet are still numerically the majority people, although with better communication by air and land (especially the new train service) and more economic development, there are increasing Han migrants in Lhasa and other urban centers.

The most common definition of indigenous people notes the fact that they have become ethnic minorities in nation-states, minorities not only numerically but also economically and politically, that is, they are economically and politically disadvantaged as a result of being incorporated into a state. As I have shown above, in some countries, such as in China and Malaysia, it may be more accurate to speak of indigenous minorities, rather than simply indigenous peoples, which may imply that the majority population is not indigenous or as indigenous. The emphasis on being disadvantaged is important, and so we can work from a definition which identifies indigenous peoples as "The disadvantaged descendants of those peoples that inhabited a territory prior to the formation of a state" (Corntassel 2003: 89).

Sociologically the term "indigenous peoples" may be understood as "indigenous minorities" for reasons outlined in the discussion above. However, social activists generally reject the term "minority", given the inferior political status defined by the majority people and the state. "Indigenous peoples" is thus the term which can be accepted by the peoples themselves. Thus indigenous peoples are disadvantaged descendants of peoples that are indigenous to particular regions in a country, who continue to identify themselves as separate ethnic categories from the dominant populations. In many countries, these people are perceived by the governments and the dominant populations as "tribal", or simply minorities. In fact even in China, it is not uncommon to hear officials and Han individuals referring to some minorities as tribal (buluo). Our definition excludes the "indigenous people" of Hong Kong as they are ethnically part of the Chinese majority.

From the above considerations we may conclude that it is acceptable to use "indigenous people" as an appropriate label for indigenous minorities, and support the usage of this term by the United Nations and other international organizations. However, in dealing with states that find it difficult to use the term "indigenous people" in their own languages, or states that already have an established or accepted label which includes our understanding of indigenous minorities, we need not insist on them adopting the exact translation of the term "indigenous people". The Republic of China already has a clear policy on "minorities" which include all its citizens other than the majority Han people. The term shaoshu minzu or "nationality minorities" includes trans-border peoples who are citizens of China, such as the E Luo Si zu (Russians) and Jing zu (i.e. Kinh or Vietnamese). Its policy on the minorities does not call for the distinction between people who are really indigenous and peoples (such as the Russians and Jing people) who have distinct civilizations outside the state of China. This should be respected. There is a need for dialogue between the United Nations (and other IGOs and NGOs) and China to reach an understanding that the term "indigenous people" can mean indigenous minorities or bendi shaoshu minzu, and in calling for China to support a convention on indigenous people, the minorities in China can be loosely recognized as "indigenous peoples". There is no intention to reclassify those who are indigenous and who are not. The spirit of the recognition of "indigenous people" is to make sure that all states and international organizations respect the dignity of the people and that their plights are not neglected. In actual implementation of economic aid, for instance, it is up to the international organizations to determine which minorities, in the case of China, deserve more assistance and monitoring of their plights. With this approach, it should be possible for all states including China to be convinced about the recognition and adoption of the term "indigenous peoples".

References

Alberts, Eli. 2006. *A History of Daoism and the Yao People of South China.* Youngstown, NY: Cambria Press

Benjamin, Geoffrey. 2002. "On Being Tribal in the Malay World", in *Tribal Communities in the Malay World: Historical, Cultural and Social Perspectives,* eds., Geoffrey Benjamin and Cynthia Chou, pp. 7-76. Singapore: Institute of Southeast Asian Studies

Corntassel, Jeff J. 2003. "Who is Indigenous? 'Peoplehood' and Ethnationalist Approaches to Rearticulating Indigenous Identity." *Nationalism and Ethnic Politics* 9(1): 75-100

Dentan, K. Robert, Kirk Endicott, Alberto G. Gomes, and M.B. Hooker. 1997. Malaysia and the Original People: A Case Study of the Impact of Development on Indigenous Peoples. Boston: Allyn and Bacon

Fei, Hsiao Tung. 1999. "Jianshu wo de minzu yanjiu jingli he sikao (My Thought and Experience of Studying Minorities)", in *Fei Xiaotong Wenji* (Collected Works of Fei Xiaotong), vol. 14, pp. 88-105. Beijing: Qunyan Chubanshe

Fei, Xiaotong. 1981. *Toward a people's Anthropology.* Beijing: New World Press.

Grunfeld, A. Tom. 1996. *The Making of Modern Tibet.* Revised edition. Armonk, NY: M.E. Sharpe

Hsu, Mutsu. 1991. *Culture, Self, and Adaptation: The Psychological Anthropology of Two Malayo-Polynesian Groups in Taiwan.* Taipei: Institute of Ethnology, Academia Sinica

Harrell, Stevan, ed. 2001. *Perspectives on the Yi of Southwest China.* Berkeley, Cal.: University of California Press

IWGIA. 2006. "The African Commission on Human and Peoples' Rights and Indigenous Peoples." Paper presented at the Workshop on Indigenous Concept, 1-3 March 2006, Chiang Mai, Thailand

Kapstein, Matthew T. 2006. *The Tibetans.* Oxford: Blackwell.

Kaup, Katherine Palmer. 2000. *Creating the Zhuang: Ethnic Politics in China.* Boulder, London: Lynne Rienner Publishers

Li, Yiyuan *et. al.* 1983 *Shandi xingzheng zhengce zhi yanjiu yu pinggu baogaoshu* (Report on the Study and Assessment of the Policy and Administration of the Hills). Taipei: Taiwan sheng zhengfu minzhengting

Nagata, Shuichi. 1995. "A Comparison of Administration of the Aboriginal Populations in Taiwan (Japanese Period), Malaysia and North America."In *Proceedings of the International Conference on Anthropology and the Museum,* ed., Tsong-yuan Lin, pp. 73-100. Taipei: Taiwan Museum

PRC State Council. 2005. "Zhongguo de minzu quyu zizhi (China's *Minzu* Autonomous Areas)". Document issued by the Department of Information, State Council, People's Republic of China, February, 2005

Schein, Louisa. 2000. *Minority Rules: The Miao and the Feminine in China's Cultural Politics.* Durham: Duke University Press

Tan, Chee Beng. 1992. "On 'Tribe'." *Sarawak Gazette* CXIX (1521) September, pp. 51-54.

————1993. "Introduction: Badeng Migration and Ethnogenesis", in *The Migration of Kenyah Badeng,* by Vom Roy, ed., Tan Chee-Beng, pp. xiii-lii. Kuala Lumpur: Institute of Advanced Studies, University of Malaya

Wu Da. 2004. *Rentong zhi jueze: Sichuan ersu ren zuqun rentong jiangou de minzuzhi yanjiu* (Selection of Identities: An Ethnographic Study of the Construction of Ethnic Identity of Ersu People in Sichuan). Ph.D. thesis, Chinese University of Hong Kong

Yang, Hui. 1997. "The Dai Tusi System and Its History in Dehong." In Wang Zhusheng, *The Jingpo Kachin of the Yunnan Plateau,* pp. 267-304. Tempe, Arizona: Program for Southeast Asian Studies Monograph Series, Arizona State University

Yazhou Zhoukan: The International Chinese Newsweekly, 21 January 2007

Yuan, Tongkai. 2004. *Zoujin zhuli jiaoshi: Tu Yao xuexiao jiaoyu de minzuzhi yanjiu* (Classrooms in the Bamboo Fences: An Ethnographic Study of Schooling among the Tu Yao). Tianjin: Tianjin Renmin Chubanshe

Notes

[1] Tan Chee-Beng is currently Chairperson and Professor in the Department o Anthropology, The Chinese University of Hongkong.

[2] I thank Dr. Christian Erni and Dr. Wu Da (himself a Yi) for giving me valuable comments on this paper. I am of course responsible for the analysis and views expressed.

[3] Under the communist system of administration, the government is not separated from the Communist Party. At each level of government administration, there is a party secretary. At the level of provincial government, for example, the Party Secretary has equal if not more de facto power than the Governor. Similarly at the county level, the county head cannot make major decision without the consent of the party secretary. While the party secretary respects, for instance, the provincial governor's position and public image, if there is a contest of power, the party secretary often has the final say.

[4] For a comprehensive study of Tu Yao and their marginality, see Yuan (2004).

[5] For a recent study of the genealogy of the label Yao, see Alberts (2006).

[6] There are now a number of studies on the Yi, see Harrell (2001) and Wu Da (2004).

[7] In the Taiwanese Government's Report on the Study and Assessment of the Policy and Administration of the Hills, *tuzhu* is rendered as aborigines in English and vice-versa. See Li *et. al.* (1983).

[8] As mentioned, indigenousness is not an issue in China, and there is no need to single out the Kinh (Vietnamese) and Russians as exceptions since before the modern state system, the border was not an issue a far as the people's homeland is concerned.

[9] See Grunfeld (1996) and Kapstein (2006) for two convenient readings in English, which have substantial academic description on Tibet and its relations to the central governments of China.

[10] During my visit to Tibet in May 2006, I learned from a Tibetan friend that despite knowing the implications, Tibetan parents (especially the educated ones) still send their children to study in cities outside Tibet because they want them to have good education. It is a decision made under the dilemma of having to decide whether to keep the children in Tibet or to send them away to study in better schools outside Tibet.

Recognition "In Kind": Indonesian Indigenous Peoples and State Legislation

John Bamba[1]

Background – The Government's Position

All this time, the Indonesian Government's attitude toward the recognition of the Indigenous Peoples' rights has been ambiguous and inconsistent. The most recent steps taken by the Indonesian government at the United Nations clearly demonstrate this. In relation to the policy concerning the Draft Declaration of the Indigenous Peoples' Rights, the Indonesian government's attitude at the Human Rights Commission level—of which Indonesia is a member—contradicts the position taken at the General Assembly level. As a member of the Human Rights Commission, Indonesia voted for the adoption of the draft while as the member of the General Assembly, Indonesia opted to support other countries that reject the inclusion of the draft as one of the agenda of the subsequent General Assembly meeting. Later on, again, it however voted in favor of the adoption of the amended Declaration by the General Assembly. This paper further highlights this inconsistency and shows how this attitude has been reflected in various national laws and regulations in Indonesia.

In the colonial era, the social status of the people in Indonesia was divided into 4 levels. On the first level were the Westerners, on the second level the local aristocrats (kings and sultans), on the third level were other foreigners/non-natives (Chinese, Arabs, Indian), and on the fourth level were the ordinary Indonesians, including those we today call the indigenous peoples.

After Soekarno and Muhamad Hatta proclaimed Indonesia's Independence on 17th August 1945, the Indonesian people were according to the constitution categorized into two main groups: the Indonesian citizens (WNI = Warga Negara Indonesia) and the foreign citizens (WNA = Warga Negara Asing). The newly formed Indonesian state also recognized what it called "Special Territories", which consisted of the former local kingdoms and sultanates that joined the Republic and the Capital City Jakarta. The local kingdoms and sultanates were thereby allowed to maintain their existence in cultural terms, but not in political terms. This, it is argued, is because the Republic is a Unitary State with a centralized government in Jakarta, leaving no room for local Kingdoms and Sultanates for self-governance. Two of the Special Territories still exist today: Aceh and Yogyakarta (along with the region of Papua which Indonesia annexed after independence in 1963). Jakarta also retains a special status as the capital city of the nation.

In the ensuing implementation of the constitutional provisions, however, both citizenship and territorial status received totally different treatment from what was originally intended in the 1945 Constitution. With regards to citizenship, the ethnic minorities have been experiencing discriminatory policies by the government. The Indonesian Chinese, for example, have long been treated as foreigners (WNA) despite the fact that they have lived in Indonesia for many generations. As a result, almost all Indonesian Chinese lost their citizenship rights and had to apply for a certificate of citizenship from generation to generation.

Under the Soekarno Government (first President, 1945-1965) this situation was not experienced by the Indonesian Chinese. Many Indonesian Chinese became high-ranking government officials, ran Chinese political organizations and became Soekarno cabinet members. This was due to Soekarno's close relationship with the Chinese government. After the Indonesian Communist Party Coup in October 1965, which later on resulted in Soekarno's loss of his presidency, Soeharto (the new President, 1968-1998) applied tough policies on the Indonesian Chinese which he accused of being supporters and followers of Communism. They were barred from joining any political activities and had to stay away from state affairs including those who had already received their certificates of citizenship (SBKRI = *Surat Bukti Kewarganegaraan Republik Indonesia* or Letter of Proof as Republic of Indonesia's citizen). Soeharto was an army general who in 1965 cracked down on what he believed was the Communist Party's coup to topple the legitimate government.[2]

During his government, Soeharto however backed some big Chinese conglomerates and granted special treatment for them in running their businesses. Soeharto used the Chinese businessmen to accumulate financial resources for his presidency, families and cronies. This partly explains why most of the successful Indonesian businessmen are Chinese. Now, after Soeharto was forced to step down in May 1998 by what is known as the people's Reformation Movement in Indonesia, many of those Chinese conglomerates have had to face prosecution on corruption cases as a result of the present government's fight on corruption, cronyism and nepotism (known as KKN = Korupsi, Kroni dan Nepotisme). On the other hand, there have been some policy changes towards the Indonesian Chinese by the present government. Confucianism, which is the major religion of the Chinese, has been officially recognized; Chinese cultural performance has been encouraged and the policy on the certificate of citizenship (SBKRI) for the Chinese has been canceled.

According to the Constitution, enacted on 18th of August 1945, one day after independence, indigenous communities were included in those "Special Territories" based on their "heredity rights". It is stated in Article 18 of the 1945 Constitution:

> The division of the territory of Indonesia into large and small regions shall be prescribed by law in consideration of and with due regard to the principles of deliberation in the government system and *the hereditary rights of special territories.* (emphasis added)

What is really meant by this "heredity rights of special territories" was further elaborated in the Elucidation of the 1945 Constitution that says:

> In the territory of Indonesia there are approximately 250 self-governing regions *(zelfbesturende landschappen)* and village communities *(volksge-meenschappen),* such as the "desa" (village) in Java and Bali, the "nagari" in Minangkabau, the "dusun" and "marga" in Palembang and other social-administrative units. These regional units have their own indigenous social systems and thus may be considered as special regions.

> The Republic of Indonesia respects the status of the special regions and any government regulation on these regions shall have due regard to their hereditary rights.

However, there have been neither further regulations nor any concrete implementation following the recognition of these special territories by the state. Words such as "indigenous social system" and "heredity rights" of the indigenous peoples just vanished in the air at the meeting rooms of the founding fathers. Fifteen years later, in 1960, this issue of indigenous communities' rights was addressed briefly in the Basic Agrarian Law. Being the first law that mentions indigenous peoples in Indonesia, the Basic Agrarian Law has set the trend in the state's interpretation of indigenous peoples' rights. Rather than giving more clarity and stronger commitment to the recognition of indigenous peoples' rights, the law weakened their position by defining special conditions for their recognition. As Article 3 reveals, one of the basic tenets of the law is that indigenous peoples' rights are rights *given by the state* rather than owned by the indigenous peoples. Since the rights are given, it is also up to the state to define, limit and put conditions on who is entitled to these rights.

Article 3 of the Basic Agrarian Law No.5/1960 states,

> Taking into account the regulations on Article 1 and 2, the implementation of *hak ulayat* (customary rights) and other similar rights of *masyarakat hukum adat* (customary-law communities), **as long as they are still existing,** should be such that **they fit in with the national and State interests,** which are based on the **nations' unity and must not against the Laws** and other higher regulations. (translation and emphasis by the author)

In the present, so-called "Reformation Era" in Indonesia, various new laws and regulations have included indigenous peoples' issues. However, the recognition of indigenous peoples in Indonesia is still ambiguous, problematic and thus prone to manipulations. The present conception of the government on indigenous peoples issues reflects the paradigm shift away from a strong and clear recognition by the founding fathers to the manipulative, ambiguous and false recognition by the present government. The conception is based on the following assumptions:

1. All native Indonesian are indigenous peoples

The most common argument found in Indonesia with regard to the concept of indigenous peoples is that all (native) Indonesians are indigenous peoples. This implies that the term is not relevant for Indonesia, and, consequently, that any discussion on indigenous peoples' rights and existence are not relevant either.

2. There are only "vulnerable groups" in Indonesia

Since all Indonesians are indigenous, the only distinction that can be made is that between the majority and the marginalized and disadvantaged groups, in Indonesia called "vulnerable groups" and "isolated communities". Thus, the Department of Social Affairs has extensive programs on what are officially called the "alienated tribal communities" *(masyarakat suku terasing)*. According to the government's conception, these communities must be freed from their alienation and be integrated into the wider modern society.

3. "Right of" not "Right to"

The government argues that if the concept of indigenous peoples, as perceived by the international community, is to be applied in Indonesia, and if special rights are granted to indigenous peoples, there is a danger of separatism or even secession, which would threaten the unity if not the basic concept of the nation state. Therefore, in order to address indigenous peoples' issues, it is the right *of* self-determination which should be applied, and not the right *to* self-determination.

Quoting Prof. Leo Gross from the Fletcher School of Law and Diplomacy, Dr. Hasan Wirajuda, an Indonesian senior diplomat and the current Minister of Foreign Affairs states that the right of self-determination is understood as the internal self-determination within the existing nation state, and not the right to form a separate state which is implicit in the concept of the right to self-determination. According to the government's view as represented by Dr. Hasan Wirajuda, the right to internal self-determination is sufficiently dealt with, for example, through the regional autonomy policies or through general election. In Dr. Wirajuda's own words:

> "The hope for [receiving] the right to self-determination, in one way or another, has given a false hope to the ethnic groups (ethnic nations) as well as developed "micro nationalism" that becomes a phenomena which erodes nation-state conception with all its consequences." (Wirajuda 1999: 125, translation by the author).

History of Concept and Terminologies

The Colonial Era

The indigenous peoples of Indonesia have a very long history, reaching back long before the feudal, colonial and present government came to rule them. Their ancestors were migrants from various parts in Asia belonging to the Austronesian linguistic stock. In the course of the long history of the archipelago's peoples, various kingdoms were established. Before Islam came to Indonesia, those kingdoms followed Hinduism and Buddhism. The first Hindu kingdom was established in Kalimantan in 400 AC under the name Kutai Kingdom with Kunduga as the first king. The two most important and biggest kingdoms in Indonesia were Sriwijaya in Sumatra and Madjapahit Kingdom in Java. As Islam came to Indonesia, most of the local kingdoms were turned into Sultanates.

Following Christopher Columbus' occupation in America, the world was divided into two spheres by the Portuguese and Spanish in the infamous Treaty of Tordesillas of 1494. The two colonial powers agreed to limit their colonial conquest to the respective sphere they were entitled to. Indonesia thus fell under the sphere of Portuguese control, who arrived there in 1511. Centuries later, Indonesia was colonized by the Netherlands (1799-1808), France (1808-1811), England (1811-1816), the Netherlands again (1816-1942) and Japan (1942-1945). The colonialists brought various local kingdoms and sultanates under their rule.

One of the regulations imposed by the Dutch, who occupied Indonesia the longest, was known as the *Domein Verklaring* of 1870, which explicitly states that all lands over which no ownership could be proven belonged to the colonial state. This regulation was met with resistance and revolts by the Indonesians, which forced the Dutch to apply the infamous divide-and-rule strategy *(devide et empera)*. This strategy had three main results:

1. Indonesia's rule was based on two systems: direct and indirect rule *(directe bestuur gebied* and indirecte *bestuur gebeid)*. Java and Madura were under the Dutch's direct rule while other territories were ruled through the local kingdoms or sultanates.

2. Serious studies on customary laws and ethnic communities were conducted to map out the territories and cultural differences. Prof. C. van Vollenhoven and Prof. Mr. B. ter Haar are the two most famous experts on *adat istiadat* (customs and traditions) and *hukum adat* (customary laws) in Indonesia even up to the present (Bahar, 2005). Based on their comprehensive studies, these two professors concluded that there were nineteen customary-law territories *(adatrechts kringen)* and they called the communities as Customary-Law Communities *(adatrechts gemeenschappen)*. This is what later on was referred to in Indonesian regulations as *masyarakat hukum adat,* the legal most widely-used term for indigenous peoples, as opposed to *masyarakat adat* currently used by Indonesia's indigenous peoples themselves. The term *Masyarakat Hukum Adat* (Customary-Law Communities) is rejected by the indigenous peoples in Indonesia because it perceives and defines indigenous peoples as related to the existing customary laws only and thus denies other characteristics that are attached to indigenous peoples' identity.

3. A comprehensive population census was carried out by the Dutch Colonial government in 1930 to identify the size of the population, and the different ethnic groups. Despite their contributions to the study of Adat Laws in Indonesia, which is still apparent up to the present, the identification and mapping-out of indigenous communities by the Dutch was done in the sphere of the divide-and-rule colonial strategy; which is to strengthen the segregation between the indigenous peoples, the Moslem/Sultanates and the migrants.

The Soekarno Era

The three initiatives by the colonial administration outlined above are very important for understanding the independent Indonesian government's attitude and policies on indigenous peoples. The Indonesian founding fathers were aware that the recognition of Indonesian indigenous peoples was crucial for creating a strong and legitimate state. It was important because, first, the indigenous peoples had been living and managing the territories *long before* any feudal, colonial and state ever existed. Secondly, those communities still existed and *practiced* their culture, traditions and way of life. Thirdly, the new republic was established in order to liberate the people from colonialism—as stated in the Preamble of the 1945 Constitution—not to bring them under a new form of colonialism.

Therefore, the recognition of the indigenous peoples was considered important and thus explicitly included in the constitution. As the term "indigenous peoples" or *"masyarakat adat"* was not known or widely used in Indonesia at that time, the term *masyarakat hukum adat* or customary-law communities, used by the Dutch, was adopted.

However, the government's awareness of the importance of the recognition of indigenous peoples' as well as their political goodwill to protect their rights in the constitution was not followed by proper action. The new-born Indonesia was more occupied with the struggle to maintain independence and gain international recognition. At the same time, the country was kept busy with various internal conflicts and the search for suitable political identity and ideology. Therefore, indigenous peoples' issues have never received proper attention during the government of the first President, Soekarno.

As mentioned above, in 1960, the Basic Agrarian Law was enacted. This law had in fact already been prepared in 1948. So many of the politicians who were involved in the drafting of the 1945 Constitution were also involved in the process, or at least aware of the concepts used in the Agrarian Law. As shown earlier, this law not only fails to properly protect the indigenous peoples, it is believed to have created a new trend: "recognition based on conditions".

The Soeharto Era

The concept and perception developed by the state apparatus and decision-makers in Indonesia during the Soeharto era treat the rights of indigenous peoples as a "gift" from the state, granted on conditions defined by the state. Thus, such recognition can best be called a recognition "in-kind". The recognition given by the state cannot be used by the indigenous peoples to exercise their rights because of the very conditions imposed on them, which contradict the fact that these rights were pre-existing. The recognition is granted insomuch as it does not sacrifice any state interests or "national development programs". The questions that arise are what are "state interests" and who defines them? Therefore, the recognition becomes very weak, amounts to not more than lip-service and thus becomes useless.

This recognition "in-kind" is obviously a false recognition. It is a manipulative recognition for the sake of diplomatic, political and legal purposes. By putting conditions before the recognition, the state allows itself to justify violation of indigenous peoples' rights committed by the state apparatus. On the other hand, these conditionalities have denied the indigenous peoples' "heredity and inalienable rights" based on the historical fact they predate the formation of the modern nation state. This type of recognition has also violated fundamental principles on which the Indonesian founding fathers based the 1945 Constitution.

The paradigmatic changes in the state's concept of indigenous peoples in Indonesia have first and foremost been driven by its interest in the natural resources that had long been managed by the indigenous peoples. Since the government intensified the exploitation of the natural resources especially through mining, logging and large-scale plantations, a number of laws and regulations had been produced that deny indigenous peoples' rights.

Since 1967, when Soeharto's Regime came to power, the government has systematically and through manipulation of the law marginalized the indigenous peoples. Ethnic and cultural identity had been suppressed under the SARA policy (an Indonesian abbreviation for Ethnic, Religion, Race and Inter-Group), since they were condemned as sensitive issues threatening national unity. Laws and regulations were produced to give business sectors access to natural resources on indigenous peoples' territories.

By completely denying the indigenous peoples' existence and rights and by treating access to land and resource as a gift from the state, the Soeharto government treated indigenous peoples' territories as *Terra Nullius,* the territories owned by the state. The government adopted the Washington Consensus[3] and granted access to land and natural resources to both foreign and domestic investors. These policies are clearly reflected in laws and investment contracts produced during the Soeharto era since 1967 and continued up to the present. The most recent controversial Law on Capital Investment No. 25/2007, signed into law on 2nd May 2007 to replace laws on foreign and domestic investment (No. 1, 1967 and No. 6, 1968) clearly show this. This new law provides three lease rights to investors[4] and permits 100%-owned foreign companies to exploit Indonesia's resources, to pay reduced levels of taxes, to use foreign staff and to transfer profits and capital overseas.

Other most important laws and their key provisions impacting on indigenous peoples' rights are:

1. Law No. 11/1967 on Mining
Article 26: "Whenever a mining authorization license is obtained over a certain area or territory based on the prevailing law, those who have the rights over the land are obliged to permit the works of the mining license holder on the said land."

2. Law No. 14/1970 on Basic Power of Judiciary
The law makes no mentioning about customary laws or customary courts and thus rejects the authority and power of customary laws in dispute settlement.

3. Law No. 5 on Village Government
This law homogenizes village government systems all over Indonesia and thus destroys diverse local and indigenous systems and institutions.

The reformation era

Two characteristics reflect the government's concept of indigenous peoples in the present reformation era. The first is the use of ambiguous terms in the legislation. Two terms are used: *Masyarakat Hukum Adat* or Customary-law Communities and *Masyarakat Tradisional* or Traditional Communities. The first term was derived from the term *Adatrechts Gemeenschappen* coined by the Dutch Colonial Government, while the second term was created from the interpretation that the indigenous peoples are the communities who are not living in modern life yet rooted from the concept of Alienated Tribal Communities. This probably has its roots in the concept of Alienated Tribal Communities used by the Department of Social Affairs during the Soeharto era.

The two terms are most likely used for the following reasons:

1. Both terms, if translated into English, are literally and by definition different from "indigenous peoples" used in international human rights instruments. This will facilitate the government's intention to escape from international legal obligations related to indigenous peoples.

2. The term "customary-law communities" could serve as the basis for the argument that it is the "customary law" that really matters. If certain communities do not have any customary laws anymore, even if their loss was caused by the government's own policies and regulations, they cannot claim to be indigenous. The Agrarian Minister Regulation No. 5/1999 clearly demonstrates this. In this regulation, any community who claims for themselves to be indigenous must meet three criteria: (1) that they have customary institution that are still in operation; (2) that they still have and implement customary laws; and (3) that they still have their customary territories.

3. The term "traditional communities" strengthens the government's argument that all native Indonesians are indigenous and that it is thus irrelevant to make special regulations on indigenous peoples. On the other hand, the term "traditional" gives the impression that it is the communities themselves who are resistant to changes, so the government's main program is .4social engineering to modernize their lifestyles.

The second characteristic is the use of conditions for the recognition of communities as indigenous, mostly to protect the government's interests in indigenous peoples' territories with all their natural resources. There are four main conditions imposed in various legislations, namely:

1. that they still exist
2. that they are in accordance with the development of societies, times and civilizations
3. that they are in accordance with the principles of the Unitary State of the Republic of Indonesia
4. that they shall be regulated by law

The rather vague concept of "development of societies" seems to mean something like the progress in the people's livelihood ("societal development" is the term used in the new Constitution). "Development of time" is even more vague, and most probably means something like "modernization". For example, government officials might say to an indigenous community "it's not the time anymore for you to maintain that tradition" (which amounts to saying: these traditions are "backward").

The Table below presents an overview of the terms used and the conditions imposed by various laws and regulations related to "indigenous peoples" in Indonesia. A compilation of the relevant articles of these laws is given in the Annex.

No	Laws (legislation)	Article	Terminology	Conditionalities
1	Amendments of 1945 Constitution	Article 18B (2)	Traditional communities	1. remain in existence 2. are in accordance with the societal development 3. and the principles of the Unitary State of the Republic of Indonesia 4. shall be regulated by law
2	Law No 24/2003 on Constitutional Court	Article 51 (b)	Union of customary-law community	
3	Amendments of 1945 Constitution	Article 281 (3)	Traditional communities	5. in accordance with the development of times and civilizations
4	MPR Decree No. XVII/MPR/1998 on Human Rights	Article 41	Traditional community	6. in accordance with the development of times
5	Law No. 39/1999 on Human Rights	Article 6 (1) & (2)	Customary-law community	7. in accordance with the development of times
6	MPR Decree No IX/MPR/2001 on Agrarian Reform and Management of Natural Resources	Article 5 (j)	Customary-law community	

By deliberately formulating conditions rather vaguely, the Indonesian state is not only taking away with one hand what the other has given, it reserves for itself the right to decide on behalf of indigenous peoples what is good for them and what is not, what can be considered "in accordance with time" and what cannot. What is actually meant here is that the state decides what is considered "developed", "modern" or "civilized", and in doing this, the Indonesian state joins all those past and present colonialist powers who have used the obligation of fulfilling a "civilizing mission" to legitimize exploitation and oppression of peoples with different cultures and histories than their own.

The concept of the "civilizing mission" *(mission civilisatrice)* was coined by the French and formed the basis of their approach to colonial rule in its colonies in Northern and Western Africa as well as Indochina in the 19th and 20th century. The French saw it as their duty to "civilize" – which means: to Westernize – peoples they considered "backward". And so did the British. Like the French, they tried to justify imperialist expansion with their self-appointed mission of spreading "civilization" – and in the process enrich themselves. The British imperial poet Rudyard Kipling in a famous poem of 1899 has called it "the White Man's Burden".

Many post-colonial governments, and among them Indonesia, continue with such an ethnocentric and oftentimes outright racist policies by which they legitimize dispossession, oppression and forced assimilation of indigenous peoples. The difference is merely that white colonizers are replaced by a native ruling elite, and that the "civilization" promoted by the state is usually a hybrid of the culture of the politically dominant group and modernist and developmentalist ideologies.

Current Efforts and Future Prospects

A clear and unconditional recognition of indigenous peoples in Indonesia will depend very much on a change of the paradigm which still sees indigenous peoples and their rights as potential problems for the state's interests. Politically, under the government's present paradigm indigenous peoples' demands for special rights are seen as a threat to the unitary state, and it is believed that treating indigenous peoples as politically distinct from other sectors in society will provoke separation and "erode the nation-state conception" (Wirajuda 1999, 125) Economically, indigenous peoples' existence in their territories are considered as a main obstacle to development and investments, and that granting special rights to indigenous peoples in natural resources management would limit the government's access to these resources and prevent foreign investment in the respective sectors . It is also believed that granting indigenous peoples their special political and economic rights will cause jealousy on the part of other members of the society and result in discrimination and injustice. Socially and culturally, indigenous peoples' way of life is seen as a symbol of underdevelopment, backwardness and the obstacles to modernization. Therefore, their culture should be "filtered" (i.e. only those traits should be maintained that are not against the laws and modernization), enhanced and modernized so that they do not leave a scar in the face of the country. Ecologically, indigenous peoples customs and traditions in natural resources management are accused of being destructive, unsustainable and the causes of man-made natural disasters such as forest fires, deforestations and soil degradation. It is perceived that the practices are highly unproductive so they must be replaced by big plantations, mining and other industries.

The struggle for the state's recognition and protection of indigenous peoples' rights has been going on both at local, national and international level. At local level, the indigenous peoples have organized themselves almost all over Indonesia. The first national congress of Indonesian indigenous peoples took place in 1999 and gave birth to AMAN *(Aliansi Masyarakat Adat Nusantara* = Alliance of the Indigenous Peoples of the Archipelago), a nation-wide network of indigenous peoples' organizations. The members of AMAN are hundreds of indigenous communities from all over Indonesian archipelago. They formed a national secretariat to do coordination for their struggle in obtaining better protection of their rights as well as building networks and collaborations with their regional and international indigenous brothers and sisters.

As far as the terms used by the state are concerned, AMAN has rejected them and uses the term *"Masyarakat Adat",* literally translated as "Adat Communities". *Adat* has a wider, deeper and more holistic meaning, emphasizing the characteristics that make indigenous peoples in Indonesia different from the mainstream society. Customary-law is only one practice of Adat, and due to various external pressures some indigenous peoples might not been able to practice it anymore. Therefore the term *Masyarakat Hukum Adat* (Customary-Law Communities) used by the government reduces the real identity of indigenous peoples on one hand and could be used to deny the existence of the indigenous peoples on the other due to the lack of customary-law practices within those particular communities. Indigenous peoples' identity is determined by the *Adat*—not only *Hukum Adat* (customary-laws). Adat is the overall beliefs, systems, practices, worldview, values and norms of the indigenous peoples governing their life from generation to generation. *Adat* makes indigenous peoples practice their own beliefs or religion; they have their own system of natural resource management; they have special attachment (sovereignty) to the territories where they have been living for generations, they have their own economic, social, cultural and spiritual value system and most of them experience some sort of oppression and marginalization from outside. AMAN defines indigenous communities as:

> "A group of people who have lived on their ancestral land for generations, have sovereignty over the land and natural wealth in their customary bounded territory, where adat law and institutions arrange the social life of the community, and carry out the social-political and economic lives of the community." (Brochure of AMAN)

Based on the above definition, there are now 777 indigenous communities that joined AMAN and another 366 communities have applied. The estimated total number of people represented by those 777 communities are about 8 million. Most of these communities are represented by 23 indigenous peoples' organizations which formed local AMAN branches. The vision of AMAN is: "The realisation of an indigenous life which is sovereign, just, prosperous, valuable and democratic".

Since the past three years, serious efforts have been undertaken by the National Commission on Human Rights (Komnas HAM) to clarify the concept of indigenous peoples. Among others, Komnas HAM together with the Constitutional Court and the Department of Internal Affairs organized the national workshop on "Inventory and Protection of Customary-Law Communities" on 14-15 June 2005. The workshop, which was attended by participants representing various stakeholders including governmental and non-governmental organizations, academics and representatives of the United Nations Development Programme (UNDP). The workshop was able to identify problems with state legislations and policies on indigenous peoples at the conceptual and implementation level. Among others, the workshop came up with the following recommendations:

1. Amendments must be done to the 1945 Constitution (Article 18B (2)), Basic Agrarian Law No. 5/1960 (Article 3), Law on Forestry No. 41/1999 (Article 1 (f) and Article 5 (1)), Law on Constitutional Court No. 24/2003 (Article 51 (1.b.)), which place conditions on the recognition of indigenous peoples.
2. Support the government's plan to draft a law on Indigenous Peoples as part of the National Program on Legislation for the Period 2004-2009.
3. That the Indonesian government ratifies the ILO Convention no. 169/1999 concerning Indigenous and Tribal Peoples in Independent Countries.
4. That Komnas HAM acts as the center for coordination/communication for various initiatives towards a better recognition of indigenous peoples

Apart from the various efforts above, it is also important to note that from a legal perspective, Law No. 32/2004 could also be used to strengthen the position of indigenous peoples. This is the law that replaces Law No. 5/1979 on Village Government which has been identified as one of the regulations that had caused serious destructions among indigenous peoples through its regulation on homogenization of village government systems.

Article 216, Law No. 32/2004 obliges local governments in Indonesia to recognize and respect the heredity rights and village's *adat istiadat* (customs and traditions) without imposing any conditions. Article 216 states:

1. Further regulation on village shall be decided in Local Regulation by holding to Government Regulation
2. Local Regulation, as meant by verse (1), has the obligation to recognize and respect heredity rights and village's *adat istiadat* (customs and traditions)

After all, the conditions of the indigenous peoples in Indonesia now and in the future depend very much on the struggle of the indigenous peoples themselves to strengthen the pressure on the government and the decision-makers so that there is more goodwill to accept the existence of indigenous peoples in Indonesia which is undeniable and has become part of the historical reality. Unfortunately, the struggle seems more and more challenging as the interests of the government and investors to take over the control on the natural resources in indigenous peoples' territories is increasing.

References

Bahar, Saafroedin 2005. Investarisasi dan Perlindungan Hak Masyarakat Hukum Adat (Investarization and Protection of the Rights of Customary-Law Communities). Jakarta: Komisi Nasional *Hak Asasi Manusia. Agust 2005.*

Wirajuda,. Hasan 1999. Indigenous Peoples and Internal Self Determination (Pribumi dan Otonomi Dalam Mengatur Urusan Sendiri); in Komnas HAM, Hak Asasi Manusia: *Tanggungjawab Negara, Peran Institusi Nasional dan Masyarakat.* Jakarta: Komnas HAM

Annex

Compilation of relevant articles in current Indonesian legislations recognizing "customary-law communitie"s or "traditional communities".

All of these articles clearly show the conditionality imposed on the recognition of "customary-law communitie"s or "traditional communities" (emphasis is added).

Amendments of the 1945 Constitution[5]:
Article 18B (1): The State recognizes and respects units of regional authorities that are special and distinct, which shall be regulated by law. (2) The State recognizes and respects *traditional communities* along with their traditional customary rights as long as these *remain in existence* and are *in accordance with the societal development and the principles of the Unitary State of the Republic of Indonesia,* and *shall be regulated by law.*

Article 28I (3): The cultural identities and rights of traditional communities shall be respected in accordance with the development of times and civilizations.

Law No. 41/1999 on Forestry:
Article 1 (6): "Customary forests are state forests located in the territory of customary-law communities."

Law No 24/2003 on Constitutional Court:
Article 51.b.: [Judicial Review can be filed by] the union of *customary-law communities* as long as they are *still in existence* and *in accordance with the development of societies and the principle of* the Unitary State of the Republic of Indonesia which shall be regulated by law.

Majelis Permusyawaratan Rakyat [MPR]⁶ f Decree No. XVII/MPR/1998 on Human Rights:
Article 41: The Identity of traditional communities, including the customary land rights are protected, *in accordance with the development of times.*

Law No. 39/1999 on Human Rights:
Article 6 (1): In upholding the human rights, differences and needs in *customary-law communities* must be paid attention to and protected by the law, society and government. (2) the Identity of customary-law communities, including customary land rights are *protected in accordance with the development of times.* (MPR Decree No IX/MPR/2001 on Agrarian Reform and Management of Natural Resources)

Article 5: Agrarian reform and natural resources management must be implemented based on the principles of: (j). recognizing and respecting the rights of *customary-law communities* and the diversity of the nation's cultures on agrarian and natural resources.

Notes

[1] John Bamba, a Dayak from West-Kalimantan, is director of the Institut Dayakologi, a community-based organization of the Dayak, based in Pontianak, West-Kalimantan.
[2] These events are still controversially and hotly debated up to now, especially on who were the men behind the gun in that failed coup attempt. Soeharto directly pointed his finger at President Soekarno, officially replaced him from his presidency in 1968 and put him in house arrest until his dead in 1972. What Soeharto did was difficult to accept by the majority of Indonesians since it is considered strange that Soekarno as a president wanted to topple his own government, as accused by Soeharto. Soeharto then moved the military and some religious groups in Indonesia

to wipe out the communists and killed an estimated 500,000 to 3,000,000 people who were members of Indonesian Communist Party or accused of being so. Some analysts believe this is one of the biggest genocide of the 20th century that qualifies Soeharto to be brought to the International Court of justice.

3 A set of ten economic policy prescriptions considered as a "standard" reform package by Washington-based institutions such as the International Monetary Fund, World Bank and U.S. Treasury Department.. Also known as Neo-Liberalism, these policies expand the role of market on one hand and limit the role of the state on the other. The policies open up less developed countries to investments from large multinational corporations and their wealthy owners in advanced First World economies. (see: http://en.wikipedia.org/wiki/Washington_Consensus)

4 1. Right of cultivation/exploitation (HGU = *Hak Guna Usaha)*: allows companies to invest in the agricultural and fisheries sector, such as plantation developers. Under the previous laws, the lease was only up to 35 years and could only be extended for maximum of a further 25 years. Under the new law, the HGU lease is for an initial 60 years, extendable for a further 35 years. Right to use (and construct) buildings (HGB = *Hak Guna Bangunan)*: the investors' right to build agricultural processing plants, pulp mills, ore processing facilities etc. Previously, these leases were for a maximum of 50 years, but under the new law the initial period is 50 years, with the option to extend for another 30 years. Right of use of land *(Hak Pakai)*: under the new law, investors could use a land for a maximum period of 70 years.. Previously the length of the lease was determined by local administrations. Source: http://dte.gn.apc.org/73fdi.htm

5 The 1945 Constitution of the Republic of Indonesia was first amended in 1999, second amendment was done in 2000, third amendment in 2001 and fourth amendment in 2002.

6 The Majelis Permusyawaratan Rakyat (People's Deliberation Assembly) is the highest decision-making body of the state in Indonesia.

Resolving the Asian Controversy:
Identification of Indigenous Peoples in the Philippines

Christian Erni[1]

My dear friend, be welcome here!
Where, perchance, did you come from?
From the seashore ebbing low?
From the bubbling water springs?
If from the water source up,
let us talk a moment here,
in a happy, friendly way.
Even whoever you are,
we like to be at your side.[2]

The Philippines one of the three countries in Asia that officially use the term "indigenous peoples".[3] Two decades of activism and lobbying by civil society organizations in the Philippines were behind the official adoption of the concept of indigenous peoples, and with it the passing of a comprehensive law on the protection of the rights of these peoples. The indigenous peoples' organizations and support groups who were most active in this and insisted on the use of the term were undoubtedly informed by the international discourse on the rights of indigenous peoples. And they, as much as the Philippine government, must have been aware of the controversy of the concept in Asia and the generally negative attitude demonstrated by other Asian governments.[4] Yet, the Philippine government did not follow the common trend of merely referring to the concept's mono-dimensional, though admittedly original, meaning of "indigenous" as being "born to, originating from a place"[5], and thus ignoring the past two decades of discussions and practice that has shaped the concept and given it a broader, more specific and more political meaning. The definition included in the Indigenous Peoples Rights Act of 1997[6] explicitly recognizes the particular developments that are the roots of the current predicament of the part of the Filipino population thus – and in line with international practice –considered to represent the country's indigenous peoples.

This article attempts to trace these historical developments that have lead to the differentiation of the Philippine population into a majority of, though ethnically diverse and equally "native", mainstream Filipinos, and an ethnically even more diverse minority which was formerly referred to as "tribal people" and today represents the indigenous peoples of the Philippines. The article will outline changes in terminologies used for these peoples over the past decades, and the identification of those ethnic groups considered to belong to this category. The article continues by showing that in spite of striking differences, particularly with respect to colonial history, the socio-political differentiation in the Philippines conforms to a pattern prevalent throughout the Southeast Asian region. It concludes with a brief discussion of the semantic evolution of the term "indigenous peoples" in international documents related to the rights of indigenous peoples and argues that it is because of this change in meaning that the term indigenous peoples is as appropriate for the Asian context as elsewhere in the world. The case of the Philippines proves that is practically applicable.

Pre-colonial Complexities

When in March 1521 Spanish explorer Magellan set foot on Limasawa island in the Western Visayas, the archipelago that later came to be named "Philippinas" was inhabited by an extremely heterogeneous and highly fragmented population. A number of large and interregionally powerful polities, like Manila, Cebu, or the Islamic sultanates of Sulu and Maguindanao, had evolved as a result of the rapidly expanding maritime luxury-goods trade in the 15th and 16th century (Junker 2000: 5, 17, 232f) and hundreds of smaller-scale chiefdoms engaged in trade were found in the coastal plains of most of the larger islands of the archipelago (ibid.: 233). The mountainous, often rugged interior was populated by ethnically highly diverse and politically autonomous peoples "ranging from small bands of hunter-gatherers to tribally organized swidden cultivators and emergent ranked societies practicing intensive agriculture" (ibid.: 221).

Like elsewhere in insular Southeast Asia, the highly fragmented geography and diverse landscape resulted in the ecological specialization of different ethnic groups linked to each other through trade and – among coastal and riverine chiefdoms – political alliances. While the coastal and lowland trading societies were engaged in intensive farming and were able to produce agricultural surplus and other goods for the local, inter-island trade, they were dependent on regular supply of those products sought after by the Chinese and other traders from further overseas: forest products like lacquer, beeswax, animal hides, or hardwood from the shifting cultivation communities or hunters-and-gatherers in the interior, as well as pearls, sea cucumbers and birds' nests from economically-specialized fishing and pearl-diver communities (ibid. 239 ff).

In the larger chiefdoms that were intensively engaged in regional trade, social stratification emerged, with a chiefly aristocratic upper class, a commoner class and at the bottom a class of dependents, comprised mostly of war captives and slaves. The politically and economically most powerful chiefdoms were those of the Islamized regions in the South, in the Sulu archipelago and western Mindanao. Manila itself was the northernmost outpost of Islam in the Philippines. Its ruler, Raja Soliman, was the son-in-law of the Sultan of Brunei, and his subject. While the emergence of hierarchical societies and the proliferation of maritime trade predated the arrival of Islam, the particular model of social organization that came along it – that of a stratified state society – had a considerable impact on the trajectory of political developments in the areas under its influence.

The first and throughout its existence most powerful Sultanate of the Philippines was founded around 1450 on Jolo in the Sulu group of islands – 70 years before the first Spaniards arrived in the archipelago. Islam quickly expanded into western Mindanao, and would probably have spread throughout the Philippines if its expansion was not halted by the Spanish in the 16th century.[7]

Except for the coastal chiefdoms, and some interior trading chiefdoms in Mindanao, by far most of the people of the archipelago lived in small, autonomous local groups, whose headmen – if they had any at all – had very limited power.

The expanding maritime trade in the 15th and 16th century led to a proliferation of the number of Philippine chiefdoms and a strengthening of the power of their elites, but they still remained only weakly centralized and basically retained their segmentary structure (Junker 2000: 59f). These chiefdoms were based on a network of continuously shifting alliances, which were maintained above all through large-scale gift exchanges of luxury goods obtained through foreign trade. The ability of the chiefs to produce or get hold of the products needed for acquiring these luxury goods in trade was therefore of crucial importance for the political economy of these polities.

Extracting tribute from subjected populations was one of the sources of the wealth needed to sustain chiefly households. Another was slave labour. At the time of European contact slave raiding was common throughout the Philippines (Gibson 1990, Junker 2000: 339 ff), and from the 16th to the 19th century some chiefdoms and sultanates in the South like Sulu, Maguindanao, and Maranao specialized in large-scale slave raiding and trading which affected much of insular Southeast Asia (Junker 2000: 342).

The challenge for the coastal chiefs and sultans was to ensure regular access to essential trade goods from the uplands in order to be able to engage in maritime trade. Due to the remoteness of these areas and the mobility of its people, direct subjugation and economic control was not a viable option. "Instead, lowland polities and adjacent upland tribal peoples generally formed extensive interactive networks that were often loosely integrated through political and social as well as economic ties" (ibid.: 221).

At the same time, however, the populations of the interior of the larger islands and the remoter corners of the archipelago, mostly being egalitarian and politically weakly-integrated societies with inferior military capacities, were also the main source of slaves for coastal peoples engaged in raiding and slave trading (Gibson 1990: 129).

The relationship between the coastal centres of power and peoples of the hinterlands were thus complex and shifting. In some cases, they were rather symbiotic as a result of mutual dependence on trade (Junker 2000: 221), although probably not always balanced, and not always voluntary either (Gibson 1990). In other cases, relations were outright antagonistic, as slave raiding polities regularly preyed on settlements in the interior.

The Magic of Colonial Alchemy

A quantum leap in the relationship between lowland coastal and highland or interior communities however occurred as a result of Spanish colonization. Although Magellan had made his first – for him ultimately fatal – step on Philippine soil already in 1521, it took another 44 years until Miguel Lopez de Legazpi managed to get a first foothold from where Spanish rule could be established over the ensuing centuries.

The strong Muslim Sultanates of Mindanao and the Sulu Archipelago as well as the dominant influence of Brunei in the Manila region were a major challenge to the Spanish.[8] Only 30 years had passed since they had managed to drive the "Moros" off the Iberian Peninsula when Magellan, on the other side of the globe, encountered communities professing the same faith which to the Spanish had become the epitome of all evil.

In the beginning the Spanish were quite successful. The "Moros" were driven off Mindoro island, and in 1571 Manila was captured. It was only now that the colonization of the Philippines really began. But the Spanish neither managed to subdue the Sultanate of Brunei nor did they ever conquer the Sultanates in the South. They thus failed in their ultimate goal of establishing control over the trade with the Spice Islands further southwest. What was worse, the Muslims did not leave them alone either. During much of the Spanish colonial era in the Philippines, the Spanish with their troops recruited among the conquered population were engaged in a low-intensity warfare with the Muslim sultanates whose elite was not willing to simply step aside. Mindoro island, right at the doorsteps of Manila, became one of the main battle grounds for the two competing powers.

To the Spanish, the Philippines was never a lucrative colony. It became important only as an *entrepôt* for the China trade. Mexican silver brought in from its colony across the Pacific was traded for Chinese silk, and this galleon trade between Mexico, Manila and China soon formed the economic bedrock of Spanish colonial rule over the Philippines. The colony was actually administered by the Viceroy of Mexico, and Spanish presence was concentrated in Manila. Only a few of the smaller towns had Spanish civil administrators. It was the various catholic monastic orders that emerged as the main agents of Spanish colonization. To provide them with better access to the "blessings of Christianity", but above all to bring them under military and eventually administrative control, the monks tried to concentrate the often scattered population in nucleated settlements *("reducciónes")* grouped around newly set-up churches.

In collaboration with the native Filipino elites, the clerics managed to establish a tribute system similar to the one applied in their Latin American colonies, and within only a few generations fundamentally remolded the local social systems. What emerged was a class of native favourites who, during the second half of Spanish rule, developed into a class of powerful landlords, a process that laid the foundations for an oligarchic political-economic order that has not changed much since.

Unlike in Latin America, there was no attempt to establish Spanish settler colonies, and the mestizo population never became numerically strong. But in spite of the small number of Spanish colonizers – there were never more than 2000 present in the Philippines at any given time (Geiger 1994: 302) –, their cultural influence was more determining than in any other Southeast Asian country brought under colonial rule. Catholicism and Spanish manners were quickly and firmly established among the subdued populations.

The conquest, however, remained incomplete. Other than in the coastal areas and lowlands, the Spanish never managed to fully subjugate the people in the uplands and impose on them tribute, *corvée,* and their culture and religion. The small number of Spanish *conquistadores* may partially explain why this was so. Other decisive factors included the inaccessibility of the hinterlands, the fierce resistance of some tribal groups, especially in the Cordillera of Northern Luzon, and the elusiveness of other groups that inhabit the mountainous interiors – much the same factors that had earlier prevented the emerging chiefdoms from extending their control over these peoples.

After the US took over as colonial power in the Philippines in 1898 as a consequence of the Spanish-American war, probably well over half of the territory of the former Spanish colony remained unconquered. Of the estimated 8 million population, about 7 million were brought under colonial control by the Spanish (Rodil 1993: 11). The remaining one million people were the Moros of the South and the inhabitants of the vast mountainous and forested interior. It was not until the Americans embarked on a protracted campaign of "pacification" and conquest that they finally managed to subdue the wayward tribes in the Cordillera or the "Moros" in the South.

Characteristic for the Spanish colonial era was a continuous flow of "refugee" populations from the plains to the uplands who sought to avoid *corvée* labor, tribute and forced resettlement. In many places, this led to a visible reduction of population in areas under Spanish control, and a corresponding increase in the hinterlands. Writes James Scott (2000: 16f, in this volume p. 171f):

"In the Spanish Philippines, the flight to the hills from Christianization and labor-bondage mimicked and overlapped a still older pattern of
flight from the Malay slaving raids that plagued the coasts. The Christian
faith and baptism were inseparable from settled life in villages and labor
bondage, and the flight from one was flight from the other. Keesing, in
his pioneering ethnohistory of Northern Luzon, concludes that the hills
were only lightly populated when the Spanish arrived and that they were
peoples by a flight from lower elevations and from the Spanish civilizational project. Living in the hills was a political and cultural choice."

Aside from the avoidance of forced labour and taxation, Scott identified
two other reasons for this phenomenon of evasive populations in the hinterlands,
which has been so common throughout Southeast Asia. One are epidemics and
famines, occurrences that were more frequent in the plains than in the hills (ibid.:
14, in this volume p. 170). The other is the rejection of lowland civilization:

"To this point, political economy and epidemiology would seem to
explain the 'reflux' of population to the hills. If it were entirely so, the
hill population might more closely resemble the valley populations except for their elevation and the shifting cultivation that such elevations
required. But they don't. The hill peoples are different: they tend to be
animists who do not follow the 'great tradition' religions of the lowland
peoples; they produce a surplus, but do not use it to support kings and
monks. What is missing from the story thus far is the cultural refusal
of civilizational projects in the valleys that characterizes hill populations
(ibid.: 15, in this volume p. 170f)[9]."

The radical transformation of lowland societies as they were brought under
Spanish colonial control had a drastic impact on the relationship between hill and
lowland peoples. It established and entrenched a powerful cognitive boundary that
separated those considered "civilized" – called *indios* – and the "heathens", called
infieles, or, if they were Muslim, *moros.* This conceptual division was internalized
by the Christianized lowland people, who henceforth treated the highlanders
with contempt and as culturally inferior. "Minorities" and "majorities" had thus
been created where none had existed before. As William Henry Scott (1985:41)
writes:

"Thus by the magic of colonial alchemy, those who changed most became
today's Filipinos while those who changed least were actually denied this
designation [   ]."

Terminologies, Lists and Figures

In the terminology of the ensuing US-American colonial administration, the people who remained uncolonized in the uplands figured as „non-Christian tribes", sometimes "wild peoples" as opposed to the "civilized peoples" of the lowlands and coastal areas. As the US government map of 1905 reprinted below shows,[10] the Moro were included in the category of "wild peoples" (left column, 9th from the top).

After independence in 1946, a range of official designations were used over the years: "Non-Christian Filipinos", "National Cultural Communities", "National Minorities", "Tribal Filipinos", "Cultural Communities" and, after the passing of the Indigenous Peoples Rights Act (IPRA) in 1997, "Indigenous Cultural Communities/Indigenous Peoples".

The IPRA, the most recent legislation on indigenous peoples that gained considerable international recognition, defines "indigenous cultural communities/indigenous peoples" as follows:

> "h) Indigenous Cultural Communities/Indigenous Peoples - refer to a group of people or homogenous societies identified by self-ascription and ascription by others, who have continuously lived as organized community on communally bounded and defined territory, and who have, under claims of ownership since time immemorial, occupied, possessed and utilized such territories, sharing common bonds of language, customs, traditions and other distinctive cultural traits, or who have, through resistance to political, social and cultural inroads of colonization, non-indigenous religions and cultures, became historically differentiated from the majority of Filipinos. ICCs/IPs shall likewise include peoples who are regarded as indigenous on account of their descent from the populations which inhabited the country, at the time of conquest or colonization, or at the time of inroads of non-indigenous religions and cultures, or the establishment of present state boundaries, who retain some or all of their own social, economic, cultural and political institutions, but who may have been displaced from their traditional domains or who may have resettled outside their ancestral domains;" (Republic of the Philippines 1997: IPRA, chapter II, sec. 3 h)

It is important to note that the IPRA emphasizes the differentiation of the Filipino population into a majority on the one hand, and the indigenous peoples on the other as a result of the latter's resistance to colonization and "non-indigenous religions and cultures". Thus, IPRA's definition of indigenous peoples is not using the term "indigenous" in its original and narrow sense (i.e. "born in/originating from a certain place"; Daes op.cit.) but follows a broader, relational understanding of the term. Such a relational understanding "focuses on the fundamental

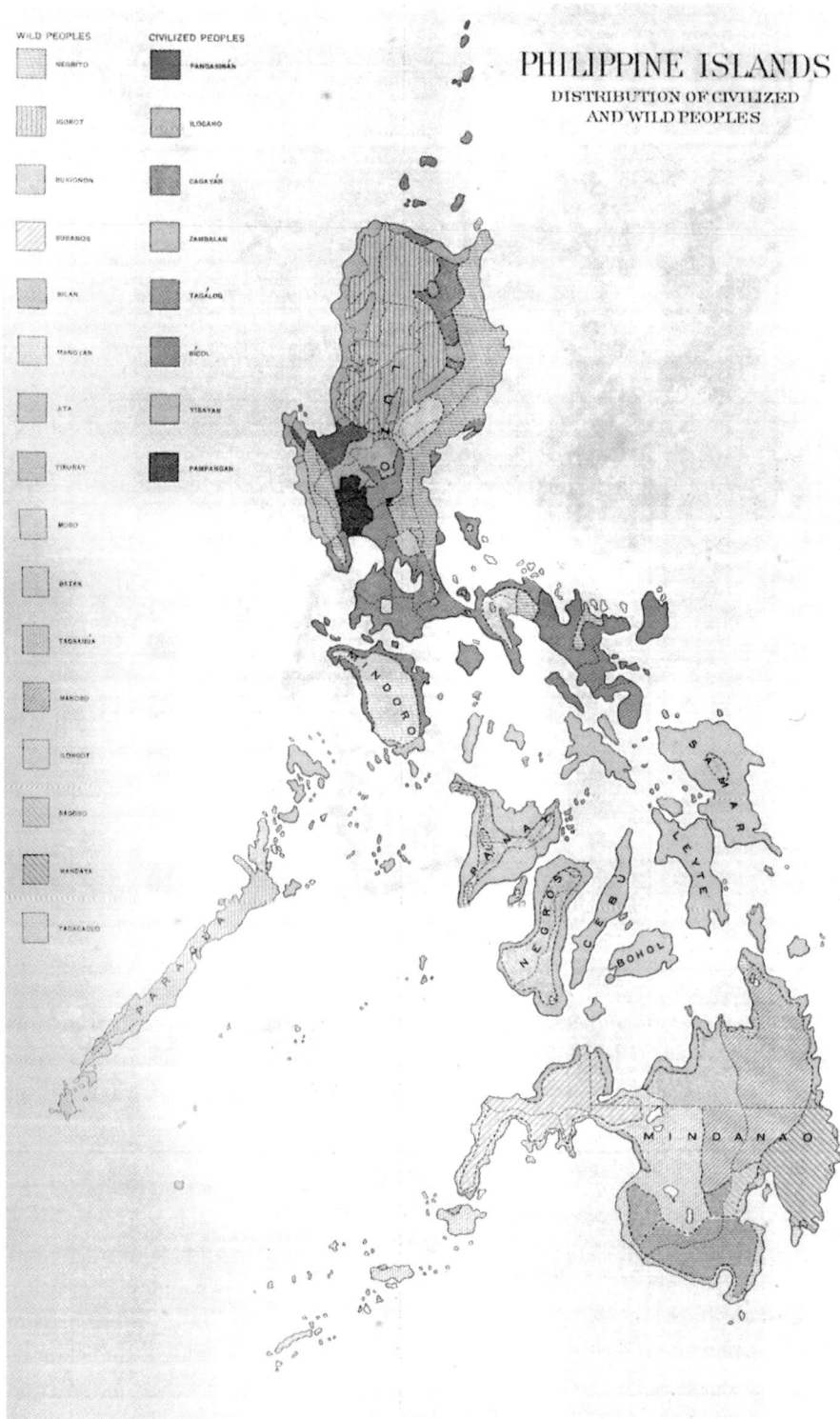

US Government map of 1905

issues of power and dispossession that those calling themselves indigenous are concerned to address, and on the enduring social, economic and religious practices that constitute their relationships with land, resources and other peoples" (Kenrick and Lewis 2004:9). The definition given in IPRA does refer to a process of past and ongoing colonization, and thus implicitly to unequal power relations, dominance and marginalization of one group by another.

According to estimates of the National Commission on Indigenous Peoples (NCIP), more than 12 million of the Philippines' total population of 76 million (census of 2000) are considered indigenous (http://www.ncip.gov.ph/resources/ethno.php). Roughly 60% of them live in the southern island of Mindanao, a third on the main island of Luzon, and the rest scattered over the central islands of the archipelago. Only guesses exist for the total number of indigenous ethnic groups with estimates ranging from 70 to over 100. The NCIP website presents a list of 91 entries (http://www.ncip.gov.ph/resources/ethno_alphabet.php). This list includes a few Islamized groups in the present Autonomous Region of Muslim Mindanao (ARMM), like Badjao, Jama Mapun, Kalagan, Kalibugan, Sama, Samal, Sangil, and Yakan, but not the main groups, such as the Maranao, Maguindanao, or Tausug, who since Spanish colonial times have been categorized as Moros.[11]

Government Policies and the Status of the Moro

As we have seen earlier, the Islamized peoples in the South, who themselves eventually adopted the generic, originally rather derogatory term "Moro" applied to them, have been included by the Spanish colonizers in the overall category of "wild" or "uncivilized" peoples in contrast to those who received the blessings of Spanish Christian "civilization". This conceptual dichotomy – and the conceptual lumping together of the Islamized groups with the "non-Christian tribes" – was continued with by the US American colonial administration. In 1901, only three years after the US took control, the Bureau of Non-Christian Tribes (BNCT) was created. It was tasked with conducting general anthropological studies in the Philippines, analyzing the situation of the "pagan" and Moslem populations, and making policy recommendations to the government on how to promote civilization and material well-being among them (Schult 1990:133).[12]

In 1936, the Bureau of Non-Christian Tribes was dissolved. While upholding an assimilationist policy, the integration of the nation was to be achieved without dichotomizing the population into Christians and non-Christians, and according to then-President Quezon the "(...) so-called non-Christian problem has been reduced to one of solidification and development" (Lao 1992:166, cit. in Wenk 2007:54). Only in 1957, after the Philippines had become independent, a new body was created tasked with taking care of national minorities: the Commission on National Integration (CNI). It pursued "a policy of appeasement by providing scholarships, loans and medical and legal services" (Lopez 1986:96), serving the government's continuing assimilationist and developmentalist agenda as well as the interest of private corporations in accessing natural resources in areas inhabited by the "national cultural minorities", as they were called those days.

The CNI's successor, the Presidential Assistant on National Minorities (PANAMIN), created in 1968, gained the reputation of being particularly effective in helping outsiders to seize its constituencies' land and resources. To serve the avarice of politicians and the business establishment and to assist the government in its fight against the communist New People's Army (NPA), PANAMIN resumed a resettlement and reservation policy similar to that practiced by the American colonial government. PANAMIN was however not in charge of the Moros. For that, President Marcos had created the Southern Philippine Development Authority (SPDA) in 1978. [13] In the early 1970s, the Moro National Liberation Front (MNLF) had taken up arms against the Philippine state to fight for independence. The creation of the SPDA was in response to the resumption of fighting after the peace negotiation initiated in 1976 had failed. For the ensuing decade the Philippine state was kept entangled in a protracted counter-insurgency war against the MNLF, and against other militant Muslim groups up to the present.[14]

Shortly before the downfall of President Marcos in 1986, PANAMIN was abolished in the wake of the disappearance of its director, Manuel Elizalde, Jr., who had secretly fled the country to escape corruption and other charges. The agency replacing it was called the Office of Muslim Affairs and Cultural Communities (OMACC). Even though again with a double mandate, the agency's name probably reflected the government's growing concern with and focus on the Moros, and the realization of the fundamentally different nature and ambitions of Moro resistance and the indigenous peoples movement.

OMACC, however, did not last long. In January 1987, following the 1986 "People's Power Revolution", it was abolished and the government under President Corazon Aquino issued three Executive Orders creating three distinct and separate offices: the Office of Muslim Affairs (OMA); the Office for Northern Cultural Communities (ONCC) and the Office for Southern Cultural Communities(OSCC). These three Offices were placed directly under the Office of the President.

Although the Office of Muslim Affairs (OMA) has been given the broad mandate of preserving and developing the culture, traditions, institutions and well-being of Muslim Filipinos, it generally limits its activities to fostering Islamic religious practices, and does not engage much in socio-economic or livelihood projects (US State Department 2006). Other state institutions have been created to directly deal with matters related to the Muslim areas, like the Committee on Muslim Affairs of the Congress.

Today, Muslim affairs and matters pertaining to the people formerly called, non-Christian "Cultural Communities" have been brought under completely separate administrations. While in the early days equally treated under the category of "uncivilized" or "wild" people, the term "indigenous peoples" is today in practice applied only to the latter, even though the definition in IPRA would allow an interpretation by which the Moro could be included.[15]

Civil society organizations and political leaders of the Moro themselves generally do not identify themselves as indigenous peoples either. The Chairman of the Bangsamoro People's Consultative Assembly[16] and executive director of the Institute of Bangsamoro Studies, Abhoud Syed M. Lingga (2002) for example, makes a clear distinction between the Moro and what he himself calls the indigenous people of Mindanao:

> "Although the whole of Mindanao, Sulu – Tawi-Tawi archipelago, the islands of Basilan and Palawan are the traditional homeland of the Bangsamoro people, the demographic reality is that they now share the territories with the Christian settler communities and the Indigenous People."

> "Having three independent states in Mindanao – for the Bangsamoro, the Indigenous People and the Christian settler communities – may be better because each can address the specific and unique needs of their citizenry."

The Moro and the indigenous peoples in the Philippines also use entirely different international platforms to make their political demands heard. The negotiations leading to the Tripoli Agreement between the MNLF and the Philippine government in 1976, for example, were facilitated by the Organization of Islamic Conference, while leaders of organizations representing indigenous peoples have since the mid 1980s been above all engaged in various processes at the United Nations related to the development of international standards for the protection of indigenous peoples' rights.[17]

Only on rare occasions and for a short time did Moro groups join the national or international indigenous rights movement. For a few years, between 1992 and 2000, the organization Kilusan Para Sa Tunay na Awtonomiya ng Bayan (KITAB) was a member of the Asia Indigenous Peoples Pact (personal communication by Jannie Lasimbang, Secretary General of AIPP). This was however not appreciated by the – then also AIPP member – Lumad Mindanaw, a federation of indigenous peoples' organizations in Mindanao (later renamed to Lumad Mindanao Peoples Federation (LMPF). In general, the leading Moro political and civil society organizations do not claim for their people the status of "indigenous peoples".

Important for Moro identity – and a crucial distinction between them and other people in the Philippines – is not only Islam, but also their history of state formation. As Lingga (2002) elaborates:

"The historical experience of the Bangsamoro people in statehood and governance started as early as the middle of the 15th century when Sultan Sharif ul-Hashim established the Sulu Sultanate. This was followed by the establishment of the Magindanaw Sultanate in the early part of the 16th century by Sharif Muhammad Kabungsuwan. The Sultanate of Buayan and the Pat a Pangampong ko Ranao (Confederation of the Four Lake-based Emirates) and other political subdivisions were organized later.

By the time the Spanish colonialists arrived in the Philippines the Muslims of Mindanao, Sulu - Tawi-Tawi archipelago and the islands of Basilan and Palawan had already established their own states and governments with diplomatic and trade relations with other countries including China. Administrative and political system based on the realities of the time existed in those states. In fact it was the existence of the well-organized administrative and political system that the Bangsamoro people managed to survive the military campaign against them by Western colonial powers for several centuries and preserve their identity as a political and social organization."

In another article (2004), Lingga classifies minorities in general into three categories: migrants from outside the present nation state (in other words: "foreigners"), indigenous peoples, and "Peoples who were incorporated into the new nation-states after the departure of the colonial powers [   ]. Before colonization these peoples had their political institutions, administrative system, and trade and international relations with other countries." What he refers to here as third category becomes clearer in his conclusions at the end of the article: the pre-colonial states that have been incorporated into post-colonial nation states.

"Within the borders of the Philippines we find Muslim minorities who identify themselves as Bangsamoro. They can be classified under the third category of minority communities. Their experience in state formation predates the formation of the Philippines as a state. They continue to occupy what remain of their traditional homeland." (ibid.)

The Muslim sultanates of the South were not only trading powers to reckon with during the pre-colonial era, but emerged as militarily dominant forces that were at the time of the arrival of the Spanish in a process of rapid expansion. The relationship between the Islamized groups under the sultanates and the people that later became known as Lumad was mostly antagonistic, as non-believers have traditionally been considered inferior and potential slaves. As mentioned earlier, some of the Islamized ethnic groups in what today constitutes the ARMM were heavily involved in slave raiding and trading, and Lumad – especially those living along the coast – were among those regularly targeted. [18]

It is on the basis of this historically antagonistic relationship, by pointing at a discriminatory and exploitative attitude among the Moro towards the Lumad, [19] that some of Lumad leaders and political activists are denying the Moro the status of indigenous peoples. They thereby implicitly assert the relational aspect (Kenrick and Lewis 2004) of the concept of indigenous peoples, i.e. its reference to the historical experience of discrimination and dispossession by more powerful groups, against its mono-dimensional interpretation as merely meaning "originating from/having been born in a place".[20]

Tribal or Indigenous: Changing Names for Persisting Peoples

It is however not just the experience of discrimination, exploitation and dispossession that is considered inherent to being indigenous. Such experiences may also be shared by people who do not consider themselves indigenous. Fundamental to the indigenous peoples' understanding of indigeneity are perceived essential differences in social organization, culture and way of life that set them apart from the dominant or mainstream society. While positively valued by the former, the same traits are negatively charged – as backward, primitive, anti-development – by the latter, thus providing them reason if not legitimacy for continuing discrimination and oppression.

Today, the Tagalog word *katutubo* (or equivalent terms in other regional linguae francae) is commonly used among indigenous organizations and support groups as translation of "indigenous" in the Philippines. Thus "indigenous peoples" in Tagalog becomes *katutubong mamamayan*. It is derived from the root word *tubo* for growth/growing, and *katutubo* is thus often also translated as "native". In everyday usage, however, the term *tribo* and its English equivalent "tribe" are still very common. For example, an informal network of indigenous activists and supporters calls its yahoo-group on the internet *inisyatribo,* described as "support initiative for rights to ancestral domain of indigenous peoples in the Philippines" (http://groups.yahoo.com/group/inisyatRibo/), and the media still frequently writes or speaks of "tribes", "tribal people" or "tribesmen" (see e.g. Inquirer of June 22, 2006 "Tribesmen as 'human carabaos'"). While the Catholic Church's Episcopal Commission on Tribal Filipinos (ECTF) in January 1995 has changed its name to Episcopal Commission on Indigenous Peoples (ECIP), [21] the Church's local (Diocese level) programs are still called "Tribal Filipino Apostolate", its bi-monthly publication retained the title "Tribal Forum" and its country-wide annual event "Tribal Filipino Sunday". Furthermore, local indigenous peoples' organizations often use "tribal" in their name, e.g. Narikdukan Manobo-Talaandig Tribal Association; Southern Bukidnon Tribal Council, Siocon Federation of Subanon Tribal Councils, the Federation of Matigsalog-Manobo Tribal Councils, or the two national-level organizations reportedly working closely with the government: the Tribal Councils of the Philippines (ATCP) and Tribal Communities Association of the Philippines (TRICAP) (www.iwgia.org/sw16786.asp).

To sum up: in the Philippines the terms applied to the peoples we today call "indigenous" changed over time, partly following international usage, but probably also out of what today would be called "political correctness". "Wild tribes" or "wild peoples" are terms that today would certainly not be acceptable any more. "Tribal Filipinos" or "cultural communities" appeared to be more appropriate two decades ago. And a decade ago, "indigenous peoples" – in tandem with "indigenous cultural communities" – was officially adopted following international practice promoted by indigenous peoples' organizations. The people whom this term is applied to, however, remain basically the same, both in the eyes of outsiders and of those referred to.

There are groups with rather dubious background and identity who have been recognized as indigenous by the NCIP,[22] but these are few and not being taken seriously by indigenous organizations and advocacy groups. Thus, in practice, self-identification alone is obviously not sufficient; it has to go along with the recognition by others. Such questionable cases however remain exceptional. More significant is the fact that the official adoption of the term indigenous peoples did not motivate any of the large Moro groups to claim this status. We can thus generalize that while terms were changing over the past decades, the scope of their application did not. In the Philippines the indigenous peoples are those formerly and sometimes still called "tribal people"; "tribal" being a term still commonly used interchangeably with "indigenous peoples" among indigenous themselves. Both in common usage as well as in academic circles it is understood that these tribal or indigenous peoples are groups which, although extremely diverse in terms of culture, social organization or livelihood patterns, have at the very least one thing in common: a historical continuity from pre-colonial *non-state* societies.

In spite of the stark difference in the trajectory and impact of Western colonization as compared to other South and Southeast Asian countries, the emergence of the socio-cultural dichotomy in the Philippines, with highland tribal/indigenous peoples on the one hand and politically dominant lowland or coastal (colonial) state society on the other, conforms to a pattern observed across the whole Southeast Asian region.

Being Tribal in Southeast Asia: The Choice for Resistance

Benjamin (2002) demonstrates that in the "Malay world", i.e. in the "various Malay kingdoms and their attendant hinterlands that have existed or still exist along the coasts of Borneo, the east coast of Sumatra, and on the Malay Peninsula" (p.7), state formation was a key factor in the emergence of a socio-political differentiation resulting in "three basic types of socio-cultural situations, where in pre-state times there had been just one" (ibid. p.8).

"Those who place themselves in command belong to what we can loosely call the ruler category, used here as a shorthand for priests, tax collectors, soldiers and so on, as well as kings. Those who allow their lives to be controlled by agencies of the state, which they provision in exchange for a little reflected glory but no counter-control, are peasants. But those who stand apart from the state and its rulers, holding themselves culturally aloof [...], are in the *tribal* category."

Thus, as Benjamin (2002:9f) continues, "[   ] those who did not become Malay peasants had to set up their own cultural and social institutions [   ]. In so doing they generated three institutionalized societal patterns – the "Semang", "Senoi", and "Malayic" – as well as some less well-defined ones [   ]. These three patterns have been aimed at retaining the people's social and cultural autonomy in the face of the state, while allowing them nevertheless to sustain relations with each other and with the civilizational centres downstream." The processes and resulting social and cultural patterns analyzed by Benjamin for the "Malay world" are very similar to the ones found in the Philippines, the difference being that whereas in the Malay case these patterns emerged in pre-colonial times in the Philippines they are a result of Spanish colonial rule.[23]

Individual agency and choice also stand at the core of Scott's analysis (2000 and in this volume) of the socio-cultural dichotomy between hill and valley societies found throughout Southeast Asia. He argues that the presence of two fundamentally different forms of societies in Southeast Asia – states in the valleys and along the coasts, tribal peoples in the hills and forested interiors – have evolved not simply as a result of the geographical isolation of the latter ("civilization didn't reach them") but also as a result of choice. As he demonstrates, there has always been intensive interaction and movement of people back and forth between the hills and valleys.

"Despite this constant exchange of populations across this permeable membrane, there is an extraordinarily stable, durable civilization discourse about hill and valley that treat each of these peoples as essentially different; one cultured, the other barbaric, one refined, the other primitive, one advanced and cosmopolitan and the other backward and parochial. These pairs, of course, are the pairs as valley elites see them. If we adopt the hill perspective we get different pairs; one is free and autonomous, the other is in bondage and subordinate; one is nominally an equal of others, the other is socially inferior; one is physically mobile, the other is hemmed in by officials and state institutions" (2000:3, in this volume, p. 162).

These two spheres remained intact in spite of the constant flow of people between them throughout history. "Hill tribes" and "valley civilization" according to Scott, constitute a "lived essentialism" that "remains intact as a powerful organizer of peoples' lives and thoughts" (ibid: 4, in this volume p. 163).

Scott identifies two antagonistic principles that underlie the mutual creation of these two spheres: Southeast Asian statecraft during the pre-colonial era, and "peasant cunning" of resistance (ibid: 8, in this volume p. 166). The pre-colonial state's main concern was to attract and often capture people and keep them in densely settled areas around the state center, as wet-rice farmers for easy taxation and source of corvée labor. People kept or took to the hills in order to avoid taxation and slavery, and during times of increased pressure, for example when taxes were increased, harvests were bad or epidemics broke out, people left the plains in large numbers and joined the "tribes" in the hills. People responded the same way to attempts by outsiders to convert them to Islam or Christianity. It was a "cultural refusal of civilizational projects in the valleys" (ibid: 15, in this volume p. 171).

For Scott "Living in the hills was a political and cultural choice" (ibid: 17, in this volume p. 172), and he quotes Tanya Li in support of his argument: "people who lived in the uplands did so not by default, bypassed by history, but for positive reasons of economy, security, and cultural style formed in dialogue with lowland agendas" (ibid: 16, in this volume p. 171; quoted from: Li 1999). For these people, the "hills" were the realms of freedom, where they could lead autonomous, self-determined lives outside the control of oppressive state power.

The International Human Rights Discourse: From Tribal to Indigenous Peoples

The situation has, however, changed drastically with the emergence of modern nation states and the creation of clearly demarcated and fixed state boundaries during decolonization. The people who see themselves as the heirs of the region's ancient kingdoms – the Thai, Lao, Kinh, Khmer, Malays, Javanese – or, in the Philippines, the successors of the colonial elite are controlling these newly formed nation states while the people in the "hills" have been largely left out. In the early years after decolonization little has changed in these remote areas and the people living there were to a large extent still able to maintain far-reaching autonomy and control over land and resource. The consolidation of state power and the rapid technological development over the past five decades, however, allowed the state to expand its control into ever remoter areas. In its wake came large-scale resource extraction, land conversion and settler colonization of these areas, resulting in dispossession, displacement and marginalization of tribal peoples. Their situation fundamentally changed as one of the key conditions for maintaining autonomy was steadily eroding: the possibility to withdraw. Today, the "basis for popular freedom" (Scott 2000: 13, in this volume p. 168), i.e. the possibility to take refuge in the "hills", is in many cases not an option anymore. Parallel to this development, state policies were framed with the aim of proactively assimilating tribal communities into national mainstream society.

Where the spirit of resistance remains unbroken, tribal communities are trying to find new ways of dealing with the state in order to withstand the pressure and maintain a certain degree of autonomy. Articulating their grievances and demands within the international discourse on "indigenous peoples' rights" is, among others, a way to do so. Through discovering that they share similar experiences with other peoples in the world who define themselves as indigenous peoples, tribal peoples in Southeast Asia have over the past two decades come to identify themselves as indigenous peoples as well.[24] New networks emerged on the national, regional and global level and along with these came the adoption of new discourses and terminologies. Locally, however, previous designations both in local languages or English are replaced only slowly and incompletely. Thus the term "tribal" is still widely used in public, by activists and some academics (see further below) throughout the region.[25] On the international level, however, the term indigenous peoples is now firmly established as a generally accepted term, and has almost completely replaced older designations like "tribal". Within the United Nations system, where standards for the protection of the rights of indigenous peoples are being developed, this can be easily traced.

General human rights instruments like the Universal Declaration of Human Rights of 1948, the International Convention on the Elimination of all Forms of Racial Discrimination of 1965, the International Covenant on Civil and Political Rights and the International Covenant on Economic, Social and Cultural Rights, both of 1966, mention neither tribal people nor indigenous peoples. In 1957, and thus fairly early in the history of the United Nations, however, Convention 107 was passed by the International Labour Organization (ILO), which specifically deals with indigenous or tribal people. It is officially called a "Convention concerning the Protection and Integration of Indigenous and Other Tribal and Semi-Tribal Populations in Independent Countries". To be noted here is that it speaks of "indigenous *and other* tribal and semi-tribal populations", which implies that "indigenous populations" are considered tribal populations.

ILO Convention 107 was replaced by Convention 169 in 1989, as a consequence of being criticized for its assimilationist thrust. In contrast to its predecessor, ILO Convention 169 is officially called "Convention concerning Indigenous and Tribal Peoples in Independent Countries", which obviously implies that a distinction is being made between indigenous peoples and tribal peoples. A comparison of the first article in the two conventions makes the semantic shift clearer.

In ILO Convention 107 Article 1 states:

> "1. This Convention applies to:
> (a) members of tribal or semi-tribal populations in independent
> countries whose social and economic conditions are at a less advanced
> stage than the stage reached by the other sections of the national com-
> munity, and whose status is regulated wholly or partially by their own
> customs or traditions or by special laws or regulations;
> (b) members of tribal or semi-tribal populations in independent coun-
> tries which are regarded as indigenous on account of their descent from
> the populations which inhabited the country, or a geographical region to
> which the country belongs, at the time of conquest or colonisation and
> which, irrespective of their legal status, live more in conformity with
> the social, economic and cultural institutions of that time than with the
> institutions of the nation to which they belong."

Here, a distinction is drawn between "tribal or semi-tribal populations ...
whose social and economic conditions are at a less advanced stage" and "tribal or
semi-tribal populations ... which are regarded as indigenous".

Article 1 of Convention 169 is more elaborate and states:

> "1. This Convention applies to:
> (a) tribal peoples in independent countries whose social, cultural
> and economic conditions distinguish them from other sections of the
> national community, and whose status is regulated wholly or partially
> by their own customs or traditions or by special laws or regulations;
> (b) peoples in independent countries who are regarded as indig-
> enous on account of their descent from the populations which inhabited
> the country, or a geographical region to which the country belongs, at
> the time of conquest or colonisation or the establishment of present state
> boundaries and who, irrespective of their legal status, retain some or all
> of their own social, economic, cultural and political institutions.
> 2. Self-identification as indigenous or tribal shall be regarded as a
> fundamental criterion for determining the groups to which the provi-
> sions of this Convention apply.
> 3. The use of the term peoples in this Convention shall not be con-
> strued as having any implications as regards the rights which may attach
> to the term under international law."

In the new Convention the rather foggy term "semi-tribal" was completely
dropped and "populations" replaced by "peoples", thus following the demand
of the indigenous representatives participating in the UN Working Group on

Indigenous Populations which at that time was already working on the draft of the Declaration on the Rights of Indigenous Peoples. Important to notice here is that in paragraph 1 b, which refers to indigenous peoples, the adjective "tribal" used in Convention 107 has been abandoned. Thus while under Convention 107 the distinction was drawn between "indigenous" and "non-indigenous" tribal peoples, it is now between indigenous and tribal peoples.

In the United Nations Declaration on the Rights of Indigenous Peoples, adopted by the United Nations' General Assembly on September 13, 2007, however, the term tribal disappeared altogether. And in all more recent international declarations and other documents of various UN bodies, such as the Rio Declaration on Environment and Development of 1992, the Cairo Program of Action of the International Conference on Population and Development of 1994, the Beijing Declaration of the Fourth Conference on Women of 1995 and the Copenhagen Declaration on Social Development of 2000 only the term indigenous (usually indigenous people or indigenous populations) is used.

The abandoning of the term tribal in the United Nations Declaration on the Rights of Indigenous Peoples is the result of the rejection of the term by indigenous representatives. In the early years of the United Nations Working Group on Indigenous Populations, the indigenous peoples' representatives were engaged in heated debates on the term to be used in the draft declaration. Not only the term "tribal" but a number of others such as "aborigines", "native", "nations" or "nationalities" were ultimately dropped when the agreement was reached to use only one instead of, as was suggested, several terms in the document (Jannie Lasimbang, personal communication). Some considered the term "tribal" as colonial and racist, others found it inappropriate since the term evokes the image of a static society while today, many of the descendants of so-called tribal peoples do not lead a "traditional" lifestyle considered typical for "tribal" people. The consensus reached was to use the term "indigenous peoples" only (Jannie Lasimbang, personal communication).[26]

In academic circles the concept of "tribe" has been heavily criticized already in the 1960s and 1970s (Fried 1966, 1975; Helm 1968; Southall 1970; Godelier 1977), and many contemporary anthropologists do not consider it an analytically useful or politically correct concept. Some, like Southall (1996: 1334) argue that the concept has been imposed on colonized peoples by imperialist nations, that it is the result of a relationship marked by oppression and a sense of supremacy on the part of the colonizers, and that it is in fact the "product of prejudice and exploitation".

Others (Winthorp 1991 and Sharp 1996, discussed in Kraus 2004 p. 42) hold that such a view is an insult for those concerned, since they are thereby being relegated to a merely passive role. The impact of colonization is not being entirely dismissed, but the authors point out that the original idea of "tribe" as clearly identifiable social units, which may have been new in many places, was taken up and adapted to local realities and needs, thus shaping and changing local perceptions and forms of collective identities. Today, as we have also seen in the case of the Philippines, many groups are rather self-consciously referring to themselves as tribes and do not seem to see it as connoting inferiority or primitivity. Kraus (2004:42f) holds that the term may still be useful as long is it is devoid of associations with archaism or primitivity and historically contextualized. In this, the focus should be on the interaction between tribal groups and other forms of political organization, above all that of state societies, and its embeddedness in more encompassing cultural contexts and with due attention to local representations of collective identity. Authors like Benjamin (2002) or Scott (2000 and in this volume) referred to above are doing precisely this, and it seems that the term has to a certain degree been rehabilitated as analytical concept.

For human rights activists working on the rights of tribal people in Asia, it could be argued, it would have been preferable if the term "tribal" had been retained in international declarations and above all the Declaration on the Rights of Indigenous Peoples – just like in ILO Convention 169 – since the long and heated debate on the applicability of the concept "indigenous peoples" in the Asian context could have been largely avoided. However, seen in another light, the terminological shift can be welcomed not simply for its being politically more correct, but because it can be understood as reflecting fundamental changes in the overall situation of the people concerned.

The replacement of the term tribal people (or whatever local equivalent was used) with indigenous peoples is not just indicating the globalization of a particular political discourse. The merging of multifaceted local tribal resistance into a global indigenous peoples' movement comes in the wake of a fundamental shift in the relationship between the state and tribal people on a global scale: the loss of autonomy and its material basis, i.e. control over natural resources as a result of expanding state power and the penetration and control of its "frontier" areas.

While pre-colonial relationships between tribal and state societies can be described as ambivalent – characterized by mutual dependence and antagonism – in post-colonial nation states the balance shifted decidedly in favor of the latter. Increased technical, military and administrative power enabled states and their elite actors to extend control over the formerly unattractive or inaccessible territories inhabited by tribal people, areas which are now increasingly recognized as repositories of key strategic resources. And control was more often than not established without any concern for the fundamental historical and human rights of the people living there. Violations of their rights have been justified by referring to their backwardness, and their need to be developed. As Nicholas (2002:124) writes on the Orang Asli of Peninsular Malaysia:

"In its simplest elaboration, the ideology that is imposed on the Orang Asli assumes that it is the duty of a people to maximize the exploitation of resources bestowed on them by nature. Failure to do this necessarily implies "backwardness". It is argued that a people ill-disposed to exploiting nature's resources have no right to stand in the way of other (external) peoples representing "higher levels" of civilization. Further, it sis assumed that the state of backwardness itself is a symptom of inferiority. Needless to say, progress is thus equated with civilization. But what is not made explicit in this ideology is the people's realization that progress in the abstract means domination in the concrete for them (cf. Devalle 1992, pp. 38-39)."

As argued above, both the concept tribe in the Southeast Asian context and the term indigenous are intrinsically contextual and relational. While the former refers to a situation in which people *chose to live apart* from the state society, *to retain autonomy* and a particular lifestyle, the latter, in its present usage, refers to a situation of *threat to or complete loss of autonomy* through *ongoing colonization* by a state.[27] The experience of colonization is highlighted in Andrew Gray's (1995: 37) understanding of the concept of indigenous peoples. For him it

" [   ] refers to the quality of a people relating their identity to a particular area and distinguishing them culturally from other, "alien" peoples who came to the territory subsequently. These indigenous peoples are "colonized" in the sense of being disadvantaged and discriminated against. Their right to self-determination is their way of overcoming these obstacles."

The right to self-determination is the core demand of the international indigenous peoples' movement, and has been most vehemently attacked by representatives of various governments engaged in the drafting process of the United Nations Declaration on the Rights of Indigenous Peoples. Since opting for withdrawal and the "tribal way of life" in the past was a way to maintain autonomy or, as Scott put it, "popular freedom" (op.cit), it should not come as a surprise that indigenous activists from Asia identify so strongly with the international indigenous peoples' rights movement. After all, self-determination was very much the *primus motor* behind the choice for the "tribal way of life", and putting the demand for the recognition of the right to self-determination at the centre of the agenda of the international indigenous peoples' movement thus struck a sensitive chord. Entering the arena of international indigenous rights activism is the continuation of self-assertion of an alternative, the "tribal" way of life under rapidly and radically changing circumstances. Therefore, it can be argued, the term "indigenous peoples", as a term reflecting this change of contexts, conditions and strategies, has become a more appropriate designation.

Over the past 20 years of international usage the concept indigenous peoples has undergone a semantic evolution that brought it far beyond its original meaning. Insisting on its original meaning would mean to ignore this development. People in Asia are using the term in international fora as self-designation precisely because of the semantic shift it has gone through. The Philippine government seems to have understood this; it has officially introduced the term and has proven that it is unproblematic in its practical application, i.e. in the identification of the people that fall under this category. There is no reason why other Asian governments should not be able to do the same.

References

Bagong Alyansng Makabayan web-site: http://www.geocities.com/CapitolHill/Lobby/4677/kamp.htm

Benjamin, Geoffrey 2002. "On Being Tribal in the Malay World", in: Geoffrey Benjamin and Cynthia Chou ed., *Tribal Communities in the Malay World. Historical, Cultural and Social Perspectives,* pp. 7-76. Singapore: Institute of Southeast Asian Studies.

Coronal-Ferrer, Miriam 2005. Institutional Response: Civil Society. A Background paper submitted to the Human Development Network Foundation, Inc. for the Philippine Human Development Report 2005. Accessed at: http://www.hdn.org.ph/bgpapers2005/Civil_Society_Assessment.pdf

Daes, Erica-Irene A. 1996. Standard-setting activities: Evolution of Standards Concerning the Rights of Indigenous People. *Working Paper by the Chairperson-Rapporteur, Mrs. Erica-Irene A. Daes. On the concept of "indigenous people".* United Nations Economic and Social Council, UN Document E/CN.4/Sub.2/AC.4/1996/2

Evans, Grant 1992. Internal Colonialism in the Central Highlands of Vietnam. Sojourn Vol. 7, number 2, p. 274-304

Fried, Morton H. 1966. On the Concept of "Tribe" and "Tribal Society". *Transaction of the New York Academy of Social Sciences* Ser. II, 28 (4)

_____1975. The Notion of Tribe. Menlo Park, CA: Cummings

Geiger, Daniel 1994. Guns n' Rosaries. Ethnische Gruppen, ihre Beziehungen und der Staat auf den Philippinen; in: Hans-Peter Müller ed., *Ethnische Dynamik in der aussereuropäischen Welt.* Zürcher Arbeitspapiere zur Ethnologie 4, pp. 295;379. Zürich: Argonaut Verlag.

Godelier, Maurice 1977. The concept of "tribe": a crisis involving merely a concept or the empirical foundations of anthropology itself?, in: Maurice Godelier, *Perspectives in Marxist Anthropology.* Cambridge Studies in Social Anthropology 18, Cambridge University Press, London.

Gray, Andrew 1995. The Indigenous Movement in Asia; in: R.H. Barnes, A. Gray and B. Kingsbury eds., *Indigenous Peoples of Asia.* Association for Asian Studies, Inc. Monograph and Occasional Paper Series 48. Ann Arbor, Michigan.

Helm, June (ed.) 1968. *Essays on the Problem of Tribe: Proceedings of the 1967 Annual Spring Meeting of the American Ethnological Society.* Seattle: University of Washington Press

International Labour Organization 1957. Indigenous and Tribal Populations Convention, 1957 (No. 107). Convention concerning the Protection and Integration of Indigenous and Other Tribal and Semi-Tribal Populations in Independent Countries. Geneva: ILO

_____1989. Indigenous and Tribal Populations Convention, 1989 (No. 169). Convention concerning Indigenous and Tribal Peoples in Independent Countries. Geneva: ILO

Kenrick, Justin and Jerome Lewis 2004. Indigenous peoples' rights and the politics of the term 'indigenous'. *Anthropology Today* Vol 20 No 2. April 2004

Kraus, Wolfgang 2004. *Islamische Stammesgesellschaften. Tribale Identitäten im Vorderen Orient in sozialanthropologischer Perspektive.* Wien: Böhlau Verlag.

Lao, Mardonio M. 1992. *Bukidnon in Historical Perspective: 1946-1985. A Tale of Growth and Progress of an In-land Mindanao Province after World War II.* Musuan, Maramag, Bukidnon: Publications Office of Research and Extension Services, Central Mindanao University, Volume II.

Li, Tania Murray. 1999. Articulating Indigenous Identity in Indonesia: Resource Politics and the Tribal Slot. *Comparative Studies in Society and History* 42(1):149-179.

Lingga, Abhoud Syed M. 2002. Understanding Bangsa Moro Independence as a Mode of Self-Determination. Paper delivered during the Forum on Mindanao Peace on February 28, Davao City. http://www.yonip.com/main/articles/determination.htm

_____2004. Muslim Minorities in the Philippines. Posted April 15, 2004. http://www.bangsamoro.com/bmoro/moro_muslim_minority.php)

Lopez, Maria, E. 1986. *The Palaw'an: Land, Ethnic Relations and Political Process in a Philippine Frontier System.* Dissertation. Harvard University. University Microfilms International.

Majul, C.A. 1973. *Muslims in the Philippines: An historical perspective.* Diliman, Quezon City: University of the Philippines Press.

Malayang, Ben S. III 2001. Tenure rights and ancestral domains in the Philippines; A study of the roots of conflict. *Bijdragen tot de Taal-, Land- en Volkenkunde* (BKI) 157-3, pp.661-76

Muehlebach, Andrea 2003. What Self in Self-Determination? Notes from the Frontiers of Transnational Indigenous Activism. *Identities: Global Studies in Culture and Power,* 10, pp.241-268

Nicholas, Colin 2002. "Organizing Orang Asli Identity", in: Geoffrey Benjamin and Cynthia Chou, *Tribal Communities in the Malay World. Historical, Cultural and Social Perspectives,* pp. 119-136. Singapore: Institute of

Southeast Asian Studies

Postma, Antoon 1981. *Treasure of a Minority.* The Ambahan: *a poetic expression of the Mangyans of Southern Mindoro, Philippines.* Revised Edition. Manila: Arnoldus Press, Inc.

Republic of the Philippines 1997. Republic Act 8372. An Act to recognize, protect and promote the rights of indigenous cultural communities/indigenous peoples, creating a national commission on indigenous peoples, establishing implementing mechanism, appropriating funds therefore, and for other purposes. Retrieved from: www.tebtebba.org/tebtebba_files/ipr/philippines/ipra.pdf

Rodil, B.R. 1993. *The Lumad and Moro of Mindanao.* London: Minority Rights Group International, Report 93/2

Schult, Volker. 1990. *Mindoro – Sozialgeschichte einer philippinischen Insel im 20. Jahrhundert. Studie eines verzögerten Entwicklungsprozesses.* Frankfurt am Main: Peter Lang.

Sharp, John 1996. Tribe, in: Adam Kuper and Jessica Kuper (eds.), *The Social Science Encyclopedia,* 2nd edition, p.883f. London: Routledge

Southall, Aidan 1970. The Illusion of Tribe. *Journal of Asian and African Studies* 5 (1-2), pp. 28-50.

US State Department 2006. Philippines. International Religious Freedom Report 2006. Released by the Bureau of Democracy, Human Rights, and Labor. http://www.state.gov/g/drl/rls/irf/2006/71355.htm

Wenk, Irina 2007. Land titling in Perspective: Indigenous-Settler Relations and Territorialization on a Southern Philippine Frontier; in: Geiger, Danilo (ed.). forthcoming. *Colonization and Conflict: Contemporary Settlement Frontiers in South and Southeast Asia.* Zürich: University of Zürich

Winthorp, Robert 1991. *Dictionary of Concepts in Cultural Anthropology.* New York: Greenwood Press

Notes

[1] Christian Erni holds a Ph.D. in Social Anthropology of Zürich University, Switzerland. He is the Asia Programme Coordinator of the International Work Group for Indigenous Affairs (IWGIA) and lives in Chiang Mai, Thailand.

[2] Ambahan # 181 (Postma 1981: 103)

[3] The other two countries are Taiwan and, since very recently, Japan. See the respective country profiles in this volume.

[4] For example, in an article on the web-site of the Embassy of the Peoples Republic of China in Switzerland the adviser of the Chinese delegation, Long Xuequn, is quoted as having stated on April 1, 1997: "The indigenous issues are a product of special historical circumstances. By and large, they are the result of the colonialist policy carried out in modern history by European countries in other regions of the world, especially on the continents of America and Oceania. [ ] As in the case of other Asian countries, the Chinese people of all ethnic groups have lived on our own land for generations. We suffered from invasion and occupation of colonialists and foreign aggressors [ ] Fortunately, after arduous struggles of all ethnic groups, we drove away

those colonialists and aggressors. In China, there are no indigenous people and therefore no indigenous issues." (http://ch.china-embassy.org/eng/ztnr/rqwt/t138829.htm)

[5] "English and Spanish share a common root in the Latin term indigenae, which was used to distinguish between persons who were born in a particular place and those who arrived from elsewhere (advenae)." (Daes 1996: para. 10; and in this volume p. 32)

[6] The law, Republic Act number 8371, is officially called "an act to recognize, protect and promote the rights of indigenous cultural communities/indigenous peoples, creating a national commission on indigenous peoples, establishing implementing mechanisms, appropriating funds therefore, and for other purposes" (Republic of the Philippines 1997: 1).

[7] On the expansion of Islam in the Philippines see Majul 1973: 35-78.

[8] The strongest adversaries of the Spanish were the Tausug of Sulu. In the early 17th century, a large alliance composed of Maranao, Maguindanao, Tausug and other Muslim groups was formed by Sultan Kudarat who led it into successful battles against several Spanish expeditions. The alliance, however, did not last long, and neither did the peace treaty concluded in 1638 between the Spanish and the Tausug (Zoilo Pascual 2003 at: http://archives.free.net.ph/message/ 20030817.134052.ad9af8fc.html).

[9] Scott emphasizes that the hills "are meant both literally and metaphorically in this context. Literally, they were the destination for those fleeing valley polities; metaphorically 'the hills' represented any space effectively outside the ambit of valley kingdoms: 'the hills' in this last sense could be marshes, mangrove swamps (sundarbans), or the sea itself as in the case of the 'sea gypsies' or 'orang laut' of archipelagic Southeast Asia (op.cit.:15, in this volume p. 171)." Groups of so-called 'sea-gypsies' have in fact survived – though sometimes rather precariously – in the Sulu archipelago and adjacent areas in the Southern Philippines and Sabah.

[10] U.S., Bureau of the Census 1905. Census of the Philippine Islands, taken under the direction of the Philippine Commission in the year 1903, Volume 2 (of 4). Washington: Government Printing Office, 1905.

[11] The NCIP list has been criticized by Filipino anthropologists as inaccurate. For example, the Sama and Samal are the same. Kalibugan is a term applied to a person of any mixed parentage (i.e. with parents that are Lumad but of different ethnicity, of mixed Lumad and Moro descent, Lumand and immigrant settler or Moro and immigrant settler). The term is best translated with "mixed parentage" or "confused ethnicity". Sangil are migrants from Indonesia. (Sabino Padilla Jr., personal communication).

[12] Interesting to note in this connection is how the colonial government actually interpreted the term "non-Christian". In a court case filed by Attorney Vicente Sotto on behalf of a group of Mangyan from Mindoro island, in which he argued that that the special laws for the Mangyan were against the principle of equality of all citizens and their forced resettlement was violating the basic right to protection of individual liberty. The Supreme Court, however, voted in favour of the legality of special laws for minorities. As Schult (ibid.) writes, the justification of the ruling was an assembly of non-specific, rather artificial, and on the whole insidious platitudes. In order to preempt charges of religious discrimination, which would have forced the court to rule in favour of the Mangyan, the term "non-Christian" was simply defined to suit the government's purpose:

> "The term 'non-Christian' refers not to religious belief, but in a way to geographical area, and more directly to natives of the Philippine Islands of a low grade of civilization (Supreme Court, Report of Cases, Vol. 39, 7, March 1919:661; cit. in Schult 1990, ibid.)"

And the ruling clearly revealed the government's true agenda behind its proclaimed mission to civilize and protect the Mangyan: to take over the land and resources of the Mangyan for national development:

> "Theoretically, one may assert that all men are created free and equal. Practically, we know that the axiom is not precisely accurate. The Manguianes, for instance, are not

free, as civilized men are free, and they are not the equal of their more fortunate brothers. True, indeed, they are citizens, with many but not all the rights which citizenship implies. And true, indeed, they are Filipinos. But just as surely, the Manguianes are citizens of a low degree of intelligence, and Filipinos who are a drag upon the progress of the State. (…) If all are to be equal before the law, all must be approximately equal in intelligence. If the Philippines is to be a rich and powerful country, Mindoro must be populated and its fertile regions must be developed. The public policy of the Government of the Philippines Islands is shaped with a view to benefit the Filipino people as a whole. The Manguianes, in order to fulfill this governmental policy, must be confined for a time, as we have said, for their own good and the good of the country. (…) Segregation really constitutes protection for the Manguianes (ibid.:719, cit. in Schult 1990:142)."

[13] See NCIP web-site at: http://www.ncip.gov.ph/agency/history.htm. The SPDA was deactivated by presidential order in 2002, and re-eactivated by another presidential order in 2006. (Government of the Philippines, Executive Order No. 560 Reactivating the Southern Philippines Development Authority. http://www.ops.gov.ph/records/eo_560.htm)

[14] In January 1987, a peace agreement was signed with the MNLF, who accepted the government's offer of semi-autonomy that lead to the passing of Republic Act 673 or the Organic Act for Mindanao, and the creation of the Autonomous Region of Muslim Mindanao (ARMM) in 1989. The creation of autonomous regions in Mindanao and the Cordilleras was provided for by the new constitution of 1986. The ARMM encompasses Maguindanao, Lanao del Sur, Sulu, and Tawi-Tawi. The Moro Islamic Liberation Front (MILF), resulting from a split within the MNLF in 1981, however refused to accept the offer, and became the largest separatist group in the Philippines. After a two years long cease fire, hostilities broke out again in 2005 and have been intermittently ongoing ever since. Along with smaller militant groups, like Abu Sayyaf formed in the early 1990, MILF has been fighting for an independen Muslim state in Mindanao.

[15] Among social scientists writing on the subject in the 1970s and 1980s it was still common to include the Islamized groups in the category of indigenous ethnic groups, and a few still continue to do so (see Malayang 2001: 663 with reference to Maceda 1974 and Lynch 1984). This has however been largely abandoned by most others, as well as by civil society organizations representing or supporting indigenous peoples. The indigenous peoples' support group TABAK, fore example, does not include any Moro group in their list of indigenous peoples (TABAK 1990; cit. in Malayang 2001:663). National-level alliances of indigenous peoples' organizations also do not have any Moro civil society organizations among their members. The Federation of Indigenous Peoples of the Philippines (Kalipunan ng Katutubong Mamamayan ng Pilipinas – KAMP) for example, lists "as members indigenous organizations from the following ethnolinguistic groups: Cordillera Peoples in Northern Luzon, Lumads from Mindanao, Mangyans of Mindoro, Agtas of Quezon, Aetas of Central Luzon, Altas of Aurora province, Atis of Antique province, Remontados of Tanay, Tagbanuas of Palawan" (http://www.geocities.com/Capitol-Hill/Lobby/4677/kamp.htm).

[16] The Bangsamoro People's Consultative Assembly "is a more organized formation of MILF supporters/mass base compared to the MNLF's Bangsamoro Congress. The Assembly has a newsletter and website, offices that are accessible to the public, allied institutions like the Institute of Bangsamoro Studies, and a set of officials and spokesperson. In effect, it is operated and structured as a "modern" CSO [Civil Society Organizations,C.E.]" (Coronal-Ferrer 2005: 22).

[17] At the first session of the United Nations Working Group on Indigenous Populations in 1982 it was the international human rights organization Amnesty International that submitted a report on "Tribal Peoples in the Philippines" (DOCIP archive WGIP 82/SEA.PHL/1). Only two years later, the first representative of an indigenous peoples (the Ibaloi of the Cordillera) submitted its "Report by a member of the Ibaloi people of the Philippines to the Working Group on Indigenous Populations, 1984. Review of Recent development in the Cordillera provinces, northern Luzon" (DOCIP archive WGIP 84/SEA.PHL/1). Since then indigenous representatives partici-

pated regularly in the meetings of the UN Working Group on Indigenous Populations and other international meetings on indigenous peoples' issues.

[18] The tradition of keeping slaves is not being denied by Moro leaders. Attorney Musib Buat, member of the MILF Peace Negotiation Panel and head of the MILF Technical Working Group, in a presentation during the National Consultation with the United Nations Special Rapporteur on the Human Rights and Fundamental Freedom of Indigenous Peoples in Manila in February 2007, elaborated his vision of how the Lumad could be part of the Bangsamoro (the Moro homeland, which, according to his view, should encompass the whole Mindanao island). He asserted that there was no intention to take over indigenous peoples' land, that the Moro have always been traders and warriors living in towns along the coast, and that they do not have any intention to farm the land. In the past, he pointed out, they had slaves who worked their land. So he suggested a kind of division of labour in a future Bangasamoro in which the indigenous could farm the land, and the Moro would "do the fighting". Attorney Buat also emphasized the fact that the Moros had been"highly organized", and that in their current struggle they were "just restoring their right". He thereby implicitly referred to one of the basic tenets of the Moro self-understanding: their pre-colonial state tradition, which forms the basis of their claim to nationhood and thus their independence or autonomy of bangasamoro, and by which they, in addition to Islam, distinguishing themselves from the lumad.

[19] As Geiger (1994: 339) elaborates, in the Tausug-dominated Sulu archipelago itself a veritable, three-tiered caste structure emerged in the wake of state formation. The nomadic non-Muslim Bajao were relegated to lowest, and the the Samal, who were Islamized by the Tausug, to the second level of cast hierarchy. Both groups occupied specialized economic niches that were crucial for the Tausug economy: the Bajao provided pearls and other sea products for trade, and the Samal were fishermen while the Tausug controlled agriculture and the maritime trade. The Tausug took every effort to keep the two groups in their subordinate position. Whole Bajau communities were considered the "property" of the Tausug elite and were prevented from adopting Islam, which would have rendered their exploitation illegitimate. Today the Bajao are generally considered Muslim and one of the smaller ethnic groups belonging to the Moro. In neighboring Sabah of Malaysia, they are the second largest ethnic group.

[20] Consequently, many traditional Lumad leaders and Lumad activists vehemently reject the proposal by the MILF to become part of the Bangsamoro homeland. This was flamboyantly expressed, for example, by the Subanen representatives during the National Consultation with the United Nations Special Rapporteur on the Human Rights and Fundamental Freedom of Indigenous Peoples in Manila in February 2007.

[21] In 1975 the Catholic Bishops' Conference created the Episcopal Commission on Cultural Communities (ECCC) (formerly just a sub-commission). It was renamed in 1977 to Episcopal Commission on Tribal Filipinos (ECTF), and in 1995 to Episcopal Commission on Indigenous Peoples (ECIP) (www.cbcponline.net/commissions /indigenous.html).

[22] An example is the Eskaya, a religious cult from Bohol island, which has received a Certificate of Ancestral Domain Claim (CADC) by the Department of Environment and Natural Resources (DENR) before the passing of the Indigenous Peoples Rights Act. The DENR was however careful and didn't include them in their list. The issuing of a CADC was allegedly just out of political exigency, following the request of the Bohol governor.

[23] The exception is the Moro area in the Sulu archipelago and western Mindanao, where a socio-cultural dichotomy already emerged in pre-Spanish times. It is very likely that if the Spanish had arrived a century or two later, the socio-politically already fairly complex societies of the coastal trading chiefdoms would, hand-in-hand with the spread of Islam, have been either brought under the rule of expanding Muslim Sultanates of the South or consolidated into more powerful and centralized polities like the trading states in the Indonesian archipelago. And along with it would probably have come a socio-political and cultural differentiation similar to the one documented in pre-colonial Malaysia and Indonesia.

[24] The first Asian indigenous organizations attending UN meetings were from the Cordillera in the

Philippines and from the Chittagong Hill Tracts in Bangladesh, who sent delegates to participate in the session of the UN Working Group on Indigenous Populations in 1984. (Muehlebach
2003: 263)

[25] This of course mainly applies to publications in English. Often, there is no equivalent term in
local languages even though the various terms used are often translated as "tribal". In Thailand,
for example, a number of designations have been coined over the years, such as chao khao
(mountain/hill people), chao thai phoo khao (mountain/hill Thai), or chon phao (tribal people),
all of which are commonly translated into English as "hill tribes".

[26] Occasionally, the term is however still lingering on in UN publications. The News and Media
Division of the United Nations Department of Public Information in an article on the 5th session of the Permanent Forum on Indigenous Issues posted on 22 May 2006 for example writes:
"Representatives of indigenous and *tribal* communities today urged the United Nations panel
charged with drawing attention to their plight to press Member States to rapidly adopt a long-
negotiated draft declaration on the rights of indigenous peoples, as the surest way to promote the
human rights of 370 million people worldwide and to protect the fragile traditional lands and
resources on which they depended for survival. (emphasis added)" http://www.un.org/News/
Press/docs/2006/hr4894.doc.htm

[27] The concept of "internal colonization" has been coined to describe colonial practices occurring
within state boundaries. (see e.g. Evans 1992)

General Considerations on the Situation of Human Rights and Fundamental Freedoms of Indigenous Peoples in Asia

Rodolfo Stavenhagen

Report by the United Nations Special Rapporteur on the situation of human rights and fundamental freedoms of indigenous people

15 May 2007[1]

Summary

This report presents a general overview of the situation of the rights of indigenous peoples in Asia, based on the information gathered by the Special Rapporteur from various sources during recent activities in the region, including activities organized by the Office of the High Commissioner for Human Rights in Cambodia and Nepal, a follow-up visit to the Philippines, and the First Asian Regional Consultation with the Special Rapporteur.

Indigenous peoples in Asian countries face similar patterns of discrimination and human rights violations as in other parts of the world. Drawing from specific examples in various Asian countries, the report focuses on issues of particular concern in the region, including the steady loss of indigenous lands, territories and natural resources; situations of internal conflict, violence and repression faced by these peoples, the implementation of peace accords and autonomy regimes, and the special abuses faced by indigenous women.

Contents   Paragraphs

Introduction

1. The mandate of the Special Rapporteur on the situation of human rights and fundamental freedoms of indigenous people was established by the Commission on Human Rights in resolution 2001/57, extended for a further period of three years in 2004 (resolution 2004/62) and renewed by the Human Rights Council in 2006 (decision 1/102). According to his mandate, the Special Rapporteur is expected to "gather, request, receive and exchange information from all relevant sources [...] on violations of [indigenous peoples'] human rights and fundamental freedoms, and to "formulate recommendations and proposals on appropriate measures and activities to prevent" these violations. The present report is submitted in accordance with the decision taken by the Permanent Forum on Indigenous Issues at its fifth session to devote half a day to the discussion during its next session to discuss the issues of indigenous peoples in Asia.

2. The situation of the human rights of indigenous peoples in Asia raises concerns at different levels. They are discriminated and victimized for their origin and identities, specially in the case of women. They are excluded from full participation in the political life in the countries in which they live. They remain at the margin of national development efforts, and they score low in all indicators in relation to their enjoyment of basic rights such as education and health. They are impoverished as a result of the loss of their traditional lands, territories and lifestyles. They suffer from violence as a result of the defence of their human

rights, often by the authorities of their own countries. While these processes are experienced by most indigenous peoples around the world, the situation of indigenous peoples in Asia presents a number of specificities.

3. These initial considerations on the human rights of indigenous people in Asia, based on the recent activities of the Special Rapporteur, do not attempt to provide a full picture of the situation. These activities include the National Consultation with the Special Rapporteur organized by local indigenous organizations and NGOs, which took place in Quezon City, Philippines, on 2-3 February 2007; the Seminar on Indigenous Peoples and Access to Land in Cambodia, organized by the Office of the High Commissioner for Human Rights (OHCHR), the International Labour Office (ILO), and the United Nations Development Programme (UNDP); and the NGO Forum on Cambodia, an and the NGO Forum on Cambodia, and the First Asian Regional Consultation with the Special Rapporteur, organized by Tebtebba and the Asia Indigenous Peoples Pact Foundation, which took place in Phonm Penh, Cambodia, on 7-8 and 9-11 February 2007, respectively; and the various meetings and on-site visits to communities organized by OHCHR in Nepal, on 23-27 April 2007.

I. Indigenous Peoples in Asia

4. Indigenous peoples in Asia are among the most discriminated against, socially and economically marginalized, and politically subordinated parts of the society in the countries where they live. Time and again disregarded in State's law and policy, they number an estimated 100 million people distributed in virtually all Asian countries, often across State borders. Their traditional territories are frequently found in remote areas where they have historically resisted the drive of colonization and nation-building, including some of the most bio-diversity rich areas of the world. The push of globalization and the State development policies in recent decades have however endangered the continuation of their traditional lifestyles, and they are victims of serious human rights violations as a consequence of the dispossession of their lands and natural resources, widespread violence and repression, and assimilation

5. Asian States differ in the legal recognition and status granted to indigenous peoples in their own countries, and also in the terminology applied to refer to these different groups in their domestic policies and legislation. Thus, depending on the specific country, they are sometimes referred as "tribals" or "tribal people," "hill tribes," "scheduled tribes", "natives", "ethnic minorities," "minority nationalities" and other similar denominations. Specific terms are also used in national languages, like Adivasis (original inhabitants) in India and Bangladesh, Orang Asli (original peoples) in Malaysia, or Janajata in Nepal.

6. In colonial times, some indigenous peoples were given special legal status, like in Bangladesh, India, Indonesia, Malaysia and Myanmar. After independence, however, many Asian countries asserted the principle of "national unity" to sup-

press any specific recognition of indigenous peoples as such, but this approach has begun to change in recent years. In a number of countries, indigenous peoples are granted constitutional recognition or are the object of special laws, as in the Constitution of India (1950) (referring to indigenous peoples or adivasis as "scheduled tribes"); the Constitution of Malaysia (1957) (including special provisions in relation to the "natives" of Sabah and Sarawak); the Indigenous Peoples' Rights Act (IPRA) of the Philippines (1997); and the Cambodian Land Law (2001). Nepal passed in 2002 the National Foundation for the Development of Indigenous Nationalities Act (NFDIN Act), and indigenous peoples are recognized in the 2006 interim Constitution. The Constitution of Pakistan (1973) recognizes federally and provincially administered Tribal Areas, and involves tribal authorities in decision-making in these areas. In other countries, indigenous peoples are referred to as ethnic minorities and given a legal treatment similar to that of other minority groups, like in the cases of China, Viet Nam, or Laos. In other countries, while not explicitly recognized as different collectivities, indigenous peoples may have a distinct legal status. In Indonesia, most peoples who fall under customary law (Adat) self-identify as indigenous peoples. In Japan, the Ainu are not officially considered as indigenous peoples in the 1997 Ainu Cultural Promotion Law, but a number of court decisions have affirmed their rights based on international indigenous rights standards. This is also the case of Malaysia, where the courts have affirmed the aboriginal title of the Orang Asli over their traditional lands.

7. In addition to the recognition in domestic legislation, three Asian countries, India, Bangladesh and Pakistan, are parties of the 1957 ILO Convention on Indigenous and Tribal Populations in Independent Countries (No. 107), and they report regularly on the implementation of the convention to the ILO Committee of Experts. Nepal has recently started the procedure to ratify the successor instrument, the 1989 ILO Convention on Indigenous and Tribal Peoples in Independent Countries (No. 169), and will thus become the first Asian country to have ratified this important instrument. Moreover, the situation of indigenous peoples in Asian countries is now routinely examined by United Nations treaty bodies in relation to the implementation of the State's general international human rights obligations.

8. Despite these varied denominations and legal treatment, some States still oppose the relevance of the discussion on the rights of indigenous peoples in the Asian context. Regardless of the controversy around issues of definition, there is an overarching consensus among Asian legal and political actors on the need to address the human rights issues faced by these groups as a result of their distinct identities, lifestyles, and histories. These issues are very similar to those faced by indigenous peoples in other parts of the world, and fall entirely within the sphere of the current international concern on the rights of these peoples, as reflected, inter alia, in the United Nations Declaration on the Rights of Indigenous Peoples. As pointed out by the Committee on the Elimination of Racial Discrimination

(CERD), the Governments concerned should provide for the protection of indigenous peoples' rights as recognized by international law, "regardless of the name given to such groups in domestic law" (CERD/C/LAO/CO/15, paras. 17). From this perspective, this report will analyze the main trends regarding the situation of the rights of indigenous peoples of Asia, putting a special emphasis on the issues of most immediate concern.

II. Issues of Special Concern Regarding the Rights of Indigenous Peoples in Asia

A. The loss of indigenous peoples' lands and territories

9. Some of the most serious forms of human rights violations that indigenous peoples' experience all over Asia are directly related to the rapid loss of indigenous lands and territories, a process that, while affecting indigenous peoples all over the world, is particularly marked in the Asian context. Development projects, plantation leases, logging concessions, and the establishment of protected areas have been major forces in the increasing loss of indigenous lands, leading to the massive displacement of indigenous peoples form their traditional territories, the degradation of their traditional environment, and rising poverty and migration. This trend is fostered by the absence in many Asian countries of precise legal regulations affirming indigenous peoples' customary rights over their traditional lands, territories and resources, as well as by the lack of adequate consultation procedures in relation to development projects taking place in indigenous territories .

10. In Thailand, despite the recognition of customary natural resource management by local communities, legal instruments adopted in recent years, such as the Land Act, the National Reserve Forests Act or the National Parks Act, have failed to recognize indigenous and tribal peoples' traditional land tenure and use patterns. The enforcement of these laws have resulted in the expulsion of many indigenous and tribal peoples, considered to be illegal encroachers on their ancestral lands, as well as in a number of unresolved disputes between state lands (including national parks, watershed areas and forestry preservation areas) and community lands. Corruption by law enforcement officers related to the forest industry is said to be rampant.

11. The development of single-crop, export-oriented plantations has involved the destruction of the natural habitat in both highlands and lowlands where indigenous peoples live, severely limiting the amount of land available for their livelihood and depleting water sources. Only in Sarawak (Malaysia), an estimate of 2.4 million hectares have been given under plantation licenses for the mono-culture of palm oil and pulp. Many of these concessions are given over indigenous traditional lands declared "development areas" and leased for prolonged periods.

Indonesia has announced its intention to become the world's largest producer of oil palm, seen as a blooming alternative source of energy, and the official target is to plant 4.6 million hectares throughout the archipelago. This has justifies the transformation of the remaining forest areas into large plantations, with devastating effects on the local indigenous communities.

12. Land grabbing in Cambodia has became a dramatic example of a trend that is also discernable in other Asian countries. Even though the 2001 Land Law incorporates a number of advanced provisions concerning indigenous communal lands, indigenous communities are losing their lands at an alarming rate as a result of economic concessions, illegal land transfer, and widespread Government corruption. This dynamic is mounting in the densely indigenous-populated provinces of Ratanakiri and Mondulkiri, where the dispossession of indigenous lands has resulted in increased rates of poverty and forced migration. Only in the last decade, an estimated 6.5 million hectares of forest have been expropriated through concessions to timber companies, and another 3.3 million hectares were declared protected areas (see the Special Rapporteur's last thematic report, A/HRC/4/32, para. 15). This critical situation is fostered by the insufficient legal development of the indigenous land provisions of the Land Law, including the lack of a procedural framework for land demarcation and titling; many observers claim that there will be little land left to title by the time the sub-decree on titling is really implemented. The Special Representative of the Secretary-General for Human Rights in Cambodia has repeatedly called attention to the seriousness of the situation, and has recommended that until the adoption of the sub-decree on collective ownership of indigenous lands, a moratorium on land sales affecting indigenous peoples should be considered by relevant authorities (E/CN.4/2006/110, para. 82 (h)).

13. In the Philippines, the Indigenous Peoples Rights Act (1997), recognizes indigenous peoples' rights over their ancestral lands and territories, and incorporates a process of demarcation and titling through the granting of Certificates of Ancestral Domain Titles (CADT). In the last six years, more than 670 CADT applications have been submitted. With an average of 4.5 titles issued per year, it has been estimated that the National Commission on Indigenous Peoples will take almost 25 years to issue titles over the existing applications. Among the reasons of the slowness of the titling process, the existence of overlap between ancestral domain areas and existing leases for mining, agro-forest, logging and pasture have been noted.

14. The loss of access to natural resources is similarly experienced by coastal peoples. For instance, the Palawan and the Molbog tribes in Bugsuk, Southern Palawan, are still struggling to regain access to their ancestral marine territory after a pearl farm was established. Fishermen who are caught in the perimeter of the farm complain about harassment, ill treatment and illegal detention by company guards. Confronted with these vested interests, the National Commission

has been accused of a weak commitment towards fully implementing its mandate. In the report on his visit to Japan, the Special Rapporteur on contemporary forms of racism described how the Ainu are still greatly limited in their capacity to fish salmon, their traditional food. This situation is "humiliating, since it puts them in a position of dependence on the public authorities in the access to their ancestral alimentary resources" (E/CN.4/2006/16/Add.2, paras. 45-47).

B. The situation of forest peoples

15. Commercial logging, both illegal and Government-sponsored, is a major source of indigenous land loss in practically all countries of the region. For instance, in Bangladesh, India, Indonesia, the Philippines and Thailand, forests are considered State-owned lands, and indigenous communities lack any legal venue to counter Government policies in these areas or seek compensation in cases in which their traditional lands are lost.

16. The Andhra Pradesh Community Forest Management Project (APCFMP), launched in 2002 in India with the support of the World Bank, has been opposed by Adivasi organizations, who claim that the procedural safeguards incorporated by the World Bank (including the establishment of forest protection committees or Vana Samrakshana Samithi) have not been adequately implemented.

17. In Malaysia, indigenous communities have denounced that the national forestry certification system run by the Malaysian Timber Certification Council (MTCC) fails to recognize and protect indigenous customary rights over the forest they have traditionally occupied or used for their subsistence. Several cases have been brought to the national courts as a result of the granting of timber certification to private companies operating in communal lands, without prior consultation of the communities concerned and with no compensation paid to the people. In some cases, indigenous communities have mobilized against logging in their ancestral territories, like the Dusun community of Terian, Sabah, which recently stopped an illegal logging road that threatened its traditional forest near Crocker Range National Park. Similarly, the Penan people in the Middle Baram region of Sarawak, who have led several peaceful blockades and have endured violence by loggers and security forces.

18. As in other parts of the world, indigenous peoples in Asia have suffered the direct consequences of the establishment of national parks. This is for instance the case of the Modhupur National Park Development, in Modhupuar, Tangail District (Bangladesh). The Eco-Park project, initiated in 1999, involved the erection of walls that cut across the Modhupur forest, ancestral land of the Garo and Koch peoples, without previously consulting them. Suspended in 2004, the Eco-Park project was resumed after the declaration of the state of emergency in January 2007, and there have been serious allegations of the detention of indigenous leaders, torture and even killings.

19. Despite international praise for its international conservation efforts, Nepal's community forests have forced many indigenous communities, like the Chepangs and the Rautes, from their traditional lands. In Sri Lanka, the Wanniyala-Aetto indigenous people were evicted in 1983 from the lands which they have occupied for centuries to give way to the Maduru Ova National Park; since then, their number has fallen to only 2,500 members, half of the original population, and they are on the verge of virtual extinction. More than 1,000 Adivasis have been expelled from the Muthanga Wildlife Sanctuary in Wayanad, State of Kerala, India. In Indonesia, the Moronene people of Southeast Sulawesi have been evicted several times since their traditional territory was declared a conservation forest in 1997. A similar case is that of the Wana people after the government announced the creation of the Morowali conservation area in their traditional territory. The Semi tribe, in Malaysia, is opposing the establishment of a National Botanical Garden in the Perak State, a project that aims at becoming a major tourist attraction but that would expel the community from the ancient rainforest in which they lived for generations, and over which they do not possess a formal title.

20. In recent years, a number of countries have started to address the legal vacuum concerning indigenous peoples' communal land rights with the adoption of new legislation. Following the example of countries like Cambodia or the Philippines, the 2003 Land Law in Viet Nam includes the category of "communal land", which has opened the possibility for indigenous people to apply for titles over their ancestral land and forest rights; some difficulties still need to be clarified concerning the interpretation of various provisions of the law. In 2006, after many massive protests by Adivasis and forest dwellers, India adopted the Scheduled Tribes and other Traditional Forest Dwellers (Recognition of Forest Rights) Bill. The bill grants extensive rights to indigenous forest dwellers, including the right to possess forest land for habitation and self-cultivation purposes, as well as the right of access to forest resources and to participate in conservation efforts. The Bill further incorporates a special procedure for the establishment of "critical wildlife areas", as well as for the informed relocation and rehabilitation of the affected communities.

21. In the absence of specific legislation, national courts have played a major role in affirming indigenous peoples' rights over their traditional forest. For instance, in Malaysia, a number of decisions by the Supreme Court, including the path-breaking Sagong Tasi v. Negeri Kerajaan Selangor (2002), have recognize the existence of Orang Asli's native title over their traditional lands even in the absence of a formal title deed, despite the lack of statutory recognition of their rights in Malaysian law.

C. Forced relocation and international resettlement

22. One of the most serious threats to indigenous peoples' survival in Asia relates to the construction of megaprojects and other forms of forced relocation or resettlement in the name of "national development", which take place in several Asian countries at a particularly alarming rate. The Special Rapporteur has expressed his concern in relation to some of these projects

23. In India, according to the Five-Year Plan (2002-7) of the National Commission on Scheduled Castes and Scheduled Tribes, 8.54 million tribals have been displaced from their traditional lands as a result of development projects in the states of Andhra Pradesh, Bihar, Gujarat, Maharastra, Madhya Pradesh, Rajasthan and Orissa, of which less than a quarter have been resettled. According to the Commission, this massive displacement has led to "loss of assets, unemployment, debt bondage and destitution." The Special Rapporteur, as well as other human rights mechanisms have repeatedly expressed their major concern about the Sardar Sarovar Dam and Power Project, a multiyear, mutipurpose project affecting areas in the states of Gujarat, Rajasthan, Madhya Pradesh and Maharashtra, involving the relocation of 320,000 people and affecting the livelihood of thousands of others. There is concern about the lack of adequate compensation or resettlement schemes of the tribal communities affected. In addition, 168 new dams are scheduled for construction in north-eastern India, without the meaningful participation by and the consent of the Bodos, Hmars, Nagas and other indigenous communities that have traditionally owned the land. These dams, it is argued, that will provide electric power to other parts of India, will create irreparable harm to indigenous peoples' traditional subsistence communities. Concern has also been expressed that these proposed dams are located in a highly seismic area.

24. Similar large scale displacement has resulted from mining. The Government of Jharkhand has open lands to 41 steel and mining companies for large scale resource extraction, which will result in the destruction of 57,000 hectares of forest and in the displacement of 9,615 families, 80per cent of whom belong to scheduled tribes. Similarly, State-sponsored mining projects in Orissa have resulted since 2004 in the displacement of hundreds of Jarene families, and 300 other families are still under threat as a result of new projects. The Khasi people of Eastern Meghalaya now face the proposed resumption of uranium mining in its traditional territory, involving the displacement of an estimate of 30,000 people, the massive influx of non-indigenous settlers, and possible health risks.

25. The 13 dam cascade project on the Chinese portion of the Nu river would have a considerable effect on the Nu, Lissu, Yi, Pumi and other ethnic minorities in the area, and its impact of the biodiversity-rich Three Parallel Rivers World Heritage Site has raised the concern of UNESCO's World Heritage Committee. Viet Nam is currently embarked in the construction of the Son Lam Dam, the largest such project in the region, involving the submersion of 24,000 hectares of land and the forced removal of 100,000 people, mostly ethnic minorities. The

Bakun Dam in Malaysia is reported to cause the forced displacement of 5,000 to 8,000 indigenous persons from 15 communities by clear-cutting 80,000 hectares of rainforest. In Laos, the construction of the Nam Theun 2 dam, in Khammouane province, involves the displacement of as many as 6,200 indigenous people. The Special Rapporteur, along with other special procedures, is currently engaged in a constructive dialogue with the Government of the Lao People's Democratic Republic, the World Bank and other donors, promoting the effective implementation of the relocation and compensation program.

26. Laos and Thailand have undertaken the resettlement of many tribal people as part of their program of eradication of drug plantations. The Government of Thailand launched in 2003 a "Master Plan for Community Development, Environment, and Narcotic Plant Control on the Highland", leading to the displacement of indigenous communities. Due to the relocation schemes, many of these communities have broken up, and they often lack alternative ways to provide for their subsistence. The Lao Government's campaign of eradication of opium poppy has been internationally praised as a success, but it has led the displacement of an estimated 65,000 hill tribe people into new villages where they are said to experience severe food shortages, disease, and mortality rates as high as 4per cent.

27. The Vietnamese Government has adopted a "Fixed Field/Fixed Residence" policy that involves the resettlement of ethnic minorities, including many indigenous and tribal communities, from remote areas into other more easily accessible locations. The purpose of this resettlement is to make social services more easily available to these communities, but also to replace their traditional slash-and-burn agriculture, viewed as inefficient by the Government, by other methods of sedentary agriculture. The resettlement has generated the social and cultural disintegration of many of these communities, as well as increased ethnic tension as a result of a state-sponsored migration program to bring non-indigenous settlers into the indigenous highlands. A similar stand has been taken in Laos, where numerous Hmong communities have been forcibly relocated by the Government from their traditional lands in the highlands and resettled in so-called "focal sites", together with other ethnic minority group or Hmong from different clans. Reports indicate that these resettlement sites are often not arable lands, and that their traditional life has been eroded. In its last concluding observations on Laos, CERD recommended the Government to avoid displacement, and if necessary, to "ensure that the persons concerned are made fully aware of the reasons for and modalities of their displacement and of the measures taken for compensation and resettlement" (CERD/C/LAO/CO/15, para. 18).

28. The Dukha (Tsaatan) people, a reindeer-herder community living in Mongolia's Darhat Valley, endured similar attempts of forceful rellocation during the 1950s. Now they are striving to retain their traditional culture against the depletion of their herds and the loss of their traditional lands. The establish-

ment of the Lake Baikal and Sayan Mountains Peace Park, in the border between Russia and Mongolia, home of the Dukha and other peoples like the Soyot and Buryat, or the 2002 adoption of the Charter Agreement on the Protection of the Transboundary Reindeer Herding Cultures of Russia and Mongolia, constitute important initiatives to promote the respect for indigenous peoples' seminomadic lifestyles with the protection of the environment in their traditional territories.

D. Conflict and repression

29. Historically, the denial of equal enjoyment of political and other rights has led to an increase in violence that, in many cases, has involved indigenous peoples directly. Internal conflict has posed an enormous burden on indigenous communities and other parties involved, and has sometimes led to massive human rights violations. Countless cases are also reported concerning abuses suffered by indigenous peoples by military and paramilitary forces in the name of public security, anti-insurgency, and counter-terrorism. Examples of these dynamics in the past decades include the armed insurgencies in north-eastern in India, in Aceh and West Papua, in Indonesia, and in Mindanao, in the Philippines, as well as the protracted conflicts in Myanmar and Nepal. In Laos and Viet Nam, some indigenous peoples still face retaliation for their involvement in armed conflicts during the American War a generation ago, and they are reportedly denied full citizen rights and persecuted as criminals.

30. Indigenous peoples (or "ethnic minorities") in Myanmar, like the Kachin, Karen, Karenni, Mon, or Shan, represent one third of the country's total population. They have endured the worst consequences of the civil war that has stricken the country for half a century, and which involved indigenous groups fighting against the military government. They experience all sorts of human rights violations in the context of counter-insurgency operations against indigenous groups, including extrajudicial killings, massacres, torture and sexual violence, and large movements refugees and internally displaced persons as a result. The ILO has also denounced the practice of forced labour, particularly in indigenous areas.

31. Different sources have documented the countless deaths of civilians, including children and elders, as a result of the continuous struggle of the Hmong with the Lao Government since 1975. It has been estimated that 20 rebel groups are surrounded by Lao military and reduced to starvation and disease in the forest where they have sough refugee. Many of them have fled to Cambodia and Thailand, where there have been reports of hundreds of deportations. Following the upsurge of military activity reported in recent years, several hundred Hmong have reportedly "surrendered" to Lao authorities, and episodes of human rights abuses have been reported, like the killing and gang rape of five girls by armed forces in 2004 (CERD/C/LAO/CO/15, para. 22).

32. The Special Rapporteur has received reports documenting hundreds of human rights violations of individual Degar (Montagnard) people in Viet Nam.

These allegations refer to cases of arbitrary arrest, ill treatment, torture and extra-judicial killing by security forces. In addition, it has been alleged that 350 Degar prisoners remain in Vietnamese prisons for human rights activism, for spreading Christianity or for attempting to flee to neighboring countries. Following the February 2001 and April 2004 protests in the Central Highland Region of Viet Nam, when numerous killings and other human rights abuses by security forces were reported, many hundreds of indigenous asylum seekers fled the country into neighboring Cambodia in fear of Government repression.

33. The massive scale of political killing of indigenous leaders and human rights defenders in the Philippines has been object of increased international concern in recent years. Leaders and member of indigenous organizations are tagged as "legal fronts" of the Communists because of their human rights related activities, and also because of their opposition to mining operations and other megaprojects that threaten indigenous communities. The Melo Commission, established in 2006 by the Parliament to investigate the situation, concluded that the majority of the killings could be attributed to members of the Philippine military. According to a report of Indigenous Peoples Watch-Philippines, 119 such killings took place in the period April 2001-January 2007. Recent examples of such acts are the killing of Rafael Markus Nagit, in June 2006, and the attempted assassination of Dr. Constancio "Chandu" Claver on July 2006, leading to his wife's death. The situation has been reported on by the Special Rapporteur during his official visit to the country in 2002 (see E/CN.4/2003/90/Add.3, para. 46); since his visit the murder of another 84 indigenous leaders has been reported.

34. Indigenous peoples of north-eastern India have repeatedly denounced the human rights violations committed by security forces under the Armed Forces (Special Powers) Act (AFSPA) (1958), adopted in the context of an armed conflict in Assam, Nagaland, and Manipur. After a 1997 decision of the Indian Supreme Court that questioned the constitutionality of several of the AFSPA provisions, a review committee appointed by the Government in 2004 proposed the amendment of the Act, but its recommendations were never publicly released, and violations of human rights continue unabated. Following the declaration of the state of emergency by the President of Bangladesh in January 2007, the Special Rapporteur have received many allegations of suppressive actions against indigenous leaders and organizations that would have involved the Joint Forces, consisting of the military, the Rapid Action Battalion (RAB), the Bangladesh Rifles (BDR), the police and intelligence servicemen, which were given special powers to control corruption. Among the alleged abuses, there are reported cases of arbitrary arrest, detention and torture of members of Jumma leaders in the Chittagong Hill Tracts and other regions. Decades of conflict in Nepal and in several Indonesian provinces, including Aceh (Nanggröe Aceh Darussalam) and West Papua (Irian Jaya), have left behind a tragic record of killings, forced displacement and other serious human rights abuses among local indigenous groups. Indigenous peoples

now demand full participation in the post-conflict political arrangements, and plead for transitional justice schemes to repair past human rights violations.

35. Local conflicts resulting from the lack of recognition of the rights of indigenous peoples to their communal lands is another permanent source of repression and abuse and often lead to violations of human rights violations of indigenous peoples. The Special Rapporteur has received many reports from countries such as India, Indonesia, Laos, Malaysia and Thailand, of arbitrary arrest or fake criminal charges made against members of indigenous and tribal peoples, as well as other forms of threats and intimidations, as a result of their mobilization to defend their rights against State authorities. Cases of ill-treatment and torture during detention, as well as extrajudicial killings have also been widely reported. In India, for instance, 15 Adivasis were killed in 2003 as a result of the use of excessive police force in the demonstrations to protest against the establishment of the Muthanga Wildlife Sanctuary. In Laos, 10 Degar people were killed as a result of the 2004 protests in the Central Highlands. In the Philippines, the lethal conjunction of militarization and large scale mining and dam projects have led indigenous peoples to coin the expression "development aggression", which is to blame for a wide range of human rights violations, including murders, massacres, and illegal detention. The critical situation faced by the various Lumad in Mindanao or the Tumandok on Panay Island, are cases in point.

E. Citizenship rights, refugees and asylum seekers

36. The lack of citizen rights has been a long-standing cause of human rights violations against members of the hill tribes in Thailand since the enactment of the Citizenship/Nationality Act in 1965. According to 2004 estimates, 90,700 original hill people are not given Thai citizenship or any enjoy other legal status, remaining stateless in their own countries. The lack of access to citizenship rights make them subject to many abuses, like charges of illegal entrance in the country and denial of freedom of movement, threats, intimidation, and bribery. They are also denied access to basic social services, including health care and education as well as income generating activities. A mix of discriminatory laws and procedures, deeply-rooted prejudices, and corruption are among the main causes of this situation, which has been repeatedly denounced by human rights bodies, including the Committee of the Rights of the Child (CRC/C/THA/CO/2, para.24), the Committee for the Elimination of Discrimination Against Women (CEDAW/C/THA/CO/5, para. 78), and the Human Rights Committee (CCPR/CO/84/THA, paras. 22-24).

37. Indigenous and tribal peoples in Myanmar face the worst consequences of the civil war that has stricken the country for decades. For instance, as a result of the large-scale offensive that took place in Karen state during 2006, 27,000 civilians were displaced, and some 232 villages destroyed. According to one independent source, between 2004 and 2006, some 470,000 Mon, Karen, Shan and

Karenni were internally displaced as a consequence of violence, military operations and human rights abuses. Others have been able to flee the country, and survival in extremely difficult conditions in formal or informal refugee camps in neighboring countries.

38. Special mention must be made of the plight of the Khmer Krom people in southern Viet Nam who complain about serious human rights violations, especially concerning citizenship, religious freedom, land rights and gender issues, as a result of complex historical and geopolitical factors.

F. Autonomy rights and implementation of peace accords

39. In a number of Asian countries, constructive arrangements, including autonomy regimes, have sought to accommodate the ethnic diversity of some regions, or to put an end to decades of armed conflict. Inasmuch many of these arrangements provide for limited autonomy in local affairs, political participation, and land and cultural protection, they represent positive steps towards the promotion of the rights of indigenous peoples. However, comparative experience suggests that these arrangements have a mixed record in terms of implementation, and that much remains to be done by the Governments concerned, and by the international actors committed to the monitoring of these arrangements, to ensure that indigenous communities are actively involved and their human rights concerns taken into account.

40. Similar dynamics are found in the Chittagong Hill Tracts (CHT), in Bangladesh, where an autonomy regime was instituted in 1997 following the Peace Accord between the Government and the Parbatya Chattagram Jana Samhati Samiti, a party representing 11 different indigenous communities of the Jumma people. Indigenous people claim that many vital provisions of the Accord have not yet been put in place, including the setting up of a functioning Land Commission (constituted in 1999 but still not fully operative); the rehabilitation of Jumma refugees and internally displaced persons, and the formation of a CHT-based police force. The policy of Government-sponsored transmigration has dramatically changed the ethnic composition of the region, and Bengalese settlers represent now more than 60 per cent of the region's population, compared to only two per cent in 1947. This influx has facilitated cultural assimilation, while creating increased ethnic animosity over diminishing land and resources. Instead of demilitarizing the area, it has been claimed that the Government has continued sending armed forces to the region under the umbrella of the Uttoran (upliftment) and Shantakaran (pacification) programs, allowing for the military intervention in civilian administration and in the establishment of settler villages.

41. In 2001, Indonesia adopted the Special Autonomy Law No. 21, aiming at finding a solution to West Papua's political status and to bring peace to the province. Similarly, a Memorandum of Understanding between the Government of the Republic of Indonesia and the Free Aceh Movement was signed in 2005,

providing for a limited autonomy to Aceh within basic sectors of public affairs, as well as for the right to consultation concerning international agreements for special interest to Aceh. While constructive arrangements have been seen as positive steps, the experience of West Papua after more than five years of the entry into force of the autonomy regime is disquieting. The Government has continued promoting the massive arrival of settlers on the island, the region is still heavily militarized, and episodes of repression and abuse in Puncak Jaya and other parts of the highlands have recently been reported.

42. Since a cease-fire was reached in Nagaland in 1997, the Government of India and several Naga insurgent groups are involved in a peace process seeking to find the political accommodation of the Naga people under the Indian Constitution. The peace process, which follows decades of violent insurgency in various north-eastern states, is subject to ongoing tensions due to the resumption of violence, internal rivalries among the Nagas and the animosity of neighboring communities and state governments at the attempt to extend the ceasefire agreement to areas beyond Nagaland. Despite the many difficulties, the Nagas favour a peaceful settlement of the conflict and demand full implementation of the 1997 agreement as a precondition to achieve this goal.

43. A deeply entrenched system of ethnic and caste-based hierarchy, along with decades of internal conflict, has led to a disproportionate part of indigenous peoples among Nepal's poor. Nepal's indigenous peoples, who represent 37 per cent of the national population, have denounced that the recently endorsed Interim Constitution fails to provide them with an equal representation in the Constituent Assembly, and they are now demanding a federal republic based on ethnic and regional autonomy.

G. The rights of indigenous women and girls

44. Gender-based violence has been recurrently used in the armed conflict in Myanmar, where numerous cases of gang-rape, sexual enslavement and killing of tribal women by members of the military have been reported. Although some of these cases have been well documented, the Military has routinely failed to investigate these abuses. In the CHT in Bangladesh, many cases of rape of Jumma girls and women by settlers backed by the military have been denounced, but in many cases the investigation of these cases is hampered by inaction on the part of the military and even of health professionals. In the Philippines, the militarization of many indigenous areas has also resulted in the sexual abuse of women of local indigenous communities. In India, the AFSFA has justified impunity of sexual violence by members of the military against tribal women, sometimes with the argument that they support insurgent groups.

45. The increasing numbers of indigenous women who have become victims of sexual trafficking and prostitution is of special concern. While systematic data is still lacking, in countries such as Mongolia, Thailand, Myanmar, Nepal, Laos,

Cambodia and Viet Nam, indigenous women and girls are prime targets for trafficking and exploitation as beggars, sex workers, domestic workers, and even child soldiers. In areas such as Chiang Mai, in Thailand, where there are thousands of indigenous women working as sex workers, 70-80per cent of these women are reportedly HIV positive. In other cases, like in Nepal, Indonesia, Bangladesh or the Philippines, indigenous women and girls are forced to leave their communities and search for jobs in other countries.

III. Conclusions

46. In recent years the plight of indigenous peoples in Asia has started to become a specific issue of concern in the international human rights agenda, as well as in domestic legislation and policies. Indigenous issues are increasingly the object of specific attention by several Asian States in key areas such as land rights, cultural protection, autonomy and self-government and development policies, thus signaling an important change of mentality regarding the recognition of cultural difference and its human rights implications. However, there is still an important implementation gap with regard to existing constitutional and legal provisions, and much remains to be done in order to mainstream indigenous rights in policies and the institutional machinery at the national level. These developments are overshadowed by the human rights violations still suffered by indigenous peoples in some countries of the region as a result of internal conflicts and insensitive official policies.

47. Indigenous peoples in Asian countries face patterns of discrimination and human right abuses similar to indigenous peoples in other parts of the world. Some of the most serious violations are related to the lack of effective protection in domestic laws and policies regarding indigenous rights over their traditional territories, lands and natural resources, as well as to the their right to participate in decisions affecting these lands and resources. This has lead to widespread violations in practically all countries of the region as result of land-grabbing and corruption, forced displacement associated with the extension of plantation economies, the construction of megaprojects, and particularly dam construction and mining; and other State development policies.

48. Forest peoples are particularly affected by these dynamics of dispossession and removal, as the forests are quickly disappearing as a result of Government-promoted and illegal logging, and other State policies often with disastrous environmental effects. Pastoralist communities similarly confront the loss of their distinct livelihoods and cultures, essential to nomadic herding, which is frequently deemed "backward" and "unecological" in official discourse and policy.

49. While militarization and State repression are frequently the source of indigenous peoples' human rights violations in many parts of the world, the recurrent and widespread character of these abuses in Asian countries gives rise to special concern. Decades-long civil conflicts, insurgency movements, political

crimes, and other abuses committed in the name of the struggle against terrorism or secessionism have taken a deadly toll in indigenous and tribal communities. Massacres, killings of social activists and human rights defenders, torture, sexual violence, and displacement are still daily realities for many such communities. While the Special Rapporteur acknowledges the complexity of the various contexts in which these violations occur, the seriousness of these violations leads to the conclusion that the indigenous peoples are widely regarded in many countries as "backward," second-class citizens.

50. A number of constructive arrangements have been put in place in order to accommodate ethnic diversity or to find a peaceful solution to decades-long conflicts. While these initiatives provide important examples of ways in which the principles of State integrity and autonomy can be combined in the Asian context, a common denominator of ongoing experiences is the lack of implementation of existing legal and political arrangements. Militarization, induced migration, unequal development policies, and resulting human rights abuses are questioning the spirit of such arrangements, while fueling the conflicts they seek to prevent.

51. As elsewhere in the world, the indigenous women of Asia experience accumulated layers of discrimination and marginalization. They are subject to human rights violations as a result of longstanding conflicts and the impoverishment of their communities. Sexual violence, trafficking and labor exploitation are daily realities for many Asian indigenous women in Asia, a problem that is just beginning to be fully understood.

IV. Recommendations

52. The protection of the rights of indigenous peoples is a human rights imperative that cannot be subordinated, nor is it contradictory, to the objectives of national unity or development. The Special Rapporteur calls upon Asian States to give priority attention to indigenous issues, regardless of the constitutional and legal status afforded to these groups in their domestic systems, taking into consideration international norms as well as the positive examples found in comparative legislation in Asia and other parts of the world.

53. Asian States should continue their efforts to enter into dialogue with indigenous peoples in order to work out constructive legal and political arrangements, within a spirit of mutual respect, autonomy, and self-determination. These demands should not be repressed or criminalized, and their basic human rights should be fully respected at all times, including in situations of conflict.

54. National legislation in Asian countries should incorporate indigenous peoples' property and use rights over communal lands, forest areas, pastures, and other natural resources, with due regard to indigenous customary laws, traditional lifestyles, and cultural values. Where such legislation exists, renewed efforts should be made in order to make indigenous rights effective, and special emphasis should be put on the demarcation and titling of indigenous lands. The system-

atic removal of indigenous peoples from their traditional lands as a public policy should be halted, and such removal of indigenous peoples from their traditional lands should be regarded as a last alternative and in cases of utmost necessity, and under condition that they be fully compensated.

55. Indigenous peoples should be involved in decision-making at all levels in the countries in which they live. They should participate in the design and implementation of all policies that may affect them directly, particularly with regard to development projects taking place in their lands and territories.

56. Asian countries should be actively and constructively involved in international discussions concerning the rights of indigenous peoples, particularly regarding the United Nations Declaration on the Rights of Indigenous Peoples and the future role of the Human Rights Council in the promotion and protection of indigenous rights. Asian states should consider the prompt ratification of ILO Convention No. 169 on Indigenous and Tribal Peoples, particularly those that are already party of the previous ILO Convention No. 107.

57. International organizations and agencies, as well as international financial institutions, should mainstream indigenous rights into their programs and activities in Asian countries, on the basis of international norms and their own policy guidelines in this area, irrespective of the level of recognition of these rights in domestic legislation and policies. OHCHR country and regional offices in Asia should further strenghen their programs of work the rights of indigenous peoples, particularly of indigenous women. UNDP and ILO should continue their efforts to promote their policies on indigenous peoples. The World Bank, the Asian Development Bank, and bilateral donors should ensure that their safeguards and guidelines in relation to indigenous peoples are fully respected in their Asian projects.

Notes

[1] Rodolfo Stavenhagen is a sociologist and professor-researcher at the El Colegio de México. From 2001 to April 2008 was the first United Nations Special Rapporteur on the situation of the human rights and fundamental freedoms of indigenous people.

Indigenous Peoples In Asia
Common Experiences and Issues

identified by the participants at the Workshop on the Concept of Indigenous Peoples in Asia Chiang Mai, Thailand, March 1-3, 2006

We are the indigenous peoples of Asia. We have lived in our territories alongside other peoples who in the course of history have come to dominate us. Our history has been questioned and our identity as indigenous peoples has been denied. As a result, our land, territories and resources have also been appropriated or made vulnerable.

We, the indigenous peoples of Asia, draw our unity and solidarity from experiences and issues that we have in common. We have jointly identified these as follows:

History and Identity

- We identify ourselves as indigenous peoples and see ourselves as being different from others.
- We have our distinct lifestyles, languages, cultures, customs and community-centric, non-centralized social and political institutions, which we inherited from our ancestors, and which we want to transmit to our future generations.
- We have a strong collective identity which is rooted in our history and territories which are the foundation of our self-respect, dignity, and freedom, and which emphasizes collective rights over those of the individual.
- We are referred to by governments and outsiders by various terms like tribals, hill tribes, highland people, ethnic minorities, indigenous ethnic minorities, aboriginal people etc.

- We are today colonized and dominated by others. We have been politically, culturally, and economically marginalized and pushed into a subordinate position especially in the wake of the formation of nation states and globalization.
- We have experienced a history of injustice, with our individual human and collective rights and fundamental freedoms being denied, and our people and resources continually exploited.
- We are looked down upon by the dominant population who misrepresents and distorts our way of life, and insists that we assimilate into their culture. As a result, some of our cultures and languages have disappeared and many have become endangered. Many of us are made to feel ashamed of our indigenous identity and try to assimilate to avoid stigma.
- Likewise, our political and justice systems have not been recognized and alien systems have been imposed on us that destroy our decision-making institutions and holistic indigenous systems and at the same time exclude us from the dominant political system.
- Most importantly, our right to self-determination has been denied. Yet we are conscious of our resilience and our dynamic adaptability that have allowed our societies to persist and we are determined to maintain our identity and regain control over our lives, land and destiny.

Land, Territories and Resources

- We have a unique historical collective connection with, and ownership of, a territory over which we maintain complex and diverse customary systems of land and resource use
- We have lived in our territories prior to the arrival of other, now dominant people, and before the formation of modern nation states. Some of us however may reside in new lands as a result of forced displacement or other circumstances.
- Our livelihoods strongly depend on natural resources and as such we have a close spiritual relationship with, and rich traditional knowledge of, our environment
- Our indigenous systems and practices are not static but flexible and dynamic; and our land and resource use systems show a high degree of adaptivity.
- We are experiencing continuing non-recognition of our rights over territory and of our customary land ownership and use systems leading to dispossession and exploitation of our land and resources.
- The imposition of land and forest laws lead to loss of our traditional lands to state forests, protected areas, commercial plantations and other uses outside our control.

- As a result, we are experiencing increasing economic marginalization and poverty.

These common experiences we share not only among ourselves but with all indigenous peoples elsewhere in the world. And as for all indigenous peoples, our situations and our problems will not be solved unless we are first recognized as indigenous peoples and thus able to regain control over our lives, land and destiny.

Part III
Country Profiles

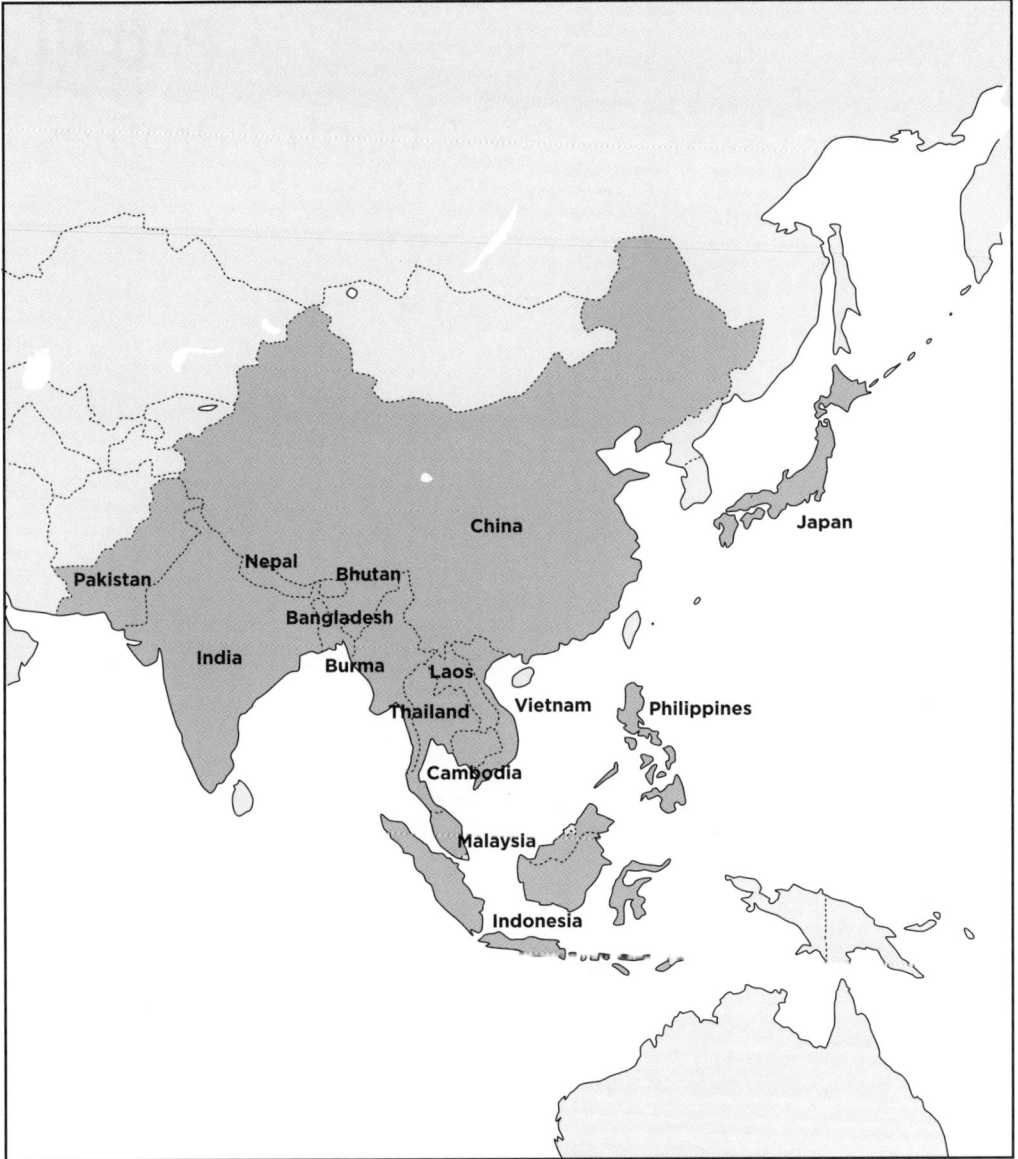

Map of Asia showing the countries for which country profiles were compiled.

Editor's note

At the Workshop on the Concept of Indigenous Peoples in Asia in Chiang Mai, Thailand in 2006 the participants unanimously agreed that a universal definition of indigenous peoples is not desirable, and that the identification of indigenous peoples has to be done separately, within the particular context of each country and with respect to the right of indigenous peoples to self-identification. Indigenous representatives at the workshop made brief presentations on the status of government recognition of indigenous peoples and relevant laws and policies, on the common terms and designations used for people who have been identified or identify themselves as indigenous peoples, and they presented lists of the groups who are commonly considered indigenous peoples in their countries. Partly based on these presentations, partly with the help of additional sources the country profiles contained in this book were written, in most cases by several authors. The area covered is South, Southeast and East Asia. Due to unforeseen editorial problems, Timor Leste and Sri Lanka could not be included.

The authors and editors do not claim that the country profiles are comprehensive, and they above all do not claim that the identification of indigenous peoples in any of the country profiles is to be considered final. The country profiles were compiled with the intention of providing basic information that can help readers to conduct further, more specific and in-depth investigations on the issues addressed.

Chakma man, Rangamati district, Chittagong Hill Tracts. Photo: Christian Erni

Country Profile

Bangladesh

Bangladesh borders India and Burma to the east, west and north, and is bordered by the Bay of Bengal to the south. It has a land area of 147,570 km². The majority of its 144 million large population are Bengalis, but it is also inhabited by approximately two million indigenous peoples, belonging to over 40 different ethnic groups. The largest indigenous population is found in the Chittagong Hill Tracts in the Southeast of the country. The parts of Bangladesh outside of the CHT are generally being referred to as the "plains" region, in contrast to the Chittagong Hill Tracts, even though these areas also contain hilly land.

The indigenous peoples remain among the most persecuted of all minorities, facing discrimination on the basis of their religion and ethnicity. In the Chittagong Hill Tracts, the indigenous peoples took up arms in defence of their rights and, in December 1997, the 25-year-long civil war ended with a peace agreement – officially called the Chittagong Hill Tracts Accord – between the Government of Bangladesh and the Parbattya Chattagram Jana Samhati Samiti (PCJSS, United People's Party), which has led the resistance movement.

Terms used for indigenous peoples

The issue of the identity of the indigenous peoples of Bangladesh has led to much debate and controversy, and on occasions has brought indigenous leaders and government officials into sharp disagreement. The aboriginal groups in the Chittagong Hill Tracts (CHT) are generally known as "Pahari" (meaning hillpeople), or as Jumma (from the common tradition of swidden or "jum" cultivation). The plains aboriginals, particularly those in the north-western greater Rajshahi-Dinajpur region, used to be generally known as adivasi (or adhivasi, adibashi), meaning aboriginal or indigenous. However, ever since 1992, when the International Year of the Indigenous People was declared by the United Nations, more and more indigenous peoples, both from the CHT and the plains, have started to increasingly refer to themselves as indigenous peoples in English, and as adivasi in the national language, Bangla.

Government perspectives on the issue, however, are varied. The Ministry of Foreign Affairs, for example, prefers the terms "tribe" and "tribal" ("upajati" in Bangla), and is opposed to the use of the words "indigenous" and "adivasi". Non-indigenous functionaries at the district and sub-district levels also generally prefer the term "tribe" and "tribal;" or their Bengali equivalent, "upajati". The terms "tribe" and "tribal" came to be applied during the British colonial rule and tend to suggest a hierarchical categorization of peoples based on their level of civilisational advancement with the tribal peoples being perceived as uncivilised and primitive.

The Government's position regarding the recognition of indigenous peoples and their rights

Officially, the government of Bangladesh rejects the use of the term "indigenous peoples". This was clearly stated for example by the representative of the Permanent Mission of the Government of Bangladesh to the United Nations at the Fifth Session of the UN Permanent Forum on Indigenous Issues, at the UN Headquarters in New York, on 26 May, 2006. And a memo dated 19.04.2006 from the Ministry of Foreign Affairs, advises the Ministry of Chittagong Hill Tracts Affairs to use the term "tribal" ("upajati") but to refrain from using the terms "indigenous" or "adivasi".

The government's reluctance to recognize indigenous peoples is largely politically motivated and has its roots in Bengali nationalism, which was the driving force in the struggle for independence from Pakistan. The country's population is overwhelmingly Bengali and there is very little understanding among the political establishment and mainstream society for diversity and multiculturalism.

The legal situation, on the other hand, is quite pluralistic, and reflects, in its totality, the currency of all the terms preferred by government officials and indigenous peoples combined. Recent legislation seems to favour the terms "tribe/tribal".[1] A 1995 law – primarily a finance law, but also containing specific references to the exemption of income tax payments by indigenous people in the Chittagong Hill Tracts – uses the term "indigenous hillmen".[2] Other laws that were framed in earlier periods, such as the Chittagong Hill Tracts Regulation of 1900 (Regulation I of 1900), use the terms "indigenous tribe" and "indigenous hillmen" interchangeably.[3] The term "indigenous hillmen" is also echoed in several references to the Finance and Income Tax Acts in the schedule to the 1900 Regulation, and in several correspondences of the National Board of Revenue. Furthermore, in a recent case in the High Court Division of the Supreme Court of Bangladesh, the court took cognisance of the fact that the petitioner was an "indigenous hillman" of the Chittagong Hill Tracts.[4]

The East Bengal State Acquisition & Tenancy Act of 1950 uses the phrase "aboriginal tribes" to refer to several groups living in the plains regions, who now identify themselves as indigenous or Adivasi.[5] In the recent National Poverty Reduction Strategy Paper adopted by the Government of Bangladesh, the term "adivasi/ethnic minorities" was used.[6] The private press and media too display divergent attitudes, but on the whole, most tend to be accommodative towards the views of the peoples concerned, and "indigenous" and "adivasi" are generally preferred over "tribes" or "tribal".

Even though Bangladesh is a signatory of Convention 107 on Indigenous and Tribal Populations of the International Labour Organisation, the constitution of Bangladesh neither recognises the cultural identities of the indigenous peoples nor specifies measures to protect and promote their rights. The Bangladeshi State however recognizes the presence of "tribal people", the adivasi. In official documents, they are often referred to as "backward segments of the population".

Although not backed by constitutional arrangements, the Chittagong Hill Tracts Accord signed in 1997 does identify the Chittagong Hill Tracts (CHT) as a tribal area and recognises their cultural rights. Under the terms of the treaty its traditional governance system and the role of its chiefs are recognized, the area was given more autonomy and a regional council was established to improve the relationship between migrants to the area from the plains of Bangladesh and the indigenous population. The Accord however remains largely unimplemented.

No official recognition comparable to that of the indigenous peoples of the Chittagong Hill Tracts is extended to indigenous groups in other regions. At the national level, the Special Affairs Division under the Prime Minister's office is responsible for the welfare of indigenous peoples in areas outside the Chittagong Hill Tracts. However, although the Chittagong Hill Tracts usually have at least a junior minister ("deputy minister") in the government, the indigenous peoples of other parts of the country do not have any direct representation, either in the Special Affairs Division or in other policy-making bodies at the national level, and demands for special representation have been ignored.

In spite of the lack of any legal recognition of indigenous peoples there are legal and constitutional provisions which can be used in defending certain rights for the indigenous peoples of Bangladesh. The Articles 28 & 29 of its Constitution makes provision of equal rights for its citizens and also stipulates affirmative measures in favour of the "disadvantaged sections" of the society[7]. More importantly, there are a number of domestic legal documents (such as the Chittagong Hill Tracts Manual 1900, Chittagong Hill Tracts Regional Council and Hill District Councils Acts, or the Bengal Tenancy Act, 1950) that have specific legal provisions for "tribal peoples", often with respect to particular geographical area, like the Chittagong Hill Tracts.

The government's Poverty Reduction Strategy Paper of 2005 is considered an important policy document since it makes explicit reference to, what is termed' "adivasi/ethnic minority communities". The strategy paper clearly acknowledges the indigenous peoples' history of exclusion and their experience of discrimination by the mainstream society.

Bangladesh has ratified all major international human rights treaties and conventions. These documents explicitly refer to the rights of indigenous peoples. The one important exception is ILO Convention 169, which was drawn up to replace Convention 107. Bangladesh was also one of the few countries of the UN General Assembly that did not vote in support of the Declaration on the Rights of Indigenous Peoples. The Bangladesh Government however did not vote against it either; it abstained.

The following are the international human rights instruments ratified by Bangladesh:

- ILO Convention No. 107 on Indigenous and Tribal Populations (1957). Ratified on 22nd June 1972
- International Convention on the Elimination of All Forms of Racial Discrimination (1965). Ratified on 11th June 1979.
- International Covenant on Civil & Political Rights (1966). Ratified on 6th September 2000
- International Covenant on Economic, Social and Cultural Rights (1966). Ratified on 5th October 1998
- Convention on the Elimination of All Forms of Discrimination against Women (1979). Ratified on 6th November 1984
- Convention against Torture and Other Cruel, Inhuman or Degrading Treatment or Punishment (1984). Ratified on 5th October1998
- International Convention on the Rights of the Child (1989). Ratified on 3rd August 1990
- Convention on Biological Diversity (1992). Ratified in May 1994

Identifying indigenous peoples in Bangladesh

Estimates on the total population of indigenous peoples in Bangladesh range from 1.7 to 3.7 million, or between 1.2 and 2.5% of the country's 144 million people. The Bangladesh Adivasi Forum (BAF) – an advocacy and human rights organization of the indigenous peoples – puts the figure of about 3 million.

The Bangladesh Adivasi Forum identifies 45 ethnic groups as indigenous peoples of Bangladesh. Devasish Roy, drawing from several sources, has compiled a more comprehensive list of 59 groups. More groups could possibly be included, like the Uchay/Usui of the Chittagong Hill Tracts (Roy refers to them in a comment as a sub-group of the Tripura). On the other hand, both lists include groups whose status as "indigenous" in Bangladesh can be questioned (like the Monipuri and Assamese, who in neighbouring India are large, economically and politically dominant non-tribal Hindu groups, and therefore sometimes not considered indigenous. The Assamese have been brought to Bangladesh by the British to serve in the government). As elsewhere in Asia, it can sometimes be difficult to decide on whether a particular group can be identified as indigenous. In by far the most cases in Bangladesh, it is however fairly unambiguous.

The majority of the indigenous peoples reside in the northwest, north-central, northeast, south and southeast of the country. The largest concentration of indigenous peoples is found in the hilly portion of the south-eastern Bangladesh, known as the ***Chittagong Hill Tracts*** region. The indigenous groups in the Chittagong Hill Tracts are: Bawm, Chakma, Khumi, Khiang, Lushai, Marma, Mro/Mru, Pangkhua, Chak, (not included in the BAF list), Tangchangya, Tripura, Uchay (not included in the BAF list).

The indigenous peoples of the Chittagong Hill Tracts differ from the majority Bengali population in physical features (they are mongoloid like the people in adjacent Burma and Northeast India), culture, social organization and religion and they have their own languages, both in written and oral forms.

Until the announcement by the British colonizers of the Chittagong Hill Tracts as "Totally Excluded Area" under the Chittagong Hill Tracts Regulation Act, 1900, which restricted all migration of non-members of the hill people into the district and centralised the administration of the region, the hill people were self-governing small entities with no formalised political structures. The special status of the Chittagong Hill Tracts was later abolished, which set in motion the internal colonisation of the indigenous peoples and subsequent emergence of a militant separatist movement.[8] A 25 year long civil war ended in 1997 with the signing of the Chittagong Hill Tracts Accord. The Peace Accord, however, has so far not been implemented and the heavy militarization of the area continues along with serious human rights violations, influx of settlers and tension between indigenous people and the Bengali settler population.

In the ***north and northeast*** of Bangladesh live the Hajong, Garos, and the Khasi. They also belong to the mongoloid stock and are linguistically and culturally closely related to Southeast Asian ethnic groups. The majority of the Hajong live in Sunamgonj (Greater Sylhet) and Netrokona (Greater Maymansingh), and fewer in number in Sherpur and adjacent districts. The Khasi mainly reside in the hilly areas of the northeastern province of Sylhet. Traditionally the have been practising shifting cultivation, with betel leaf being one of the main products today. The Khasi have also traditionally been involved in trading across the Indian border, where a much larger Khasi population lives. The majority of Garos live in the Garo hills in the north of the country and across the border in India, and there is also a large number residing in the Modhupur Forest in ***central Bangladesh.*** They belong to a matrilineal society and were traditionally practising shifting cultivation, but government prohibition made many adopt wet rice and cash-crop cultivation. Lack of land rights, grabbing of land by outsiders, harassment as well as the education and job prospects have lead a large number of Khasi and Garos to migrate to the cities.

The non-mongoloid indigenous groups of Bangladesh are the Adivasis of the **north-western plains districts** and, in smaller numbers, in the **southern coastal districts** of Barguna and Patuakhali. They include several ethnic groups such as, Santal, Banais, Bhuiya, Bhumijie, Ho, Kharia, Kharwar, Kora, Oraon, Munda, Mahali, Munija, Turi, Mal Paharia, Sauria Paharia. The Santals are the largest group, numbering over 200,000 people. Much larger population of these adivasi groups live across the border in neighbouring India.

The adivasi have a distinct culture and social organization that are essentially different from Bengali culture. Most of them still have their own language, communal land ownership and their traditional knowledge of resource management or medicinal plants. Adivasis have been structurally marginalised by the mainstream society at all levels of society. Their specific cultural identity and rights are not recognised and alienation of adivasi lands is taking place at an alarming rate. Adivasis are among the poorest of the country. Participation of Adivasis in education is very low, and almost zero at the higher levels of education.

This country profile was written by and Christian Erni and Christina Nilsson (both IWGIA), with contributions from Binota Moy Dhamai, Asia Indigenous Peoples Pact (AIPP) Foundation.

Sources
Printed Sources

Bleie, Tone 2005. *Tribal Peoples, Nationalism and the Human Rights Challenge. The Adivasis of Bangladesh. Dhaka:* The University Press Limited

Chittagong Hill Tracts Commission 1991. *"Life is not ours" – Land and Human Rights in the Chittagong Hill Tracts, Bangladesh.* Copenhagen: International Work Group for Indigenous Affairs (PDF available at: http://www.iwgia.org/sw28374.asp)

_____"Life is not ours" – Updates 1992, 1994, 1997, 2000 (PDF available at: http://www.iwgia.org/sw28374.asp)

Drong, Sanjeeb (ed), 2005. "Solidarity, 2005", Bangladesh Indigenous Peoples Forum. Dhaka

Government of People's Republic of Bangladesh 2005. Unlocking the Potential: National Strategy for Accelerated Poverty Reduction. General Economics Division, Planning Commission, October 30, 2005

International Work Group for Indigenous Affairs 2005 to 2008. *The Indigenous World* (Chapter on Cambodia). Copenhagen: IWGIA

Minority Rights Group 1992. *The Adivasis of Bangladesh.* Minority Rights Group

International Report, 92/1. London: Minority Rights Group

Singh, Rajeen 1996. The Chittagong Hill Tracts of Bangladesh; in: Colin Nicholas and Rajeen Singh 1996. *Indigenous Peoples of Asia. Many Peoples, One Struggle.* Bangkok: Asia Indigenous Peoples Pact

Roy, Raja Devasish 2005. *Traditional Customary Laws and Indigenous Peoples in Asia.* Report March 2005. London: Minority Rights Group International

_____2006. The ILO Convention on Indigenous and Tribal Populations, 1957, and the Laws of Bangladesh: A Comparative Review. International Labour Organization. Mimeo

Roy, Rajkumari Chandra 2000. *Land Rights of the Indigenous Peoples of the Chittagong Hill Tracts, Bangladesh.* IWGIA Document No. 99. Copenhagen: International Work Group for Indigenous Affairs

Internet Sources

Various reports and documents on the Chittagong Hill Tracts are available at: http://www.iwgia.org/sw28374.asp

Notes

[1] See for example, Chittagong Hill Tracts Regulation (Amendment) Act, 2003 (Act XXXVIII of 2003), and the CHT Regional Council Act, 1998 (Act XII of 1998).

[2] The Finance Act, 1995 (Act XII of 1995), paragraph 27.

[3] CHT Regulation, 1900, especially, rules 4, 6 and 52 (since repealed), and the Schedule to the Regulation.

[4] Sampriti Chakma v. Commissioner of Customs & Others (5 BLC, AD, 2000, 29)

[5] The "aboriginal castes and tribes" referred to in this law (Act XXVIII of 1950) include the following: Santhals, Banais, Bhuiyas, Bhumijies, Dalus, Garos, Gonds, Hadis, Hajangs, Hos, Kharias, Kharwars, Kochs (Dacca Division), Koras, Maghs (Bakarganj District), Mal Paharias, Sauria Paharias, Maches, Mundas, Oraons and Turis.

[6] Unlocking the Potential: National Strategy for Accelerated Poverty Reduction, General Economics Division, Planning Commission, Government of People's Republic of Bangladesh, October 30, 2005

[7] The CHT Peace Accord refers precisely to these two articles of the Constitutions for legal and legislative validation.

[8] Singh 1996: 123ff

Rawang girl, Kachin State. Photo: Colin Nicholas

Country Profile

Burma

Burma, officially the Union of Myanmar is 676,578 km² the largest country in mainland Southeast Asia. It borders China in the north, Laos in the east, Thailand in the southeast, Bangladesh in the west, and India in the northwest.

Burma is one of the ethnically most diverse countries in the world and this diversity has played a major role in defining the country's politics, history and demographics. Burmans make up between 60 and 70% of Burma's 50 million people. The remaining are a plethora of ethnic groups, the exact number of which has not been determined. It is usually the non-Burman ethnic groups that are considered Burma's indigenous peoples. The country is divided geographically into seven, mainly Burman-dominated, divisions and seven ethnic states named after the dominant ethnic groups: Chin, Kachin, Karen, Karenni, Mon, Rakhine and Shan. These states also constitute the mountainous frontiers of the country covering about 55 percent of the geographical area of Burma.

Burma has been ruled by a succession of military regimes dominated by ethnic Burmans since the popularly elected government was toppled in 1962. After decades of low-intensity conflict in indigenous peoples' areas, the military regime negotiated a series of ceasefire agreements with various groups in the early and mid 1990s. The military regime has justified its rule, which is characterized by the oppression of indigenous peoples, by claiming that the military is the only institution that can prevent Burma from disintegrating along ethnic lines.

Terms used for indigenous peoples

Even though representatives of many ethnic groups from Burma have since many years regularly participated in international meetings dealing with indigenous peoples' issues, like for example those of the former United Nations Working Group on Indigenous Populations or at present the United Nations Permanent Forum on Indigenous Issues, and even though many of them have come to identify themselves as indigenous peoples, the term is still not very common among political and civil society groups in Burma. The terms "ethnic nationalities", "ethnic minorities", and "indigenous ethnic minorities" are predominantly used. "Indigenous peoples" is generally translated to Burmese as *Taiyinta Lumyomya*.[1]

The Burmese government regards only the Indian and Chinese communities as having a "non-national" or "minority" status, while the native groups, including the Burmans, are considered as "nationalities", "national races" or "nationality groups".[2] For the government this implies that everyone is "indigenous" in Burma and therefore the issue of indigenous peoples' rights does not arise.

The Government's position regarding the recognition of indigenous peoples and their rights

The position of the Burmese government regarding the concept of indigenous peoples and its use in international law is expressed in the statement made by Ambassador U Tin Kyaw Hlaing, permanent representative and leader of the observer delegation of the Union of Myanmar, at the 44th session of the Sub-Commission on Prevention of Discrimination and Protection of Minorities, in Geneva on August 26, 1993:

> "Permit me to state at the outset that we in Myanmar (Burma) do not have any problems of indigenous populations. Neither there is discrimination against them. The reason for this fact is simple. All the 135 national races residing in Myanmar are indigenous national races in the true sense of that word. We have lived through weal and woe throughout the ages. There were no distinct early arrivals or late comers."

In the same year, the Chairman of the State Law and Order Restoration Council summarized the government's view on the country's ethnic diversity and identities on Burma's Union Day on 12 February 1993:

> "In the Union of Myanmar where national races are residing, the culture, traditions and customs, language and social systems may appear to be different, but in essence they are all based on the common blood of Union Kinship and Union Spirit like a hundred fruits from a common stem... There can be no doubt whatsoever of the fact that our national races have lived together unitedly in the Union of Myanmar since time immemorial.[3]"

Many of the non-Burman ethnic groups reject this view, arguing that before the British annexation in the 19th century they had never been brought under the direct rule of any "Burman" government.

During World War II, while many Burman joined Japanese forces, many non-Burman ethnic groups remained loyal to Britain. This reflected a genuine desire for independence on the part of both groups; Burmans struggling to be free of the British colonial yoke, and ethnic minorities wishing to escape Burman domination.[4]

However, before its independence, General Aung San persuaded the non-Burman ethnic nationalities to join the Union that was being negotiated with the British. An agreement popularly known as the Panglong Agreement was signed to this effect on 12th Feb. 1947, and the spirit of which was incorporated into the constitution proclaimed in the same year and which came into effect on January 4, 1948 despite the assassination of Aung San in July in 1947.

Under the 1947 constitution, a federal system of governance was envisaged with non-Burman areas organized as the Shan, Kachin, Kayin, Kayah, and Chin states; each possessing a degree of autonomy. The failure to fully respect constitutional guarantees lead to conflicts immediately after independence. Since the much-promised Karen State remained undemarcated and they felt excluded, the Karen began their struggle for a separate Karen nation

In 1958, as the ten-year opportunity for non-Burmans to secede from Burma (granted as part of the Panglong agreement) approached, and amidst growing discontent over the civilian government and fears of a communist takeover, the military under General Ne Win was invited to take over the government. In 1962 he staged a military coup, after which the constitution was abandoned and with it the constitutional guaranteed right of ethnic nationalities agreed on in the Panglong Agreement.

Over the past five decades, armed groups fighting for autonomy had operated among virtually all the larger indigenous peoples, predominantly in the mountainous border regions. Since the military coup in 1962, each successive military junta has subjected indigenous peoples to violent repression. A "Burmese Way to Socialism" and a two-fold strategy was embarked upon: to run an all-out counterinsurgency campaign in the rural countryside while at the same time trying to establish a centralised, one-party system of government. In 1974 a new constitution was adopted, which centralised every aspect of political, economic, social and cultural life and abolished the right of secession.

Counter-insurgency operations by the army have been intensified since 1984. The army has imposed harsh restrictions on indigenous communities in an effort to eliminate grassroots support for the insurgents, and human rights violations are rampant.

The State Law and Order Restoration Council (SLORC), later renamed to State Peace and Development Council (SPDC), seized power in 1988. By the mid

1990s, many of the armed ethnic groups had entered into ceasefire agreements with the SPDC. In consideration for signing the ceasefire agreements, the SPDC granted the various groups territories over which they could exercise political and economic control. The ceasefire agreements are thought to serve mainly the economic and political interests of the leaders and members of the armed ethnic groups, and the SPDC which was able to increase its military presence in the ceasefire areas. In some cases, the SPDC was also able to take over the economic activities originally given to the groups in exchange for ceasefire agreements.[5]

Several armed groups have however not made ceasefire agreements with the SPDC. These are[6]:

- Arakan Liberation Party/Arakan Liberation Army (ALP/ALA)
- Arakan Rohingya National Organization (ARNO)
- Chin National Front/Chin National Army (CNF/CNA)
- Hongsawatoi Restoration Party
- Karen National Union (KNU)
- Karenni National Progressive Party (KNPP) - broke previous ceasefire agreement with the SPDC
- Lahu Democratic Front
- Lahu National Organization
- Mergui-Tavoy United Front
- National United Party of Arakan (NUPA)
- Shan State Army – South (SSA-S)
- Wa National Army

In general, the ruling military government severely restricts basic rights and freedoms of all citizens, but indigenous peoples suffer from all forms of discrimination and oppression and a deliberate policy of Burmanisation. In spite of the cease fire agreements that have been negotiated with the junta, the human rights abuses perpetrated by the Burmese army have not abated. Arbitrary killings, forced labour, rape, forced relocation, destruction and forceful alienation of property and other forms of human rights abuse continue to be committed against indigenous peoples.

In mid-1992, military junta announced a plan to convene a National Convention, or Constituent Assembly, to lay down guidelines and basic principles for a new constitution. On 9 April 2008, the junta released its proposed new constitution for the country to be put to a vote in a public referendum. On May 10 the referendum was held and the regime announced that the constitution had been overwhelmingly approved. The constitutional referendum has however been widely dismissed as a sham and was conducted amid accusations of massive cheating at the polling stations and reports of a very low turnout.[7]

The charter was drafted by the generals without inputs from the pro-democracy opposition. The process is meant to culminate in multi-party elections in

2010 and bring to an end nearly five decades of military rule in Burma. However, the new charter gives the military an automatic 25% of seats in both houses of parliament, which makes it impossible to alter the constitution without their support. It guarantees the military control of key ministries and the right to suspend the constitution at will.[8] With the new constitution Burma also remains a highly centralized state, which runs against the demand of ethnic nationalities for federalism and greater autonomy of the respective states.

Burma has ratified only few international conventions: The Convention on the Elimination of All Forms of Discrimination against Women (CEDAW) and the International Convention on the Rights of the Child (CRC). It has signed the Convention on Biological Diversity in 1992, but has not yet ratified or acceded to it.

Identifying indigenous peoples in Burma

The military junta estimates the percentage of non-Burman ethnic groups to be around 30%. This figure is contested by non-Burman ethnic groups, some suggesting even a figure as high as 50%. However, most estimates put the figure between 30 to 40% of the total population. It has been suggested that existing population data is distorted to "exaggerate the number of Burmans who form the largest single ethnic group,"[9] and in other cases the population of ethnic groups may be exaggerated to "conceal the true scale of the physical destruction"[10] of these people.

The indigenous peoples live throughout Burma, but are concentrated mainly in seven states and divisions named after the dominant ethnic groups there: Chin, Kachin, Karen, Karenni, Mon, Rakhine and Shan. Groups like the Chin, Kachin or Karen are very comprehensive ethnic categories that include a number of distinct ethnic groups each. The Summer Institute of Linguistics, for example, distinguishes between 20 different Chin languages and 14 Karen languages. [11]

Lack of a reliable census makes it impossible to more than roughly estimate the composition of Burma's ethnic mosaic, the populations or percentage of each non-Burman ethnic group. The last recorded official census of ethnic groups was conducted by the British in 1931, and this identified 135 linguistic groups from 13 "ethnic families". They belong to five linguistic families (Tibeto-Burman, Mon-Khmer, Tai-Kadai, Hmong-Mien and Malayo-Polynesian).

The share of the major ethnic groups (or, rather, "ethnic families") in the overall population given in the census of 1931 are 65% Burman, 9% Karen, 7% Shan, 2% Chin, 2% Mon, 1% Kachin, and 1% Wa. But this census also seems to have conflated many smaller groups into the bigger ones as their differentiation was based on the language a person may speak, which is not necessarily equal to ethnic identity. [12] In addition to the difficulty of any outsider distinguishing and identifying the numerous groups, some smaller groups who assert a separate identity may be considered by a bigger group a part of itself.

This country profile was written by Christina Nilsson and Christian Erni (both IW-GIA), with contributions from Sui Khar, Chin Human Rights Organisation.

Sources
Printed sources

Economist Intelligence Unit 2005. *Country Profile: Myanmar (Burma)*. London: The Economist Group

Horton, Guy 2005. *Dying Alive: A Legal Assessment of Human Rights Violations in Burma*. Chiang Mai: Images Asia Inc.

International Work Group for Indigenous Affairs 2005 to 2008. *The Indigenous World* (Chapter on Burma). Copenhagen: IWGIA

Smith, Martin in collaboration with Annie Allsebrook 1994. *Ethnic Groups in Burma: Development, Democracy and Human Rights*. Anti-Slavery International Human Rights Series No 8. London: Anti-Slavery International. PDF version available at: http://burmalibrary.org /docs3/Ethnic_Groups_in_Burma-ocr.pdf

Internet sources

On history, the political situation and human rights in Burma:
The Burma Campaign UK Website: http://www.burmacampaign.org.uk/
Human Rights Watch Website: http://hrw.org/doc/?t=asia&c=burma
Amnesty International Website: http://www.amnesty.org/en/region/asia-and-pacific/south-east-asia/myanmar
Alternative Asean Network on Burma (ALTSEAN Burma) Website: http://www.altsean.org/
On linguistic groups in Burma:
http://www.ethnologue.com/show_country.asp?name=MM

Notes

[1] *Tar (tiang)* means state or country, *Yin* means origin or aborigine, *Tha* min son or citizen, *Lumyomya* means peoples.
[2] Minority Rights Group International, 2002
[3] Smith and Allsebrook 1994: p. 19
[4] http://www.burmacampaign.org.uk/
[5] http://www.altsean.org/Key%20Issues/KeyIssuesEthnic.htm
[6] Ibid.
[7] http://www.burmacampaign.org.uk/Last%20Month/Last%20Month_May_08.pdf
[8] http://in.reuters.com/article/topNews/idINIndia-33587120080515. See also the report "The May 2008 Constitutional Referendum in Burma" published by Human Rights Watch (http://hrw.org/reports/2008/burma0508/)
[9] http://www.burmacampaign.org.uk/
[10] Horton 2005: p. 87.
[11] http://www.ethnologue.com/show_country.asp?name=MM
[12] Economist Intelligence Unit 2005: p. 17

Tampuen woman with her grandchild. Ratanakiri province. Photo: Christian Erni

Country Profile

Cambodia

Cambodia covers a land area of about 181,035 km² and borders Thailand, Lao PDR and Vietnam. Estimates of the population range from 11 million to 14.8 million people. It is ethnically fairly homogeneous, with roughly 90 percent of the nation's population represented by Khmers. The rest are made up of groups including Vietnamese, Cham, Lao, Thai, Chinese, and indigenous peoples. The indigenous peoples, mainly considered to be the highlanders, are estimated to constitute about 1% of the overall population.

Cambodia is considered by the UN to be one of the poorest countries in the world, with about 35 percent of the population living below the poverty line. The prolonged history of war and political instability after independence from French colonial rule in 1954 has been a major impediment to achieving economic recovery and development that respects human rights. In Cambodia, the judiciary is weak and under the control of politicians, political violence, intimidation of the media, and human rights violations are common. Indigenous peoples are among the most marginalized groups in Cambodian society.

Terms used for indigenous peoples

In Khmer, the most appropriate term for "indigenous people" is *chuncheat daoem pheak tech,* which means literally "minority original ethnicity". This term is used officially by the Government. It is not clear whether the meaning is "indigenous people" or "indigenous peoples." The word *chuncheat,* though commonly used, is not found in standard Khmer dictionaries. The word *chuncheat daoem pheak tech* appears to have been coined just recently, during development of the 2001 Land Law. It is generally accepted that this term refers to all the indigenous people of Cambodia, and does not apply to the Khmers, Chams, Chinese, Laos, Thais, or Kinh (Vietnamese), although some of these people may indeed contest not being considered indigenous in the future.

Other terms used in Khmer are:

- *Khmer loe,* meaning "highland Khmer".
- *Kol sampoan phnum,* meaning "hill tribes."
- *Chun antao kream,* meaning "people within the region".
- *Neak eysan means* "northeastern people."

The following two terms are widely used but considered offensive by indigenous people:

- *Chuncheat,* meaning "ethnicity", or literally "national people"
- *"Phnong",* or more correctly *"Bunong",* is the name of one ethnic group who mostly lives in Mondulkiri province. However, Khmer people often mistakenly use the term "Phnong" as a pejorative to refer to all indigenous people. "Samre" has a similar meaning.

To refer to indigenous people, Kreung, Tumpuon, Brao, Lun, and Kavet people all use the term *son sat,* which means, roughly, indigenous people who live in a specific place, have indigenous blood, traditions, and culture similar to other indigenous people.

A distinction is made between *chuncheat deum pheak tech* used for indigenous peoples (deum means "original"), and *chuncheat pheak tech,* which refers to other ethnic minority groups like the Cham, Vietnamese, Chinese or Khmer Krom (Khmer from the Mekong delta of neighbouring Vietnam). In the Land Law, the former is used, i.e. indigenous peoples are distinguished from ethnic minorities, while in the recent draft "National Policy on Minority People Development" the term khmer loe has been replaced by *chuncheat pheak tech.*

The Kreung, Tumpuon, Brao, Lun, and Kavet people of Ratanakiri province all use the term *son sat* in their own languages to refer to indigenous peoples. *Son sat* originates from the Lao language and literally means the same thing as chuncheat in Khmer.

The Government's position regarding the recognition of indigenous peoples and their rights

The terms "indigenous people" *(chuncheat daoem pheak tech)* and "indigenous community" *(sahakom chuncheat daoem pheat tech)* are officially used by the Cambodian Government, although Prime Minister Hun Sen recently declared that *chuncheat Khmer daoem* ("original Khmer ethnicity") should not be used to define someone's ethnicity, since there has been a trend in many parts of the country to do that in recent years, in order to try to reclaim ethnicity-based land rights. Some government officers from the Ministry of Interior have emphasized that "indigenous people are all Khmers."

Article 32 of the Constitution of the Kingdom of Cambodia states:

> Khmer citizens shall be equal before the law and shall enjoy the same rights, freedom and duties, regardless of their race, color, sex, language, beliefs, religions, political tendencies, birth origin, social status, resources and any position.

In the debate on the Constitution in the National Assembly, the representatives discussed and debated the definition of Khmer citizens. It was agreed that the term included some Cambodian ethnic minorities, such as the *khmer loe and the khmer islam* ("Muslim Khmer", which are mainly the Cham, some of whom however claim to be indigenous).

In 1994 the Inter-Ministerial Committee (IMC)[1] for Highland Peoples Development was formed by the Government, at the same time as the Highland Peoples Programme of the United Nations Development Programme (UNDP) was established. At present, IMC is the main body representing the Government in coordinating activities with those national and international institutions and NGOs working in the northeastern provinces, where the vast majority of the indigenous population lives.

Despite the guarantees in the Cambodian Constitution and the existence of the IMC, there is no current active policy in Cambodia concerning indigenous peoples. The "General Policy for Highland Peoples Development", drafted in 1997, has been reviewed and the final draft, now called "National Policy on Minority People Development", was made by the Ministry of Rural Development. In its introduction, the policy refers to at least 24 groups of indigenous peoples of living in Cambodia. It uses the same definition as the one given in article 23 of the Land Law of Cambodia 2001.

A Department of Ethnic Minority Development (DEMD) was created under the Ministry of Rural Development . The DEMD has led the process of drafting a "National Policy on the Development of Indigenous Peoples", and with support of the United Nations Development Programme (UNDP) has developed a "Strategic Plan for the Development of Indigenous Peoples 2006-2008". The strategic plan has however never been implemented.

General laws affecting indigenous peoples in Cambodia include the Land Law (2001) and the Forestry Law (2002). Chapter 3, Section 2 of the Land Law (2001) is entitled "On immovable property of indigenous communities". It describes the rights of indigenous communities *(sahakom chuncheat daoem pheak tech)* to register their communal lands. Article 25 states that "Indigenous community land is all the land on which the community set up residence and undertake traditional agriculture." Official pilot projects to title indigenous communities' lands were done in three villages and the by-laws being developed by the Ministry of the Interior are expected to serve as the basis for guidelines, to be applied across the country. It is unclear when the by-laws will be completed, and there may be some foot dragging in the government. During 2007 the Ministry of Land Management, Urban Planning and Construction (MLMUPC) focused on finalizing two other pieces of legislation relevant to indigenous peoples' land rights: the Policy on Indigenous Peoples Communal Land Registration; and a yet un-named sub-decree also addressing communal land registration. Civil society groups have been involved in ongoing negotiation with relevant government agencies to ensure the policies' content are in line with existing legislation. By the end of 2007 the draft sub-decree had however not yet been publicly released.

The Forest Law recognizes community forests and indigenous communities' right to forest products in concession areas. Article 37 of the Forestry Law (2002) says: "Local communities who conduct traditional swidden farming can do so on land belonging to indigenous communities that has already been registered with the state...."

Cambodia is a signatory to a number of international instruments that are designed to protect the rights of indigenous peoples. This includes the following:

- International Covenant on Economic, Social and Cultural Rights (ICESCR)
- International Covenant on Civil and Political Rights (ICCPR)
- International Convention on the Elimination of All Forms of Racial Discrimination (CERD)
- Discrimination (Employment and Occupation) Convention, 1958 (No. 111) of the International Labour Office (ILO)

Cambodia is a party to the Convention on Biological Diversity (1992), which recognizes the role of indigenous peoples in protecting biodiversity. The Cambodian Government also voted in favour of the UN Declaration on the Rights of Indigenous Peoples in the UN General Assembly .

Identifying indigenous peoples in Cambodia

There are no recent census data on the population of indigenous peoples in Cambodia. In 1997, the Inter-ministerial Committee on Highland Peoples Development estimated the total population of "indigenous minorities" in Cambodia to be about 120,000 people, which represented only 0.95% of the total population of Cambodia. Bourdier (1996) gave a figure, based on census data, of 142,700 people for 1995. Generally, it is assumed that indigenous peoples in Cambodia make up over 1% of the total population. The largest concentrations of indigenous peoples are found in the four north-eastern provinces of Ratanakiri, Mondolkiri, Steung Treng, and Kratie. Over 90% of Cambodia's indigenous peoples live there. They form the majority of the population in Ratanakiri (66%) and Mondulkiri (71%). In Steung Treng they make up 7%; and in Kratie 8%.[2] Indigenous peoples also live in eleven other Preah Vihear, Kampong Thom, Siem Reap, Koh Kong, Sihanoukville, Kampong Speu, Kampong Cham, Battambang, Bantey Mean Chey, Odar Mean Chey and Pursat. Some were dispersed to other parts of the country during recent wars.

These 15 provinces are mentioned in the draft "National Policy on Minority People Development" recently finalized by the Ministry of Rural Development.

Among the ethnic groups identified as indigenous are the Brao, Chong or Khmer Daoem, Jarai, Kachak, Kanchruk, Kavet, Khaonh, Kraol, Kreung, Kui, Lun, Mil (Mel), Por (Poar, Pear), Phnong (Punong), Rhade (Ede), R'ong, S'och (Saoch), Stieng, Suoy, Thmon, Tumpuon. However, the Lun, Kavet, Kreung and Brao are considered by many to all be Brao sub-groups.

The territories of some groups go beyond the Cambodian border. The Jarai and Rhade in Ratanakiri, and the Bunong in Mondulkiri and Kratie, may be found respectively in the provinces of Pleiku and Dalat in Viet Nam; the Kui, present in Preah Vihear and in Kampong Thom, are also found in Thailand and in Lao PDR; and the Brao and Kavet in Ratanakiri are related to those in southern Lao PDR.

Most indigenous communities have undergone traumatic times during the past decades. The aftermath of Cambodia's independence in 1954 saw the implementation of government policies that sought to integrate them into the mainstream Khmer society. Khmer soldiers and their families were posted to these provinces with the responsibility of implementing the policy of integration. This assimilationist policy involved the expropriation of indigenous communities' lands and villagers were forced to work on plantations. Several indigenous communities and villages in the highlands were displaced and relocated to new places along the river, with the aim of encouraging wet rice cultivation. The Khmer language was taught with the education model focused on transforming the "backward" social system of these groups. This policy of Khmerization was met with considerable resistance and occasionally let to clashes, revolts, and armed confrontations.[3]

Situated close to the Lao and Vietnamese border, the indigenous peoples in the northeast were heavily affected by the second Indochina War. Livelihood was disrupted and many were forced to leave their land. Bomb craters are still found all over their territories.

The coming of the infamous Khmer Rouge saw a lot of indigenous communities again relocated to work in lowland rice fields. The Khmer Rouge also began with their own assimilation program. Entire villages were resettled, indigenous communities were forbidden to speak their languages and forced to learn Khmer; their traditional rituals, dress and hair style were also forbidden. Some indigenous communities living near the border fled to neighbouring countries. After the defeat of the Khmer Rouge, these relocated and displaced indigenous communities returned to their ancestral lands, reverting to their traditional farming methods.

The 1980s again saw resurgence in government policy to integrate the indigenous communities into the mainstream Khmer society through its policy of encouraging indigenous communities to reside along the river and close to the road, partly to avoid the Khmer Rouge which was still active in remote places.

Around the same time, lowland Khmers were encouraged to go settle in less populated and remote areas such as Ratanakiri. And with them they brought into these areas new practices of resource use which were directed toward benefiting commercially. Industrial logging, large-scale plantation development, commercial farming and mining began to be extensively practiced in these areas. Large tracts of land under the traditional control of the indigenous communities were given away as concessions to individuals and commercial companies for exploitation of resources leading to environmental degradation and the denial of access for indigenous communities to resources that were traditionally under their control. The trend continues with more and more cases of conflicts over land coming to the fore.

The indigenous peoples concentrated in the north-eastern provinces of Cambodia "represent perhaps the most disadvantaged population group in the country". The report mainly refers to lack of access to education and health services. The loss of land and access to forest due to illegal land transaction, the issuing of mining concessions and land concessions for plantations are currently however the main threat to the well-being and future survival of Cambodia's indigenous peoples.

This country profile has been compiled and edited by Christian Erni and Christina Nilsson based on a presentation by Nun Sokunthea and Peter Swift, and further inputs by Sophorn Sek, ILO Phnom Penh, Ian Baird of the Global Association for People and the Environment (GAPE), and Suo Vansey of the Indigenous Community Support Organization (ICSO).

Sources
Printed Sources

Asian Development Bank [ADB] 2002. *Indigenous Peoples/Ethnic Minorities and Poverty Reduction. Cambodia.* Environment and Social Safeguard Division, Regional and Sustainable Development Department. Manila: Asian Development Bank

Baird, Ian G. 2008. Various forms of colonialism: The social and spatial reorganisation of the Brao in southern Laos and northeastern Cambodia. Ph.D. dissertation, Department of Geography, The University of British Columbia, Vancouver, B.C., Canada.

Bourdier, F. 1996. *Provincial Statistics and Statistics of Ministry of Interior, 1995.* Phnom Penh

Colm, Sarah 1996. The highland minorities and the Khmer Rouge in Northeastern Cambodia 1968-1979. Phnom Penh: Document Center of Cambodia

International Work Group for Indigenous Affairs [IWGIA] 2005 to 2008. *The Indigenous World* (Chapter on Cambodia). Copenhagen: IWGIA

Ironside, Jeremy 2005. *Overview of the History and Distribution of Pear (Por) Groups in Cambodia.* http://www.ngoforum.org.kh/Land/Docs/Indigenous/Overview.htm

NGO Forum on Cambodia. 2005. *Rethinking Poverty Reduction to Protect and Promote the Rights of Indigenous Minorities in Cambodia.* Phnom Penh: NGO Forum on Cambodia

Ovesen, Jan. and I.-B Trankell, 2004. Foreigners and Honorary Khmers. Ethnic Minorities in Cambodia. In: Duncan C.R. (ed.): *Civilizing the Margins. Southeast Asian Government Policies for the Development of Minorities,* pp. 241-269. Ithaca: Cornell University Press

Sugiarti, Sri 1997. *A Preliminary Socio-Economic Study of Rotanak Kiri Province of Northeast Cambodia.* Phnom Penh: IDRC/ CARERE

Taylor, P.M. 2006. Ethnic minorities and indigenous peoples of Cambodia. Pages 128-141 in World Bank Inspection Panel, Investigation Report (March 30, 2006), *Cambodia: Forest Concession Management and Control Pilot Project (Credit No. 3365-KH and Trust Fund 26419-JPN).* Washington DC.

White, Joanna 1996. The Indigenous Highlanders of the Northeast. An Uncertain Future, in: Center for Advanced Study, Interdisciplinary Research on Ethnic Groups in Cambodia. Final Draft Report Phnom Penh: Center for Advanced Study

Internet sources

Human Rights Watch web-site on Cambodia: http://www.hrw.org/doc?t=asia&c =cambodThe NGO Forum on Cambodia web-site: www.ngoforum.org. kh

Notes

[1] Members of the IMC are the Ministry of Rural Development; the Ministry of Agriculture, Forestry, and Fisheries; the Ministry of Education, Youth, and Sport; the Ministry of Health; the Ministry of Public Works and Transport; the Ministry of Social Affairs, Labors, Vocational Training and Youth Rehabilitation; the Ministry of Women's and Veterans Affairs; the Ministry of Environment; and the Cambodian Mines Action Center.

[2] Asian Development Bank 2002: 5

[3] On the Khmer Rouge period in Ratanakiri province see Baird 2008 and Colm 1996

Yi woman, Yunnan Province. Photo: Christian Erni

Country Profile

China

China occupies a vast continental landmass in East Asia. With its 9.6 million km² it is the third largest nation by area. It is bounded in the north by Russian Siberia, to the east by Korea and the East China Sea, to the west by the Central Asia nations, and to the south by Pakistan, India, Nepal, and the countries of Mekong Southeast Asia.

For the sake of current international convention and expediency, we shall in this article refer to the present recognized international boundary of China. As it is, we shall therefore also include the ethnic groups living in Tibet, Uighur Xinjiang, Inner Mongolia, and other "autonomous regions" of ethnic minority peoples.

In spite of possessing the world's largest population of 1.3 billion, China's demographic distribution is very uneven. Most of the population, dominated by Han Chinese (at over 90 %), live in the coastal and eastern half of the country, in the urban centers and rural villages of the plains and hills along the Yangtze River, the Yellow River, the Pearl River and their tributaries. Low population density is found in China's central and western regions, as these are dominated by loess hills, arid grasslands, deserts, mountains and alpine plateaus. It is also in these more harsh environments, and in the higher uplands and mountains, that most of the non-Han Chinese, the so-called "ethnic minorities" of China, live. These peoples have been incorporated into the expanding Chinese empire through military conquests and vassal state subjugation over the centuries.

The Chinese government officially recognizes a total of 55 "ethnic minority groups" in the country, which according to the census of 2000 comprised of 105,226,114 persons, or 8.47 % of the total population.

Terms used for indigenous peoples

The Chinese government does not recognize the term, "indigenous peoples", and does not agree to its concepts and definition as accepted in international fora. The official terminology and preferred usage is "ethnic minorities" or "minority peoples". At the international level, Chinese officials have stated that, "In China, there are no indigenous people and therefore no indigenous issues."[1]

In Chinese language and culture, there are various terms used for non-Chinese tribes, or people of foreign lands, with words such as "Fan" (番 or 蕃), and "Man"(蠻). These carry the connotations of "barbarian", "primitive", "backward", or "uncivilized people". The words still have the derogatory meanings in modern-day usage.

Besides general and inclusive term of "Fan" (番 or 蕃), the Han Chinese throughout historic times have a familiar stock phrase when talking about the "enemy peoples" or "the uncivilized tribes" living in the hinterlands or outside of the Middle Kingdom - 「東夷、西狄、南蠻、北戎」(Dong Yi, Si Di, Nan Man, Bei Rong).

Dong, Si, Nan, and Bei (東西南北) are the Chinese words for the four cardinal directions of East, West, South, and North. Yi, Di, Man, and Rong (夷狄蠻戎) originally referred to specific nomadic or tribal peoples in the regions outside of the Chinese heartland of Yellow River Basin.

As Chinese dynasties and empires expanded through the historic periods, these terms later evolved to describe what the Chinese regarded as the uncivilized, primitive nomadic or tribal peoples who are found further outwards in the hinterlands, and also for those ethnic peoples who had yet not been conquered and not yet brought under Chinese imperial rule.

"Dong Yi" (東夷) is associated with the coastal and island peoples outward from the East China Sea. Scholars generally agreed that at one time it referred to the sea-faring peoples and islanders of Japan, Okinawa, and Taiwan.

"Si Di" (西狄) means the nomadic people of China's western frontiers, and is associated with the Uighurs, Kazaks, and other Turkic-speaking peoples of Central Asia, and it also refers to the Tibetans.

"Nan Man" (南蠻) refers to the ethnic peoples living in the hills and mountains in a large belt from China's southeast to the southwest regions. In historic times, all areas south of Yangtze River are regarded as lands of the Nan Man tribes. These included today's Yunnan, Guizhou, Sichuan, Guangdong, Fujian provinces, and the Guangxi Zhuang Autonomous Region. Most of the historic Nan Man peoples are related to the "hill tribes" or ethnic groups of Mekong Southeast Asia, or are ancient Austronesian-speaking peoples.

"Bei Rong" (北戎) is taken to refer to the non-Chinese peoples inhabiting the northern frontiers outside of the traditional Chinese homeland. It has been historically used to refer to the Mongolians, Manchus, Koreans, and other ethnic minorities of the north. Another term commonly used throughout history for the northern nomadic tribes is "胡" (Hu).

The Government's position regarding the recognition of indigenous peoples and their rights

When the PRC was established in 1949, a national project on "Ethnic Minority Identification (or Classification)" was initiated. At that time, Yunnan province in the southwest, for example, reported to the national government that there were around 260 "ethnic groups or minority peoples" within the province. On a national level, a total of 400 groups were reported. The government simplified this complexity by merging and classifying various ethnic groups under the 55 ethnic groups that were subsequently officially recognized.[2]

These official ethnic minority groups include Tibetans, Uighurs, Mongolians, along with those that outsiders would consider as "foreign minority peoples" living within the current Chinese borders, such as Russian, Korean, Kirgiz, Kazak, and Tajik. Interestingly, Hui (a term for Moslem), a religious minority of western China (mostly descendents of Uighur, Kazaks, and other Turkic-speaking nomadic peoples) is also recognized as one of the 55 ethnic minority groups in the country.

Other, more well-known Chinese ethnic minorities are the tribal communities living in the mountains, hills, and upland valleys of south and southwest China, such as Lisu, Lahu, Miao, Hani, Jingpo, Jino, Dai, Naxi, Bai, Wa, Yi, Dulong, Deang, Blang, and others, whom have close historic, ethnic, and linguistic links to the indigenous peoples of neighboring countries of Southeast Asia.

It must be noted that official PRC government also included "Gaoshan" (meaning "high mountain" people) in its 55 ethnic minority groups. "Gaoshan" is a collective term for the ethnic groups of the Austronesian linguistic family now recognized as the indigenous peoples of Taiwan.

China passed the "Law on Regional Ethnic Autonomy" in 1984, which was revised in 2001 to keep up with new developments. This law is the most important basis for policies on ethnic minority autonomy. According to article 73m, "The People's Congresses and their Standing Committees in autonomous areas and in provinces and municipalities with autonomous prefectures and autonomous counties should determine concrete implementation guidelines".[3]

In those areas where there were concentrations of one or more ethnic minorities, autonomous regions, counties and prefectures were established, in accordance with population concentration, local ethnic relations, and economic development as well as historical conditions. At the provincial level, five autonomous regions were established, namely, Inner Mongolian Autonomous Region (1947), Xinjiang Uighur Autonomous Region (1955), Guangxi Zhuang Autonomous Region (1958), Ningxia Hui Autonomous Region (1958), and Tibet Autonomous Region (1965). Aside from the five autonomous regions (provinces), there are 30 autonomous prefectures, and 120 autonomous counties.[4]

China has signed the following international human rights conventions:

- Convention on the Elimination of All Forms of Racial Discrimination;
- Convention Against Torture and Other Cruel, Inhuman or Degrading Treatment or Punishment;
- Convention on the Elimination of Discrimination Against Women;
- Convention on the Rights of the Child;
- International Covenant on Economic, Social and Cultural Rights;
- International Covenant on Civil and Political Rights.

China has however not yet to ratified the latter two, signed in 1997 and 1998 respectively.[5]

Identifying indigenous peoples in China

By historic records and official school textbooks, the Han Chinese have their origin in the amalgamation of several tribes in the Yellow River basin areas of the present northern China provinces of Henan, Shanxi, and Shaanxi. Originally known as the "Hua-Sia" tribes (華夏民族), these ancient tribes were united by the legendary Yellow Emperor (黃帝 "Huang Di") during the third millennium B.C.

Throughout history, the Chinese people referred to their country as "Middle Kingdom" (中國Zhong Guo). They regarded themselves as inhabiting the "centre of human civilization", as they were bounded by the ocean to the east and south, and the wide expanse of mountains, uplands, and deserts to the north and west. In the course of the advance of Chinese civilization through the millennia the Chinese people came to regard themselves as culturally superior to the nomadic peoples, the forest-dwelling hill tribes, and other "less advanced" or "backward" peoples of these hinterlands.

In contrast, the ethnic minority groups of China have different cultural and linguistic origins, and originate in their own homeland areas. In general, they mostly still live in their traditional territory, which are in the hills and mountainous regions, and the western hinterlands of present-day China.

They are regarded as having different "ethnic" and "cultural" characters from the Han Chinese. Nevertheless, after the communist revolution and the establishment of modern China after 1949, the government of the People's Republic of China (PRC) and the communist party hold that the ethnic minority peoples have also been "liberated", and officially they are regarded as "members of the big family of Chinese people" in modern China.

Although it has not been clearly established which of the ethnic minority groups can be considered as indigenous peoples, it is generally understood that they mainly comprise the ethnic minority groups living in the south and southwest of the country, along with some groups in the hinterlands of north, northeast, and the west regions. Most of them are subsistence farmers or nomadic herders belonging to the poorest segment of the country and they have illiteracy rates of over 50%.

South and Southwest China

Through their historic experience and varying ways of cultural contacts, the Chinese people have quite different concepts about "ethnic minority peoples" when they talk about the "Nan Man" (南蠻), southern tribal peoples, as compared to Si Di (西狄) and Bei Rong (北戎), the mostly nomadic peoples of China's northern and western hinterland regions.

In modern-day understanding, the "Nan Man" (南蠻) or China's southern tribal peoples would come closest to what are elsewhere identified as "indigenous peoples". They comprise a large number of ethnic groups, like the Lisu, Lahu, Miao, Hani, Jingpo, Jino, Dai, Naxi, Bai, Wa, Yi, Dulong, Deang, Blang, etc. They have their traditional homeland in the hills and mountains of present-day south and southwest China. They are now in greatest concentration in Yunnan, and to lesser extent in Guizhou, and Sichuan provinces.

The indigenous peoples of South and Southwest China live in tribal communities, usually rural villages, and have their own distinct culture, language, traditional customs, and beliefs. They are mostly engaged in subsistent agriculture, while some groups still practicing shifting cultivation, and they depend much on natural resources of forests and mountains. Some of these groups live in remote isolation, are still engaged in traditional hunting, fishing, and gathering lifestyles. Most of these "Nan Man" (南蠻) or China's southern tribal groups are related to the Mon-Khmer and Tibeto-Burman speaking peoples in the neighboring countries of Vietnam, Laos, Cambodia, Thailand, Burma and Northeast India.

North and West China

The Tibetans, Mongolians, Uighurs, and other ethnic groups found in the western and northern regions have historically been referred to by the Han Chinese as "Si Di" (西狄) and "Bei Rong" (北戎). They are undoubtedly "minority peoples" vis-à-vis the dominant Han Chinese population and when referring to the present internationally recognized national boundary of the People's Republic of China. while some people do not regard them as true "ethnic peoples" of China proper.

The Tibetans, Mongolians, Uighurs, and other China's ethnic minority groups of the western and northern regions mostly inhabit the arid to semi-arid lands. Traditionally, a large proportion of their populations have been nomadic pastoralists, with seasonal migrations to different locations.

In contrast to the "Nan Man" groups mentioned above, it has been argued that Tibetans, Mongolians, and Uighurs cannot be considered as "indigenous peoples" in the present understanding, because they are not "non-dominant" peoples, but in the past were builders of kingdoms and dynastic empires themselves.[6] The Tibetans, Mongolians, and Uighurs controlled large territories after expansion and military conquest arising from their traditional homeland. The Mongolian Empire, founded by Genghis Khan, at its peak in the 13th to 14th century had conquered all of China, much of central Asia and Eastern Europe. Tibetan King Songtsen Gampo founded the Tibetan Kingdom in the 7th century, which built upon earlier dynasties that can be traced to the first century BC. The ethnic Uighur people maintained their historic and cultural links to the Uighur East Turkestan Kingdom, which was in existence through the Middle Ages, but fell to the invading Manchurian army from China in 1759.

In times when the Chinese Empire was strong, the Tibetans, Mongolians, and Uighurs came under subjugation by military conquest. In other periods, they signed peace treaties, with agreed annual offering and gifts, as conditions to become protected vassal states at the border of the Chinese Empire proper.

It is with reference to this historical context and the particular relationship with past Chinese dynastic empires that some have argued that Tibetans, Mongolians, and Uighurs are only now, within the modern Chinese nation state, minority peoples. They once were powerful people with their own states. Today, only "Outer" Mongolia exists as independent nation state.

It should also be mentioned that the Tibetan and Uighur political movements seeking independence from China have hardly ever used the international discourse on indigenous peoples' rights as a forum to voice their aspirations.

There are however small ethnic groups with lifestyles, cultures and social organizations distinct from those of the dominant groups in these areas. An example is the Oroqens in present-day Oroqen Autonomous Banner in the forests of the Greater and Lesser Hinggan Mountains in Inner Mongolia Autonomous Region. Today, they number around 7,000 people. Traditionally, the Oroqens had lived a life of hunting and fishing in the forests, but have been resettled by the government in the 1950s.

Another example are the Ewenki of the Ewenki Autonomous Banner in the Greater Hinggan Mountains of Inner Mongolia and Nahe County of Heilongjiang Province. The Ewenki have traditionally been nomadic reindeer herders. There are larger Ewenki populations in Russia. In China they number around 26,000 people.

In Tibet, several smaller ethnic groups, like the Nu, Dulong, Moinba, Lhoba, Naxi, Deng, and Sherpa live among the dominant Tibetan population. They comprise of less than 8% of the population. Many of these ethnic groups are also found in neighbouring provinces of Southwest China or in countries bordering Tibet.

It is therefore argued that the concept of "indigenous peoples" should rather be applied to such small peoples living among the dominant Tibetans, Uighurs and Mongols.[7]

This country profile has been written by Jason Pan, director of TARA – Ping Pu, with inputs from Christian Erni, along with Prof Lim Siu-Theh, Huang Chi-Ping, and Ong Nga-Ping of the Ethnology Department of the National Cheng-Chi University (Taiwan).

Sources
Printed sources

Li Xing, Peijin Lan, Qin Wang, and Weiping Ouyang 2003. *China's Ethnic Minorities.* University of Michigan: Foreign Languages Press,

Snelgrove, D. and Richardson, H. 1968. *A Cultural History of Tibet.* Boulder, Colorado: Prajna

Internet sources

Ethnic Minorities in China: http://english.peopledaily.com.cn/data/minorities/ethnic_minorities.html;
http://english.hanban.edu.cn/english/features/EthnicGroups/126822.htm
http://china.org.cn/e-groups/shaoshu/

Ethnic minorities in Tibet: http://www.tibet.cn/tibetzt/ssmz_en/minzu.htm

Cultural and Religious History of Tibet: Alexander Berzin, 1996. http://www.berzinarchives.com/web/en/archives/study/history_buddhism/buddhism_tibet/details_tibetan_history/history_early_period_buddhism_tibet/Part_1.html

Ethnic minorities in Xinjiang: http://french.china.org.cn/english/139389.htm

Uighurs and China's Xinjiang Region: Washington Post article retrieved at: http://www.washingtonpost.com/wp-dyn/content/article/2008/08/01/AR2008080100933.html

Regional Autonomy for Ethnic Minorities: Information Office of the State Council of the People's Republic of China (February 2005, Beijing) http://english.gov.cn/official/2005-07/28/content_18127.htm

Human rights: Moore, Greg 2001. China's Cautious Participation in the UN Human Rights Regime. A review of China, the United Nations, and Human Rights: The Limits of Compliance, by Ann Kent. Philadelphia: University of Pennsylvania Press, 1999. http://www.du.edu/korbel/hrhw/volumes/2001/1-1/kent.pdf

Ancient history of China: http://www.stockton.edu/~gilmorew/consorti/1heasia.htm

Mongol History: http://mongolempire.4t.com/h2_steppesbefore.htm

Notes

1   The Adviser of the Chinese delegation Mr. Long Xuequn, speaking at the 53rd session of the United Nations Commission on Human Rights in 1997. Website of the Embassy of the Peoples Republic of China in Switzerland. http://ch.china-embassy.org/eng/ztnr/rqwt/t138829.htm
2   Huang Chi-ping 2008. China, in: IWGIA. The Indigenous World 2008. Copenhagen: IWGIA, p. 263
3   Huang Chi-ping 2007. China, in: IWGIA. The Indigenous World 2007. Copenhagen: IWGIA, p. 294
4   Tan Chee Beng. The Concept of Indigenous Peoples and Its Application in China, Paper presented at the Workshop on the Concept of Indigenous Peoples, Chiang Mai, 2005, p. 7
5   Moore 2001
6   References to this are hard to find. Few academics in China would officially espouse such views, as it a very sensitive issue.
7   In Xinjiang Autonomous Region, the situation is somewhat more complex. The Uighurs are the largest ethnic groups and historically have been politically dominant. There are smaller ethnic groups and nomadic tribes that are distinct from the dominant groups, but the authors of this article do not have sufficient information to elaborate further on the subject in this article.

Angami elder, Nagaland state. Photo: Christian Erni

Country Profile

India

India covers an area of 3.3 million km² and with just over one billion people India ranks right after China as the second most populous country in the world. Although only few areas of India remain uninhabited and unused by humans, the population is very unevenly distributed. More than three fifth live in the fertile Indo-Gangetic plains, the deltas of the eastern coast, and along the western coast. Population densities in these areas reach up to 800 persons per square kilometres, and it is here where most of the multi-million mega cities are located. Although urbanisation due to massive rural-urban migration is proceeding fast, with the present 28% urban population India remains a largely rural society. It is estimated that between 33 and 40% of the world's absolute poor live in India. About 35-37 % of India's population has an annual income below the national poverty line.

India's indigenous and tribal peoples are officially called "Scheduled Tribes" and remain outside the caste system. The tribal peoples have resisted integration and maintained their own cultures and social organisation. This does however not mean that there has not been any interaction with Hindu society. In many tribal areas life is very much and increasingly determined by this interaction.

Terms used for indigenous peoples

While the government of India refers to indigenous peoples as "Scheduled Tribes", *Adivasi* has become the popular term for India's indigenous or tribal peoples. It is a Sanskrit word, which means "original people". Contrary to the official government position, this term reflects the widely recognised fact that the people in question are the earliest known settlers on the Indian subcontinent and North-East India. The indigenous or tribal peoples of India's North-Eastern region (in the seven states Arunachal Pradesh, Assam, Manipur, Meghalaya, Mizoram, Nagaland, and Tripura) do not call themselves, nor are they normally referred to in the literature, as Adivasi in spite of the fact that the meaning of the term very much applies to the respective people as well. Representatives of these peoples prefer to use the English term "indigenous peoples".

The Government's position regarding the recognition of indigenous peoples and their rights

The government of India adamantly rejects the discriminative use of the term "indigenous" for any of the people living within its boundary. It is argued that the complex and millennia long history of migration and exchange and mixing of cultural and physical traits makes it impossible to distinguish any group as "indigenous" in relation to other groups, therefore everyone in India is indigenous.

What indigenous activists in India, their local and outside supporters, some Indian and foreign academics as well as overseas development agencies like the World Bank refer to when they speak of indigenous peoples in India is in official parlance called "Scheduled Tribes". Indeed, and contrary to the government's position, the so-called "Scheduled Tribes" possess many characteristics which, according to internationally accepted definitions sufficiently qualify them to be called "indigenous peoples".

The government of India uses the term *Scheduled Tribes* for those communities specified under article 342 of the Constitution. However, no definition of "tribe" is included in the Constitution. "It is an administrative term, which is area-specific and envisaged to reflect the level of socio-economic development rather than a distinct ethnic status".[1] Criteria like geographical isolation, distinctive culture, "primitive traits", 'shy of contact with community at large", "relative isolation" or "economic backwardness" are used to identify "Scheduled Tribes" (STs). The lack of a clear definition and the application of rather vague (and partially questionable) criteria for the identification of groups as Scheduled Tribes have lead to considerable arbitrariness. A group may therefore be officially recognised as tribe in one state, but not in another. An example is the Lambadas of Andhra Pradesh who are not considered as tribe in neighbouring states. This resulted in the migration of Lambadas to Andhra Pradesh in order to take advantage of privileges granted to Scheduled Tribes.[2] More people have been included in the scheduled tribe population due to area expansion for the respective STs each year. On the other hand, cases of non-tribals' fraudulent claims to tribal status in order to benefit from the constitutionally granted privileges are also on the increase.[3] This is partly responsible for the high "growth rates" of the tribal population in some states. There are still many tribal communities who have not been recognised as such. As Bhengra et.al.[4] conclude, "Many believe that arbitrariness and political expediency are often factors in determining the recognition or non-recognition of Adivasis as STs".

The *Constitution of India* provides for specific measures for the protection and promotion of the social and economic interests of the Scheduled Tribes. They include among others: reservation of seats in legislature, educational institutions, services and posts; tribal development program and provisions for autonomy.

Reservation in the Legislature: The Constitution of India ensures the political representation of Scheduled Tribes in the Lower House *(Lok Sabha)* of the Parliament and in the State Legislative Assemblies through reserved seats.

Reservation in Educational Institutions and Services: Article 15(4) of the Indian Constitution provides for the reservation of seats in the educational institutions for Scheduled Tribes. In order to improve the social situation of the tribal people, the government has, in addition to quotas in education, also designed a reservation policy in employment in government services. Depending on the respective positions, posts reserved for members of Scheduled Tribes are either in proportion to the tribal population of the state in question, or – in most cases – comprise of 7.5% of the total number of government jobs.

Constitutional Provisions for Tribal Self Rule: Geographical areas designated as Fifth and Sixth Schedule areas by independent India are almost identical to those already delineated by the British as Partially Excluded Area and Excluded Area respectively. Article 244(i) provides for a *Fifth Schedule* that can be applied to any state other than those in North-East India. This Schedule has been termed a "Constitution within the Constitution". Under this Schedule, the Governors of the concerned states have been given extensive powers, and may prevent or amend any law enacted in the parliament or the state assembly that could harm the tribals' interests. The *Sixth Schedule* is supposed to be informed by the ethos of self-management. Presently, the Schedule operates in the tribal dominated areas of the North East India: Karbi Anglong and North Cachar districts in Assam; Khasi Hills, Jaintia Hills and Garo Hills districts in Meghalaya; Chakma, Lai and Mara districts in Mizoram; and Tripura tribal areas in Tripura state. Each Tribal area covered by the Sixth Schedule has an Autonomous District Council, which has legislative, executive and judicial powers.

Provisions of the Panchayats (Extension to the Scheduled Areas) Act, 1996: This act is directed primarily at promoting village level democracy through the Panchayat Raj institutions. It has been carried out with suitable changes to transform a system established for the general areas of the country to the Scheduled Areas (Fifth Schedule area) having a different socio-economic as well as politico-administrative setting. There are significant ST majority areas that have not been included in the Fifth Schedule despite strident demands for the same.

The National Commission for Scheduled Casts and Tribes: Article 338 of the Constitution provides for the appointment of a Commissioner for Scheduled Tribes and Scheduled Castes by the President who is to investigate and report to the President on all matters relating to the constitutional safeguards on Scheduled Tribes and Schedule Castes. In 1992, a National Commission for Scheduled Casts and Scheduled Tribes was created to take over these responsibilities. In 2004, this was bifurcated with a separate National Commission for Scheduled Tribes.

The promotion of the economic and educational interests of the Scheduled Tribes and their protection from social injustice and exploitation are enshrined as a national goal in article 46 in the constitution. Realizing that earlier programs under the central government's Five-Year Plans failed to address development needs, marginalization and exploitation of tribal communities, the *Tribal Sub-Plan (TSP)* was devised as a new strategy in the Fifth Five-Year Plan in 1973. It is still the approach guiding development programs in tribal areas. Its main objectives are to eliminate exploitation; to speed up social and economic development; and to promote and to improve the organisational capability of tribal people.

There are now 194 Integrated Tribal Development Projects (ITDPs) in the country, where the ST population is more than 50% of the total population of the blocks or groups of block. During the Sixth Plan, pockets outside ITDP areas, having a total population of 10,000 with at least 5,000 Scheduled Tribes were covered under the Tribal Sub-Plan under Modified Area Development Approach (MADA). So far 252 MADA pockets have been identified in the country. In addition, 79 clusters with a total population of 5,000 of which 50 per cent are schedule tribes have been identified.

Wide ranges of sector programs in tribal areas development programmes have been implemented since the launching of the TSP by the different line agencies with both state and central government funds. The focus has so far clearly been on the development of physical infrastructure and on establishing and improving service institutions.

On the state level, the departments in charge for tribal affairs vary, i.e. not in all cases a separate department has been created. Earlier, tribal issues fell under the Ministry of Welfare, but later a separate Tribal Department were created. On the national level, a separate ministry, the Ministry of Tribal Affairs, was constituted in October 1999.

The most recent legislation with special reference to tribal people is the *Scheduled Tribes and Other Traditional Forest Dwellers (Recognition of Forest Rights) Act*, passed in December 2006. The act was passed against stiff resistance of the Forest Department and environmentalists. It provides for the recognition of the traditional and customary rights (including land rights and community forest reserves) of Scheduled Tribes and "other forest dwellers" to the forests, both collective and individual, which have hitherto remained unrecognised with the village assembly being authorised to determine these rights.

The following are some of international human rights and other instruments ratified by India which are most relevant for indigenous peoples:

- ILO Convention No. 107 on Indigenous and Tribal Populations – ratified in 1955
- The Universal Declaration of Human Rights
- The International Covenant on Economic, Social and Cultural Rights (ICESCR) – ratified on 10th April, 1979
- The International Covenant on Civil and Political Rights (ICCPR) – acceded on 10th April, 1979.
- The International Convention on Elimination of all forms of Racial Discrimination – ratified on 3rd December, 1968.
- The Convention on Rights of the Child – ratified on 2nd December 1992
- The Convention on Elimination of all Forms of Discrimination Against Women – Signed on 30th July, 1981.
- The Convention on the Prevention and Punishment on the Crime on Genocide – Ratified on 27th August, 1959.
- Slavery Convention ratified 18th June, 1927.
- Supplementary Convention on the Evolution of Slavery, Slave Trade and Institutions and Practice similar to Slavery – Ratified on 23rd June, 1960.
- Convention on Biological Diversity – signed in June 1992.

Identifying indigenous peoples in India

In the 2001 census 84.32 million persons were classified as members of Scheduled Tribes, which corresponded to 8.32% of the total population. In the Schedule of the Constitution of 1950 212 tribes were included and thus officially recognized as Scheduled Tribes. In the amendment of 1976 there were nearly 300 tribes. There are 622 tribes recognised as STs today.[5] Estimates of the actual number of tribes living in India go as high as 635.

There are many ethnic groups that claim the status but have not been officially recognized as Scheduled Tribes under Constitution of India. Also, in some states an ethnic group may be recognized while it is not in the neighbouring state. Thus, while there is a strong correspondence between the officially recognized Scheduled Tribes and the ethnic groups that are generally consider indigenous peoples, the official list cannot be considered authoritative. References to the Scheduled Tribes list and other statistical information are provided further below.

Some of the tribes, like the Gonds, Santals, Oraon, or Bhils have large populations of several million people. Others, like the Onge or the Great Andamanese are on the brink of extinction.

The majority of India's indigenous peoples live in an almost contiguous belt stretching from Gujarat in the West to the seven states in the North-East. 85% of these are concentrated in the central and western region, in the nine states of Orissa, Madhya Pradesh, Chattisgarh, Jharkhand, Maharashtra, Gujarat, Rajasthan, Andhra Pradesh and West Bengal. About 11% inhabit the north-eastern region, 3% the southern, and about 1% the northern region. The highest ethnic diversity among the indigenous peoples is found in the seven north-eastern states where 220 distinct groups have been identified.

India's tribal people are among the poorest of the country. The Scheduled Tribes have the highest poverty rate of the three categories of people officially distinguished. 52.17% live below the poverty line, while among the Scheduled Castes it is 48.14%, among the other people 31.29% (the overall figure for India given in the same survey is 37.09%). The dismal situation is reflected in the health and nutritional status of tribal villagers. Especially where access to forest products to supplement their diet and to provide additional cash income is not possible anymore – either because the forests have been destroyed or their rights of access are being denied – under-nourishment and malnourishment is widespread.

About 89% of the labour force among Scheduled Tribes is engaged in the agricultural sector (the figure for all India is 66.84%). This means that almost nine tenth of tribal families rely on natural resources for their livelihood. The majority of these are engaged in permanent agriculture, but shifting cultivation still forms the mainstay of the domestic economy in many upland areas, particularly in the Northeast. A few small groups in Central and South India and on the Andaman Islands live almost entirely from hunting, gathering and fishing.

This country profile was written by Christian Erni and Christina Nilsson (both IW-GIA), with inputs from C.R. Bijoy.

Sources
Printed sources

Bhengra, R., C.R. Bijoy, S. Luithui 1998. *The Adivasis of India.* Minority Rights Group International Report 98/1. London: Minority Rights Group

Burman, B.K. Roy 1995. *Tribal Situation and Approach to Tribal Problems in India. A Preliminary Appraisal.* New Delhi: Rajiv Gandhi Institute for Contemporary Studies

Fernandes, Walter 1999. Tribal and indigenous Peoples of India; in: Minority Rights Group International (ed.). *Forests and Indigenous Peoples of Asia.* London: Minority Rights Group International

Karlsson, Bengt G. and Tanka B. Subba (eds.) 2006. Indigeneity in India. London: Kegan Paul

Kothari, Smitu 1997. Whose Independence? The Social Impact of Economic Reform in India. *Journal of International Affairs,* Summer 1997

Kulkarni, Sharad 1998. Fraudulent Claims to Tribal Status; in: B.K. Roy Burman/B.G. Verghese (eds.). *Aspiring to Be. Tribal/Indigenous Condition.* Commonwealth Human Rights Initiative. Delhi: Konark Publishers

Rao, Biyyala Janrdhan 2000. *Adivasis in India. Characterization of Transition and*

Development. Warangal: Adhyayana Publications

Satish, S. 1999. *The World Bank Policy on Indigenous Peoples. India Consultations on the Approach Paper for Revision of Operational Directive 4.20.* South Asia Sector Social Development (SASSD). New Delhi: The World Bank

Schechla, Joseph 1993. The State as Juggernaut: The Politics of India's Tribal Nations. In: Marc A. Shills and G.T. Morris (eds.). *Indigenous Peoples' Politics: An Introdcution.* Vol. I. The Fourth World Center for the Study of Indigenous Law and Politics. University of Colorado

Singh, Amar Kumar and M.K. Jabbi 1995. *Tribals in India. Development, Deprivation and Discontent.* New Delhi: Hr-Anand Publications

Verma, R.C. 1990. *Indian Tribes through the Ages.* New Delhi: Government of India Publication

Sharma, B.D. 1997. *Tide Tiurned. The Makings of Tribal Self-Rule in the First Central Law in the Wake of the Bhuria Committee Report.* Whither Tribal Areas? Supplement 1. National Front for Tribal Self-Rule. New Delhi: Sahyog Pustak Kutir

Upadhyay, Vijay Shankar, and Gaya Pandey 2003. Tribal Development in India. A Critical Appraisal. Ranchi: Crown Publications

Internet sources

Laws and policies
1. The Constitution
    A. Articles 46 http://www.constitution.org/cons/india/p04046.html,
    B. 244(i), 244(2) http://www.constitution.org/cons/india/p10.html,
    C. 330 http://www.constitution.org/cons/india/p16330.html,
    D. 332 http://www.constitution.org/cons/india/p16332.html ,
    E. 342 http://www.constitution.org/cons/india/p16342.html
    F. 366(25) http://www.constitution.org/cons/india/p19366.html
    G. 338 http://www.constitution.org/cons/india/p16338.html
2. The Provisions of the Panchayats (Extension to Schduled Areas) Act 1996 [PESA 1996] http://panchayat.nic.in/
3. Scheduled Tribes and Other Traditional Forest Dwellers (Recognition of Forest Rights) Act, 2006: <http://tribal.nic.in/actTA06.pdf>
4. Ministry of Tribal Affairs: http://tribal.nic.in
5. Ministry of Home Affairs, Human Rights Division: http://mha.nic.in/uniquepage.asp?Id_Pk=235

Population figures and other statistical information:
http://www.censusindia.net/t_00_005.html

Notes

[1] Bhengra et.al. 1998: 4
[2] Satish 1999: 11

3 Kulkarni 1998

4 1998: 5

5 The Ministry of Tribal Affairs of the Government of India on its web-site provides an alphabetical list and a state-wise list of the recognized Scheduled Tribes; http://tribal.nic.in/index1.html

Jelai Dayak man, West-Kalimantan province. Photo: Christian Erni

Country Profile | # Indonesia

Indonesia consists of more than 17, 000 islands, covers a land area of 1,919,440 km² and has a population of around 220 million people. Indonesia is an ethnically extremely diverse country. Over 700 different languages have been identified.[1] Indonesia is still a unitary state with a strong central government, even though political and governmental structures have been decentralized after the resignation of President Suharto in 1998.

The government officially recognizes 365 ethnic and sub-ethnic groups as so-called *komunitas adat terpencil* (isolated *adat*[2] communities). They number about 1.1 million. However, there are many more ethnic groups that consider themselves, or are considered by others, as indigenous peoples. The nation-wide indigenous peoples' organization, Aliansi Masyarakat Adat Nusantara (AMAN), uses the term *masyarakat adat* to refer to indigenous peoples. A conservative estimate of the number of indigenous peoples in Indonesia amounts to between 50 and 70 million.

Terms used for indigenous peoples

Terms used to refer indigenous peoples in Indonesia change from time to time. During the General Soeharto regime (1967-1998), various terms were used to refer indigenous peoples such as *masyarakat terasing* (isolated people), *suku-suku terasing* (isolated tribes), *masyarakat terkebelang* (backward people), *masyarakat terpencil* (remote community) etc. These terms usually represent negative connotations and were use to emphasize the backwardness of indigenous peoples, that had led to discrimination, marginalization and exclusion of indigenous peoples.

The term *Masyarakat Adat* was initially introduced by JAPHAMA[3] in 1993 and later on endorsed by Indigenous Peoples Congress in 1999. *Masyarakat Adat* is more accepted and has been consistently used by indigenous peoples as well as NGO, Academics and some government official.

After the fall of Soeharto, Indonesian Government has been using several terms. *Masyarakat hukum adat*[4] *and masyarakat tradisional*[5] are used in Indonesian Constitution (second Amendment, 2000). *Masyarakat adat* is also used consistently in the Act No 27/2007 on Coastal and Small Islands Management.

The Department of Social Welfare of Republic Indonesia uses *komunitas adat terpencil* (remote indigenous community) to replace *masyarakat terasing* (isolated community) which was used prior to the implementation of Presidential Decree no.111/1999 on the Establishment of the Social Welfare of Isolated Indigenous Communities.

The Government's position regarding the recognition of indigenous peoples and their rights

In the early days of Indonesian independence, the Department of Social Affairs was put in charge of what came to be called *masyarakat terasing.* Its work was limited to relief projects for a few small and impoverished groups, which however had little impact.[6] The government's policy was to integrate these people, who were considered backward, into mainstream society. This was to be achieved by rather drastic means such as prohibiting traditional ways of life (like living in communal houses) or forced resettlement. Indigenous people's right to land and resources were not recognized, they were considered illegal occupants of state forest land which the government wanted to open up for logging, mining, plantation and transmigration projects. The latter involved the settlement of hundreds of thousands of migrants on indigenous peoples' lands, above all in West Papua, Kalimantan and Sumatra.

The third amendment of the Indonesian Constitution of 2001 recognizes indigenous peoples' rights in Article 18 Para 2 (concerning regional government) *"The State recognizes and respects indigenous communities along with their customary rights as long as they are still exist, in accordance to the society/cultural development and civilization within the Unitary State of Indonesia, and they are recognized legally by law".*

Article 28I Para 3 (regarding Human Rights) respects the cultural identity of indigenous peoples.[7] These two articles use two terms to refer indigenous peoples, namely masyarakat hukum adat (Article 18 Para 2) and *masyarakat tradisional* (Article 28I Para 3). In addition, these two article emphasize the recognition of indigenous peoples shall apply *as long as they still exist, in accordance to the society/cultural development* and *civilization within* the *Unitary State of Indonesia,* and *they are recognized legally by law.*

However, the Indonesia government at international fora persistently argues that the concept of indigenous peoples is not applicable in Indonesia, as almost all Indonesians (with the exception of the ethnic Chinese) were indigenous and thus entitled to the same rights. Consequently, the government rejected all calls for special treatment by groups identifying themselves as indigenous, which prevented indigenous peoples from maintaining their distinct identity and control over their territories, land and resources.

There are several Indonesia's laws and policies that at least implicitly recognize or are in other ways related to indigenous peoples' rights:

1. Act No. 39/1999 on Human Rights
2. Act No. 10 /1992 on Population and Prosperous Family
3. Act No. 22/1999 on Local Government
4. Act No. 5/1960 on Basic Regulations on Agrarian Principles (or Basic Agrarian Law)
5. Act No. 41/1999 on Forestry
6. Act No. 5 of 1990 on the Conservation of Biological Resources and the Ecosystem
7. Act No 27/2007 on Coastal and Small Islands Management.
8. People's Assembly Decree 17/1998 on Human Rights,
9. People' Assembly Decree 9/2001 on the Agrarian Reform and Natural Resource Management.
10. Act number 24/1992 on the Spatial Layout Planning
11. Act No. 23/1997 on the Environmental Management
12. Act No. 10/2004 on the Law-Making Process
13. Act No. 32/2004 on the Local Government
14. Government Regulation No. 76/2001 on the Local Government Implementation Guidelines
15. Ministerial Regulation of the Agrarian Minister and the Head of the National Land Agency number 5/1999 on the Guidelines on Dispute Resolution of the Communal Title of the Indigenous peoples.

In addition, there are many district-level or provincial legislations and policies relevant for indigenous peoples.

Indonesia voted for the adoption of the UN Declaration on the Rights of Indigenous Peoples (UNDRIP) at the UN General Assembly on 13 September 2007. This shows commitment by the government for the protection of Indonesia's indigenous peoples. The UNDRIP added on to a set of the core international human rights instruments that Indonesian has, although in several cases with reservations, become party to. They are as following:

1. International Convention on the Elimination of All Forms of Racial Discrimination, Party since 25 June 1999 (Reservation)
2. International Covenant on Civil and Political Rights, Party since 23 February 2006 (accession)
3. International Covenant on Economic, Social and Cultural Rights, Party since 23 February 2006 (accession)
4. Convention on the Elimination of All Forms of Discrimination against Women, Party since 13 October 1984
5. Convention against Torture and Other Cruel, Inhuman or Degrading Treatment or Punishment, Signatory since 23 October 1985 , Party since 28 October 1998
6. Convention on the Rights of the Child, Signatory since 26 January 1990, Party since 5 September 1990
7. International Convention on the Protection of the Rights of All Migrant Workers and Members of Their Families, Signatory since 22 September 2004.

Identifying indigenous peoples in Indonesia

The number of ethnic groups in Indonesia is not known and estimates very considerably. Leo Suryadinata et. Al. in 2003[8] reported that there are 100 ethnic and sub-ethnic groups (including the Chinese descendants). The Joshua Project[9] in 2007 estimated that Indonesia has some 758 ethnic and sub-ethnic groups, while the Summer Institute of Linguistics Ethnologue reports that there are 737 living languages in Indonesia. According to a rough classification suggested by Noer Fauzi 45% of the people in Indonesia are Javanese, 14% Sundanese, 8% Maduranese, 7% Malay, and the remaining 26% belong to numerous small ethnic groups.[10]

The Ministry of Social Welfare officially recognizes 365 groups as *masyarakat adat* terpencil ((isolated *adapt* communities) with a total population of 1.1 million.[11] The national alliance AMAN estimates that out off the 210 millions of Indonesia's population, around 50-70 million are indigenous. This prediction is established based on the working definition endorsed in March 1999 by the Congress of Indigenous Peoples of the Archipelago (KMAN-Kongres Masyarakat Adat Nusantara) as *"the people who live in a community unit descendent from specific generation over a territorial area, has sovereignty over the land and natural resources, their distinct socio-cultural system is ruled by customary law and governed by indigenous institution"*[12] (KMAN 1999). Indigenous Peoples live mostly in the so-called "outer islands", i.e. the archipelago outside Java, and in the eastern part of Indonesia. The main groups consist

With the high diversity of ethnic groups and the fact that most of them are ethnic groups with small populations, the identification of indigenous peoples based on the ethno-linguistic approach alone is difficult and problematic. It has therefore been suggested to us a the community approach. Using this approach in practice means that among the Javanese, for example, who are the biggest ethno-linguistic group in Java, small communities like the Orang Kanekes (also known as Baduy people), the Kasepuhan in Banten Kidul and the Orang Osing in East Java can be identified as indigenous peoples since they identify themselves as such in distinction to the majority Javanese. This situation has created challenges in the effort to identify the numbers and the populations of indigenous peoples in Indonesia. A similar situation is also found in the Malayu territory which concentrated in west coast of Sumatera. In that area, we can find indigenous communities like the Orang Rimba, Nias, Mentawai and Orang Talang Mamak who maintain a distinct identity vis-à-vis the majority.

This country profile was written by Rukka Sombolinggi, AMAN, with inputs from Abdon Nababan (Executive Secretary of AMAN) and Christian Erni (IWGIA).

Sources
Printed Sources

Duncan, Christopher R. 2007. Mixed Outcomes: The Impact of Regional Autonomy and Decentralization on Indigenous Ethnic Minorities in Indonesia. *Development and Change,* Volume 38, Number 4, July 2007

Fauzi, Noer 2005. *Memahami Gerakan-gerakan Rakyat Dunia Ketiga* Yogyakarta: Insist Press

International Work Group for Indigenous Affairs 2007. Indonesia, in: *The Indigenous World 2007.* Copenhagen: IWGIA

Li, Tania Murray. 1999. Articulating Indigenous Identity in Indonesia: Resource Politics and the Tribal Slot. *Comparative Studies in Society and History* 42(1):149-179

_____(ed.). 1999 *Transforming the Indonesian Uplands: Marginality, Power and Production.* London: Harwood Academic Publishers

_____2001. Masyarakat Adat, Difference, and the Limits of Recognition in Indonesia's Forest Zone. *Modern Asian Studies* 35, pp 645-676

Persoon, Gerard 2004. Indonesia: Reformulating indigenous identity. *IIAS Newsletter* no. 35, November 2004

Suryadinata, Leo, Evi Nurvidya Arifin, Aris Ananta 2003, *"Indonesia's Population: Ethnicity and Religion in a Changing Political Landscape".* Singapore: ISEAS

Internet sources

AMAN Web-site: http://aman.or.id/
On linguistic diversity:
Ethnologue web-site: http://www.ethnologue.com/show_country.asp?name=id

Notes

[1] http://www.ethnologue.com/show_country.asp?name=id
[2] Wikipedia defines adat as follows: *"Adat (Arabic عادة ādah)* is a set of local and traditional laws and dispute resolution systems in many parts of Nusantara. In older Malay language, adat refers to the customary laws, the unwritten traditional code regulating social, political, and economical as well maritime laws." http://en.wikipedia.org/wiki/Adat
[3] JAPHAMA - *Jaringan Pembelaan Hak-Hak Masyarakat Adat* (Network of Indigenous Peoples' Rights Defender)
[4] Article 18B(2)
[5] Article 28I (3) – Human Rights Section
[6] Persoon 2004: 11
[7] The Second Amendment of the Constitution of 2000 uses two terms to refer indigenous peoples. Article 18B-2 uses *masyarakat hukum adat* while Article 28I-3 uses *masyarakat tradisional.*
[8] Suryadinata, Leo, Evi Nurvidya Arifin, Aris Ananta 2003
[9] http://www.joshuaproject.net
[10] Fauzi 2005
[11] International Work Group for Indigenous Affairs 2007: p. 322
[12] Kongres Masyarakat Adat Nusantara (KMAN) I, Jakarta 1999

Young Ainu woman at the United Nations in Geneva. Photo: David Pearson

Country Profile

Japan

Japan is an island country and in the Pacific Ocean east of China, Korea and Russia. Japan has over 3,000 islands, the largest of which are Honshu, Hokkaido, Kyushu, and Shikoku. Together they make up a land area of 377,873 km².

Japan has until recently been officially projected as a homogeneous nation while in fact the population of 127.4 million people consists of several groups who differ culturally, linguistically and biologically from the ethnic Japanese population. These other groups include the Ainu and the Okinawans (also called Uchinanchū or Ryūkyūans), who are generally considered the indigenous peoples of Japan.

Terms used for indigenous peoples

The Ainu have only recently come to identify themselves as "indigenous peoples". In line with dominant discourse and Japanese government policy, many Ainu have denied their Ainu identity and at best identified themselves as "Japanese of Ainu descent". Others have continued to assert their Ainu identity and use *Utari,* which is how the Ainu actually refer to themselves.[1] Ainu just means "human" in Ainu language. The Ainu concept *un kur,* meaning "person who lives in (place name)" is used to refer to specific local identities in the sense of "belonging to" e.g. a group or a place. Hence, people living in Nibutani for example call themselves *Nibutani un kur.*[2]

Very few Okinawans self-identify explicitly as "indigenous peoples" *(senjū minzoku).* The reason for this seems to stem from preconceptions of the term "indigenous peoples" as a descriptor of a particular way of life, namely the *hunter-gatherer* tradition, rather than as a political position vis-à-vis states. At present the term "indigenous peoples" is used consistently only by self-identified indigenous rights activists within Okinawa.[3]

However, terms of self-identification used by Okinawans imply recognition of themselves and their territory as historically distinct from Japanese and Japan. The most prevalent example is Okinawans' everyday use of the word *Uchinanchū*. This is the Okinawan language term for both a person and the people of Uchinaa, which refers to Okinawa Island, the largest and most populated island of the Ryūkyū Archipelago. It should be noted that the inhabitants of other islands in the Ryūkyūs do not readily identify as Uchinanchū. Because the Ryūkyū Islands were, upon their reincorporation into the Japanese state in 1972, subsumed under the political label "Okinawa Prefecture," the archipelago's entire population came to be labelled "Okinawans" in Japanese and in English. This obscures the fact that the Ryūkyū Islands are multicultural and multilingual. Recognizing this themselves, mainland Okinawans, particularly those in the activist community, will sometimes refer to themselves or the entire population using the more inclusive "person/people of the Ryūkyūs" *(Ryūkyūjin)*. Similarly, some Japanese and English-language scholars have begun using the term Ryūkyūans.

As with the Ainu, Ryūkyūans' self-identification has a complex history and has also included deliberate subordination of their distinct identity. In the Okinawan context, the increasing politicization of Okinawan/Ryūkyūan identity in recent decades marks a shift away from their deliberate self-identification as *Japanese* nationals in the decades after World War Two. For 27 years, the United States' military formally occupied and controlled the Ryūkyū Islands. During this time Ryūkyūans were a stateless people. Seeing reincorporation into the Japanese state as the most promising and expedient way to oust the US military, the majority of Ryūkyūans asserted a Japanese identity and pushed for unification with Japan in the popular movement to end US occupation.[4]

The Government's position regarding the recognition of indigenous peoples and their rights

In June 2008, the Ainu were recognized as indigenous people of Japan. Before that, the attitude of the authorities toward the Ainu was largely based on an assimilationist ideology. According to this conception, all peoples native to present-day Japan are Japanese, and thus are to be addressed by the term *Nihonjin* (Japanese). This is still the stance of the Japanese government with regard to Ryūkyūans. To date, the government has consistently rejected the notion that Ryūkyūans are indigenous peoples.

In 1899, the Japanese government enacted its "Former Aboriginals Protection Act". The act designated the Ainu as "former aborigines" and made the clear distinction between the Japanese and the Ainu. Despite its declared purpose of assisting the impoverished Ainu, this law, which was effective until 1997, was in fact used to force the Ainu to assimilate into Japanese society. The Ainu had no secure rights to land or natural resources and were encouraged to abandon their customs, culture and language.

Futile attempts to raise the living standard of the Ainu resulted in 1974 in the establishment of a welfare policy on behalf of the Ainu called "The Hokkaido Ainu Welfare Policy". This welfare policy, which aims at eliminating the difference in living standards between the Ainu and the Japanese, has regional limitations though by only covering Ainu living in Hokkaido. Measures include the promotion of education and culture, the maintenance of livelihood opportunities, and the promotion of industries. For example, the government offers entrance allowances and grants (loans for college students) to encourage Ainu students to attend high school and college to eliminate the existing gap in educational opportunities between the Ainu and other residents.[5]

Once Ainu indigenous rights activists began participating in United Nations fora, the Japanese government gradually shifted its stance regarding the Ainu, but stopped short of recognizing them as indigenous. This was evident in its periodic reports required by the International Covenant on Economic, Social and Cultural Rights. But Japanese authorities managed to draw out its reformulation of its official position over nearly twenty years, from the mid-1980s to the early 2000s. Initially denying their existence as a distinct people, the government then acknowledged the Ainu but claimed they were no different from Japanese. In its 2001 report the government recognized Ainu as a distinct ethnic minority, but still insisted that Ainu territory had forever been inherently part of Japan.[6]

In 1997 the Law for the Promotion of the Ainu Culture and Dissemination and Advocacy for the Traditions of the Ainu and the Ainu Culture (hereafter the Ainu Culture Promotion Law) was enacted. The law provided for the protection the Ainu language and culture and in Article 1 it proclaims that it "aims to realize a society in which the ethnic pride of the Ainu people is respected and to contribute to the development of diverse cultures in our country". However, because the government did not recognize the Ainu as an indigenous people, the law offered nothing in terms of actual rights. The government did not recognize, for example, their right to establish a system for Ainu education.[7]

Supplementary provisions in the 1997 Ainu Culture Promotion Act stipulate that all remaining communal property should be returned to the Ainu. However, the government did not consult with the Ainu. Instead it unilaterally established procedures to address the communal property claims and limited the entire restoration process to just one year. Without properly evaluating the assets or their management, the government was offering only a fraction of the real value of the communal property lost. The communal property issue highlights the inability of the Ainu Cultural Promotion Act to address the most pressing problems facing the Ainu in any fundamental way. Although it recognizes the Ainu people as an ethnic group, the content of the law provides for only limited and indeed government-defined promotion of Ainu culture.

In September 2007, the Japanese government voted in favour of the passing of the UN Declaration on the Rights of Indigenous Peoples in the UN General Assembly. In response to this, the Ainu organizations, including the Ainu Association of Hokkaido, petitioned the Japanese Parliament *(Diet)* to implement the Declaration domestically. Ainu organizations demanded that the Japanese Government recognizes the Ainu people as an indigenous people, establishes a governmental organ concerning Ainu rights and policies; and introduces comprehensive measures concerning the Ainu people[8]

As a result, the Japanese Parliament passed a resolution on June 6, 2008, calling for the recognition of the Ainu as an indigenous people of Japan. On the same day, the Chief Cabinet Secretary made a statement recognizing that Ainu people are indigenous to the northern part of the Japan archipelago, especially Hokkaido, and that they, as an indigenous people, possess a unique language, religion and culture. He further announced the establishment of a "Governmental Panel of Experts on Ainu Affairs". At the same time, an Ainu Policy Promotion Unit was established under the direction of the Chief Cabinet Secretary.[9]

To what extent this considerable shift in the Japanese government's official stance on the indigeneity of the Ainu will impact its position with regard to Ryūkyūans is unclear. Rather than explicitly rejecting the notion that Ryūkyūans are indigenous, or asserting their equality under Japanese law, as it did regarding the Ainu for nearly two decades within UN fora, the Japanese government appears to have adopted a strategy of silence when it comes to the Ryūkyūans. Despite Ryūkyūan activists' participation in UN indigenous rights and other human rights fora, for example, the Japanese government has not made any formal statements in these meetings in reference to the Ryūkyūans. Nor has it mentioned Okinawa or the Ryūkyūans in its periodic reports as a signatory to human rights instruments pertaining to minority and indigenous rights. Recent examples include its 2001 report to the UN as a signatory to the Convention on the Elimination of All Forms of Racial Discrimination, and its 2002 report to the International Covenant on Civil & Political Rights.

What is clear is that a key intervening factor in Japan's relations with and policies regarding Ryūkyūans is Japan's security arrangements, specifically its commitment to the US-Japan Security Treaty. Instead of the end of US military presence as Ryūkyūans had hoped, reincorporation of the Ryūkyūs into the Japanese state in 1972 meant the automatic extension of the two country's security treaty to the islands. Indeed, the very terms of Ryūkyūans' citizenship in the Japanese state were negotiated and determined *bilaterally* between the two countries in the late 1960s, and predicated on continued US military presence in the Ryūkyūs. As a result Ryūkyūan issues, particularly problems and demands related to US military presence, are treated as bilateral diplomatic matters between the US and Japan. Given the widespread desire among Ryūkyūans to either close the US bases immediately or reduce their number systematically over time, any recognition by Japan of Ryūkyūans' indigenous rights would have serious implications for US military presence, and by extension the two countries' security relationship. All of this profoundly complicates Ryūkyūans' ability to seek redress and to exercise their right to self-determination.[10]

Japan is a state party, either by ratification or accession, to the following international human rights and other instruments most relevant for indigenous peoples:

- International Convention on the Elimination of All Forms of Racial Discrimination (1996)
- International Covenant on Civil & Political Rights (1979)
- International Covenant on Economic, Social and Cultural Rights (1979)
- Convention on the Elimination of All Forms of Discrimination against Women (1985)
- International Convention on the Rights of the Child (1994)
- Convention on Biological Diversity (2004)

Identifying indigenous peoples in Japan

The Ainu

The Ainu are now officially recognized as an indigenous people of Japan. The traditional Ainu territory stretched from Sakhalin and the Kurile Islands (now both Russian territories) to the northern part of present-day Japan, including the north of Honshu and all of Hokkaido Island, which constitutes 20% of Japan's current territory. The Ainu were incorporated into the Japanese state in 1868, without any negotiations.[11] The Ainu were treated separately as "native" colonial subjects, with very limited civil rights and were not granted full citizenship until 1933. They became targets of an assimilation policy of which central features were outlawing Ainu language and the removal of people from their small, scattered traditional communities, and their resettlement in larger villages where their ways of life could more easily be monitored and transformed.[12] According to research conducted in 1996 only 15 fluent speakers of the Ainu language remained. Most Ainu today are native speakers of Japanese or Russian.[13]

The traditional Ainu way of life was characterised by hunting, fishing and gathering in egalitarian communities. Today, the majority of the Ainu are engaged in agricultural, tourism, fishing, mining etc. Although most Ainu still live in Hokkaido, over the second half of the 20th century tens of thousands Ainu migrated to Japan's urban centres for work and to escape from discrimination which has been most prevalent in Hokkaido. Poverty is widespread, unemployment high and education levels well below the Japanese average.

The number of Ainu living in Japan is not known, as many Ainu hide their origins or in many cases are not even aware of them, their parents having kept it from them due to the discrimination they experienced. The total number may lie between 50,000 and 100,000 people, with a majority of them now living on the main island Honshu. [14] Estimates including people of mixed ancestry go a high as one million. [15]

The Ryūkyūans

Japan's present-day Okinawa prefecture and the Amami Islands of Kagoshima prefecture were once an independent territory unified in the 15th century under the Ryūkyū Kingdom. The 160 or so islands that make up the Ryūkyū Archipelago are located 560km south of Japan, extending some 1,100 km southwestward toward Taiwan.

Both China and Japan considered the kingdom a tribute territory, and the Ryūkyūan court obliged by maintaining tributary relations with both. In practice, however the Ryūkyū Kingdom retained its political autonomy over the islands. Japan invaded the Ryukyus in 1871 and forcibly annexed the territory in 1879. Establishing a colonial administration in the kingdom's former capital city of Naha, Tokyo imposed its national education system and the Japanese language, and redirected economic outputs toward Japan. In contrast to the experience of the Ainu, however, Ryūkyūans did not see massive state-initiated immigration of ethnic Japanese to their territory after annexation.

Their colonization set the stage for Ryūkyūans' experience of the Pacific War and their treatment in its aftermath. Towards the end of the war Japanese leaders designated the Ryūkyūs as a strategic buffer zone, to be sacrificed in order to protect the "mainland", and after the War Japanese leaders relinquished the islands to the US in exchange for its own independence. Although America's formal occupation of Okinawa ended in 1972, the US military remained. Currently 75% of all US forces in Japan are located in Okinawa prefecture, a mere 0.6% of Japan's territory. 50,000 US service members and their dependents occupy 37 military bases on Okinawa Island, home to 90% of the Ryūkyūs' 1.3 million people. Moreover, the Japanese government stations its own military forces in Okinawa, making it a doubly-militarized society.

The Ryūkyūs' distance from Japan and low rates of ethnic Japanese immigration to the islands contributed to Ryūkyūans' relative ability to practice and maintain a range of distinct cultural traditions. However the reintroduction of Japan's national education system in 1972, as well as media-driven cultural influences, has led to an increasing identification with Japan and Japanese culture among young Ryūkyūans. While elderly Ryūkyūans can still speak their native language (particularly those in more remote islands) and most Ryūkyūans' daily speech contains some indigenous language expressions, Japanese has become the native language for most.

Traditionally a fishing- and agriculture-based economy, the Ryūkyū Kingdom was known throughout the region as a vibrant maritime trading society. Today employment revolves around tourism, fishing, agriculture, and, on Okinawa Island, the US base presence. Okinawa's GDP and per capita income levels are lowest among Japan's forty-seven prefectures, while its rate of unemployment ranks highest.

This country profile is based on contributions provided by Kelly Dietz (on the Ryūkyūans), Kanako Uzawa, Yuuki Hasegawa and Christina Nilsson (on the Ainu). It has been compiled and edited by Christina Erni.

Sources
Printed Sources

Ainu Resource Centre 2008. Additional information in relation to the fifth Japanese report submitted under Article 40 paragraph 1(b) of the International Covenant on Civil and Political Rights, September 8, 2008. Retrieved at: *www2.ohchr.org/english/bodies/hrc/docs/ngos/ARCJapan94.doc*

Dietz, Kelly. 1999. "Ainu in the international arena"; in: W. Fitzhugh. *Ainu: Spirit of a Northern People.* Washington, DC: Smithsonian Institution & Seattle: University of Washington Press

———(forthcoming). "Demilitarizing Sovereignty: Self-Determination and Anti-Military Base Activism in Okinawa" in Critical Struggles: Conflicts over Rights, Resources and Representation

Siddle, Richard. 1996. *Race, Resistance and the Ainu of Japan.* London and New York, Routledge.

Siddle, Richard. 2003. Return to Uchinaa: The Politics of Identity in Contemporary Okinawa. R. Siddle. *Japan and Okinawa: Structure and subjectivity.* London: Routledge

Sjöberg, Katarina 1990. "Mr. Ainu" in the Japanese culture. Indigenous Affairs 60-61/1990

———1995. Practicing Ethnicity in a Hierarchical Culture: The Ainu Case. In R.H. Barnes, A. Gray and B. Kingsbury (eds.) *Indigenous Peoples of Asia.* Association for Asian Studies, Inc. Monograph and Occasional Paper Series 48. Ann Arbor, Michigan

Uzawa, Kanako 2008. Ainu today: Challenges in the Process of Self-Recognition. (What it takes to be recognized as Ainu). Draft report prepared for the ILO Project to Promote ILO Convention No. 169

Internet Sources

International Labour Organization web site, Indigenous and Tribal Peoples: http://www.ilo.org/public/english/indigenous/index.htm

The Ainu Museum web site: http://www.ainu-museum.or.jp/english/english. html

Wikipedia web site on the Ainu: http://en.wikipedia.org/wiki/Ainu_people

Yuuki Hasagawa: Ainu People in Japan. CTC Bulletin: http://www.cca.org.hk/ resources/ctc/ctc02-02/ctc02-02i.htm

Minority Rights Group International, report on the Ryūkyūans:

http://www.minorityrights.org/5363/japan/ryukyuans-okinawans.html

Wikipedia web site on the Rykyuan People: http://en.wikipedia.org/wiki/ Ryukyuan_people

Notes

[1] Sjöberg 1990
[2] Ibid.
[3] See Dietz, *forthcoming*.
[4] Dietz, ibid.
[5] First and Second report by the Japanese government submitted to the CERD committee 1999
[6] Dietz 1999
[7] Yuuki Hasegawa n.d.
[8] Ainu Resource Centre: Additional information in relation to the fifth Japanese report submitted under Article 40 paragraph 1(b) of the International Covenant on Civil and Political Rights, September 8, 2008
[9] Ainu Resource Centre: Additional information in relation to the fifth Japanese report submitted under Article 40 paragraph 1(b) of the International Covenant on Civil and Political Rights, September 8, 2008
[10] Dietz, *forthcoming*.
[11] Sjöberg 1995: 375
[12] See Sjöberg 375 ff; Uzawa 2008
[13] Wikipedia web-site: Ainu
[14] In 1988 the official figure for the Ainu population on Hokaido was 24,381 people (Sjöberg 1995: 373), and the population on Honshu was estimated at 50,000 to 60,000 (ibid.).
[15] Uzawa 2008: 5

Akha mother, Luang Nam Tha province. Photo: Christian Erni

Country Profile

Laos

The Lao People's Democratic Republic (Lao PDR) is a landlocked country bordering China, Vietnam, Cambodia, Thailand and Burma. It is one of the few remaining politically socialist countries and, following the communist takeover in 1975, opened up to the world only at the end of the 1980s. According to the UN, the Lao PDR is one of the Least Developed Countries. In spite of its relatively small population of about 6.3 million, Laos is the most ethnically diverse in mainland Southeast Asia.

Terms used for indigenous peoples

The concept of "indigenous peoples" is not used by the government in Lao PDR. It is considered too broad and is associated with the French term *indigènes,* used pejoratively during the colonial regime.[1] The main reason may, however, be that it is a political term that gives special rights to ethnic minorities, including land and resource rights, something that the Lao government does seem to be ready to provide. Since the passing of the 1991 Constitution, the Lao government uses the term *Son phao Lao,* usually understood as meaning "non-ethnic Lao", or, more general, "ethnic group" or "ethnic people".[2] Before the 1991 Constitution, the term *phao* was often used alone, which has been translated as "tribe". It is however often used in connection with *Lao* as well "to emphasize an ethnic distinction".[3]

The constitution of 1991 refers to Laos as a "multi-ethnic society" with many "ethnic groups." The government also prefers not to use the term "ethnic minority", as some believe that the term makes people in less populous ethnic groups feel inferior because they are only represented with a relatively smaller number of people. The categorization and terminology used for ethnic groups is rather ambiguous. At present the government officially recognizes 49 ethnic groups and a large number of sub-groups. It is the non-Lao which are usually referred to as the indigenous peoples of Laos.

In the 1991 constitution the government abolished the official classification of the population into highlanders *(Lao Soung)* living on the mountain tops, up-landers *(Lao Thoeng)* living on the mountain slopes, and lowlanders *(Lao Loum)*. These terms are however still used quite often through the country.

The Government's position regarding the recognition of indigenous peoples and their rights

The Constitution of 1991 is the general framework of the State's policy with respect to indigenous peoples. According to the 1991 Constitution, Lao PDR is defined as a multi-ethnic state, with "equality among all ethnic groups." Article 8 of the Constitution reads:

> "The State pursues the policy of promoting unity and equality among all ethnic groups. All ethnic groups have the rights to protect, preserve and promote the fine customs and cultures of their own tribes and of the nation. All acts of creating division and discrimination among ethnic groups are forbidden. The State implements every measure to gradually develop and upgrade the economic and social level of all ethnic groups."

It is assumed here that the intention of the Constitution is to grant equal status to all ethnic groups, and to this end no reference is made to the previous distinction between highlanders *(Lao Soung)* and lowlanders *(Lao Loum)* and midlanders *(Lao Theung)*. The constitution guarantees a number of fundamental rights, including the right to work (Article 26), and the freedom of assembly and association (Article 31).

The 1992 ethnic minority policy, Resolution of the Party Central Organisation Concerning Ethnic Minority Affairs in the New Era, focuses on gradually improving the lives of ethnic minorities, while promoting their ethnic identity and cultural heritage. It is the cornerstone of current national ethnic minority policy. The general policy of the Lao People's Revolutionary Party, the ruling communist party, concerning ethnic minorities can be summarised as follows:

- Build national sentiment (national identity).
- Realise equality between ethnic minorities.
- Increase the level of solidarity among ethnic minorities as members of the greater Lao family.
- Resolve problems of inflexible and vengeful thinking, as well as economic and cultural inequality.

- Improve the living conditions of the ethnic minorities step by step.
- Expand, to the greatest extent possible, the good and beautiful heritage and ethnic identity of each group as well as their capacity to participate in the affairs of the nation.

The implementation of the Party's policy on ethnic groups is tasked to the Lao Front for National Construction (LFNC).

The Ethnic Minorities Committee under the National Assembly is charged with the responsibility to draft and evaluate proposed legislation concerning ethnic minorities, lobby for its implementation as well as implementation of socio-economic development plans. Ethnic minority research is the responsibility of the Institute for Cultural Research under the Ministry of Information and Culture. The lead institution for ethnic affairs is the LNFC.

In 2005, the National Assembly declined to approve a new list of ethnic group names proposed by the Central Lao Front for National Construction. This was after the Central Party Politburo (the leadership committee within the Central Party) had sanctioned the list in principle in late 2000. In 2005, the Lao Front decided to counter their setback at the National Assembly by successfully reaffirming the list's validity with the Politburo. The Lao government thus adopted the new list for classifying people by ethnicity during the 2005 National census. The list presently includes 49 ethnic groups and a large number of sub-groups, but this figure is likely to change in the future as there is still not enough known about the diverse peoples of the country.[4]

The following are the international human rights and other instruments most relevant for indigenous peoples that have been ratified by Laos:

- International Convention on the Elimination of All Forms of Racial Discrimination
- International Convention on the Rights of the Child
- Convention on the Elimination of All Forms of Discrimination against Women

Laos has signed but not yet ratified:
- International Covenant on Civil & Political Rights
- International Covenant on Economic, Social and Cultural Rights
- Convention on Biological Diversity

The Lao government has also voted in favour of the adoption of the Declaration on the Rights of Indigenous Peoples by the United Nations General Assembly.

Identifying indigenous peoples in Lao PDR

The last revision of the list of officially recognized ethnic groups by the Lao Front for National Construction in 2005 included 49 ethnic groups, and over 160 subgroups. Linguistic anthropologists have however identified over 200 different ethnic groups belonging to four different linguistic families: Tai-Kadai, Mon-Khmer, Tibeto-Burman and Hmong-Mien.

Around 30% of Laos' population are ethnic Lao, who dominate the country both politically and economically. The non-Lao ethnic groups are usually considered the indigenous peoples of Laos.

The 49 ethnic groups included in the Lao Front's list of in 2005 are:

Xaek, Nhouan, Tai, Thaneua, Phouthay, Yang, Lao, Lue, Khmou, Katang, Katu, Kriang, Kri, Khmer, Ngouan, Cheng, Samtao, Sadang, Xuay, Xingmoun, Nhaheun, Ta-Oy, Triang, Tri, Toum, Thaen, Bit, Brao, Pakoh, Pray, Phong, Makong, Moy, Yrou, Yae, Lamet, Lavi, Oy, Oedou, Harak, Singsily, Sila, Lahu, Lolo, Hor, Akha, Hanyi, Hmong and Ieumien.[5]

So far, only in two provinces has a detailed survey of the ethnic groups based on self-identification been conducted, one in Bokeo in 2003, and one in Xekong in 2007. In Bokeo a total of 27 ethnic groups (including sub-groups) were identified in the province: Lao, Tai Dam, Leu, Yang, Tai Neua, Kalome, Nhouan, Kheun, Keummou Ou, Keummou Khven, Keummou Nhouan, Keummou Roke, Keummou Roke Khrong, Lamet, Samtao, Akha Ahcha, Akha Bieng Lae, Akha Louma, Akha Ho, Lahu Fou, Lahu Akha, Lahu Xi, Pana, Ieu-Mien, Mon (Lenten), Hmong Khao, Hmong Dam. In Xekong a total of 13 ethnic groups were identified: Katu, Katu Trieu, Katu Dak Kang, Kriang (Nge), Chatong, Ta-Oy (Brou Ta-Oy), Lao, Triang (Taliang), Yae, Harak (Alak), Lavi, Xouy, Yrou (Laven).

As diverse as Lao PDR's indigenous peoples are in cultural and linguistic terms, as diverse are their adaptive response to the natural and social environment in which they live. The livelihood systems found range from hunting and gathering (like the Mlabri in the North-western, the Atel, Thémarou, or Mlengbrou in Central-eastern Lao PDR) to various forms of swidden farming, in the uplands (generally classified into pioneer swidden like that of the Hmong and the rotational swidden farming of most of the members the Mon-Khmer and Tibeto-Burman ethnolinguistic family) and wet-rice farming in the plains (mostly by members of the Tai-Kadai ethnolingusitic family). Often, one finds a combination of these basic patterns, supplemented by minor cash-crop production, the collection of non-timber forest products for trade, fishing, animal husbandry, etc.

Most of the people in Lao PDR still live in rural areas and depend on various degrees on forest products, serving a wide range of subsistence needs and opportunities for income generation. Lao PDR has a low population density compared to other countries in Asia, with about 20 persons per sq km, and the country still has extensive natural forests, which allows people to live a life in what has been called "benevolent poverty": a subsistence economy with little cash-flow but providing the people with amply basic necessities.

This simply means that there is still relatively limited resource scarcity compared to other countries in the region. However, in some areas, like in the North, critical levels of resource degradation have been reached. With 2.4%, Laos' population growth rate is among the highest in Asia. Large-scale commercial resource exploitation (logging, industrial plantations, hydro-electric dams, mining, etc.) is diminishing the resource base of the rural people, and especially the forest dependent indigenous peoples. This makes the indigenous peoples less resilient than before to the impact of extreme weather conditions, like droughts.

For years, the Lao government has pursued a policy of internally resettling indigenous communities from the highlands to the lowland areas and along roads. The reasons given are varied, but resettlement is often justified due to the difficulties of providing access to services and concern for the environment, i.e. forest conservation. The Government has recently toned down its rhetoric in support of resettling villages, probably due to the increased recognition that much of the previous resettlement has resulted in serious problems for the affected people. Criticism of internal resettlement by donor agencies and others working in Laos has probably also contributed to government sensitivity regarding this controversial issue. However,, some internal resettlement is still continuing and more is planned for the coming years.[6]

This country profile has been compiled and edited by Christian Erni and Christina Nilsson with advise and inputs from Ian Baird, Director of the Global Association for People and the Environment (GAPE).

Sources
Printed Sources

Asian Development Bank 2001. Participatory *Poverty Assessment: Lao Peoples' Democratic Republic.* Manila: ADB

Chazée, Laurent 1999. *The Peoples of Laos: Rural and Ethnic Diversities.* Bangkok: White Lotus,

Lebar, Frank M., Gerald C. Hickey and John K. Musgrave 1964. *Ethnic Groups of Mainland Southeast Asia.* New Haven: Human Relations Area Files Press

Government of Lao People's Democratic Republic/Asian Development Bank 2006. Lao PDR-Northern Region Sustainable Livelihoods Development Project. Ethnic Groups Development Plan. Asian Development Bank Indigenous Peoples Development Planning Document

International Work Group for Indigenous Affairs [IWGIA] 2006. *The Indigenous World*, issues 2002-2003, 2004, 2005, 2006, 2007. Copenhagen: IWGIA

International Labour Office 2000. Policy Study on Ethnic Minority Issues in Rural Development. (LAO/98/551/A/08/ILO) Project to Promote ILO Policy on Indigenous and Tribal Peoples. Geneva: ILO

Ian Baird 2006. Laos; in: International Work Group for Indigenous Affairs [IW-GIA] 2006. *The Indigenous World,* p. 338-346. Copenhagen: IWGIA

Lao Front for National Construction 2005. The Ethnic Groups in Laos. Vientiane

Schliesinger, Joachim 2003. *Ethnic Groups of Laos.* 3 volumes. Bangkok: White Lotus

Internet Sources

On indigenous peoples in Laos in general:

IWGIA web-site: Laos country profile. http://www.iwgia.org/sw16162.asp

On classification and the situation of ethnic minorities http://www.h7.dion.ne.jp/~yokoyama/ethnic_minority.pdf

Notes

[1] International Labour Office 2000: 6

[2] Ibid. The latter is a grammatically more correct translation than the former (Ian Baird, personal communication).

[3] Ibid.

[4] Baird 2006: 345

[5] Lao Front for National Construction 2005

[6] See the chapter on Laos by Ian Baird in IWGIA: The Indigenous World, issues 2002-2003, 2004, 2005, 2006, 2007

Che wong boy, Pahang state. Photo: Colin Nicholas

Country Profile

Malaysia

Malaysia is a federation of 13 states, covering an area of 329,847 sq. km. The country consists of two geographical regions divided by the South China Sea: Peninsular Malaysia (or West Malaysia) on the Malay Peninsular which shares a land border with Thailand to the north with Singapore to the south, and Malaysian Borneo (or East Malaysia) occupies the northern and western part of the island of Borneo, bordering Indonesian Kalimantan and surrounding the Sultanate of Brunei. The latter consists of the states of Sabah and Sarawak and the federal territory of Labuan.

The Malay states were successively colonized by Portugal, Holland and Great Britain from the16th century before being occupied by Japan from 1942 to 1945. Sabah and Sarawak on the other hand were ruled by the North Borneo Chartered Company and the Brooke Rajahs until the Japanese Occupation whereupon they became colonies of Great Britain. While Peninsular Malaysia gained its Independence in 1957, the nation state of Malaysia was created when the Malay states, Singapore, Sabah and Sarawak formed a federation in 1963. Singapore eventually withdrew from Malaysia in 1965 to become an independent country.

In 2006, the total population of Malaysia was estimated at 26.64 million. Indigenous peoples account for about 12% of the total population. On Peninsular Malaysia, the Orang Asli account for only 0.6% of the population. In Sarawak, the indigenous peoples represent about 50% and in Sabah, about 60%.

Terms used for indigenous peoples

Malaysia has a multicultural and multiracial population consisting of Malays, Chinese, Indians, Eurasians and various ethnic groups including the indigenous communities.

The following terms are used to collectively describe the indigenous groups in the different regions of Malaysia:

- Orang Asli, which translates as "original peoples" or "first peoples", is used for the indigenous minority peoples of Peninsular Malaysia;
- Anak Negeri, which translates as "child of the state" or "native", is used for the indigenous peoples of Sabah; and
- Dayaks and Orang Ulu, which translates as "native' or "interior people", is used for the indigenous peoples in Sarawak.

In the Federal Constitution of Malaysia, however, the indigenous peoples of Sabah and Sarawak are referred to as "Natives". Together with the Malays of Peninsular Malaysia, they have been accorded a special position (Article 153) vis-à-vis the other ethnic groups. The Orang Asli, however, are not expressedly included in this categorisation.

Nevertheless, with the implementation of the New Economic Policy in 1970, the term "Bumiputera" was introduced. Translated as "prince of the soil", the generic term refereed to the Malays of Peninsular, the natives of Sabah and Sarawak *and* the Orang Asli. Such categorisation was meant to accord these groups with special rights and privileges in various speheres (e.g. employment, economic opportunities, protection of culture and traditions) but in reality the non-Malay bumiputera groups were left out in the distribution of the largesse afforded by this policy.

The Government's position regarding the recognition of indigenous peoples and their rights

Article 161(A) of the Federal Constitution of Malaysia 1957 provides for the recognition of the indigenous peoples (called "natives") of the States of Sabah and Sarawak. It defines the meaning of "native" in paragraph 6 and lists the peoples to be considered "natives" in paragraph 7:

(6) In this Article "native" means-
(a) in relation to Sarawak, a person who is a citizen and either belongs to one of the races specified in Clause (7) as indigenous to the State or is of mixed blood deriving exclusively from those races; and
(b) in relation to Sabah, a person who is a citizen, is the child or grandchild of a person of a race indigenous to Sabah, and was born (whether on or after Malaysia Day or not) either in Sabah or to a father domiciled in Sabah at the time of the birth.

(7) The races to be treated for the purposes of the definition of "native" in Clause (6) as indigenous to Sarawak are the Bukitans, Bisayahs, Dusuns, Sea Dayaks, Land Dayaks, Kadayans, Kalabit, Kayans, Kenyags (Including Sabups and Sipengs), Kajangs (including Sekapans,. Kejamans, Lahanans, Punans, Tanjongs dan Kanowits), Lugats, Lisums, Malays, Melanos, Muruts, Penans, Sians, Tagals, Tabuns and Ukits.[1]

In paragraph 5 of the same article, state-level laws in Sarawak and Sabah on customary land rights are explicitly recognized and protected:

(5) Article 89[2] shall not apply to the State of Sabah or Sarawak, and Article 8 shall not invalidate or prohibit any provision of State law in the State of Sabah or Sarawak for the reservation of land for natives of the State or for alienation to them, or for giving them preferential treatment as regards the alienation of land by the State.

Sabah and Sarawak have several state laws specifically on indigenous peoples. In Sabah, the Interpretation (Definition of Native) Ordinance of 1952 defines who is a "native" and the procedure to get a declaration of native status through the Native Courts. The Native Court Enactment 1992 is an important piece of legislation that recognises legal pluralism and the indigenous juridical system. Other laws with special reference to indigenous peoples include the Land Ordinance 1930 (defines native customary tenure rights) and the Rural Administration Ordinance 1951 (outlines the powers and duties of Native Chiefs and Village Heads). Several other laws that also have direct references to indigenous peoples are the Inland Fisheries and Aquaculture Enactment 2003[3], Wildlife Conservation Enactment 1997[4], and the Biodiversity Enactment, 2000[5].

There are also disputes over the definition and extent of Native Customary Rights (NCR) between the indigenous, who want to expand rights under NCR, and the states governments who want to limit the application of NCR. In theory, laws pertaining to NCR and other similar laws protect the right to land of the indigenous peoples of Sarawak and Sabah. In practice, however, the state has been able to alienate large tracts of land for logging, development projects and commercial purposes. For example, about 12% of the total area of Sabah has been reserved for commercial plantations to government statutory bodies. In Sarawak, by 2001, a total area of 1.5 million hectares of land was already used for development projects including hydroelectric dam projects and monocrop plantations.[6] Many indigenous communities have moved to establish settlements and farms in forest reserves as more lands are being taken for oil palm plantations. The growing number of incidents in the country reflects the slow process of demarcation and recognition of customary lands, compared to the alienation of large areas for plantations, logging and protected areas.

In Sarawak, amendments to the Land Code over the years have been passed to make it more difficult for indigenous communities to hold on to or protect their land. Such amendments empower the Minister to extinguish NCR to all land. The Sarawak Land Code Amendment Bill 2000 restricted the NCR claims over NCR land to farmland, burial grounds or shrines. This would not allow them to claim rights over the ancestral domains or communities, territory, communal forest and forest area for hunting-gathering purposes. Before the amendment indigenous communities could claim and prove their rights in accordance with the provisions of the Land Code and the *adat* (customary laws and practice).[7] This shrinking of rights has led to indigenous communities resorting to more blockades to protect their land. However the Forest Ordinance in 1987 makes such protests and action criminal and therefore subject to arrests and remand fines.

In a significant judgment in May 2001, the High Court of Kuching, Sarawak, ruled in the Rumah Nor land case that NCR of the indigenous people of Sarawak do not exist because of statute; rather, they are historically recognized rights which existed long before independence. Prior to the ruling, only farmlands actively cultivated by forest dependent communities could be considered native customary land but the judgment recognized that forests, rivers, and streams adjacent to indigenous communities are also included under native customary rights. Unfortunately in 2005, the appeal by the state government of Sarawak and the other parties who lost the case resulted in the appeal court overturning the original ruling.[8] However, this was on a legal point of evidence and not on the concept of the right of the native peoples to their customary land.

Often the laws that govern sale and transfer of land require only token safeguards such as notifications in land and survey offices, which in many instances, indigenous people may have no access. The result is that many indigenous people were deprived of their traditional lands with little or no legal recourse. The power of the Sabah and Sarawak state governments to change the status of the land from NCR and even freehold native titles to other types of leases leaves the rights of indigenous peoples over their land insecure and shaky.

In Peninsular Malaysia, the Aboriginal Peoples Act (1954, revised 1974) was initially enacted to prevent the communist insurgents to get help from the Orang Asli, and vice-versa. The Act is unique in that it is the only piece of legislation directed at a particular ethnic community. It defines the basic rules for the treatment of Orang Asli and their lands. The law is also seen as granting the Minister concerned or the Director-General of the Department of Orang Asli Affairs (JHEOA) with the authority over all matters concerning the administration of the Orang Asli. It also recognizes the authority of the state government over matters concerning land inhabited by the Orang Asli.[9] However this authority has been challenged in courts, notably in the *Sagong Tasi* case wherein the High Court and the Court of Appeal had ruled that the principles of the Federal Constitution and that of Common Law provide more rights to the Orang Asli over their traditional lands than does the Aboriginal Peoples Act.

The Act after all was enacted to erode support for the communist insurgents during the Emergency of 1948-1960 and was in essence a 'security legislation'. For this reason, there are provisions in the Act which allow the Minister concerned to prohibit any non-Orang Asli from entering an Orang Asli area, or to prohibit the entry of any communication medium capable of conveying a message, and even to overrule the choice of the community as to who should be their village-head!

Malaysia has ratified only a few international conventions that are important for indigenous peoples namely the Convention on the Elimination of All Forms of Discrimination Against Women (CEDAW), the Convention on the Rights of the Child (CRC) and the Convention on Biological Diversity (CBD). While the active lobby for these Conventions to be implemented, including a strong lobby to protect indigenous peoples rights by the Malaysian Human Rights Commission or SUHAKAM, has resulted in some positive actions, the Malaysian government continued to dodge appeals to also ratify the ILO Convention 169 and the two international human rights covenants. In September 2007, however, Malaysia along with many other Asian states adopted the UN Declaration on the Rights of Indigenous Peoples (UNDRIP).

Identifying indigenous peoples in Malaysia

Peninsular Malaysia

The total Orang Asli population numbers around 150,000 people, representing a mere 0.6% of the national population and consists of 19 ethnic sub-groups officially classified for administrative purposes under three groups viz. Negrito, Senoi and Aboriginal Malay.

Negrito: Kensiu, Kintak, Jahai, Lanoh, Mendriq and Bateq.
Senoi: Semai, Temiar, Chewong, Jah Hut, Semaq Beri, Mah Meri and Temoq
Aboriginal Malay: Temuan, Semelai, Jakun, Orang Kanaq, Orang Kuala and Orang Seletar.

Sabah

Indigenous peoples in Sabah make up about 60% of the population. Sabah is characterized by ethnic pluralism with people speaking more than 50 languages and 80 dialects. The Indigenous Peoples Network of Malaysia distinguishes between four main classificatory groups, each of which consists of several ethnic groups:

Dusun: Bisaya, Dumpas, Kujiau, Kadazandusun, Kimaragang, Lotud, Rungus, Tatana, Tinagas, Tobilung and Gana
Murut: Baukan, Kalabakan, Nabai/Ambual, Okolod/Kolod, Paluan, Selungai, Sembangkung, Serudung, Tagal/Tagol, Tidung and Timugon
Paitan: Abai Sungai, Lobu/Rumanau, Tampias Lobu, Tombonuo, Makiang, Kolobuan, Sinabu, Segama

Others: Banjar, Brunei/Kedayan, Ida'an/Begahak, Iranun, Cocos, Melayu Sabah, Tausug/Suluk, Bugis, Wolio, Chavacano, Sama/Bajau, Yakan, Bonggi and Molbog

Sarawak

The indigenous peoples in Sarawak make up about 50% of the State's population. Officially there are 28 indigenous groups listed, however there are many more groups and sub-groups. The Indigenous Peoples Network of Malaysia distinguishes the following five classificatory groups, each of which with a number of groups identified as indigenous peoples:

Bidayuh: Selako, Lara, Jagoi, Singgai, Krokong, Bilo'ih, Biperoh, Biatah, Benuk, Pinyowah, Bengoh, Braang, Tibiak, Bianah, Bukar, Sadong, Tringgus, Bigumbang, Bikuyab, Barieng, Bikutud, Bisepug, Biemban and Bisitang

Iban: Iban, Iban Sebuyau

Orang Ulu: Kelabit, Lun Bawang, Kayan, Kenyah Sambob, Kenyah Badeng, Kenyah Lepo Ke, Kenyah Nyurik, Kenyah Uma Pawa, Kajang Sekapan, Kajang Kejaman, Kajang Lahanan, Kajang Punan Bah, Penan, Sa'ban, Ukit, Baketan, Bisaya, Lakiput, Berawan, Tring, Seping, Punan Vuhang, Tagal, Tabun, Vai'e, Sihan

Melanau: Mukah and Dalat, Bintulu, Matu, Daro and Afaik

Others: Kadayan, Bakong, Tanjong, Remun, Kanowit, Rajang, Mirie, Dalek, Melayu Sarawak

This country profile was written by Jannie Lasimbang (Asia Indigenous Peoples Pact Foundation), Colin Nicholas (Center for Orang Asli Concerns) and Christian Erni (IWGIA).

Sources
Printed Sources

Nicholas, Colin 2000. *The Orang Asli and the Contest for Resources: Indigenous Politics, Development and Identity in Peninsular Malaysia.* IWGIA Document No. 95. Copenhagen: International Work Group for Indigenous Affairs/Center for Orang Asli Concerns (2000, reprinted 2004)

Nicholas, Colin 2007. The Orang Asli: Origins, identity and classification. In *Encyclopaedia Malaysia,* Vol. 12: 'Peoples and Traditions', Volume Editor: Hood Salleh. Singapore: Archipelago Press

Center for Orang Asli Concerns, Cordillera Peoples Alliance & PACOS Trust 2005. *Indigenous Peoples and Local Government: Experiences from Malaysia and the Philippines.* IWGIA Document No. 113. Copenhagen: IWGIA

Lasimbang, Jannie, et. al. 2007. *Bridging the Gap: Indigenous Peoples and Natural Resource Management in Asia.* Chiangmai, Thailand: UNDP Regional Indigenous Peoples Programme & Asia Indigenous People's Pact

Internet Sources

Web-site of the Center for Orang Asli Concerns (COAC): www.coac.org.my
Blog of the Indigenous Peoples Network of Malaysia or Jaringan Orang Asal Se-Malaysia (JOAS): http://orangasal.blogspot.com/

Notes

[1] These various different indigenous groups are also known together as the Dayaks.
[2] Article 89 regulates the declaration of Malay reservations.
[3] Under Part V of the Enactment, Sections 35, 36 and 37 relate to Community Fisheries Management Zones, including the declaration and recognition of indigenous system of resource management.
[4] The Wildlife Conservation Enactment 1997 recognises community hunting areas (Section 32) and honorary wildlife wardens (Section 7) from the community.
[5] The law contains eight important sections that are relevant to indigenous peoples. Section 9(1)(j) of the Enactment provides for a system to ensure that the indigenous peoples and other local communities are, at all times and in perpetuity, the legitimate creators, users and custodians of traditional knowledge, and collectively benefit from the use of such knowledge. It also recognizes rights to biological resources in land claimed under NCR [Section 16(b)], and has provisions to ensure that any activities related to the collection of biological resources do not negatively impact the livelihood, quality of life and the way of life of indigenous peoples [Section 20(3) and Section 25(1)(b)].
[6] Wong Meng Chuo. Racial Discrimination in Economic Development: The Denial of Indigenous Peoples Rights and Choice of Livelihood in Sarawak. paper presented at the Conference on Anti Racism, Racial discrimination, Xenophobia and Related Intolerance on 16-20 May 2001, Bangkok, organised by the World Council of Churches and Christian Conference of Asia.
[7] See M.C.Wong, Sarawak Land Code Amendment Bill 2000 Does Not Recognise Indigenous Rights Over Customary Land.
[8] The judgment can be accessed at Rengah Sarawak website at www.rengah_c2o.org
[9] Colin Nicholas *The Orang Asli Of Peninsular Malaysia,* available at: www.coac.org.my
[10] Orang Asal Malaysia – Indigenous Peoples of Malaysia. Poster produced by Jaringan Orang Asal SeMalaysia (JOAS), 2008

Tharu woman, Western Terai,. Photo: Colin Nicholas

Country Profile

Nepal

Nepal is a land-locked country of 147,181 km^2, bordered by China in the North and by India in the South, East and West. Nepal is a pluralistic country with many castes and ethnic groups, cultures, languages and religions. The total population of Nepal is 22.7 million, and over one hundred castes/ethnic and religious groups, and ninety-two mother tongues were listed in the Census 2001. Indigenous peoples, often referred as "indigenous nationalities" *(Adivasi Janajati)* comprised 8.4 million, or 38 % of the total population. However, indigenous peoples' organizations claim they have been under-represented in the census, and their actual populations comprise more than 50%. Indigenous peoples are highly marginalized, and have been excluded from the nation building process, which has been largely in then hands of the non-indigenous *Bahun* and *Chetri* castes, who still hold dominant positions in political, economical and social life of the country. Indigenous peoples are among the poorest of the poor, and their marginalization has been the reason for the broad support which the Maoist Party enjoyed during the 12 years long armed conflict. The inclusion of hitherto excluded groups like indigenous peoples in the process of restructuring the state was an important agenda of Twelve-point Agreements between the government and Maoists, which has been consistently reflected in subsequent agreements as well as in the Interim Constitution of 2007.

Terms used for indigenous peoples

Indigenous peoples are recognized constitutionally[1] as well as legally. They are officially called *"Adivasi Janajati"* (indigenous nationalities). The National Foundation for Development of Indigenous Nationalities Act 2002 defines *Adi-*

vasi Janajati as a group or community with own mother tongue and traditional customary practices, distinct cultural identity, social structure and oral or written history.[2] 59 indigenous nationalities have been legally enlisted in the NFDIN Act 2002. The definition more or less incorporates cultural identity rather than political entity of indigenous peoples, ignoring the recommendation made by the working group that was commissioned to make recommendations to the government for the establishment of NFDIN.

The Government's position regarding the recognition of indigenous peoples and their rights

Indigenous peoples have the right of Social justice thus they have a right of proportional representation in the State Structure.[3]

Until 1990 indigenous peoples' separate identities and concerns had been completely denied by government. The government's policy was to assimilate indigenous peoples into the dominant Hindu hierarchical caste system. This position changed in the wake of the political change of 1990, which was reflected in the government's new plans and policies (e.g. Ninth Five-Year Plan and subsequently reflected into the Tenth-Five Year Plan as well as in the Three Year Interim Plan). The government was compelled to address indigenous peoples' issues due to overwhelming pressure from indigenous peoples, scholars and academic institutions who pointed at the vast discrepancies between the dominant groups (*Banhun and Chettri* castes) and indigenous peoples. As a result, for the first time in history, the Constitution recognized the diverse nature of the state [4]and provided rights to language, culture and religion [5]. However the demand for secularism expressed by various excluded groups including indigenous peoples was denied, and Nepal continued to be a Hindu Country[6]. Importantly, the Constitutional provision for equal protection gave avenue to have special measure for the protection and educational, economic and social development of marginalized groups, which was considered to be applicable to indigenous peoples. However, these provisions were never really implemented, and were even made ineffective by the Supreme Court in the name of judicial interpretation for example with respect to some educational institutions.

In 2002 the NFDIN Act, 2002 was promulgated to establish a semi-governmental focal institution with mandate of working in the area of social, educational and cultural development of indigenous peoples. The purpose of the Act was also to legally define and identify indigenous peoples. The Act refers to indigenous peoples as *Adivasi Janjati*. The Act however neither stipulates the rights of indigenous peoples nor has the NEFDIN been given a sole and clear mandate to work in the development sector. With this rather blurry mandate, the Foundation has been facing problem of addressing all issues and concerns including human rights and fundamental freedoms of *Adivasi Janajati*. Similarly, as a semi-governmental institution the Foundation is bound by and dependant on the government.

Recently, the government's position on the recognition of indigenous peoples and their rights has moved in a positive direction due to relentless pressured by the organized indigenous peoples' movement. A Twenty Point Agreement was made between indigenous peoples and the government in 2007 which emphasized the inclusion of indigenous peoples in the process of restructuring the state. The agreement was however severely criticized by some indigenous groups as failing to address some of their main concerns and demands, e.g. autonomy and federalism in connection with the right to self-determination. Indigenous peoples have also been denied direct representation in the Constituent Assembly, which represents a huge challenge for them to address their aspirations and concerns in the Constitution making process.

At present, Nepal is in the process of writing a new Constitution after holding the Constituent Assembly election to institutionalize the restructure of the State introducing a federal republic system[7] replacing the Unitary System. As part of this process, an Interim Constitution was promulgated in 2007. The Interim Constitution recognizes indigenous peoples and their rights to some extent. It guarantees the right to social justice, including the right to participate in the state structure on the basis of the principle of social inclusion[8]. Poverty among indigenous peoples is supposed to be addressed by special measures including reservations in education and employment for a certain time period.[9] However, these provisions have only a moral force and their implementation depends on the political will of the political parties in power. Even though Article 63.4.3(a) provides for proportional representation of indigenous peoples' in the Constituent Assembly it is up to political parties to select indigenous representatives.

The *National Foundation for Development of Indigenous Nationalities (NFDIN) Act 2002* is the only national law that specifically deals with indigenous development issues. It has a unique structural framework where 92 out of the 125 members of the governing council are selected upon recommendation of indigenous peoples' organizations and the others are nominated by the co-chairperson. Both the recommended and nominated members are indigenous. The Prime Minister is the chairperson of the Council. The vice-chairperson is the main executive post and only and indigenous is eligible. Indigenous peoples' organizations are demanding to convert the foundation into a commission with the provision of overseeing the implementation of laws on indigenous peoples' rights.

The *Self-Governance Act 1998* triggered the passing of the NFDIN Act. For the first time a law recognized that indigenous peoples are excluded and need to be brought into the national mainstream (Preamble). There are provisions for indigenous peoples' representation in Village, Municipal and District Development Councils. However, these bodies had been non-functional which lead to the demand by indigenous organizations for a specific law, resulting in the passing of the NFDIN Act.

Section 2 of the Scholarship Act 2006 has been amended to ensure scholarships for indigenous and other excluded groups. There is however still a lack of regulations to translate this provision into practice.

The law with the severest negative consequence for indigenous communities is the Land Reform Act 1964 and Land Maintenance Act of 1963. They abolished traditional communal land rights and as a consequence displaced indigenous communities from their lands as they were taken over by members of the dominant Hindus of the *Bahun and Chetri* casts.

Nepal is a signatory to the number of international instruments and conventions including the International Covenant on Civil and Political Rights 1966, International Covenant on Economic, Social and Cultural Rights 1966, International Convention on the Elimination of All Form of Racial Discrimination 1969, UN Convention on the Rights of Child 1989, the Convention on Biological Diversity 1992.

In 2007, the Nepal parliament ratified ILO Convention No. 169 "concerning Indigenous and Tribal Peoples in Independent Countries", and Nepal voted in favour of the passing of the United Nations Declaration on the Rights of Indigenous Peoples in the UN General Assembly on 13 September 2007.

Identifying indigenous peoples in Nepal

Nepal is an ethnically highly diverse country with over spoken 120 languages[10] of four main linguistic families – Dravidian, Indo-European, Sino-Tibetan and Austro-Asiatic. Most of the Indo-Arian speakers have migrated to the present territory of Nepal since the 12th and 13th century, while the Sino-Tibetan speakers have lived there much longer. The Dravidian and Austro-Asiatic speakers are very few and also more recent migrants.

After the annexation of the native principalities by King Prithvi Narayan Shah in the second half of the 18th century, the native groups were forced into the Hindu cast system and their traditional cultures, social practices and institutions were discriminated against and forbidden. It is within the context of suppression and marginalization by the dominant Hindu groups that the indigenous peoples of Nepal are identified. Most of the indigenous ethnic groups are speakers of languages belonging to the Sino-Tibetan linguistic family, but there are a few groups – such as the Tharu in the plains region (called Terai) – who speak languages belonging to the Indo-European linguistic family.

59 indigenous nationalities have been legally enlisted in the National Foundation for Development of Indigenous Nationalities Act 2002 and are thus officially recognized in Nepal. These are categorized according to four major geographical regions:

Mountain Region (Himalaya): 17 groups: Barah Gaunle, Bhote, Byansi, Chhairontan, Dolpo, Larke, Lhomi (Shingsawa), Lhopa, Marphali Thakali, Mugali, Siyar, Sherpa, Tangbe, Thakali, Thudam, Topkegola and Walung.

Hills: 24 groups: Baramu, Bhujel, Chepang, Chhantyal, Dura, Fri, Gurung, Hayu, Hyolmo, Jirel, Kusunda, Lepcha, Limbu, Magar, Newar, Pahari, Rai, Sunuwar, Surel, Tamang, Thami, Kumal, Yakkha and Tin Gaunle Thakali.

Inner Terai: 7 groups: Bankaria, Bote, Danuwar, Darai, Majhi, Raji and Raute.

Tarai: 11 groups: Dhanuk (Rajbanshi), Dhimal, Gangai, Jhangad, Kisan, Kushbadia, Meche, Rajbanshi (Koch), Satar (Santhal), Tajpuria and Tharu.

There are however several ethnic groups, like the Ghale, Kulung, Bahing, Karani etc., that have been left out and are demanding to be included. The National Foundation for Development of Indigenous Nationalities (NFDIN) has initiated the enlistment of more groups within the Act

This country profile was written by Shakar Limbu, Secretary of the Lawyers' Association for Human Rights of Nepalese Indigenous Peoples (LAHURNIP).

Sources
Printed sources

Bhattachan, Krishna B. 2003. Expected Model &Process of Inclusive Democracy in Nepal. Paper presented in a International Seminar on the Agenda of Transformation: Inclusion in Nepali Democracy organized by the Social Science Baha in Kathmandu.

International Work Group for Indigenous Affaris 2007. *The Indigenous World.* Copenhagen: IWGIA

IIDS, 2000. *The Fourth Parliamentary Election: A Study of the Evolving Democratization Process in Nepal.* Kathmandu : IIDS

Interim Constitution of Nepal 2007. Nepal Kanoon Kitab Byawastha Smeetee, Kathmandu, Nepal

ILO and NEFIN 2005. *ILO Convention No.169 and Peace Building in Nepal,* Joint Publication. Kathmandu

LAHURNIP 2005. Comparative Analysis of National Laws and ILO Convention on Indigenous and Tribal Peoples, 1989(No.169)

Nepal Act Collection Supplementary Part 2063(C)

Pairabi, Prakashan 2005. *Nepal Ain Sangrah Bhag 1. Pairabi Publication:* Kathmandu Nepal

Internet sources

National Foundation for Development of Indigenous Nationalities (NEFDIN) web-site: http://www.nfdin.gov.np

Nepal Federation of Indigenous Nationalities (NEFIN) web-site: http://www.nefin.org.np

Notes

1 Article 3 of the Interim Constitution 2007
2 Sec. 2 a of the NFDIN Act 2001
3 Article 21 of the Interim Constitution 2007
4 The Constitution of Kingdom of Nepal 1991. Art 2
5 *Ibid Art. 18,19 and 26(2)*
6 *Ibid Art. 4*
7 Article 159 of the Interim Constitution
8 Interim Constitution 2007, Art. 25
9 *Ibid Art. 35*
10 Summer Institute of Linguistics. Ethnologue. Languages of the World http://www.ethnologue.com/

Kalash sisters, North-West Frontier Province. Photo: Imran Schah/imranthetrekker@yahoo.com

Country Profile

Pakistan

Officially called the Islamic Republic of Pakistan, the country shares borders with India in the East, China in the North, Afghanistan and Iran in the West, and has a 1046 km long coastline along the Arabian Sea in the South. Pakistan covers 881,640 km² and has a population of 172,800,000 as of July 2008.

Pakistan has four provinces, namely Sindh, Punjab, North-Western Frontier Province (NWFP) and Balochistan. The government of Pakistan classifies the country's population on the basis of these administrative units – those who live in Sindh province are called Sindhis, those from Punjab province Punjabis, in Balochistan live the Baloch tribes and in the NWFP the Pashtun tribes. Aside from these major "ethnic nationalities" there are many other nationalities which the government does not recognize and for which no separate administrative regions have been created. Some of these groups are Seraikis, Pothoaris or Birahvis which demand their separate administrative region and their right over their lands and other resources.

A large number of people are immigrants and their descendents, mostly Muslims who have come to Pakistan at the time of partition of Indian sub-continent in 1947, and those who migrated from Afghanistan in the early 1980s.

Peoples of Sindh province and the tribal peoples of Balochistan and NWFP have a long history of dispute and conflict with the federal government (dominated by the Punjabi political establishment) over the discriminatory resource distribution among provinces.

Terms used for indigenous peoples

The concept of "indigenous peoples" has made its way into Pakistan only recently. The government does not use this term officially, and there is thus no official definition of the term in Pakistan. A distinction is made between the mainstream population and tribal people. In Urdu, the official language of Pakistan, the term for tribal people is *qabaili log* or just qabail[1]. The tribal peoples and their areas are well defined in Pakistan. In current local literature, among various ethnic groups and in some local right-based movements, however, the term adi vaas ("son of the soil"), meaning "original people", is used. *Adi vaas* (sometimes also adivas or adivasi) is used with a cultural, ecological and political connotation. As *adi vaas* refers to people who have inhabited the region long before any intruder, they are understood to have a time-tested relationship with their ecosystem and natural resources.

The Government's position regarding the recognition of indigenous peoples and their rights

Since the government does not use the term "indigenous peoples", but only speaks of and identifies "tribal people", the respective national and international legal instruments have only limited scope. An example is ILO Convention 107, of which Pakistan is a signatory. It is applied only to the tribal peoples that live in the "Tribal Areas" of Baluchistan and the North-West Frontier Province, the former States of Amb, Chitral, Dir and Swat. Article 246 of the Constitution defines the so-called Tribal Areas, which are sub-divided into the Provincially Administered Tribal Areas (PATA) and the Federally Administered Tribal Areas (FATA).

The Provincially Administered Tribal Areas comprise:[2]
The districts of Chitral, Dir and Swat, the Tribal Areas of Kohistan and Mansehra districts; Malakand Protected Area; the former states of Amb; Zhoub district, Loralai district (except Duki Tehsil), Dalbandin Tehsil of Chagai District and Marri and Bugti tribal territories of Sibi district.

The Federally Administered Tribal Areas comprise: [3]
Tribal Areas adjoining Peshawar district; Tribal Areas adjoining Bannu district; Tribal Areas adjoining Kohat district; Tribal Areas adjoining Dera Ismail Khan district; Bajau Agency; Mohmand Agency; Khyber Agency; Kurram Agency; North Waziristan Agency; South Wasiristan Agency.

At national level, Pakistan has no official policy or legislation for indigenous peoples, except The Frontier Crime Regulation (1930), enacted during the last days of British India, which is a brief definition and administrative guidelines towards the tribal areas and peoples. The late president Mohtarma Benazir Bhuttu of the Pakistan People's Party, assassinated on 27th December 2007, has terminated this law since it was considered discriminatory.

As a result of the lack of legal protection in Pakistan, indigenous peoples' resources like the lands, water, fish and forests are appropriated for development and revenue purpose without their consent and hence without any benefits. Thus the indigenous peoples are fast loosing there livelihoods base. Huge tracts of indigenous peoples' lands are considered "state-land".

The only legal instrument protecting the rights of indigenous peoples is ILO Convention No.107 (which was replaced by ILO Convention on Indigenous and Tribal Peoples No.169 of 1989, which was however not ratified by Pakistan). As mentioned, there is however only limited application of Convention 107 in Pakistan. The government of Pakistan as well as the ILO Pakistan, through ILO Convention 107, only deal with the tribal peoples of Balochistan and North Western Frontier Province. The scope of the convention is not extended to other indigenous peoples.

Among the international human rights instruments ratified by Pakistan are:

1. Convention on Elimination of Discrimination against Women (CEDAW).
2. Convention on the Rights of the Child (CRC).
3. International Convention on Elimination of Racial Discrimination (ICERD).Pakistan has signed, but not ratified:
4. International Convention on Economic, Social and Cultural Rights.

Identifying indigenous peoples in Pakistan

As there is no formal definition and classification of indigenous peoples in Pakistan, the identification of which ethnic groups can be considered indigenous in Pakistan is difficult. It relies on a combination of criteria including their assertion of their distinct identities, the possession of livelihood systems, cultures and social organization distinct from the mainstream society, and their relative political, economic and social marginalization.

The indigenous peoples of the North-West Frontier Province

The North-West Frontier Province (NWFP) was created in 1901, and currently consists of seven divisions and 22 districts and the Provincial Administered Tribal Areas (PATA). About ¾ of the territory is under the administration of the provincial government, the remainder under the federal government (Federally Administered Tribal Areas).[4] The Pukhtun, (or Pakhtun, Pushtun, Pathan) represent the largest indigenous ethnic group in the NWFP. They also live in a vast area of adjacent Afghanistan. The Pukhtun are Muslim, and are sub-divided into three main branches (the Sarbani Pukhtun, the Ghilzai Pukhtun and the Gurghush Pukhtuns), each of them consisting of several tribes, which are again divided into khels (clans).[5] There are around 60 tribes and 400 khels.[6] The Pukhtun are basically farmers or herdsmen, or a combinations of both.

The people of Chitral in the North of the NWFP, like the Kohwar, have a different language and culture. And in three small valleys in Chitral live the Kalash, who have their own indigenous belief system, but who are now increasingly converting to Islam.[7]

The forests dwellers of Malakand division i.e. Swat Kohistan and Dir Kohistan valleys, and in Mata and Shangla districts, have been struggling for their forest royalty since the early 1990s. The area is inhabited by five major ethnic groups, namely Kohistanis, the Pukhtun, the Gujjars, Swatis and Syads. Local rulers and landlords traditionally exercised control only to the extent of collecting taxes on certain animals and plant species. The British control, however, change the land use pattern, property rights and tenure system of the region. Various colonial forests acts, such as the Hazara Forest Conservancy Rules of 1857, the Forest Act of 1865 and the Forest Act of 1927, declared all forests as property of the government and opened them for commercial exploitation

The Baloch

The Baloch inhabit Balochistan province in the west of Pakistan and the adjacent areas in Iran and Afghanistan. There are three branches of the Baloch: the Makrani, Sulemani and Brahui (the latter speaking a different language)[8]. The major Baloch tribes include the Bugtis, Maris, and Mengals. Other Baloch tribes were forcibly included in Punjab province. Among them are the Ligharis, Mazaris, Gorchanis, Dreshaks, Khosas, Qaisranis, Khitrans, and Buzdars who live in the Suleiman Mountains.

The Baloch live by a mixture of dry and irrigated agriculture and pastoralism. Their community organization varies between extremes of highly stratified villages and small egalitarian nomadic groups. These nomadic pastoralists play a significant social role. Their continued activity provides a communication network among the settled village communities and symbolizes for those communities the values that support traditional Baloch identity.

The *Buzdars,* one of the largest Baloch tribes with a number of sub tribes, live in area called Andar Pahar in the Sulaiman Mountain, which lies between Balochistan and the South Punjab. Detached from Balochistan, this large Baloch zone is part of District Dera Ghazi Khan of Punjab as "De- Excluded Area". This arrangement was made by the British government before partition while during British colonial times these tribes had enjoyed an independent status and were administered as "Special Area". Compared to other Baloch tribes in the area, *(Ligharis, Khosas, Qaisranis, Nutkanis, Khitrans),* the *Buzdars* have been less-visible on the local and national political scene.

Indigenous peoples of the Indus River

The Kihals and Mors are considered indigenous peoples of the Indus River. They depend on fishing and the forests of the Indus delta. Most of their population is concentrated between Chashma Barrage and Taunsa Barrage.

Fishing, basket weaving and agricultural labour are major sources of livelihood for the Kihals and Mors for which they entirely depend on the Indus. Their livelihood is however under threat due to mega water development project like dams and barrages, project-induced flooding, increased agricultural activities on riverine lands and contract fishing.

Instead of following one single religion in strict, the Kihals kept to a flexible system of believes. Due to their increasing dependence on neighboring Muslim population, Kihals and Mors are fast converting to Islam and adapt a Muslim life style. They now call themselves Sheikhs (new Muslims), and Khokhar (a sub-caste of Muslims), and want their women to wear scarfs and stay at home.

The indigenous peoples of the Northern Areas

The Northern Areas is a Federally Administered Area (officially called Federally Administered Northern Areas - FANA). It became a single administrative unit in 1970 through the amalgamation of the Gilgit Agency, the Baltistan District of the Ladakh Wazarat, and the states of Hunza and Nagar. According to Pakistan's constitution, the FANA is not part of Pakistan, and its people have no representation in Pakistan's parliament. The United Nations considers the whole area of the former princely state of Kashmir and Jammu, including the present-day FANA, as disputed territory which is still awaiting resolution of the long-standing conflict between India and Pakistan.

The extremely rugged terrain with high mountains and isolated valleys has a highly diverse population with many linguistic, ethnic, and religious groups. Urdu is the lingua franca of the region, but many indigenous languages are spoken which again often have several local dialects. Shina is the language of 40% of the population, spoken mainly in Gilgit, Diamer, and in some parts of Ghizer. The Balti language, part of the Sino-Tibetan language family, is spoken by the people of Baltistan. Smaller language groups are Wakhi, spoken in upper Hunza, and in some villages in Ghizer, and Khowar of Ghizer. Burushaski is an isolated language spoken in Hunza, Nagar, Yasin (where Khowar is also spoken), in some parts of Gilgit and in some villages of Punyal.[9]

At present, the people of the Northern Areas have no participation in the governance of their territories. Their resources, above all timber, are rapidly exploited and poverty levels are extremely high. The Gilgit Baltistan United Movement (GBUM) and the Balawaristan National Front (BNF) are two local movements calling for the establishment of a fully autonomous state.

This country profile was written by Wasim Wagha, Programme Manager, Research and Advocacy, & Executive Officer DAMAAN (Development through Awareness and Motivation) based in Southern Punjab, Pakistan, with inputs from Christian Erni (IWGIA).

Sources
Printed sources

Shaheen Sardar Ali and Javaid Rehman 2001. *Indigenous Peoples and Ethnic Minorities of Pakistan. Constitutional and Legal Perspectives.* Nordic Institute of Asian Studies Monograph Series No. 84. Curzon Press

Internet sources

Wikipedia web-site, Pakistan: http://en.wikipedia.org/wiki/Pakistan;
on the Northern Areas: http://en.wikipedia.org/wiki/Northern_Areas_(Pakistan);
On Federally Administered Tribal Areas: http://en.wikipedia.org/wiki/Federally_Administered_Tribal_Areas;
On North-West Frontier Province: http://en.wikipedia.org/wiki/North-West_Frontier_Province;
On Balochistan: http://en.wikipedia.org/wiki/Balochistan_(Pakistan)

Notes

[1] *Qabila* - tribe / *Qabail* - plural of tribe i.e. tribes (also used for people of the tribes). *Log* - people.
[2] Ali and Rehman 2001, p. 45
[3] Ibid.
[4] Ibid.: p. 78f
[5] Ibid.: p. 79
[6] http://en.wikipedia.org/wiki/Pashtuns#Modern_era
[7] Ali and Rehman 2001: p. 79
[8] Ibid: p. 61
[9] http://en.wikipedia.org/wiki/Northern_Areas_(Pakistan)#Demographics

Buhid man, Occidental Mindor. Photo: Christian Erni

Country Profile   # Philippines

The Philippines is a tropical mountainous archipelago of 7,100 large and small islands, covering an area of 300,000 km². As of July 2006 the population was 89.5 million. Colonized by Spain for 350 years, the modern Filipino nation was born in the Revolution of 1896-98, came under U.S. occupation for 45 years, and regained its independence in 1946.

More than 170 native languages are spoken in the Philippines, most of them belonging to the Austronesian (Malayo-Polynesian) linguistic family. 110 ethnic groups are officially recognized as indigenous peoples.

Terms used for indigenous peoples

Officially, indigenous peoples are referred to as "Indigenous Cultural Communities/Indigenous Peoples". These are also the terms used in the constitution, laws and other official documents.

In Filipino (Tagalog), the national language, the word *katutubo* is used as translation of "indigenous", and the term "indigenous peoples" is translated as *katutubong mamamayan*. The term *tribo* (tribe) or n*itibo* (native) are also still very commonly used, both by non-indigenous and among indigenous peoples themselves.

The following four terms are used to refer to the indigenous groups in different regions of the Philippines:

- *Lumad* is used for the indigenous peoples in Mindanao, the country's second largest island found in the south. It is a Visayan term meaning native, indigenous, "of the land".

- *Igorot* is used as a generic term for the indigenous peoples of the Cordillera mountain range in the north of Luzon, the largest island of the Philippines located in the north. It is derived from the word *i-golot* or *gulod* meaning "people from the mountain". It used to have a negative connotation but is increasingly accepted by the indigenous peoples of the Cordillera themselves.
- *Mangyan* is the generic designation for the indigenous peoples of Mindoro island in the central part of the archipelago. It is also used for the indigenous communities on Sibuyan Island ("Sibuyan Mangyan").
- *Negrito* is used as generic term for indigenous peoples with distinct physical features (dark skin, curly hair) living across the Archipelageo. The word *Negrito* is the Spanish diminutive of negro, i.e. "little black", and was coined by early European colonizers and explorers who thought that the Negritos were from Africa.
- *Bukidnon* or *Remontados* is used for the indigenous peoples in Panay, Negros and Sibuyan island group who withdrew to the mountains to escape and resist Spanish colonization. They are also referred to as *Sulod* or *Tumandok*. In Luzon, particularly in the province of Isabela, they are referred to as *Kalinga* while in Rizal and Quezon provinces the Remontados have been grouped with the Agta due to the high degree of intermarriages among them.

The Government's position regarding the recognition of indigenous peoples and their rights

Indigenous peoples and their rights are fully recognised by the Philippine government. The Indigenous Peoples Rights Act (IPRA) uses both the terms "Indigenous Cultural Communities" and "Indigenous Peoples", while the Constitution refers to "indigenous cultural communities" (ICC).

The 1987 Constitution has several provisions of relevance for indigenous peoples. In Article XII Sec. 5, the state commits to protecting the rights of indigenous cultural communities (ICC) to their ancestral land, "subject to the provisions of this Constitution and national development policies and programs". This provision gave Congress the task of defining "the applicability of customary laws governing property rights or relations in determining the ownership and extent of ancestral domain". In Article XIV Sec. 17, the state recognizes and guarantees the rights of the ICC "to preserve and develop their cultures, traditions, and institutions".

In 1997 the Philippine government enacted the Indigenous Peoples Rights Act (IPRA), which is an interpretation of the constitutional provisions governing indigenous peoples' rights. IPRA has been recognised as one of the world's most progressive laws specifically dealing with indigenous peoples. The IPRA recognizes, protects and promotes the rights of Indigenous Cultural Communities/

Indigenous Peoples (ICC/IP). Apart from provisions guaranteeing social justice and human rights, recognizing and protecting cultural integrity, and recognizing "the inherent right of ICC/IP to self-governance and self-determination", the IPRA contains important provisions concerning the right to ancestral domain and ancestral lands. IPRA also provides for the creation of the office of the National Commission on Indigenous Peoples (NCIP) as implementing agency of the IPRA, as well as for the Consultative Body, consisting of traditional leaders, elders and sectors of the different indigenous peoples, which is supposed to oversee and advise on the implementation of the IPRA by the NCIP.

NCIP is an independent agency under the office of the President and is composed of seven Commissioners representing seven ethnographic regions that have been identified and delineated by the NCIP and are not identical to the administrative regions of the state. NCIP is in charge of implementing the IPRA and for that has developed a Medium Term Philippine Development Plan for Indigenous Peoples (2004-2008), which includes indigenous peoples in several sectoral plans.

On occasion of the 10th anniversary of the passing of IPRA, civil society organizations have undertaken assessments of how the IPRA had fared.[1] It was found that indigenous peoples' concerns have not been sufficiently mainstreamed within government agencies. In most cases, there is a continuing conflict between different laws and their implementing agencies, for example, between the National Commission on Indigenous Peoples (NCIP) and the Department of the Environment and Natural Resources (DENR) regarding access to and management of forests. Sometimes the problem is indifference rather than conflict, as with the Department of the Interior and Local Governments (DILG) regarding the responsibilities of local government units (LGUs) in upholding indigenous peoples' representation in local bodies.

Regarding the NCIP, the observation is that this institution is still in great need of institutional strengthening. Frequently, the NCIP is perceived as addressing the interests of government or of business rather than those of indigenous peoples' communities, resulting in many expressions of disappointment from them and indigenous peoples' support groups. Instead of following the spirit of the law, the NCIP is seen to have succumbed to a more bureaucratic interpretation of the law's provisions.

This can clearly be seen in the NCIP's performance in one of its three core programs: the delineation and titling of ancestral land. By end of 2007, five years after the first Certificate of Ancestral Domain Title (CADT) was granted, the NCIP has processed only 57 CADTs, which is 9% of the titling applications it has received. The titling procedures have been criticized for being unnecessarily costly and lengthy, and lacking in cultural sensitivity. These criticisms were also levelled at the NCIP projects aimed at assisting indigenous peoples' communities to develop their community development plans which, according to the IPRA's

Implementing Rules and Regulations (IRR), come under the Ancestral Domain Sustainable Development and Protection Plan (ADSDPP).

While the NCIP has been rather slow in dealing with applications for CADTs, it has been found to be quick in issuing "Certificates of Compliance to the Free Prior Informed Consent (FPIC) Process" and "Certification that the Community Has Given Its Consent" for development projects, including for mining claims and for plantations to produce bio-fuels. A total of 118 such certificates have been issued since 2004, when the first one was granted. In 2007 alone it has issued 62 such certificates. [2]

The Philippines has, among others, ratified the following international instruments relevant for indigenous peoples:

- International Convention on the Elimination of All Forms of Racial Discrimination
- International Covenant on Civil and Political Rights
- International Covenant on Economic, Social and Cultural Rights
- International Convention on the Protection of the Rights of All Migrant Workers and Members of Their Families
- Convention on the Elimination of All Forms of Discrimination against Women
- Convention on the Rights of the Child

Identifying indigenous peoples in the Philippines

The ethnic divide between indigenous and non-indigenous peoples emerged during the colonial period during which there came about a segregation within the population into those who were hispanized and those who resisted and withdrew to remote and inaccessible areas where they retained their original ways of life. It is the latter group who is referred to as indigenous peoples.

Without having a clear basis, the government usually identifies 110 indigenous groups with population estimates that range from 6.5 million to more than 12 million, or between 10 and 15% of the total national population. According to NCIP, 60% of the total indigenous population live in Mindanao, 30 % in the Cordillera-Northern Luzon, and 10% in the rest of Luzon and the Visayas (central) islands.

The Cordillera

The majority of the Cordillera peoples, also collectively known as *Igorot*, are the indigenous groups living in the highlands, foothills and river valleys of the Cordillera mountain ranges of Northern Luzon and extends to the Ilocos and Cagayan Valley regions.

The Isneg are found in the Apayao province. There are seven ethnolinguistic groups of Tingguian or Itneg. These are the Adasen, Banao, Binongan, Inlaod, Masadiit, Maeng and Moyadan Itneg, who occupy the province of Abra.

There are 50 Kalinga *bogis,* traditionally-defined territories among the eight ethnolinguistic groups within the province of Kalinga. In the Mountain Province live the Bontok (Central Bontok), Finallig (Southern Bontok), and in Bontoc Province live the Bontok, and the Balangao or Gad'ang (in eastern Bontoc) who extend their territories to Isabela and southeastern Kalinga.

The Kankana'ey inhabit Benguet and Mountain Province. The Northern Kankana'ey are also known as Lepanto or Sagada Igorot. A group of Kankana'ey in the La Union and Ilocos Sur extent of the Cordilleras have in recent years asserted a separate identity as Bago.

The Ikallahan or Kalanguya are generally from Tinoc, Ifugao and extend their territories to Benguet and Nueva Vizcaya, and in recent years their population movement have brought them within the borders of Nueva Eicja. The Ibaloi inhabit the areas of Benguet and Nueva Vizcaya. The territories also stretch to the highlands of La Union, Pangasinan, and Nueva Ecija. The I-wak is the smallest group in the Cordillera, living in Benguet province.

A population of Atta Negrito live in the fringes of the Cordillera, in the provinces of Abra and Apayao (Villa Viciosa, Pamplona, Faire and Pudtol).

North, Central and Southern Luzon

The Negrito, of which up to 30 groups have been identified, are mostly distinguished by their Australoid physical features. They live in dispersed groups throughout the major islands, usually in the less accessible forested areas. Prehistorians suggest that one migration stream (with groups now called Alta, Arta, Agta) settled the northern part of Luzon and moved down the eastern part, along the Sierra Madre and Pacific coast down to the Bondoc and Bicol mountains. Another branch (with groups now called Aete, Ayta, Atta, Ita, Ati, Sinauna) settled in western and southern Luzon, with larger populations now found in the Zambales-Bataan mountains and Southern Tagalog foothills, while others settled on Palawan (Batak), Panay, Negros and northern Mindanao (Mamanwa).

The non-Negrito groups in these areas are the Bugkalot or Ilongot in Nueva Vizcaya, Quirino and Nueva Ecija and two Remontado groups, the Sierra Madre Kalinga in Isabela and the Remontado of Rizal and Quezon.

Island Group

"Mangyan" is the collective term for the indigenous peoples of Mindoro island, which are usually clustered into the Northern Mangyan (Tadyawan, Alangan and Iraya) and the Southern Mangyan (Buhid, Taobuid *and* Hanunuo). A small group of people who have so fare considered to belong to the Taobuid is now identifying itself as Bangon, a term otherwise used by neighbouring groups with negative connotation. Another small group, the Ratagnon on Mindoro's southernmost tip, is closely related to the Cuyonin of Palawan. Generally, the Mangyan of Mindoro practise swidden agriculture combined with hunting, fishing, gathering and trade.

Several groups in Palawan are considered as indigenous: the Tagbanwa (Kalamianen), Palaw'an, Molbog and Batak (a Negrito group). The Agutaynen, Cuyonin and Kagayanen are no longer considering themselves an indigenous group, having long been assimilated into the mainstream culture. Some traits of their traditional indigenous way of life however remain and some groups are asserting their indigenous identity.

The Negrito (Ati and Ata) and various groups of Bukidnon or Remontados largely populate Panay, Negros, Guimaras and Romblon islands. The Bukidnon are also called Sulod in Panay. In Negros, they are also referred to as Magahat or Karol-an. In Sibuyan, the non-negrito indigenous population are called Sibuyan Mangyan.

Mindanao

The spread of Islam in Mindanao-Sulu created a differentiation among its native peoples between those who became Muslim (also called *Moro*) and those who did not (now called Lumad). There are seven major Islamized ethnic groups in the Mindanao-Sulu area (the Maranaw, Maguindanao, Tausug, Yakan, Samal, Iranun and Kalagan). The Sangil who are long time residents in the coastal areas of Davao and Sarangani have migrated from Indonesia. Kolibugan is used for any group married to another group or the offspring of mixed parentage.

The *Lumad,* or non-Moro indigenous peoples of Mindanao, are a complex patchwork of indigenous groups. The Lumad stress that they are different from the Moros and many do not recognize the Moros as being indigenous. To simplify, Lumad groups may be clustered into (a) the Manobo cluster, (b) the B'laan-T'boli-Tiruray cluster, (d) the Mandaya-Mansaka cluster, (e) the Subanen, and (f) the Mamanwa. There is much inter-penetration among these groups. The term Bagobo refers to two Manobo ethnolinguistic group (Ubo and Tagabawa) and Klata, a B'laan related linguistic group. The popular term Bagobo is derived from Bago and Obo or "new person", largely referring to new Christian or in Spanish as *Nuevos Cristianos.* For the most part, the indigenous peoples in Mindanao basically subsist through swidden and wet rice cultivation, hunting, fishing, gathering and the trade in locally manufactured items.

This country profile was written by Christian Erni, Ma. Teresa Guia-Padilla, Dr. Sabino Padilla Jr. and Christina Nilsson.

Sources
Printed Sources

Coalition for Indigenous Peoples' Rights and Ancestral Domains, International Labour Organisation, BILANCE-Asia Department *1999. Guide to R.A. 8371. Indigenous Peoples' Rights Acto fo 1997 (IPRA).* Manila: PANLIPI/ECIP

Gatmaytan, Augusto B. (ed.) 2007. *Negotiating Autonomy. Case Studies on Philippine Indigenous Peoples' Land Rights.* IWGIA Document 114. Quezon City/Copenhagen: LRC-KsK/IWGIA

Guia-Padilla, Ma. Teresa and Mybabel T. Pomarin 2008. Philippines; in: International Work Group for Indigenous Affairs [IWGIA] 2008. *The Indigenous World 2008.* Copenhagen: IWGIA

National Commission on Indigenous Peoples (NCIP) 2003. *Medium-Term Philippine Development Plan for Indigenous Peoples (2004-2008).* Manila: NCIP

Padilla, Sabino Jr G. 2003. *Mindanao Indigenous Peoples Mapping Project.* University of the Philippines, Center for Integrative and Development Studies. 30 July 2003

_____2005. The Indigenous Peoples of the Visayan Island Groups. Paper presented at the Regional Seminar-Workshop on Philippine Studies in the Visayas. Golden Peak Hotel and Suites in Cebu City. September 9-10, 2005.

PANLIPI 2007. *Initial Assessment of the Extent of the Implementation of IPRA.* Manila: International Labour Organization (ILO) for South East Asia and the Pacific

Rodil, B.R. 1993. *The Lumad and Moro of Mindanao.* London: Minority Rights Group International, Report 93/2

Indigenous Peoples Rights Monitor 2007. The Situation of Human Rights and Fundamental Freedoms of the Indigenous Peoples in the Philippines: January 2003 to November 2007 Manila: Indigenous Peoples Rights Monitor

Tuyor, Josefo B., et al. 2007. Philippines Indigenous Peoples Rights Act: Is It Protecting the Rights of the Indigenous Peoples? Study commissioned by the World Bank. Manila: World Bank

Quilaman, Masli A. 2007. "Status: Issuance of CADTs/CALTs, ADSDPP Formulation, & CP Issuances", report presented to the "Subanen Elders and Leaders General Assembly and Environment and Indigenous Peoples' Concerns", Springland Resort, Pagadian City, 18-20 November 2007

Internet Sources

AnthroWatch: http://anthropologywatch.blogspot.com/

International Work Group for Indigenous Affairs [IWGIA]. Country profile Philippines. http://www.iwgia.org/sw16701.asp

National Commission on Indigenous Peoples: http://www.ncip.gov.ph/

Republic of the Philippines 1997. Republic Act 8372. An Act to recognize, protect and promote the rights of indigenous cultural communities/indigenous peoples, creating a national commission on indigenous peoples, establishing implementing mechanism, appropriating funds therefore, and for other purposes. Retrieved from: www.tebtebba.org/tebtebba_files/ipr/philippines/ipra.pdf

Tebtebba Foudation web-site: www.tebtebba.org

Notes

[1] The paragraph on the assessment of IPRA has been previously published in Guia-Padilla and Pomarin 2008: 278f. The major sources of information regarding the assessment are the following: PANLIPI 2007; Indigenous Peoples Rights Monitor 2007); Tuyor et al. 2007; Quilaman 2007.

[2] Ancestral Domains Office, NCIP, "List of Issued Compliance Certificate as of February 2008 (Certificate of Compliance to FPIC Process and Certification that the Community Has Given Its Consent)".

Thao elder, Nantou County. Photo: Peingamla Luithui

Country Profile

Taiwan

Taiwan, also known as Formosa, is located off the southeast coast of mainland China, south of Japan and north of the Philippines. Part of the Wesern Pacific chain of volcanic island arcs, Taiwan has a total area of 36,000 square kilometers. The Taiwan Island is elongated in the north-south axis with a length of 395 kilometers, and width of 145 kilometers along its east-west axis.

The history of the indigenous peoples of Taiwan has been dominated by foreign powers since at least the seventeenth century, although competition and conflict existed long before then. All or parts of their traditional lands have been conquered at various times throughout history by Dutch, Spanish, Manchu China, Japanese and Chinese (the Chinese Nationalist government, or Kuomintang) rulers.

The indigenous population of Taiwan currently numbers 469,000 people, or 2.1% of the total population of 23 million. Thirteen indigenous peoples are officially recognized. In addition, there are at least nine Ping Pu (平埔 "lowland plains") indigenous peoples who are denied official recognition. Most of the recognized indigenous peoples live in the central mountains, on the east coast and in the south of Taiwan.

Terms used for indigenous peoples

The indigenous peoples of Taiwan have been referred by various names in history. In the western literature and early anthropology papers, they were called "Formosan Aborigines". The Han Chinese settlers and Chinese administrators during the Manchu dynasty era used the term "fan" (番 *or* 蕃), which denoted the indigenous peoples as barbarian, primitive or backward. This term was further divided into two major categories: "Seng fan" (生番 the unfamiliar primitive people), and "Sou fan" (熟番 the familiar primitive people). These two terms referred to the degree of "familiarity", or cultural contact with the early Han Chinese settlers from mainland China. Later it also referred to the subjugation under military conquest of Manchu Chinese rule. Used extensively in historic documents and official records (Manchu Chinese and Japanese periods), the two terms roughly corresponded to the two major divisions of Taiwan's indigenous peoples: "Seng fan" for the mountain indigenous peoples, and "Sou fan" for the Ping Pu plains indigenous peoples.

Later the indigenous peoples living in upland areas were referred to as "*Shan-bao*" (山胞 mountain compatriots or mountain people), a term inherited from the categories used by the Japanese colonial regime. In the mid-1980s a group of indigenous activists initiated a campaign to demand a respectful name. After 10 years of struggle, the name proposed by indigenous peoples, "*Yuan-zhu-min*" (原住民 literally meaning "people who have originally lived here"), was used to refer to indigenous peoples in an official Presidential speech. In 1994, the Constitution was amended and the term gained legal status.

Each indigenous tribal group has their own way of referring to themselves, in many cases simply the designation "human being" in their own language. The term "*Yuan-zhu-min*" is used in pan-indigenous activism and refers to the pan-indigenous identity that indigenous communities have used to differentiate themselves from the Chinese Taiwanese majority.

The Government's position regarding the recognition of indigenous people and their rights

A number of national laws protect the rights of Taiwan's indigenous peoples, including the Constitutional Amendments (2005) on indigenous representation in the Legislative Assembly and protection of language and culture, the Indigenous Peoples' Basic Act (2005), the Education Act for Indigenous Peoples (2004), the Status Act for Indigenous Peoples (2001), the Regulations Regarding Recognition of Indigenous Peoples (2002) and the Name Act (2003), which allows indigenous peoples to register their original names in Chinese characters and to annotate them in Romanized script.

The Indigenous Peoples' Basic Act recognises indigenous rights to land and resources and states that the government must safeguard the status of indigenous peoples and work toward providing self-rule of each tribe. However, the drive towards self-governance, inspired by the call for self-determination by indigenous activists, has been stalled by the intervention of national legislation and administration. One of the problems is that the Council for Indigenous Peoples (CIP), a ministry-level body under the Executive Yuan (the executive branch of the government), must propose amendments to certain of the nation's other laws before the Act can be used to provide regional self-government systems to the indigenous groups and no progress in passing such key amendments by the Legislature has been made. Another problem is that although the "tribal community", the fundamental unit for self-governance in the Basic Act, can be interpreted broadly as covering everything from tribal settlements to indigenous nations, the CIP took a conservative stance, adopting the narrower interpretation that it applies to tribal settlements only.

At present, a constitutional reform is ongoing. The new Constitution will contain a chapter on indigenous peoples and the Draft Constitutional Chapter on Indigenous Peoples proposed by the CIP defines and guarantees indigenous peoples' rights, which cover sovereignty, land and natural resources, education, culture, language, traditional knowledge, customary law, participation in national policy-making, as well as the recognition and protection of other collective rights. Unfortunately, due to the top-down nature of the reform process and the resulting lack of participation by indigenous peoples, the draft has yet to receive wide recognition or support from indigenous peoples.

Identifying indigenous peoples in Taiwan

Since the period of Japanese colonization, the indigenous peoples have been categorized into "Ping-pu" (those who live in the plains) and "Kao-sa" (高砂those who live in the mountains). Thirteen indigenous peoples are officially recognized. In addition, there are at least nine Ping Pu indigenous peoples who are denied official recognition.

The thirteen officially recognized indigenous groups are the Amis (aka Pangcah), Atayal, Paiwan, Bunun, Pinuyumayan (aka Puyuma or Beinan), Tsou, Rukai, Saisiyat, Tao (aka Yami), Thao, Kavalan, Truku and, since January 2007, Sakizaya.

The nine non-recognized indigenous Ping Pu groups are the Ketagalan, Taokas, Pazeh, Kahabu, Papora, Babuza, Hoanya, Siraya and Makatao.

Most indigenous peoples traditionally live in the central mountains, on the east coast and in the south of Taiwan, while according to the latest census it was found that about 1/3 of them now live in the cities (primarily in Taipei and Kaohsiung) as a result of migration for employment and better living conditions).[1.]

For centuries the indigenous peoples experienced economic competition and military conflict with a series of conquering foreign powers and many of the indigenous groups have been linguistically and culturally assimilated. Like indigenous peoples in many other areas of the Asian region, Taiwan's indigenous peoples face threats to their culture and way of life, and a continual encroachment on their traditional areas of residence. Although the indigenous peoples are not subject to any official discrimination, they find it difficult to influence policies and programs that affect their ways of life. Thus, the main challenges facing indigenous peoples in Taiwan today include rapid erosion of cultures and languages, low social status, high unemployment rate, and weakened political or economic influence.

Mountain indigenous peoples

The mountain indigenous peoples were known as "Fan" (Manchu Chinese era), "Kao-sa" (Japanese era), and "Shanbao" (Nationalist Chinese - Kuomintang era). It is known that they are native Austronesian peoples, and are related to Malay-Indonesians, Polynesians, Maoris, and other Pacific islanders. Their Austronesian origin was established by well-documented research and scientific studies on their language, culture, and genetic affinities. As the term denotes, Taiwan's mountain indigenous peoples traditionally live in the mountainous regions, among the cutivated slopes, forest woodlands, and river valleys of the upland areas. They live in mountain villages or in isolated settlement of family clans. The only exceptions are the Tao people (living in the offshore Lanyu Island, having an oceanic culture and dependency on fishing and marine resources), and the Amis Kavalan, and Sakizaya peoples who live in the valleys and coastal areas of Taiwan's eastern region (Ilan, Hualien, and Taitung counties) with a mix of traditional marine fishing and land-based lifestyle practices.

Despite the fact that the traditional territories of four groups (Tao, Amis, Kavalan and Sakizaya) lie in the eastern coastal valleys and islands, Taiwan's thirteen recognized indigenous peoples together were referred to as "mountain peoples", which is a leftover legacy of the colonial times and it is a common term found in historic documents. In the past, they were generally referred to as the "nine tribes of mountain people" (the traditional categorization into nine ethnic groups by anthropologists). After years of fighting against discrimination and for recognition of their rights, the "nine tribes of mountain peoples" won a major battle in 1994 when they collectively gained legal status as "indigenous peoples", and achieved further empowerment with the establishment of the Cabinet-level ministry, the Council of Indigenous Peoples" in 1996.

Plains indigenous peoples

The indigenous plains peoples are collectively known as the "Ping Pu". Like the other indigenous groups in Taiwan, the Ping Pu are native Austronesian peoples. Traditionally they mainly lived in village settlements.

There are nine major indigenous groups living in the plains of Taiwan who, up until now, have been denied official recognition by the government. They do not identify themselves as Ping Pu but as nine distinct peoples, each with its own language and cultural affinities. Estimated to number between 150,000 and 200,000, these Ping Pu indigenous peoples are not even recognized as ethnic groups, and thus have no minority group status in Taiwan. As a result of a loss of land, culture, language and group identity, and their total exclusion from government and the social welfare system (the above mentioned laws and legislations recognizing the rights of indigenous peoples do not apply to the Ping Pu indigenous peoples), they are among the most marginalized groups in the country and it is feared that they will cease to exist as distinct indigenous ethnic groups within the coming decade. Ping Pu indigenous activists are still fighting against pervasive discrimination, and the total neglect and exclusion by the government. Their demands for Ping Pu peoples to be recognized as indigenous people of Taiwan, and for inclusion under the rights protection and services of the Council of Indigenous Peoples have been ignored to this date.

This country profile has been written by Jason Pan, director of TARA – Ping Pu, with inputs from Christian Erni.

Sources
Printed Sources

Bellwood, Peter, 2000. Formosan Prehistory and Austronesian Dispersal; in: D. Blundell (ed.). *Austronesian Taiwan.* Taipei: SMC Publishsing, Inc.

Diamond, Jared M. 2000. Taiwan's Gift to the World. *Nature,* Vol. 403, 17 February 2000

Hsieh, Jolan 2006. *Collective Rights of Indigenous Peoples: Identity-Based Movement of Plain Indigenous in Taiwan.* New York, London: Routledge

International Work Group for Indigenous Affairs [IWGIA] 2008. Taiwan; in: *The Indigenous World 2008.* Copenhagen: IWGIA

Li, Paul Jen-kuei 2001. The dispersal of the Formosan aborigines in *Taiwan. Language and Linguistics* 2.1

Shepherd, John R. 1996. From Barbarians to Sinners: Collective Conversion Among Plains Aborigines in Qing Taiwan, 1859-1895; in: D.H. Bays (ed.). *Christianity in China.* Stanford: Stanford University Press

Internet Sources

On Taiwan Indigenous Peoples (recognized groups): http://www.tacp.gov.tw/tacpeng/home02_3.aspx?ID=$3001&IDK=2&EXEC=L

On Ping Pu Plains Aborigine Peoples (website information in Chinese only): http://140.109.4.130/~pingpu/museum/introduction/01/01.htm

On Indigenous and Ping Pu Aborigines, and Taiwan Identity: http://taiwanjournal.nat.gov.tw/ct.asp?CtNode=122&xItem=22970

Minorities At Risk (MAR) web-site: www.cidcm.umd.edu/mar/

Notes

[1] Minorities At Risk (MAR) web-site

Karen woman and boys, Chiang Mai province. Photo: Christian Erni

Country Profile

Thailand

The Kingdom of Thailand lies in the heart of Southeast Asia, with Laos and Cambodia to its east, the Gulf of Thailand and Malaysia to its south, and the Andaman Sea and Myanmar to its west. Thailand comprises of 76 provinces and since 1932 the country has had a constitutional monarchy. It covers an area of 513,115 km^2 and has a total population of 64.6 million people.

The indigenous peoples of Thailand live in three geographical regions of the country: indigenous fisher communities and a small population of hunter-gatherers in the south of Thailand, the many different highland peoples living in the north and north-west of the country, and a few groups in the north-east. According to the official survey of 2002, there are 923,257 "hill tribe people" living in 20 provinces in the north and west of the country. There are no figures available for the indigenous groups in the south and north-east.

Terms used for indigenous peoples

Ten ethnic groups have been granted official recognition as *chao khao* (meaning "hill/mountain people" or "highlanders"). The term *chao khao* or hill tribes has been used since the late 1950s and is linked to the term *chao pha* ("forest people"), which was used to denote the non-Thai minority groups before the term *chao khao* came into use. For the Thais, *pha* – meaning "forest" – has the connotation of "wild", "savage" and is generally conceived in opposition to *muang* – "town", "city", "country" – with the connotation of "civilized" or "human domain". The adoption of the term *chao khao* was part of a nation building process in which national identity and definition of "Thai-ness" was linked to cultural traits, particularly Buddhism, language and monarchy. With the negative stereotyping of the hill tribes as destroying the forest, opium cultivators and communist sympathisers, the social category of the *chao khao* came to be defined as being "non-Thai", underdeveloped and environmentally destructive. Other terms with a very similar meaning and connotation have been used, like *chao khao oppayob* ("migrant hill people") or *chao thai phukhao* ("mountain Thai people"). Other terms used in Thailand are more or less equivalent to terms commonly used in English for the region, like *klum chat tiphan* ("ethnic groups") or *chon klum noy* ("ethnic minorities")

The negative connotation of the official designation *chao khao* has led a number of indigenous activists in Thailand to oppose it and its translation "hill people". The term *chon phao* ("tribal people" has become more common, and recently indigenous organisations and indigenous rights advocacy groups have begun to promote the term *chon phao phuen mueang* (ชนเผ่าพื้นเมือง) as translation of "indigenous peoples".

The fishing communities of the South (who call themselves Moken) are called in Thai *chao thale* (meaning "sea people"), and in English often "sea gypsies". The (former) hunter-gatherer groups along the Malaysian border are still often referred to by the derogatory term *sakai* (literally meaning "slave").

The Government's position regarding the recognition of indigenous peoples and their rights

The term indigenous peoples has been rejected by the Thai government who has stated that the hill-tribes of Thailand "are not considered to be minorities or indigenous peoples but as Thais who are able to enjoy fundamental rights and are protected by the laws of the Kingdom as any other Thai citizen."[1]

The widespread misconception of indigenous peoples as being drug producers and posing a threat to national security and the environment has historically shaped government policies towards indigenous peoples in the northern highlands. Although over the past decade there have been positive developments away from this approach, it continues to underlie the attitudes and actions of government officials.

Thailand does not have laws recognising and protecting the rights of indigenous peoples. The new Constitution passed in 2007 does not explicitly recognize the identity of indigenous peoples. This is despite the fact that, during the drafting of the new Constitution, indigenous peoples' representatives participated in different constitution-drafting discussion forums at provincial as well as national level. Even though the Constitution does not specifically mention indigenous peoples' rights, Part 12 on Community Rights refers to the "traditional community" and indigenous communities can benefit from the recognition of economic, social and cultural rights guaranteed to "local" or "traditional" communities under articles 66 and 67 of Part 12 of the Constitution.

Policies and programs specifically addressing "hill tribes" have been implemented since the late 1950s after the creation of the Central Hill Tribe Committee, which later saw the creation of the Hill Tribe Welfare Division within the Ministry of Interior. Until the 1980s, Thai policies towards indigenous peoples was dominated by concerns about opium cultivation and communist insurgency and some of the major programs addressing these concerns included the National Economic and Social Development Plans, Self Help Settlement Projects, opium substitution programs, and Highland Development Projects initiated by the King.[2]

By the 1980s, deforestation and control of resources in the uplands became important national issues and in 1982, the "Committee for the Solution of National Security Problems involving Hill Tribes and the Cultivation of Narcotic Crops" was established to coordinate and realize policies aimed at the indigenous peoples, including the Master Plans for Development of Highland Populations, Environment and Control of Narcotic Crops (Master Plans for Highland Development) and the National Economic and Social Development Plans. The objectives of these policies, which are still valid today, include the integration of the indigenous peoples into Thai society, requiring the reorganization of their way of life accordingly (meaning particularly giving up shifting cultivation, and resettlement into the lowlands), elimination of opium cultivation and consumption, reduction of population growth, and improvement of living standards.[3]

Aside from the policies directed specifically at indigenous peoples, a number of laws affect their livelihood. The Nationality Act of 1965 granted Thai citizenship to people belonging to indigenous groups who were born in the Thailand providing both their parents were Thai nationals. These limits on citizenship qualifications slowed or impeded citizenship approval for many indigenous peoples and continue to pose a great problem. It is estimated that about 50% of indigenous peoples with a legitimate claim to Thai citizenship do not have it because they do not have birth registers or other means of proof.

Since the passing of the Forest Act 1941 the Thai state has enacted various laws and launched policies to protect and conserve forests and wildlife. As a result, it brought virtually all forest land under its control. These laws – the objective of which was essentially to curb illegal logging – have effectively de-legitimized and disenfranchised the indigenous peoples who had been living in the forests but had no title deeds to their land. Subsequently, other laws have declared more areas as national parks, reserved forests or wildlife sanctuaries and have restricted the use of such land by communities. Today, 28.78% of Thailand is categorized as protected areas.

In 2005 a range of government-led projects were initiated such as the "Forest Village Reform", the "25 River Basins Management Initiative" and the "Joint Management of Protected Areas" (JoMPA) project which claim to promote and ensure the involvement and participation of local communities and their leaders.

However, in the execution of these projects, participation is practised merely in the form of consultations, with no access to decision-making power.[4]

On 21 December 2007, the Community Forest Act was passed, in the face of much opposition from civil society. The law has been long awaited. But the final version deviates substantially from the original proposal of civil society organisations. Many provisions de-facto abolish the rights of numerous forest communities. The contents of Sections 25 and 34 are considered to be not much different from the conventional forest laws aimed at curbing people's rights to use forests and which, in fact, led to conflicts of interest and the demand for a Community Forest law in the first place. According to indigenous rights advocates, the law will make it impossible for most indigenous communities to participate fully in community forest management and it thus contradicts the provisions for community resource management rights included in the new Constitution.

Thailand has, among others, ratified the following UN Conventions relevant for indigenous peoples:

- International Covenant on Civil and Political Rights
- Convention on the Elimination of All Forms of Discrimination against Women
- International Convention on the Elimination of All Forms of Racial Discrimination
- International Covenant on Economic, Social and Cultural Rights
- Convention on the Rights of the Child
- Convention on Biological Diversity

Identifying indigenous peoples in Thailand

With the drawing of national boundaries in Southeast Asia during the colonial era and in the wake of decolonization, many peoples living in remote highlands and forests were divided. There is thus not a single indigenous people that resides only in Thailand. The indigenous peoples of Thailand belong to five linguistic families: Tai-Kadai (like e.g. the various Tai groups in the North, the Saek, or Shan, also called Thai Yai,), Tibeto-Burman (like e.g. the Akha, Karen, Lahu, Lisu), Mon-Khmer (e.g. Lua, Khmu, Souei, Mlabri) and Hmong-Mien (Hmong, Mien), and Malayo-Polynesian (Moken)

Ten ethnic groups living in the north and west of the country are officially recognized "hill tribes": the Akha, Hmong, H'tin, Karen, Khmu, Lahu, Lisu, Lua, Mien and Palaung.[5] The directory of ethnic communities of 20 northern and western provinces of the Department of Social Development and Welfare of 2002 also includes the Mlabri and Padong. There are however several other, mostly small groups that reside in the North: several so-called tribal Tai groups (Tai Lue, Tai Khuen, Tai Yong), Kachin (Jingpaw and Rawang ethnic groups) and Shan. With exception of the Lua, Karen and Mlabri most of the indigenous groups in the North migrated to Thailand from China, Burma or Laos in the 19th and 20th centuries. The indigenous groups in the highlands traditionally planted rice and wide range of other crops in shifting cultivation fields or terraced wet rice fields. Many continue to rely heavily on forest products while others started to grow cash crops encouraged by government programs.

On the Korat plateau of the north-east and especially along the border with Laos and Cambodia live various ethnic groups that bear characteristics common with others that are considered indigenous peoples in Thailand. There are several Tai speaking groups (Saek, Phuan, Phuthai and Black Thai) the Mon-Khmer speaking Suoi (also called Kui or Kuoy) and the So. Larger populations of these peoples live in the respective countries across the border. In Chauiyaphum province lives a group known as Nyahkur, Niakkuoll, Niakuolor or Chao Bon and are considered to speak the old Mon language.

In Trat Province and Chanthaburi Province of eastern Thailand (as well as then adjacent areas in Cambodia) live the Chong. They are a Mon-Khmer speaking group. They also call themselves Chong-Samré in the former, or Chong la and Chong heap in the latter province. In the literature they are often referred to as Pear or Por.[6] The Sa'och of Trat province and neighbouring Cambodia speak the same language as the Chong but are physically very different, i.e. have negroid features. Both groups used to live mainly from swidden farming, hunting and gathering.

In the very South, along the border with Malaysia live people who across the border in Malaysia are classified as belonging to the negrito group of the Orang Asli. In Thailand they are sometimes called Ngo, Ngko, Ngok Pa or Sakai, a term which in Malaysia has a negative connotations, which seems to be less the case in Thailand. In some records they are also called Semang, which is the generic term for the negrito groups of the Orang Asli in Malaysia. Records from the first half of the 20th century refer to four different groups of Sakai living in Thailand, but little is know about actual self-identification of these people who number only a few hundred.

Along the coast and the islands of the Andaman Sea, from Malayasia though Thailand into the Mergui archipelago of Burma live the Moken, the so-called "sea gypsies or, in Thai, *chao thale* ("sea people").

This country profile was written by Christian Erni (IWGIA) with inputs from Dr. Chayan Vaddhanaputi and Dr. Colin Nicholas.

Sources
Printed Sources

Buergin, Reiner 2000. '*Hill Tribes' and Forests: Minority Policies and Resource Conflicts in Thailand*. SEFUT Working Paper No. 7. Freiburg: Albert-Ludwigs-Universität Freiburg

UNDP-RIPP Natural Resource Management Country Studies: Thailand Report, AIPP

Dutta, Kalpalata and Pronpen Khongkachonkiet 2008. *Reclaiming Rights in Forests. Struggles of Indigenous Peoples.* Bangkok: Highland Peoples Taskforce (HPT) Thailand and IWGIA

Luithui, Chingya and Jannie Lasimbang. Thailand. The Challenges of Joint Management in the Northern Hills; in: Helen Leake (ed.) 2007. *Bridging the Gap. Policies and Practices on Indigenous Peoples' Natural Resource Management in Asia.* Chiang Mai: UNDP-RIPP/AIPP Foundation

Nagata, Shuichi 2006. Subgroup 'names' of the Sakai (Thailand) and the Semang (Malaysia): a literature survey. *Anthropological Science* Vol. 114, 45–57, 2006

Internet Sources

Virtual Hilltribe Museum: http://www.hilltribe.org

Princess Maha Chakri Sirindhom Anthropology Centre: http://av.sac.or.th/SAC_E/databases.html

Notes

[1] UNHCR, Sub-Commission on Prevention of Discrimination and Protection of Minorities. WGIP 10th session. E/CN.4/Sub.2/AC.4/1992/4.

[2] UNDP-RIPP Natural Resource Management Country Studies: Thailand Report, AIPP & Reiner BUERGIN (http://www.sefut.uni-freiburg.de/pdf/WP_7e.pdf)

[3] Reiner BUERGIN (http://www.sefut.uni-freiburg.de/pdf/WP_7e.pdf)

[4] YB 2006

[5] Sometimes only nine are mentioned, i.e. the Palaung are excluded. The inclusion of the Palaung is considered problematic because of their comparably late arrival. Dr. Chayan Vadhanaputi, personal communication.

[6] http://en.wikipedia.org/wiki/Pear_(people)

Hmong girls, Lao Cai province. Photo: Christian Erni

Country Profile

Vietnam

Vietnam, officially known as the Socialist Republic of Vietnam, is the easternmost nation on the Indochina Peninsula. It borders China to the north, Laos to the northwest, and Cambodia to the southwest. It covers an area of approximately 331,688 km² and has a population of over 86 million, which makes it the most densely populated nation in Southeast Asia.

Vietnam officially has 54 ethnic groups, with the Kinh (ethnic Vietnamese) accounting for the majority. The remaining 53 groups are classified by the government as ethnic minorities. Most of these ethnic minorities reside in mountainous or remote areas.

Terms used for indigenous peoples

In official wording indigenous peoples in Vietnam are referred to as ethnic minorities *(dan toc thieu so, dan toc it nguoi)*. The government has invested considerable resources in identifying the exact number of ethnic groups. The present official figure of 54 ethnic groups (including the Kinh) is considered definitive, and the government reacts quite sensitively to critique from – mainly foreign – scholars with respect to the criteria and methods applied.[1]

The Government has defined ethnic minorities as "those people who have Vietnamese nationality, who live in Viet Nam but who do not share 'Kinh' characteristics such as language, culture and identity."[2]

While many indigenous communities in Vietnam define themselves as "indigenous" with respect to their ancestral territories which are being invaded by settlers, reference to the international discourse on indigenousness and the definitions used is not very likely, simply because few of them has had access to that discourse yet. And even if some individual scholars or social workers, either indigenous or Kinh, are aware of and sympathize with the international indigenous movement and its concepts and demands, they avoid using the term or furthering the spread of the concept in public.

The Government's position regarding the recognition of indigenous peoples and their rights

Indigenous peoples are full citizens of the Vietnamese state and enjoy constitutionally guaranteed rights to their languages and cultural traditions. Hence, the legal rights of indigenous peoples in Vietnam compare favourably with those of other Southeast Asian countries. On the legislative level, the "Council on Ethnic Minorities" has the mandate to advise the National Assembly on ethnic minority issues and to supervise and control the implementation of the government's ethnic minority policies and development programs in ethnic minority areas. On the executive level, the Committee for Ethnic Minority Affairs (CEMA, formerly called Committee for Ethnic Minorities and Mountainous Areas – CEMMA) is responsible for co-ordinating all activities and overseeing the implementation of programs specifically targeting or impacting on indigenous peoples and mountain areas.

All constitutions of the Vietnam nation since its creation have spelled out a number of broad principles relating to indigenous peoples, including respecting the interests, traditional cultures, languages, customs, and beliefs of all ethnic groups; and matching socioeconomic policies with the special characteristics of the regions and ethnic groups, particularly ethnic minorities. The 1992 Constitution affirms the rights of ethnic minorities. Article 5 states that the government forbids all acts of ethnic discrimination and guarantees the rights of ethnic groups to use their own language and writing systems, preserve their ethnic identity, and promote their own traditions and culture. Articles 36 and 39 authorize preferential treatment for national minorities in education and health care. Article 94 mandates the establishment of the Nationalities Council of the National Assembly to "supervise and control" the implementation of policies and programs in regard to ethnic minorities.[3]

A number of policies and programs have since the 1960s been designed specifically for ethnic minorities but these have mainly aimed at integrating them into mainstream society rather than enabling them to strengthen their own institutions. Most likely the largest impact on indigenous peoples has so far been exerted by the Fixed Cultivation and Permanent Settlement Program (now part of the national Program 135, see below). It is a program specially targeting indigenous peoples and its main goal has been to eradicate shifting cultivation by creation of permanent, fixed cultivation followed by sedentarization of the population. In the still well forested areas of the southern highlands, shifting cultivators are resettled in new villages, where they grow subsistence and cash crops on allocated land

and sometimes are employed in forest work. In the northern mountains with its much smaller forested lands, a modified approach, focusing on plantation of commercially valuable tree crops is being implemented. Other polices and programs include: the Program for Socioeconomic Development in the Most Disadvantaged Communes (Program 135) – focusing mainly on building infrastructure; the Hunger Eradication and Poverty Reduction Program (which merged with the former Program to Support Ethnic Minorities with Special Difficulties), and the Program of Forest Development (also called "5 million hectares program", referring to the target of establishing forest plantations on 5 million hectares). [4]

While not specifically targeting indigenous peoples, a number of policies, such as the land and forest policies, have inevitably affected the indigenous population. For example, the present legislation in Vietnam allows for obtaining use right certificates for land and forest. In 2004, the National Assembly passed a new land law which, most relevant for indigenous peoples, now includes the category of "communal land". So far land use certificates could only be issued to individuals, households, mass-organizations, state enterprises, or companies. By introducing the concept of communal land the new law provides for the possibility of communities to apply for certificates over communal land. However, the law does not define what communal land means and it is thus unclear under which conditions and for what types of land a community can receive a communal land use certificate. Like the concept of "communal land" the term "community" itself has not been clearly defined either and can therefore be interpreted in different ways.[5]

The Vietnamese government has also introduced a quota system in order to ensure minimal access for indigenous students to higher education. There are also protected political representations at the national and local level.

The provisions and decrees potentially beneficial to the ethnic minorities are, however, often little known and there is an enormous gap between theory and practice, intentions and results. For example, a selective education and recruiting system ensures Kinh dominated party control. Furthermore, while local government offices in communes and districts with a majority of indigenous peoples are also held by members of the respective indigenous groups, the more powerful positions at province level or, if a considerable number of Kinh are present, at the district level are usually held by Kinh. In terms of education, the government has recognized the language problem in indigenous education. The present policy explicitly permits the use of local languages in teaching and the reform of the curriculum in schools. But this is rarely put into practice. Lack of indigenous teachers or Kinh teachers speaking the local languages, and a general priority given to infrastructure rather than to capacity development and improvement of curriculi has been characteristic of the education policy.

The following are the most relevant international human rights and other instruments ratified by Vietnam:

- International Covenant on Civil and Political Rights
- Convention on the Elimination of All Forms of Discrimination against Women
- International Convention on the Elimination of All Forms of Racial Discrimination
- International Covenant on Economic, Social and Cultural Rights
- Convention on the Rights of the Child
- Convention on Biological Diversity

Identifying indigenous peoples in Vietnam

According to the 1999 census, the 53 officially identified and recognized ethnic minorities in Vietnam total about 10 million people, accounting for 13.8% of the total population of the country.[6] These ethnic groups differ markedly from the majority people, the ethnic Vietnamese or Kinh. Language, culture, social organization and mode of production set them clearly apart from the dominant ethnic group. And even among them, differences are often very pronounced.

The size of the indigenous groups varies between groups with a total population of over one millions (like the Tay, the Thai and the Muong; all live in the northern provinces), and those with only a few hundred people (like the Si La, Ro-Mam, O-du or Brau). While some of the small indigenous groups extend across boundaries into neighbouring China, Laos or Cambodia, and therefore have a much larger total population, a few live only in Vietnam. Very little is known about the small groups and some are considered to be severely threatened with cultural extinction.

Official list of ethnic minorities in Vietnam

1	Ba-na	15	E-de	29	Lao	43	Ro-mam
2	Bo Y	16	Giay	30	Lo Lo	44	San Chay
3	Brau	17	Gia rai	31	Lu	45	San Diu
4	Bru-Van	18	GieTrie	32	Ma	46	Si La
5	Cham	19	Ha Nhi	33	Mang	47	Tay
6	Cho-ro	20	Hmong	34	Mnong	48	Ta-oi
7	Chu-ru	21	Hoa	35	Muong	49	Thai
8	Chut	22	Hre	36	Ngai	50	Tho
9	Co	23	Khang	37	Nung	51	Xinh-mun
10	Cong	24	Khome	38	O-du	52	Xo-dang
11	Co-ho	25	Kho-mu	39	Pa Then	53	Xtieng
12	Co Lao	26	La Chi	40	Phu La		
13	Co-tu	27	La Ha	41	Pu Peo		
14	Dao	28	La Hu	42	Ra-glai		

Source: ADB 2002: p. 6f

It has been estimated that 75% of the ethnic minorities live in eleven provinces in the Northern Mountains and four provinces in the Central Highlands. It is usually the ethnic minorities in these mountains and uplands who are referred to as the indigenous peoples of Vietnam. This means that ethnic groups such as the mostly urban Chinese (in Vietnam called Hoa) or the Cham, descendents of the ancient empire of the same name, who live in the coastal plains of the South, are ethnic minorities but not considered indigenous peoples.

The great majority of indigenous peoples are poor, marginalized, subsistence farmers, supplemented by petty commodity production of cash crops, sale of forest products or handicraft, animal husbandry, hunting, gathering and fishing.

The relocation process of Kinh into the highlands has caused significant changes in the population composition of the highland regions. In 1945 Kinh accounted for 5% of the total population in the Central Highlands while today they account for more than 70%. In other areas previously dominated by indigenous peoples, Kinh have also become the majority inhabitants. Fertile valley bottoms where wet rice cultivation is possible were often taken over by Kinh, and alternatives like production of perennial cash crops are difficult to adopt due to lack of capital and market access. Therefore, food shortage and, consequently, malnutrition is widespread among indigenous peoples. This results in weakened resistance to communicable diseases, which again are more widespread due to poor sanitation and lack of safe potable water.

This country profile was written by Christian Erni and Christina Nilsson (both IW-GIA).

Sources
Printed Sources

Asian Development Bank 2002. *Indigenous Peoples/Ethnic Minorities and Poverty Reduction. Viet Nam.* Environmental and Social Safeguard Division, Regional and Sustainable Development Department. Manila: Asian Development Bank

Asian Indigenous and Tribal Peoples Network (AITPN) and International Work Group on Indigenous Affairs (IWGIA) 2001. Discrimination Against Indigenous Mountain Peoples of Viet Nam. An Alternate Report to the CERD Committee to the sixth to ninth Periodic Report of Viet Nam (CERD/C/357/Add.2). Unpublished report. New Delhi/Copenhagen: AITPN/IWGIA

Erni, Christian 1999. Indigenous Peoples in Vietnam. Background Paper and Report on the Networking Trip to Vietnam. Unpublished report. Copenhagen: IWGIA

International Work Group for Indigenous Affairs 2005. *The Indigenous World 2005.* Copenhagen: IWGIA

Rambo, A. Terry 1997. Development Trends in Vietnams Northern Mountain Region; in: Donovan, Deanna et. al.: *Development Trends in Vietnams Northern Mountain Region.* Vol. 1. An Overview and Analysis. Hanoi: National Publishing House

Zankel, Stanley 1996. A Health Strategy for Ethnic Minorities Living in Vietnam. Draft Consultancy Report Population and Family Health Project

Internet Sources

Human Rights Watch Web-site: http://hrw.org

Notes

[1] Rambo 1997: 7
[2] Asian Indigenous and Tribal Peoples Network 2001: p. 10
[3] Human Rights Watch - http://www.hrw.org/reports/2002/vietnam/viet0402-05.htm
[4] Asian Development Bank 2002: p. 13 ff
[5] IWGIA 2005: p. 350f
[6] Asian Development Bank 2002: p. 8

Annex

Definitions of Indigenous Peoples by International Organizations and Governments

José Martínez Cobo, Study of the Problem of Discrimination against indigenous populations, UN Doc. E/CN.4/Sub.2/1986/7/Add.4, paras 379-80

"Indigenous communities, peoples and nations are those which, having a historical continuity with pre-invasion and pre-colonial societies that developed on their territories, consider themselves distinct from other sectors of the societies now prevailing in those territories, or parts of them. They form at present non-dominant sectors of society and are determined to preserve, develop and transmit to future generations their ancestral territories, and their ethnic identity, as the basis of their continued existence as peoples, in accordance with their own cultural patterns, social institutions and legal systems.

The historical continuity may consist of the continuation, for and extended period reaching into the present, of one or more of the following factors:

(a) Occupation of ancestral lands, or at least part of them;

(b) Common ancestry with the original occupants of these lands;

(c) Culture in general, or in specific manifestations (such as religion, living under a tribal system, membership on an indigenous community, dress, means of livelihood, life-style, etc.);

(d) Language (whether used as the only language, as mother- tongue, as the habitual means of communication at home or in the family, or as the main, preferred, habitual or normal language;

(e) Residence in certain parts of the country, or in certain regions of the world;

(f) Other relevant factors."

ILO Convention No. 169, June 27, 1989, 28 ILM 1382, 1384-85 (1989)

Article 1(1) of the Convention applies to:

"(a) tribal peoples in independent countries whose social, cultural and economic conditions distinguish them from other sections of the national community, and whose status is regulated wholly or partially by their own customs or traditions or by special laws or regulations;

(b) peoples in independent countries who are regarded as indigenous on account of their descent from the populations which inhabited the country, or a geographical region to which the country belongs, at the tie of conquest or colonisation or the establishment of resent state boundaries and who, irrespective of their legal status, retain some or all of their own social, economic, cultural and political institutions."

World Bank Operational Directive, No. 4.20, 1991 (p.19)

"The term 'indigenous peoples', 'indigenous ethnic minorities', 'tribal groups', and 'scheduled tribes' describe social groups with a social and cultural identity distinct from the dominant society that makes them vulnerable to being disadvantaged in the development process. For the purpose of this directive, 'indigenous peoples' is the term that will be used to refer to these groups."

"Because of the varied and changing contexts in which indigenous peoples are found, no single definition can capture their diversity. Indigenous people are commonly among the poorest segments of a population. They engage in economic activities that range from shifting agriculture in or near forests to wage labor or even small-scale market-oriented activities. Indigenous peoples can be identified in particular geographical areas by the presence in varying degrees of the following characteristics:

(a) a close attachment to ancestral territories and to the natural resources in these areas;

(b) self-identification and identification by others as members of a distinct cultural group;

(c) an indigenous language, often different from the national language;

(d) presence of customary social political institutions; and

(e) primarily subsistence-oriented production.

Task managers (TMs) must exercise judgment in determining the populations to which this directive applies and should make use of specialised anthropological and sociological experts throughout the project cycle."

Government of the Republic of the Philippines. Republic Act 8371 (Indigenous Peoples Rights Act)

In Chapter II, section 3, the law defines indigenous peoples as follows:

> "h) Indigenous Cultural Communities/Indigenous Peoples - refer to a group of people or homogenous societies identified by self-ascription and ascription by others, who have continuously lived as organized community on communally bounded and defined territory, and who have, under claims of ownership since time immemorial, occupied, possessed and utilized such territories, sharing common bonds of language, customs, traditions and other distinctive cultural traits, or who have, through resistance to political, social and cultural inroads of colonization, non-indigenous religions and cultures, became historically differentiated from the majority of Filipinos. ICCs/IPs shall likewise include peoples who are regarded as indigenous on account of their descent from the populations which inhabited the country, at the time of conquest or colonization, or at the time of inroads of non-indigenous religions and cultures, or the establishment of present state boundaries, who retain some or all of their own social, economic, cultural and political institutions, but who may have been displaced from their traditional domains or who may have resettled outside their ancestral domains;"